Praise for *The Black Atlantic's Triple Burden*

"Sweeping across continents and centuries, this volume offers a deeply important collection of essays on the experiences and impacts of slavery and colonialism, as well as the possibilities and challenges of reparative justice. With its roster of some of the world's finest and most distinguished scholars addressing these topics, *The Black Atlantic's Triple Burden* should be required reading for academics and a general audience alike."
– Caroline Elkins, author of *Legacy of Violence: A History of the British Empire*

"Professor Adekeye Adebajo, an astute scholar of African affairs, has brought together a talented cast of scholars to produce an encyclopaedic work on the triple challenges that confront the people of the Black Atlantic. This tour de force has probed the innards of its subject, thereby helping readers to understand the battles that lie ahead."
– Selwyn R. Cudjoe, Professor Emeritus, Wellesley College, USA

"Beginning with Adekeye Adebajo's magisterial introduction, this volume canvasses the successive calamities for Africa of slavery and colonialism, their contemporary legacies, and the reparations movement's efforts to interrupt their future transmission. This extraordinary collection is essential reading for anybody seeking to engage with the world-leading scholarship on these critical themes."
– Professor Thula Simpson, author of *History of South Africa: From 1902 to the Present*

"The editor, Adekeye Adebajo, and his multi-disciplinary group of contributors to *The Black Atlantic's Triple Burden* must be commended for this work. These academics and advocates not only rehearse familiar themes, but also add new perspectives which together form a welcome addition to the

body of work explaining the justification for reparations for historical crimes against humanity and the lingering legacies of colonialism."
– Professor Verene A. Shepherd, University of the West Indies and member of Jamaica's National Council on Reparations

"This book is of uniformly high-quality scholarship and writing. It contains good variation in emphases and discusses a wide sweep of historical and contemporary issues surrounding enslavement and colonialism. The collection marks a significant increase in information, insights, and public conversation about the legacies of enslavement and colonialism from authoritative scholars, many from or based in Africa. It is vital that we have books like this to provide concrete facts, concepts, and perspectives based on accumulated research. It is compelling reading."
– Professor Colin Samson, Essex University, England

The Black Atlantic's Triple Burden

Slavery, Colonialism, and Reparations

Edited by Adekeye Adebajo

Manchester University Press

First published in South Africa by Jacana Media in 2024

This edition published by Manchester University Press, Oxford Road, Manchester M13 9PL is available in North America (excluding the Caribbean), United Kingdom, Europe, Asia, Africa (excluding South Africa), Australia and New Zealand

www.manchesteruniversitypress.co.uk

British Library Cataloguing-in-Publication Data
A catalogue record for this book is available from the British Library

ISBN 978 1 5261 9302 5 hardback
ISBN 978 1 5261 9303 2 paperback

EU authorised representative for GPSR:
Easy Access System Europe, Mustamäe tee 50, 10621 Tallinn, Estonia
gpsr.requests@easproject.com

Contents

Acknowledgements

THIS BOOK IS A DIRECT outgrowth of my 38-chapter edited volume *The Pan-African Pantheon: Prophets, Poets, and Philosophers* (2020–1), which won the Cambridge University Press *African Studies Review* (ASR) prize in 2022 for best edited volume or anthology of the African Studies Association (ASA) of the United States. It was through researching and editing that book that I first noticed the close connections between slavery, colonialism, and reparations, with which this current volume on *The Black Atlantic's Triple Burden* is concerned. This new book seeks to bring the study of slavery, colonialism, and reparations – which are often examined in separate silos – into mainstream discourses, so that connections can be drawn between all three subjects and the issues do not remain the parochial domain of scholars in ivory and ebony towers. This study thus deals centrally with the 'Black Atlantic', which emerged as a result of transatlantic slavery in Africa, the Caribbean, the Americas, and Europe.

Our edited volume also seeks to make a substantive contribution to contemporary global transformation debates in an era of Rhodes Must Fall and Black Lives Matter, as well as to efforts to transform fossilised Eurocentric curricula. The book demonstrates the continuities of European-led slavery and colonialism in Africa, the Caribbean, the Americas, and Europe, examining calls for reparations in all four regions for what most now acknowledge to have been crimes against humanity. The volume is authored by some of the most eminent scholars in the field, who appropriately represent citizens of the geographical Black Atlantic. The book thus seeks to be comprehensive and multidisciplinary, and to enable cross-regional comparisons to be drawn in these important areas, thus ensuring that important global events are read from diverse perspectives. The volume is further aimed at subject area experts, as well as students in diverse areas of the humanities and beyond who seek a sound introductory reference book for these important historical subjects, which was not available to us when we entered our diverse social sciences fields. The authors represent an interdisciplinary group encompassing varied fields such as history, international relations, politics, economics, sociology, anthropology, literature, and languages.

I would like firstly to acknowledge the enormous patience, passion, and encouragement of all the committed scholars of the Black Atlantic who contributed so richly to this volume, consistently and enthusiastically supporting the process throughout the three years that it lasted. Their hard work has been richly rewarded through this book, which was truly a collective effort.

I would also like to thank the external reviewers who took the time to provide substantive comments that were very useful in revising this volume, as well as Russell Martin for his meticulous editing skills, and Ali Parry for her thorough indexing. The first edition of the book for the African market was produced by Jacana Media in South Africa. I would like to thank its dynamic publishing director, Bridget Impey, for believing in the project from the start, as well as Jacana founder Maggie Davey. At Manchester University Press (MUP), I would like to acknowledge the impressively patient punctiliousness of editorial director, Emma Brennan, as well as the sterling efforts of senior commissioning editor, Shannon Kneis, and editorial co-ordinator, Laura Swift, which all ensured that the book reaches a wider global audience outside Africa through this new edition.

This three-year project was supported by the University of Johannesburg (UJ) and the University of Pretoria (UP), both in South Africa. I am grateful to the former Vice-Chancellors, Professors Tshilidzi Marwala and Tawana Kupe, as well as the current UJ Vice-Chancellor, Letlhokwa Mpedi, for their joint support. I would also like to thank my former colleagues at UJ's Institute for Pan-African Thought and Conversation in Johannesburg (IPATC) – which I directed between 2017 and 2021 – as well as UP's Centre for the Advancement of Scholarship (CAS) – where I am currently a senior research fellow – who contributed to the success of this project over three long years. They also deserve to share in the credit for the publication of this book. I particularly note the project coordination assistance of Ratidzo Makombe at UJ, and Mwansa Mwansa and Samuel Igba at UP.

We hope that this volume will be read not just by scholars, but also by members of civil society and the general public across Africa and its diaspora and beyond. The five-century struggles against the European-led transatlantic slave trade and colonialism have eventually triggered a global battle for reparations across the Black Atlantic of Africa, the Caribbean, the Americas, and Europe, which has deep roots in the church-based civil society activism in the United States and the Caribbean from the eighteenth century. As has often been noted, the movements to abolish slavery and colonialism took generations to succeed, and so also will the contemporary movement to achieve reparations for slavery and colonialism. We hope that this book can make a modest contribution to this noble struggle, and also provide empirical and historical research for these worthy activist efforts.

Adekeye Adebajo

Johannesburg, October 2024

List of Contributors

ADEKEYE ADEBAJO is a professor and senior research fellow at the University of Pretoria's Centre for the Advancement of Scholarship (CAS). He was director of the Institute for Pan-African Thought and Conversation (IPATC) at the University of Johannesburg for five years (2017-2021), and executive director of the Centre for Conflict Resolution (CCR) in Cape Town between 2003 and 2016. He is the author of ten books, including *The Curse of Berlin: Africa after the Cold War*; *Global Africa: Profiles in Courage, Creativity, and Cruelty*; and *The Splendid Tapestry of African Life: Essays on a Resilient Continent, its Diaspora, and the World*. He is also the editor of ten books including *The Pan-African Pantheon: Prophets, Poets, and Philosophers*. Professor Adebajo holds a doctorate from Oxford University, where he studied as a Rhodes Scholar.

ROSE MARY ALLEN is an anthropologist, and Professor (by special appointment) of Culture, Community and History at the University of Curaçao. She is the author of, among other works, *Di ki manera: A Social History of Afro-Curaçaoans, 1863-1917* and co-editor of *Staat en slavernij: Het Nederlandse koloniale slavernijverleden en zijn doorwerkingen* (Slavery and the State: Dutch Colonial Slavery History and Its Legacies). She is the recipient of numerous awards, most recently the Cross of Merit from the Government of Curaçao in 2023 in recognition of her contributions to research on the Dutch Caribbean.

JAIME ARAGÓN FALOMIR is a Research Associate in Latin American Studies at the Roger Toumson Faculty of the University of the Antilles in Guadeloupe. He was assistant professor at the Martinique Pôle at the same university. Professor Aragón was a Latin American post-doctoral fellow at the National University of Rosario in Argentina. He is co-coordinator of the ConnecCaribbean programme (Horizon Marie Curie), and holds a doctorate from the Sorbonne University in Paris.

HILARY BECKLES is Vice-Chancellor and Professor of Economic History at the University of the West Indies (UWI). He is an editor of volume 9 of the United Nations Educational, Scientific, and Cultural Organization (UNESCO) *General History of Africa*. Professor Beckles was Vice-President of the UNESCO Slave Route project, and served as a science adviser to UN Secretary-General Ban Ki-moon's committee on sustainable development. He is President of the Association of Caribbean Universities, has been awarded several honorary degrees, and received the Martin Luther King Award for global justice in 2021. He is widely known for his many books on the globalisation of chattel slavery and reparatory justice such as *Britain's Black Debt*, and is chair of the Reparations Commission of the Caribbean Community (Caricom).

ADAM A. BLACKLER is an Associate Professor of History at the University of Wyoming in the US. He is the author of *An Imperial Homeland: Forging German Identity in Southwest Africa*, which appeared in the Pennsylvania State University Press's series "Germans beyond Europe" in 2022. Among Dr Blackler's other recent publications are: the anthology *After the Imperialist Imagination: Two Decades of Research on Global Germany and Its Legacies*, and a chapter in the multi-volume collection *A Cultural History of Genocide*. Dr Blackler is currently researching a new book that explores how imperial adherents publicly assuaged their humiliated national ego against a backdrop of military defeat and political collapse during Germany's Weimar Republic from 1919 to 1933.

BRIDGET BRERETON is Emerita Professor of History at the University of the West Indies, St Augustine campus, Trinidad and Tobago. She is the author of several books on the history of the Caribbean and of Trinidad, including standard works such as *Race Relations in Colonial Trinidad, 1870–1900* and *A History of Modern Trinidad, 1783–1962*. She is the editor or co-editor of several more (including volume 5 of the UNESCO *General History of the Caribbean*), and the author of many journal articles, book chapters, book reviews, and newspaper columns. She has served as Deputy Principal and Interim Principal of UWI's St Augustine campus.

DANIEL J. BROYLD is an Associate Professor of African American History at the University of Massachusetts Lowell in the US. He earned his doctorate in nineteenth-century United States and African Diaspora History at Howard University in Washington DC. His work focuses on the American–Canadian borderlands and issues of black identity, migration, and transnational relations, as well as oral history, material culture, and museum–community interactions. Broyld was a 2017–18 Fulbright Canada scholar at Brock University, and his book *Borderland Blacks: Two Cities in the Niagara Region during the Final Decades of Slavery* (2022) was published by the Louisiana State University Press.

ALAN COBLEY is Professor of South African and Comparative History at the University of the West Indies on the Cave Hill campus in Barbados. He was Pro-Vice-Chancellor for Undergraduate Studies (2013–19) and co-director of the UWI–University of Johannesburg Institute for Global African Affairs (2018–22). He is author, editor, or co-editor of 12 books, and has written numerous articles and book chapters on South African and Caribbean history. He serves on the editorial board of the *Journal of Caribbean History*. His recent works include *Ann Gill: The Making of a Barbadian National Hero*, and *RV Selope Thema: A Forgotten Founder of the ANC*.

CATHERINE COQUERY-VIDROVITCH is Professor Emerita of Modern African History at the University of Paris in France,. and Adjunct Professor at Binghamton University, State University of New York (SUNY) in the US. Over the years, she has trained a large number of African historians. Four of her books were translated into English: *Africa South of the Sahara: Endurance and Change*; *African Women: A Modern History*; *The History of African Cities South of the Sahara: From the Origins to Colonization* (which was selected by *Choice* as one of the best books of the year); and *Africa and the Africans in the 19th Century: A Turbulent History*. Her last books were *Les routes de l'esclavage africain*, and *Le choix de l'Afrique*. Professor Coquery-Vidrovitch won the Distinguished Africanist Award of the African Studies Association (ASA) of the US in 1999.

NICOLA FRITH is a Senior Lecturer in French and Francophone Studies at the University of Edinburgh, Scotland. Her research focuses on grassroots activism linked to the legacies of African enslavement, the politics of memory and commemoration, and the work of activists within the International Social Movement for Afrikan Reparations. She has published many articles, chapters, and collections linked to the history and memory of slavery and reparations, and her book *Legacies of Slavery in the French Republic: Politics, Activism, Reparation* is forthcoming. She is one of the co-founders of the International Network of Scholars and Activists for Afrikan Reparations (INOSAAR).

MIA FULLER is Gladyce Arata Terrill Distinguished Professor of Italian Studies at the University of California, Berkeley, in the US. A cultural anthropologist, she writes on Italian colonial and fascist architecture and urbanism, and the legacies of Italian colonialism and fascism. Her book *Moderns Abroad: Architecture, Cities, Italian Imperialism* won an International Planning History Society book prize. She is section editor of the *Routledge Companion to Italian Fascist Architecture*; and co-editor with Ruth Ben-Ghiat of *Italian Colonialism*. Professor Fuller is currently completing a book provisionally titled *Monuments and Mussolini: A Cultural History of Fascist Memory*, based on long-term field research in Italy's Pontine Marshes area.

SHELENE GOMES is a Lecturer in Social Anthropology and Sociology at the University of the West Indies, St Augustine campus, in Trinidad and Tobago. She is also a Senior Research Associate at the University of Johannesburg's Department of Anthropology and Development Studies. Her monograph *Cosmopolitanism from the Global South* explores Caribbean migratory movements, specifically of Rastafari spiritual repatriation to Ethiopia, tracing the connections between African diasporic imaginings and Caribbean cosmopolitan sensibilities.

SAMUEL IGBA was a Postdoctoral Research Fellow at the Centre for the Advancement of Scholarship (CAS) at the University of Pretoria. He was also a Research Associate at the Centre for Mediation in Africa, University of Pretoria, where he worked as a researcher for three years focusing on peace-building and state-building in Africa. Dr Igba holds a doctorate in political science from the University of Pretoria.

JEFFREY KERR-RITCHIE is Professor of History at Howard University in Washington DC, where he directed the graduate history programme for eight years. His books include *Freedpeople in the Tobacco South: Virginia, 1860–1900*; *Rites of August First: Emancipation Day in the Black Atlantic World*; *Freedom's Seekers: Essays on Comparative Emancipation*; and *Rebellious Passage: The Creole Revolt and America's Coastal Slave Trade*. He is writing a biography of the Pan-Africanist Dusé Mohamed Ali. He completed his doctorate in history at the University of Pennsylvania in the US, and holds fellowships from Fulbright-Hays, the Schomburg Center in New York, and the National Humanities Center in North Carolina.

Martin A. Klein is a Professor Emeritus of the University of Toronto. He is the author of three books and over seventy articles and book chapters. Most of his research is on the history of slavery and the slave trade in Africa. His books include *Historical Dictionary of Slavery and Abolition*; *Slavery and Colonial Rule in Africa*, edited with Suzanne Miers; *Breaking the Chains: Slavery, Bondage, and Emancipation in Modern Africa and Asia*; and *Women and Slavery in Africa*, edited with Claire C. Robertson. His book *Slavery and Colonial Rule in French West Africa* earned an honourable mention from the Herskovits Award Committee of the African Studies Association of the US. He has been president of both the Canadian Association of African Studies and the African Studies Association (ASA) of the US, received the ASA US's Distinguished Africanist Award in 2012; and had a prize in African history named after him by the American Historical Association (AHA).

Andrew Maginn is a Visiting Assistant Professor of History at Sewanee: The University of the South in the US. He has served as the Senior Research Associate and Programme Coordinator for Sewanee's Race and Reconciliation programme. Professor Maginn was a contributing editor of the book *The Haiti Reader: History, Culture, Politics*, and holds a doctorate from Howard University in Washington DC.

Butholezwe Mtombeni is a Lecturer in History at the University of South Africa (UNISA) in Pretoria. His research interests are focused on African history, spanning the pre-colonial and post-colonial eras; Zulu history; gender history; religion and slavery; social history; and agrarian history. Dr Mtombeni holds a doctorate in history from UNISA.

Gustau Nerín holds a doctorate in anthropology and teaches African history at the University of Barcelona in Spain. He specialises in Spanish colonialism in Equatorial Guinea, and has taught at the Universidad Nacional de Guinea Ecuatorial, the Paul Valéry University of Montpellier (France), the Universitat Pompeu Fabra in Barcelona, and the Universidad Federal de Integración Latinoamericana in Foz do Iguaçu, Brazil. Professor Nerín is the author of nine monographs including *Guinea Equatorial: Història en blanc i negre*; *La última selva de España*; *Blanc bo busca negre pobre*; and *Corisco y el estuario del Muni*.

Kwame Nimako is the founder and director of the Black Europe Summer

School (BESS), based in Amsterdam since 2007. He lectured in International Relations in the Department of Political Sciences at the University of Amsterdam, and held visiting professorial positions in the Department of African American Studies at the University of California, Berkeley, and at the University of Suriname. He is the author or co-author of more than thirty books, reports, and guidebooks, including *The Dutch Atlantic: Slavery, Abolition and Emancipation* (with Glenn Willemsen). Professor Nimako obtained his doctorate in economics from the University of Amsterdam in the Netherlands.

PATRIZIA PALUMBO is a senior lecturer in the Department of Italian at Columbia University in New York, where she obtained her doctorate. She is the author of a number of articles on the history of Italian culture from the Middle Ages to the present, the main focus of which has been the representation of Africa. Professor Palumbo is also the editor of and contributor to *A Place in the Sun: Africa in Italian Colonial Culture from Post-unification to the Present*. Her current research project deals with the specifies of Italian Orientalism in the nineteenth and twentieth centuries.

SUSAN ELIZABETH RAMIREZ taught for nineteen years at Texas Christian University in the US where she held the Penrose Chair of History. Her major books include *Provincial Patriarchs: Land Tenure and the Economics of Power in Colonial Peru*; *The World Upside Down: Cross Cultural Contact and Conflict in Colonial Peru*; *To Feed and Be Fed: The Cosmological Bases of Authority and Identity in the Andes*; *Al servicio de Dios y Su Majestad: Los orígenes de las escuelas públicas en Perú*; *Colonial Latin American History from First Encounters to Independence*; and *In Praise of the Ancestors: Names, Memory, and Identity in Africa and the Americas*. Professor Ramirez obtained her doctorate from the University of Wisconsin in the US.

CARLOS DA SILVA JR has worked as an Assistant Professor at the State University of Feira de Santana in Brazil since 2018. He obtained his doctorate from the Wilberforce Institute for the Study of Slavery and Emancipation (WISE) at the University of Hull in England, as well as a master's degree in social history from the Federal University of Bahia. He studied history with an emphasis on the history of colonial Brazil, mainly working on slavery, the African diaspora, and the history of Bahia. His main areas of interest are the African diaspora and the construction of ethnic identities in eighteenth-century Bahia.

STEPHEN SMALL is a Professor in the Department of African Diaspora Studies, and Director of the Institute for the Study of Societal Issues, both at the University of California, Berkeley, where he has taught since 1995. He has been a visiting scholar at universities in Brazil, England, France, the Netherlands, Spain, and Zimbabwe. He is the author of five books and co-author or co-editor of eight books. His most recent publications are *In the Shadows of the Big House: Twenty-First Century Antebellum Slave Cabins and Heritage Tourism in Louisiana*; and *1981: Black Liverpool, Past and Present* (co-written with Jimi Jagne). Professor Small earned his doctorate in sociology from the University of California, Berkeley. He was born and raised in Liverpool, England, the city with the longest-standing black population in Britain.

JUNE SOOMER worked at the University of the West Indies, universities in the US, and the Eastern Caribbean Central Bank. She was St Lucia's Ambassador to the Organisation of Eastern Caribbean States (OECS) and the Caribbean Community (Caricom), and the secretary-general of the Association of Caribbean States. She is chair of the Global Campus Council of UWI, a member of the St Lucia Reparations Committee, and a member of the UN Permanent Forum on People of African Descent. She was awarded the St Lucia Cross, and the Order of José de Marcoleta from Nicaragua. Dr Soomer also holds a doctorate in history from the University of the West Indies.

SANDRA SOUSA is an Associate Professor in the Modern Languages and Literatures Department at the University of Central Florida in the US, where she teaches Portuguese language, Lusophone Studies, and Latin American Studies. She is the author of *Ficções do outro: Império, raça e subjectividade no Moçambique colonial*; and *Portugal segundo os Estados Unidos da América;* and co-edited *Visitas a João Paulo Borges Coelho: Leituras, diálogos e futuros*; and *The Africas in the World and the World in the Africas: African Literatures and Comparativism*.

SCOTT TIMCKE is a sociologist working on the political economy of development, economic history, and imperialism. He is a Research Associate at the University of Johannesburg's Centre for Social Change and affiliated with the Center for Information, Technology, and Public Life at the University of North Carolina at Chapel Hill in the US. His third book was titled *The Political Economy of Fortune and Misfortune: Prospects for Prosperity in Our Times*.

IÑAKI TOFIÑO, a linguist by training, has worked for many years as a secondary school teacher. He was a Juan de la Cierva post-doctoral research fellow at the Institució Milá y Fontanals of the Spanish Research Council. He is the author of the book *Guinea, el delirio colonial de España* on the cultural history of Spanish Guinea through literature. Dr Tofiño is currently studying Equatorial Guinean literature, as well as European literature about the former Spanish colony, which is often full of stereotypes and colonial nostalgia.

GUY VANTHEMSCHE is Professor Emeritus of Contemporary History at the Free University of Brussels. He is the secretary of the Belgian Royal Historical Commission, and a member of the Belgian Royal Academy of Overseas Sciences (RAOS). Professor Vanthemsche has published several books on contemporary Belgian history including *Belgium and the Congo, 1885–1980*; and *A Concise History of Belgium.*

ESTHER XOSEI is Executive Director of the Maangamizi Educational Trust. She is a Motherist and decolonial Pan-Afrikanist Jurisconsult, Reparationist, Community Advocate, and 'Ourstorian' specialising in the critical legal praxis of 'law as resistance' as an approach to social movement lawyering. She also focuses on Mother Earth Jurisprudence and eco-socio-legal transformation 'from below'. Ms Xosei is engaged in reparations policy development, research, and movement building under the auspices of the Pan-Afrikan Reparations Coalition in Europe, the Stop the Maangamizi: We Charge Genocide/Ecocide Campaign, the International Network of Scholars and Activists for Afrikan Reparations, and the Extinction Rebellion Internationalist Solidarity Network.

DOUGLAS YATES is a Professor of Political Science at the American Graduate School in Paris (AGS), and director of the Anglo-American Law programme at the Law School of Cergy Paris University (CYU). He has published several books on French Africa, including *The Rentier State in Africa: Oil-Rent Dependency and Neocolonialism in the Republic of Gabon,* based on his doctoral research at Boston University in the US, and *The Historical Dictionary of Gabon; The French Oil Industry and the Corps des Mines in Africa;* and *The Scramble for African Oil: Oppression, Corruption and War for Control of Africa's Natural Resources.*

Part One

Introduction:
Setting the Scene

1

The Black Atlantic's Triple Tragedies: Slavery, Colonialism, and Reparations

Adekeye Adebajo

The caged bird sings
with a fearful trill
of things unknown
but longed for still
and his tune is heard
on the distant hill
for the caged bird
sings of freedom
– Maya Angelou, "Caged Bird" (1983)

THE UNITED NATIONS WORLD Conference Against Racism, Racial Discrimination, Xenophobia and Related Intolerance, which took place in South Africa's port city of Durban in August–September 2001, provided a rallying point for contemporary racial struggles for reparations for the twin crimes against humanity of slavery and colonialism.[1] The summit was hosted by South Africa's president, Thabo Mbeki, who more than any other contemporary African leader, as president, demonstrated a deep engagement with the Black World. As a young student, he had imbibed the activism of Martin Luther King Jr, the scholarship of Frantz Fanon, and the poetry of Langston Hughes. As president of South Africa (1999–2008), he preached black solidarity from Atlanta to Bahia, from Havana to Haiti.[2]

Durban declared slavery to be "a crime against humanity". The transatlantic slave trade was termed an "appalling tragedy" of "abhorrent barbarism" that "should always have been" a crime against humanity. Durban also argued that colonialism had resulted in racism and suffering that have endured into the contemporary age. The Durban Declaration therefore pushed for the inclusion of the history and contributions of Africans in educational curricula, as well as fully integrating into public services, and increasing social services to, "communities of primarily African descent" in places like the United States, Brazil, and Cuba.[3]

#Black Lives Matter Global Network, Rhodes Must Fall, and other civic movements built on this foundation to mobilise anti-racism protesters around the globe in 2020 more effectively than at any other time in living memory. In 2024, the African Union (AU) declared its key theme for 2025 to be "Justice for Africans and People of African Descent through Reparations".[4] Democrats in the US Congress have now embraced the cause of reparations. Oppressive statues in America and Europe have been toppled. In May 2021, the German government apologised and announced reparations of €1.1 billion for a century-old genocide in Namibia, while the Netherlands government apologised for the Dutch role in the transatlantic slave trade in December 2022, establishing a €200 million fund to address its impact.

In January 2023, Justin Welby, the Archbishop of Canterbury, announced a £100 million investment fund for communities afflicted by slavery, after researchers had discovered that the church's £9 billion endowment fund had benefited from the transatlantic slave trade. Welby disingenuously dismissed accusations of "post-colonial guilt", arguing instead that his conversion to reparations demonstrated "the presence of the risen Christ alive in the church".[5] The 335-year-old insurance conglomerate, Lloyd's of London, was pushed by reparations protesters to apologise for slavery in June 2020, before the company announced a £40 million fund, in November 2023, to invest in communities impacted by slavery. This was after an independent report had earlier exposed Lloyd's role in the "sophisticated network of financial interests and activities" that had made the transatlantic slave trade possible.[6] Harvard, Yale, and Oxford universities have established programmes of restitution for their involvement in the slave trade.[7] Barbadian historian Hilary Beckles has identified reparations for slavery and colonialism as the defining battle of the 21st century (see Beckles in this volume).

This book – which builds directly on my edited volume *The Pan-African*

Pantheon: Prophets, Poets, and Philosophers (2020)[8] – seeks to bring the study of slavery, colonialism, and reparations – which are often examined in separate silos – into mainstream discourses, so that connections can be made between all three subjects and these issues do not remain the parochial domain of scholars in ivory and ebony towers. One cannot understand colonialism without comprehending transatlantic slavery from the fifteenth to the nineteenth centuries, while the quest for reparations cannot be effectively pursued without exposing how slavery was used to promote and justify colonialism and racism. This volume thus deals centrally with the Black Atlantic – Africa and its diaspora – which emerged as a result of transatlantic slavery in Africa, the Caribbean, the Americas, and Europe. It is also worth noting that the European-created nation-state that resulted from the 1648 Treaty of Westphalia constitutes the main unit of analysis of this volume, though the struggles of civil society activists and scholars are also highlighted, particularly in the final section on reparations.

This Introduction will explain the terms "Global Africa" and "Black Atlantic", before examining comparatively the practice, impact, and legacy of the transatlantic slave trade on Africa, the Caribbean, and the Americas. I then assess the origins of European colonial rule in Africa, highlighting the German genocide in Namibia (1904–1908), before analysing the more contemporary practice of neo-colonialism, using the negative treatment of Africans and Caribbeans in France and Britain – and neo-colonial scholarship in Britain – as case studies. After a summary of the remaining 27 chapters in the book, this Introduction concludes with an examination of calls for reparations for slavery and colonialism by Caribbeans (37 million people), North Americans (47.9 million African Americans and 1.5 million black Canadians), South Americans (130 million people of colour), and Africans (1.4 billion people).[9]

The Black Atlantic and Global Africa: A Resilient Continent and Its Diaspora[10]

The Black Atlantic's "triple burden" involves efforts by Africa and its diaspora to alleviate the devastating impacts of slavery and colonialism through achieving reparatory justice. This strategy is being pursued by addressing the historical and structural damage caused to black and brown people in Africa, the Caribbean, and the Americas. This book acknowledges the continuing legacies and impacts of the twin scourges of transatlantic slavery and colonialism, and the fact that the culmination of Africa's liberation struggles was mirrored by similar battles in the Caribbean as well as the American Civil Rights Movement. Both involved citizens of Global Africa.

The use of the term "Global Africa" in this chapter is consistent with Kenyan scholar Ali Mazrui's definition of the term as involving both geography and movement. As he noted: "Global Africa ... is divided between the Black Atlantic and the Black Indian Ocean. The Black Atlantic combines the African continent with the part of the African Diaspora that is located in Europe and the Western hemisphere ... Four continents thus constitute the Black Atlantic – Africa, Europe, North America, and South America, accompanied by neighbouring islands, especially the islands of the Caribbean. The Black Indian Ocean, on the other hand, consists mainly of Africa and Asia."[11]

The "Black Atlantic", used in the title of this volume and Introduction, is a term popularised by Guyanese-British scholar Paul Gilroy in a 1993 study. Gilroy's central organising symbol is "ships in motion across the spaces between Europe, America, Africa, and the Caribbean". He explains that "ships immediately focus attention on the middle passage, on the various projects for redemptive return to an African homeland, on the circulation of ideas and activists as well as the movement of key cultural and political artefacts".[12] Gilroy sees the Black Atlantic as representing an amalgamation of the cultures of the four regions of the Middle Passage, which transcends ethnicity and nationality to produce something new and modern. For him, modernity is the result of a hybridity to which the black dispersal has contributed substantively.[13] The Atlantic world economy emerged from these interactions. The triangular transatlantic trade involved the export of textiles, arms, and wine from Europe to Africa; the forced migration of slaves by European ships from Africa to the Americas; and the export of coffee and sugar from the Americas to Europe. This is thus the story of the birth of the modern capitalist world that has shaped global trade, finance, consumer tastes, lifestyles, and fashion for five centuries (see Nimako in this volume).

While acknowledging Gilroy's contributions to the concept, in this book I define the Black Atlantic in the sense used by Ali Mazrui, which is narrowly focused on a political geography of race. The Black Atlantic is thus a child of the transatlantic slave trade from the fifteenth to the nineteenth centuries,[14] while the Black Indian Ocean emerged largely out of the Arab slave trade from 652 CE until the 1960s. Mazrui adds a more recent "diaspora of colonialism" to his analysis, which he defines as "the dispersal of Africans which continues to occur as a result of colonization and its aftermath".[15] This newer diaspora is particularly well represented in present-day Europe and America. Mazrui argues that the United States historically forced its enslaved Africans to forget their African ancestry, and focus instead on their racial identity. Global Africa thus represents an effort to "re-Africanise" the diaspora in the Americas, the Caribbean, and Europe.[16]

As part of the Black Atlantic struggle from the eighteenth century, black churches and civil society groups in the United States, the Caribbean, and Europe mobilised against European slavery and colonialism. After the birth of the global Pan-African movement in 1900, at a conference in London led by the Trinidadian lawyer Henry Sylvester Williams and black South African activist Alice Kinloch, African American and European civil society groups criticised the barbaric brutalities of Belgian king Leopold's rule in the Congo; opposed the Italian fascist dictator Benito Mussolini's occupation of Ethiopia between 1936 and 1941; and, from 1948, vociferously condemned the inhumane treatment of the black population in apartheid South Africa.[17] One of the most practical manifestations of Global Africa occurred in 1986 when the Congressional Black Caucus (CBC) and African American lobby group TransAfrica had their greatest success in forcing the Ronald Reagan administration (by overriding a presidential veto) to impose economic sanctions on South Africa's racist regime in October 1986.[18]

The cultural aspects of the Black Atlantic are also important to stress. As the African American intellectual Amiri Baraka notes, "blues could not exist if the African captives had not become American captives".[19] Blues and jazz both emerged directly from slavery, based on the rhythmic West African traditional work songs that the slaves sang on southern US plantations. The improvisational nature of jazz is also tied to this same slave culture.[20] It is no exaggeration to note that American popular music – from jazz to Motown to hip-hop and rap – had its roots in this very slave tradition. It is also no surprise that some of the saddest and most humiliated people in the world invented the singing of the blues, underlining the African American writer Maya Angelou's insight in the poem, quoted at the beginning of this Introduction, about "why the caged bird sings".[21] Most of the enslaved in the Americas brought traditional religions that were later fused with Catholicism. The pantheon of Yoruba gods is now arguably more widely preserved in Brazil and Cuba than in its Nigerian homeland.

Slavery: Europe's Original Sin[22]

The Transatlantic Slave Trade

Slavery was undoubtedly Europe's "original sin" against Africa. European locusts – explorers, slavers, merchants, missionaries, imperialists – arrived in Africa in the fifteenth century, and for the next five centuries ravaged the continent. The Portuguese were transporting enslaved Africans to Cape Verde and Madeira islands by the 1480s, while Spanish *conquistadors* shipped Africans to the Caribbean from 1502. In the process, they spread destructive plague and pestilence. As with biblical locusts, the agricultural sector, in which most Africans found employment, was destroyed; famines proliferated; and the greatest migration in human history was enforced, with enchained human cargo being transported to the Caribbean and the Americas as chattel in totally degrading circumstances. In comparing European slavery to a plague, this crime can be likened in its destructive socio-economic impact to the Black Death (1346–1353), which killed over 50 million of medieval Europe's 80 million people: an astonishing 60 per cent of the population.[23] But there is an important distinction: while the Black Death was a natural disaster that lasted eight years, the slave trade was a human act that endured for over four centuries.

Colonialism was the continuation of slavery by other means, with enslavement dehumanising Africans globally and providing the racist justifications and economic methods to implement colonial rule on the basis that black people could not yet stand on their own feet in the difficult conditions of "Western civilisation". Slavery often existed alongside colonialism, and both were inseparable. Portugal, for example, occupied Angola in 1574, having been trading in slaves from contemporary Mauritania, São Tomé, Nigeria, and Angola for 133 years. Lisbon started exporting slaves to Brazil by the 1530s (see Coquery-Vidrovitch and Silva Jr in this volume). France established settlement colonies and trading posts in Madagascar in 1642 and Senegal from 1659, while simultaneously exporting African slaves to Haiti, Martinique, and Guadeloupe. England established a settler colony on James Island in the Gambia River in 1661 and colonies in Sierra Leone in 1787 and the Cape of Good Hope in 1806, even as it exported slaves from Africa to plantations in Barbados, Jamaica, and Antigua from the seventeenth century.

France, Spain, England, Portugal, the Netherlands, and Denmark occupied and traded with territories in the Caribbean and South America from the sixteenth century.[24] European imperial powers also sold and seized stolen property to and from each other: England annexed Jamaica and Trinidad from Spain in 1655 and 1797 respectively; the French seized Louisiana from Spain in 1802, before selling it to the United States for $15 million a year later. Spain was forced to cede Florida to the United States in 1819, and to surrender Guam and Puerto Rico to Washington, while selling the Philippines to America for $20 million in 1899. The Danes sold the Virgin Islands to the United States for $25 million in 1917[25] (see also Kerr-Ritchie and Brereton in this volume).

Four centuries of European enslavement of Africans (1450–1888), who were sent to work on plantations in the Caribbean and the Americas, thus created the Black Atlantic, and flowed seamlessly into a century of European imperialism on the African continent. Both systems involved profit-driven exploitation – cloaked under the perverse justifications of a *mission civilisatrice* – which blamed their African victims for their own misfortunes, while the whole enterprise was legitimised by Western politicians, monarchs, capitalists, churches, slavers, and scientists.

Aside from numerous slave revolts in the Caribbean and the Americas, there were many cases of African resistance to European colonialism. One of the most famous was the seventeenth-century Queen Njinga, who ruled the Ndongo kingdom in what is now Angola, for three decades. She bravely resisted Portuguese colonisers through adroit diplomacy and military prowess, and by forging effective alliances.[26] Pan-Africanist movements also emerged by the eighteenth century to provide African resistance to the evils of slavery. It is no coincidence that Pan-Africanism was born in the United States and the Caribbean as a response to European enslavement. This struggle (assessed in greater detail later in this chapter) was led by the descendants of African slaves in the diaspora, fighting for both their freedom and that of Africans on the mother continent. The Haitian Revolution, which created the world's first black republic – and only the second republic in the hemisphere after the United States – was achieved in 1804, as the result of a slave revolt.

During the transatlantic slave trade, between 12 and 15 million Africans were transported to the Caribbean and the Americas.[27] The slavers involved mostly European states and included merchants and plantation owners from England, France, Portugal, Spain, the Netherlands, Denmark, and Sweden. By the seventeenth century, slaves were being exported by these European nations to work on sugar plantations in Caribbean islands like Jamaica, Cuba, Haiti, Trinidad, Tobago, Martinique, and Barbados, as well as South and Latin American countries such as Brazil, Mexico, Peru, and Colombia (see Brereton, Aragón Falomir, Nimako, Silva Jr, and Ramirez in this volume).

The United States, which had been born out of the European genocide of indigenous Indians, was also deeply involved in the trade, having inherited sugar, tobacco, and rice-growing slave plantations, with 700,000 enslaved people, from former English overlords at the country's independence (for the white population) in 1776. Slavery eventually spread through Virginia, North Carolina, South Carolina, Georgia, Arkansas, Kentucky, Tennessee, Alabama, Mississippi, Louisiana, and Texas, where cotton plantations were established by the eighteenth century to feed British textile factories, alongside plantations producing coffee, sugar, tobacco, rice, olives, and grapes. Cotton became the heart of the American economy, greatly enabling US industrialisation (see Kerr-Ritchie in this volume).

These slaves came mostly from such modern-day African countries as Senegal, Gambia, Ghana, Nigeria, Benin, Côte d'Ivoire, Mali, Guinea-Bissau, the Democratic Republic of the Congo (DRC), Congo-Brazzaville, Cameroon, Gabon, Angola, Tanzania, Malawi, Mozambique, and Zambia (see Coquery-Vidrovitch, Mtombeni, and Klein in this volume). The captives were often kidnapped in wars between African kingdoms and principalities, while some had been convicted of domestic crimes of a sometimes dubious nature. About 80 per cent of the slaves were exported to the Americas in the eighteenth and early nineteenth centuries.[28] An estimated 25–35 per cent of these slaves died en route, while about 30 per cent were thrown overboard to their deaths in aquatic Atlantic graves.[29] Widespread abuse of female bodies took place throughout the Middle Passage, both in the Americas and in Africa, as well as on slave ships.[30]

On their arrival in the New World, the surviving slaves were typically branded with a hot iron, given European names, and – in the United States especially – often denied the right to speak their own languages or practise their own indigenous African religions. They were also prevented from learning to read and write. Within three years, 25 to 33 per cent of the slaves taken to Jamaica had died from the inhumane 16–18-hour work days, and few lived for more than nine years, as they were literally worked to death.[31]

Millions of the most productive African men and women (typically between the ages of 15 and 35) were enslaved in their prime, and an entire continent was depopulated of some of its most productive workforce. Africa's population stagnated between 1650 and 1850, and ecological damage was caused in some depopulated areas, where the tsetse fly forced populations to migrate. African agriculture suffered greatly, and famines increased in some areas, as slave hunters and warriors were prioritised over farmers and entrepreneurs.[32] Slavery effectively arrested human and socio-economic development and intra-regional trade across Africa. The inhuman trade provided the capital for Europe's and America's industrial revolutions. The West's industrialisation was thus literally built on the back of African slavery resulting in the emergence of the contemporary global capitalist economy.[33]

The Portuguese were among the earliest slave traders from the fifteenth century. England, however, soon became the largest slave-trading nation after establishing colonies in the Caribbean by the middle of the seventeenth century (along with France and Spain), based largely on exports from slaveholding sugar plantations. As they had done in the United States, Europeans annihilated most of the indigenous Amerindian population in the Caribbean by the seventeenth century in another genocidal act. England's Royal African Company was created in 1672, and was granted a monopoly of the African slave trade, transporting on average 5,000 enslaved Africans a year to Caribbean plantations between 1680 and 1686. This monopoly ended 26 years later under pressure from the "plantocracy" of English merchants and planters in the Caribbean, who pushed for free trade in slaves. In 1750, the Company of Merchants – slave traders based largely in Bristol, London, and Liverpool – took over this sordid commerce, and greatly accelerated it. Between 1680 and 1786, over 2 million African slaves were shipped to British colonies in the Caribbean in vessels with names like *Enterprise*, *Fortune*, and *Lottery*.[34]

This slave trade laid the foundations of modern British industry and banking, and had widespread support within society. As the Trinidadian scholar-politician Eric Williams noted in his seminal 1944 study of slavery and capitalism, until 1783 "the monarchy, the government, the church, [and] public opinion in general supported the slave trade".[35] Slave traders also included British parliamentarians, the Barclay and Baring banking families, and several prominent Boston families in the United States such as the Seavers, the Shirleys, the Eustices, the Lamberts, and the Welds. The English further supplied an estimated 500,000 slaves to Spanish and French sugar plantations in the Americas. British colonial rivalry with the French in the eighteenth century revolved largely around African slaves and Caribbean sugar. French slave traders operated out of the ports of Nantes, Bordeaux, La Rochelle, and Le Havre.

Aside from the Caribbean, Portugal established the first African slave plantation in São Tomé in 1500, while a French slave presence was established on plantations in Mauritius and the Seychelles. European priests blessed slaves boarding vessels. The British government and British churches went along with their planters' insistence on denying slaves the right to religious worship, while Moravian missionaries in Jamaica themselves held slaves. The church also marched in lockstep with the Devil in Spanish colonies, being involved in both slaveholding and sugar-growing. Catholic missionaries in Brazil exploited the indigenous Amerindian population for two centuries until the eighteenth century (see Silva Jr and Ramirez in this volume). But the system of slavery contained the seeds of its own destruction, as the industrial capitalism of the nineteenth century, which had been financed by the proceeds of slavery in the preceding four centuries, rendered the slave trade anachronistic.

Although there was internal slavery in African societies, this phenomenon had never formed the basis of the social system, and there was often social mobility within this structure. These were not "slaves" in the European sense, in which human beings totally lost their freedom and became the property of slave masters.[36] Though many African chiefs, warlords, and merchants from kingdoms such as Oyo, Benin, Dahomey, and Asante shamefully took part in providing slaves to European slavers and greatly profited from this trade,[37] they were not its main beneficiaries and were a tiny cog in a much larger European wheel. Most African leaders also eventually opposed the slave trade, and some were killed and their territories destroyed for obstructing the trade.[38] Furthermore, the goods that some of these African traders obtained in exchange for slaves were often of inferior quality: old pots and kettles, substandard gunpowder, cheap gin, trinkets, cloth, alcohol, and beads.[39]

This was a grossly unequal exchange, and slavery's main profiteers and the trade's initiators and promoters were based in Europe and America, not in Africa. Chiefs who were unwilling to provide slaves were put under tremendous pressure, and European slavers often used force against uncooperative Africans.[40] The insatiable Western demand for slaves in fact fuelled and exacerbated conflicts in African societies, as chiefs sought to capture prisoners of war to sell into serfdom. Pressure also led to more widespread kidnapping and wider definitions of crime in African societies in order to provide sufficient slaves to satisfy the gluttony of white slavers.[41] Formal slavery was thus not abolished out of any moral conscience on the part of European slavers and governments but because industrialisation rendered it inefficient. Perversely, after the end of formal slavery, it was slave-owning planters who were compensated by their American, British, Dutch, and other European governments, not the victims of four centuries of unpaid labour or their descendants.

African Resistance to Slavery

Despite the horrors of the transatlantic Middle Passage, there were many acts of African resistance during the four and a half centuries of slavery, which represent the first stirrings of Pan-Africanism in the Black Atlantic. Mutinies and revolts occurred throughout the age of slavery, while many enslaved escaped, particularly from the American South to the North. Slave revolts started in the Americas as early as 1522. In the Caribbean, the famous maroon community in Jamaica (descended largely from Ghanaian slaves) resisted English colonialism right from its start in 1655. They launched major rebellions from their hilltop dwellings in 1673 and 1685, which involved waging guerrilla warfare to destroy plantations and to free slaves. An estimated 400 slave revolts occurred in Jamaica, England's richest Caribbean colony. The Maroon War (1729–39) saw local guerrillas launch hit-and-run strikes against British colonisers and their local militias. London was eventually forced to sue for peace, and agreed a treaty allowing the maroons to continue ruling themselves in their enclaves – and not shelter escaped slaves – in exchange for a British pledge not to enslave them.[42]

There was another major confrontation in Jamaica in 1760 when over a thousand slaves confronted the British planters for six months, resulting in the deaths of about 60 white inhabitants and the execution of an estimated 600 black slaves. The second Maroon War erupted in 1795 when London sought to renege on the previous accord. The maroons again killed members of the local British-backed militia, and 556 maroons were deported to Canada. Three major slave rebellions erupted in Jamaica, Suriname, and St Vincent in the early 1770s; the Bussa rebellion was staged in Barbados in 1816; while other slave rebellions took place in Trinidad and Tobago in 1819, 1825, and 1829, and in Antigua and Jamaica in 1831.

The success of the Haitian Revolution (1791–1804) gave Africa's enslaved populations throughout the Caribbean and the Americas a sense of dignity and self-worth, and struck great fear in white plantation owners throughout the hemisphere. This was the most famous black rebellion and the only successful one. At the same time as European revolutionaries were rising up against the absolutist rule of monarchs in countries like France, Haitian revolutionaries rose up against the arbitrary and brutal reign of terror of French and Spanish slave masters. The revolt was led by figures such as Toussaint L'Ouverture and Jean-Jacques Dessalines. The Trinidadian author Cyril Lionel Robert (C.L.R.) James memorialised the revolution in his seminal book, *The Black Jacobins* (1938).[43] Several thousand African Americans migrated to Haiti from

Philadelphia and other cities soon after the revolt. On the cultural front, Haitians used their African roots to develop the religion of Voodoo, which played a part in the revolution. Furthermore, a large slave rebellion took place in Cuba in 1812, while over 200 Muslim slaves in the Brazilian city of Salvador – inspired by the Haitian Revolution – staged the Revolt of the Malê in 1835.

In the United States, slave revolts took place throughout the 246-year period of the existence of this institution. A large rebellion occurred in Virginia in 1800. Twenty-two years later, slaves revolted in South Carolina. In 1831 the black preacher Nat Turner's slave rebellion in Virginia became the bloodiest black revolt in American history, in which over 60 white inhabitants were killed, before it was halted and its perpetrators executed. The draconian Fugitive Slave Act of 1850 forced Americans in the slave-free North to hand over any escaped slaves to their Southern masters, thus making free black slaves everywhere vulnerable to kidnapping and enslavement. The notorious 1857 Dred Scott decision saw the US Supreme Court argue that black slaves were not American citizens, and upheld the Fifth Amendment, which stated that the enslaved were the property of their owners. About 500,000 slaves risked their lives to escape from Southern plantations to the North during the American Civil War (1861–1865), with an estimated 200,000 joining the Union army. During their own war of independence, black soldiers suffered about 40,000 fatalities fighting for the Union.[44]

The African American abolitionist Harriet Tubman was born into slavery in the American South but escaped in 1849 by walking a hundred miles from Maryland to Pennsylvania. She then joined the Anti-Slavery Society to become a "conductor" on the Underground Railroad, an intricate network used by escaping slaves. She returned 19 times to free at least 70 slaves. During the American Civil War, Tubman became the first female commander, leading an all-black battalion to liberate over 700 slaves in South Carolina. This pioneering activist also campaigned for women's rights as part of the suffragette movement (see also Broyld in this volume).[45]

The Cultural Impact of Slaves on Societies in the Americas

Resistance to slavery also took cultural forms. The Kenyan intellectual Micere Mugo has highlighted the importance of orature – the art of the spoken word – which was used by artists and activists to bring about social change in society. As she noted: "When Africans were taken into slavery in the Americas and the Caribbean islands, they not only utilised orature across the Middle Passage to resist and survive terror, but recreated it, emerging with new oratures that spoke to the realities they were encountering and wrestling with under enslavement. Song, dance, music, stories, myths, legends, proverbs, ritual incantations and oracy were the most commonly used genres ..."[46]

Much of this orature was reflected in the "Negro" spirituals characteristic especially of slaves in the American South and captured so eloquently by the African American intellectual W.E.B. Du Bois in his book *The Souls of Black Folk* (1903).[47] Such songs as "Go Down, Moses", "Deep River", and "Swing Low, Sweet Chariot" evoked slaves seeking succour in Christian tales of deliverance from the bondage of autocratic European pharaohs. These lamentations thus represented a call for a black Moses to lead Africans from the clutches of slavery back to the Promised Land of their ancestral homelands.[48]

On the cultural front, slaves in Jamaica sought, to the extent possible under their difficult circumstances, to maintain their African cultures by enacting religious rituals and by reciting folktales. The enslaved believed that they would return to the ancestral homeland after death, and their funeral rites involved African drumming, dancing, and singing. The practice of African religions was eventually banned in Jamaica. Black Baptist preachers emerged by the eighteenth century, and African religions were then often incorporated into their preaching, while literacy among slaves was increasingly encouraged.[49]

In the slave system in countries such as Brazil and Cuba, slaves were sometimes allowed to remain with their families and ethnic groups, and mostly mixed-race and female enslaved could buy their freedom.[50] This enabled some of them to retain more of their African cultures. Portuguese-ruled Brazil imported about 5.1 million slaves, the largest number in the Americas. Cuba imported about 778,000 enslaved people, which was the largest for any Spanish colony. Both countries thus accounted for around 40 per cent of all Africans who were forcibly transported during the transatlantic slave trade (see also Silva Jr, Ramirez, and Nerín and Tofiño in this volume).[51] Slavery was not abolished in Cuba and Brazil until 1886 and 1888 respectively, and both countries used slaves to produce sugar and coffee. Most of these slaves came from West and Central Africa, bringing traditional religions that were later fused with Catholicism. In both countries, slaves were baptised, and many joined Catholic lay brotherhoods.[52]

In Brazil, plantations had been established from Rio de Janeiro to Porto Alegre, and enslaved populations also produced much of the craft in the country.[53] African cultures greatly influenced Brazilian religion, the arts, literature, music, and social institutions. In 2024, the more than 100 million

African-descended Brazilians represented the third-largest such population in the world after Nigeria and Ethiopia.[54] Yoruba cosmology and *orishas* (deities) like Obatala, Shango, Ogun, and Yemoja (Yemanja) were fused with Catholic saints to form the Afro-Brazilian religion of Candomblé, which is still strongly practised in the 1,100 temples in Salvador, the capital of the black-majority Bahia state. A similar syncretism occurred in Trinidad (see Brereton in this volume), while African religion, music, and oral traditions also continued to shape the Dutch Caribbean islands of Suriname and Curaçao (see Allen in this volume).

The Brazilian music and dance form of Capoeira was originated by African slaves, who used it as a disguised form of self-defence. In 1832, the Society for the Protection of the Needy was founded by free black Brazilian slaves as a civil society movement, which purchased the freedom of fellow enslaved people. But, despite the prominence of black Brazilian footballers such as Pelé, Garrincha, Ronaldinho, and Vinicius Jr, black youths in impoverished *favelas* (ghettos) like Rio de Janeiro's "City of God" – immortalised in a 2002 movie – continue to be gunned down in disproportionate numbers by security forces: a constant reminder of the racial inequalities that continue to prevail in this mythical "racial democracy". Affirmative action programmes for blacks in Brazilian universities were only initiated in 2003.[55]

In Cuba, the enslaved worked plantations, from Havana province to La Isabelica. These African slaves contributed to national religions such as Santeria, Palo-Monte, and Voodoo, with African deities – as in Brazil – fused with Catholic saints to produce a Cuban national identity. The Abakuá male secret society (originating from south-west Cameroon and Nigeria's Old Calabar) became one of the country's most important social institutions. Its members were prominent in social events like carnivals, and many of these black Abakuá took part in rebellions and other demonstrations throughout the nineteenth century.[56] Enslaved individuals fought in Cuba's war of independence (1868–1878) but were marginalised after the war by a racist Spanish-descended elite. African religious and cultural expressions were banned until the 1920s, when *son* music – a blend of African percussions and vocals with Spanish strings – became popular again. Afro-Cubans benefited from Fidel Castro's 1959 revolution in terms of free education and health care, but prejudice against blacks still remains rife on the island.[57]

A century after the formal abolition of slavery in the Caribbean, the Rastafarian movement emerged out of Jamaica in the 1930s as a religious and spiritual movement swearing allegiance to the divinity of Ethiopian Emperor Haile Selassie. Its adherents were heavily influenced by the Bible, Garveyism,

Ethiopianism, and Pan-Africanism. They sought to move out of the Western hemisphere (Babylon) to a paradisiac Africa (Zion). Rastas wore dreadlocks, maintained a strict diet of vegetarianism, and smoked marijuana. From the 1960s, reggae music became closely linked to the movement largely through Bob Marley and the Wailers, who did much to maintain the bridge between Africa and its diaspora, starring in the concert that celebrated Zimbabwe's independence in April 1980.[58]

Marley's visit to Ethiopia in 1979 reinforced his Pan-African identity, and shortly afterwards he recorded the liberation song "Zimbabwe". The song appeared in his 1979 *Survival* album with flags of African countries and a slave ship, as Marley increasingly made connections between the struggles in Africa and its diaspora. Other songs on the *Survival* album included "Africa Unite". The 1976 song "War" was an anti-apartheid lament, while albums such as the 1977 *Exodus*, the 1980 *Uprising*, and the posthumous 1983 *Confrontation* championed similar themes of black emancipation. Marley's astonishing legacy was confirmed by the fact that his music, involving about 20 major albums, still accounted for half of all reggae records sold by 2008.[59] *Time* magazine voted *Exodus* the album of the century in 1999. Other popular reggae artists included Jimmy Cliff, Burning Spear, Steel Pulse, Culture, and the Mighty Diamond.

Despite four centuries of European dehumanisation and the enslavement of Africans on their continent and in the Caribbean and the Americas, African slaves showed incredible resilience just to have survived these horrors. Not only did they survive, however, but they also left an indelible mark on the mainstream cultures of countries across the Western hemisphere.

Colonialism: How Europe Underdeveloped and Brutalised Africa[60]

The link between slavery and colonialism is inextricable. As the Nigerian historian Jacob Ade Ajayi noted: "The Trans-Atlantic slave trade paved the way for colonialism in several ways. It integrated the economy of several African peoples into that of the Americas and Europe, and thus into a capitalist world economy dominated by western Europe ... The overall result was underdevelopment ... The legacy of wars ensured that Africans could not unite to protect their interests in the way that Europeans were able to coordinate their plans for the partition of Africa at the Congress of Berlin."[61]

Scholars like Guyana's Walter Rodney, in his 1972 classic, *How Europe Underdeveloped Africa*, have also shown how European powers created the economic dependence of the "periphery" on the metropolitan "core" in order to perfect the system of colonial rule in the Caribbean and the Americas during two centuries of imperial slavery, before formally applying it to Africa for a century. European plantation owners in the Caribbean and the Americas used their wealth to increase consumer demand at home, which in turn fostered greater economic activity in the metropolis (see Timcke and Gomes in this volume). Rodney – who taught at the University of Dar es Salaam in Julius Nyerere's Tanzania – traced the roots of African underdevelopment to the 1884–1885 "curse of Berlin",[62] the conference at which European powers set the rules for an orderly partition of African territories. He lamented the consumerist rather than productive nature of African economies and the general lack of savings across the continent. Rodney further bemoaned Africa's declining terms of trade, unequal exchange, and exploitation by both European colonial powers and the United States, which he argued integrated African economies into their capitalist systems on vastly unequal terms in a structure built during the slave trade. Rodney thus called for African self-reliance and self-sustainability to reverse the harmful impact of these Western designs.[63]

Africa was notoriously declared a *res nullius* – a no man's land – conquered by brutal European imperialists such as Britain's Cecil Rhodes and Belgium's King Leopold II. The Scottish missionary-explorer David Livingstone described colonialism in the apparently benign terms of the "three Cs": Commerce, Christianity, and Civilisation. The more malign "three Ps" may, in fact, have been more accurate: Profit, Plunder, and Prestige. The search for new markets amidst a global Great Depression in the early 1880s was a widespread concern that spurred on European imperialism in Africa. Scientific techniques were introduced into colonial territories that led to the extraction of minerals like diamonds and gold and the production of cash crops like cocoa, coffee, palm oil, rubber, cotton, and tobacco. African economies were thus structured – as the economies in the Caribbean and the Americas had been for two centuries – to produce crops to meet European consumer needs. This both increased African dependence on metropolitan economies and, in many cases, negatively impacted on their ability to produce their own food. Africans – like Caribbeans and Latin Americans – thus typically imbibed Western consumption patterns without acquiring Western production methods.

The Berlin Conference of 1884–1885, which was overseen by Germany's "Iron Chancellor", Otto von Bismarck, dealt with the issue of free trade in the Congo and the Niger as well as the status of protectorates, effectively setting the rules for the partition of Africa. Berlin represented the compromises of European imperialists rather than the political and economic interests of Africans. The European curse of artificial nation-states has thus caused untold suffering in post-colonial Africa, resulting in unviable, dependent economies, 16 land-locked countries, artificially imported political systems, weak and balkanised states, and insecure borders. Bismarck was undoubtedly the Grand Wizard of the Berlin Conference. The German sorcerer and his European apprentices employed the Western wizardry of the technology of the industrial revolution – scientific and technological advances, mass production of goods, global finance, expansion of railways and roads, the telegraph, and the Maxim gun – to set the rules for the "Scramble for Africa". Bismarck used his political magic wand to cast a spell on Africa, having earlier done the same in Europe.[64]

The "New Imperialism", which erupted into the "Scramble for Africa" by the 1880s, saw European powers seeking their own "place in the sun", an African sun that, it was said, would never set on the British Empire. As late as 1880, relatively few African territories had come under direct European rule (though Portugal had occupied Angola since 1575, and France and Britain had established settler colonies in Africa from the seventeenth century), and 80 per cent of the continent was still ruled by its own leaders. In 1830, the French colonisation of Algeria started.[65] In 1881, Paris declared a "protectorate" over Tunisia, and a year later over Porto-Novo in Dahomey (now Benin).[66] The British occupied Egypt in 1882. Even before sending out invitations to the Berlin Conference in October 1884, Bismarck himself had extended the *Reichsschutz* (the protection of the Reich) to South West Africa (now Namibia) and acquired that territory along with Cameroon and Togo by August 1884. A day after the end of the Berlin Conference in February 1885, Bismarck acquired German East Africa: clear evidence, if any were needed, that the Berlin Conference was indeed about how to ensure an orderly partition of Africa.[67]

These events triggered the start of one of the most barbaric episodes in European imperialism, with widespread atrocities and forced labour on rubber plantations overseen by Belgian colonial authorities, resulting in an estimated 10 million African deaths.[68] This landmark conference would prove to be a watershed in African history: it had set the rules for trade, navigation, and control of Africa to avoid conflicts among European nations. Berlin had fired the starting gun for the imperial partition, and in the next two and a half decades almost the entire landmass of Africa would be parcelled out among

European colonial powers. Africa was often described in culinary terms as food to be devoured by greedy imperialists in juicy morsels at the avaricious imperial banquet in Berlin. The continent was frequently compared to a big fruitcake to be shared out: Tunis was described as a 'ripe pear', and terms like 'plums' and 'cherries' were bandied around to describe the compromises struck by European imperialists over African territories. Berlin represented a grandiloquent banquet at which gluttonous European imperialists feasted on territories that clearly did not belong to them. They sought in the process to cloak the fraudulent scheme under the patronising and paternalistic moral platitudes of a "civilising" mission.

The German Genocide in Namibia

One of the most repugnant episodes of European colonial rule in Africa was the German genocide in its colony of South West Africa (modern Namibia) in 1904–1908 (see also Blackler in this volume). A decade after Otto von Bismarck declared a protectorate over South West Africa in 1884, the ruthless military commander Curt von François launched an unprovoked massacre of indigenous people. In January 1904, reacting against the theft of their land and cattle by German citizens, the Herero – led bravely by guerrillas like Samuel Maharero – killed a hundred white settlers during an uprising. Nine months later, the German commanding general, Lothar von Trotha – known as "the human shark" – issued a *Vernichtungsbefehl* for the extermination of the Herero for having had the temerity to rebel against the dispossession of their own land and cattle. Trotha was chilling in his savagery: "Any Herero found inside the German frontier, with or without a gun or cattle, will be executed. I shall spare neither women nor children."[69]

The Herero waged a courageous resistance but were simply overpowered by German machine guns, cannons, and bayonets. They were defeated at the Waterberg in August 1904, resulting in floggings, mass executions, and hangings. Forced into the Kalahari desert, many died of starvation and thirst. The survivors were carted off in cattle trucks to concentration camps in Swakopmund, Lüderitz, and Windhoek, where many were beaten and raped, and thousands died from slave labour. Some were deliberately infected with tuberculosis, typhus, and smallpox. Eugenics policies were initiated, with inmates forced to scrape the flesh of kinsfolk and boil human skulls, about 3,000 of which were sent back to Germany for pseudo-scientific experiments.[70]

The Nama uprising – courageously led by Hendrik Witbooi – was equally ruthlessly quashed, with the rebels locked up in cold death camps on Shark Island. By 1908, an estimated 90,000 people – 80 per cent of the total Herero population and 50 per cent of the Nama population – had been massacred in the twentieth century's first genocide. Many unmarked mass graves of Herero remain in Swakopmund and in railway yards in the capital of Windhoek. Many historians regard the Namibian genocide as having been a grisly dress rehearsal for the Jewish Holocaust two decades later.[71]

Neo-colonialism: The Lingering Impacts of European Imperialism

Having provided the background to European slavery and colonialism, it is important to stress the continuities of this colonialism across the Black Atlantic, which have been widely dubbed "neo-colonialism".[72] This involves the phenomenon of former colonial states continuing patterns of paternalistic political, economic, and/or cultural thought and action with their former colonies after these states gained formal independence. France and Britain provide useful case studies, especially since the two largest imperial powers in Africa also now host 4 million African-descended populations (about 2 million in each country), which are the most sizeable such populations in Europe.[73] Four examples suffice to illustrate this point: the French role in its former African colonies, and the brutalisation of its Arab, African, and Caribbean populations; and a continuing portrayal by some British academics of its empire as benign, as well as continuing British maltreatment of its Caribbean citizens.

France: The Myth of Liberté, Egalité, and Fraternité[74]

Modern-day France often likes to pride itself as the heir of progressive regicidal revolutionaries as enshrined in its national motto: *liberté, égalité*, and *fraternité* (liberty, equality, and fraternity). Former French president François Mitterrand prophetically noted in 1957: "Without Africa, France will no longer have a history in the twenty-first century."[75] For the next six and a half decades, an intricate network of political, military, economic, and cultural ties – known as *Françafrique* – has been used to promote what French leaders regarded as a *politique de grandeur*. All French presidents of the Fifth Republic from Charles de Gaulle have continued this neo-colonial Africa policy.

After the independence of most African colonies, French *coopérants* continued to provide technical assistance to African ministries, sometimes overruling national ministers. In a clearly corrupt system, African leaders in Côte d'Ivoire and Gabon funded the political campaigns of Gaullist parties in France. For nearly three decades, highly personalised relations with African rulers were entrusted to Jacques Foccart, an *éminence grise* and master of the *secret du roi*, who established his infamous *réseaux africains*: clandestine networks of spooks and soldiers, priests and policemen, and murderers and mercenaries.[76]

During the Cold War, Washington considered France's role useful in keeping the Soviet Union out of Africa. For six decades, the French *gendarme* acted like a pyromaniac fireman, intervening over 50 times in Africa. The franc zone saw 13 francophone African states tying their CFA (*Communauté financière d'Afrique*) franc to the French franc – and later the euro – with the French treasury holding all of their foreign reserves. French industrial giants such as CFAO, SCOA, Elf Aquitaine and Bouygues continued to monopolise markets they had cornered during the colonial era. France's "cooperation agreements" gave it priority access to Africa's strategic minerals: Gabon and Niger provided Paris with 100 per cent of its uranium, Guinea with 90 per cent of its bauxite, and Cameroon, Congo-Brazzaville, and Gabon with 70 per cent of its oil.[77]

With the end of the Cold War, the idea of an exclusive French *chasse gardée* (private hunting-ground) in Africa came under increasing challenge. French policy reversals left its Africa policy in disarray: it trained and armed Rwandan *génocidaires* in 1993–1994,[78] and supported Zaire's Mobutu Sese Seko long after he had passed his sell-by date, with his regime collapsing in ignominy in 1997. By 1990, pro-democracy demonstrations in Benin, Côte d'Ivoire, Gabon, and Niger forced many francophone states to adopt various forms of multiparty democracy. But France continued to apply democracy inconsistently, sanctioning sham elections in Burkina Faso, Chad, Côte d'Ivoire, Cameroon, Gabon, Niger, and Togo between 1992 and 1996, and resuming aid to fraudulent, undemocratic regimes.

Having periodically rigged elections in its African possessions during colonial times, it has been easy for France to condone undemocratic behaviour in Africa. Former French president Jacques Chirac described democracy as a "luxury" for Africa, demonstrating a paternalism that is all too typical of the French political class, many of whose members – including Chirac himself – have themselves often been embroiled in sleaze and scandals. Paris's unilateral 50 per cent devaluation of the CFA franc in 1994 further dealt a devastating blow to its Africa policy.[79] In May 1996, angry protesters burned down the French cultural centre in the Central African Republic (CAR). (An angry crowd had similarly burned down the French consulate in Bangui, resulting in the intervention of French legionnaires in 1991.) In CAR in January 1997, a bloody French reprisal in revenge for the killing of two French officers left 100 civilians and 50 mutinous African soldiers dead.[80] Proving further that old habits die hard, in October 1997 Paris helped Denis Sassou-Nguesso use military means to topple the elected government of Pascal Lissouba in Congo-Brazzaville.[81] France intervened militarily to save Chadian autocrat Idriss Déby in 2006 and 2008.

Perhaps nothing better symbolises the death of *Françafrique* than the spectacular collapse of France's failed decade-long counter-terrorism war in the Sahel. Paris – already expelled from its military bases in Mali in 2022 and Burkina Faso in 2023 – was asked by putschists in Niger to withdraw its 1,500 troops from the country in 2023. French intervention on the continent has thus become a costly relic of a bygone age of imperial delusion.[82]

France: Brutalising Arab, African, and Caribbean Citizens

Closer to home, the riots by Maghrebi and African and Caribbean citizens in France in June–July 2023 glaringly exposed the profound socio-economic fault lines and dyed-in-the-wool racism of a country in deep denial. The last six post-independence decades have witnessed an obstinate and often abusive neo-colonial relationship with Africa and the Caribbean, which is now fraying at the edges, as the Gallic Emperor's nakedness is increasingly exposed.[83]

Following the emergence of a video of the execution-style killing in June 2023 of a 17-year-old Algerian-Moroccan-French youth, Nahel Merzouk, in broad daylight, by a French policeman at a traffic stop in a Parisian suburb, six nights of rioting erupted across Paris, Marseilles, Lyons, Lille, Dijon, Toulouse, and Strasbourg. These attacks resulted in 3,700 arrests; 5,000 burned cars; 11,000 lit fires; 2,000 looted shops;[84] and attacks on police stations, town halls, tax offices, and post offices: all seen by the protesters as symbols of state oppression. The damage from these attacks reached an estimated €1.1 billion.[85] The officer who killed Nahel was charged with homicide, only because of video evidence of a motorist showing Nahel driving away from the policeman who pointed a gun at his head to shoot him. Before the video emerged, the French police publicly claimed that Nahel had driven straight at the policeman, who it alleged had acted in self-defence.[86]

These events once again highlighted the pent-up anger of brutalised and marginalised black and brown populations in France's destitute *banlieues* (suburbs), which continue to lack basic social services and decent schools, hospitals, and housing, despite half-hearted efforts at urban renewal and failed entrepreneurial projects.[87] Also pertinent is the institutional racism of the French police and the constant harassment of Maghrebi and black African and Caribbean youths living in impoverished housing estates. A culture of impunity is widespread among the French police in these communities, fanned by mainstream politicians, led by President Emmanuel Macron.

The anger of the rioters was raw, as black and brown youths know that, like Nahel, they could easily have been the one shot dead by the police. So many Africans, Caribbeans, and Maghrebi youths have died at the hands of French police under suspicious circumstances. Nahel's death was therefore not unusual, which helps to contextualise the rage of the rioters. Between January 2020 and June 2023, French police killed 21 people in similar circumstances.[88] Most of them were black and brown citizens, who are 20 times more likely to be stopped by police than their white compatriots.[89] The trigger-happy French police are thus regarded in these communities as a dangerous source of insecurity and terror, and not as public protectors. They serve the state, not local communities.

Rather than show sympathy and solidarity with the victim of this ghastly killing, France's self-styled Jupiterian president Emmanuel Macron instead publicly embraced police chiefs, praising their apparent "professionalism".[90] Macron, in his usual macho manner, deployed 45,000 heavily armed police to deal with a situation that was treated like a war against citizens wielding stones and fireworks. The French president was tone-deaf to demands to call off his "mad dogs" unleashed against angry citizens in poor ghettos. Following the riots, fast-track judges in "kangaroo courts" were encouraged to dish out rapid jail sentences in sham trials in which the most basic tenets of the rule of law did not seem to have been observed. Over 380 people were jailed in the first two days of the riots: one 28-year-old man was imprisoned for ten months for stealing a can of Red Bull from a looted supermarket.[91] This "expedited justice" has been contrasted with the five to ten years it can take to achieve any prosecution of policemen who have killed unarmed black and brown French citizens.

Rather than addressing the root causes of the genuine grievances that have triggered this violence, the French government instead tried to distract attention away from the real issues. Playing the populist politician, Macron inanely suggested that video games and social media among youths had catalysed these events, and he threatened to cut off social media, which he accused of spreading hate. He patronisingly put the responsibility on Maghrebi and black parents to keep their children at home.[92] The French president thus used a dog whistle to reinforce widely held stereotypical beliefs among the white majority, of cultures that lack good morals in a society that already widely considers black and Maghrebi citizens "backward" and unrepresentative of "enlightened" French cultural values.

In 2005, French police chased three Maghrebi and black teenagers, who were walking home after playing football, into an electric substation, where two of them – Zyed Benna and Bouna Traoré – were electrocuted, triggering three weeks of riots. The uncouth and insensitive French interior minister, Nicolas Sarkozy – sentenced to three years in prison in March 2021 for corruption and influence-peddling – implied that the teenagers were thieves, as they were running from the police. He also described rioting Maghrebi and black youths as "scum".[93] After the 2023 riots, French politicians again fell over themselves to put out a tough "law and order" message. Interior minister Gérald Darmanin noted: "It's the republic that will win, not the rioters"[94] – language dripping with vulgar jingoism, clearly intended as a coded message of a "civilised" republic under threat from foreign "barbarians". Darmanin later made the extraordinary statement: "police violence doesn't exist."[95] The right-wing head of the French Senate, Bruno Retailleau, also condemned the behaviour of second- and third-generation French migrants, in racist tones, as "regression towards their ethnic roots".[96]

Not to be outdone, two of France's police unions described rioters as "vermin" and "savage hordes" with whom they were "at war".[97] The ill-disciplined French police appear to have inherited the colonial policing culture of the savage Algerian war (1954–1962), when torture and wanton murder of innocent civilians were widespread, eventually resulting in one million Algerian deaths.[98] The highly militarised police – long cited for human rights abuses and discriminatory behaviour by the European Court of Human Rights (ECHR), the Office of the UN High Commissioner for Human Rights (UNHCR), the Council of Europe, Amnesty International, Human Rights Watch,[99] and a plethora of domestic civil rights organisations – responded characteristically to the rioters with armoured personnel carriers, helicopters, stun grenades, and projectiles. A 2017 law making it easier for the police to use their weapons, without necessarily having to justify this on the basis of self-defence, has virtually given the French police the sense that it has a licence to kill.[100]

Furthermore, it is important to note that 41 per cent of the French population – a staggering 13 million people – voted for the openly racist, anti-immigration far-right Marine Le Pen and her National Rally (RN) party in April 2022 presidential elections. Parts of the mainstream French media are also guilty of criminalising black and brown people in their reporting. Many supposedly progressive French academics often condone police brutality against foreigners. In stark contrast to the prejudiced narratives of many Gallic politicians and police, scores of French civic groups and left-wing politicians have demonstrated more understanding and sympathy for the plight of oppressed communities. Almost a hundred trade unions, associations, and left-wing parties – including the Greens and Unbowed France – marched in solidarity to demand police reforms after Nahel's killing. Civil society groups such as SOS Racisme, the Defender of Rights, Mother's Front, and Community House for Solidarity Development have gallantly fought for the voices of the marginalised to be heard, and for institutionalised racism within the French police to be addressed through concrete reforms such as establishing an independent investigative body and conducting an independent audit of police racism. Their marches, letters, and petitions have, however, often gone unheeded.[101]

The fundamental problem of the French social model is that it insists on the myth of imaginary "universalist" values, and as a result bans the collecting of any race-based data, while pretending that racism does not exist.[102] This is despite voluminous research showing the ever-widening gulf between downtrodden Maghrebi and black populations and the rest of society. France insists on a "colour-blind" society and derides Anglo-Saxon "multiculturalism" but has ended up entrenching institutional racism and turning politically invisible and culturally marginalised African, Caribbean, and Maghrebi minorities into second-class citizens. Its assimilationist policies have clearly proved counterproductive, as many black and brown communities continue to reject a mainstream culture that they feel has criminalised them and stripped them of their dignity and humanity. These events clearly demonstrate that the French model of citizenship is completely broken.

Britain's Imperial Apologist

If we turn to another former colonial power, though Britain has not sought to maintain the extensive political, economic, military, and cultural ties with its former colonies as France has done, some of its scholars still demonstrate a colonial mindset, and its government has often adopted a neo-colonial stance towards its Caribbean citizens. England shipped 3.3 million African slaves from its ports to the Caribbean after 1680 (see Brereton and Small in this volume), and introduced slavery into, and colonised, 20 Caribbean countries for nearly three centuries. As earlier noted, Eric Williams demonstrated in his seminal 1944 study *Capitalism and Slavery* that the main beneficiaries of the transatlantic slave trade were the "plantocracy" of British merchants and planters in the Caribbean,[103] while slavery laid the foundations of modern British industry and banking.

Given this sordid history, it is hard to imagine that there are still diehard defenders of Cecil Rhodes, the racist nineteenth-century British imperialist, whom I "tried" in an imaginary African after-life in a 2021 novella, *The Trial of Cecil John Rhodes*.[104] Oxford University's theology professor, Nigel Biggar, has recently made a career out of defending Rhodes's atrocities and attacking what he deems to be politically correct "woke" academics and activists who challenge the arch-imperialist's racism.

In a March 2016 article in the conservative *Standpoint* magazine, "Rhodes, Race and the Abuse of History", Biggar demonised as "zealots" Oxford University's Rhodes Must Fall student-led movement, which called for the removal of the imperialist's statue from Oxford's Oriel College.[105] He flippantly tried to justify Rhodes's description of non-whites as "the most despicable specimens of human beings" by noting that the ruthless imperialist made this comment as a 24-year-old, and "young men often say reckless things".[106] Biggar then went on to argue that the man who pursued a "scorched earth" policy in what is now Zimbabwe in the 1890s – in which his white mercenary hired guns burnt kraals, raped women, plundered cattle, and eventually stole 3.5 million square miles of African real estate – "had a record of good relations with individual Africans", condemning instead the "abominable practices of the Zulu and Ndebele".[107]

Our pseudo-scientific eugenicist then helpfully tells us that "Rhodes thought that blacks were generally inferior, but in terms of cultural development, not biology. He believed they could become civilised."[108] Using the racist trope of "the noble savage", Biggar then reassures us that blacks can be brought up to the "civilised" standards of whites, who massacred and looted in the name of racial superiority. The Oxford don ahistorically attempts to present Rhodes as seeking to establish trust between whites and blacks, implausibly portraying a dyed-in-the-wool racist as a prophet of racial reconciliation. Biggar ultimately discredits himself by making the extraordinarily absurd claim that Rhodes "must be credited with early support of the African National Congress",[109] by – according to him –

providing financial support to the *Izwi Labuntu* newspaper, which promoted black political aspirations. Rhodes, though, was widely known to have paid journalists in a bid to influence and corrupt them.[110]

Biggar next carelessly unmasks his own prejudices in noting: "It is also true that Rhodes saw the British as civilised and African people as not. But he had good reason to think that."[111] As justification for dismissing blacks as barbarians, Biggar cites "science or technology or communications or commerce or liberal policies",[112] thereby revealing his own historical ignorance of how civilisations develop: Christianity arrived in Ethiopia as early as the fourth century when much of Europe was still under the sway of the Roman Empire.

Biggar erroneously accused this author in a May 2021 *Sunday Telegraph* article of making up three Rhodes quotes in a review of Paul Maylam's book *The Cult of Rhodes* (2005), which was published in the *Times Literary Supplement*.[113] He claims that the quote "I prefer land to niggers" appeared in an 1897 novel by Olive Schreiner. But two renowned South African biographers of Rhodes, Paul Maylam and Antony Thomas, have both attributed this statement to Rhodes, as did a 1956 biographer, Felix Gross.[114] Biggar claims that a second Rhodes quote, "the natives are children. They are just emerging from barbarism" was "misleadingly torn from its proper context".[115] However, both Maylam and the Zimbabwean historian Stanlake Samkange[116] confirmed that these words were uttered by Rhodes in a racist July 1894 speech to the Cape parliament.[117]

Finally, Biggar argues that the quote "one should kill as many niggers as possible" is "a mixture of distortion and fabrication". This statement is, however, cited by Maylam.[118] It is shocking that an Oxford don could make such scurrilous charges and consistently peddle prejudice without proper research. Perhaps Biggar should stick to his own field of theology, rather than wallowing in tendentious history. A much more authoritative and rigorously researched study is Caroline Elkins's magisterial study of the British Empire, *Legacy of Violence: A History of the British Empire* (2022).[119]

Britain's Windrush Scandal

A further example of the continuing British colonial mindset was evidenced in the 2018 scandal relating to Caribbean immigrants in the country. The "Windrush generation" are Caribbean nationals whose parents had migrated to Britain between 1948 and 1971 and welcomed by the British government to fill post-Second World War labour shortages. They were guaranteed the right to British citizenship. Between 1948 and 1963, an estimated 300,000

Caribbean immigrants from Jamaica, Trinidad and Tobago, Guyana, St Kitts and Nevis, Antigua and Barbuda, and other islands arrived in Britain. They worked as teachers in Croydon, welders in Leeds, nurses in Manchester, bus drivers in Bristol, motor workers in Luton, seamstresses in Birmingham, seamen in Ipswich, slum landlords in Notting Hill, and Carnival Queens in Chapeltown. These are all people who have been largely rendered invisible to their British hosts, whose lives have never been properly documented, and whose significant contributions to the making of contemporary Britain has never been properly acknowledged.[120]

The West Indians soon felt the hostility of British society. Within a decade, they were greeted with headlines such as "Our Jamaica Problem" and "Racial Troubles in Notting Hill". Nativist British politicians started talking about controlling the "influx" of West Indians, fanning the flames of anti-immigrant xenophobia. Many white British citizens disparaged the immigrants as "savages", "monkeys", and "coons". Official government reports described West Indian workers as "unsuitable for heavy manual work" and "slow mentally". Caribbeans faced open discrimination in employment, housing, and accessing loans and mortgages. Many West Indian Britons thus held on to low-paying, unskilled, menial jobs as if their lives depended on them. Having been denied employment opportunities in most sectors, the exiles subsequently endured the double indignity of being derided as lazy spongers off the British welfare system. They, however, showed resourcefulness in setting up self-help associations and communal funding schemes that helped pay for rent, mortgages, and cars.[121] Caribbean Britons eventually discovered that they kept journeying but somehow never arrived. Never accepted as full citizens, they found themselves permanent exiles in a strange, cold, and inhospitable land.

Many of this "Windrush generation" who had sailed from the Caribbean as infants on their parents' passports did not have travel documents. Between 2014 and 2018, the British Home Office – acting like a Dickensian "Circumlocution Office"[122] – required these arrivals from half a century before to prove that they had not left Britain for two consecutive years, and to produce four pieces of documentary evidence for every year they had resided in Britain, while the ministry inexplicably destroyed an archive of old landing slips that could have helped prove the arrival of many of these migrants.

As home secretary and later prime minister, Theresa May set out deliberately – with overwhelming support from both Conservative and

Labour parliamentarians – to pass draconian immigration Acts in 2014 and 2016 in order to create a "hostile environment". In a reversion to the worst Orwellian tactics of the Nazi era, employers, landlords, banks, schools, and hospitals were turned into border guards, and asked to check the papers of immigrants under the threat of hefty fines or even jail terms. A brutal "deport first, appeal later" policy was adopted. In an action more befitting a banana republic than a democratic state, the government had vans drive into immigrant areas with billboards bearing the sign "Go Home or Face Arrest".

May spoke, in xenophobic tones, about "citizens of nowhere". She set out mechanistically to reduce the number of immigrants to Britain to the arbitrary figure of 100,000 annually, regardless of the human cost. She also bizarrely insisted that students be included in these numbers. Home Office bureaucrats were set targets for deportations, and sometimes broke the law to achieve their quotas. These policies have had a devastating impact on the lives of over 5,000 law-abiding Caribbean immigrants who have lived in Britain for decades. Many faced Kafkaesque situations in which they lost overnight their citizenship, jobs, homes, benefits, pensions, and access to public services, and were jailed and then sometimes deported to countries many had never lived in.

The British government's response to this scandal was as inept as its initial handling of it. Tory home secretary Amber Rudd followed in May's draconian footsteps until forced to resign in April 2018 under relentless parliamentary questioning from the Labour Party after having misled Britain's Home Affairs parliamentary select committee on deportation targets. She was brought back into cabinet by May, seven months later, in a move further underlining the impunity and lack of accountability of British officialdom. A reasonable request from Caribbean leaders at the Commonwealth summit in London in April 2018 for May to discuss the Windrush scandal was contemptuously turned down by the mother country, again demonstrating the inequities of a club in which the wealth has always been far from common.

This was not Britain's finest moment. These events ironically coincided with the fiftieth anniversary of racist Conservative politician Enoch Powell's notorious "rivers of blood" speech in which he warned of race wars if immigration to Britain was not urgently curbed. This is despite 2021 census figures showing that 81.7 per cent of the population of England and Wales was white.[123] The immense contributions of Caribbean citizens to British life – in the arts, politics, literature, food, and sports – have rarely been properly acknowledged, except superficially through annual Notting Hill and Chapeltown carnivals. Boris Johnson, the British prime minister between 2019 and 2022, had earlier epitomised the continuing prejudice at the heart of the British establishment when he noted that "West Indians were allowed to immigrate after the war, multiply like flies and then the great state apparatus took over the care of their multiplications". He also noted, after the shooting of two girls in Birmingham in 2003, that disaffected West Indian youths in the city were "black thugs, sons of black thugs and grandsons of black thugs".[124]

The tired cliché about Britain's "sense of fair play" has never been evidenced by a nation that colonised a quarter of the earth's surface, populating countries with its citizens uninvited, while ruling over them without their consent as a supposed "heaven's breed" of imperial supermen. The irony of the hostility towards citizens of countries that Britain had colonised (and benefited greatly from for nearly three centuries) is thus rather rich. The sun did finally set on the British Empire, but its neo-colonial cultural prejudices continue to linger.

Reparations: Global Africa's Quest for Justice[125]

Only by first explaining the scourges of European slavery, colonialism, and neo-colonialism as we have just done, can we focus in the next section on the critical issue of reparations. It is important to start by noting that it was the cumulative efforts, over nearly two centuries, of Pan-African activists, beginning in the diaspora, that would eventually liberate Africa and the Caribbean from European colonial rule and lay the foundation for the successful African American struggle for civil rights. These were early prophets of reparatory justice for the crimes of slavery and colonialism. It was no coincidence that the contemporary Pan-Africanist movement was born in 1900, 15 years after the partition of the continent was sealed and 24 years after black Americans had had their rights revoked after the brief period of Reconstruction.[126]

The quest for reparations for enslavement and colonialism can thus be traced back to eighteenth-century civil society activism in the African diaspora. It is always important to stress that Pan-Africanism was born in America and the Caribbean, and not in Africa. This section thus examines the emancipation efforts of Pan-African activists from the eighteenth century through figures such as Edward Blyden, widely considered to have been the greatest theoretician of Pan-Africanism. We then assess the Pan-African Conference of 1900 and the five Pan-African Congresses between 1919 and 1945, which led to the movement being handed over from Africans in the diaspora to Africans on the continent. This final section further highlights the contributions of other African Americans, francophone, South American, and lusophone civil society activists to the struggle. Only after having provided this background can we examine more recent reparations struggles in Africa, the Americas, the Caribbean, and Europe.

The Emergence of Pan-African Civil Society

Pan-African civil society activism can be traced back to the 1770s, when an African Baptist Church movement became active in the US, the Caribbean, and Canada. These early reparationists sought to challenge the pervasive racism towards Africans around the globe. In 1773, Phillis Wheatley, a former slave purchased from West Africa by a Boston family, became the first African American woman to publish a book of poetry, which was widely read and helped to promote a more positive image of the black world.[127] As she wrote:

> Some view our sable race with scornful eye
> Their colour is a diabolical die.
> Remember Christians, Negros black as Cain
> May be refin'd, and join th' angelic train.[128]

In the 1780s, Olaudah Equiano and Ottobah Cugoano – Nigerian and Ghanaian former slaves, respectively – established the Sons of Africa organisation in Britain to campaign for the abolition of slavery. Even at this early stage, Cugoano demanded reparations for enslavement.[129] The Sons of Africa lobbied the British Parliament, wrote to newspapers, and worked with like-minded groups. In the American city of Boston, African American activist Prince Hall established the first African Masonic lodge in North America in 1784 to fight racism in the United States, and to build bridges to Africa. By 1787, an African church movement – eventually involving the African Methodist Episcopal (AME) Church – had emerged out of Richard Allen and Absalom Jones's Free Africa Society in Philadelphia and Baltimore. By 1793, George Liele had established the Ethiopian Baptist Church in Jamaica. All these civil society groups sought to challenge racist Western tropes about Africans and to portray a positive image of their homeland.[130]

One of the most significant figures in Pan-Africanism, who came to symbolise its return to the ancestral continent, was Edward Wilmot Blyden. His Trinidadian-American biographer Hollis Lynch described Blyden as "the greatest Negro champion of his race in the nineteenth century".[131] Originally from St Thomas, which was part of the Caribbean colony of the Danish Virgin Islands (now the US Virgin Islands), Blyden had an advantage over other Pan-African prophets like W.E.B. Du Bois and Marcus Garvey in that his ideas were based on actual lived experiences on the continent in Liberia and Sierra Leone, leading to often more nuanced perspectives.

Blyden has sometimes been referred to as the "father of Pan-Africanism" and is widely considered to have been the single most important conceptualiser of the Pan-African ideology. He championed the concept of "Ethiopianism", which envisioned an African regeneration based on biblical scriptures. He urged African Americans in the diaspora to return to Africa to help develop the continent. Blyden was further credited with having coined the concept of the "African personality", which he saw as "the sum of values of African civilisation, the body of qualities which make up the distinctiveness of the people of Africa".[132] Through this idea, African cultures would take their equal place among global cultures, African people would make a unique contribution to the world, and Africans would rediscover their own "soul" by returning to their indigenous values.

The Pan-African Conference and Congresses, 1900–1945

Fifteen years after the Berlin Conference of 1884–1885, the Pan-African movement was born when the Trinidadian lawyer Henry Sylvester Williams – who is credited with having coined the terms "Pan-African" and "Pan-Africanism"[133] – became the moving force behind the first Pan-African Conference in Westminster Town Hall in London in July 1900. Williams had co-founded the African Association in London in 1897 with the black South African activist Alice Kinloch to lobby the British Parliament and public opinion in order to oppose the violence of European colonial rule in Africa, the lynching of black men in America, and Western economic exploitation of the Caribbean.[134] They were assisted by an African American bishop of the AME Zion Church, Alexander Walters. By this time, African American and Caribbean churches were also inspiring Africa's Ethiopian Church movement to set up their own independent churches on the continent.

The 1900 London Conference was the occasion where W.E.B. Du Bois uttered the remarkably prescient prophecy: "The problem of the twentieth century is the problem of the colour line."[135] The attendees of the conference from the United States, the Caribbean, and Africa addressed a message to

Queen Victoria at the end of their deliberations, complaining about the ill-treatment of blacks in South Africa and Rhodesia (modern Zimbabwe). They also called for reparations to Africa and Africans for slavery and colonialism, self-government, and the recognition of the rights of women. Two female activists – Catherine Impey and Jane Cobden Unwin – spoke at the conference.

Between 1919 and 1945, five Pan-African Congresses took place in various European capitals and New York, led by W.E.B. Du Bois.[136] The powerful Western media mostly heaped derision, scorn, and ridicule on these efforts.[137] The First Pan-African Congress was held in Paris in February 1919, simultaneously with the Versailles Peace Conference after the First World War (1914-1918). Du Bois was a dominant figure in Paris, along with the Senegalese-born French parliamentarian, Blaise Diagne, and the 57 delegates also included black American soldiers and black African public office-holders in the French government. The Congress called for the abolition of slave labour and the passing of laws to protect Africans and their land, demanding that Africans have the right to education and to take part in their own government.[138]

Even as the supposedly liberal American president Woodrow Wilson, meeting with European statesmen in Versailles to redraw the map of Europe after the First World War, passionately championed the right to self-determination of subjugated Central European minorities, Pan-Africanists meeting nearby sought to remind him of his denial of the most basic rights to his own African American subjects, whom he steadfastly refused to acknowledge as full citizens.[139]

The Paris Pan-African Congress of 1919 occurred at a time when Jamaica's Marcus Garvey – "the Black Moses" and one of Pan-Africanism's most charismatic and controversial figures – was, through his Universal Negro Improvement Association and African Communities League (UNIA-ACL), mobilising huge crowds of black Americans, along with his wife Amy Ashwood Garvey, in New York's Harlem and across the country through his "Back to Africa" movement and his evocative slogan of "Africa for the Africans".[140] Both Garvey and Du Bois implicitly demanded reparations for European slavery and imperialism.[141] The UNIA was greatly inspired by, and in turn also influenced, the New Negro Movement, which spawned the Harlem Renaissance of the 1920s. This epoch witnessed an era of great literary, cultural – including the music of the "jazz age" – and political activities linked to Africa. Its main prophets included Langston Hughes, Claude McKay, A. Philip Randolph, Alain Locke, and Hubert Harrison. Some 380,000 African Americans had fought in the First World War, while 100,000 Caribbeans migrated to the United States in the first two decades of the twentieth century. They helped to create a critical mass of the Americo-Caribbean leadership of the New Negro Movement.[142]

The Second Pan-African Congress took place simultaneously in London and Brussels in August–September 1921. The main demand made on behalf of the "Negro race" by "their thinking intelligentsia" was "local self-government for backward groups".[143] Other demands also included establishing indigenous political institutions and democracy. The Third Pan-African Congress took place simultaneously in London and Lisbon in 1923. The meetings mainly called for Africans to "have a voice" in running their own affairs. The Fourth Pan-African Congress was held in New York in 1927. It was at this meeting that the towering intellectual prophet of Pan-Africanism, Trinidad's George Padmore, lambasted white communists for trying to discredit black Pan-African organisations which they could not control.[144]

By the time of the Fifth Pan-African Congress in Manchester in October 1945, the movement had shifted its centre of gravity from the diaspora to Africa. The conference was now dominated by future African leaders such as Ghana's Kwame Nkrumah, Kenya's Jomo Kenyatta, and Malawi's Hastings Banda. Other Africans in Manchester included Joe Appiah (Ghana); H.O. Davies and S.L. Akintola (Nigeria); I.T.A. Wallace-Johnson (Sierra Leone); Peter Abrahams and Mark Hlubi (South Africa); C.L.R. James (Trinidad); and Amy Ashwood Garvey (Jamaica). Among its 200 delegates were representatives of African trade unions, farmers, cooperative societies, and students.[145]

Africans were now speaking directly for themselves in a Western idiom of self-determination, and their demands were unequivocal: immediate self-government and independence for African states, and the waging of armed struggles to liberate colonial territories, if necessary.[146] At Manchester, the 73-year-old Du Bois symbolically passed the torch of Pan-Africanism to a 36-year-old Nkrumah. Both Du Bois and George Padmore subsequently worked as advisers to Nkrumah's government in independent Ghana after 1957, living out their last days in the country where both now lie buried.

A Brief History of US Reparations

From the 1940s, the US-based Nation of Islam demanded reparations to compensate black Americans for the crimes of slavery. The African American civil rights stalwart Audley "Queen Mother" Moore created the Reparations Committee of Descendants of United States Slaves in 1955 to secure similar reparations. Fourteen years later, the former Black Panther and Student Non-Violent Coordinating Committee (SNCC) activist James Forman, pushed for reparations from churches and synagogues, issuing a *Black Manifesto*. In 1987, the National Coalition of Blacks for Reparations in America (N'COBRA) was established to seek reparations for African Americans "for the genocidal war against Africans that created the TransAtlantic Slave Trade".[147] The National Association for the Advancement of Colored People (NAACP) also embraced reparations, as did the African American congressman John Conyers, who tirelessly tabled the issue annually in Congress from 1989 (see Maginn in this volume). Across the Atlantic in Britain, Conyers's fellow legislator, the Guyanese-British parliamentarian, Bernie Grant, created the African Reparations Movement in Britain in 1993 (see Small, and Frith and Xosei in this volume).[148]

Francophone, Lusophone, and South American Contributions to Pan-Africanism[149]

Pan-Africanism was also promoted in the francophone and lusophone worlds. In 1890, two Haitians, Anténor Firmin and Benito Sylvain, launched the journal *La Fraternité* to protect black interests in Europe. The First World War resulted in an estimated 15,000 Africans, Caribbeans, and South Americans – mostly from West and Equatorial Africa, Madagascar, and the Maghreb (Algeria, Tunisia, and Morocco); Haiti, Guadeloupe, Martinique, and other Antillean French territories; and French Guiana – migrating to France, after some had fought for the mother country in the global conflict. Many of this population considered assimilationist black members of the French National Assembly to be sell-outs of the liberation struggle. African and Caribbean activists during this period included René Maran, Kojo Tovalou Houénou, Lamine Senghor, Tiemoko Garan Kouyaté, Stéphane Rosso, Thomas Ramananjato, and Messali Hadi. The Martinican sisters Jane and Paulette Nardal were instrumental in these activities and often acted as a bridge between Paris-based African American activists and French-based liberation fighters.

These civil society activists formed groups to combat racism in France and to liberate Africa, forging uneasy ties with the French Communist Party to fund journals and mobilise support. By the 1930s, Paris-based Africans and Caribbeans – Aimé Césaire (Martinique), Léopold Senghor (Senegal), and Léon-Gontran Damas (Guyana) – founded the concept of Négritude, which affirmed the worth and dignity of African culture. The idea of the

"African personality" was borrowed from Edward Blyden, while the prophets of Négritude were inspired by the poets of the Harlem Renaissance such as Claude McKay, and spread their message to Cuba, Brazil, and lusophone Africa. In Lisbon, future leaders of Portuguese Africa such as Amilcar Cabral, Agostinho Neto, and Mário de Andrade created the Centre for African Studies in 1950. Its aim was to promote the growth of African culture, literature, and history. The movement sought to "re-Africanise the mind", and was inspired by both the Afro-Brazilian cultural movement and Négritude.

Aside from Brazil, 44 per cent of whose population has African ancestry, countries in Latin and South America with large African populations include Uruguay, Colombia, Peru, Mexico, Costa Rica, Panama, Cuba, the Dominican Republic, and Puerto Rico (see also Silva Jr, Ramirez, and Soomer in this volume). An estimated quarter of South Americans are estimated to be descendants of 12–15 million enslaved Africans: ten times more than in the United States. The Partido Independiente de Color was established in Cuba as early as 1908, the Brazilian Black Front in 1931, and the Partido Autóconto Negro in Uruguay in 1936. Brazil's Black Front was inspired by Garveyism, and fought to end segregation and institutional racism. Other Afro-Brazilian interest groups active in the 1930s and 1940s included the Socialist Black Front, the Association of Brazilian Blacks, and the Afro-Brazilian Democratic Committee. A vibrant Afro-Brazilian press, centred around the *Quilombo* newspaper – founded by the Black Experimental Theatre (BET) – covered African and African American news, as well as cultural developments in France and Senegal. They pushed the "Black is beautiful" message in the 1950s even before it had reached the United States. These anti-racism messages were somewhat curtailed by Brazil's repressive military regime, which banned discourses on racism in the 1960s and 1970s.

Contemporary Pan-African Prophets of Reparations

The UN World Conference Against Racism, Racial Discrimination, Xenophobia and Related Intolerance held in Durban in August–September 2001 mobilised support for black reparations. For example, black Spaniards who attended the summit used it as a catalyst to organise conferences in Spain on the situation of its black citizens, demanding reparations for Madrid's exploitative colonisation of Africa. This activism has also spawned groups such as the Black African and Afro-descendant Community of Spain, which fights for the political, social, and cultural rights of black Spaniards (see Nerín and Tofiño in this volume).

In the light of the contemporary global anti-slavery and anti-colonial protests led by the US-based Black Lives Matter movement, a burning issue that has not been adequately addressed is that of reparations for the victims of these two evil scourges in the Americas, the Caribbean, and Africa. When the 400th anniversary of American slavery was commemorated in 2019, calls for reparations for descendants of this exploitative system grew louder.

Similar campaigns also exist in Africa, the Caribbean, and Europe. Rather perversely, it was slave owners – and not the enslaved themselves or their descendants – who were compensated by the American, British, and other European governments for the loss of their "property". The British government, for example, paid £20 million (the equivalent of £20 billion in 2024)[150] to 46,000 slave owners after the abolition of slavery across the British Empire in 1833.

The most articulate African American crusader of reparations has been the late civil rights activist Randall Robinson. He consistently argued for reparations to close the 250-year gap between white and black Americans created by plantation slavery. The late African American Nobel laureate Toni Morrison persistently talked of "the layers of scar tissue that the black-body has grown in order to obscure, if not annihilate, the slave body underneath".[151] As Robinson correctly noted: "the black holocaust is far and away the most heinous human rights crime visited upon any group of people in the world over the last five hundred years".[152] He noted that Germany paid individual Jewish survivors and the state of Israel reparations – estimated at $98 billion – for the Holocaust (1933–1945), while 82,250 Japanese Americans interned in concentration camps by President Franklin Roosevelt during the Second World War were compensated with a $1.2 billion payment.[153] The US Federal Government awarded Native American groups about $2.2 billion in compensation for their stolen lands between 1924 and 1987 (see Maginn in this volume).

To understand the continuing structural impact of slavery in the United States, one need go no further than the "Great Plague" of the 2020–2021 Covid-19 pandemic. Despite accounting for only 14.4 per cent of the US population at the time, black Americans were hospitalised at rates 2.9 times higher than white Americans, and died from the disease at rates 1.9 times faster.[154] Further afield, in Canada, the government has, for two decades, paid a total of $60 billion (Canadian dollars) by 2023 to members and groups of indigenous First Nations. These involved settlements relating to the adoptions of indigenous children, improvement of drinking water on reserves, the involuntary sterilisation of indigenous women, and the attendance of residential schools by First Nation children.[155]

In the Caribbean, the Barbadian historian and chair of the Caribbean Community's (Caricom's) Reparations Commission, Hilary Beckles, similarly noted that "slavery and genocide in the Caribbean are lived experiences despite over a century of emancipation".[156] Modern ailments common among Caribbean citizens like diabetes and hypertension can be traced directly to the bad diet and sugary drinks inherited from the era of European slavery and colonialism. A 2004 estimate of the cost of slave imports in the Caribbean arrived at a figure of £7.5 trillion. A more recent *Report on Reparations for Transatlantic Chattel Slavery (TCS) in the Americas and the Caribbean*, led by Jamaican judge Patrick Robinson, estimated in June 2023 that former slaveholding European nations owed 31 countries in the Americas $107.8 trillion.[157] Beckles therefore urged European slaving nations to pay reparations to Caribbean countries in order to repair this damage (see also Beckles in this volume).[158]

Under Beckles's leadership from 2013, national committees were established in each Caricom country to pursue restitution from former European slaving nations through the regional body's ten-point plan for reparatory justice: making a full apology; creating an indigenous people's development programme; repatriating willing Caribbean nationals back to Africa, and returning looted West Indian cultural heritage; building cultural institutions; addressing the regional public health crisis; eradicating illiteracy; initiating an African reconnection and African knowledge programme; supporting psychological rehabilitation; transferring technology; and annulling regional debt; as well as returning to the region the £20 million compensation paid by European governments to Caribbean slave owners.[159]

The Jamaican scholar Verene Shepherd has perceptively examined some of the criticisms of, and opposition to, the Caricom reparations strategy. The Caribbean diaspora – especially in Britain – accused West Indian governments of having hijacked a grassroots civil society reparations movement through a top-down government-led initiative. They noted that indigenous and enslaved people in the Caribbean had started the restitution agenda, which was then extended by movements, like the Rastafarians, that had kept the reparations flame alive for decades. Indigenous groups such as the Taino, Kalinago, and Garifuna also felt marginalised from national committees, thereby forcing several committees belatedly to include members of these groups in their deliberations.

More controversially, Indo-Caribbeans – particularly in Trinidad and Tobago, and Guyana – many of whose ancestors had migrated to the region as indentured workers, also claimed marginalisation from the Caricom reparations movement, forcing its Reparations Commission to revise the justificatory narrative accompanying its ten-point plan to include their grievances. Many in the region, however, opposed the inclusion of descendants of indentured nineteenth- and twentieth-century Indo-Caribbeans in an initiative which they felt strongly should focus solely on the black victims of three centuries of transatlantic chattel slavery.[160]

During a visit to Lisbon by Brazilian president Luiz Inácio Lula da Silva in April 2023, the Portuguese president, Marcelo Rebelo de Sousa, appeared partly to heed Caricom's call for reparations, when he urged his country to apologise and accept full responsibility for its profits from the transatlantic slave trade, in which Lisbon had exported 6 million enslaved Africans to the Americas for four centuries: a past that Portugal has scarcely acknowledged or taught in its school curricula. Sousa repeated this call a year later.[161]

In Latin America, Colombia has started to recognise its Afro-descendant communities by creating a reparations commission, while its environmental campaigner Francia Márquez became the country's first black vice-president in June 2022. Reformed land rights laws have also recognised collective land titles for Afro-Colombian communities.[162] In July 1993, black activists of Surinamese and Antillean ancestry based in Amsterdam pushed for an apology for three centuries of Dutch slavery in the Caribbean, and their demand for a monument and annual commemoration of this sordid trade was finally heeded in 2002. The descendants of Dutch slavery and colonialism in the Caribbean have further campaigned for the decolonisation of Dutch political, socio-economic, and cultural institutions in Holland as well as in their homelands (see Nimako and Allen in this volume). Using the Caricom ten-point plan, the island of St Maarten claimed reparations from the Dutch government that included a formal apology, commitments to cooperation deals, and recognising ancestral rights.

Responding to such pressures, the prime minister of the Netherlands at the time, Mark Rutte – himself a trained historian – apologised for the Dutch role in the transatlantic slave trade in December 2022, and established a €200 million fund to address its impact. Rutte noted: "On behalf of the Dutch government, I apologise for the past actions of the Dutch state; to enslaved people in the past, everywhere in the world, who suffered as a consequence of these actions, as well as to their daughters and sons, and to all their descendants, up to the present day."[163] On the 160th anniversary of the abolition of slavery in Dutch territories, the King of the Netherlands, Willem-Alexander, similarly offered an apology to victims of the slave trade at the national slavery monument in Amsterdam's Oosterpark, noting: "On this day that we remember the Dutch history of slavery, I ask forgiveness for this crime against humanity."[164] The king went on to note that racism remained a challenge in modern Dutch society. It was also revealed in June 2023 that the House of Orange – the Dutch royal family – had profited from the slave trade through the Dutch East India Company, between 1675 and 1770, to the tune of $600 million (in present-day terms).[165]

In August 2019, Scotland's Glasgow University agreed to raise £20 million to establish a joint Centre for Development Research at the University of the West Indies (UWI) in order to start to atone for its sins in having benefited from Scottish slave traders in the Caribbean. Oxford University's All Souls College also announced an annual scholarship for West Indian students, and provided a £100,000 grant to Codrington College in Barbados, for having received funding from an eighteenth-century slave trader, Christopher Codrington, after whom the main college library was named until November 2020. King's College London further benefited from proceeds from slave labour at the Codrington estates in Barbados (see also Timcke and Gomes in this volume).

In the African context, the late Nigerian historian Ade Ajayi was a member of the Organisation of African Unity's (OAU's) Group of Eminent Persons (GEP) on Reparations in 1992–1993, and along with his colleagues (particularly Nigerian philanthropist-politician Moshood Abiola, Kenyan intellectual Ali Mazrui, and Jamaican scholar-politician Dudley Thompson) demanded that the West recognise its moral debt to Africa and its diaspora for slavery and colonialism, and pay these populations full monetary compensation. The long-time reparations advocate, Guyanese-British parliamentarian Bernie Grant, also attended the meeting. The OAU's 1993 Abuja Declaration was visionary in calling for the return of looted African artefacts to their rightful owners, which the French, German, British, and Belgian governments belatedly started to do two decades later. Inspired by Ajayi, the proclamation called on African governments to establish national committees to study the damage of slavery and colonialism, while promoting dissemination and education.

The document further implored the OAU to grant observer status to diaspora groups working on restitution. Abuja also requested African states to accede to the "right of return" of all diaspora citizens wanting to resettle in their ancestral homelands. Building on this work, the African World Reparations and Repatriation Truth Commission, held in Accra in August 1999, made similar demands as the Abuja proclamation. The meeting was attended by civil society representatives of 15 African and Caribbean countries, as well as diaspora delegates from the United States and Britain. Accra called specifically for compensation of $777 trillion as reparations from the West for slavery and colonialism, and for African traditional leaders to make land available for diaspora returnees.

More recently, the 55-strong African Union and the 20-member Caricom held a four-day conference in Accra in November 2023 to forge a united front in order to persuade European nations to repair "historical mass crimes". The summit established an Africa-based global fund to catalyse the reparations movement. The AU pledged to collaborate with the UN to investigate "mitigation options" for slavery and colonialism, and to determine whether enslavement constituted crimes against humanity at the time that they were committed (see also Adebajo in this volume).[166]

AU delegates travelled to Barbados before the November 2023 summit to coordinate the AU–Caricom strategy. Caricom's ten-point plan for reparatory justice remains one of the most comprehensive initiatives, calling for such measures as a full formal apology for enslavement, and debt annulment, as well as European colonial powers to invest in the Caribbean's health and education sectors. The University of the West Indies-commissioned Brattle report further estimated that Britain alone owed the region £18.8 trillion for centuries of unpaid labour.[167] As Carla Barnett, Caricom's secretary general noted at the November 2023 Accra summit: "We are at an important inflection point in the global movement for reparatory justice." She thus urged the movement to "speak with one voice to advance the call for reparations".[168]

German Reparations for the Namibian Genocide

There are increasingly more efforts by a few European governments to provide reparations and to acknowledge past crimes. From 2015, the governments of Germany and Namibia took six years to negotiate a joint agreement to atone for Berlin's century-old genocide in South West Africa between 1904 and 1908. In May 2021, Germany agreed to pay €1.1 billion over 30 years in "reconstruction and development" aid – in the key areas of land reform, rural infrastructure, health care, energy, education, water, and vocational training – as a "gesture to recognise the immense suffering inflicted on the victims". These crimes were, however, described as genocide "from today's perspective", suggesting that international law – effectively made by, and for, European states[169] – did not apply to African victims. Much of this money is to benefit primarily descendants of the Herero and Nama. German foreign minister Heiko Maas quickly added that the accord should not open the door to any "legal request for compensation", out of fear of similar claims from Poland, Greece, and Italy for Nazi war crimes committed during the Second World War.

Despite many monuments to German soldiers in Namibia, there are barely any memorials to the victims of the Herero and Nama genocide. On the centenary of the start of the massacres in 2004 – pushed by left-wing German scholars and politicians – Berlin offered an apology to the Herero and Nama for these crimes. Only as recently as 2011 did museums in Germany start to send the skulls of victims back to Namibia for decent burials. After 108 years of denial and equivocation, German foreign minister Frank-Walter Steinmeier finally conceded, in July 2015, that the events in Namibia constituted "a war crime and a genocide". Museums in Berlin started holding exhibitions on Germany's colonial history in Africa.

Berlin refused to include the word "reparations" in the joint declaration. Though Namibian officials described the payment as a "first step in the right direction", Windhoek was widely seen to have been outmanoeuvred in these negotiations of unequals between the government and its largest aid donor. The main challenge in implementing this historic accord remained how to persuade Herero and Nama leaders to accept it. Several of them have complained that they were not represented at the negotiation table. They thus voiced vociferous hostility to the deal, which some dismissed as a "public relations coup" rather than a genuine act of reparation. Vekuii Rukoro, leader of the Ovaherero Traditional Authority, and Gaob Isaack, head of the Nama Traditional Leaders Association, condemned the bilateral agreement as "a construct of a racist mindset", portraying it as a "total sell-out". The distrust of indigenous groups also derives from what many see as their continuing marginalisation within Namibian society, as well as their criticism of what they regard as a corrupt elite in Windhoek that cannot be relied on to spend aid money honestly and equitably.

Germany's recent history has often been overshadowed by the brutalities of the Third Reich's crimes, which resulted in the death of six million European Jews. Berlin instituted one of the most impressive processes of restorative justice thereafter, involving paying compensation of $98 billion to Israel and

Jewish groups. Post-war Germany has sought to become a model of global citizenry, impressively taking in one million Syrian, Iraqi, and Afghan refugees during the 2015–2016 European refugee crisis, with 17 per cent of its population now consisting of immigrants (though this has also resulted in the rise of the extreme right Alternative for Germany [AfD] party). The country's colonial genocide in Namibia has, however, only recently become more widely known, and only two memorials in Berlin and Bremen commemorate these African massacres.[170]

Unmasking Anglo-Saxon Anti-Reparationists

Further complicating efforts to achieve reparations are many Western media institutions which continue to rubbish and ridicule Pan-African liberation aspirations, as their forerunners had done during the five Pan-African Congresses between 1919 and 1945. A good illustration appeared in the Anglo-American establishment mouthpiece, the London-based *Economist* magazine, which in June 2023 published a leader ("How Not to Repair America") and an accompanying main article ("The Tide Goes Out") on the reparations debate in the United States.[171] Both exposed the magazine's illiberal ideology and consistent misreading of race issues in America. *The Economist* crudely caricatures this important issue, making lazy arguments that are often put forward by conservative analysts: reparations are unpopular and backed by only 30 per cent of Americans; most living whites played no part in Jim Crow segregation, and so none can be held responsible for its legacies; black Americans are not the only disadvantaged group in America; resources are finite and should go towards better schools and health care for all Americans, and not just to descendants of slaves.

The argument that reparations are not popular needs to be disaggregated. Explaining complicated historical issues to voters also requires strong and courageous leadership, as America's partisan media space is often deluged by stereotypical arguments presented by conservative outlets similar to this *Economist* perspective. Many Americans tend to think differently once the issue of reparations has been sensibly explained as a structural one in which the country benefited from two and a half centuries of unpaid labour, which facilitated America's industrialisation, using 450,000 enslaved Africans, who only won their basic voting rights from the 1960s. Such an approach would also note that, as *The Economist* itself concedes, the lingering effects of this legacy remain with America today, as many of the victims still alive have inherited these socio-economic disadvantages. *The Economist* itself observes that the median net worth of black families in 2019 was only 13 per cent of that of white families.[172]

Such gross racial inequalities are also evident in the lower levels of life expectancy and health, as well as continuing discrimination against African Americans. During the 2020–2021 Covid-19 crisis, black Americans accounted for 30 per cent of deaths, despite constituting only 14.4 per cent of the population.[173] Today, members of this group are less likely to have health care and are more prone to police brutality, while 26 per cent of black men have been incarcerated in what the scholar-activist Angela Davis dubbed America's "prison industrial complex".[174] Many African Americans also live in ghettos, suffering the effects of bad housing, bad diet, and bad schooling, with 34 per cent of black children born on or below the poverty line.[175] These stark realities all constitute the continuing legacies of two and a half centuries of slavery.

In terms of the *Economist*'s argument that African Americans are not the only group discriminated against, this is scarcely an excuse for not paying reparations. After the Second World War in 1946, the US government's Indian Claims Commission paid $1.3 billion (worth $20 billion in 2024) in reparations to indigenous Americans who had historically been victims of widespread land dispossession and genocide. As earlier noted, Japanese Americans incarcerated in camps during the Second World War were also compensated through a $1.2 billion payment (worth $18 billion in 2024). Though *The Economist* cites the Japanese case, attempts to repair historical crimes should not be turned into a hierarchy of suffering. Historical injustices with far-reaching and continuing consequences should be repaired regardless of the groups involved.

The *Economist*'s argument that no living whites are responsible for slavery ignores the structural issues of those who continue to benefit from 246 years of free labour, in stark contrast to those who continue to suffer from it. This statement is akin to saying that no one is responsible or should be held accountable for America's contemporary racism, which was consolidated over two and a half centuries of black exploitation, dehumanisation, and disenfranchisement. Governments in Canada, Australia, and Germany have paid reparations for crimes committed against indigenous populations and European Jews, for which many of their living citizens were not directly responsible. Between 2021 and 2022, the governments of Germany and the Netherlands announced similar reparations for past colonial crimes. As for the *Economist*'s argument that resources are finite, the fact that Washington continues to spend more on its military than the next ten countries combined[176] is the clearest sign of the distortion of socio-economic priorities through its lobbyist-fuelled legislative process of legalised corruption. America can thus clearly afford to pay compensation to repair its past.

The Economist then cites the case of two commissions in the "golden state" of California, which in 2023 recommended reparations for descendants of American slavery, as an example of how "it is impossible to create an actuarial table of injustice ... to determine how much cash is owed and to whom".[177] The reparations commission recommended that the maximum cost of reparations for each African American citizen should be $1.2 million as a down payment, while a similar reparations commission in San Francisco suggested $5 million per person. *The Economist* notes that California is focused more on repairing current racial disparities, which the magazine concedes remain considerable across the country. It further cites 2016 figures showing that black Angelenos had 1 per cent of the wealth of their white compatriots in Los Angeles.

The Economist then suggests that the sum of the proposed reparations would cripple California's finances. However, its own British government had paid the country's slave owners – and not the exploited enslaved themselves or their descendants – £20 million for the loss of their "property" after Westminster abolished slavery in 1833. This sum was fully paid out only in 2015. If the British government could take out a loan worth 40 per cent of its Treasury's annual income and 5 per cent of its gross domestic product (GDP) at the time, to make perverse payments to 46,000 slave owners and their descendants over a 182-year period, why can the government of California not have the ingenuity to devise a similar long-term compensation scheme for a more just cause? The *Economist*'s alternative suggestion that race-neutral anti-poverty programmes be put in place, instead of reparations, seems utterly insensitive given that the institution of slavery itself was based solely on race. The magazine's suggestion that the governor of California, Gavin Newsom, and mayor of San Francisco, London Breed, oppose cash payments is clearly mean-spirited.

In seeking to nuance the *Economist*'s views, I consulted two mainstream American newspapers. The *Los Angeles Times* noted that California had been requested by its reparations commission to issue a formal apology for the persistent damage of slavery and discrimination: an important fact that *The Economist* omitted in its rush to discredit the case for reparations. The California-based newspaper further explained that monetary losses for the descendants of enslaved African Americans had been calculated based on the three categories of health disparities, mass incarceration and over-policing, and housing discrimination, making these sums appear less arbitrary than was portrayed by the *Economist*'s superficial analysis.[178] The *New York Times* further nuanced the 30 per cent of Americans that the *Economist* claimed were opposed to reparations, by citing disaggregated figures from the same Pew Research Center survey: 77 per cent of African American adults support reparations, as do 39 per cent of Hispanics, 33 per cent of Asians, but only 18 per cent of whites. Unsurprisingly, the main beneficiaries of slavery are the most opposed to its redress, while the main victims of this crime against humanity are the most supportive. Significantly, the *New York Times* also exposed the ideological disparity in this debate, with 50 per cent of Democrats backing reparations, in contrast to 8 per cent of Republicans: a camp into which *The Economist* falls.[179]

The Economist – not renowned for its cultural diversity, and notorious for a Eurocentric gaze on the non-Western world – tends to view race relations in America through the jaundiced lens of its own British society, which is often in denial about widespread prejudices against black and brown people. This is despite clear evidence of institutional racism in its policing, public health, and, more recently, even its cricket. *The Economist* supported the slave-owning Confederacy during the American Civil War (1861–1865) and has been criticised by several scholars for having a "slavery problem".[180] A magazine living in a London glasshouse should clearly not throw stones.

Synopsis of the Book

Having assessed the Black Atlantic's triple burden of slavery, colonialism (including neo-colonialism), and reparations, I will next summarise the rest of the 27 chapters in this book. This edited volume demonstrates the continuities of European slavery and colonialism in Africa, the Caribbean, and the Americas, examining calls for reparations in all three regions for what most now acknowledge to have been crimes against humanity. The book is authored by some of the most eminent scholars in the field from Africa, the Caribbean, the Americas, and Europe. The authors are largely based in these regions, thus contributing substantively to efforts to transform educational curricula across the globe. The book seeks to be comprehensive and multidisciplinary, and to enable cross-regional comparisons to be drawn in these important areas, thus ensuring that important global events are read from diverse perspectives. The volume is also aimed at subject area experts, as well as students in diverse areas of the humanities and beyond who seek a sound introductory reference book for these important historical subjects to which they are often not exposed. The authors thus represent a multidisciplinary group encompassing diverse fields such as history, international relations, politics, economics, sociology, anthropology, literature, and languages.

This book is divided into six sections and is written by scholars who introduce readers to French, German, Spanish, Portuguese, Italian, and Dutch historical and other sources that are often not accessible to an English-speaking audience. An introductory section has four framing chapters, which provide a broader context for understanding the complexities of slavery, colonialism, and reparations. This introductory chapter by the Nigerian international relations scholar Adekeye Adebajo sets the three key issues of slavery, colonialism, and reparations in historical perspective in Africa, the Americas, the Caribbean, and Europe. Another essay by the British-Barbadian historian Alan Cobley provides a detailed comparative examination of the degradations of Master and Servant laws in Barbados and South Africa. These laws proliferated after the abolition of chattel slavery across the British Empire in 1834, and were a means to control labour during the subsequent apprenticeship era, which did not bring about much fundamental change in the conditions of the previously enslaved. Some 800,000 former slaves in the Caribbean continued to work for a pittance with few or no political rights (see also Small and Brereton in this volume).

Demonstrating how totalising and systematic imperialism was, Cobley reveals how lawfare was used as a system by plantation owners – who often dominated local legislatures – to oppress the enslaved. European imperialism operated sophisticated methods of governance, which were often imported from the metropolis and adapted to local conditions. Riots and labour disruptions occurred throughout the British Empire in reaction to these often draconian laws. There were efforts at "amelioration" made as a result of the 1833 Act of Abolition to abolish the whipping of workers and establish courts to regulate labour relations. The separation of families was also ended. Some field workers were now remunerated for overtime. Apprentices could finally have free time for a quarter of their work hours, and they were allowed to buy their freedom. But even after apprenticeship, unpaid labour remained ubiquitous, as did physical punishment. Planters in Barbados refused to provide allowances to the 14,000 liberated slave children. Dutch-speaking farmers (Boers) in South Africa also treated the former enslaved similarly at the Cape. Underlining the continuity between slavery and colonialism highlighted throughout this Introduction, these Master and Servant laws laid the foundation of labour laws in British colonies in southern, central, and eastern Africa over the next 70 years.

In her rich chapter, the Italian cultural scholar and linguist Patrizia

Palumbo reveals some of the cultural mechanisms behind colonialism. She demonstrates how propaganda was used in Italian colonial children's literature in an effort, during the *ventennio* of the fascist regime of Benito Mussolini (1922–1943), to indoctrinate the country's youth. Italian writers and artists were encouraged to present an eastern Africa (Ethiopia, Eritrea, and Somalia) where supposedly virgin lands and fields were turned into blooming green farms through the efforts of intrepid and hard-working Italian migrants, using their superior technology. Brave Italian soldiers were depicted as fighting a "just war" during the invasion of Ethiopia in 1935–1936. In contrast, helpless Africans were portrayed as being freed from misery and slavery by benevolent European conquerors.

The Jamaican-British sociologist Stephen Small then rounds out the introductory section with an insightful essay on the need for reparations for British colonialism. Unlike much advocacy for reparations which focuses on British slavery, Small argues that reparations for imperialism are equally important. Using a rich case study of his childhood city of Liverpool – the "slaving capital of the world" – Small shows how British companies run by John Holt, William Lever, Alfred Lewis Jones, and Elder Dempster made huge profits from palm oil, soap, margarine, and shipping derived from often exploited African land and labour. He also examines the widespread discrimination against black African and Caribbean citizens living in "the empire's second city".

A second section contains three essays examining the legacies of slavery in central, eastern, western, and southern Africa. The French historian Catherine Coquery-Vidrovitch provides a detailed historical exposition of slavery in central and eastern Africa (including internal African enslavement), ranging from the Indian Ocean slave trade with the arrival of Muslim Arabs in the eighth century, to the north-east African slave trade through eastern Africa (involving the Berber and Swahili slave trade), and the Sahara route to the transatlantic slave trade involving Portuguese and Spanish sailors from 1492 who transported slaves from Africa to Brazil. She then investigates slavery in the Kongo kingdoms from the fifteenth century, involving largely Portuguese slave traders who also ran sugar plantations in São Tomé. Coquery-Vidrovitch concludes with an examination of the transatlantic slave-trading ports in the present-day Congos – Kinshasa and Brazzaville – and Angola.

The American historian Martin Klein then examines the practice of slavery from the seventeenth century in West Africa's Saint-Louis-du-Senegal, the Gold and Slave Coasts (Elmina, Whydah, and Lagos), and the Bight of Benin

(Niger Delta and Calabar). This commerce also involved Portuguese, English, French, and Dutch slavers. Klein examines the role of powerful African *signares*: women traders who were married to European men in trading companies. Along with *métis* (mixed-race) families, these were active slave owners and slave traders in eighteenth-century Senegal. The enslaved in Saint-Louis also worked as sailors, masons, cooks, blacksmiths, laundresses, and traders. From the seventeenth century, an Afro-Dutch community emerged in what is now Ghana, which played important roles in the Dutch trading company-led slave trade in Elmina Castle. These slaves also worked as carpenters, bricklayers, coopers, cooks, and stonebreakers. Whydah had French, English, and Portuguese settlements involved in the slave trade, while slavery in British-dominated Lagos continued into the colonial era. Enslaved labour in Lagos was involved in fishing, crafts, manufacturing, and transport, while the Bight of Benin's slavery was largely indigenous-led.

The South African historian Butholezwe Mtombeni concludes the section by covering the topic of slavery in southern Africa, focusing largely on debates about the economic benefits from slavery of the Dutch East India Company's exploits at the Cape of Good Hope between 1652 and 1795. Slave labour was imported from Madagascar, Indonesia, and India, as well as West, southern, and East Africa, with Asia supplying 81 per cent of the enslaved that entered the Cape. Mtombeni argues that slaves used religion – largely Islam for men, and Christianity for women – to alleviate the worst consequences of their plight, and he regards slave rebellions against the brutal Dutch settler regime as having planted the seeds of future black nationalism.

The three essays in the third section cover the impacts of slavery in the British, French, and Dutch Caribbean. The British-Trinidadian historian Bridget Brereton elegantly and unflinchingly assesses English colonisation of the Caribbean (St Kitts, Barbados, Nevis, Montserrat, Antigua, and Jamaica) between 1624 and 1670. Starting with tobacco and sugar plantations, indentured English, Scottish, and Irish labour was eventually replaced by enslaved Africans, following the launch of the "Sugar Revolution" in Barbados from the 1640s. Britain exported about 3.3 million slaves from Africa to the Caribbean to grow sugar, cotton, cocoa, and coffee. Brereton also exposes the dreary life – with diverse but rigidly assigned roles – of the enslaved, particularly the widespread abuse of female slaves, on brutal plantations across the Caribbean, which destroyed and dislocated African families. She nevertheless highlights the rebellions and resistance of slaves across the region, particularly from the eighteenth century.

The French political sociologist Jaime Aragón Falomir then examines the history of France in the Caribbean, focusing particularly on Saint-Domingue (modern Haiti), Martinique, and Guadeloupe. The author explains the methods through which Paris colonised and enslaved these countries, establishing sugar cane plantations with exploited African slaves. He further assesses the social polarisation between dominant and dominated groups based on race and rank, before using the concept of *habitus* to show how imperial dominance was ensured in time and place. France formally abolished slavery in its Caribbean colonies only in 1848.

The Amsterdam-based Ghanaian economist Kwame Nimako then examines the institutionalisation of Dutch slavery in the Caribbean in the eighteenth century, led by the Dutch East India Company, which was firmly entrenched in the Asian market. The Dutch West India Company prioritised the enslavement of Africans to make goods for exports to Asia. Nimako notes that the Dutch often acted as intermediaries (transporting more than 500,000 slaves to the Americas) with the larger European imperial powers – England, France, and Spain – with which they could not directly compete. Suriname became a sugar-producing Dutch colony by the middle of the seventeenth century, before later producing coffee and cotton. In the eastern Caribbean, Curaçao, Aruba, Bonaire, Sint Eustatius, Saba, and Sint Maarten also came under Dutch dominion, with African slaves transported to work on plantations there. Nimako further exposes myths about Dutch slavery within the country's scholarship. Like the British and Americans, after the abolition of the formal slave trade in 1863 the Dutch government paid compensation to slave owners rather than to the enslaved and their heirs.

The fourth section covers slavery in Brazil and the US, as well as the contributions of female activists to anti-slavery efforts in the US and Canada. The Brazilian historian Carlos Silva Jr examines slavery in Brazil, starting in the 1530s with sugar plantations in Pernambuco and Bahia. These events were characterised by the horrendous brutality of whippings by slave masters. Silva notes that 45 per cent of the enslaved between the mid-sixteenth and mid-nineteenth centuries were transported by Portugal to Brazilian mines, plantations, and urban settings. He traces the history of the country to Portuguese colonialism in the sixteenth century, starting with the extraction of red wood called brazilwood. Lisbon had earlier enslaved Amerindian indigenous groups to work on sugar plantations. Facing resistance from the native population, Portugal imported African slaves from the sixteenth century. But Silva also notes the widespread resistance by the enslaved, many of whom created runaway maroon communities (*quilombos*). Brazil was the last state to abolish slavery in the Americas by 1888.

The African American historian Jeffrey Kerr-Ritchie then provides an insightful examination of slavery in the United States, noting that five of the first seven American presidents – starting with George Washington – were slaveholders. The notorious 1857 Dred Scott decision confirmed in law the stripping of citizenship from the country's black population. Louisiana, Mississippi, Alabama, Missouri, Arkansas, and Florida all legalised chattel slavery – solely from Africa – between 1812 and 1845. Kerr-Ritchie highlights the huge economic benefits of slave labour to the country, with cotton exports earning the US treasury $192 billion by 1860, four times the federal government's revenues. Between 1770 and 1831, cotton production increased from 2 per cent to 22 per cent of the American economy.

Kerr-Ritchie also notes how the indigenous Amerindian population were forced off their land in genocidal military campaigns by European settlers, thus enabling the development of America's cotton and slave empire across the Mississippi Valley, fuelled by European – particularly British – demand. The enslaved were further exploited in America's lucrative tobacco trade, with Kerr-Ritchie detailing the diverse tasks performed by slaves. He then focuses on the exploitation of the body of enslaved women to increase fertility rates, as well as on the widespread rape of black slave women by white slave owners. Kerr-Ritchie, however, also highlights the 250 black slave revolts and conspiracies from the seventeenth century, noting that the American Civil War (1861–1865) was less a civil conflict and more of an uprising of the enslaved. He concludes by examining the damaging impacts of slavery on present-day African American life.

The African-American historian Daniel Broyld then examines the role of women in the emancipation of North America, noting their major contributions to abolitionist movements in the United States and Canada. He particularly highlights the role of Harriet Tubman, Mary Ellen Pleasant, Mary Bibb, and Caroline Elizabeth Loguen, who were all involved in freeing the enslaved (through the Underground Railroad), protecting runaway slaves, protesting, newspaper publishing, and writing. Broyld seeks to debunk the myth of the "Great Man in History" and to move women activists from the periphery to the centre of abolitionist struggles.

The seven essays of the fifth section assess the legacies of colonialism in British, French, Belgian, Portuguese, German, Spanish, and Italian colonies in Africa. The Nigerian political scientist Samuel Igba examines Britain's role in the "Scramble for Africa" from the 1880s, through which London annexed colonies in western, eastern, southern, and North Africa. He notes that British colonialism had already began in Sierra Leone from 1787. Igba argues that the British-led capitalist expansion of the industrial revolution from the eighteenth century swapped the need for slaves for markets through which to consume surplus goods. He highlights British colonial atrocities in Kenya, Sudan, and South Africa, as well as the racist views of historical imperial figures such as Cecil Rhodes and Christian missionaries like David Livingstone, which were used to justify Pax Britannica.

The Paris-based American political economist Douglas Yates then examines the history of French colonialism in Africa, providing a general overview of its activities in West, Central, East, and North Africa, before providing a case study of the construction of the Congo-Ocean Railway from Pointe-Noire to Brazzaville in modern-day Congo-Brazzaville. Relying on French journalist Albert Londres's 1929 book *Terre d'ébène* (Land of Ebony) – based on four months of reporting from the site of the railway construction – Yates exposes the brutal slave labour and exploitation that characterised Gallic colonialism on the continent. Workers were starved, randomly shot, and forced to work 12-hour days, resulting in high mortality rates, and triggering the Kongo-Wara rebellion (1926–1931), which was fuelled by indigenous resistance to the French recruitment of forced labour.

The Belgian historian Guy Vanthemsche then assesses Belgian colonial rule in Burundi and Rwanda between 1916 and 1962, as well as, more extensively, in the Democratic Republic of the Congo between 1885 and 1960. Vanthemsche shows how Belgian colonial engineering – and particularly the atrocities of King Leopold's Congo Free State – left a damaging legacy of genocide, mass atrocities, and anarchy in all three countries. He notes that the Congo had only 29 university graduates at independence in 1960 owing to deliberate Belgian colonial policy.

The Portuguese decolonial scholar and linguist Sandra Sousa next eloquently examines Portuguese colonial rule in Africa, noting that its citizens first arrived in the Moroccan town of Ceuta in 1415, before establishing settlements in Arguin in Mauritania (1445) and Elmina in Ghana (1482). The late sixteenth and mid-seventeenth centuries saw the unified Portuguese–Spanish crowns leading the way in the transatlantic slave trade, to which the rise of Luanda in 1575 can be attributed. Brazil – which Lisbon had colonised from 1500 – was the main destination of this commerce in human chattel. Brazil's independence in 1822 would switch Portugal's focus to creating "new

Brazils" in Africa, with colonial settlements mushrooming in Cape Verde and São Tomé and Príncipe and, increasingly, in Angola and Mozambique. Though Portugal often portrayed itself as a "multiracial and pluri-continental nation", its administration in Africa involved forced labour and slavery, as well as the exploitation of mineral and agricultural resources. Sousa notes that Lisbon was widely seen – even by other Europeans – as one of the most incompetent and corrupt colonial administrations in the world.

The American historian Adam Blackler examines imperial Germany's African empire between 1884 and 1914. Pushed by commercial interests, Berlin's empire encompassed modern-day Cameroon, Togo, Tanzania, part of Kenya, Burundi, Rwanda, and Namibia. Blackler reminds readers how violent and culturally damaging Germany's colonial rule was. Like similar European settler-colonialism, German imperialism was based on "hyper-masculinity, nationalism, and hierarchical world views". Blackler focuses particularly on Berlin's genocidal conquest of South West Africa (modern Namibia) between 1904 and 1908, and the "race thinking" and apartheid segregation that characterised Germany's imperial rule. He also highlights African resistance to the genocide of the Herero and Nama led by figures such as Hendrik Witbooi and Samuel Maharero.

The Spanish co-authors, anthropologist Gustau Nerín and comparative literature expert and linguist Iñaki Tofiño, then examine Spanish colonialism in Africa. From the fifteenth century, the kingdom of Castile was involved in military interventions in North Africa before occupying enclaves such as Oran and Bugia in Algeria. Melilla was seized in 1497, while Ceuta was transferred from Portugal in 1640 and incorporated into Madrid's system of overseas territories. Morocco continues to challenge these annexations. Spain returned the occupied coastal town of Ifni to Rabat only in 1969. Madrid ruled Western Sahara from 1900, before irresponsibly ceding the territory to Morocco and Mauritania in 1975 without the self-determination referendum that the UN had demanded. Portugal ceded Fernando Po and Annobón to Spain in 1777, while Spanish Guinea was declared independent in 1900. The authors note the absence of any substantive public debates in modern Spain about its colonial past, as well as any acknowledgment by Madrid of the country's colonial crimes.

The American cultural anthropologist Mia Fuller next provides a succinct assessment of Italian colonialism in Africa between 1869 and 1947. She notes the ubiquitous recognition of Rome as "the least of the great powers", controlling Eritrea and Somalia in the nineteenth century. Libya was settled in the 1930s, before fascist dictator Benito Mussolini invaded Ethiopia in 1935.

Fuller identifies "demographic colonisation" (*colonizzazione demografica*) as the distinguishing feature of Italian imperialism in Africa. This idea held that finding space for Italian settler farmers on fertile soil in Africa would resolve the country's domestic problems. Rome thus focused on the cultivation of cotton, tobacco, grapes, and bananas in its African possessions. In pursuing these exploits in Africa, there was a consistent delusional nostalgia seeking to restore the glory of the Roman Empire. The realities of Italian imperial rule, however, involved the use of chemical weapons in the eastern Libyan region of Cyrenaica in the 1920s in a brutal attempt to exterminate the Bedouins, followed by the establishment of inhumane concentration camps. Forced labour was also widely used by Rome in Somalia. Furthermore, there was widespread rape of local women by Italian soldiers across Italy's colonies.

The three essays in the sixth section then examine the lingering impacts of colonialism in the British and Dutch Caribbean, as well as in Iberian America. The South African political economist Scott Timcke and the Guyanese socio-cultural anthropologist Shelene Gomes examine the history of British colonialism in the Caribbean between 1609 and 1814, encompassing Bermuda, Barbados, the Bahamas, the Leeward Islands, Jamaica, Dominica, Grenada, St Vincent, Tobago, Trinidad, and British Guiana. Britain's rivalry with France and the Netherlands is also assessed. The authors note that the Caribbean was among the first laboratories for English colonial expansion, with its methods thereafter being exported to other parts of the world. They further examine both these colonial techniques and post-emancipation cultural practices in the British Caribbean relating to family and kinship. Enslaved Africans were massively exploited on sugar plantations for nearly three centuries.

The black Curaçaoan anthropologist Rose Mary Allen then assesses Dutch conquest (1631–1667) – through the Dutch West India Company, which exploited slave labour from West Africa – and colonisation of the Caribbean: Suriname, Aruba, Bonaire, Curaçao, Saba, Sint Eustatius, and Sint Maarten. She analyses the diverse experiences of Dutch colonisation through instruments such as commercial links, education systems, economic models, language, and culture. Her chapter further examines the ways in which the colonised resisted and challenged Dutch rule. From the eighteenth century to the end of Dutch slavery in 1863, 5.2 per cent of the Dutch economy was derived from this sordid commerce in human chattel. Slavery thus coexisted with colonialism. Allen further demonstrates the ways in which European slavery and colonialism set out deliberately to destroy indigenous cultures and impose in their place imported systems on people considered inferior and in need of "civilising".

The Hispanic American scholar Susan Ramirez next examines Portuguese and Spanish colonialism in the Americas. Both imperialisms started in the fifteenth century as trading relationships, with a particular obsession with finding gold-rich El Dorados. The Italian explorer Christopher Columbus was sponsored by the Catholic Spanish crown, but his explorations ended in the genocide of indigenous people. Both Lisbon and Madrid used profits derived from commerce, agriculture, and mining to establish tax-collecting and judicial bureaucracies through which they ran their empires. Royal decrees, forced labour, segregationist policies, and forcible conversion of indigenous people to Catholicism characterised Spanish rule in the Americas. After the Bourbons inherited the Spanish throne from the Habsburgs in 1700, governance reforms increased revenues (mostly from silver and tobacco), and a more traditional army was established to reduce smuggling of contraband. Ramirez further examines Portugal's colonisation of Brazil from 1500. Lisbon exploited the territory's agricultural and fishing resources, especially its brazilwood, sugar cane, cotton, and tobacco. By 1550, the Portuguese had originated the transatlantic slave trade, exporting human chattel to Brazil until 1888. Gold was also mined from 1695.

With this background to five centuries of European enslavement and colonialism, the seventh and final section of the book then examines the global struggle for reparations that emerged directly from these two crimes against humanity. Starting in the Caribbean, the Barbadian historian and chair of the Caribbean Community's Reparations Commission, Hilary Beckles, describes the activities of the region's governments and civil society since 2013 to coordinate their efforts with similar groups in the United States, Colombia, Canada, Europe, and Africa in order to achieve reparations for European slavery and colonialism in the Caribbean and the Americas. Beckles outlines the Caricom ten-point reparations plan with its demands for a sincere apology and admission that slavery had been a "crime against humanity". He notes the progress of reparations in forcing Western governments, universities, companies, churches, monarchies, and British families like the Draxes and the Trevelyans to apologise to Caribbean citizens and make amends for their historical links to slavery in the region. He argues that despite some progress, success remains limited.

The American historian Andrew Maginn then examines the reparations struggle in the United States during four key phases: early American reparations (1783–1915); the re-emergence of the reparations movement (1950–1989);

the growth in US reparations discourse (1989–2014); and contemporary reparations debates since 2014. He makes the startling point that though Presidents Bill Clinton (1993–2000), George W. Bush Jr (2001–2008), and Joe Biden (2021–2024) apologised to Africans on the continent for slavery, no American president had ever apologised directly to their own black citizens for two and a half centuries of enslavement. Maginn notes that conservative scholars like America's David Horowitz have sought to discredit the reparations movement with arguments that slavery occurred too long ago; only very few benefited from it; the issue divides rather than unites; and civil rights-era laws had corrected the crimes of the past.[181] From 2019, American states and cities such as Evanston, Asheville, and Amherst started to implement reparations projects in black communities, as well as equal housing schemes. Universities and religious organisations that had benefited directly from slavery joined in, but the US federal government is yet to secure political consensus to enact legislation for substantive reparations.

In their joint chapter, British linguist and post-colonial scholar Nicole Frith and Caribbean-British legal scholar, historian, and activist Esther Xosei demonstrate the diverse strategies and ideologies used by British-based activists in pushing for reparations for slavery and colonialism. They criticise the fact that reparations are often reduced to monetary compensation for individuals, and argue that the crucial role of grassroots activists in Britain such as the International Social Movement for Afrikan Reparations has often been ignored. They stress the importance of the British alliance between reparationists and environmentalists propagating "holistic repairs", and promoting concepts such as "Planet Repairs" and "rematriation", involving a spiritual and cultural return to African indigeneity.

In his chapter, Adekeye Adebajo examines reparations efforts in Africa through the intergovernmental-led efforts of the Organisation of African Unity, the African Union, and the UN, as well as civil society-led activists, which produced the Abuja Declaration of 1993, the Accra Declaration of 1999, the Durban Declaration of 2001, and the Accra Proclamation of 2023. He then assesses the thinking and contributions of four important African prophets of reparations: Kenya's Ali Mazrui, Nigeria's Ade Ajayi and Wole Soyinka, and South Africa's Thabo Mbeki. He briefly analyses more recent efforts led by the Ghanaian president, Nana Akufo-Addo – involving the African Union and Caricom – to coordinate Afro-Caribbean reparations struggles more effectively.

The St Lucian historian-diplomat June Soomer then concludes the volume by arguing forcefully for reparations for the people of Latin America in order to atone for European slavery and colonialism, which she notes are still denying victims the opportunity to participate equally in the political, social, and economic life of the region. She argues that truth commissions in Argentina, Chile, and Colombia in the 1990s – with a focus on contemporary atrocities – have complicated issues of reparations for historical injustices. She details the efforts of reparations movements across South America in confronting European governments for reparations for indigenous people across the region. Soomer focuses particular attention on the resistance of the Black Caribs (Garifuna) against European oppression from the eighteenth century. She also examines the whitening and *mestizaje* (miscegenation) policies of Brazil's Portuguese-descended elite, who imported nearly 4 million white Europeans to the country between 1884 and 1939, and notes similar issues of "colourism" evident in Mexico and the Dominican Republic. Soomer further analyses the varying degrees of success of affirmative action programmes in Brazil, Cuba, and Colombia, before assessing Caricom's reparations struggle and its impact on contemporary South and Latin America.

Concluding Reflections

In concluding this Introduction, it is important to note that five centuries of European slavery and colonialism have clearly brought massive political, economic, social, and cultural destruction to indigenous peoples across Africa, the Caribbean, and the Americas. Commercial companies such as the British South Africa Company, the Royal African Company, the Dutch West India Company, and the Dutch East India Company were all used to enslave and exploit black and brown peoples and territories, greatly benefiting European imperial powers and enabling the West's industrialisation. European planters often dominated parliaments across the Caribbean and the Americas, even after slavery formally ended in the nineteenth century. It was these slave owners rather than the enslaved who were compensated for these heinous crimes. The rape and abuse of indigenous women by European colonisers was very much an ubiquitous feature of this brutal four-century subjugation.

These events have eventually triggered a global struggle for reparations across the Black Atlantic of Africa, the Caribbean, the Americas, and Europe, with deep roots in the church-based civil society activism in the United States and the Caribbean. European imperialists exported their systems of government to Africa, the Caribbean, and the Americas, but failed spectacularly to build viable institutions and extensive infrastructure, as well as provide social services and promote socio-economic development in their colonies. The silver lining in this grim four-and-a-half-century history of European imperial slavery is that enslaved and colonised black and brown people in Africa, the Caribbean, and the Americas survived against all odds. Indigenous populations in the Americas and Australia were not always as fortunate, with their populations decimated to a far greater extent by genocidal European holocausts.

About 40 million Africans currently live outside the continent.[182] An estimated 10.6 million reside in Europe,[183] while sizeable Afro-Caribbean minority populations continue to live in Britain and France (around 2 million each), and similar Antillean populations reside in the Netherlands. Africans are still estimated to constitute only around 1 per cent of the total European continental population.[184] Yet many vulnerable Africans in Europe continue to suffer from racist stereotyping. A key source of tensions between Africa and the 27-member European Union (EU) has involved the migration of Africans across the Mediterranean. Several European governments and populations continue to view the phenomenon as a security threat, often scapegoating and criminalising African migrants. "Fortress Europe" has thus resulted in EU governments strengthening border security and sometimes violating refugee rights.

Europe's free movement principles have often been restricted.[185] In 2021, 151,417 migrants arrived in the EU, with 72,425 of them coming from African countries such as Tunisia, Morocco, Algeria, Libya, Sudan, Somalia, Eritrea, Ethiopia, Côte d'Ivoire, Nigeria, Niger, Senegal, Guinea, and Mali. Tragically, 3,224 of the total migrants perished in the Mediterranean or were declared missing.[186] Hungary, Poland, and Greece have been particularly concerned about African migrants, and xenophobic sentiments are widespread in all three countries and across the EU bloc, as well as among many political leaders. African governments, in stark contrast, view migrants as a vital source of remittances, and have thus opposed forced migrant returns from Europe. They have often noted that most African migration occurs within the continent itself, with 32 million Africans forcibly displaced in June 2021, 75 per cent of them within their own national borders.[187]

Across the Atlantic, the African-born population in the United States doubled every decade between 1970 and 2020 to reach 2.4 million: most are from Nigeria, Ethiopia, and Ghana.[188] The most effective recent African American civil rights organisation, Black Lives Matter, seeks to "connect Black people from all over the world who have a shared desire for justice to act together in their communities".[189] The group effectively led global anti-racism protests in 2020, and has great potential to forge links with similar movements across Africa and its diaspora. In the Caribbean, identification with Africa has grown tremendously as a result of Nigeria-produced Nollywood movies, and consequently West Indian populations experience cultures and people with whom they can readily identify. Netflix had 112 Nollywood films and television shows in 2023.[190]

But the level of social interaction and trade between both Africa and the Caribbean remains abysmally low, despite periodic high-level inter-governmental summits between leaders of the AU and Caricom. The geographical pull of the United States – where many Caribbean students study, and even more desire to go – and the overwhelming American cultural pull still remain strong influences, especially among the region's youth. Having united to attain the political kingdom from the 1960s, Africa and its neglected diaspora in the Caribbean, the Americas, and Europe must, however, now collaborate to pursue contemporary struggles for reparations by rebuilding diasporic bridges to achieve a new people-driven Pan-Africanism.

In concluding this Introduction on the Black Atlantic's continuing triple tragedies of the lingering impacts of slavery and colonialism and the unfulfilled quest for reparatory justice, it is important to pose the fundamental question: how can European nations who enslaved and colonised black and brown populations for nearly five centuries repair this pernicious damage that has left Africa, the Caribbean, and the Americas with the triple burdens of a lack of development and crippling debt; diseases; and deadly conflicts? As has often been noted, the movements to abolish slavery and colonialism took generations to succeed, and so also will the contemporary movement for reparations for slavery and colonialism. As African-American civil rights activist, Frederick Douglass, famously observed in 1857: "Power concedes nothing without a demand. It never did and it never will."[191] We hope that this book can make a modest contribution to this noble struggle.

2

Masters and Servants in Barbados and South Africa: From Enslaved Labour to Coerced "Free" Labour in the British Empire

Alan Cobley

IN THE EARLY 1990s, Douglas Hay and Paul Craven – a legal historian and a legal scholar respectively at York University in Toronto, Canada – embarked on a project to investigate the law of Master and Servant, which had its origins in England in the fourteenth century. Their work demonstrated that, as England launched into a process of overseas territorial expansion from the seventeenth century onwards, the law of Master and Servant was exported and adapted as one of the key legal mechanisms to define labour relations between employer and worker in its new colonies. As Hay and Craven noted in the introduction to their edited volume, *Masters, Servants, and Magistrates in Britain and the Empire, 1562–1955*, published in 2004: "Master and Servant was one of the many legal ligaments that helped make the British Empire a thinkable whole by the eighteenth century."[1]

Masters and Servants in the British Empire

In the course of their research, Hay and Craven identified over 500 Master and Servant laws in more than a hundred different jurisdictions worldwide, all of which contained three core elements. First, these laws regulated employment between the employer and worker through a private contract, which gave the employer the right to command and required the worker to obey. Second, these laws provided for the enforcement of such contracts by the criminal justice system. Third, they allowed punishments to be meted out to workers who were deemed to have breached their contracts. As the Indian scholar Ravi Ahuja explains: "'master and servant law' constructed employment relationships as contractual relationships between formally unequal parties, parties who were bound by the contract in divergent ways. Medieval concepts of the asymmetrical legal status of master and servant were preserved by giving them new expression in the language of contract law, which unilaterally criminalized servants who breached the contract."[2]

When chattel slavery was abolished throughout the British Empire after the Act of Abolition of 1833, former slave masters scrambled to redefine their relationships with their formerly enslaved workers to ensure that they would retain control over this labour. The British Colonial Office assisted this transition from enslaved labour to "free" labour, by offering advice based on precedents found in British labour law as well as on comparisons with evolving labour practices found in various imperial jurisdictions. The first phase of this transition involved the institution of forced apprenticeship, followed within a few years by the near-ubiquitous application of Master and Servant laws.

One important consequence of the legal definition of labour relations as between "master" and "servant" was that it made labour combination by workers to agitate for improved pay and conditions illegal and practically impossible to organise. This delayed the development of trade unions in many colonial societies. The result was numerous episodes of worker militancy in the form of riots and uprisings in these territories during the latter half of the nineteenth and the first half of the twentieth centuries.[3]

This chapter will consider, in comparative perspective, the impact of the replacement of slavery in the British Empire with this form of coerced labour relations in two geographically widely separated jurisdictions: Barbados in the British Caribbean and the Cape Colony in South Africa. How was the law of Master and Servant used to perpetuate and entrench coercive labour practices and unequal power in these societies? What was the impact of these laws on their social, economic, and political development in the nineteenth and early twentieth centuries?

Ameliorating Apprenticeship

When the Act of Abolition formally brought the institution of chattel slavery in the British Empire to an end effectively from 1834, the change in labour relations was not as dramatic as many had anticipated. In the British West Indies, the Act came into effect on 1 August 1834. In Barbados, the House of Assembly refused to implement the suggestion by Governor Lionel Smith to make the day a public holiday. However, the day passed off peacefully, with many former slaves attending church in the morning and participating in organised festivities in the afternoon.[4] Some white plantation owners provided meat and rum for the celebrations. In South Africa, the Act came into force four months later, on 1 December 1834. As in the West Indies, celebrations were orderly, with many former slaves attending thanksgiving services in the mission churches.[5]

The muted response to the 1834 emancipation reflected the fact that, in most cases, the formerly enslaved experienced little or no change in their material circumstances. This was due to two reasons. First, measures to ameliorate the harshest aspects of slavery had been implemented progressively since at least 1823, in anticipation of its ultimate abolition. These measures had been mandated by the British House of Commons and implemented in the various colonies through directives from the Colonial Office – despite efforts by many slave owners in the colonies to derail or delay these reforms. These initiatives included provision for the moral and religious instruction of slaves, the abolition of Sunday markets, the ending of the practice of separating enslaved families, the abolition of whipping as a form of punishment, and the removal of several restrictions on manumission.[6]

The second reason for the low-key response to the emancipation was that the formal institution of slavery was replaced immediately by a system of forced "apprenticeship" for a minimum period of four years for non-field workers ("non-praendials") and six years for field workers ("praendials"). The 1834 Act, however, provided for field workers to receive some remuneration for overtime work. Another important provision was that former masters were no longer allowed to punish their formerly enslaved workers directly. Instead, courts were established to manage the relationship between masters and "apprentices", and these were presided over by specially appointed stipendiary magistrates.[7] The degree of protection from abuses afforded to the apprentices depended largely on the interpretation of their role by individual magistrates.[8] A quarter of the apprentice's normal working time (15 out of 60 hours) was designated "free time", and they were granted the right to "buy" their freedom, if they could muster the means to do so – even if their master objected. On the other hand, the labour services of the "apprentices" could still be mortgaged, bought, and sold – as under slavery. Apprentices were also still required to perform unpaid labour for their former slave masters, and could still receive physical punishments for disobedience or other offences against the master (though administered by order of the magistrates), while their civil rights – including their freedom of movement – remained strictly limited. As the Barbadian scholar Woodville Marshall remarked: "there is a strong case for saying that the Apprenticeship was merely amelioration of slavery – the last phase of the amelioration policy".[9]

The apprenticeship system included one further concession of note: children six years or under were exempted from forced apprenticeship, as were children born after the date on which the Act had come into force. However, this left many parents with the unenviable choice of having to find the means to support their children without any provision from their former masters, or voluntarily contracting these children as apprentices to their former masters until the age of 21. As the American scholar William Green notes, the situation was particularly acute in Barbados because apprentices were largely dependent on food provided by their masters for their survival: "Interpreting the Emancipation Act with self-serving rigidity, Barbados Planters refused to supply customary allowances to the island's 14,000 free children. An appeal by Governor Lionel Smith to the humane instincts of assemblymen, a group already bristling over their capitulation on the slavery question, proved unavailing."[10] Nevertheless, many apprentices in Barbados were "magnificently adamant" that they would rather see their children starve than bind them to another 15 years or more of servitude.[11] At the other end of the age spectrum, some employers abandoned all responsibility for the aged and infirm on their estates. These people were left to fend for themselves as part of a growing category of vagrants and destitute persons on the island.

In Barbados, the total formerly enslaved population in August 1834 was 83,150. Of these, 52,193 were categorised as "praendials" (field labour) and 14,732 as "non-praendials" (non-field labour). The remaining 16,225 were classified as children under six or "worn-out" or infirm persons.[12] By comparison, the enslaved population in the Cape Colony in 1833 on the eve of the 1834 emancipation was 38,427, of which 35,843 were classified as "apprentices" by November 1838. One key difference between apprenticeship as applied in the Cape Colony and that in Barbados was that none of the apprentices at the Cape were categorised as "praendial". This was because the distinction between field labour and non-field labour was much less clear in a colony with no plantations, and the Cape colonial administration decided that any attempt to impose these labels would lead to endless disputes. Though this meant that white farmers were guaranteed labour from their "apprentices" for a shorter period than was the case in Barbados, it also meant that they were not required to pay them for overtime work.

The period of apprenticeship was intended as a transitional stage during which both former slave masters and former slaves would have time to adjust to a system of wage labour. Unfortunately, many former slave masters treated apprenticeship as the continuation of slavery by other means, and took the opportunity to extract the maximum possible labour and profit from their workforce before the period of apprenticeship ended. In Barbados, the situation was particularly acute because all the available agricultural land was owned by the planters, so there was little opportunity for former slaves to escape their control. Many found themselves in a worse position than they had been under slavery: they were still tied to the plantations, but the planters now refused to pay for many of the customary benefits (such as providing food for children) that had applied under the old system, arguing that under the new system of wage labour, they no longer had any obligation to do so.

In the Cape Colony, instances of resistance to the system of apprenticeship were more common than in Barbados, mainly because the size and topography of the colony, as well as its proximity to free black African societies, increased the possibility of desertion and escape. According to an analysis by the South African historian Nigel Worden of the apprenticeship offences brought before the stipendiary magistrate in Cape Town between the implementation of the Act of Abolition in December 1834 and November 1835, 229 – or 64.3 per cent – were for desertion or unauthorised absence. Other offences included "insolence", "negligence", "theft", and "malicious damage", suggesting that desertion was just one of several forms of resistance that persisted in the Cape Colony from the era of slavery into apprenticeship.[13]

Eventually, the numerous complaints and petitions from apprentices, missionaries, and abolitionists about abuses of the apprenticeship system by masters – supported by reports from stipendiary magistrates and several colonial governors – remobilised the anti-slavery lobby in London to call for the termination of the period of apprenticeship in the British House of Commons. By April 1838, the original scheme for a "staggered emancipation" for non-field and field slaves was abandoned by the British Colonial Office, not only because of the campaign waged in parliament, but also because of correspondence from the Governor of Barbados, E.J. Murray MacGregor, which pointed out the practical difficulties of administering the policy in the light of the heightened expectations of freedom among apprentices in both groups. Termination of the system for all apprentices after four years now became the preferred policy.[14] Meanwhile, the white planters in the British West Indies had become increasingly impatient with what they perceived as the persistent meddling in their affairs by the British government that the apprenticeship system allowed. They also feared that the anti-apprenticeship agitation in London would force other, even more unfavourable changes in labour relations upon them. Spurred by these pressures, Montserrat voted to abolish apprenticeship in 1837, followed by Nevis, St Kitts, the Virgin Islands, and Barbados the following year. In Barbados, the Assembly voted to abolish apprenticeship in May 1838.[15] Apprenticeship was officially terminated in the remaining territories across the British West Indies three months later.

Similar frustrations to those being felt by planters in the West Indies were experienced by many of the Dutch-speaking farmers (or "Boers") in the Cape Colony. Anger over what they regarded as British interference in their control over black labour since the imposition of British colonial rule at the Cape in 1806 was compounded by a policy to "anglicise" the colony, especially after the introduction of British settlers from 1820. This left the Boers feeling marginalised and powerless. For many of them, the imposition from London of the abolition of slavery, and the efforts by the colonial authorities in Cape Town to administer the apprenticeship system which replaced it, were the last straw. As early as February 1834, the colonial administration was receiving reports that some Boers were planning to quit the colony "with the view of preventing the liberation of their slaves".[16] Beginning in late 1835, the Boers began to migrate in organised groups beyond the eastern colonial frontier in search of new lands to colonise, taking many of their "apprentices" with them. This migration, which eventually involved about 12,000 Boers, became known as the Great Trek.[17] Although the Boers did not reinstate slavery in their own independent republics – the South African Republic (Transvaal) and the Orange Free State – fearing that it would provoke the British to pursue them into the interior, they created a class of black and brown servile labour based on their own version of apprenticeship, known as *inboekselings* and *Oorlams*.[18] Meanwhile, the decision to end apprenticeship in the Cape Colony was implemented with effect from 1 December 1838. These developments are indicative of the complexities of the transition from slavery to "freedom" across the British Empire and the differing perceptions of what constituted black liberation. The date of 1 August 1834 is commemorated as Emancipation Day in Barbados, while the event is marked at the Cape on 1 December.[19]

Masters and Servants in Barbados

In response to the abolition of slavery and the anticipated ending of apprenticeship in 1838, various Caribbean colonies passed laws that reflected the preoccupation of the former slave owners with maintaining control over their labour, rather than establishing the principle of wage labour on an equitable basis. Officials in the British Colonial Office, led by the Under-Secretary of State, James Stephen, tried to impose order, logic, and a measure of common humanity on this legislation, which had to be submitted to them for vetting and approval.[20] Where legislation was disallowed, the Colonial Office proposed its own model legislation, promulgated in London in the form of an Order-in-Council, which drew on Master and Servant laws in England. According to the British scholar Mandy Banton:

> The essential features of the model were that contract periods should be limited to four weeks if made orally, or one year if written, and written contracts were to be attested by a stipendiary magistrate. Breaches of contract subject to criminal penalties should be limited to three: failure to perform stipulated work; negligent or improper performance of such work; and causing damage to the employer's property by negligence or improper conduct. Maximum penalties should be a fine of one month's wages, fourteen days' imprisonment, or dismissal. Claims for nonpayment of wages or compensation for ill-treatment, as in England, could be made before a magistrate for summary settlement.[21]

Lord Glenelg, the Secretary of State for the Colonies, sent this model to the Cape Colony in December 1838 but indicated that it could be adapted to suit local conditions in South Africa.[22] In the case of Barbados, a new Master and Servant law (or the Contract law, as it was more commonly known) was passed by the legislature in Barbados in June 1838. However, the law was immediately referred to London by Governor MacGregor, who believed that it was designed to continue the practice of coercion of black labour on the island, rather than move towards a system of "free" wage labour, as intended. Under the terms of the legislation, a worker who provided five days of continuous labour to a planter was deemed to have entered a contract with the employer for a minimum of a year. The contract included the provision of housing for the worker and his family on the plantation, and allowed the termination of the contract by either party at one month's notice. However, a worker who terminated a contract, or who was dismissed, was no longer entitled to housing and faced eviction. The law also replaced the role of stipendiary magistrates (who were at least notionally independent) in mediating labour disputes between employers and workers with local Justices of the Peace, who were, almost invariably, planters. The Contract law was accompanied by a companion piece of legislation – a "vagrancy" law – which prescribed severe punishments for those found to be "idle" and "disorderly". Although both the Master and Servant law and the Vagrancy law initially came into force after the ending of apprenticeship in August 1838, both were disallowed by the Colonial Office in London two months later, owing to their draconian conditions.[23]

Barbados had already made special provisions for the control of the formerly enslaved population by becoming the first British colony in the West Indies to create a police force. An Act passed on the eve of emancipation on 14 July 1834 "for the Establishment of a Rural Police for this Island, and for the erection of Houses of Correction" was also disallowed by the British Colonial Office. However, a separate Act passed two weeks later to establish a police force in the island's capital of Bridgetown was allowed to stand. A revised version of the disallowed law, entitled "An Act to provide for the building of House of Correction, and Police Establishments", was later passed in September 1835.[24] Eventually, the disallowed labour and vagrancy laws were replaced by two Acts passed in Barbados on the same day, 7 January 1840. These were a revised Contract law, entitled "An Act to Regulate the Hiring of Servants and to Provide for the Recovery and Security of their Wages", and a new companion Vagrancy law, entitled "An Act for the Suppression and Punishment of Vagrancy".[25]

The new Contract law appeared more even-handed in its provisions and in its language than its predecessor, since it dropped the presumption that five days of continuous work for an employer would constitute a contract, and instead provided that any contract longer than a month had to be in writing, entered into voluntarily, and signed by both parties before a Justice of the Peace. The period of one month's notice of termination of the contract on either side was retained, and the hours of work and the nature of the work to be undertaken were to be specified in the contract. The law also included detailed provisions for workers to recover wages owed to them by recalcitrant employers. The core element of criminal prosecution and punishment for workers who breached the terms of their contract remained in place, though the stipulated breaches and penalties were now in line with those proposed in Glenelg's model legislation.

In Barbados, the planters increased their coercive power over black workers after the end of slavery by exploiting their virtual monopoly over land and living space on the island. They inserted clauses in the contracts of many of their workers that meant that part of their wages was paid in kind, in the form of access to housing and provision grounds on the plantation. These "customary allowances" had existed under slavery, but now they were reinvented in the post-emancipation period as additional means to control "free" black workers. As the Barbadian historian Hilary Beckles explains: "The law ... transformed the free wage worker into a 'located' plantation tenant."[26] This strategy had been carefully planned by the white planters to keep a firm grip on their black workers after emancipation. As one Barbadian planter, George Carrington, told a British House of Commons select committee in 1848, "A considerable time before emancipation took place, I thought the only chance of securing labour was to encourage a system of tenantry."[27]

The rise of the "tenantry" system in Barbados resulted in cash wages for field labourers that were among the lowest in the West Indies, at around 10 pence per day in 1840. To compound the misery of the workers, one of the standard provisions in such contracts was a monetary penalty of between 5 and 10 pence per day for every day of work that they missed. As the Barbadian scholar Bentley Gibbs noted:

Under this arrangement, therefore, the level of rent payable to the estate was a function, not of the value of the house and piece of land the tenant occupied, but of the quantum of labour he gave to the estate. In short, the less labour he provided, the higher his rent. The operation of this renting arrangement was applied, not only to the labour of the tenant himself, but also to the potential labour of those he sheltered in his home and who shared the benefits which his spot of land offered.[28]

The wording of the Contract law of 1840 spelt out the additional coercive power accorded to employers by the tenantry system, and made clear the invidious situation in which workers had been placed as a result. Clause 6 of the Act stated:

That in case any servant after dissolution of his or her contract of service ... shall refuse to quit and deliver up possession to his or her master, mistress, or employer, ... of any house, room or land which he shall be permitted to occupy as an incident to such service, or shall continue the possession thereof after twenty-four hours' notice to quit the same ... it shall and may be lawful for any Police Magistrate or Justice of the Peace ... to remove and expel any such servant from such premises; and in case any such servant shall refuse to quit, or in case such servant should return and occupy such house, room or land ... it shall be made lawful, and [the Magistrate] is hereby required to commit every such servant to prison with or without hard labour for any time not exceeding one calendar month; and such servant shall also pay the costs [incurred in the prosecution].[29]

An added refinement of the system further reduced the cost to planters: over time, most labour tenants built their own homes on the land provided to replace the "slave huts" provided by the planters. Thus, the "chattel house" – a movable wooden structure built by the tenant on a rented house spot – became one of the most notable features of Barbadian vernacular architecture over the next 200 years. These "movable" houses are portrayed to tourists today as one of Barbados's quainter and more picturesque features, but their existence is eloquent testimony to the intensely coercive nature of labour relations on the island in the post-emancipation era. In 1839, Samuel Jackman Prescod, a leading Coloured (mixed-race) advocate of rights for black Barbadians after emancipation, explained how lack of security of tenure militated against the efforts of labourers to lift themselves out of poverty:

The labourer is far from being as comfortable as he might be – he has no security for his comfort – cannot be sure of its continuance for another day. Liable every moment to ejectment from a bit of hired land he tills for his benefit, from the hut that he, perhaps, or his father built and has kept in repair for years, he has no certain home; his industry is, as far, a venture – a mere game of chance in which the probabilities, number and weight are against him.[30]

Prescod summed up the role of the tenantry system in perpetuating control over black field labourers by their erstwhile slave masters, in this way: "Ejectment", he wrote, "is the grand instrument of coercion which has succeeded the cowskin

[whip]." The sense that formerly enslaved workers in Barbados were "trapped" on the plantations by the terms of their labour contracts was compounded by the simultaneous passage of the Vagrancy Act in 1840. The Act declared that "every person being able either by their labour, or by other lawful means, to maintain himself or herself, or his wife, or his or her children, who shall wilfully refuse or neglect to do so ... shall be deemed an idle and disorderly person."[31] Any individual suspected of vagrancy was thus subject to arrest by the police and, on conviction, was liable to a maximum of 14 days' confinement with hard labour. "Incorrigibles", who were repeat offenders, were liable to six months in prison with hard labour.[32] The Contract law and the Vagrancy law of 1840, together with the widespread use of the tenantry system, formed the tripartite basis of labour relations in Barbados over the next century.

Masters and Servants in South Africa

The remaking of coercive labour relations after the end of slavery in the Cape Colony was complicated by the existence of a residual indigenous black South African population within the colony known as the "Khoikhoi", or – in colonial parlance – "the Hottentots". The British administration that took control of the Cape in the early nineteenth century was lobbied by missionaries who worked among this group to provide them with various legal protections. Eventually, this led in 1828 to the passage of a measure known as Ordinance 50, which gave this indigenous population and other "free Persons of colour" various legal protections. The ordinance stated: "no Hottentot or other free Person of colour ... shall be subject to any compulsory service to which other of His Majesty's Subjects ... are not liable, nor to any hindrance, molestation, fine, imprisonment or punishment of any kind whatsoever, under pretense that such Person has been guilty of vagrancy or any other offence, unless after trial."[33] Among other provisions, the 1828 Ordinance freed the Khoikhoi from the obligation to carry passes while moving about the colony, confirmed their right to own land, and regulated their employment through the issuing of contracts for a period of up to a month if oral, or up to a year if written. The Ordinance was celebrated by missionaries as the "emancipation of the Hottentots" but was bitterly resented by many Boers.[34]

To counteract the perceived threat of increased vagrancy following emancipation, a new vagrancy law was drafted at the Cape in 1834. The Acting Governor, Lieutenant Colonel T.F. Wade, informed the British Colonial Office that the legislation would secure "a sufficiency of labourers to the colony by compelling not only the liberated apprentices to earn an honest livelihood, but all others who, being capable of doing so, may be inclined to lead an idle and vagabonding life".[35] The Vagrancy Ordinance passed by the Legislative Council in May 1834 allowed local magistrates to detain any Hottentots and persons of colour who might "reasonably be suspected of having no honest means of subsistence".[36] However, the Colonial Office disallowed the law in 1835 on the grounds that it was incompatible with the provisions of Ordinance 50, and because "the proposed enactments were at variance with the most established principles of personal freedom".[37]

The first draft of a Master and Servant Ordinance for the Cape, submitted to London in June 1839, tried to achieve the same result as the failed 1834 Vagrancy Ordinance, by redefining labour relations at the Cape after the end of slavery in overtly racist terms. The declared purpose of the new ordinance was to provide "for the improvement of the labouring classes, and more particularly for that class composed of persons of colour". The new measure imposed longer contract periods and heavier penalties, and granted the power to regulate contracts to resident district magistrates, who were part of the white settler community. For good measure, the proposed ordinance added several new criminal offences such as "behaving to the master with violence or insolence", "scandalous immorality", "drunkenness", and other "gross misconduct". James Stephen, the Under-Secretary of State in the Colonial Office in London, rejected the proposed ordinance as replicating the conditions of slavery, since "much of the essence of slavery consisted, and must always consist, in the power of summary punishment for offences either wholly indefinite or defined merely by vague and general words".[38] Stephen also specifically rejected the notion that "immorality" and undefined "gross misconduct" could be considered criminal offences.[39]

A revised version of the ordinance was submitted in January 1840. This was eventually approved by the Colonial Office – but only after the Governor, George Napier, had insisted that some of the clauses – such as the use of resident magistrates for enforcement – were necessary owing to "local circumstances". The ordinance was implemented at the Cape in August 1842. Though the revised ordinance was supposedly "race-neutral", one of the core assumptions in the Act remained that the masters would be white, while the bulk of the "servants" or "labouring classes" would be "coloured" (mixed-race) or black. This same assumption applied in Barbados. As the Canadian scholar Elizabeth Elbourne succinctly put it: "The Masters and Servants Act was essentially racially biased legislation disguised as legislation to control class relations."[40]

One of the interesting parallels between the Caribbean and South Africa in the nineteenth century was the use of the terms "coloured" and "persons of colour" to describe segments of the population. According to the American scholar John Mason, these terms "seem to have entered the Cape from usage in the British West Indies, by way of the Colonial Office: in the West Indies, they distinguished free people of mixed ancestry from those of purely European or African descent".[41] This was the beginning of a process that led to "legally defined and self-identified" coloured communities under segregation and apartheid in South Africa in the twentieth century. As Mason noted: "In practice, in speech and, indirectly, in law, the colonists were inventing a racially defined, subordinate working class."[42]

In 1853, the Cape Colony became a crown colony with a form of representative government. The new Legislative Assembly took advantage of the reduced role of the British Colonial Office to draft a new, much more stringent Masters and Servants Act, which came into effect in 1856. This Act was a comprehensive piece of legislation, containing 76 sections, many of which were punitive in nature. Penalties were increased for breaches of contract, and the list of possible offences was increased from three to eight "minor" and six "major" ones. "Minor" offences included failing to commence an agreed contract, unauthorised absence from the workplace, negligent performance of work, drunkenness, abusive language, insubordination, and making a "brawl or disturbance." "Major" offences included causing damage or loss to the employer's property; assault or attempted assault on the employer, his family, or fellow servants; and desertion. Punishments ranged from terms of imprisonment from a month to six months with or without hard labour, to solitary confinement and a reduced diet. In the case of imprisonment, the term would be added to the length of the contract, while in the case of damage or loss of property, compensation was to be paid from the worker's wages. The law also made provision for sick pay and for the feeding and proper housing of domestic servants. However, it made no provision to enforce these ameliorative clauses.[43]

As Mandy Banton noted, the effects of the 1856 Masters and Servants Act were far-reaching: it became the basis for labour laws enacted in British colonies throughout southern, central, and eastern Africa over the next 70 years. In South Africa, the Act was used as a model for similar laws passed in the Transvaal in 1880 and in Natal in 1894. The legislation was also invoked to extend the principle of coercion and control to black mine workers in the diamond and gold mining industries in South Africa, as these industries became established in the late nineteenth and early twentieth centuries. By these means, the law provided a foundation for racially discriminatory labour laws under segregation and apartheid. Such was its utility and ubiquity in South African labour law that aspects of the 1856 Masters and Servants Act would remain in force in South Africa until finally repealed in 1974.[44]

Masters and Servants in Comparative Perspective

Master and Servant laws were used throughout the British colonial world in former slaveholding colonies to re-engineer labour relations after the end of slavery. At heart, the perpetuation of coercion in employer–employee labour relations from the era of slavery was predicated on the fear that, if given the choice, formerly enslaved workers would refuse to work for their former slave masters. This was also justified by the racist assumption that black workers were, by nature, indolent. The racist overtones of the law of Master and Servant in the colonial world became increasingly clear in the latter half of the nineteenth century, when more stringent versions of these laws were applied in British colonies, even as the principle of criminalisation of labour contracts was being abandoned in the metropole.[45]

There are many striking points of comparison in the application of Master and Servant laws in Barbados and South Africa, although there was no equivalent in Barbados of the sweeping Masters and Servants Act passed at the Cape in 1856. A more stringent version of the law on this model was unnecessary in Barbados owing to the Vagrancy law of 1840 allied to the operation of the labour tenantry system.

One strategy to control black labour that was common to both territories was the use of alcohol as a means of payment and control of workers. In the case of South Africa, the "tot" or "dop" system, which had been established as a device to control labour in the winelands of the Western Cape during the era of slavery, continued long after emancipation. White farmers argued that the "tot" was a form of refreshment and a reward for hard labour which was both demanded and much appreciated by the workers as part of their customary remuneration. However, critics noted the resulting high level of alcohol abuse among "coloured" (mixed-race) workers, and argued that the true purpose of the tot system was to create a dependency on alcohol which helped to tie workers to their employers in a situation of permanent dependency.[46] The tot system was officially banned in South Africa in 1960 but continued largely unchecked until after the end of apartheid in 1994. The practice was finally ended by the passage of the Liquor Act nine years later.[47]

Alcohol was used in a similar way in Barbados. A visitor to the island in the 1640s reported that a crude early form of rum known locally as "Kill-Devil" was given routinely to slaves who worked on the plantations:

> This drink is of great use, to cure and refresh the poor negroes, whom we ought to have a special care of, by the labour of whose hands, our profit is brought in; so it is helpful to our Christian Servants too; for, when their spirits are exhausted, by their hard labour, and sweating in the sun, ten hours every day, they find their stomachs debilitated, and much weakened in their vigour every way, a dram or two of this spirit is a great comfort and refreshing to them.[48]

After the formal end of slavery in 1834, workers on the plantations continued to receive alcohol, or the molasses with which to make it, as one of their "customary allowances".[49]

Another measure common to both colonies as a means to consolidate the labour force was a Marriage Act, based on a model supplied by the British Colonial Office and passed in both Barbados and the Cape Colony in 1839. This legislation established a form of civil marriage, the purpose of which was to stabilise the formerly enslaved population by creating permanent family units. This was considered necessary not only on moral grounds, but as one of the means by which to establish a permanent free wage-labouring class in former slaveholding colonies.[50]

Concluding Reflections

While the use of Master and Servant laws in Barbados and South Africa was similar, in the end the trajectories of development of these two societies were quite different. In Barbados, the plantation economy, based on sugar cane, went into depression in the 1870s, before settling into a long-term decline. By the early twentieth century, many plantations on the island were mired in debt. Dwindling sugar production reduced the demand for labour on the plantations and the need for stringent measures to control it. The result was that fears of labour shortages in Barbados were thereafter replaced with complaints about a labour surplus. Nevertheless, the Contract law passed in 1840 was still being enforced in Barbados in the 1930s. As a result, as E.R. Darnley, head of the West Indian Department in the British Colonial Office, remarked in 1931: in

Barbados, "'Mary Jane' could be imprisoned for breaking a teacup".[51] The continuing application of this law delayed and stunted the growth of political and labour organisations among the Barbadian working class. It took a major upsurge in worker-led militancy, culminating in the riots of 1937, to hasten the end of the law of Master and Servant in Barbados, and to open up a new era establishing workers' rights.[52]

At the same time, pressure was mounting internationally on the British government to bring an end to the use of this archaic and coercive form of labour relations throughout the British Empire. The report of the Committee of Experts on Native Labour appointed by the International Labour Organization (ILO) went to the nub of the issue by calling for the immediate abolition of the use of penal sanctions in labour contracts in 1935.[53] The death knell of Master and Servant laws in much of the British Empire was finally sounded when the Penal Sanctions (Indigenous Workers) Convention (no. 65) was promulgated by the ILO in Geneva in 1939, although it was not ratified and did not formally come into force until after the Second World War ended in 1945. This was followed by a second ILO convention calling for the immediate removal of all remaining penal sanctions in employment contracts in 1955.[54]

In South Africa, meanwhile, the effective achievement of Dominion status (alongside Australia, New Zealand, and Canada), following the passage of the Statute of Westminster in 1931, ensured that its labour laws were at last insulated from further British oversight or interference. Already committed to a segregationist path under successive white governments since the birth of the Union in 1910, South Africa under the National Party after 1948 began the process of instituting a modernised system of racial domination known as apartheid, in which racialised labour relations empowered the white minority at the expense of the black majority. These developments represented the culmination of a long process of creating coercive and racist labour relations that had first been sketched out throughout the British Empire in the post-emancipation era from 1834 by Master and Servant laws.

3

Colonialism: Mamma Italia and Her Imperial Orphans

Patrizia Palumbo

ITALIAN COLONIALISM IN AFRICA emerged as the subject of an animated debate in the late 1980s.[1] In those years, the scholarly attention given to Italian expansionism in Africa was made urgent by the intensifying flow of African immigrants into the Italian peninsula. Together with the diffusion of post-colonial studies, immigration from North and sub-Saharan Africa triggered a discussion about Italy's expansionist wars on the African continent, as well as on Italian colonial culture and propaganda, in which these wars had figured as "civilising missions" and expressions of the ambitions of a young nation seeking to emulate and compete with much older and more established European powers.

Following its unification in 1870, Italy started to expand its territory, colonising parts of Eritrea.[2] Less than a decade later, Italy invaded the territory south of the Horn of Africa, establishing first what would become Italian Somaliland, and subsequently the new colony of Eritrea. In 1911, through a war against the Ottoman Empire, Italy acquired Tripolitania and Cyrenaica, which together constituted Italian Libya. Italy's expansionism into Africa ended with the 1935 invasion of Ethiopia and Benito Mussolini's proclamation of his African "empire" in 1936. It is important to stress that Rome's colonisation of African countries did not start during the fascist *ventennio* (1922–1943). It was not the brainchild of a dictatorship but started as the objective of a new nation which, unlike other European nations with their vast colonial empires, could only boast the "glories" of Rome's ancient past (see Fuller in this volume).

Corrupting the Children

Decades of scholarly work on Italian colonialism in Africa have debunked myths of political and military strength that, according to Italian governmental propaganda, had defined its colonial campaigns since their inception. This work also exposed the economic fantasies and miscalculations of a succession of Italian governments, as well as many of the atrocities committed and, consequently, the unsustainability of the self-proclaimed myth of Italians as *brava gente* (good-hearted people). Nevertheless, there is an aspect of Italian colonialism that has not been sufficiently studied: the propaganda relating to Italian children. In general, Italian colonial propaganda directed at children ranged from an exaltation of aggression to a sentimentalisation of expansionist aims. This is what this chapter seeks to demonstrate, although its scope is limited to the fascist era of *ventennio*.

The political socialisation of Italian youth was at the very core of the fascist project after the party assumed power in Italy in 1922. Throughout the *ventennio*, the fascist regime systematically fed young Italians with its ideological doctrines by taking control of their schools and their textbooks, as well as youth organisations and radio programmes that provided them with social outlets.[3] Even immediately prior to and after the Ethiopian War, when the fascist government intensified its propagandistic efforts, Italian children as well as adults were widely exposed to imperialist indoctrination.

As the American scholar Edward Tannenbaum shows, the Ethiopian campaign was the primary topic of discussion in Italian elementary and secondary schools. In 1936, many teachers read an adaptation of the popular song "Faccetta nera" (Little Black Face) to first-graders. They also taught basic notions of "aggressive patriotism" by, for example, assigning their students compositions with titles such as "Italy is powerful and feared" or dictation exercises that stressed the greatness of the Italian nation, while condemning other European nations that had joined the embargo against Rome following its invasion of Ethiopia.[4] Even mathematics provided an opportunity for imperial propaganda. One of the puzzles that eight- or nine-year-old third-graders had to solve during this period was: "The glorious war in Africa lasted seven months. How many days is that?"[5] Between 1935 and 1936, moreover, half of all radio broadcasts for children dealt with the Ethiopian campaign.[6]

Conforming to the dictates of the regime, Italian publishers of children's and young adult literature filled their lists with texts on the Italian colonisation of East Africa just after the beginning of the Ethiopian War of 1935–1936.[7] Before that period, although Italy had already occupied African territories for four decades, children's literature did not show much interest in Italian colonial endeavours. A romantic, adventurous spirit also permeated novels written for very young Italians between 1925 and 1935 that dealt with the Italian colonial campaigns. For instance, in *Il piccolo Brassa: Romanzo coloniale per giovani*, written by Rosolino Davy Gabrielli and published in 1928, the main desire of Italian soldiers in Cyrenaica is to experience the "spell" of the desert, the oasis, and the nomadic life of the Bedouins. The description of the soldiers' adventures in a highly exoticised Africa effectively obscures the gruesome details of their military operations (see Fuller in this volume).

Fascist educators and officials were instrumental in the move away from this literary cliché of a mysterious and dangerous Africa. They encouraged Italian writers and artists instead to represent Africa as a cultivated land marked by the dignified white houses of the Italian colonists, the flowing steel ribbons of railway tracks, and imposing dams. In 1935, the Italian author and pedagogue Giuseppe Fanciulli produced a radio programme for young children entitled *Coi nostri soldati in Africa orientale* (With Our Soldiers in East Africa) to familiarise young Italians with the colonial environment. In addition, during this same year, Fanciulli published the novel *Dalla Nievole a Bargal: Avventure di un ragazzo nella Somalia italiana*. As Adolfo Scotto Di Luzio observes, in this novel Fanciulli carefully erases the fearful and exotic image of Africa that had characterised much of previous children's literature, and replaces it with a space filled with the reassuring signs of Italian "civilisation".[8] In *Dalla Nievole a Bargal*, the story of a father and son's arrival in an African colony and their search for a friend is nothing but a pretext to offer a reading tour of the much-celebrated Italian agricultural enterprises in Africa where indigenous people worked under the supposedly benevolent supervision of Italian colonists.

Although a wealth of imperialist fantasies can be traced in narratives and texts written for children in the mid-1930s – these images were intended to revive notions of imperial Rome – my concern in this chapter is to assess specifically the values and role models propagated by authors of children's literature who, in Fanciulli's wake, responded to the Mussolini regime's appeal for the creation of a new colonial literature for children immediately prior to or after the establishment of the empire. I will first devote my attention to texts that, like Fanciulli's, faithfully reproduced fascist imperial propaganda. Second, I will discuss the Italian writer Arnaldo Cipolla's *Balilla regale*: this is a more complex novel that breaks through what is a relatively homogeneous field by articulating scepticism about the dominant myths of Italian imperialism, as well as discomfort with contemporary ideals of masculinity.[9]

In dealing with cultural material produced during fascism, it is important not to take for granted popular acceptance and replication of the values promoted by such material. In spite of the combined efforts of the fascist regime and the publishers and authors who supported it, children's colonial literature of the time did not achieve great success among Italian children. According to critics and historians of literature for children, one of the favourite books among children in the 1930s was Salvator Gotta's *Piccolo alpino*, which dealt with Rome's participation in the Great War (1915–1918).[10] In addition, remarkable enthusiasm was aroused by the Italian writer Emilio Salgari's novels. Edward Tannenbaum observes that children liked Salgari's adventure stories, American movies, and comics because they "formed a spicy 'counterculture' to the discipline and moralizing tendencies they experienced at home, in school, and in the Balilla [youth organisation]".[11]

Children's Literature in the Imperial Climate

Much of the children's literature of the mid-1930s responded enthusiastically to the fascist imperial appeal and sought deferentially to serve it. This is certainly true of works by Olga Visentini, an Italian author, critic, and historian of Italian children's literature, who expressed obsequious adherence to the fascist regime in many of her books.[12] Visentini's personal celebration of fascist imperial politics as a writer came only after the invasion of Ethiopia, in *Africanelle: Fiabe*, published in 1937.[13] Her embrace of the colonial cause is demonstrated in a few stories in *Africanelle* in which blond fairies and mermaids leave their idyllic environments in order to find a more "noble mission". In "Mirta's Mission", for example, the fairy Mirta leaves behind her home of "silvery summits", gnomes, and elves and ends up in a modest Italian home where she helps a child to write a letter to his father, who is labouring in East Africa to build Rome's imperial infrastructure.

The same pedagogical change is dramatised in Visentini's "The Goblin on the Roof", in which the goblin Aldane interrupts his trip to fairyland with other fabulous creatures, to provide a child with the uniform he needs to march with other children in Rome after the declaration of the Italian empire.[14] Visentini's employment of classical fairy-tale structures for the ideological ends of Italy's fascists may be usefully compared to the use of such tales by the Nazis to socialise children in the party's images of the stable German family and *Heimat* (homeland).[15]

Besides Visentini's *Africanelle*, the books for children that publishers rushed to put on the market at the time were texts that recalled the history of Italian colonialism since its inception: the creation of the Eritrean colony, the war against Ethiopia, and the exploration and commercial penetration of Italy's African colonies. Exemplary texts of this genre include, respectively, *Volontario in Africa*, *Piccolo legionario in Africa orientale*, *Genietti e sirenelle in Africa orientale*, and *Balilla regale*. *Volontario in Africa: Racconti di guerra per ragazzi* (War Stories for Boys) – written by an author with the militaristic nom de plume Tenente Anonimo (Anonymous Lieutenant) – illustrates the heroism of a now aged Italian soldier during the conflicts that led to the creation of the Eritrean colony in the previous century.[16] Motivated by the transparent intention of justifying the imminent invasion of Ethiopia, the author depicts the Abyssinian population as brutal, fearful, and mischievous.

One of the few exceptions to this uniformity of purpose is y *Balilla regale: Romanzo africano per giovinetti*. As I will demonstrate, its representation of Italian colonialism is much more complex than that of the other texts discussed above. *Volontario in Africa*, *Piccolo legionario*, and *Genietti e sirenelle* simply depict a Manichaean world in which brave Italian soldiers were fighting a necessary war against an evil and uncivilised enemy: a representation that *Balilla regale* distorts in a particularly interesting manner. Although the publication of this book, diverging greatly from the imperial fascist propaganda, seems surprising at first, it actually confirms that fascist censorship – like many of the directives of the party – was not always consistent, efficient, and infallible.[17]

The author of *Balilla regale*, Arnaldo Cipolla, was born into an Italian family with strong military traditions. He went to Africa first as a soldier in the Congo, and later as an explorer and a correspondent for several Italian daily newspapers. Although Cipolla wrote several works of youth fiction set in Africa, *Balilla regale* is his only book for children that refers to Italian colonialism. This intricate novel recounts the many adventures in East Africa of Omar, the child of an Italian explorer and an African queen, and of Irenetta, the daughter of an Italian entrepreneur who meets Omar on her way to establish an Italian colony in Africa.

Boys, Girls, Empire, and Mamma Italia

Like nationalism, its derivative, imperialism, is gendered. Indeed, as British-Turkish author Deniz Kandiyoti has argued, control of women is central to processes of nationalisation and ethnicisation. In times of social stress or upheaval such as those that generally accompany imperial projects, the female element of the nation is usually confined to a symbolic role and excluded from political agency.[18] As South African scholar Elleke Boehmer suggests, the male role is, by contrast, "typically 'metonymic'; that is, men are represented as contiguous with each other and with the national whole".[19] In other words, they are ascribed active roles in constituting the nation.

Although a fixed line cannot be drawn between literature for girls and boys – girls may have had access to stories addressing boys – there is a rigid distinction in the gendering of roles, both factual and metaphoric, in literature for children set in colonial environments. In the texts written in response to the 1935–1936 Ethiopian War and the creation of the empire, girls are often absent, as in the case of *Volontario in Africa* and *Piccolo legionario in Africa orientale*. In such literature, girls are portrayed as embodiments of continuity and national integrity: in other words, of conservative principles that militate against any form of agency among young women. Indeed, when in these narratives girls are called to be part of the national colonial project, they are socially static, and no real evolution occurs in them from the beginning of the stories to the end. The tales narrated in these works focus instead on the social transformation of boys, on their evolution into brave soldiers and conquerors, and – in the case of indigenous Africans – on their liberation from misery and slavery. Usually, the role of African boys is that of faithful helpers of the Italian colonial enterprise.

As a result of such loyalty, these African boys are offered access to Italian "civilisation". In other narratives, the painful condition of the African child as a slave, orphan, or homeless person provides a moral justification for the Italian invasion. Extraordinary physical vigour and technological superiority are at the core of the first part of *Genietti e sirenelle*, in which the function of its acrobatic protagonist – the *genietto* Nano 48 – is to demonstrate the military advantages that Italian technology provides. Thanks to his dexterity in controlling emblems of modernity as diverse as planes, radios, and motor vehicles, Nano 48 is able to coordinate the Italian colonial forces, which then annihilate their enemies with extraordinary speed. An essentially similar role is played by Pierino Marra in *Piccolo legionario*. In the novel, little Pierino's first mission is to maintain the technological disparity between the Italians and

Ethiopians by ensuring that a load of weapons, which the despised French plan to sell to the Ethiopians, never reaches the enemy. In addition to his courage, which allows him to thwart the French plan, it is his technical skills that are emphasised in the novel. Pierino, the son of an engineer, knows how to handle explosives and repair the engines of motorboats, and is capable of learning, in no time, how to use a machine gun to slaughter his Ethiopian adversaries.

As the American scholar Michael Adas has noted in *Machines as the Measure of Men*, technological advancement formed an integral element in arguments concerning the broader civilisational superiority that legitimated European colonial expansion from the nineteenth century (see Introduction to this volume). European technological pride was obviously manifested even in children's literature: the stories of the exploits of "heroic" British aviators on colonial missions that have proliferated since the beginning of the twentieth century constitute a good example of the value attached to technology by European imperialists.[20] However, the "belatedness" and limited extent of Italy's industrialisation and its colonial enterprises, in comparison with the two major European colonial powers, Britain and France, confer a megalomaniac mode to the literary representation of Italy's national and technological strength, which diffuses and counteracts fears of inadequacy at an international level. Nano 48's distinctive trait, for instance, is a Napoleonic pose that accompanies every planning phase of his military life.

Volontario in Africa and *Piccolo legionario in Africa orientale* are war stories that – conforming to a long-standing tradition of the gendering of the public and private spheres – were addressed to an audience of young boys in order to instil military spirit and national pride. In contrast, *Balilla regale*, *Genietti e sirenelle in Africa orientale*, and *Africanelle* catered to girls as well. In *Balilla regale*, Irenetta and Omar are both enjoined by the author to build a "*nuova Italia*" (new Italy) in Africa. Similarly, the involvement of both female and male imaginary creatures – although in different degrees and forms – in the conflict between Italians and Ethiopians is represented by Nonno Ebe in *Genietti e sirenelle in Africa orientale*. In all these works, girls are the bearers of national honour and its boundary markers, preserving the integrity of the fatherland in a metaphorical role that is visibly signified in *Genietti e sirenelle*.

In the first and second part of his book, Nonno Ebe deals with the *genietti*. With disproportionately large heads because they have "a lot of brains", the *genietti* are defined as the embodiments of the intelligence of Italian boys. In the third part of his book, in which the Italian soldiers have already prevailed over their African adversaries, Ebe turns to the *sirenelle:* creatures who are the graceful priestesses of national rituals. After receiving the news of the Italian advance in the area of the lake that they inhabit, the *sirenelle* rush to sing the praises of the Italian soldiers and to don the Italian flag. These little female creatures are "natural" and ahistorical: their origins go back to a mythical time, as does the motherland for which they stand. By contrast, *genietti*, their male counterparts, are "historical" figures whose past is proudly traced in the narration by their leader.

The social mobility of boys and the correlative metaphoric fixity of girls in this imperial imaginary are well exemplified in *Balilla regale*. Irenetta, the daughter of an Italian entrepreneur, is journeying with her father in East Africa towards the kingdom of Ghera, where a new Italian colony will be founded. In a port on the Red Sea, she meets a lovely boy, Omar, who is initially presented as a *meticcio*, or a mixed-race child. Omar's sole dream is to reach Italian shores to find his Italian father. It is through his devotion and demonstration to Irenetta of physical strength and moral nobility that, in the beginning of the novel, Omar proves himself worthy of being included in the Italian national narrative. As a result, Omar is allowed to journey to Italy on board the ship of Irenetta's father. Later, after Omar has successfully endured a series of trials and gained the recognition of Irenetta, his new goal is to protect the physical integrity of the little girl, which, if preserved, will guarantee the Italian presence and its continuity in Africa. Because of her tender age, Irenetta is indeed the perfect incarnation of imperial Italy in the making. Omar's longing for the grandeur of Italy is therefore figured by his courtly love for little Irenetta.

The homogeneous character of the representations of girls in the children's literature of the imperial age is confirmed by Visentini's *Africanelle*. The first fairy tale of the collection, "The Olive Grove in the Sands", attempts to sustain the morality of the Italian colonisation of Somalia. Indeed, Italian expansion through conquest is represented as the peaceful journey of the diligent Italian people in search of land to cultivate. The protagonist of this fairy tale is Fioralisa, the daughter of an Italian explorer. During her father's exploration of Somalia, in which she does not seem to participate, she meets Red Assam, a little Abyssinian orphan kept as a slave by a cruel local *ras*, or chieftain. The encounter of the two children is very brief, but they meet again at the end of the story, when Fioralisa welcomes Red Assam to her father's house. Here, the boy will live next to the Italian labourers and be able to learn how to turn the desert land of his country into olive groves. The metaphor contained in the story could not be more transparent: the Italian nation liberates the Abyssinians and provides them with a "civilised" manner of living.

The metaphoric role of girls is even more apparent in another fairy tale of *Africanelle*: "Reginetta Imperiale". Its protagonist, Imperiale, a fairy wearing Italian colours, cheerfully labours day and night for the well-being of her empire. Both "Reginetta Imperiale" and "The Olive Grove in the Sands" make clear that Visentini fully subscribed to the imperial propaganda that the fascist regime addressed to schoolchildren. A reader for 10-year-old fourth-graders in state-controlled schools exemplifies this political indoctrination. In this text, the war against Ethiopia is presented as the duty of a nation intending to help a country where "there were slaves to liberate, children, men and women to clothe, diseases to cure".[21]

Naturally, this sentimentalised representation of the nation was an effective means of indoctrination, particularly of the youngest children of both sexes, who could identify with the neediness and dependency of the youngest Ethiopians, and who had not yet developed strong ties other than familial ones. The position of Italian girls in relation to the motherland was, however, complicated by the dominant gendering of social roles. As many studies of fascist school programmes have shown, girls were inculcated with "motherly sentiments" from their earliest days in state-controlled schools. In addition, the "recreational" organisation Piccole Italiane, which was attended by very young girls, contributed to this indoctrination. In the statutes of this organisation, "*la patria*" is represented as "*la mamma più grande, la mamma di tutti i buoni italiani*" (the greatest mother, the mother of all good Italians).[22]

As was reported by Cicely Hamilton, an emancipated and wealthy Englishwoman travelling in Italy in the early 1930s, among the activities conceived by the organisation for Italian girls were doll drills in which the little Italians publicly simulated "maternal" gestures.[23] Because of this orientation of girls towards motherhood and the equation of mother with the nation, Italian mothers were the ideal signifiers of the expanding nation. This, as I have argued above, is perfectly exemplified by Irenetta in *Balilla regale*.

However, in addition to providing a symbolic figuration, children's literature of the time offered Italian girls models of feminine virtue that they could emulate as future settlers in the colonial environment. In "Reginetta Imperiale", for example, Visentini turns the symbol of the maternal nation of the first story of the collection, "The Olive Grove in the Sands", into a domestic figure who performs simple daily rituals:

She would gather in a big basket now rose petals, now fragrant leaves, or the sugary dates, or banana tufts ... She would see the little fairy

squeezing flowers, distilling essences, putting them in certain vials …
For those children, Imperiale would open the vials filled with flower
essences saved in the warm season, would remove the tops from the
jars full of date or banana jam so that the little ones would plunge in
their spoons and their fingers.[24]

"Reginetta Imperiale" turns the African landscape into a manicured garden
where Imperiale gathers succulent fruits and herbs to feed the orphaned
indigenous children, and where diligent domesticity is enlivened with exotic
diversity and plenty. Conversely, the tropical produce is familiarised by being
incorporated into reassuring Italian decor signified by glass jars and vials. This
image reflects interesting pedagogic elements that need to be discussed and
contextualised. Christian ideals, in particular, humility and charity, certainly
inform all of Visentini's *Africanelle*. In "Reginetta Imperiale", in spite of her
high status, Imperiale works tirelessly to feed famished Abyssinian children.
The other young protagonists of Visentini's stories are equally humble and
charitable: they include Fioralisa, who introduces the Abyssinian orphan to
edifying Italian values, and the fairies who assist the poor Italian children.
Furthermore, humility is embodied in the very title chosen by the author for
her collection, the diminutive word *Africanelle*.

Although Imperiale is also animated by Christian virtues, her story presents
an element of leisure that is not evident in "The Olive Grove in the Sands"
and that points to the picturing, on Visentini's part, of a different audience.
Baskets of roses and jars and vials of flowery essences redesign in the colony an
Italian bourgeois interior in which domesticity is a cult, and charitable work a
redeeming and pleasurable pastime. Visentini thus reveals her desire to appeal
to girls from two different social groups: the working class and the middle
class. At the same time, she aspires to create for both a pastoral picture of
colonial living in which tensions and economic disparities are smoothed away
by a common involvement in a Christian mission sanctioned by the presence
of the indigenous orphans.

Visentini's charitable sensibility also shows that she inherited some of the
piousness and sentimentalism that characterised children's literature of the
nineteenth century, a mode that culminated in *Cuore* and *Pinocchio*. *Cuore*, in
particular, was often the object of harsh criticism from fascist intellectuals and
educators, who rejected its tearful and pathetic ethos in favour of the "male
vigour" of the new fascist pedagogy.[25] In spite of this, in the 1930s *Cuore* was –
together with Salgari's novels and Salvator Gotta's *Piccolo alpino*, which dealt

with Italy's involvement in the Great War (1915–1918) – among the most beloved literary works for children.[26] Not only did fascism fail to eradicate *Cuore*'s tearful spirit, but sentimentalism came to permeate fascism's official pedagogy as well as the works of its declared supporters. Another manifestation of the legacy of the nineteenth century's pathetic ethos in children's literature is the figure of the orphan, present both in Visentini's fairy tales and in contemporary works celebrating the empire, to which I now turn.

Orphans for the Empire

Whether the protagonists of children's literature written during the mid-1930s are boys or girls, their mothers are always deceased before the narrative begins. As I have mentioned, the bulk of this literature deals with Italian exploration and subsequent military campaigns in East Africa rather than with the daily life of Italian settlers. Such narratives are therefore antithetical to the depiction of domestic and familial life, which would have required the figure of the Mother. Actually, although Italy had already governed African colonies for four decades, there are few texts for children that portray the life of the Italian settlers. In this respect, it is essential to recall that, in spite of the fascist discourse presenting the expansionist Italian campaigns as providing an outlet for an over-populated nation, the Italian population in the African colonies was always quite thinly spread. This was particularly true in the case of women. The paucity of Italian civilians in the colonies, and the brevity of Italian domination in East Africa, partially explain the dearth of Italian fictional works representing the daily life of Italian settlers, both in adult and in children's literature. Even Italian colonial cinema limited its horizon, for the most part, to Italian military enterprises or to romantic or commercial adventures.[27]

In children's literature of the imperial period, however, the orphanhood of the Italian protagonists is also a prerequisite for adventure. It frees them from the sentimental ties that would hinder their departure from home. For example, having lost his mother, Pierino Marra of *Piccolo legionario* can throw himself into his search for his father who has joined the Italian soldiers in the Ethiopian War as a volunteer. Similarly, the motherless Irenetta of *Balilla regale* can follow her father on his business adventure in Africa. The same is true for Fioralisa in "The Olive Grove in the Sands" in *Africanelle*: the little Italian girl accompanies her father in his exploration of Somalia. If the motherlessness of Italian boys and girls in these children's stories allows them to leave the domestic space of Italy and participate in the colonial adventure, the motherlessness of the many indigenous children in Visentini's fairy tales serves as an ethical foundation for Italian colonial endeavours. It also incarnates, as I will show, the fantasy of a virgin land, of a blank space upon which the author can project her own values.

In "The Olive Grove in the Sands", the Somali orphan Red Assam is taken from his mother at a tender age to be sold as a slave to a ruthless *ras*, who entrusts to him his flock. In one of his solitary wanderings as a shepherd, the orphan meets a sorcerer who predicts that he will find peace when he sees "the sands of the desert verdant with trees".[28] Instead of going back to his hut, Red Assam decides to try to find the miracle foretold by the sorcerer. One day, lying on a dune, the little boy sees an Italian girl with dazzling blond hair who overwhelms him with her grace. After this brief encounter with Fioralisa, he wanders for years through mountains, forests, and deserts. At last, he finds himself back in the region of his birth. Here, instead of the arid land he was familiar with, there is an expanse of silvery olive trees. At the edge of this olive grove is the white house of the little Italian girl he had met long before. She has now turned into a beautiful young woman.

This story, in particular, contains a significant misappropriation of the structural forms of popular fairy tales, a field of expertise for Visentini. This misappropriation reveals Visentini's inability fully to reconcile popular tradition with colonial ideology. In spite of the many significant cultural and historical differences between fairy tales, the *fabula* of each, the basic plot that underlies every tale, shares structural similarities. The prototypical young protagonist of fairy tales has always to go through a series of trials before obtaining his final reward – a bride or a kingdom, for example – and being reintegrated into society, or whatever other form his social transformation takes. Although Visentini suggests in her title, *Africanelle: Fiabe,* that the form of her stories is that of popular fairy tales, she cannot help delivering the happy ending that her story sets the reader up to expect.

Red Assam's final compensation is not Fioralisa, the beautiful daughter of the Italian explorer, but a less palpable prize: access to the values of the Italian colonists, the most paradigmatic of which is a diligent work ethic. At the end of his story, Red Assam is in fact shown the green olive grove cultivated on Somali desert land by hard-working Italians. Although Red Assam's race annuls his narrative potential, his status as an orphan makes him the most malleable of propagandistic materials. Indeed, this status deprives him of his own history and traditions. His cultural blankness is a sort of utopian space, a *tabula rasa* on which the presumed values of the Italian settlers divulged by the author will not collide with his own cultural values, which were, of course, never transmitted to him by his missing family.

Racial Ambiguity and the Foundation of a New Nation

Presented at the beginning of the novel *Balilla regale* as a *meticcio* child, Omar comes to provide the Italian girl Irenetta with access to Africa by describing the land to her, taming the wild beasts that populate it, and escorting her to her destination: a region in East Africa where her father will find the "*nuova Italia*" (new Italy). The *meticcio* boy is therefore represented as an intermediary between the colonising nation and the colonised in a manner that accords with theories elaborated in the colonial period about children born from the union between Italian men and indigenous African women.

The *meticcio* Omar seems at first to conform to ideas circulating among anthropologists, missionaries, and colonial officials in the first decades of the century, and then disavowed by Italy's racial legislation of 1938. In short, it was believed by some that mixed-race people, because of their intermediate position, could serve the colonisers' interests.[29] First, the *meticcio* was thought to belong to the two cultures involved in the colonial encounter: the Italian and the indigenous African. It was also believed that, in genetic terms, *meticcio* children demonstrated their Italian fathers' intelligence and their indigenous mothers' physical strength and adaptability to the African physical environment. These were ideas with which *Balilla regale*'s author, Arnaldo Cipolla, an educated man with a long-term interest in the African continent, must have been familiar.

In Cipolla's novel, however, the narratological position of the *meticcio* boy, the protagonist, is not motivated by the services he offers to the Italian nation. On the contrary, later in the novel, Omar's status and racial connotation turn out to be different from that of the mendicant *meticcio* who introduces the superior Italian "race" to its new dominions. As suggested earlier, *Balilla regale* differs from the highly propagandistic children's literature of the epoch. Its publication is in fact evidence that fascist censorship and directives were not very consistent during the period of the regime's power.

In addition to complicating the racial identity of Omar, Cipolla attributes to the young boy an anachronistic form of manliness. In spite of the fascist appellation of *Balilla* granted to him in the novel by the enamoured Irenetta, Omar provides a model of masculinity that is almost antithetical to that which the fascist youth organisation, Opera Nazionale Balilla, tried to inculcate in its young members. As has been well documented, the primary task of this youth organisation was to create "fascist soldiers" who would preserve the new Italy and provide it with military strength.

In his novel, nevertheless, Cipolla seems to fantasise about an alternative world to the actual reality of Italian imperialism in East Africa and, in general, undermine the militaristic spirit of the fascist regime. A look at the plot is enough to indicate its surprising divergence from the expansionist ideology of Italian fascism. Although, at the beginning of the novel, reaching the shores of Italy and finding his Italian father is the protagonist's only dream, this objective is later deferred, and Omar decides to escort the Italian expedition to their final destination. While he is travelling with the Italians, Omar's father has returned to live with his wife, the queen of Ghera.[30] It is at this point that the boy and the reader also learn that his father had left Africa long before to fight for the independence of Ghera, and that Il Congresso Romano – an imaginary Italian political body – has granted it this status. At the end of the novel, Omar receives the crown and the newly independent kingdom which hosts "*la nuova Italia*", constituted by Irenetta, her father, and his retinue and attendants.

Through protecting Irenetta in her journey to the foundation of the "*nuova Italia*", Omar certainly helps to preserve the Italian nation, and thus assure the reproduction of future Italian generations in their African colonies. However, Omar is not representative of the martial spirit that fascism sought to inspire in Italy's children of his age. In the novel, Omar's manliness and the bravery that, according to fascist discourse, accompanies it are not tested and proved through violent actions and rituals such as war and hunting. In *Balilla regale*, the enemies and the marauders that he comes across while accompanying Irenetta and the other Italians through the desert are neutralised by Omar with his shrewdness and rhetorical skills. In the novel, moreover, there are no safari scenes in which Omar might demonstrate his courage. Hunting is even criticised as a practice dictated by cruelty and greed. This stance further distinguishes Cipolla's work from more orthodox fascist texts. In novels such as *Africa mia! Un balilla nell'Oltre Giuba*, for example, hunting appears as one of the testing grounds of the Italian protagonists' virile heroism as well as the means - as Scotto Di Luzio points out – to locate fascist colonisation within an aristocratic European tradition.[31]

Equally important is the fact that in his novel, Cipolla creates a distinction between the ordinary Italian *balillas* who "believe, obey, and fight" without much thought and a more noble youth who is above such uniformity and does not subscribe to the militaristic spirit of the former. Cipolla writes in his novel that the inhabitants of Ghera, where Omar comes from, "had never manifested any desire to enlarge the borders of their kingdom".[32]

The racial ambiguity of the book's protagonist reveals Cipolla's fascination with the racial and cultural "Other" and distinguishes his work from numerous contemporary portrayals of East Africans as cruel and uncivilised. In the colonial children's literature of the mid-1930s, *Balilla regale* also stands out for its idea of technological progress. As I previously argued, in *Genietti e sirenelle* and *Piccolo legionario in Africa orientale*, imperialism was represented as the necessary consequence of Italian technological superiority. In *Balilla regale*, by contrast, the technological superiority of the kingdom of Ghera makes expansionist politics obsolete.

Concluding Reflections

The ideological indoctrination to which Italian children were subjected during the 1930s was not simply passively absorbed by them. Fascist schools, youth organisations, and a complacent popular culture, for example, did not fully succeed in inculcating maternal attitudes in girls. The results of a survey conducted among girls between 6 and 18 years of age in 1938 revealed that the majority of the interviewees lacked any interest in domestic work and did not aspire to marriage and family.[33] Boys, for their part, did not all uniformly identify with the military culture to which they were being exposed during the *ventennio*.[34]

Imperialistic propaganda, disseminated by fascist education and by many of the "African" texts for children, was resisted by young Italians because, I would suggest, they could not identify with the complexities of its discourse. The "Africa" of Salgari's novels, which clearly exercised a powerful pull on the fantasies of Italian children during the colonial era, figured visibly as the land of exciting and liberating adventures. By contrast, the Africa found in children's literature and imperial propaganda of the mid-1930s was the object at once of desire, contempt, and compassion. It was a multifaceted, highly conflictual space that must have disoriented members of the young Italian audience that this discourse was courting.

Children's literature of Italy's imperial epoch is perhaps an ideal means for shedding light on the Italian nation as a colonial power. The intricacy and ideological contradictions of the colonial discourse circulating in such literature powerfully illuminate the national uncertainties about Italian involvement in Africa. Furthermore, its relevance for our understanding of colonial discourses during fascism necessitates a revision of such literature's traditionally marginal position in scholarly work on Italian culture. Finally, children's reception of such literature demonstrates their active participation in the creation of the national archive, and places them in a position that is less peripheral than is generally accorded to them by cultural critics.

4

Reparations for Imperialism: Legacies beyond Slavery in the British Empire

Stephen Small

IN MODERN BRITAIN, MOST discussions of reparations for colonialism focus on slavery and its legacies. They focus on the families, individuals, and companies that benefited economically from slavery; the shipowners, banks, investors, and ancillary businesses; the politicians that rose in power and prestige, and the military and naval officers who conquered territories across Africa and the Americas. These are the men for whom portraits were painted, after whom streets were named, and whose statues and country mansions are now being consistently targeted by protesters. British imperialism is mentioned in some of these discussions – as with diamonds and gold in southern Africa, the British Commonwealth, statues of Winston Churchill and Cecil Rhodes, and the plunder of Nigeria's Benin bronzes in the nineteenth century. But British imperialism does not figure in discussions to the same extent that slavery does, and we almost never hear the demand for "reparations for imperialism". Scholars of slavery say little or nothing about the distinct reparations needed for imperialism, while scholars of imperialism say little about reparations per se. There are few systematic attempts to compare legacies of slavery with legacies of imperialism, or to consider their implications for reparations. In other words, imperialism is mentioned but not in a robust or analytically insightful way, as it is with slavery. British slavery lasted from at least the 1560s until the 1830s, and, after that, British imperialism lasted for more than another century, during which time Britain consolidated and expanded the economic exploitation, political domination, and social subordination of Africa and of Africans in the diaspora. Today, we are confronting the legacies of both in a far more systematic and informed way than ever before.

In this chapter, building on the tremendous insights gained in analysing reparations for slavery, I describe and evaluate why it is necessary and beneficial to carry out similar work on British imperialism. I argue that in terms of reparations, the legacies of British imperialism are as important as those of slavery. I suggest that, in many instances, these legacies provide greater insights into Britain's current relations with Africa and the West Indies, and with the black British population today, than do legacies of slavery. Some of the most fundamental British imperial developments and their legacies – economic, political, and social – cannot be explained by a focus primarily or exclusively on British slavery. Demands for reparations for these developments must therefore focus on the period after British slavery was legally abolished in 1834. I exemplify many of these issues with a case study of the city of Liverpool – the "slaving capital of the world", which later became "the second city of empire".[1] And the case of Liverpool indicates some of the ways in which different cities require our attention, as we examine reparatory demands. I focus mainly on the period leading up to, and including, the "new imperialism" from the 1830s to the 1950s.

British Imperialism and Its Legacies

There are several reasons to regard British imperialism and its legacies as distinctive from British slavery and its legacies. The British abolition of slavery in the 1830s did not free black people. It was a single legal act, did not cover the entire British Empire, established a vicious system of so-called apprenticeship, and lacked an economic, political or social process designed to lead to equality for black people (see Cobley and Brereton in this volume).[2] Black people received no apology and no compensation, while the owners of black bodies obtained £20 million compensation[3] (worth £77 billion by 2015 when it was fully paid). After legal abolition, more than 800,000 previously enslaved people of African descent across the West Indies continued to labour for highly exploitative wages, with few or no political rights, and in socially subordinated conditions rationalised by state-sponsored racist beliefs.[4]

Britain continued trade and expanded commercial deals with the largest slaving nations of the time – the United States, Brazil, and the Spanish Caribbean (see Kerr-Ritchie, Silva Jr, and Ramirez in this volume) – importing cotton, coffee, and sugar grown by the enslaved, and exporting products and goods to those countries.[5] Slavery remained legal in the United States until the 1860s, and in Cuba and Brazil until the 1880s, and Britain maintained diplomatic posts and remained engaged in mining, railroads, banks, and insurance in the slaving countries. For example, in the 1840s, as much as 20 per cent of the British market in sugar came from Cuba and Puerto Rico.[6] The world's biggest mine for copper production at the time – El Cobre in Cuba – was taken over by the British in the 1830s. British workers and mining machinery like steam engines were imported there from Cornwall. Britain also expanded trade with Argentina and Chile.[7] British residents lived and worked in these countries, too.

Cotton imports and exports in Britain grew massively after the 1830s. For example, in 1861 there were more than 500,000 workers "directly employed in the cotton industry", and as many as four million workers in Britain depended on cotton manufacturing.[8] British companies had made profits from the labour and land of African territories during the period of slavery, not least from the extraction of gold and ivory in West Africa, but they were less lucrative than the financial rewards from transporting millions of Africans into slavery.[9] That fiscal balance changed after slavery was abolished. Far more territory in Africa was acquired, the Suez Canal was completed in November 1869, and diamonds and gold were mined in southern Africa from the late 1860s. By 1913, 74 per cent of all cotton exported from Africa to Europe came out of British colonies.[10] The production of palm oil, palm kernels, and other products in West Africa dramatically increased too, playing an indispensable role in Britain's second industrial revolution.

Scandinavian nations also played a major role in British imperialism. During slavery, Denmark–Norway, and Sweden produced raw materials like timber, iron ore, cereals, and fish that were indispensable to the operations of slaving nations like Britain, the Netherlands, and France (see also Brereton, Nimako, and Aragón Falomir in this volume).[11] These countries also consumed products like coffee, sugar, and cotton produced by the enslaved in colonies across the Americas. During imperialism the Nordics massively expanded production of these and other products, including grain, pork, and butter from Denmark, fish from Norway, and oats and electronics from Sweden.[12] The economic activity involving Scandinavian shipping expanded greatly too, as it was transformed from sail to steam, and most of it concerned the British Empire, the largest in the world at the time.

British politicians strongly supported imperial economic activity, while the army and navy continued to play their role as Britain sought to maintain its global lead and keep at bay nations like the United States, Germany, and France (see Igba, Blackler, and Yates in this volume). As a result of imperial activities, most nation-states that exist today across the former British Empire were expanded and consolidated. This was true of the "white dominions" – Australia, Canada, New Zealand, and South Africa. It was also true of countries like Nigeria and Ghana (the Gold Coast) as well as Zimbabwe (Rhodesia) and Kenya. These countries began to take their final form after the Berlin Conference in 1884–1885.[13] British territories in the West Indies also went through a series of political status changes, with some being categorised as "protectorates". Finally, the populations of Indian descent that exist in the Caribbean today arrived after slavery was legally abolished. This was the case, for example, in British Guiana and Trinidad and Tobago in the 1830s, and in Kenya, Uganda, and South Africa in the late nineteenth century.[14]

British imperialism also changed the demographics of black Britain as well as population movements across the African diaspora. British slavery had forced Africans into the Americas, while simultaneously keeping their numbers tiny in Britain. For example, British ports were responsible for transporting more than 3.3 million Africans into slavery, and Liverpool was responsible for 1,171,171 of them.[15] The number of black people in Britain during slavery, however, remained negligible, never more than 15,000.[16] Imperialism brought this flow of black people to an end, and new patterns developed. Increasing numbers of blacks travelled from the Americas – and from Africa – to England from the start of the twentieth century and beyond. Almost all were men, most were sailors, while some were students.[17] These numbers dramatically increased in the twentieth century during the two world wars (1914–1918 and 1939–1945) and afterwards, as did the number of women. Hundreds of blacks settled in Britain each year at the start of the twentieth century, reaching the thousands, tens of thousands, and hundreds of thousands by the 1960s.[18]

During imperialism, black people in the British Empire – and in Britain – generated far more written analysis, empirical evidence, and insights into British domination under imperialism than they had done under slavery.[19] And we have far more insights by and for black women. There are nineteenth-century writings by black people who visited Britain like African Americans Ellen Craft and Anna Julia Cooper, and by Caribbeans like Henry Sylvester Williams, Amy

Ashwood Garvey, and Marcus Garvey.[20] Writings also exist by visitors, students, and others from Africa,[21] and by people born, raised, or resident in Britain.[22] Later in the twentieth century, writings emerged from Pan-Africanists and leaders of anti-colonial struggles such as Nigeria's Nnamdi Azikiwe, Ghana's Kwame Nkrumah, Trinidad's George Padmore, and Jamaica's Una Marson. Those fighting anti-racism, such as Jamaica's Harold Moody, also added their voices.[23] These first-hand experiences and analyses provide a more accurate, comprehensive, and inclusive understanding of this era.

Imperialism and Its Legacies in Liverpool

The people, ideologies, institutions, and processes that made Liverpool the "slaving capital of the world" continued to oppress and exploit black people long after slavery had legally ended across the British Empire in 1834. The British abolition of slavery changed the legal and economic system, and politicians and economic power brokers in Liverpool adapted accordingly, often with great success. That was how and why Liverpool earned the reputation of being the "second city of empire".[24] Merseyside was directly involved in all of the imperial developments described in the previous section, and the city led some of the most profitable of them. To begin with, many men who had become rich under slavery received so-called financial compensation for giving up their "property", and continued to extract labour from the former enslaved who were forced to remain on their plantations.[25] Owners of plantations in the West Indies who lived in Liverpool received significant amounts of compensation for the loss of their human property.[26] The British scholar Anthony Tibbles relates: "Among nearly ninety Liverpool residents who were compensated were John Gladstone (over £106,000), West Indian merchants Philip Tinne (over £90,000) and Samuel Sandbach (over £35,000), and banker and railway investor John Moss (over £40,000). Not one of the enslaved received any redress, financial or otherwise."[27]

The money received from the British government by John Gladstone – the owner of seven plantations in Demerara (a territory in what later became British Guiana) – was more than that awarded to anyone else in Britain.[28] He and his family continued to extract profits from their plantations and other post-slavery businesses afterwards, which included the use of indentured workers from India. One son in particular, William Ewart Gladstone, went to Eton and Oxford, opposed abolition, inherited much of his father's wealth, and became British prime minister on four separate occasions between 1868 and 1894.[29] He played a major role in imperial Britain. Many other men from Liverpool continued to prosper on the backs of black populations in Africa, the Caribbean, and the Americas.

Many planters became far richer working with other nations still involved in slavery at the time of abolition such as the United States, Cuba, and Brazil. Liverpool merchants were at the forefront of British trading with American slave owners from the 1830s through to the 1860s. They built ships for, and strongly supported, the slave-owning Confederacy. The US consulate in Liverpool, established in the 1790s – and located in a building that became part of the University of Liverpool – actively backed the Confederacy during the American Civil War (1861–1865). The number of cotton brokers in Liverpool had reached 320 by 1860.[30] Liverpool was also at the forefront of the cotton business as it expanded globally. The American scholar Sven Beckert noted that, after slavery, "For once and future cotton lords … the true center of the world was Liverpool."[31] Furthermore, "Liverpool's merchants had accumulated unprecedented wealth and influence by connecting a nascent European manufacturing complex with an ever more martial and expansive cotton hinterland." Beckert concluded: "Liverpool's port was the epicenter of a globe-spanning empire. Its merchants sent ships all over the world."[32]

Individuals, families, and companies in Liverpool who had not been directly involved in slavery entered imperial trade in the Americas, Africa, and elsewhere. Many became immensely wealthy. Shipbuilders and ship company owners like Alexander Elder, John Dempster, and John Holt were in the foreground. Two of the most enormously successful in financial terms were William Lever and Alfred Lewis Jones. Lever attained unprecedented levels of international business success, above all in West Africa.[33] He developed extensive industrial operations; became the world's most successful seller of soap, margarine, and candles; and had astounding success with palm oil and palm kernels from West Africa, ingredients essential for industrial lubrication and factories.[34] Alfred Lewis Jones became the owner of multiple shipping companies, banks, and numerous other financial and commercial interests in West Africa.[35] He also emerged as the owner of the Elder Dempster shipping company, massively expanding its operations across West Africa, where it became the single biggest company. In Liverpool, trade with other regions of the world, like China, was led by Alfred Holt, and the world's most luxurious ocean liners were also built there.[36]

A unique and little-explored development relevant to imperial economic activity in Liverpool was the opening, in 1898, of the Liverpool School of

Tropical Medicine (LSTM). An initiative of the British Colonial Secretary, Joseph Chamberlain, and several Liverpool shipping magnates, especially Alfred Lewis Jones, the school was designed to investigate diseases and reduce morbidity and mortality in the tropical regions of the British Empire, especially in West Africa.[37] Before the discovery of quinine, the mortality rate of British expatriates in Africa was extremely high and, even after its discovery, remained high, especially in West Africa, which was then known as "the white man's grave". Chamberlain, Jones, and others funded LSTM – and its counterpart, the London School of Tropical Medicine – to turn the "white man's grave" into the "white man's garden" for the extraction of raw materials utilising cheap African labour. And they succeeded spectacularly. Rates of morbidity and mortality dropped dramatically. For example, the US historian Philip Curtin reports that death rates across West Africa decreased from as high as 40 per cent in the first half of the nineteenth century to "the range of 6 to 24 deaths per 1,000 per year" in the period 1909–1913.[38] And "death rates for British West Africa dropped by 99 per cent from those reported for Sierra Leone at the earlier period".[39] Many white scientists who discovered treatments and cures won international awards.[40] Trade and economic activity rose too, along with the infrastructure of roads and rail, as well as banks and businesses.[41]

Liverpool University emerged during this period, with funds and political support from many of the men who had become rich during slavery and even richer during imperialism. Apologists for British imperialism suggest that the school – and other activities – developed for the benefit of Africans, as part of the British "civilising" project, and was established for the economic development of Africa. This is a complete falsehood, as the American academic John Farley has noted. He argued that the evidence reveals "that tropical medicine from 1898 to the 1970s was fundamentally imperialistic in its assumptions, its methods, its goals, and its priorities; it was the age of imperial tropical medicine".[42] He continued:

> the basic goal of Tropical Medicine was to render the tropical world fit for white habitation and white investment. Its practitioners were members of colonial services, armies of occupation, and mining and fruit companies. What, if anything, should be done about the health of the native inhabitants was determined by the policies of these Western agencies without reference to the needs of the indigenous communities. Not surprisingly their health needs became a priority only when their diseases were felt to threaten the health or profits of

the white man, or when imperial policies demanded that the health needs of the indigenous populations be addressed.[43]

Trade with Scandinavia was central to Liverpool's success, and Nordic nations traded more with Merseyside than they did with any other single port in Britain. Cargo included timber, iron ore, and fish, as well as matches and pulp.[44] In part, this was because of Liverpool's extensive railway network throughout the region, which linked the port to the Manchester and Leeds textile factories, and to Birmingham, renowned as a leading arms manufacturing centre.[45]

Liverpool also became the primary port in Britain for millions of emigrants to the Americas and for immigrants from Ireland and Europe.[46] Tens of thousands of jobs directly involved in imperialism were located there, even if many of them were low-paid. Needless to say, Liverpool's politicians were strong supporters of all these business activities, and some owned businesses and were themselves significant employers.

Army and naval officers continued to play their role, bringing firepower and muscle to ensure that might made right in pursuit of the Pax Britannica. Many of the soldiers and sailors who took part in imperial wars and conquests – like the Ashanti wars in West Africa, and the Zulu and Boer wars in southern Africa in the nineteenth and early twentieth centuries – came from Liverpool.[47] Liverpool recruits and volunteers were also involved in imperial punitive expeditions in Ethiopia in 1867 and Nigeria (in Benin) in 1897. In fact, Admiral Sir Harry Rawson, who led the punitive British expedition to Benin city in 1897, was born in Walton, at that time a district on the edge of Liverpool and now firmly inside the city's boundaries.

The black population in Liverpool during the entire imperial period was continuously exploited and oppressed.[48] Black people faced incessant prejudice and stereotypes, discrimination, and institutional racism. Most low-paid work was done by poor whites, including Irish immigrants, and black people were thus at the bottom of the ladder. Liverpool has the longest-established black population and community in Britain, dating back to the 1700s.[49] Blacks in Liverpool numbered no more than a couple of thousand by the end of the 1700s.[50] According to various records, this number declined by the late nineteenth century, and then increased again in the early 1900s, mainly owing to male sailors from West Africa.[51] The lack of reliable statistical data on race means there are no definitive figures. The city's total black population was estimated by the end of the First World War to be around 5,000, but the British scholar John Belchem, an expert on the history of Liverpool, argues that this is an exaggeration.[52] The black population in Liverpool began to rise rapidly in the twentieth century, as the result of black settlement during the two world wars. At all times black men outnumbered black women.

The ethnic composition of the black population in Liverpool changed over time too, and this has implications for reparations. While most blacks born abroad who lived in Merseyside during the era of slavery came from the Americas and were not British citizens, most blacks in Liverpool from around 1900 born outside Britain came from Africa and were British citizens. In both cases, the majority were once again men. This is at variance with population patterns elsewhere in Britain throughout the twentieth century, which show far more Caribbean than African immigrants and many more British-born Caribbean-descended children.[53] By the time Caribbeans arrived in Liverpool, there were far fewer job opportunities in the city than elsewhere in England. Most therefore left for other cities like Manchester, Birmingham, and London. In other words, Liverpool became an African city, while all the other major cities became West Indian.

None of these differences mattered – whether immigrant or British-born; West Indian or West African; male or female. All black people faced stereotypes, discrimination, and institutional racism. Black people in Liverpool had the highest rates of unemployment and poverty and the worst jobs. When they got jobs at all, they were often paid the worst, hired last, and fired first. Jobs on ships were the worst and lowest-paid and attracted immigrants from Africa, who were often fired and replaced by white men.[54] Trade unions constantly discriminated against blacks, and the Seamen's Union played a key role in securing racist legislation against black British citizens.[55] Black men were confined to the worst housing – in a city where housing was especially poor – and many of them lived in segregated hostels.[56] They were restricted, at the risk of violence, brutality, or death, to the "sailor-town" district near the docks. Given the shortage of black women, relationships between black men and white women became common, and a population of mixed-race children grew quickly. There was widespread verbal abuse and violence by white men against both black men and white women associated with them. White men attacked black men for any and all reasons, often just for being black. Overall, the British police failed to protect them, and often abused them too.

This hostile environment and these harsh experiences intensified after the First World War: black people were randomly and viciously attacked in the streets and in their lodgings and homes, while the police stood idly by or even took part in the violence.[57] A local black resident and former member of the

British navy, the Bermuda-born Charles Wootton, was murdered in 1919 – a crime for which no one was ever prosecuted.[58] Wootton's name has become an important symbol in Liverpool's black community. Given limited jobs, black British citizens were encouraged to "go back" to Africa. When they refused, they were often persuaded, cajoled, or forced to do so, frequently with the support of the British government.[59]

Connecting Slavery to Imperialism

In this chapter I have sought to demonstrate that, in addition to an analysis of reparations for British slavery, discussions of reparations today can benefit substantially from an analysis of reparations for British imperialism. Like slavery, imperialism – its derivative – was a multifaceted system of political domination, economic exploitation, and social subordination. It continued processes begun during slavery and transformed them during the lengthy period that followed the era of enslavement. Both systems oppressed and exploited black people, and they shared much in common. But they also revealed differences which need to be identified and examined, especially in terms of reparations. While slavery is the foundation upon which imperialism built its structures and institutions, slavery did not determine the specific form or function of those structures or the immediate consequences for the twenty-first century. It was the dynamics of imperialism – political, economic, and social – that shaped these outcomes.

British slavery transported 12 to 20 million Africans to the Americas and the Caribbean, and it was the extraction of labour from enslaved Africans in British North America that produced the greatest economic activity and profits for Britain, compared with investments in Africa. After the legal abolition of slavery in the British Empire in 1834, British imperialism continued to derive profits from subordinated labour in its former colonies, as well as in countries that continued slavery such as the United States, Cuba, and Brazil. Beyond that, British imperialism extracted greater profits from the appropriation of land and the coercion and subordination of African labour within Africa itself after slavery than it had done during slavery. Later on, throughout the twentieth century, for economic reasons Britain actively recruited or invited West Indians – and some Africans – into Britain, especially between the two world wars and following labour shortages after 1945 (see Introduction in this volume). In stark contrast, both Caribbeans and Africans were systematically kept out of Britain during the period of slavery.

Slavery denied sovereignty to Native Americans when the British conquered lands and set up colonies across the Americas, where successor states continue to exist today. Furthermore, British imperialism denied sovereignty to Africans as it expanded its territories across the continent and created colonies and then nation-states that continue to exist today. The British Commonwealth – which emerged from a series of imperial conferences between the 1880s and the 1920s – was founded in 1931, long after slavery had legally ended.

Throughout the four centuries of European slavery, Liverpool engaged in extensive economic activity and earned substantial profits with the ideological support of Britain's leading businessmen and politicians and the backing and support of the army and navy. The most powerful people involved in this enterprise embraced and disseminated racist ideologies as justification for their exploitation. Liverpool's involvement in imperialism expanded the scope and geographical focus of its economic activities and profit-making, from enslaved labour across the Americas to subordinated and exploited labour across Africa.

We cannot understand the origins and development of British imperialism without understanding slavery. But there are many aspects of the relationship between Britain and Africa, and between an imperial power and its black subjects, that cannot be explained solely by slavery. This is because the vectors and trajectories of these relationships were shaped by the unique features of imperialism. Therefore, to understand the legacies and implications of these forces for reparations in Liverpool, we need to examine the particular trajectories that imperialism took in that city itself.

Concluding Reflections

Three more points need to be made for Britain as a whole and for Liverpool specifically. First, racist ideologies and institutional practices were transformed during imperialism – from biological and so-called scientific racism to Social Darwinism and eugenics. These racisms have more in common with, and can provide far more insights into, institutional racism in modern Britain than the racisms that prevailed during slavery. Second, most of the statues, monuments, and buildings currently being targeted by protesters across Britain – and in Liverpool in 2020 – are actually imperial creations, even though some were dedicated to men involved in slavery. These include the statue of Edward Colson in Bristol, erected in 1895; the statue of Winston Churchill in London, unveiled in 1973; and the statue of William Ewart Gladstone in Liverpool city centre.[60] The statue of Alfred Lewis Jones at the waterfront in Liverpool (the Pier Head) has yet to attract attention. These physical memorials are an important reason for examining imperialism, especially its legacies in the built environment. This holds true for many museums, a topic I have covered elsewhere.[61] And, third, there have been dramatic public announcements recently by the white descendants of slaveholding families and imperialists – including the Gladstone family – acknowledging that they profited from slavery and imperialism, with several families making financial and other forms of restitution to descendants of the enslaved (see Beckles in this volume).[62] These are unprecedented developments and shift the demand for reparations and restitution to another level.

Many of the issues described in this chapter about slavery, and most of those about imperialism, were almost entirely absent from the literature and from popular knowledge in Britain until at least the 1970s. This is mainly because they were neglected or ignored by scholars and universities. Most of what we know about British slavery and imperialism – and about the role that Liverpool played in both – was written by elite white men. And they told a very different story – of British magnanimity in Africa, and economic prosperity and racial harmony in Liverpool, bestowing accolades on the city's shipping magnates. Scholars of that period wrote biased, self-serving narratives which asserted British magnanimity engaged in a civilising mission, while universities and schools provided stereotypical and caricatured accounts of Africa and Africans. For example, in the first decades of the twentieth century, Ramsay Muir of Liverpool University extolled the virtues of the British Empire, insisting that it had put an end to savagery and barbarism around the world and that "the more the British Empire has grown the more freedom has been established on the face of the earth".[63] He added that British colonialism was better than the colonialism of any other nation. Many of his contemporaries across the nation said the same. Newspaper accounts, glowing profiles, and biographies of Liverpool's shipping magnates showered these men with praise for their contributions to the British Empire. Many received medals and awards, were knighted, or entered the House of Lords. Museums throughout the nation, like the British Museum and Oxford's Pitt Rivers Museum – and in Liverpool, the Derby Museum and Mayer Museum – also played their part in propagating these narratives of a benevolent "white man's burden".[64] All this is what protesters and reformists in Britain in 2022 referred to as "colonised education and knowledge production".

Fortunately, we no longer have to rely on biased white voices alone to provide accurate or comprehensive information about the past. We now know of multiple writings in Liverpool from people born and raised there: from those who visited and settled there for weeks, months or years, and from prominent Pan-Africanists passing through the city. We have nineteenth-century writings by African Americans such as Frederick Douglass, Samuel Ringgold Ward, and Ida B Wells; Caribbean citizens such as Edward Wilmot Blyden and Amy Ashwood Garvey.[65] We have work from the early twentieth century written by people born, raised, or resident in Liverpool like John Archer, reputedly the first black mayor in England, elected in 1913. Other writers include Ernest Marke and Pastor Daniels Ekarte, who arrived in Liverpool around 1915 and remained there for the rest of his life.[66] And as the twentieth century developed, there were writings by Pan-Africanists and leaders of anti-colonial struggles like Nigeria's Ladipo Solanke (of the West African Students' Union) and the Trinidadian scholar-activist George Padmore.[67]

The nature and extent of these different approaches to the evidence is captured in a quote in a volume of 37 Pan-African writers, edited by the Nigerian academic Adekeye Adebajo. When contemplating what has been done and written about Africa, he says: "British explorer David Livingstone described colonialism in the apparently benign terms of the 'three Cs': Commerce, Christianity, and Civilisation. The more malign 'three Ps' may, in fact, have been more accurate: Profit, Plunder and Prestige."[68] In my view, the evidence we now have available strongly suggests the "three Ps" are indeed more accurate. The comprehensive evidence currently available repudiates just about every assertion made at that time by white scholars and politicians, and provides a necessary corrective to their biases and partiality. This data should also silence the loud and unsubstantiated assertions by prominent white politicians and public figures that racism did not exist in the city.

A focus on British imperialism has one other benefit: it can move our attention away from the American experience (see Kerr-Ritchie, Broyld, and Maginn in this volume) and more towards the black experience in Europe. Although a lot is known about slavery in the West Indies, many people in Britain, including many scholars, spend an inordinate amount of time focusing on slavery and post-slavery in the United States. We thus know far more about the United States than we do about all the rest of the Americas combined, especially countries outside the anglophone world like Brazil, Colombia, Cuba, Puerto Rico, and Haiti. Yet slavery in the United States – and especially post-slavery (from the 1860s to the 1960s) – is unrepresentative of black people's experiences in the British West Indies during and after slavery. Take, for example, such features as legal racial segregation, the formation of so-called ghettoes (Jim Crow) enforced by a racist Supreme Court, a substantial black population outnumbered and dominated by a large white majority, and the Ku Klux Klan and the lynching of blacks. This was followed from the 1950s by the Civil Rights, Black Power, and Black Feminism movements.

In fact, black people in the British Empire share far more in common with other European nations, and British experiences post-slavery were shaped far more by these conditions and by European imperialism. British imperialism also shaped these experiences in Britain in ways that are unparalleled in the United States. This difference is demonstrated by the tiny black population in Britain, mainly immigrant or transient; the way that racisms developed through administrative fiat, bureaucratic obstruction, subterfuge, and political denial; the flow of black migration and settlement in Britain; and their minuscule numbers before the 1950s. The harsh realities of immigration, legal status, and citizenship for black people in Europe – the idea that black people are "permanent strangers" – are also more immediate in black British lives than in the lives of most black people in the United States. Demands for reparations in Britain will thus have very different components from demands for reparations in the United States. This is a compelling reason why we need to give far more attention to imperialism. This does not mean we should forget black America. The truth is, however, that black Britons can develop inspiration, motivation, determination if they are tactical and attentive, and can borrow and transform what they need from the United States while adapting it to their own specific needs in Britain.[69]

The case for reparations for slavery in general – and Liverpool in particular – has already been convincingly made. We have significant scholarly research and widespread public discussion and support for this cause. These debates have become more multidimensional and more sophisticated, and address far more issues than ever before. But we still lack detailed information and insights into vast swathes of black experiences under both slavery and imperialism (see Frith and Xosei in this volume). The knowledge we lack about imperialism is far greater than the information that we lack about slavery. And while Africans and black scholars across the diaspora have written about their experiences during British slavery, they left far more substantive, analytically rich, and compelling writings during British imperialism. This information will help us repair the damage done by colonial education, and enable us to acquire better and more comprehensive knowledge and understanding of the nature, scope, and range of both slavery and imperialism. Until we use this information to pursue reparations, our financial and political demands will remain underdeveloped.

Everyone is familiar with the public call for "reparations for slavery". But the case for reparations for British imperialism is yet to be convincingly made. We need to build this case effectively in order to develop more scholarly research on imperialism and reparations, cultivate more widespread awareness of its distinctive features, and foster greater support and mobilisation. Only then will we hear the call more often for "reparations for imperialism".

Part Two

Slavery in Africa

5

Slavery in Central and Eastern Africa

Catherine Coquery-Vidrovitch

THIS CHAPTER FOCUSES largely on slavery in Central Africa, while also covering aspects of East Africa. Like the rest of the world, African people have historically engaged in the use of slaves. As technology was scarce, humans were used as the main means of production. To possess slaves was the best guarantee of greater output. Unfortunately, we know very little about this remote period due to a lack of historical sources. This is especially true for Central Africa, whose ancient periods are known only from a few, scarce sources.

Our knowledge is extremely limited before the sixteenth century. We can make inferences from similar societies in other parts of the world, for slavery existed everywhere. These societies were mostly organised as social and familial groups, which does not mean that they were equal: members of the lineage were highly structured. At the top of the pyramid were chiefs, the ancestors and living elders, among whom were aristocratic leaders. Then came ordinary free people, and at the bottom of the pyramid were slaves. They were regarded as domestic slaves, meaning that they were owned by the lineage, from elders to youths. Being the inferior section of the lineage, these slaves were used for the heaviest and most demanding tasks. As they were owned, they could be exchanged, given, sold, or buried – in the case of funerals of important chiefs. They were regarded as having no honour, no dignity, and no rights. In short, they were slaves, who were used to work the soil or mine the ground, or as eunuchs or soldiers (often taken as prisoners of war). Women slaves were more numerous and valuable than men; they were mostly used as concubines and servants.

It is necessary not to confuse slavery – a social status – with the slave trade, which is a commercial affair aimed at making profit. A slave was not a slave by nature, even if their masters thought they were: they were born from slaves who had previously been enslaved through war or pillage, or because of a debt or a crime. Their fate was to remain slaves by birth, depending on their fathers' status: a slave man's child was a slave; a slave woman's child was free if his or her father was free.

Pre-modern Times

Our knowledge of slavery improves from the sixteenth century onwards thanks to relatively recent historical research, especially of the Buganda kingdom in the east, and the Kongo area in the west, which has been meticulously researched by the Belgian historian Jan Vansina[1] and others.

The Slave Trades

Slave trading had a long history in the Indian Ocean world. It reached Africa with the arrival of Muslim Arabs in the eighth century. It is probable that the path had already been opened from the beginning of the Christian era with the arrival of camels, possibly originating from Arabia and introduced to North Africa by the Romans between the first and third centuries AD. In north-east Africa, the first known slave trading occurred between Arabs occupying Egypt and southern Nubia. The Arabs long tried to conquer Nubia. A treaty was finally concluded in 652, by which the Arab conqueror, Abd Fallah ben Sayd, forced the Nubians to pay him an annual tribute of 365 slaves. This continued for several centuries, and probably stopped only with the emergence of the Ottoman Empire from the thirteenth century. For this tribute, slaves were imported from eastern Africa and also along the eastward Saharan route from the Lake Chad area to Cairo (also known as Fustat in ancient times).

This commerce was much older than the Atlantic trade, which only became possible when Portuguese and Spanish sailors crossed the Atlantic Ocean in 1492 and began organising slave trading between Africa and Brazil at the very beginning of the sixteenth century. As the Portuguese sailed along the Senegambia coast, they became aware of African Islam and Muslim traders.

Ca' da Mosto, a Venetian traveller in the service of Henry the Navigator, visited the Senegal area twice in 1454–1455, and eloquently described in his written account the early presence of Islam and the importance of the mullahs. Near the Mauritanian coast, he met Africans selling slaves and gold among themselves as well as to Muslim traders from the north. They were associated with the Mali Empire, which collapsed around 1560 and which was succeeded by the Songhai empire centred on Gao. Europeans were also involved in this trade.[2] Of course, the Portuguese knew about Arab slave trading. Neither the Portuguese slave trade nor the Arab, Berber, and Swahili slave trades operated separately in Africa south of the Sahara. From the beginning, these trades were connected. This is culturally important not only because of Euro-African cultural hybridisation but also, simultaneously, Arab–Berber–European–African cultural blending. There was thus an encounter not only between Europeans and Africans, but also between Christian and Muslim influences, and, in addition, traders from North and East Africa connected with Africa south of the Sahara as well as with Europeans. From the beginning, these cultural influences were very complex.

In the Indian Ocean world, there had long been maritime contacts between India (and perhaps China) and the East African coast. We know very little about the first African slaves abroad: there were a few of them in ancient Rome, perhaps imported from Carthage. As for Asia, there was a huge and violent revolt of slaves, most of them black "Zendj" people imported from the eastern coast of Africa, which occurred in Mesopotamia (modern Iraq, eastern Syria, and south-east Turkey) in the second half of the ninth century.[3] These slaves were needed to develop the land for agriculture. The revolt, which has been relatively well studied, lasted for nearly 20 years, from 869 to 883, and the slave army threatened Baghdad. According to local testimonies, between 500,000 and one million slaves were massacred. This dramatic event may explain why there were few large slave plantations in the Muslim world before the eighteenth century.

A painted silk cotton cloth from the tenth century has been found in Canton (south China) representing a black youth, probably a slave. We also have medieval paintings representing black slaves in the Near East. The slave trade increased from the eighth century with the arrival along the East African coast of Arabs from Arabia and Egypt. Their presence gave birth to a new mixed culture and language – the Swahili culture – which emerged from the eighth century onwards. The centre of the slave trade was the island of Zanzibar, which received slave caravans from the African hinterland. It is difficult to know how many slaves were involved before the nineteenth century. Historians have suggested perhaps two million, not taking into account slaves used for domestic roles or on plantations in Africa, which developed only from the eighteenth century.

Slavery and the Slave Trade in the Ganda Area

Caravans organised by slave traders supplied an active internal African trade, reaching further and further westward. New trading people gradually emerged within Africa, such as the Buganda kingdom (in present-day Uganda) from the sixteenth century. This small state was built on two main activities: agricultural production and trade. Previous small kingdoms, such as the Bunyoro and Ankole, were progressively absorbed by the most powerful of them, the Buganda. We know today that the role of non-coastal Africans living in the Great Lakes region in the slave trade was more complex than has hitherto been recognised.[4] Much more is known about slavery in Buganda than in any other part of the region thanks to Protestant missionaries in the nineteenth century; the records of French White Fathers missions in this region and also around Lake Tanganyika;[5] and early research by anthropologists such as the French scholar Henri Médard.[6]

Buganda's wealth was derived from its cattle and agriculture combined with international trade and pillage, both based on slavery. Annual military raids were conducted to capture people outside the kingdom, who were sold as slaves, either for use at home or for sale to caravans. Similarly, enslaved people were sold to kingdoms that developed on or in the hinterland of the West African coast from the mid-seventeenth to the mid-nineteenth century, thanks to the Atlantic slave trade. The growing power of the Buganda was strictly related to the growth of the slave trade from the early eighteenth century until as late as the end of the nineteenth century, when the British conquered the area. Slave trading had probably existed there for a long time, but it increased from the eighteenth century, even before the growth of the Swahili slave trade from the Indian Ocean coast, especially in the nineteenth century. It was perhaps at this time that the slave trade transformed these societies from communities in which slavery was incidental to ones in which slavery was central. The East African hinterland possessed a number of regional trading networks in which local products like salt or iron were exchanged with goods coming from the coast, everything changing hands many times, with a surplus of slaves flowing eastward. This is evidenced by the discovery of glass beads in pre-eighteenth-

114

century archaeological sites in Uganda and Rwanda.[7] During the nineteenth century, through territorial expansion the Buganda kingdom became linked to the international trade in ivory and slaves. The Buganda army and its ships on Lake Wamala claimed tributes when it imposed its authority on increasing numbers of people until as late as the British arrival in 1900.

Slaves and the Slave Trade in the Kongo Kingdom

The issue of slavery is better known in West Africa thanks to Portuguese writings as they began to trade in slaves in the Atlantic Ocean. The Portuguese landed in North Africa in 1410; and in Ceuta, north of Morocco, in 1415; they progressively explored the western coast of Africa, further and further southwards. The Portuguese then reached Mauritania, where in about 1441 a Portuguese captain bought the very first slaves. In 1482, the Portuguese built an important trading port on the Gold Coast in São Jorge da Mina (which later became Elmina in modern Ghana), where they arrived in 1471, and they landed at the mouth of the Congo river in 1482. There, a powerful king, with the title of Manikongo, ruled the Kongo kingdom (in what is now Angola). They met him in 1483 in his hinterland capital city of Mbanza Kongo – later renamed São Salvador by the Portuguese – and offered him European goods such as alcohol, cotton cloth, guns, powder, and beads. They also brought missionaries with them in 1480. The Kongo kingdom had existed for several centuries, probably originating in the twelfth century. Like other local rulers, the king's power was based on agriculture, hunting elephants, collecting ivory, and capturing slaves, thanks to his military organisation. The kingdom had a hierarchical organisation with subordinated military chiefs. An internal trading network had also developed.

After encountering the Portuguese, King Nzinga Nkuwu and the ruling elite were attracted by the new and fascinating European goods on offer. They wanted to obtain more. The king was persuaded to adopt Christianity, and he converted in 1491, thinking that it would help develop his country with the agreement of Portugal's King Philip I. Nkuwu's successor, Mvemba Nzinga, who became king in 1506, adopted a Christian name, Afonso I, and the kingdom converted to Christianity three years later.[8] At first, there was no difficulty for an African polytheistic religion to adopt a single deity. Nevertheless, Christianity was monopolised by the Kongolese aristocracy, as the king wanting to protect his privileged relationship with his new friends. He exchanged letters with the king of Portugal, first using the mediation of Portuguese missionaries, but then directly after studying the Portuguese language. He also opened a school, assisted by Jesuit priests. This royal correspondence can be found in the Portuguese archives. Afonso I sent one of his sons to Portugal, who went on to Rome and became the first African bishop, with the name of Henrique. At first, Philip sent artisans to the Manikongo, such as builders, carpenters, and craftsmen. Afonso I was probably a clever politician, hoping to use the opportunity of his links with Lisbon to develop his country.

Unfortunately, the Portuguese began to trade in slaves and, after a dozen years, became increasingly rapacious, and began to enslave Kongolese subjects. The reason for this was clear: Portuguese traders had come to Africa to find gold. They had known that gold mines were located in West Africa since 1375, when a famous portolan or nautical chart – the Catalan Atlas – was gifted by the king of Aragon, Peter IV, to the French king, Charles V. This chart had been compiled by a Mediterranean Jew, Abraham Cresques, who used information derived from Muslim sailors. It depicted the king of Mali, Mansa Musa, as a major fourteenth-century gold producer. The Portuguese needed Kongolese slaves to sell in West Africa to the Akan people of the Gold Coast, where, as the name suggests, gold arrived from the hinterland, which was obtained by the sale of slaves. After a while, Afonso realised that his kingdom had been devastated. In 1526, he wrote a moving letter to the Portuguese king John III, asking him urgently to put an end to the slave trade.[9] But it was too late: the Kongo kingdom was already trapped in a vicious circle. Internal wars occurred, and the king's power was progressively weakened until it disintegrated. Portugal occupied Angola in 1574,[10] one year before Lisbon helped King Alvaro of Kongo repel Jaga invaders.[11]

The Era of Slave Plantations

São Tomé Island

Slave plantations were an invention of Portuguese merchants in Africa, hastened by their discovery of sugar cane. This plant probably came from India. It was introduced by Arabs to Egypt, and then adopted by the Portuguese. Lisbon first tried to introduce the culture into the Atlantic islands such as Madeira and Cape Verde. The climate was, however, too dry and unsuitable. The Portuguese were, however, successful at the lower end of the Bight of Benin, around modern-day Equatorial Guinea. There, the inhabited island of São Tomé proved to be perfect: rainy, because of the equatorial climate, and sunny, with favourable soils. Around 1485, its first settlers were Portuguese by language and by faith, most of them of mixed blood through intermarriage with Africans. They bought slaves from the coast, first from the Benin coast (in modern Nigeria), then, from 1515 onwards, they purchased 4,000 slaves a year from Kongo. In 1500, there were already 2,000 slaves on the sugar plantations.

The slave trade in São Tomé was complex: it was regional and international, being connected to Antwerp, where a slaving station had been created in 1493, which received more than a hundred ships a year. By the sixteenth century, there were 12,000 slaves on São Tomé as well as 2,000 or, at most, 3,000 free people; they produced half of the sugar sent to Europe. This "marriage" between slavery and sugar, cemented by fear and violence, resulted in several slave revolts. The last one, in 1595, involved about 5,000 rebels. Plantations were set on fire, the capital city was nearly occupied, and settlers fled from the island, taking with them their slaves, technicians, and sugar mills. They sailed to Brazil, where the production of sugar began in 1560. From there, production expanded to the Caribbean islands during the eighteenth century. By the end of the century, the main sugar producer was Saint-Domingue, a French colony.

The Atlantic Slave Trade

Sugar cane plantations needed an enormous number of workers. Portuguese and Spanish planters began to use Indians from South America. But they were ill-treated, and vulnerable to imported European diseases, to which most of them succumbed. A Spanish priest, Bartolomé de Las Casas, campaigned to protect them, and in 1542 the Holy Roman Emperor Charles V forbade the enslavement of American Indians. This ban had already been proposed in 1537 by Pope Paul III,[12] and it was reinforced by a famous debate, organised by a meeting of prominent theologians, lawyers, and imperial officers convened by Las Casas, at Spain's Valladolid University in 1550–1551.[13]

Nothing was actually discussed about African people. They had proved that they were expendable since the São Tomé experience. In 1492, the Italian explorer Christopher Columbus had already taken slaves on board his ship. By 1503 the first African slaves were imported to Brazil by the Portuguese, who had "discovered" the country in 1500. This marked the beginning of a huge trade in slaves, first to Brazil and the Caribbean islands. About 45 per cent of the total number of Atlantic slaves were imported across the South Atlantic, most of them enslaved people from the west-central African coast, from Cameroon to Angola, mainly from about 1550 to 1750, and then again in the nineteenth century after the British banned the Atlantic slave trade in the North Atlantic.

Slave Trading in Central Africa

Two main African ports exported slaves: Loango, the capital city of a small kingdom dependent on Kongo, on the right bank of the Congo River, and Luanda in present-day Angola. These ports gave rise to important cities based exclusively on the slave trade. Loango, which has nearly disappeared today, was once an opulent city in the seventeenth and eighteenth centuries. Luanda is much better known. The city, occupied by Lisbon since the sixteenth century, included many Portuguese traders, as well as growing numbers of Brazilian traders. A famous example was Francesco Honoraria da Costa, who arrived in 1777. He created a firm with his Angolan associate, Antonio José da Costa, one of the main local slave traders. He settled in Kasanje in 1794 and became famous for sending two of his trading slaves (or *pombeiros*) on an expedition from Luanda to Mozambique: they were the first to cross the continent, following the slave trading routes.[14]

Since there were very few white women, local and foreign slave traders married African women, mostly aristocratic daughters of important chiefs from the hinterland. These marriages strengthened slave-trading relationships, which were reinforced by military expeditions across the heart of the continent backed by Portuguese imports of guns and gunpowder. The marriages gave rise to larger *métis* populations. Moreover, European merchants, weakened by the local climate and diseases, frequently died at a younger age than their spouses. Angolan women thus inherited their wealth, and became important businesswomen – the so-called *senhoras*. One of them, Dona Ana Joaquina dos Santos e Silva, still had powerful connections with the hinterland in the nineteenth century. They lived in modern storeyed houses with a balcony – called *sobrados* – in an aristocratic district of the city, in a luxurious style, and themselves possessed several slaves. The Catholic Church owned many slaves too. From 1693 onwards – the Portuguese slave trade was forbidden only in 1836 – the Church had a right to buy 700 slaves a year.

In the Central African hinterland, new states emerged from the sixteenth century. The main ones were to develop into the Luba and Lunda empires. Before the eighteenth century, their emergence was probably favoured by the increasing production of maize, introduced from America by the Portuguese.

Maize culture played a part in the increase in population density, which, in turn, gave rise to powerful states. The earliest Lunda mostly lived on food cultivation and production of cloth (raffia and cotton). Maize and cloth were the main trading goods across Central Africa; slaves were then probably not so important. Only between the 1720s and the 1750s did these empires – increasingly, military powers – also became important providers of slaves. Capturing slaves for sale to the West made possible foreign exchange earnings for the importation of swords and, later, guns. These kingdoms also bought salt and copper from the East. The whole region was occupied by a series of smaller states, all in competition with each other, and engaged in incessant conquests and military campaigns, which provided more and more slaves.[15]

The Nineteenth Century

In the nineteenth century, there were 86,000 slaves in Luanda, half of them 40,000 women slaves.[16] There were also 5,800 *métis*, around 300,000 free black people, and only 1,000 white men in the whole of Angola. This meant that Luanda – a centre of slave trading – was a creolised city and a centre for Western cultural diffusion. As a result, within Central Africa, there was a progressive diffusion of European manufactured goods, language, and culture, which transformed local ideas and political life.

Slavery and the slave trade increased enormously throughout the nineteenth century. This was especially so in Central Africa because of major changes in the Indian Ocean world, which resulted from global economic exchanges. In the Atlantic world, the Haitian Revolution (1791–1804)[17] and the European industrial revolution (roughly 1780–1840) were powerful factors that led to the progressive abolition of the Atlantic slave trade: from 1803 for Denmark, 1808 for Britain, and 1831 for France. The Atlantic demand for new African slaves steadily declined.

As a result of the industrial revolution, armament production techniques developed, and guns used by European armies became obsolete every 20 years or so. The question of what to do with the old stocks became a major problem. A few industrial cities like Leuven in Belgium specialised in transforming these arms into "trade arms", for use by African partners for their internal needs. Then, at the end of the nineteenth century, Europeans eager to conquer Africa began to reduce the sale of their armaments in the Atlantic Ocean world in order to avoid assisting African resistance. They discovered the opportunity to sell these arms further east, when in 1869 the Suez Canal was opened, connecting the Mediterranean world to people in the Indian Ocean. Arab and Swahili traders were increasingly eager to buy European armaments. The Muslim and Swahili slave trade developed hugely in the Indian Ocean in the second half of the nineteenth century. This was a time when the Oman empire (south-east of Arabia) had already extended its reach to East Africa. In 1840, the Sultan of Oman settled on Zanzibar Island, which progressively became, in the second half of the nineteenth century, the main centre of slave trading in the Indian Ocean.

Swahili and creolised Arabs developed a number of slave ports on the African coast. From the Swahili coastal ports, military and trading caravans began operating into Africa, while creolised Portuguese and Brazilians did the same from Angola and Kongo. Thus, in the second half of the nineteenth century, there was a convergence of slave trading from the eastern and western coasts. Slave networks were thus fully established across Africa. The use of these slaves was twofold: first, local planters mainly employed slaves on plantations that developed on a global scale: for sugar cane, cloves (introduced in Zanzibar around 1835), sisal, and coconut palms. Most slaves were women, used as much as men were for portage and plantations, and also for sex.

Other slaves were used for wars. Swahili and Arab traders not only competed for power in the coastal towns and cities, like Mombasa, but they also established themselves forcefully in the hinterland, with rape and enslavement commonplace. Local slave-trading polities emerged – similar to what occurred on the western coast – such as the Nyamwezi kingdom, the town of Pangani, and Lake Tanganyika or, further westward, in southern Kongo.

The west coast of Central Africa was a major "producer" of slaves for the Atlantic slave trade from the beginning of the sixteenth century. This role increased tremendously when sugar cane plantations expanded to the Americas: first, in Brazil as early as the mid-seventeenth century, then the Caribbean islands throughout the eighteenth century, and again in the first half of the nineteenth century. The Atlantic slave trade was progressively forbidden by the European powers. The British banned the trade for several reasons. First, they understood early on, from the time of the Haitian Revolution which resulted in the first modern black republic, that the end of slavery was imminent. Second, the Napoleonic Wars had begun. The main economic purpose for the British was to destroy the French economy, and France's main international wealth still lay in the Atlantic slave trade, while the industrial revolution had already emerged in Britain. The profits of the Atlantic slave trade in Britain had been surpassed by those of the coal and textile industries at home.

In 1815, with the Congress of Vienna bringing an end to the Napoleonic Wars, the British tried to obtain a comprehensive ban on the European slave trade. The only pledge London received, however, from its allies – and France too – was that they would put an end to the trade "as early as possible". In spite of British control, the clandestine slave trade continued as late as the mid-nineteenth century. A law forbidding the slave trade was passed in France only in 1831, and the last slave ship left the French port of Nantes in 1832. Meanwhile, on the West African coast, the contraband slave trade was increasingly suppressed in the Bight of Benin by the British navy. Portuguese and Brazilians from Angola consequently reactivated their contraband slave trade all along the Central African coast – from Cameroon to Benguela. Most of the four million slaves traded in the first half of the nineteenth century came from active ports that had long been settled: mainly Loango (north of the Congo River), Luanda, and Benguela (in Angola). The first European explorers entering the hinterland, such as Savorgnan de Brazza in Gabon from 1877 to 1885, wrote accounts of this intense internal trade, and often bought slaves to assist their caravans. The pretext was to buy the freedom of the enslaved, after they had been used as ill-paid and ill-fed porters and workers (see also Klein in this volume).[18]

Within Africa, a major change occurred throughout the nineteenth century. Until then, a large number of slaves had been sent abroad. Across the Atlantic Ocean, some 12 to 15 million African slaves were transported to the Americas from the beginning of the sixteenth to the mid-nineteenth century: 45 per cent from Central Africa (including Mozambique) by Portuguese and Brazilian slave traders across the South Atlantic, most of them at the beginning and at the end of the Atlantic slave trade. From the beginning of the nineteenth century, owing to the progressive abolition of the Atlantic slave trade and, above all, to the abolition of slavery, which closed the market – in 1835 for British colonies, in 1848 for French colonies, in 1883 for the United States, in 1886 for Cuba, and in 1888 for Brazil – Atlantic slave-trading activity gradually disappeared in the second half of the century.

The contraband slave exports were as important in the first half of the nineteenth century as the "legal" exports in the second half of the eighteenth century. Meanwhile, within Africa itself, slave trade routes and networks were strongly reinforced. In Central Africa, slave trade routes crossed the middle of the continent from east to west. There are a number of narratives of slave women who, at the end of their wretched lives, found refuge with Protestant missions in Central Africa from the mid-nineteenth century. One of these life stories reveals that a young girl born on the border of Tanganyika – her name was Bwanika – was raped, married, and enslaved from place to place a dozen times. She was beautiful and clever, and she fled several times. Around the 1850s, she was taken in a caravan towards the Indian Ocean, and some years later she was again enslaved in a caravan travelling westward to the Atlantic Ocean. She ended her life as an old woman, a convert to Christianity, in a mission station, where her life story was recorded.[19]

Throughout the nineteenth century, internal slavery greatly increased. Slaves, who were no longer exported, were used locally: many were employed as workers on slave plantations. Others were used as soldiers for new conquering empires or kingdoms that emerged in the nineteenth century, such as the Kuba kingdom in west-central Africa.[20] There were probably ten times more African slaves on the continent at the end of the nineteenth century than a century before.[21] While slave contraband was intense on the western coast, in Central and East Africa slave plantations appeared and developed throughout the nineteenth century. One famous Swahili slave owner created plantations in the upper Congo River area. His name was Hamed bin Mohammed el Marjebi (1837–1905), nicknamed "Tippu Tip". He negotiated with Zanzibar's sultan, as well as with the American explorer Henry Morton Stanley, who was hired by King Leopold II of Belgium to explore the upper Congo River (see Vanthemsche in this volume). King Leopold even nominated Stanley in the 1890s as his agent in the area, but eventually Tippu Tip preferred to approach the Zanzibar sultan directly. El Marjebi retired and died in Zanzibar in June 1905, probably of malaria.

Concluding Reflections

Although European slave trading was forbidden and disappeared in the second half of the nineteenth century, internal slavery remained ubiquitous in pre-colonial and colonial Central Africa. Colonial officers were reluctant to ban it, on the pretext of not interfering with local traditions. It was useful for colonial Europeans to request workers from local chiefs, without knowing their social status: most of them were slaves until late into the twentieth century. Until today, social slavery, although legally forbidden, still remains present in many African societies, as an international conference on "African Slavery in Africa: Past, Present and Future", held in Nairobi in October 2014, revealed.[22]

6

Slavery in West Africa

Martin A. Klein

IN EXAMINING THE ROLE OF slavery in cities, Africanist scholars have begun to move beyond models derived from the literature on European colonialism and American plantation systems.[1] In the former approach, African slavery was characterised as largely domestic or kin-oriented – in any case, based less on direct exploitation than elsewhere. The classic formulation of this approach is Suzanne Miers and Igor Kopytoff's *Slavery in Africa* (1977),[2] a collection of articles on slavery in African societies during the colonial period. In the latter approach, Africanists looked for characteristics of plantation slavery (labour organisation, harsh treatment, lack of reproduction, connections to international trade) in larger-scale agriculture enterprises that aligned with patterns of plantation slavery in the New World. Here, early and influential work on the continent includes studies by Frederick Cooper[3] and Paul Lovejoy.[4] This comparative, plantation-focused framework also continues to have resonance, as recent work by Mohammed Bashir Salau[5] demonstrates.

However, neither of these models well represents the practice of slavery in urban Africa.[6] Enslaved people generally had more autonomy and opportunities in town as compared with plantation agricultural settings. Yet they were usually better treated, not because the system itself was more "benign", but because of the way their labour was exploited. Enslavement was in all cases based on acts of violence. However, the ways in which slaves were used varied greatly. In societies based on slavery, enslaved people were used both to produce more slaves and to control and oversee other enslaved workers. Thus, slaves themselves were a crucial part of the servile social order, and they provided a dependable and sometimes unusually loyal labour force. One result of the centrality of the slaves in slave-dependent economies was that the cities of the slave trade were populated mostly by enslaved people – indeed, in some cases, overwhelmingly so.

This chapter uses a case study of slavery in Saint-Louis-du-Sénégal – a settlement established by the French at the mouth of the Senegal River in 1659 – to raise issues that are then drawn upon to shape discussion of broader regional patterns of urban slavery in West Africa. Following the case study analysis, I revisit selected literature focused on coastal towns and settlements from the Gold and Slave Coasts (Elmina, Whydah, Lagos) and the Bight of Biafra (Niger Delta ports, Calabar). As so much historical research focuses increasingly on narrowly defined themes, it is important that historians try to pull things together and place such specialised research into broader contexts. My concluding observations seek to contribute to the growing and significant literature on forms of servitude.

Saint-Louis, Senegal

History of the Town, Rise of the Signares

The European presence and the slave trade at the mouth of the Senegal River date back to the first Portuguese expeditions during the second half of the fifteenth century (see also Coquery-Vidrovitch and Silva Jr in this volume).[7] Though there does not seem to have been a Portuguese settlement where the French later established Saint-Louis, other Luso-African settlements along the coast provided a model for social relationships in the trade.[8] The Portuguese monopoly of the slave trade was challenged by the English, Dutch, and French in the late sixteenth century (see Brereton, Nimako, and Aragón Falomir in this volume). After having settled on the island of Saint-Louis, the French seized Gorée Island from the Dutch in 1677. In both settlements, the number of Europeans was always very small. As late as 1738, there were 231 Europeans in Saint-Louis, Gorée, and the upriver post at Galam. Trading operations in the upper Senegal River – the major source of slaves – were costly in terms of French lives. The French slave-trading company thus decided that it was more economical to rely on African sailors and artisans.[9] European soldiers, sailors, and artisans were paid more than Africans and had a much higher mortality rate. By 1835, the population of Saint-Louis and Gorée had multiplied about ten times, but at that time there were still only 151 Europeans in Saint-Louis. Even well into the nineteenth century, the colonial economy of Saint-Louis was largely managed by Africans and staffed by slaves.

During most periods, trade in Senegal was in the hands of companies granted a monopoly by the French state. These companies regularly failed because of interlopers and European wars, and they were always under financial pressure. Such companies were thus not eager to create a larger and more costly colonial establishment. Nevertheless, they found it difficult to control the growth of Saint-Louis and the behaviour of the men they sent out to it. Central to that growth were the mostly African women with whom company officials cohabited. By the 1680s, there were persistent complaints of employees using such women to trade privately; employees also often provided the best merchandise to these women, called *signares*, rather than to the companies for which they worked.[10] Although company employees were forbidden to trade on their own, none of the monopoly companies could control the actions of *signares*. Both officials of the trading companies and some subsequent authors have viewed these women as seductive temptresses. However, the reality is that they filled a variety of functions in the lives of the men they married *à la mode du pays*, and many proved to be very astute entrepreneurs. There were few French women in the colony. European males sought African female partners, but not solely for sex. They also wanted cooks, companions, care-givers for when they were sick, and (as noted above) trading partners.[11] It was, however, the high mortality rate of European men that was the source of much of the wealth of the *signares*. Since their trading relations were illegal, they were also secret. It was often difficult for a deceased man's French family to get its hands on whatever he had accumulated through clandestine private trade. Some *signares* outlasted a number of husbands in the course of a lifetime. Their businesses with their husbands or male partners were also collaborative, with the *signares* often providing capital and local contacts for their joint enterprises. Thus, even in those cases where men returned to Europe, they often left property or a bequest to their African wives and families.[12]

Slavery in the Regional Economy of Saint-Louis

By the middle of the eighteenth century, the economy was dominated by a number of *métis* families in Saint-Louis, all with the names of their French progenitors.[13] These families and their *signares* were major slave owners who provided enslaved captives for use in Saint-Louis and in Gorée's coasting trade. Gorée Island – another slave export point – is about 180 kilometres south of Saint-Louis, just off the Cap-Vert peninsula where the city of Dakar is found today. For French companies, it made more sense to rent slaves from *signares* than to acquire their own. British colonists similarly found *signares* to be essential economic partners. When the British occupied Saint-Louis in 1758, they reported that there were between 30 and 40 influential *métis* families. The *signares* by this time were perhaps the most visible part of a system in which these influential families controlled both the city of Saint-Louis itself and the Senegal River economy more broadly. The British quickly found they could best manage this economy by working through *signares*. Samuel Swan, an American visitor, described Saint-Louis elite households and their use of enslaved workers in 1815. The larger compounds had high walls with enslaved guards controlling access. Inside were two-storey houses, with storerooms and living quarters for enslaved workers on the ground floor and the family apartments as well as a large hall on the upper floor:

> Each house may in fact be considered a Fortress where the master on his sofa views & directs from the piazza his numerous slaves below. These all have their huts ranged around the wall within the yard & it is not uncommon to see carpenters, coopers, Blacksmiths, weavers, Tailors, &c. all in operation at their respective works belonging to the same yard.[14]

Indeed, Gorée Island's "House of Slaves" museum is an example of such a configuration. Its restoration included the creation of an information centre that replicates in words and drawings exactly such a scene as described by Swan. Certainly, enslaved people sometimes lived in separate compounds, but many lived in structures along the outer compound wall or in rooms on the ground floor of the owner's main house.

In this section and the one that follows, I explore three characteristics that distinguished the enslaved communities of coastal urban Senegal, including those in Saint-Louis. First, many enslaved workers were highly mobile, moving freely in and out of the city in the service of their owners. Some of this movement was associated with the gum trade. Gum arabic, much in demand in France, was harvested from acacia trees by slaves working under the direction of Bidan slave owners in the desert areas north of the Senegal River. This natural gum was economically important to Saint-Louis in the eighteenth century. French posts up the Senegal River were accessible only during the rainy season when the river waters were high. There were thus two trading seasons: February to May, when there were trade fairs in middle river ports called *escales*, where gum was purchased; and June, after the rains began, when the whole trading community moved upriver in a convoy. The boats were pulled by workers known as *laptots*, a term that came from the Wolof word for sailors, which described a variety of people in the French service.[15] The convoy itself was made up of different groups, free and enslaved, *métis* and African, and an occasional French trader.[16] However, until at least the mid-nineteenth century, the vast majority of people in the convoy were slaves.[17] The convoy bought enslaved captives and gum for export, as well as gold, wax, ivory, and hides. Grain and other foodstuffs were also purchased in the middle and lower Senegal River area to feed Saint-Louis and supply incoming ocean-going vessels; some was also sold to the Bidan to feed themselves and their slaves.

During the 1820s, there were about 1,200 *laptots* working in the annual convoy. Over 85 per cent of them were enslaved.[18] Though steam navigation had been introduced on the Senegal River by this time, most boats were still pulled physically upstream. This meant that in the post-Napoleonic era, over a thousand slaves went up the river every year for over four months. This was between a quarter and a half of Saint-Louis's entire enslaved male population. If we deduct children, the old, and the sick, it means that the vast majority of the town's able-bodied male slaves participated in the river trade. To allow such participation in commerce and regional movement on the part of enslaved men, slave owners had to be confident that they would not flee. Enslaved *laptots* were paid, they were fed, and they could trade for themselves.[19] Thus enslaved life in Saint-Louis very likely offered greater economic security and autonomy than that in many more rural locales in Senegal.

Composition of the Slave Community

The mobility of enslaved men in Saint-Louis was similarly apparent on Gorée Island, where there were about 325 sailors working in the coasting trade during this period. Over 90 per cent of them were enslaved. This was a larger percentage of the total slave population of 3,731 recorded in 1835 than in Saint-Louis.[20] When age and gender are taken into consideration, able-bodied men were also a larger proportion of the local enslaved population in Gorée as compared with Saint-Louis. Furthermore, their work was probably less seasonal. Gorée was totally barren. Grain, wood, water, and livestock all had to be brought from the mainland throughout the year. Though there is some evidence of slave flight, the *laptots* at Gorée often demonstrated a high degree of loyalty to slave owners. *Laptots* could be recruited for defence or even for permanent militia positions. They were also used to guard other slaves and protect merchant households. However, this is not to say that they did not also sometimes act collectively in their own interests. For example, when British vessels entered the Senegal River in 1758, *laptots* blockaded the fort until the British signed a written agreement guaranteeing their protection.[21] This behaviour of the *laptots* was similar to so-called slave warriors such as Bambara *tonjon* and the Wolof *ceddo*, who served the state loyally because they were part of the social order and profited from it.

Beyond their mobility, the autonomy of enslaved workers in Saint-Louis and in Gorée was supported by their specialised work skills. This was particularly true for enslaved men. I have not seen an occupational census from Saint-Louis, but one taken on Gorée in 1847 lists occupations for enslaved people.[22] Of the 983 male slaves, less than 10 per cent were listed simply as labourers and less than 5 per cent as "without profession". In contrast, almost a third consisted of sailors; the rest were masons, weavers, ship's carpenters, cooks, servants, blacksmiths, and traders. The occupations listed for female slaves were less specialised: 68 per cent were *pileuses* (pounders), while 19 per cent were laundresses. *Pileuses*, however, did more than pound millet. They were set to a variety of tasks by their owners, including spinning thread. It generally took about eight hours to spin enough thread to keep a weaver busy for an hour.

If the 107 male weavers listed in the census were working full-time, almost all of the listed *pileuses* were spending a large percentage of their time spinning – indeed, probably more than they spent pounding. It is possible that some of the thread used by Gorée's male weavers was produced in nearby villages, but textile production was, clearly, economically important. Enslaved people also worked as servants. When wealthier *signares* went out, they were often accompanied by a servant with an umbrella and followed by several others. Some French officials were bothered by the extravagant display. However, census records suggest that most of the labour of enslaved people in Gorée was put to full economic use by their owners. Training enslaved workers in various crafts not only gave their owners higher revenues, but also meant that male *laptots* could be fruitfully employed even during the trading off-season. Moreover, cloth production could use the time of male and female slaves even as these workers aged, and some other forms of labour became less feasible.

In addition to their mobility and work skills, enslaved people in Saint-Louis were distinguished by their living situation. They lived in the households of their owners. Thus, they were involved in constant face-to-face relationships with one another, as well as with their masters. They were involved in performing varied tasks rather than gang labour. Only 10 households on Gorée and 17 in Saint-Louis had more than 50 slaves. The biggest in 1779 belonged to a *signare* with 69 slaves. Enslaved communities rarely got any bigger. In fact, the vast majority of slave-owning households in Saint-Louis and Gorée had less than 10 slaves. Many had only one or two. Generally, the enslaved who resided in Saint-Louis and Gorée seem to have been acquired from the 1,000 to 2,000 captives annually destined for export. The number kept in any year was probably small, and they were most likely children young enough to be trained over time. After all, an enslaved worker with specialised skills was valuable.

In 1828, a healthy slave with no specialised work skills cost about 300 francs and could be rented out for 60–90 centimes a day. In contrast, an enslaved worker with specialised skills could cost as much as 1,500 francs and was hired out for up to 3 francs 60 centimes a day. Slaves who were hired out generally kept half of what they earned.[23] Slave owners had different strategies for how they directed the labour of their enslaved workers, depending on their own economic activities and enterprises. Some rented out most of their slaves. Some seem to have had businesses. Most probably did both. Marie Legrose, for example, owned 39 slaves, of whom 9 were laundresses. In addition, there were 3 pileuses, 4 masons, 3 carpenters, 2 cooks, a sailor, and a dressmaker. Others invested heavily in pileuses. The American historian Michael Marcson cites a household that had 5 pileuses and 6 children among 17 slaves. Another slave owner clearly had a clothing operation: 3 tailors and seamstresses and a cloth dyer in a household of only 13.[24]

Some enslaved people earned enough money to buy slaves of their own or to buy their own freedom. For a slave to buy another slave rather than his own freedom may seem surprising, but my rural informants also reported that it was a frequent strategy.[25] Male slaves in the river trade were sometimes able to buy their freedom and a boat. They could also rent slaves and start out in business as marigotiers, working the creeks that fed the Senegal River. Even some pileuses managed to buy slaves of their own. Like workers on boats, pileuses could trade. Mbaye Guèye has suggested that some also worked as prostitutes.[26] Slaves were sometimes manumitted with a commitment to serve for several years before becoming free. The rate does not seem to have been very high, though it was increasing during the last years of slavery. Indeed, 500 slaves were freed during the decade before 1848.[27]

Life Cycles of Urban Slaves

Though the process is not without difficulty, we can reconstruct the life cycles of Senegalese urban slaves. Most were either born in coastal towns or came to them as enslaved children. Among their servants, *signares* often had young boys called *rapasses* or *raparcilles*, which is a Portuguese term for small boys, again demonstrating Portuguese influence in the region.[28] Child captives were often preferred since many slave owners believed that children could be taught to accept their status. Coastal Senegal differs from the spatial and social expectations of American slavery. This was not a "big house" and "slave quarter" culture. Indeed, while young enslaved children most likely mixed socially and played with free children, they were only increasingly separated as free children advanced in their education. From the point of view of a slave owner, the education of enslaved children served a specific purpose: foremost, to enable enslaved children to accept their ascribed role under slavery. Additionally, because a skilled slave was worth so much more than an unskilled one, slave owners often pursued training for the children they enslaved.

In Saint-Louis, as elsewhere in Africa, enslaved women were almost always more numerous than enslaved men. I have previously argued that women were the cement of African slavery: elite men took the prettiest among them as companions, slave warriors depended on their wives to farm, and there were always enough women to serve as partners for enslaved men.[29] While these statements and the research underlying them were not directed solely at urban contexts, I see no reason to think that the towns would have been different. Enslaved women's expected contributions would inevitably have been influenced by sexuality and involved with reproduction. For enslaved females, I hypothesise a trajectory from child servant to wife and worker. If widowed, a woman could depend on her children or return to her owner's household as a servant, a spinner, or a nanny. Indeed, enslaved women were useful to their owners at almost all ages.

For male slaves, reproduction was less central to their experiences. Their life trajectory seems to have involved not sex, but work. They undoubtedly started working within the household when very young, possibly as servants like the girls. In their early teens, most of them would then begin working as apprentices to senior craftsmen or sailing in the convoys up the Senegal River. Indeed, many very likely did both. Many craftsmen would have continued taking part in the annual expedition, though that probably depended on their speciality. House construction generally took place in the off-season. Artisans were also capable of working into old age, though with decline and illness they undoubtedly reached a point where they were totally dependent.[30]

In French Senegal, flow-through and amelioration were important to the functioning of the system of slavery. By flow-through, I mean the progression of enslaved individuals through a series of stages from initial captivity to integration in their captors' households, and eventually to manumission. The percentage of enslaved people manumitted in Saint-Louis does not seem to have been very high. However, manumission as an idea was just as important as manumission as an act. The possibility of manumission, however remote, was probably important to the morale of slaves, particularly the most economically ambitious. In 1848, one ex-slave, Samba Agui, had become one of the biggest slaveholders in Saint-Louis and one of the most resolute defenders of slavery.[31]

In Saint-Louis, manumission was probably less important than amelioration, which involved enslaved people's differential access to more privileged positions within slavery (see Cobley in this volume). There were slave ship's captains, slaves who traded for their masters, and *maîtres de langue*, who worked as interpreters and diplomatic agents on colonial commercial expeditions. In town, there were also positions of authority, people who directed the work of others, and there were always confidential relationships in which the slave's knowledge and advice were important. Ship captains were responsible for merchandise and for buying and selling. Enslaved workers counselled their masters, undertook missions on their behalf, and were often reportedly more important and trusted than sons. Slaves who worked in such positions could accumulate wealth. However, they also had to maintain the confidence of their owners.

Cities of the Slave Trade

The case study of Saint-Louis provides a vivid picture of slavery that departs strongly both from the understandings of Americanists of the institution and from more kin-based models of indigenous African contexts. In Saint-Louis, slavery was defined by the mobility and specialised work skills of enslaved people. There also tended to be less social and spatial separation between slaves and slave owners than in plantation contexts, as they lived in combined households and frequently interacted face to face. These features contributed to the relative autonomy of enslaved people in Saint-Louis. To understand slave life more fully in the town, we must also discard the notion that being a "slave" was a single, static and immutable status. Enslaved people occupied a variety of social positions, some with greater autonomy and power, such as ship captain. The amelioration of the slave system in Saint-Louis meant that an enslaved person could achieve greater personal economic prosperity and social status over time, even under slavery. Such features should not be read as indicative of an inherently more "benign" form of slavery. Rather, they reflect the ways in which enslaved people were used in Saint-Louis – for example, as part of the annual trading convoy upriver – and the strategies that slave owners used to ensure that their slaves would be less likely to abscond altogether. That is, the amelioration of slavery that we observe was driven by economic factors more than by moral ones. What follows are brief reviews of slavery in several other coastal urban contexts in West Africa. I include these summaries as part of an attempt to draw the increasingly specialised research of historians into conversation with one another, and to seek broader regional patterns of slavery as practised in coastal urban West Africa.

Gold Coast (Ghana)

The structure of slaving on West Africa's Gold Coast (and, as follows, on the Slave Coast) differed from Senegal in that trading posts operated under African states and the economic role of women was much less developed. On the Gold Coast (modern Ghana), slavery was very important in the communities that grew up around the castles built by European slave traders – important to both the traditional elites and those linked to the castles.[32] An interesting example of slave accumulation was the Afro-Dutch community of Elmina.[33] Elmina was a town of 15,000–20,000 people in the early nineteenth century, one of the largest on the African coast. The adjacent castle had been built in 1482 by the Portuguese to tap the gold trade. It was occupied by the Dutch in 1637. Towards the end of the seventeenth century, the town shifted its economic focus from gold to slave exports.

Like other Europeans, the Dutch formed relationships with local women. The result of these unions was the emergence of a series of Afro-Dutch families who played a major role in the slave trade as brokers. Though descendants of these first European–African unions generally married Africans, they clung to their Dutch names and Dutch legal identity, using their ambiguous position to accumulate wealth. While they were able to exploit the slave trade for their own economic benefit, these families did not control the means of coercion, which lay in the hands of the castle and the traditional state.

Much of these families' wealth was in the form of slaves. Indeed, some

Afro-Dutch families owned over 200 enslaved workers. In the larger holdings, enslaved men predominated by a 2:1 ratio, probably because many worked on farms outside Elmina. A majority of enslaved workers, however, were artisans or labourers. When Carel Ruhle, one of Elmina's largest slaveholders, died in 1818, he owned 205 slaves, who included 17 carpenters, 13 bricklayers, 4 smiths, 4 coopers, 4 stonebreakers, 4 shepherds, 3 cooks, 2 canoemen and 16 house servants.[34] The varied skill sets of Ruhle's workforce meant that he could move slaves from one task to another and, when their skills were not necessary to his own enterprises, he could hire them out. There were other African merchants in Elmina with similar slaveholdings, and those also included a high percentage of artisans who were hired out, as well as petty traders.[35] The specialised work skills observed in enslaved artisans at Elmina echo patterns we have previously observed at Saint-Louis, where these skills contributed to the relative autonomy of enslaved people. In Elmina, however, a degree of autonomy is observable even among labourers in agricultural settings. Though agricultural slaves were certainly worse off than enslaved artisans, they nonetheless had the right to take action against their owners. For example, they resisted regimentation and any effort to deprive them of their wives; most interestingly, when Ruhle died, they also resisted the division of his estate.[36]

In contrast to Saint-Louis and the Senegal coast, the Gold Coast had numerous company slaves – that is, workers owned by companies rather than individuals. About 300 company slaves resided at Elmina and another 300 were scattered across other Dutch forts and lodges on the Gold Coast. An 1808 list of Elmina castle slaves includes 421 persons. A majority were men, with 59 being disabled. The others included 30 house carpenters, 15 ship's carpenters, 22 bricklayers, 4 stonebreakers, 8 masons and 19 garden workers. Many of those not listed with a craft skill probably worked as guards, messengers, labourers, and servants.[37] They did a lot of heavy labour, loading and unloading ships, quarrying, rowing canoes, and farming experimental crops like indigo. They guarded the trade slaves – that is, captives bound for the transatlantic trade – who flowed through the castle or were kept there until a ship arrived. Like enslaved people owned by individual local families, company slaves maintained a diverse skill set. Strategically, these slaves were purchased from outside the region, mostly from the Slave Coast, so they would have no social ties with those captives whom they were expected to guard. While historical records provide limited insight into the relative autonomy of company slaves, there is evidence of some manumission. Also, like people enslaved by Afro-Dutch entrepreneurs, company slaves had a strong sense of collective interest and were willing to unite in order to protect it. For example, Dutch–American scholar Johannes Postma reports at least two occasions in the eighteenth century when the enslaved stopped work because they were dissatisfied with their food allowances.[38]

Slave Coast (Bight of Benin)

During the eighteenth century, Whydah (on the Slave Coast, in modern Benin) was the most important slave port in West Africa. It was a small city of between 6,000 and 8,000 people, though it grew to about 20,000 by the mid-nineteenth century. Whydah was the major port of trade for the kingdom of Dahomey. In general, its merchants did not go into the interior to acquire enslaved captives; rather, the slaves were brought to town from neighbouring Oyo or from the Dahomey interior for export. But some of them remained. "In Ouidah [Whydah]," British historian Robin Law tells us, "as throughout West Africa, the growth of internal slavery was closely linked to that of the export trade in slaves, the same mechanisms of slaving serving both markets."[39]

Whydah was largely a slave city, though there is disagreement about what percentage of its population consisted of enslaved individuals.[40] It was also a majority-female slave city. Slaves were protected by Dahomean law, which prohibited the export abroad of enslaved individuals who were born in Dahomey and provided recourse for those who were mistreated. There was a nucleus of slaves in and around Whydah's three European settlements – French, English, and Portuguese forts established to service the slave trade. These forts' personnel were largely African and enslaved. About 20 Englishmen resided in the English fort alongside 100 slaves, for example. The female slaves were largely house servants and market women. Many of the slaves worked on their own, paying their owners a monthly remittance from their wages.[41]

Further east again was Lagos, also an important centre of the slave trade, though only beginning in the late eighteenth century. The British established a consulate there in 1851 and occupied it in 1861. Although they intervened in order to end the slave trade, slavery remained important in Lagos well into the colonial period. Regardless of British law, the British in Lagos both acknowledged and tacitly accepted the practice of urban slavery. Indeed, even British citizens illegally owned and hired slaves.

There were a number of ways captives were acquired and enslaved. The Yoruba civil wars of the late eighteenth and nineteenth centuries in what is now south-west Nigeria, which fed the Lagos slave trade, also created a body of unattached men willing to align themselves with the more powerful households.[42]

Yoruba patriarchal households expanded their offspring through polygyny, as well as by adopting orphans. Slaves, however, were their most important source of labour. Moreover, slavery was a model for other forms of dependency, as American historian Kristin Mann explains:

> slaves had fewer competing allegiances and loyalties than most other kinds of non-kin who could be incorporated into households and retinues. Wives, wards, strangers, and clients remained members of their own lineages and, if born outside Lagos, also of their natal communities. Many of them felt obligations to their own kin groups and hometowns that could conflict with those of the head of the household under whose authority they lived. Slaves, on the other hand, had normally been torn from their families and hometowns and sold afar. Once they began to settle into their owners' households, they had fewer competing loyalties than other dependants, which opened the possibility of a closer and more complete identification with their owners' interests.[43]

Slave-ownership was widespread in Lagos. Some free families owned only one or two individuals, but more important and established households typically held numerous slaves.

Most Europeans believed that the majority of the population in Lagos was slaves. Enslaved labour was important in fishing, transport, crafts, and manufacturing. Canoes commanded and rowed by the enslaved brought goods to Lagos Island, where they could be used or trans-shipped. Some enslaved people lived in the master's compound or in a nearby free-standing house. However, many were allowed to work or trade on their own and to live independently. Moreover, many had supervisory or leadership roles within the household itself. Indeed, some enslaved people were able to accumulate enough wealth to buy slaves of their own.

To tamp down any threat of insurrection and to motivate their industriousness, slave owners provided slaves with considerable freedom in their movements and actions through the practice of hiring them out. Hired slaves typically received their wages directly and passed on a portion of this money to their owners as a remittance. One result of this policy was that both the British colonial regime and European missionaries were reluctant to attack slavery since they depended on hiring slaves themselves when they needed labour. While British colonialism may have tempered the practice of slavery in

135

Lagos, it did not abolish the institution. A court was set up to deal with master–slave disputes soon after British occupation in 1861 (see Cobley in this volume). In 1874, the government abolished slave dealing and emancipated "persons holden as slaves" in order to create the "illusion of legal abolition".[44] Yet, while some enslaved people certainly absconded from their captivity, there was also continuing importation of enslaved captives to meet the labour needs of what had become West Africa's most important port. As in other West African regions, slave owners at times struggled to keep control of their slaves and, to do so, they had in fact to loosen their control and allow enslaved people more autonomy and control over their labour and their lives.

Bight of Biafra

In the Bight of Biafra, slaves were only accumulated by men, not by women as in Senegal. Unlike in the regions discussed above, the slave trade here involved a very limited European presence. What is similar is the degree of autonomy that enslaved people achieved. Slaves were objects of economic activity, but they also played important roles in shaping that activity. Local people originally moved into the coastal mangrove swamps to obtain salt and fish, which were exchanged for yams and other food crops from the hinterland that the Niger Delta communities could not produce. When the slave trade developed, these trading networks were easily converted to serve that market, trading partners in the interior readily finding ways to deliver slaves – at first, alongside food and, later, in place of it.[45]

There were two problems. One was that the Niger Delta was poorly populated. To deal with the shortage of people and acquire enslaved workers capable of manning the well-armed canoes that visited interior markets, Delta communities turned to the same slave trade that provided captives for export. The second problem was that conflict between the dispersed ports was intense. Here, one does not find the development of work-for-hire practices for enslaved workers that existed in other slave ports. Instead there was a system that was trade-based – one that attempted rapidly to acculturate slaves and give them opportunities to excel. Enslaved workers not only paddled the canoes, but also commanded them, conducted trading expeditions, and (if successful) became heads of canoe houses themselves. Only the top offices in this social hierarchy were limited to the freeborn, and even that restriction was sometimes broken in the nineteenth century. A former slave named Jaja broke away and founded the city-state of Opobo in 1869 (see Igba in this volume).[46] Because of opportunities for social and economic advancement, the system won the loyalty of many slaves by making the ablest among them key players in its functioning.

The Biafran towns of Calabar and Douala lay east of the Delta and had access to agricultural land on which were settled enslaved agricultural workers. These settlements became particularly important after the rise of "legitimate commerce" – here, trading switched from enslaved people to palm oil in the first half of the nineteenth century. Both settlements had depended heavily on the slave trade and incorporated enslaved people into their urban structures. As the economies of these settlements developed from trading fish, to trading ivory, to trading captives and, then, to producing palm oil, enslaved people continued to make up a majority of the population. However, they were less likely than their counterparts in the Niger Delta (in modern Nigeria) to achieve the highest offices. Nevertheless, some pathways to social and economic advancement remained open. For example, enslaved workers made up the crews of profitable trading expeditions here. In addition, many of them were privileged household retainers who played major, often independent, roles in these expeditions.[47]

Concluding Reflections

When comparing Saint-Louis with other West African cities of the slave trade, we must account for a variety of factors. One was that Saint-Louis was not populated prior to the French settling there. The city was French and remained French except for several interludes of British occupation. In addition, Saint-Louis and the Niger Delta lacked nearby arable land, which meant that residents bought grain from farmers in the interior; the necessity of these transactions contributed to the overall complexity of their trading systems. In the other African cities of the slave trade we have reviewed, there was good cultivable and easily accessible land nearby, and a market for agricultural produce in the town and on the visiting ships. This difference meant that the transfer of enslaved workers between city and farm was not important in Saint-Louis, but it could be and often was significant elsewhere.

This observation links to a second factor we must analyse: the ways in which enslaved people were exploited. How enslaved people laboured was related to a town's economic hinterland, certainly. But it was also a function of the economic structure of the town itself – hence the significance of slave-trading cities. These cities developed structures to serve the needs of their ruling elites and of the Atlantic slave trade more broadly. Slavery was not simply an abstract legal category. Rather, it was a practice and an institution that evolved in different ways in response to the economic needs of specific communities.

And, finally, a third issue to consider is the extent to which the nature of the Atlantic trade drew Europeans into the urban environment and encouraged commercial, political, and marital links with African partners. With the exception of the Biafran ports, the European presence was integral to how slave-trading cities in West Africa evolved over time. Clearly, European domestic and business needs were distinctive, as exemplified by the "castle settlements" of the Gold Coast and the Lagos merchant community. But, as the Saint-Louis and Ghanaian case studies here highlight, the longer-term social impact of early European–African sexual and marital relations was the creation of and subsequent reliance on intermediary groups, led at first by the *signares* and *donas*. These relationships produced groups, like Luso-Africans, who facilitated European activities, who were Atlantic in orientation, and who often identified themselves as European. Their greater resistance to tropical maladies as compared with newly arrived Europeans made them particularly indispensable to slave traders and colonisers.

Significant differences existed between the cities of the slave trade in terms of their size and their occupational, racial, and ethnic composition, but urban slave systems had some elements in common. The first is that they involved fairly small groups of enslaved people. Urban populations generally ranged from about 4,000 to 20,000 people, but many settlements along the Gold and Slave Coasts were much smaller than that. Slave owners managing enslaved populations in the hundreds or even thousands were more likely to be found in rural areas deeper in the interior. Many of these more massive slaveholdings emerged in West Africa when the export of enslaved captives across the Atlantic declined and then ended.

The second shared characteristic of the urban case studies I have highlighted is the importance placed on the development of specialised skills among enslaved workers in a variety of fields. They included masons, carpenters, bricklayers, smiths, and seamstresses. Whereas there was some demand for such skills in rural areas, most plantation labour was routine and sometimes collective. In contrast, in the cities, a skilled enslaved man or woman could generally earn significantly more money for a slave owner and him- or herself by being hired out. Thus, there was an incentive for slave owners to apprentice younger captives or slaves born in their households. Slave owners could profit from the development of those skills directly within the household, they could rent the slave out, or they could permit him or her to look for work independently – but still expect in return a percentage of his or her wages as a remittance. In any case, many people enslaved in urban areas kept part of their income and, in some cases, lived independently of their owners.

A third congruence we should note in the urban case studies reviewed is enslaved people's relatively greater freedom of movement. Urban slaves often moved freely as agents of their masters and had greater autonomy as compared with their counterparts in the countryside. This greater autonomy and freedom of movement also provided more opportunities for escape. Certainly, the opportunity to escape was present for enslaved people who left the city in the course of their labour, like the *laptots* of the Senegal River, the canoemen of the Niger Delta, or the slave sailors of the South Atlantic. Such slaves were often away from home for long periods of time, sometimes trading for their masters, at other times carrying messages or commanding boats. However, a greater opportunity to abscond was also true on a local level for those who worked as street vendors or who hired out their own labour.

The primary strategy of slave owners to limit escape attempts was amelioration. The labour system in West African urban contexts was set up to allow the potential accumulation of some degree of wealth and status even within slavery. Through the practice of hiring out, relationships between enslaved people and their enslavers were highly monetised. The ability to earn money led to the manumission of some enslaved artisans, but also made it possible for them to improve their status both by seeking education and by accumulating wealth while still enslaved. Thus, enslaved people in urban West Africa had differential access to more privileged positions within slavery. Because of the potential for economic and social advancement within slavery, these "urban options" often trumped the benefits of "breaking free" for enslaved people. That is, even with greater opportunity to escape, most enslaved people did not attempt to do so. This was not because this version of slavery was somehow more benign. Rather, it was because both slave owners and slaves had a vested interest in each other. An enslaved person's decision to remain either "in" slavery or closely associated with it by staying in or near their owner's household as a freed slave or client was influenced by the types of "advancements" open to them. These included the accumulation of wealth, a rising social position, and sometimes even the achievement of political power, as in the Biafran towns.

Still, in such circumstances, master–slave disagreements did exist. Enslaved people pushed the boundaries of the system to achieve some degree of personal autonomy, as the Saint-Louis case study and the history of the former slave Jaja in the Niger Delta most dramatically illustrate. Within urban slave systems, there was a lot of room to push these boundaries. This resistance and negotiation on the part of enslaved people should influence our understanding of slavery overall. The experience of enslavement and of the slave trade was always brutal and dehumanising. It always originated in an act of violence and inevitably began with an effort to reduce a person to an object. However, enslaved people also inevitably sought to push the boundaries of their enslavement. Thus, slave owners found themselves pressured to recognise the humanity of enslaved people and to afford them some degree of both dignity and autonomy – extending in some circumstances as far as manumission. This was especially true where the slave was part of the household. This was true even in the age of the Atlantic trade and even in the very port towns through which African captives moved en route to a more brutal servitude in the Americas.

7

Slavery in Southern Africa

Butholezwe Mtombeni

RICH ACADEMIC SCHOLARSHIP has been produced on the history of slavery at the Cape of Good Hope in South Africa. Despite this diverse literature, which stresses the origins and social aspects of slaves, not much has been published on the economic benefits of slavery and the enslaved to European imperialists as well as the issue of religion before emancipation at the Cape. Slavery is the most brutal system of labour coercion or labour extraction.[1] Slaves were not allowed to share in the fruits of their own labour and were treated as human property. The slave trade, though an inhumane practice, was a lucrative business for the Dutch East India Company from the seventeenth century until it went bankrupt in 1795 (see Nimako and Allen in this volume).

According to the American scholar Markus Vink, the Dutch Indian Ocean slave trade included the movement of people, cultural diffusion, and economic exchange.[2] Vink further noted that the Dutch enslaved people from fragmented micro-states and stateless societies in Southeast Asia outside the "House of Islam" – those lands in which a Muslim government rules and the holy law of Islam prevails – for its plantations and agricultural estates. Company slaves were imported to the Cape in the seventeenth and eighteenth centuries from Madagascar, Indonesia, and India, as well as from southern, West, and Central Africa. They were used in a wide variety of occupations at the Cape, on farms and as semi-skilled artisans. The indigenous communities in South Africa were not enslaved. However, in the eighteenth century, the Khoisan people were dispossessed and employed by the Dutch as indentured labourers.[3]

This chapter deals with slavery in southern Africa, with a particular focus on slavery at the Cape. It investigates the introduction of slavery at the Cape, the economic benefits of slavery, slave religion, and the abolition of slavery in 1834. I argue that while slavery robbed the enslaved of their humanity, religion often provided them with purpose and community. The chapter concludes by noting that the intertwined Cape and Dutch economies were built on and nourished by slave labour. This history legitimises the calls for the compensation and monumentalisation of slaves and their history.

Introducing Slavery into the Cape

Dutch scholar Herman Nieboer and Russian-American scholar Evsey Domar's hypothesis has become a vital tool for identifying and explaining the economic conditions that were used to justify slave labour.[4] According to this argument, the use of slavery became an alternative to increased production where there was an abundance of land and shortage of labour.[5] Such conditions characterised the Cape in the eighteenth and nineteenth centuries.[6] Given the lack of alternative sources of labour, settler farmers at the Cape resorted to slavery and other forms of coercion to ensure a constant supply of labour. In contrast, others have argued that slavery at the Cape did not emerge from the labour demands of settler farmers but was already an established practice of the Dutch East India Company.[7] According to this view, it was the Company's monopolistic nature, coupled with its insatiable demand for high profit margins with minimum expenditure, that better explains the rise of slavery at the Cape. The fact that only the Company and wealthy landowners could afford slaves refutes the Nieboer–Domar hypothesis.[8]

In 1652, the Dutch East India Company decided to establish a refreshment station at the Cape for its passing ships. The Cape was a strategic location because it was halfway between the Netherlands and Dutch territories and trading posts in the East Indies. But already in 1657 the station began to expand when freehold farms were granted to so-called free burghers, often former employees of the Company, in an attempt to stimulate agricultural production and meet the growing demand for fresh meat and vegetables. However, a chronic shortage of labour handicapped the new farmers. From as early as the 1650s, slaves were imported to the Cape to meet the acute shortage of labour, thus laying the foundations of a slave society at the Cape.

The British South African historian Nigel Worden provides an extensive analysis of the origins of the Cape slave population.[9] Table 7.1 shows the number and proportion of slaves in Cape Town according to region of origin between 1695 and 1807.

Table 7.1

Place of Origin	Number	Percentage
South Asia	498	40.6
Southeast Asia	501	40.8
Madagascar and Mascarenes	87	7.1
Southern, West, and East Africa	139	11.3
Total	1,225	100

Source: Worden, "Indian Ocean Slaves in Cape Town, 1695–1807", p. 395.

South Asia and Southeast Asia accounted for the greatest number of Cape Town slaves (81.4 per cent) while Madagascar and the Mascarenes contributed 7.1 per cent of the total. This confirms the Cape's deep involvement in the Indian Ocean world and its commerce. The links between the Cape and Indian Ocean can also be found "in the memory of slave descendants and in wider popular awareness through the identification of Cape Islam and 'Cape Malays' with a heritage from Southeast Asia".[10]

Table 7.2 shows the number of Dutch East India Company slaves at the Cape at intervals between 1693 and 1826. The number of those enslaved declined sharply towards the end of the eighteenth century, and especially at the beginning of the nineteenth century, when the British Parliament passed the Abolition of the Slave Trade Act in 1807.[11]

Table 7.2

Year	Number
1693	337
1731	566
1752	506
1784	625
1807	283
1826	171

Source: Armstrong and Worden, "The Slaves, 1652–1834", p. 124; Worden, "Indian Ocean Slaves in Cape Town, 1695–1807", p. 392.

Table 7.3 shows the total number of privately owned slaves at the Cape from 1727 to 1827. Privately owned slaves increased steadily during Dutch East India Company rule.[12]

Table 7.3

Year	Number
1727	742
1731	767
1749	1,038
1774	2,373
1806	9,367
1822	7,160
1827	6,222

Source: Worden et al., *Cape Town: The Making of a City*, p. 50; Worden, "Indian Ocean Slaves in Cape Town, 1695–1807", p. 392.

Economic Benefits of Slaves

Once we consider slaves as both suppliers of labour and capital to the production process, how does our understanding of agricultural output at the Cape change?[13] It is difficult to understand and quantify the economic benefits of slavery at the Cape. Some economic historians have questioned the profitability of slave labour and argued that slavery, in fact, stalled economic development. According to this view, the Dutch settlers did not attempt to implement efficient labour-saving methods of production because they were overly dependent on slave labour. Moreover, more capital was invested in purchasing slaves than in developing farming techniques, infrastructure, and/or roads.

However, all this does not mean that slave labour at the Cape was not profitable. There is evidence to suggest that slave labour increased the productivity and profitability of the Cape for the Dutch. The expansion of farming in the south-western Cape region depended on a steady supply of slaves, though this was sometimes erratic. Wealthy Dutch settlers with large farms who could afford to buy slaves lived a life of leisure and comfort. It is on this basis that scholars have argued that personal wealth, land size, and slave numbers were closely linked.[14]

Slaves boosted agricultural and industrial production at the Cape, thereby nourishing the Cape economy, which was ailing before the introduction of slave labour. Both the Cape urban and rural agricultural sectors depended heavily on slave labour. According to South African scholar Johan Fourie, and Swedish scholars Ellen Hillbom and Patrick Svensson, while slave labour led to high inequality, slavery transformed the Cape Colony into one of the most successful regions in the world.[15] Slaves became the backbone of the Cape economy.[16] That slave owners were opposed to amelioration and manumission was clear proof that slavery was a profitable business. Slave owners were not willing to part with their profitable human property. Slaves were valuable commodities. Since there were no banks in the early Cape, slaves became a means of accumulating capital. Slaves were treated as valuable capital goods and used as collateral for loans. By 1834, slave mortgages were valued at £400,000.[17] In short, slave labour was profitable, transforming the economic face of the Cape and expanding agriculture into the interior.

Slaves and Religion at the Cape before Emancipation, 1652–1820

Christianity and Islam at the Cape are as old as the establishment of the settlement itself.[18] European settlers brought their Christian heritage with them. The Cape also served as a penal settlement or place of banishment for political leaders from Southeast Asia whom the Dutch had caught and sentenced. Most of them subscribed to the Muslim faith. Furthermore, most of the slaves imported to the Cape during the Dutch period originated from South Asia and Southeast Asia, where Islam was predominant.[19] Later, other slaves came from Angola, Mozambique, Guinea, Dahomey (modern Benin), and the East African coast, where Islam had a strong presence. Most slave men thus remained faithful to the Prophet. According to the American scholar John Edwin Mason: "Islam accompanied their [the Dutch] prisoners, servants, and slaves."[20] However, it is important to note that the two faiths came to the Cape in the same ships: Dutch East India Company vessels.[21]

Before 1795, the Dutch Reformed Church monopolised the spread of the word of God at the Cape. In places where congregations of the church already existed, ministers baptised converts, including some enslaved, but were often reluctant to make converted slaves full members of the church. Slave owners were also opposed to allowing evangelisation among slaves because they believed they might have to free any converted slaves and thus lose their labour. Converted slaves were clearly not treated as equals of their masters, nor did

Christianity provide much improvement to their lives.

The Dutch East India Company operated schools for its own slaves until 1795. Slaves were taught the basics of the Dutch language and the rudiments of Reformed Christianity.[22] This had less to do with religious enthusiasm, and was born more out of a desire to maintain Dutch cultural and political hegemony. Company schools led to the baptism of slaves.[23] Between 1665 and 1795, the Dutch Reformed Church baptised more than 2,000 slaves: an average of more than 15 slaves a year. Most of these slaves were children and were the "property" of the Company itself. Moreover, the Company granted no civic rights to its baptised slaves during the period of its rule.

At the end of the eighteenth century, Protestant missionaries from Europe began evangelising work among the slaves at the Cape, spreading the gospel of salvation. This movement was heralded by the arrival at the Cape in 1799 of the Dutch medical doctor and missionary, Johannes Theodorus van der Kemp, of the London Missionary Society. His arrival marked the beginning of a new era in the history of Christianity at the Cape. However, slave men who converted to Christianity were not granted civic rights nor treated as social equals. Maart from Mozambique, a slave convert "owned" by the London Missionary Society in the early nineteenth century, was neither freed nor treated as an equal.[24]

It is worth noting that a number of slave women were converted to Christianity during the period of Company rule.[25] These women were attracted by the civic promises of Christianity, which were closely linked to status and freedom. Thus, between 1652 and 1795, some privately owned slave women were baptised because male settlers wanted to marry them. A European male settler wishing to marry an enslaved woman had to instruct her in the Dutch language and then have her baptised. Thereafter, he had to pay a manumission bond to the deaconry.[26] The missionary Johannes Theodorus van der Kemp is a good example of someone who bought the freedom of a slave woman – Sara Janse – whom he made his wife. This made him unpopular with the Cape settlers. In February 1814, George Thom, a Scottish missionary, described Van der Kemp's marriage as "disgraceful".[27]

Enslaved women discovered in Christianity other opportunities that could break their chains of bondage. Christian marriages were often a path to freedom for slave women and their children. This path was only open to women. An ex-slave woman in a Christian marriage was accepted by the white community, and her children were brought up as freed slaves. Enslaved women in Christian marriages could not be separated from their children, and their children could not be sold into slavery.

The beginning of Islam at the Cape was marked by the arrival in 1667 of three exiled Sufi sheikhs from present-day Indonesia. In the course of the seventeenth and eighteenth centuries, Muslim communities coalesced around religious leaders such as these.[28] They attracted followers from among slaves and free blacks, initiating them into the Islam faith. They thus laid the foundation of the Islamic faith in the Cape. Islam was largely concentrated in Cape Town, and spread by word of mouth. It was practised secretly because the Company punished those who embraced it. Thus, Islam started as an underground faith that was detested by the colonial authorities. According to a 1712–1713 court case, Santrij, a Muslim "priest", was sentenced to having his tongue cut from his mouth and burnt alive for preaching to a group of convicts and slaves at the Cape. Islam had powerful appeal to slaves, particularly slave men. According to South African academic Robert Shell, "Muslim universalism was extended into the domestic sphere; some Muslim slaves ate at the same table with their Muslim masters."[29] The local imam Taun Guru, himself a slave owner, offered slaves the possibility of upward social mobility within the Muslim community and protection from harsh treatment by Muslim masters.[30]

By the 1790s, Islam had grown into a widespread faith with a great following in the Cape. The first Islamic school was opened in Cape Town in 1793, and the first mosque between 1795 and 1804.[31] Three decades later, the Cape became home to several Islamic schools. The schools and mosques provided energetic sheikhs and imams with the institutional infrastructure needed to attract more converts from the slave population in and around Cape Town. While most slave men preferred the Muslim faith, it did not afford them civic rights. It is for this reason that slave masters ended up warming to the idea of their slaves converting to the Muslim faith. The conversion of slaves to Islam faith did not threaten the labour pool of the slave owners.

Visiting Europeans were often surprised by the strength and inclusivity of Islam at the Cape, and were impressed by the reverence Muslim converts felt for their mosques and kramats (shrines of holy men).[32] Islam gave slave men a sense of belonging and revived their spirituality. Mosques were physical spaces within which faithful slaves became full members of the Islamic community. Thus, Muslim converts experienced belonging instead of alienation, respect instead of degradation, and love instead of domination.[33] Conversion to Islam therefore represented an attempt by the enslaved to find meaning and value in their lives, despite their suffering as slaves.

Slave women had another avenue for escaping slavery: getting married to Muslim men, even though Muslim marriages were not viewed officially as legal. Muslim men practised abstinence from alcohol, as required by Islam, and as a result, many became themselves overseers of slaves. Alcoholism in the slavery era was considered an evil practice that affected mostly European men. This was why Muslim men were often attractive to European immigrant women at the Cape. According to Robert Shell, "the marital conversion of slaves changed twice, benefiting Christianity and Islam at different times".[34] At first, slave women converted to Christianity before entering marriage with European settlers. In the nineteenth century, slave women embraced Islam because their Muslim husbands had bought their freedom.

While slavery dislodged people from their homeland and further stripped them of their rights and humanity, leading to their social death, Cape slaves defied the odds, using religion as a source of survival and a means of creating a sense of community and belonging.

Slave Resistance and Revolts

The ill-treatment of slaves and their desire for freedom sparked sporadic, small-scale slave revolts at the Cape in the nineteenth century. They were often motivated by the frustration of slaves at the slow pace of amelioration and emancipation.[35] Slave resistance was, however, localised and poorly coordinated. Cultural diversity, coupled with the distances between farms, often undermined the solidarity and organisational capacity of the enslaved. However, the absence of large-scale slave revolts does not mean that there were not everyday forms of resistance.

Such resistance was widespread and frequently took several forms including breaking farm equipment, stealing, go-slows, arson, poisoning of masters, suicide, assault, and disobeying orders[36] (see Brereton in this volume). On rare occasions, slaves resisted oppression by taking their masters to court. Available court records reveal that urban slaves rarely poisoned or murdered their masters, while the rural enslaved in the agricultural districts sometimes resorted to these forms of resistance because of the brutality of their masters. The presence of the British army garrison at the Cape in the early nineteenth century reduced the likelihood of urban slave revolts. Non-violent forms of resistance increased during this period, as slaves became more aware of the possibility of their own emancipation.

The most common form of resistance was marooning or desertion. Company records are littered with complaints of slaves who either temporarily or permanently disappeared. Desertion was the main problem for the Dutch East India Company. Anthony from Madagascar was the first runaway slave;

he escaped in 1655 and was never found. Most desertions were unplanned but were more an immediate response to a crisis such as punishment or fear of punishment.[37] Runaway slave communities grew up in the Cape, and survived on the mountains at the margins of nearby settlements or farms by means of poaching, stealing, raiding, and trading for food, clothing, and weapons.[38] The largest maroon community was a group of 50 runaway slaves near Cape Hangklip, led by a slave from Indonesia. The maroons were unable to exploit their environment efficiently and optimally. Wisdom born of experience and deep knowledge of their environs nevertheless ensured their survival. The Hangklip maroon community was established around the 1720s and existed until the emancipation of the enslaved in 1834.

In October 1808, 300 slaves and servants staged a revolt in the Swartland district that took European farmers by surprise. Louis, a slave tailor from Mauritius, organised local slaves and attacked more than 30 grain farms in the Koeberg and Swartland areas. He took farmers prisoner, and persuaded their labourers to join the revolt. However, in less than 48 hours, the rebellion was crushed by government troops. The 300 slaves and their leaders were arrested, and 47 were put on trial, including Louis. A total of 250 slaves were pardoned and returned to their owners.[39] The rebels were influenced by the revolutionary ideas then sweeping the Atlantic world. Thus, the American (1776), French (1789), and Haitian (1791–1804) revolutions played a pivotal role in shaping the ideas of slaves at the Cape. The enslaved were not separated by difference but were tied to an underclass network that connected them to other slaves and servants. These connections cut across ethnic divides.[40] The participation of Khoikhoi in the rebellion confirmed that class solidarity had replaced earlier conflicts between runaway slaves and Khoikhoi herders. The revolt was not an isolated event: it took place at a time when the British Empire was seeking to reform the system of slavery.[41]

In 1825, in response to maltreatment by his master, the slave Galant organised a revolt which included 12 slaves and Khoisan servants from the Koue Bokkeveld area. They killed Galant's master and two other white people, before escaping to the nearby mountains. However, they were captured and prosecuted. Although in most cases, the slave revolts were ruthlessly crushed, their attempt to challenge their masters and free themselves from slavery proves that the slaves were politically conscious. They laid the foundation for future resistance to colonial rule. While the bodies of the enslaved were in chains of bondage, their consciousness was free: they developed a consciousness of freedom.

The End of Slavery at the Cape

Most historians have long agreed that emancipation at the Cape was not a specific moment but a process.[42] In 1807, the international slave trade formally ended when the British government made the trans-shipment of slaves illegal. The Emancipation Act of 1833 heralded the end of slavery. However, the enslaved continued working for their masters for no pay as apprentices. Apprenticeship contracts could be bought and sold in the same manner that slaves had been bought and sold.[43] The second and final phase of emancipation came in December 1838 when the apprentice system was abolished. Slaveholders tried in vain to launch a counter-discourse.[44] The freed slaves were not given land on which to settle and thus remained unwillingly in the employ of their former masters (see Cobley in this volume).

With the emancipation of slaves, former slaveholders were compensated through the Office of the Slave Compensation Commission. The Cape Colony was apportioned about £1.2 million of the £20 million fund that had been set aside for the compensation of former slave owners.[45] Money from successful claims could be collected from the National Debt Office in London. This was an inconvenience to the Cape slave owners, who had to travel long distances to obtain their compensation.[46] Former slaveholders criticised the emancipation of slaves as unjust, and argued that it was likely to create unprecedented economic and social crises. More than four-fifths of the value of Cape slave property was eroded in the process of emancipation and compensation.[47] The Dutch-speaking farmers' dissatisfaction with emancipation was one of the major causes of the Great Trek in the 1830s (see Cobley in this volume).[48] This shows how important the institution of slavery was to Cape farmers.

Concluding Reflections

If the slave masters were compensated soon after the emancipation of their slaves, the slaves themselves also deserved to be compensated for their long and unpaid labour. The Dutch and the British governments thus owe the descendants of former slaves at the Cape compensation for their labour. To address this historical injustice, the South African government's land redistribution programme must prioritise the descendants of former slaves. Land is a vital resource of human development which can be used economically to empower people. Failure to agree on reparations would be a dereliction of duty to humankind.

Part Three

—

Slavery in the Caribbean

8

Slavery in the British Caribbean

Bridget Brereton

THE GREAT GUYANESE historian Elsa V. Goveia wrote in 1970: "The slave society is one of the most fundamental experiences shared by the West Indies, and its understanding must be of significance for our future as well as for our past."[1] Goveia was the first historian to use the concept of "slave society" in relation to the Caribbean, and she noted that it "refers to the whole community based on slavery, including masters and freedmen as well as slaves", a society dependent on enslaved labourers as opposed to a "society with slaves", such as Canada before 1834.[2] Undoubtedly, Goveia's concept of a slave society applies to most of the British Caribbean in the period between the 1620s – when the English first colonised some islands in the region – and the 1830s – when Britain abolished slavery in its own colonies.[3]

There have been many definitions of the Caribbean by scholars and others over time, but this chapter will accept the one most commonly used by modern historians: all the islands in the Caribbean Sea (and the Bahamas), along with a few territories on the mainland of South and Central America whose history has more in common with that of the islands than with the surrounding lands.[4] In the case of the British Caribbean, the colonies that became modern Guyana and Belize fall into this last category.

The Map of Slavery in the English Caribbean

English colonisation in the region began in the 1620s in the small islands known as the Leewards, which had been ignored by Spain: St Kitts (1624),

Barbados (1627), Nevis (1628), Montserrat (1632), and Antigua (1632). There was resistance in some islands, notably St Kitts, from the indigenous Kalinago people. Barbados, which soon became the most important English colony, was uninhabited in 1627 because its native population had been killed or removed by Spanish slave traders. In 1655, the larger island of Jamaica, in the Greater Antilles, was seized from Spain by an English expeditionary force and ceded by treaty in 1670.[5] In that year, a rather tenuous English occupation of Honduras (Belize) also began.

The settlers in the Leewards initially developed small tobacco farms with indentured English, Scottish, and Irish labourers. Tobacco was, however, soon overtaken by sugar, which involved larger concentrations of land and considerable capital outlay. Barbados took the lead in what historians have called the Sugar Revolution in the second half of the 1600s. The other Leeward islands followed, while Jamaica developed large sugar plantations from the 1680s onwards. It was the emergence of big sugar plantations and the related decline in the traffic in indentured Britons that led directly to the enslavement of captured Africans as the main form of labour on the island. This followed the precedents already set by the Spanish and Portuguese in the Caribbean and Central and South America (see Nerín and Tofiño, Silva Jr, and Sousa in this volume). As early as 1655, Barbados already had about 20,000 enslaved workers, rising to 46,500 by 1684. About 15,000 enslaved inhabited the Leewards by 1690. Jamaica developed as a plantation economy more slowly, but by 1696 it had about 30,000 enslaved Africans. As early as 1660, the Barbadian scholar Hilary Beckles writes, "the African slave trade was the 'lifeline' of the Caribbean economy".[6]

Barbados pioneered the Sugar Revolution from the 1640s. It also became the "model colony" for the rest of the English Caribbean (and indeed for North American colonies such as the Carolinas) with respect to legislation governing the status and treatment of enslaved Africans: lifelong, hereditary (through the mother), and chattel slavery. Widely copied slave codes were enacted by the island's planter-dominated elected assembly from 1660 onwards (see Cobley in this volume). In addition to formal legislation, Beckles writes, "English planters quickly became experienced in slave organisation, and their management policies were brutal."[7] Both formal codes and informal modes of "managing" enslaved Africans spread from Barbados to the Leeward Islands and Jamaica.

In the eighteenth century, as Jamaica consolidated its plantation economy and slave society to become Britain's most important Caribbean possession,

London acquired more colonies in the region. The many scattered islands of the Bahamas (strictly speaking, beyond the Caribbean Sea) became a formal colony, though they never developed a viable plantation sector. Four of the Windward Islands – previously sparsely settled by the French or left to the indigenous Kalinago – were ceded to Britain at the end of the Seven Years War in 1763: Grenada, Dominica, St Vincent, and Tobago. These islands were rapidly developed by London as sugar plantation economies dependent on enslaved labour in the last decades of the eighteenth century. Finally, during the Revolutionary and Napoleonic Wars between 1793 and 1815, Britain acquired important colonies in the southern Caribbean: Trinidad, seized from Spain in 1797 and ceded by treaty in 1802; St Lucia, ceded by France in 1814; and the mainland territories of Demerara–Essequibo and Berbice, seized from the Dutch in 1796 but not formally ceded until 1814. These late entries into the British Empire made possible an equally late Sugar Revolution based on enslaved labour well into the 1820s. This took place, above all, in the mainland colonies, which were united as British Guiana in 1831.[8]

In the British Caribbean, the majority of enslaved Africans and their locally born descendants laboured on sugar plantations, and their lives were shaped by the brutal work regimes of that crop. But we should note that many had different experiences. Some small and marginal colonies – for example, the Bahamas, the Turks and Caicos, the Cayman Islands, British Honduras, and others – never developed sugar plantations. Enslaved people instead worked on cotton and cocoa estates, grew food crops, and harvested timber. Even in a big sugar producer like Jamaica, many of the enslaved worked on coffee estates, or on "pens" raising livestock and provisions as well as other food crops. Some were "jobbing slaves", hired out to planters and others who needed to supplement their own labour force. And everywhere across the British Caribbean, the enslaved worked in towns in a wide variety of urban occupations.[9]

Numbers and Demographic Structures

British slavers shipped around 3.3 million captured Africans – most of them between 1713 and 1807 – when Britain was a leading slave-trading nation over the four centuries of the transatlantic trade, second only to Portugal (see Silva Jr in this volume). Not all the enslaved ended up in British colonies, however, as some Caribbean colonies had a thriving re-export trade, notably Jamaica and Barbados. Jamaica received more captured Africans than any other British Caribbean colony, at over one million, with Barbados next with around

500,000. Tiny Antigua and the even smaller St Kitts received about 138,000 and 134,000 respectively. Trinidad and Tobago hosted around 44,000 enslaved directly from Africa. Many of Trinidad's initial enslaved population came from nearby French and British islands. The British Guianese colonies took some 73,000 enslaved in the last years of the legal British slave trade.[10]

It is unnecessary in this chapter to dwell on the horrors of the Middle Passage as it is dealt with elsewhere in this book (see Introduction in this volume). Most crossings to the Caribbean took around two months on average. Mortality rates on the ships averaged 12–13 per cent as a result of diseases, violent resistance, and at times deliberate murder, as in the infamous British-owned *Zong* massacre in November–December 1781. Uniquely, in pre-twentieth-century migrations, probably a quarter of all those on slave ships were children torn from their homes and kinships. In the sober words of the Canadian historian David Eltis: "the human misery generated by the forced movement of millions of people in slave ships cannot have been matched by any other human activity ... [It was] likely the most costly in human life of all long-distance global migrations."[11]

Britain made participation in the African slave trade illegal for its subjects in 1807 – but abolished slavery across its empire a generation later, between 1834 and 1838. We know much more about the enslaved people of the British Caribbean in the years between 1807 and 1834 than in the longer earlier period, because detailed British records have survived in archives in London and have been fruitfully studied by several historians, notably the Australian scholar Barry W. Higman. The enslaved populations of these colonies grew steadily during the eighteenth century, fuelled by imports rather than by natural increase, with particularly large arrivals from Africa in the 1790s and continuing right up to 1807. In that year, Higman estimates the total slave population of the British Caribbean to have been about 775,000: around 25 per cent of all enslaved people in the Americas, and about 66 per cent of those in the Caribbean. By 1834, when Britain formally ended slavery in its colonies, the total population had decreased to about 665,000: a significant decline at a time when other New World slave populations, such as Cuba's, were increasing (see Ramirez in this volume). This population now accounted for only about half of all enslaved people in the Caribbean. Clearly, this sharp decline, following the end of imports from Africa, was due to an excess of deaths over births across British colonies.

It is well known that Caribbean planters had a preference for male Africans for field labour. This was demonstrated in the higher prices paid for young adult men. As long as most of the enslaved were survivors of the Middle Passage, the relevant colony's demographic structure showed a male majority. But as the Creole (locally born) populations grew, gender ratios gradually evened out. The decline in the proportion of African-born people was the most obvious result of the abolition of the slave trade, but this varied considerably from colony to colony, depending on when each territory had begun to develop a plantation economy. In Barbados, the earliest to do so, only about 7 per cent of the enslaved were African-born in 1817; in Jamaica the figure was about 35 per cent; in late-developing Trinidad and British Guiana, it was over 50 per cent. But nearly everywhere across the British Caribbean, the early 1800s saw a shift to Creole majorities and an even gender ratio. By 1817, the overall ratio was 101 men to 100 women, regardless of variations between colonies.

As British colonies in the Caribbean shifted to Creole majorities, the proportion of mixed-race enslaved people also increased. Legal status stemmed from the mother, and so the many children generated from sexual unions between white men and enslaved women were born into slavery. Some wealthier whites freed their mixed-race children and sometimes their mothers too, but the great majority could not or would not. One estimate puts the mixed-race enslaved in Jamaica at about 10 per cent of the entire enslaved population in 1832.

The slave populations of the British Caribbean declined significantly (though with variations) between the end of the slave trade in 1807 and the end of slavery in 1834. This was due to high mortality rates, especially for infants and children, and low fertility: a striking contrast with the demographic performance of enslaved people in North America in the same period (see Kerr-Ritchie and Broyld in this volume). It was, above all, in the colonies dominated by plantation sugar production that the decline occurred most precipitously. The brutal work regime and living conditions on the sugar estates almost guaranteed this outcome. In the smallest islands such as Anguilla or the Grenadines, and marginal colonies like British Honduras and the Bahamas – where sugar never developed significantly – natural increase emerged fairly early. Urban occupations and non-plantation agriculture also favoured natural increase when compared with the economies based on sugar. But since the majority of the enslaved in the British Caribbean endured the harsh conditions of life and labour on the sugar plantations, the overall population decline after the abolition of the African slave trade in 1807 was inevitable. Efforts by the more far-sighted sugar planters after 1807 to provide greater care for pregnant and nursing mothers, and to offer incentives for live births and infant survival, generally failed. Only the withdrawal of women of reproductive age from the field gangs could have helped to increase fertility and live births, something the planters never even contemplated.[12]

The Dreary Lives of the Enslaved

Most enslaved people in the British Caribbean were labourers on medium-sized and large sugar plantations. By the 1790s, women often outnumbered men in the main field gangs. In Antigua, for example, as early as 1751, on one large plantation, there were 42 "able" field men and 59 women, while in Jamaica, by the 1790s, women made up the majority of field labourers on the sugar estates. The daily life of most of the enslaved – male and female, African-born and Creole – was consumed in the harsh work regime of regimented gangs pushed by "drivers" – "elite" slave men – and "overseers" freely using the whip. Men and women aged between 18 and 40 made up the "first gang", doing the back-breaking tasks of "holing" (preparing the soil for new plants), planting, manuring, weeding, cane-cutting, loading the cut canes, and carting them to the mills. During the crop or harvest season, lasting several months, it was common for these enslaved to work six 12-hour days and three nights in the mill each week. Managers had no qualms about giving women these physically demanding jobs, even pregnant and nursing mothers. At least with respect to field labour, one can say that Caribbean slavery was "gender blind". As sugar consolidated its grip across most of the British colonies, the enslaved, and especially adult women, were increasingly occupied in harsh gang labour under the whip.

If the managers were gender-neutral when it came to the field, this was not the case when the skilled jobs were allocated. A sugar plantation was like a factory in the field, which called for diverse skills in the mill (boilermen, mechanics) and elsewhere: coopers, carpenters, smiths, carters, wheelwrights, men who cared for livestock, watchmen, boatmen, coachmen, and fishermen. Nearly all these jobs – which enjoyed some prestige, a little more freedom of movement, and some opportunities for earning cash – went to men. Males also occupied nearly all the supervisory positions open to the enslaved. Only two jobs – the "housekeeper" in the manager's or owner's house, and the "doctress" in charge of the so-called plantation hospital – were usually held by women. Except for the housekeeper, nearly all the "elite" or "confidential" slaves on the plantation were men.

On most plantations, around 10–15 per cent of the enslaved were domestics, employed in and around the Great House. Most were women, and typically they were Creole and often mixed-race. While the domestics escaped gang labour in the field, most of them worked hard as washerwomen, cleaners, water carriers, and kitchen drudges. A few, such as the housekeeper, the head cook (often a man), and the nannies, had an easier life. At best, domestics were generally better fed, clothed, and housed than field workers. At worst, they endured cruel treatment, sexual abuse, and constant surveillance by the white family, as well as less personal autonomy than the field slaves. Exceptionally, some light-skinned Creole domestics lived lives of relative privilege. On Newton plantation in Barbados in the early 1800s, a family of such women did little besides some sewing. One of them, Polly Williams, was described to her absentee owner in Britain: "Since her birth she has never as much as turned over one straw for you, she is as white as either of us and in fact I could not find an occupation for her."[13] But this was very far from the reality for the vast majority of enslaved domestics.

An important aspect of the lives of enslaved plantation workers in the British Caribbean was the informal domestic economy which emerged by the early 1700s, known to historians as the "provision grounds complex". Nearly everywhere, though more so in some colonies than others, the enslaved were allowed to cultivate food crops on plots of land, both small kitchen gardens around their huts and larger areas situated away from the cane fields. Of course, this was an attempt by owners to reduce the cost of feeding their workers by making them grow much of their own food, and also using lands unsuitable for planting sugar. But the provision grounds soon became a key part of the lives of the enslaved and a jealously guarded "right". They allowed slave families to eat better by supplementing the miserably inadequate rations doled out to them and, crucially, selling surplus produce to earn a little cash. An internal marketing system soon developed in all the colonies, dominated by enslaved women who travelled many miles to district markets to sell their produce, foodstuffs, and small livestock. Cultivation of the grounds and related marketing by enslaved families became central to their lives, creating what have been called "proto-peasants" long before emancipation made an actual peasantry possible.[14]

We should note that a substantial minority of the enslaved in the British Caribbean lived in towns, where women nearly always outnumbered men. Most urban slaves were domestics, working for their owners or hired out to others: wet nurses, nannies, cooks, cleaners, seamstresses, washerwomen, maids, and prostitutes. Some sold goods on the streets for their owners. Others were carters, coachmen, grooms, valets, general labourers, and skilled artisans; nearly all were men. In general, the urban enslaved had greater mobility and personal freedom than the plantation people, and the towns always sheltered runaways trying to merge into the urban free black community.[15]

The transatlantic slave trade in captured Africans, if they survived the Middle Passage, irretrievably dislocated family lives. Arriving enslaved, they had lost their status as son or daughter, sister or brother, husband or wife. They were torn apart from their dense kinship networks, and arrived in the Caribbean as isolated individuals, the great majority cut off forever from their kith and kin. Of course, family ties did develop in the places of captivity; and as slave populations became more "creolised", kinship was invented and re-established, and family life developed. In Trinidad in 1813, many of the enslaved lived in households with both parents present, though mother–children units were more common and the majority of enslaved children lived only with their mothers. In Jamaica, Higman's study of three large plantations between 1807 and 1834 revealed that just over half of all households were "nuclear", with both parents resident. Probably the role of the enslaved father and husband was not as "marginal" as historians had always assumed. But mother–children units overall were more common, though a non-resident father might still play an important role, and most enslaved children knew their fathers. Male authority was a reality across the slave communities, with patriarchal traditions imported from West Africa and Britain.

Men and women in the plantation villages formed unions, sometimes co-residential, sometimes not. Couples often belonged to different estates, and stable relationships – involving at least female fidelity – were normative. All the evidence points to very strong mother–child bonds, and to the centrality of motherhood to enslaved women. Of course, slavery rendered a stable family life extraordinarily difficult. Apart from the punishing work regime, above all on sugar plantations, forced separation by sale and removal were a reality. So was the constant risk of sexual exploitation of girls and women by owners, managers, overseers, and elite enslaved men. Enslaved females were seen as always available, with sexual coercion often re-enacting the power relations of the gendered system of enslavement. Sexual relations between white and sometimes brown men and enslaved women ranged from violent rape, to coerced and generally unwanted sex in the fields or the Great House, to relatively stable unions that might offer advantages to the women and their children. The notorious diaries of the Jamaican-based Thomas Thistlewood, in the later 1700s, show how frequent and routine coerced sex was, though he also had a 30-year affair with Phibbah, an African woman whom he clearly cared for.[16]

We have already noted that fertility rates of enslaved women in the British Caribbean were low. Combined with appalling rates of infant and child mortality, this meant that – with exceptions such as Barbados and the Bahamas – populations declined when imports of enslaved Africans were cut off after 1807. Some historians, such as the British scholar Barbara Bush, as well as white contemporaries, such as the English plantation owner Matthew Lewis, have suggested that women refused to bear enslaved children through such means as contraception, deliberate abortion, and even infanticide: a kind of "gynaecological resistance". Though contraception and abortion must often have been attempted, and infanticide occasionally carried out by midwives or desperate mothers, the evidence points elsewhere. Factors beyond the control of enslaved women and men were the leading causes of low fertility, probably aided by some voluntary control. The punishing labour by women of reproductive age in the first gang of the sugar plantations damaged their health. Diseases of all kinds, including dysentery and other gastro-intestinal disorders, smallpox, leprosy, yaws, venereal diseases, and many others, sapped their strength and, of course, that of men too. Malnutrition was an everyday reality for most plantation labourers. Miscarriages and still births were also common owing to all these factors, and children succumbed to a host of infections and diseases. It was not until after emancipation in 1834, when most women of child-bearing age withdrew from gang labour on the sugar plantations, that the fertility of Afro-Caribbean women began to recover.

Slavery distorted family life and rendered motherhood a tragic experience for most enslaved women (and fatherhood, perhaps less directly so, for men). Yet women managed to rear their children against all odds. They took the lead in the slave community's attempts to create a viable family life and a network of kinship ties, efforts which were largely successful by the time of emancipation in the 1830s. Women were the major socialisers of children, and they helped to transmit key aspects of African culture and religion.[17]

The enslaved Africans who were brought to the British Caribbean came from many ethnic and linguistic groups throughout West and Central Africa, but beliefs relating to the spirits of ancestral kin were powerful across these divides. Theirs was a densely populated spirit world in which the worship of the ancestral dead and the manipulation of supernatural powers for material or earthly ends were crucial to daily life. In the British colonies, this complex was called "Obeah": a catch-all word to designate a wide range of religious and magical beliefs and practices. "Myal" was another term for the African-derived religion of enslaved Jamaicans.

Of course, Christianity eventually came to exert a powerful influence on the enslaved, especially from the late 1700s. In those British islands which had previously been colonised by the Spanish or French – Trinidad, Dominica, Grenada, and St Lucia – Catholicism was the predominant variant. In general, Catholic slave owners in these territories arranged for mass baptisms of their enslaved, but little else in terms of religious instruction. Syncretism with African belief systems became widespread, creating mixed faiths such as Sango in Trinidad, which combined the Yoruba Orisha with Catholic saints.

In most of the British colonies, Protestant missionaries were the main agents of Christianisation of the enslaved. From the mid-1700s, Quakers, Baptists, Moravians (from Germany), Methodists, and Presbyterians all worked to "save the souls" of the enslaved, often in the face of strong planter hostility. Later, the established Church of England also began some missionary activities. In the British Leeward Islands, as many as a quarter of the enslaved were claimed as converts by the Moravian and Methodist missions. By around 1800, Antigua was the centre of their work. In Jamaica, the Baptists were especially strong, but the Moravians, Methodists, and Presbyterians were also active, and, together, these missions claimed some 10 per cent of the Jamaican enslaved by the time of emancipation. Baptist congregations – led, not by British missionaries, but by literate enslaved men known as "Native Baptists" – had emerged in Jamaica by the early 1800s. Their strength was revealed in the Great Rebellion there of 1831–1832, known as the Baptist War, led by Sam Sharpe, a Native Baptist leader.[18]

The Two Hundred Years War

Resistance to enslavement was endemic in the slave societies of the British Caribbean. Historians have coined the phrase "the Two Hundred Years War" to capture this reality of the period from the 1630s to the 1830s. The period was longer for the Spanish Caribbean, where Africans had been enslaved since the early 1500s (see Nerín and Tofiño in this volume). Though no single rebellion succeeded in ending slavery, unlike the Great Revolt that started in Saint-Domingue in 1791 and ended with an independent Haiti,[19] the many uprisings fatally weakened the slave system and eventually helped to bring about emancipation. In addition, a wide range of other modes of resistance had the same cumulative effect.[20]

Rebellions took place in small islands like Antigua, as well as Barbados, and in larger territories such as Jamaica and Demerara (British Guiana). They occurred early and late during the 200 years of enslavement. At first, these uprisings tended to be led by African-born men, such as the revolt in Antigua in 1736, the huge rebellion in Jamaica in 1760 known as Tacky's Revolt, and the rising led by the recently enslaved African known as Sandy in Tobago in 1770.[21] Later revolts were more often led by Creoles, especially the three major rebellions of the last 20 years before emancipation: Barbados in 1816, Demerara in 1823, and Jamaica in 1831–1832. This last event, which was brutally suppressed at the cost of hundreds killed in the field or executed after it was over, decisively swung public and parliamentary opinion in Britain in favour of emancipation. The Act freeing the enslaved in the British Empire was passed in Westminster a year later, in 1833.[22]

Less spectacular than the great rebellions, but equally debilitating to the slave regime, was marronage, or running away. Small islands like Barbados and Antigua, which lacked mountains and which were almost entirely covered with sugar plantations, offered less refuge for runaways than Jamaica with its mountain ranges and its largely undeveloped interior, or Trinidad, with its unusually high proportion of urban slaves and free blacks. Yet enslaved people ran away everywhere, as is revealed in the many advertisements for absconded slaves in the colonial newspapers and the registration records after 1813, which referred to "absent" people.[23] Some ran away after an especially severe punishment or some other crime against them. Others fled to meet up with relatives or partners elsewhere on the island. Not all intended to stay away forever, if they were not captured and returned to their plantations for punishment. Family ties on the estate brought many back, especially women with children, which probably explains why men outnumbered women among runaways.

But some runaways succeeded in escaping permanently and forming semi-autonomous communities far from the plantations. The outstanding example in the British Caribbean is the Maroons of Jamaica. In the mountainous interior of that island, two separate communities succeeded in defeating British troops and winning a grudging treaty commitment from London in 1739, which guaranteed their autonomy and permanent freedom, albeit at the price of agreeing to send back future runaways who joined their villages. Jamaica's Maroons have retained their autonomy and their unique culture to this day.[24]

Another mode of resistance, especially important in the late slavery period, saw the enslaved bargaining with managers and owners for what they regarded as their "rights": hours of work, delineation of field tasks, modes of punishment, and time off to cultivate their provision grounds. Behaving more like proletarians than enslaved workers, on many plantations these enslaved groups succeeded in winning some control over their working conditions, at the risk always of severe punishment, and even sometimes securing the dismissal of overseers who violated established practices. During the period of Amelioration in the last decade before emancipation (1824–1834), the enslaved had some recourse to Protectors of Slaves and to magistrates for the redress of wrongs against them. Studies of Berbice (British Guiana) and Trinidad during this period show that the enslaved eagerly took advantage of these legal procedures, even though they were often unsuccessful in gaining redress and were sometimes punished for lodging complaints.[25]

What has come to be known as "day-to-day resistance" constantly chipped away at the slave system. It took many forms: "malingering"; feigning illness (though actual ill health was a constant in the lives of the enslaved); damaging plantation equipment, machines, and livestock; stealing food; and "insolence" and verbal "rudeness" to plantation staff. Owners and managers were haunted by the fear that enslaved cooks and domestics might poison or otherwise harm them and their families, and no doubt this did occasionally happen. Cultural resistance – holding on to African religious beliefs and practices, beating drums, singing rebellious songs, insisting on naming children, and rejecting imposed names – was part of this insidious daily defiance of the brutal slave regime.[26] These were the veritable "weapons of the weak" across the British Caribbean.[27]

Women were less likely to be runaways, and the great rebellions were led by men. Nanny, a member of Jamaica's Maroons, was an outstanding exception. But women were actively involved in everyday resistance and more prone than men to acts of verbal defiance and "insolence". Overseers and managers everywhere considered female slaves more "troublesome" to deal with than men. Specifically, "gendered resistance" included using menstruation, pregnancy, and lactation to win concessions and time off from work, though this had more chance of limited success in the period after the abolition of the African slave trade in 1807, when managers were anxious to promote births and infant survival. Enslaved women often claimed the right to breastfeed infants long past the expected 12 months, and to be given work breaks for this, which was a constant source of conflict with managers and overseers. This act can also be regarded as a form of gendered resistance, as well as adherence to African practices of prolonged lactation. As we have seen, "gynaecological resistance" through contraception, voluntary abortion, and infanticide was a reality, though such acts are unlikely to have been the leading cause of the notoriously low rates of fertility and live births among enslaved women on slave plantations across the British Caribbean.[28]

Concluding Reflections

Ever since the publication in 1944 of the classic work by the Trinidadian scholar-politician Eric Williams, *Capitalism and Slavery*, there has been a vibrant historiographical debate about the causes of British abolition and emancipation, which has generated an enormous and still growing scholarly literature. No attempt can be made in this chapter to summarise the debate and the literature. Instead, a brief timeline of events will be provided in concluding this chapter.[29]

Three major, interrelated developments combined to make British abolition possible. First, multifaceted resistance by the enslaved, briefly outlined in the preceding section, helped to persuade many in Britain that maintaining the African trade and slavery itself was dangerous and counterproductive. Everyday resistance and marronage chipped away at the system, and the great rebellions – especially those in the last decades of slavery – made it clear that a legislated and controlled emancipation was better than the very real possibility of a Haiti-type revolution, which created the first independent black republic in the world in 1804 (see also Aragón Falomir in this volume).[30]

Second, fundamental shifts in Britain's economy associated with the early industrial revolution made the British West Indies, and the associated sugar and African trades, far less important than they had been before the 1780s. The economic and political clout of the "West India Interest" – the sugar barons and their financial backers in Britain – thus declined, and, concomitantly, their ability to influence the British Parliament and policymakers had significantly shrunk by the early 1800s.

Third, important changes in British public opinion, starting in the 1770s and accelerating over the next 50 years, created the ideological opening for abolitionism. This movement had a religious dimension. Many Quakers, Nonconformist Protestants, and evangelical Anglicans came to believe that the slave trade and slavery were sins which should not be tolerated by a Christian nation. The more secular dimension of the new ideology involved the conviction that slavery was an irrational and unproductive form of labour unsuited to a modern, industrialising economy: a view influentially propounded particularly by the Scottish political economist Adam Smith. Whether religiously inspired or persuaded by secular arguments, Britain's middle classes had broadly become anti-slavery by 1830.

The transatlantic trade in captured Africans, with all its blatant brutalities and its massive loss of human life, was the first target for the abolitionists. Their attack began in earnest in the 1790s but only succeeded by 1807. The imports of Africans to newly acquired British territories – Trinidad and the Guiana colonies – were first prohibited, and then the parliamentary Act of 1807 made the whole trade illegal for British subjects.

The abolitionists had hoped that the end of the African slave trade would prompt significant improvements in the lives of the enslaved, as planters attempted to encourage a natural increase of the enslaved population through better treatment. Failing this, they pushed for a system of "registration" between 1812 and 1834, according to which owners and managers were obliged, by law, to make detailed returns about their enslaved labourers on a regular basis. This enabled the abolitionists to amass hard evidence about the excessive deaths found in nearly all British plantation colonies.[31]

Between 1823 and 1824, the British government, under increasing pressure from the abolitionists, embarked on a policy known as Amelioration, an attempt to improve the lives of the enslaved without altering the fundamental character of chattel slavery (see Cobley in this volume).[32] By around 1830, the overall failure of this policy was clear, and the abolitionists pushed for legislation to eliminate slavery. With the reform of the British Parliament in 1832 resulting in fewer lawmakers who supported the West India Interest, and more who reflected middle-class anti-slavery opinion, the path was clear for the passage of the 1833 Act of Emancipation. This legislation called for the formal end of slavery throughout the British Empire to take effect on 1 August 1834.

Notoriously, the Emancipation Act included two huge concessions to former slave owners. First, they received the enormous sum of £20 million as compensation for their "lost property", paid out in the 1830s according to the going price of the enslaved in the different colonies at the time of emancipation.[33] Needless to say, the former slaves received nothing at all for their two centuries of unpaid labour. Second, a quasi-slavery "apprenticeship" system was put in place. For several years, every former slave over the age of six had to work for his or her former owner without wages for a stipulated number of hours per week. This absurd scheme was bitterly resented by the formerly enslaved, and their resistance, combined with abolitionist pressure, resulted in the end of the practice by 1838. The date 1 August 1838 marked the final abolition of slavery across the British Caribbean, resulting in what liberated people dubbed "full free".

The slave system was much the same throughout the plantation colonies of the British Caribbean, where most of the enslaved laboured on sugar (and other) estates. In the non-plantation colonies, mainly very small islands such as the Bahamas, the Turks and Caicos, the Cayman Islands, and others, the experience of the enslaved was different and generally less harsh. A significant difference, however, lay in the temporal duration of the slave society, ranging from just under 200 years in Barbados and the Leeward Islands (1640s–1830s) to around 50 in Trinidad (1780s–1830s). But everywhere, the aftermath of slavery shaped the trajectory of these colonies in the century that followed emancipation and into the present (see Timcke and Gomes in this volume). What the American journalist William E. Sewell referred to as "the ordeal of free labour in the British West Indies" in 1861 – the struggle of the newly freed and their descendants to survive and carve out autonomous lives – became the grand theme of British Caribbean history after emancipation.[34]

9

Slavery in the French Caribbean

Jaime Aragón Falomir

The past is never dead. It's not even past.
William Faulkner, *Requiem for a Nun* (1951)

The slave system has been replaced with indentured servitude.
Raphaël Confiant, *Commandeur du sucre* (1994)

THE ARRIVAL OF EUROPEAN empires in the Americas from the sixteenth
century onwards provoked an unprecedented transformation in multiple
areas – demographic and territorial – that impacted on all the actors involved.[1]
According to the Brazilian anthropologist Darcy Ribeiro,[2] the "witness"
people ("modern representatives of the old autonomous civilisations on which
the European expansion fell"[3]) have been uprooted and replaced in some places
by the "transplanted" peoples, or descendants of Europeans. Ribeiro omitted
to say that the enslaved Africans were equally uprooted. In fact, the Caribbean
is a region where "new" peoples, made up of indigenous, black, and European,
have emerged.[4] Ribeiro's statement is at the root of the problem, since it brings
together a category of the conquerors, skin colour, and a continental origin. At
the same time, it leaves aside the variety and density of the indigenous peoples
of the region – Tainos, Caribs, and Arawaks – as well as the impact of the
different types of slave systems on the construction of present-day peoples.

This orientation demonstrates a need to focus on the impact of the slave
trade, from a historical point of view,[5] as a driver of the Western capitalist

system.[6] We should also examine the need for restitution for these four centuries of damage. Likewise, recent proposals have identified the impact of slavery through a study of different variables: prosperity, dependence, poverty, inequality, population growth, and ethnic stratification.[7] Similarly, other researchers have delved into the link between modern structural inequalities – racial and economic – and the slave trade.[8]

I begin this chapter with a literature review that allows me to approach the subject through the theoretical framework of my speciality: political sociology. This is how I identify the common denominators among the mechanisms of domination and power structures that some groups – elites and slave masters – exercise, reproduce, and justify over indigenous majorities ("native" peoples and slaves).[9] Beyond denouncing the slave system, my aim is to merge the analysis of politics and society in order to contribute to the debate on the functioning and organisation of power relations in the context of slavery. For this purpose, I focus on the territories located in the French Caribbean: Saint-Domingue (modern Haiti), Martinique, and Guadeloupe.

The chapter is divided into three parts. The first introduces the particularities of French colonialism in the Caribbean, and the importance of sugar cane as part of structuring, regulation, and social codes. The second examines the social polarisation between dominant and dominated through skin colour and rank, which involved differentiation, racialisation, and segregation. The third addresses, through the use of the concept of *habitus*,[10] the impact that interactions (on the plantation–habitation) had on the agents involved (in terms of spatial segregation).

My theoretical approach argues that societies can be viewed through the lens of dominant and dominated, which was clearly appropriate to slavery. However, few studies have applied the modern concept of elites to slave masters.[11] Therefore, we turn to the notion of "elite" as conceived by the American scholar John Scott. These are groups that possess a degree of power and exercise it. Power is defined as the capacity to produce causal effects that influence the behaviour of agents.[12] In other words, power consists in making someone do something that he or she would not otherwise have done without an incentive. Such power projects the illusion that it does not belong to anyone, and can also be understood as an evolving process that is far from static.[13] This imposition is executed through coercive mechanisms,[14] or by internalising such domination as representing the natural order of things, as a phenomenon that is valid and legitimate.[15] I seek to answer the question: to what extent do such theories explain the establishment of a lasting domination?

France and Slavery: When Sugar Cane Saved the Colony

The cane is what makes the richness of the White Creole. It's what gives him sugar and rum. Without sugar cane, he'd be as useless as a zero in front of a number in front of Blanc-France ... Sugar cane is what keeps the colony on its feet.

Raphaël Confiant, *Commandeur du sucre* (1994)

According to John Scott, domination requires the internalisation of values and rights for subalterns to accept orders and carry out obligations.[16] For him, elites have the capacity to influence subaltern groups through the use of force (repression) or by inducing the latter to carry out the actions the former desire.[17] In our case, the subaltern groups are those who are in a position of physical inferiority, as was the case during slavery. The French sociologist Luc Boltanski argues that dominant groups realise it is indispensable to have rules – rights, procedures, and norms – since in a world governed by uncertainty, they would not be able to secure the benefits of such rights.[18] My chapter aims to weave together different strands of the vertical links between the French overseas colonised territories and the metropolis (Continental France), on the one hand, and relations between masters and enslaved people, on the other.[19]

To demonstrate the first verticality, I have transcribed a few statements. An eighteenth-century French merchant called Jean Pellet noted that "the colonies were founded only for the utility of the metropolis".[20] Others have asserted that although natural conditions determined where to set up plantations, the decision was also determined by the ability to generate rents for the metropolis.[21] Similarly, for the American scholar Robert Stein, "political reason insists that the colonies are always dependent on the mother country".[22] Among the regulations imposed on the colonies was the French system of exclusivity held by the metropolis, which indicated a dual monopoly, both commercial and manufacturing. It was forbidden in the colonies to sell products to, buy them from, or transport them to or from other countries besides France.[23] In addition, it was assumed that slavery was morally wrong, since it was forbidden in France itself, even though it was permitted in the colonies. This again demonstrates the differentiation between the metropolis and the overseas colonies.

The second verticality in question was governed by the Code Noir of 1685, which stipulated the rights of slaves and the duties of masters, even though these were rarely respected.[24] Within the code, we find the French duty to Christianise slaves through baptism, consecrate marriages, provide proper food rations and clothing, and, above all, observe the prohibition on the "excessive" use of force to punish locals.[25] For Guadeloupean French literary theorist Roger Toumson, the Code Noir served to justify the enjoyment by masters of their "white" status, and the respect that every individual of colour owed them for their dual status as white and master.[26] We will next examine how the colony, slavery, and social differentiation were established.

Settlements: Why Slaves?

The first French settlement was created in 1630 by the French sailor, buccaneer, adventurer, and settler Pierre Belain d'Esnambuc on the island of Saint-Croix (present-day St Kitts), from which French settlers were eventually expelled by the British in 1713.[27] From there, settlements were extended to Martinique and Guadeloupe and neighbouring islands. Although the Caribs, the indigenous people, hindered colonisation of both islands, French settlement was quickly completed by the extermination or expulsion of the locals.[28] The choice of these islands was not fortuitous, but circumstantial, since for the Spanish empire (see Ramirez in this volume) they were useless lands, lacking minerals.[29] By 1670, the colonial enterprise expanded to the island that would become the most important in the French Empire: Saint-Domingue.[30] By this time, the indigenous peoples, the Tainos, had almost been wholly exterminated during two centuries of the Spanish imperial presence.

After the first settlements were established, there began what the Barbadian novelist George Lamming described as "an immense human migration to the new world of the Caribbean [where] everyone found themselves in a strange land".[31] This was an influx of poor Europeans called *engagés* (in indentured servitude) who sold their freedom for 36 months to pay for moving to Martinique and Guadeloupe.[32] Many of these people could not physically adapt to the climate and diseases such as malaria.[33] For this pragmatic reason, as well as a religious one – "to save the pagan souls brought to the islands for baptism", according to the French king Louis XIII – the French began to promote slavery. For the French scholar Frédéric Régent, there were two other reasons for this migration. The first involved tradition, since African slaves had been used on plantations in the Canaries, Madeira, and São Tomé and Príncipe since the fifteenth century; and the second was a matter of convenience, since the uprooting of Africans also facilitated their control. But what was the purpose of importing slaves from the African continent?[34]

Sugar Cane and African Slaves: What for?

In the early stages of settlement, the poor whites (*engagés*) exploited the land to produce mainly tobacco, indigo, cotton, and coffee: these primary products required small patches of land and a limited labour force. However, after the expulsion of the Dutch from Brazil by the Portuguese in 1640, French labourers from Brazil resettled in both Barbados and Guadeloupe in 1654, bringing with them sugar cane and the techniques to produce sugar; these would gradually spread to all the Caribbean islands. The arrival of French migrants and the decline of the tobacco cycle – which ended by 1690 – caused a total transformation of labour and territorial relations, since sugar cane required capital investment to acquire land, machinery, and slave labour.[35]

As a consequence, there emerged a monoculture concentrated among fewer owners. By 1671, an estate in the French Caribbean averaged 50 hectares, while during the tobacco cycle it had averaged 15 hectares. In the same year, 74 per cent and 89 per cent of the surface of Martinique and Guadeloupe respectively was covered by sugar cane plantations.[36] According to the US scholar Philip Boucher, "sugar was crucial in Martinique and Guadeloupe in the 1680s, but not to the extent it would be in 1750".[37] After 1763, Saint-Domingue overtook the Lesser Antilles to become the largest sugar producer in the world.

The consequence of this paradigmatic shift was a growing need for labour. This explains the disproportionate growth in the slave population between 1700 and 1730: the number of African enslaved increased by nine times between 1700 and 1730.[38] It is estimated that between 1650 and 1848, French territories in the Caribbean received about 1.5 million slaves – 20 per cent of whom died during the Middle Passage.[39] The number of slaves arriving in the different French territories is estimated at 864,000 (Saint-Domingue), 366,000 (Martinique), and 291,000 (Guadeloupe).[40]

Likewise, the so-called white gold – sugar – had an impact on the vertical economic links established between the colony and the metropolis, bearing in mind the system of exclusivity. In fact, exports of products – mainly sugar – to France grew from £221 million to £500 million between 1735 and 1752, reaching almost £750 million in 1777.[41]

Social Polarisation: Between Skin and Rank

Race and class relations were as prevalent as ever, dividing society between Creole whites, mulattoes (offspring of whites with female slaves) and blacks: a veritable "pigmentocracy".

Raphaël Confiant, *Commandeur du sucre* (1994)

The double verticality already mentioned compels us to identify the ways in which a society is organised that has, from its genesis, involved racial inequality, a fractured social structure, and a rigid hierarchy. The notion of "social race" is defined by the American anthropologist Charles Wagley as "the way in which the members of a society tend to categorise each one according to their physical aspects".[42] Each country has its own ways of classification: in the United States, the one-drop rule assigns African origin to any individual with a drop of blood from that continent, while in Brazil a "white" drop assigns that individual to European stock.[43]

We will now examine the ways in which "social race" was constructed in the French Caribbean. Colour distinction ("social race") and rank respond to a need for differentiation, domination, and maintaining positions of superiority. Most slave codes had three elements in common: the status of slave was life-long; and it also had a racial and a property component.[44] The racial component was a guarantor of colonial control through the identification of superiority (rank) with colour ("white"). In fact, Louis XV's prime minister Étienne-François de Choiseul noted in 1766: "legitimate unions of whites with coloured women must be discouraged. If through these alliances the whites ended up getting along with free blacks, the colony could easily escape the authority of the king."[45]

To justify domination, the dominant must possess the capacity to restrict the access of other groups to their own.[46] Although French sociologist Luc Boltanski does not use ideas of race, skin colour, or slavery in his work, his theory echoes the link between the dominant and dominated in the Caribbean. It is important for dominant groups to establish complicity with some subordinate actors (generally those of a lighter skin) by permitting them access to the middle levels of subalternship as opposed to the lowest levels (the *esclaves*). I next examine both dimensions of differentiation – "social race" and rank – in the productive hierarchy.

Social Race: Status, Colour, and Origin

From the demographic point of view, French immigrants to the colonies were mainly male, which meant that miscegenation was inevitable. However, when the colonial society was firmly established, access to the white caste became restricted.[47] Miscegenation forced the dominant minority to establish mechanisms of differentiation linked to skin colour in order to preserve the power structure vis-à-vis the dominated. This prevented the children of slaves from achieving social mobility.

What the French West Indian scholar Raphaël Confiant defines as "pigmentocracy"[48] seems to have originated from the racial caste system of the Spanish empire (see Ramirez in this volume). An ethno-social pyramid allowed each individual to identify his or her location within the hierarchy, based on the origins and racial classification of his or her progenitors.[49] In the French Caribbean, there were limits that could never be crossed by a *mestizo* (mixed race), no matter how white he was: he would always be considered "bleached" (*mal-blanchi*). This distinction occurred because, quantitatively speaking, the masters were always in the minority, and the only mechanism to prevent others from diluting their power was to differentiate by origin.

In Saint-Domingue there was a clear division between whites, freedmen, and slaves. The last were sometimes called blacks, which reveals a mix of racial (white vs black) and legal categories (slave owner, freedman, or slave).[50] Between 1681 and 1789, there was an uneven population growth in the three French territories. Freedmen grew tenfold in number within a century in all the territories; whites fourfold in Saint-Domingue and Guadeloupe, and twofold in Martinique. In stark contrast, the number of slaves increased 200, 20, and 5.5 times respectively on each island.[51] At the dawn of the nineteenth century, as an obvious consequence of the Haitian Revolution (1791–1804),[52] the number of slaves decreased in each territory both absolutely and as a proportion of the total population, causing a significant proportional increase in Martinique and Guadeloupe.

In the French territories, a complex system of colour categorisation and distinction was established, with the supremacy of every European and "white" individual residing in multiple nuances, although with an emphasis on white skin colour, straight hair or the shape of lips and nose, in a context in which even aesthetics could be transposed to intelligence. Thus, there was a desire to create societies that would justify the "superiority" of some[53] and trigger competition among others. This system was maintained through the differentiated treatment of slaves, a condition mentioned in other contexts as necessary for establishing the domination of some over others.[54] This is confirmed by many scholars. As Richard Burton notes: "To be light-skinned still confers definite social and sexual advantages in Martinique (especially) and Guadeloupe, and, despite the rise of a substantial black middle class since 1946, a high degree of correlation still obtains between class and colour."[55] For French sociologist Michel Giraud, the supremacy of whites is the *sine qua non* of the inferiority of blacks, which is, in turn, the reflection of a social structure imposed by the colonisers.[56]

This hierarchy was not only organised according to skin colour, but was also linked to place of birth (West Indies or Africa), knowledge of the Creole language,[57] and miscegenation.[58] However, for Guadeloupean French literary theorist Roger Toumson, miscegenation is a myth that serves as a mechanism of domination and a means of identification of any "non-white" individual. For this reason, there was a "delirious hierarchisation of races and colors" that involved a "paranoia of classification" distinguishing 128 types without any biological reality.[59] Table 9.1 shows some examples of racial division in the French Caribbean.

Table 9.1: "Paranoia of classification"

Male	Female	Result
White	Negress	Mulatto
White	Mulattress	Quadroon
White	*Métis*	Mameluk
White	Mameluk	Quadroon
White	Quadroon	*Sang-mêlé*
White	*Sang-mêlé*	*Sang-mêlé* (close to white)

Source: Médéric Louis Élie Moreau de Saint-Méry, *Description topographique, physique, civile, politique et historique de la partie française de l'Isle Saint-Domingue* (Philadelphia: Société de l'Histoire des Colonies Françaises, 1789); Roger Toumson, *Mythologie du métissage* (Paris: Presses Universitaires de France, 1998), p. 111.

Indeed, as Michel Giraud notes: "for non-whites (married to whites) it tends to be socially advantageous and a sought-after means of upward mobility, as a capital resource that has to be acquired or defended".[60] Beyond the paranoia of classification, a third group (which also existed in Spanish territories) was established: that of the mulatto. Members of this group were somewhere between masters and slaves since, often free, they were regarded as people who had "rejected their black African origins and, therefore, slave",[61] because "as soon as a mulatto owned a horse, he denied that his mother was black".[62] At the same time, according to Roger Toumson, a mulatto woman had a customary destiny: to be the master's mistress.[63]

Differentiation: Rank and Skin Colour

In slave society, another type of division was established according to activity (rank) within the plantation-habitation. This hierarchy was created to organise the work process on the sugar plantation and discipline the workers.[64] To reinforce domination, it was necessary to be able to demonstrate that there was a measure of convergence between actors dispersed in space, exercising different activities, occupying very diverse positions in relation to the authorities, and endowed with unequal powers in terms of property and capital.

At the top of the pyramid were the slave masters or planters (white Creoles, *békés*) who personified power on the estate. The landowners of Saint-Domingue resided in France, though this absenteeism was less common in Martinique and Guadeloupe. At their side, there was a group of superior and free subordinates such as the administrator (*géreur*), the superintendent or inspector (*économe*), and the slave driver or slave foreman (*commandeur*), who enjoyed infinitely better conditions than the rest. Except for the *géreur*, the latter two were generally mulattoes. The *commandeur* has been described by Confiant as that person who "is not made to be loved, but to be obeyed and to make the blacks walk straight".[65]

Subsequently, the slave population was divided into three main groups. The first-level subalterns included the "domestic slaves" (*esclave de case*) who worked in the master's house. At the second level were the "talent slaves" (*esclaves de talent*), who exercised a trade as carpenters, refiners, coopers, blacksmiths, and masons. At the bottom of the hierarchy were most of those who worked in the mill (*esclaves du moulin*) or in the fields (*nègres de jardin*). The latter were in turn divided according to gender and physical strength: the men who cut (*coupeurs*), the women who tied the canes (*amarreuses*), and the cane transporters (*muletiers* and *cabrouettiers*).[66]

This pyramid should be seen in terms of racial implications: the lighter the skin, the greater the possibility of promotion. All this division within the plantation was accepted and justified as a social process based on personal and imaginary attributes that legitimised domination. Following the American scholar Dale Tomich, Table 9.2 shows how slaves were distributed among the various occupations and activities of the sugar plantation.[67]

Table 9.2: Hierarchy of plantation staff

TOP (white)		
Planter	Top of the plantation hierarchy	He personified power on the estate
Administrator (*Géreur*)	Responsible for the overall operation of the estate	He lived on the plantation, either in the big house or in a separate house with his family
MIDDLE TOP (mulatto)		
Overseer (*Économe*)	Engaged in the practical day-to-day work of the plantation. He was directly responsible for the slaves (for keeping records of births, deaths, and accidents).	He was familiar with the individual condition of every slave. He had to carry out the master's demand for surplus and for the maintenance of social control.
Slave commander	The soul of the plantation. He was responsible for controlling the slaves who were field hands.	A slave himself, he symbolised both authority and exemption from physical labour
Domestics	Considered the most "pampered" slaves	They were better fed, better clothed, and better treated because they did not have a supervisor
Head sugar refiner	The most important slave on the plantation	The entire crop was in his hands
MIDDLE (black)		
Mill master	*Maître du moulin*	Great prestige

Talented slaves	Those who stood out for their knowledge of a trade	Carpenters, coopers, smiths, and masons
BOTTOM (black)		
Slaves of the mill	Their work was exhausting, dangerous, and hazardous	Many slaves had their arms crushed in the mills or were burned in the boilers
Mule driver and cart driver	Transporting sugar cane to the mills or refineries	
Amarreuses *Coupeurs*	Women who bind the canes cut into bundles Men who cut the canes	

Source: Dale Tomich, "Slavery in the French Martinique", in Verene Shepherd and Hilary Mc D. Beckles (eds.), *Caribbean Slavery in the Atlantic World* (Kingston: Ian Randle Publishers, 2000), p. 418 and pp. 428–429; and Raphaël Confiant, *Commandeur du sucre* (Paris: Ecriture, 1994).

The Habitus: "Sugar Cane Fields Forever"

The Negro is a race that is condemned. The condemnation is sugar cane. Nobody likes sugar cane. Neither the white man, nor the mulatto, nor the Negro

Raphaël Confiant, *Commandeur du sucre* (1994)

Having studied how slave society was ordered in the French Caribbean, we can now analyse the influence of the place in which a community interacts. As already noted, sugar cane transformed the Caribbean, socially, territorially, and architecturally. This was how the plantation–habitation was built, structuring and differentiating the life of each individual. The French sociologist Pierre Bourdieu sought to understand the influence of the environment on the way agents evolve as generators of behaviours, by developing the concept of *habitus*.[68] Other works allude to the social conditioning and signals associated with belonging to a *habitus* that are linked to the practices of each agent.[69]

Although developed to examine a social world without enslavement, the idea of *habitus* can be used for any other apparatus of control. In fact, the devices of domination that we observe in the plantation–habitation can give the illusion that power is systemic – in the sense that it belongs to no one – and that

179

control partially escapes each of the actors. According to Bourdieu, there is a connection between the structure of natural, social, and property spaces which symbolically binds these actors.[70]

Needless to say, outside the plantation–habitation the slave had no value as a "good": outside the plantation–habitation he, in fact, had no "utility". Therefore, the bond between the slave and the plantation–habitation was inseparable from the slave system of domination. In fact, the uprooting suffered by enslaved people makes the plantation–habitation act as the new "home" environment to which they are forced to adapt.

As for the facilities of the plantation–habitation, different areas converge, such as the economic-productive (harvest, refinery); residential (houses of masters, foremen and different levels of slaves); carceral or punitive; socialisation (central courtyards); cultural (halls and entrances); and sometimes hospitals.[71] There were three sets of residential buildings: first, the master's house (*grand-case*), where the domestics lived, generally close to where the superior subalterns resided; second, at some distance and sometimes hidden from the master's view were the slaves' houses (*cases nègres*); and, third, the buildings for processing sugar (the mill, boiling house, infirmary, distillery, and the workshops of artisans). There were also fields that were cultivated (the plantation) and others that were not (the savannah).

Although the master's house served primarily as a shelter, for the French scholar Danielle Bégot, it had behind it a symbolic element: to impose its power and build a binary social world between settler and slave.[72] The determining element, which Bégot unfortunately does not fully develop, was the "symbolic violence" applied to all the agents that interacted in this architectural and productive organisation. Racial segregation was evident here too, since spaces were rigorously divided and separated between whites and blacks. In fact, the plantation–habitation has been described as a totalitarian institution where spaces had a double function: on the one hand, they were built by, and for, sugar production; on the other hand, they exerted a coercive pressure on slaves for the benefit of the French state, sugar planters, and white Creoles.[73]

The arrangements, boundaries, and prohibitions existing between the different structures shaped the interacting agents. According to Roger Toumson, each space implied a set of practices that were attributed so as to differentiate individuals but, at the same time, to unite them around a relationship of mutual need (i.e. producing sugar).[74] Places of socialisation common to all the actors were non-existent. The enslaved carried out their labours according to their rank, and when they finished, they returned to their huts. This organisation and differentiation was the result of the construction of a sense of belonging to a rank, so that the architectural structures had an underlying element, intended to reinforce the power of the master (elitism) and perpetuate traditions (inheritance).

Such social spaces provide an abstract representation that reveals an overall picture of the set of social unions and social divisions in the world of slavery. Indeed, they inevitably served as a physical barrier that maintained social and symbolic positions.[75] For this reason, *habitus* is the generating principle that defines and differentiates the social practices and roles of each actor. Roger Toumson notes that the relation between plantation and habitation space can be explained by two structures governed by the same principles: each space has a *habitus* that is respected, which allocates hierarchical differences that cross natural, social, and architectural spaces.[76] This is why he considers the plantation–habitation as the reference space of the master–slave dialectic.

Although the plantation–habitation is found in other large agricultural estates systems, it differs from them because it is involved in extensive exploitation (monoculture) which is speculative and destined for export.[77] For a significant time (1635–1848),[78] the plantation–habitation functioned as a closed fiefdom and was relatively autonomous from the rest of the villages on the island,[79] since production generally ended up in Europe. For this reason, the French Caribbean scholar Maurice Burac believes that sugar marks the beginning of a purely capitalist and foreign-dependent production cycle.[80]

The architectural structure (of residence, work, production, and forbidden zones) linked to other elements (inheritance, tradition, and fortune) determines a sort of class consciousness that is essential to transmitting the intrinsic elements of domination. This spatial segregation is both effective and symbolic, and allows individuals to identify themselves and be identified by others as belonging to a group according to their tasks. This has been demonstrated for other contexts.[81] In this way, socialisation links are established in which individuals locate and identify their peers. To be part of a social group, one has to be able to identify oneself by rank, colour, and origin, and to accept the norms which these attributes imply. In this way, the plantation–habitation was in tune with the whole system of coordination, organisation, and hierarchisation which implied that French slavery was based on a strong feeling of belonging to a group or community.

Concluding Reflections

This chapter has analysed some of the mechanisms of domination which, according to political sociology, have been studied by the specialised literature. It goes without saying that, in the context of slavery, identifying common threads with "free" societies reveals the complexity of the various gradations of such a system of exploitation. However, I have demonstrated that domination does not impose itself all at once, as slavery would have us believe, but is an evolving, metamorphosing, and changing process that always seeks to perpetuate and preserve structures.[82]

I have highlighted the principle of verticality between territories and actors, which shows how there is a market and a captive labour force. Likewise, in the first part, I showed the evolution of the colonial system towards a European system of sugar cane monoculture using African slave labour. In the second, through the analysis of social polarisation, I revealed how a key differentiation was introduced to guarantee domination, identification, and racialisation. In the third and final section, the chapter examined – through the lens of *habitus* – how domination is guaranteed in time and space. I demonstrated that the dual role of both masters (economic) and whites (social race) reinforced the sense of "superiority". Nevertheless, the masters established some horizontal links, such as by speaking Creole with the slaves, which allowed them to use French with the metropolitans.[83] This domination converged in the descendants of both groups, since infants learn affinities, convergences, and divergences in terms of skin colour and rank, thereby guaranteeing the perpetuation of the system.

We cannot ignore the fact that capitalism influenced the implementation of this pre-industrial system of exploitation and domination. However, the industrial revolution showed that slavery was an obsolete production system, and it also guided the new productive horizons linked to the systematisation of processes, the purchase of Western machinery, and the proletarianisation of labour. Studies of slavery, restitution, and racialisation are at present in vogue. However, such literature still does not go to the heart of the political economy debates that reveal the burdens of some and the benefits of others. Fortunately, a couple of decades ago, a new strand of research began to demonstrate the extent to which modern economic performance correlates with a slaveholding past, for all the actors involved.[84] In this way, comparative studies are being carried out between and within countries to identify the impacts of regions where slavery existed. These initiatives must continue to verify empirically the damage suffered by enslaved populations and territories in order to propose effective economic, political, and symbolic remedies and forms of restitution.

10

Slavery in the Dutch Caribbean

Kwame Nimako

CHATTEL SLAVERY IN THE Atlantic world was initiated, designed, and planned from Europe under the direction of European monarchs, and executed by their subjects in the Americas. Not only were European monarchs – both men and women – bonded through Christian religion and marriage, but they also responded to reports about the voyage of Italian explorer Christopher Columbus across the Atlantic in 1492 and Portuguese explorer Vasco da Gama's voyage around Africa to Asia in 1497. Through competition and cooperation, European conquistadors gained direct access to human and natural resources in Africa, the Americas, and Asia. In this context, chattel slavery must be understood as part of a worldwide system of European activities involving state formation.[1] These activities created opportunities for personal enrichment and for escape from class domination and religious persecution in Europe. There was thus intense competition between European nations over who should have the best access to these resources, resulting in frequent antagonism, conflicts, and wars. But their common ancestry, religion, and culture as Europeans, and increasingly their racial beliefs and shared identity, resulted in these imperialists signing treaties and making agreements collectively that privileged all Europeans over all non-Europeans, especially Africans.[2]

In the case of the Netherlands, the monarch was foreign – Spanish – and ruled through intermediaries, edicts, and decrees (see Ramirez in this volume). The strategic location of the province of Holland was also significant. According to the Dutch scholar Pieter Geyl, geography made it possible for the Netherlands to pursue trade during the war against the King of Spain. According to Geyl, Dutch harbours gave access to all seas and oceans, and thus created conditions that made it difficult for King Philip to do without the ships of his rebellious subjects.[3] Once Antwerp was shut off from the sea, the towns of Holland and Zeeland – and, in the long run, particularly Amsterdam – assumed the role which the great city of Antwerp had hitherto played in Europe's economic life.[4] As will be demonstrated below, the Dutch were involved in the transatlantic slave trade before they became a sovereign nation in 1648, an involvement that facilitated state formation.[5] This chapter reflects on Holland's involvement in chattel slavery in the Caribbean.

The next section discusses the emergence of the Atlantic world economy out of the plunder and expropriation of the lands of native populations. This occurred simultaneously with the appropriation of African labour through enslavement to produce silver, sugar, cotton, coffee, tobacco, salt, and other products. The third section describes the institutionalisation of chattel slavery in the eighteenth century on territory expropriated by the Dutch in the Caribbean. We should not lose sight of the fact that in the literature, enslavers are often referred to as "planters". In the real world, however, these individuals planted nothing: the work was all done by enslaved labour. It is equally clear that the coordination and control of enslaved labour required active intervention in the social life of the enslaved: from the production process to reproduction and family life. These interventions, and resistance to them, still form a vital part of the memories of the descendants of the enslaved,[6] which will be discussed below in more detail. Thus, for European populations, the colonies offered escape routes from persecution – including the Spanish Inquisition, by means of which Catholic monarchs suppressed heresy within the Church – and thus provided far more freedom, mobility, access to land, and wealth for Europeans. However, expropriation of land and enslavement led to unfreedom and servitude for many Africans and most Native American populations.

The fourth section discusses the circumstances that led the Dutch to abolish slavery in the nineteenth century. In contrast to the dominant explanation in Britain with its emphasis on philanthropy and abolitionism (see Brereton in this volume), we argue that the Napoleonic occupation of the Netherlands between 1795 and 1813 provides a far better frame for understanding the decline and end of Dutch involvement in Atlantic slavery. We conclude the chapter by arguing that one of the legacies of Dutch slavery is the unfinished business of emancipation.

On Land, Labour, and Kidnappings

The current worldwide economy is a convergence of two world economies: the Afro-Eurasia world economy, which has been in existence for millennia, and the Atlantic world economy, built on slavery and colonialism, which emerged in the sixteenth century after the voyages of Christopher Columbus and Vasco da Gama. Spain and Portugal led the way, while other European countries followed. Many European nations created East India companies to insert themselves into existing trade networks in Asia, while West India companies were also established to initiate the Atlantic slavery system (see also Mtombeni in this volume). Both sets of companies complemented each other in an interlocking network of economic activities. The importance of Atlantic slavery to the European economy developed in several phases, involving the production of silver, sugar, cotton, tobacco, and salt. In the process, European imperialists also brought vital American crops such as maize and tobacco to Europe and even China. By the eighteenth century, the East India and West India companies had created a global market, with London as the financial hub, underpinned by silver extracted from the Americas.[7]

Resistance is dialectically linked to enslavement, since no human being gives him- or herself voluntarily to be enslaved. This is why the Guyanese scholar Walter Rodney noted that the African in Africa was a free person before she or he was captured; remained a captive in Africa and during the transatlantic crossing; and only became enslaved when he or she reached the Americas.[8] This is often forgotten by scholars who write that Europeans took slaves from Africa. Viewed in this context, chattel slavery was a legal institution created and supported by European states.[9]

The slavery-based economy and societies in the Caribbean and the Americas gave rise to free Europeans and unfree Africans, and made race the organising principle of the institution of chattel slavery. This also explains why the enslaved resisted captivity and enslavement from the very beginning. But resistance has passive and active elements. Passive resistance is permanent and occurs daily, and involves language development. Active resistance translated into major revolts and, in some cases, the overthrow of slavery, as in Haiti (see Aragón Falomir in this volume).[10]

Salt is indispensable in understanding Dutch slavery. Its various sources of supply were of major importance to the Dutch for centuries. It was used to conserve meat and fish, and was important for Holland's international shipping and fishing, especially herring, industries. During much of the sixteenth century, Dutch foreign trade hinged on exchange with the Baltic countries, as well as France, Spain, and Portugal. The outbreak of the Eighty Years War with Spain (1568–1648) led the Dutch to intensify their search for salt in Africa and the Caribbean. The first three Dutch ships from Vlissingen arrived in Panama in 1569. Twelve years later, several Dutch ships appeared in the Caribbean in search of salt. Initially, the Dutch obtained salt from Punta de Araga, an island that is now part of Venezuela. By 1600, more than a hundred ships had obtained salt from Punta de Araga. Each ship carried an estimated 300 tonnes of salt to Holland: this amounted annually to 30,000 tonnes.[11]

In 1590, for the first time, Dutch merchantmen passed through the Strait of Gibraltar and entered the Mediterranean. As Pieter Geyl succinctly noted: "Stimulated by the overseas trade, and by the money it brought into the country, prosperity increased by leaps and bounds on all sides."[12] In other words, trade in salt and its related industries made it possible for the Dutch to compete with larger countries such as England, France, Germany, and Spain, and emerge as a small, influential nation within the global system. However, it took a while for the different provinces to come together in a closer union and present a common front by asserting sovereignty. According to Geyl, the mutual jealousies and fierce competition between France and England worked in favour of the Netherlands, and the leaders of the two provinces of Holland and Zeeland made "tireless attempts to move France and England to come to their aid [against Spain]".[13] In these ways, Dutch trade and commerce facilitated state formation.

In 1615, 94 per cent of the value of exports by the Dutch East India Company consisted of gold bullion. From 1660 to 1720, silver and gold bullion constituted, on average, 87 per cent of the Dutch East India Company's exports to Asia.[14] According to the Dutch scholar Karel Davids: "Most of the coins struck in the United Provinces did not come into circulation at home, however, but were used as trade coins in international transactions, especially after about 1660. Between 1660 and 1750, nearly 20% of all coins struck in the Netherlands were exported to Asia alone."[15] The sale and resale of gold, silver, and copper became essential to the financial dealings of the Dutch East India Company.[16] Silver quickly became the monetary standard of the world economy, although gold and copper were also regarded as legal currency.[17] Enslaved labour played a significant role in the mining of silver in the Americas.

Prior to the rise of silver as the most important medium of exchange between Asia and European traders in the global economy, it was impossible for one country to dominate and control all markets at the same time or to extract profits in an efficient manner. However, the key to European domination of markets was the steady supply of bullion from colonies in the Americas. Europeans shifted huge amounts of bullion across Asia and managed to position themselves as middlemen in intra-Asian trading circuits, most notably those between China and Japan in the period from the late 1500s to the early 1600s. This meant that, while Europe was importing large quantities of goods from Asia, the only major commodity it was able to export was currency. To do this, it was completely dependent on enslaved labour in the Americas. Without the Caribbean and American slave colonies, Europe would never have been able to maintain its position as a major trading partner with Asian countries and as an intermediary in the intra-Asian trade.[18]

In other words, whereas the East India company inserted itself into the already developed Asian market, the West India company specialised in the enslavement of Africans to produce goods that could be exchanged in Asia. This system also supported consumption at home and re-export abroad. Silver became the medium of exchange in Asia, and sugar the main product for consumption.

On the Institutionalisation of Chattel Slavery

The primary purpose of transporting Africans into slavery was the production of goods by the enslaved under the supervision of the enslavers.[19] Most scholars still refer to the enslavers as planters, though, as earlier noted, in practice they planted nothing.[20] It was the enslaved who chopped, planted, and harvested, and who carried, cooked, served, washed, and cleaned, so as to support the life and well-being of the enslavers on the plantations.[21] The enslaved, however, did not accept their condition and status without a fight. Some resisted passively, others collectively and actively. Where possible, some left the plantations to form their own maroon communities and, in the process, developed their own languages as forms of communication (see Brereton in this volume).

Dutch slavery shared many common elements with that in other societies established in the Americas, including the brutal transportation and enslavement of Africans, along with economic exploitation and political domination (see Allen in this volume). All slave societies developed or shared racist ideologies born out of daily practice and philosophical writings. European ideologies defined Africans and black people as mentally and intellectually inferior but physically superior, all the better to work in the burning tropical sun all day long.[22] But Dutch colonies also had their distinctive features. There were far fewer plantations and far smaller enslaved populations than in the Caribbean, the United States, and Brazil (see Brereton, Aragón Falomir, Silva Jr, and Kerr-Ritchie in this volume). This was simply because the Dutch could not outcompete the larger European nations. They therefore positioned themselves to spend far more of their energies and gain far more of their money and wealth from acting as intermediaries with larger nations. That meant transporting Africans and exporting and importing a wide range of products for the Spanish, the British, and other European imperial powers. By the time slavery was legally abolished by the Netherlands in 1863, the Dutch had transported more than 500,000 Africans into slavery.[23]

In the Caribbean, sugar is the product most closely associated with Atlantic slavery.[24] Under Dutch control, Suriname became a sugar-producing colony, though coffee was later introduced. Before this, the Dutch imported sugar from Brazil, where they had first controlled large swathes of land in the country's north-east. These lands were ceded to Portugal in the 1650s. Holland eventually secured control of Suriname, and the island became host to the largest enslaved population of any colony controlled by the Dutch. Some of the slavers in Brazil – especially a small but significant number of Jews – left Brazil, and became an influential presence in Suriname and the Dutch Antilles.[25]

Sugar industries had already been established in the Netherlands and were largely dependent on Brazilian sugar plantations before Suriname was acquired. In 1607, Amsterdam had three sugar refineries. This increased to 40 in 1650, declined to 20 in 1680, and jumped to 103 in 1787. Behind the refineries lay the enslaved labour of Suriname. Available evidence indicates that in 1713 an estimated 171 plantations were registered in Suriname. This grew to 294 plantations by 1745, and an estimated 406 in 1770, the number remaining relatively stable until the end of the eighteenth century. In the nineteenth century, the number of plantations fluctuated but always remained below 300.[26]

Sugar plantations dominated the Suriname economy until the mid-eighteenth century. Then, from 1745 onwards, coffee plantations emerged. Of the estimated 294 plantations recorded in 1745, 154 (52 per cent) were sugar plantations while 140 (48 per cent) were coffee plantations. In 1770, of the 406 plantations recorded, 295 (73 per cent) were producing coffee while 111 (27 per cent) produced sugar. Of the 389 plantations recorded in 1795, about 102 (26 per cent) were given over to sugar, 248 (64 per cent) to coffee, and 39 (10 per cent) to cotton. On the eve of the abolition of slavery, in 1862, there were 131 plantations in Suriname, of which 86 (66 per cent) were devoted to sugar,

30 (23 per cent) to coffee, and 15 (11 per cent) to cotton.[27]

Between 1701 and 1725, 45 tonnes of coffee were exported from Suriname to the Netherlands. This increased to 26,000 tonnes between 1726 and 1750, reaching a peak of nearly 138,000 tonnes, before declining to 30,000 tonnes between 1826 and 1850, and then to 3,000 tonnes between 1851 and 1863.[28] By 1820, there were no less than 416 plantations in Suriname producing coffee, sugar, cotton, and mixed crops.[29]

The Dutch also controlled six islands in the eastern Caribbean: Curaçao, Aruba, Bonaire, Sint Eustatius, Saba, and Sint Maarten.[30] Just as the Atlantic world became complementary to the Asian world, so the Antilles islands became complementary to Suriname in the larger slavery system. On these islands, physical conditions – including soil composition and drought – prevented the development of a plantation economy in the conventional sense of the word. In so far as one could speak of plantations, production was principally aimed at the Curaçao domestic market.

These islands, especially Curaçao, became key entrepôts for the transport of Africans to mainland South America. For example, between 1670 and 1730, the Dutch transported 100,000 African captives through Curaçao to be enslaved elsewhere – under the control of other European nations – in the Americas. Curaçao evolved into an important human bondage market and depot. Here, the enslaved economy had a transit function, not a production one: its intention was to import "seasoned" captives – which meant Africans "broken in" physically and mentally to make them pliable for enslavement – and forward them to plantations in other parts of the Caribbean and South America. The island was also notorious for its active contraband trade in weapons and captives.[31] This partly explains why the Dutch transported more African captives to the Americas – over 500,000 – than the Africans that they themselves enslaved. In this regard, the horrors of slavery under the Dutch were of a different kind from those under the British, the Portuguese, or the Spaniards.

Curaçao did produce some small-scale agricultural output for the domestic market. Maize, vegetables, and fruit were grown, and livestock included goats, sheep, cows, pigs, and some poultry. The owners of these territories could hardly be called "planters"; they were instead dairymen and greengrocers. When times were difficult and the enslavers did not have the necessary means to sustain the enslaved, the slave owner gave his slaves permission "to go work for a living".[32] Many of the enslaved worked as domestic slaves or were hired out by their enslavers as artisans and craftsmen and even as sailors.

These economic and ecological realities impacted on the composition of the population, as well as on enslaver–enslaved relations. "Coloured people" and the "free black" population lived on small parcels of land which they rented from the owners, on condition that they work a number of days every year for the landowner without pay (the so-called *paga-terra* system).[33]

On the islands of Sint Maarten and Sint Eustatius, sugar cane and cotton were cultivated on a small scale, but the salt pans were far more important. In fact, the production of salt was one of the major reasons that the Dutch sought colonies in the Caribbean. Both islands also produced some tobacco. Salt extraction involved heavy, seasonal work. On the island of Bonaire, too, the enslaved primarily worked on salt plantations belonging to the Dutch government.[34]

As we have noted, none of this implied that the enslaved accepted their position and status without a fight. Some resisted every day, while others left the plantations to form maroon communities and developed their own culture and languages, such as Papiamentu and Sranan Tongo, as a means of communicating with each other. We are still learning about the full nature and extent of this resistance.

There are three myths that can be found in Dutch scholarship about slavery.[35] All three are disingenuous.[36] First, some Dutch scholars insist that the country did not have many slaves. While it is true that the numbers enslaved in Dutch territories were far smaller than those in the United States, Brazil, and Jamaica, this is surely not the point. The fact is that the Dutch tried to develop large-scale plantations in Brazil, Suriname, and elsewhere – including New York – but were unable to compete with the British, Portuguese, and other empires. So, instead, Holland settled on an intermediate role vis-à-vis these larger nations, as described above. The Dutch also consumed significant amounts of the products produced by the enslaved in these other nations.

Second, some scholars insist that the Dutch did not make profits from the slave trade or slavery, that they even suffered losses. The evidence they provide for this argument is unconvincing. Besides, the issue is not one of profit and loss, but economic activity. Many companies fail to make profits – at least on the books – but, as with Dutch ships, plantations, and factors involved in slavery, they produced thousands of jobs, hundreds of thousands of products, and millions of guilders of income for Holland. This bounty was not just for those directly involved, but also for all the ancillary businesses in Amsterdam, Rotterdam, Middelburg, and elsewhere.[37]

Third, some Dutch scholars even insist that slavery was mild. This evokes all kinds of stereotypes of kind and gentle masters. The idea of "mildness", however, has no analytical value, and was invented merely to assuage Dutch guilt. In Curaçao, for example, the enslaved were worked to death, beaten, whipped, and sexually assaulted. After a slave rebellion in the territory led by Tula in 1795, he was brutally tortured and killed. If Dutch slavery really was so mild, why did so many enslaved run away, rebel, or revolt? (See Cobley and Brereton in this volume.)

On Legal Abolition and Progressive Control

The Napoleonic military occupation of the Netherlands in 1795–1813 sowed the seeds of the ending of Dutch involvement in the European slave trade and chattel slavery in the Caribbean. The French occupation denied the Dutch the opportunity to operate independently on the international stage. However, when Napoleon invaded and occupied the Netherlands in 1795, the Dutch National Assembly was confronted with two problems. The first was how to define and delineate the "new" nation under occupation. This raised the question of whether the nation should be limited to the territory agreed under the 1648 Treaty of Westphalia, or whether it should include the territories that had been acquired for slavery in the West Indies as well as for trade in Asia. As a result, a member of the Dutch National Assembly, Pieter Vreede, suggested that the issue of slavery and colonial possessions should be placed on the agenda. However, the issue disappeared as quickly as it had appeared.[38]

Available data indicates that between 1751 and 1775 the Dutch transported 118,200 kidnapped Africans for enslavement to the Caribbean and the Americas. However, between 1776 and 1800, this figure declined to 34,200. The opposite trend took place in France in the same period: France transported 321,500 Africans for enslavement between 1751 and 1775, and 419,500 between 1776 and 1800. This suggests that the French increased their share of transported slaves at the expense of the Dutch.[39]

The Napoleonic occupation took place against the backdrop of two developments: the successful anti-slavery revolt in Haiti in 1791–1804, and the suppression of a rebellion in Curaçao in 1795. The latter represented the culmination of previous anti-slavery revolts in Curaçao in 1745, 1747, 1748, and 1751. The French occupation also extended the wars of mainland Europe to the colonies in the Americas and the Caribbean. Thus, in the same period, Britain occupied Bonaire in 1804 and Curaçao in 1805. As part of its negotiations to regain its sovereignty and install a constitutional monarch, the Dutch were obliged to end their participation in the slave trade in 1814. Britain, however, kept Ceylon (Sri Lanka) and the Cape of Good Hope, and financially compensated the new Dutch king, Willem I.[40] The second major development was the declining "enslaved" population in Suriname owing to the British suppression of the slave trade. The number of enslaved people registered in Suriname in 1849 was 40,311; this declined to 36,501 by 1859.[41]

When Britain formally abolished the slave trade in 1807, it encouraged and persuaded other European countries to do the same. It was, therefore, not surprising that when London abolished chattel slavery in its Caribbean territories in 1838, the Dutch took Britain as a model, and started to prepare itself for abolition. Thus, in 1844, the Dutch established a commission to report on the state of the slave colony of Suriname. One of the conclusions of this report was that the enslaved population was in decline. The authors thus advised that, if the Dutch government wanted to maintain Suriname as a colony, it had first to abolish slavery. Holland heeded this advice and set in motion a process to end chattel slavery in Suriname and the Antilles.

Like the British, the Dutch also sought compensation for slave owners rather than the enslaved.[42] To justify their claims, the planter lobby in Suriname presented a petition to the Dutch Parliament that partly read:

> In the past, and not even very long ago, the government not only encouraged and protected but also made compulsory keeping and purchasing of slaves in the colony. Moreover, manumission was made difficult, and slaves were even forbidden to buy themselves free. So, slavery was then not only considered legal, but also protected; thus, the slave is the property of his master recognised by law.[43]

Chattel slavery was thus a state-sponsored institution in Dutch territories, and the enslavers were protected by their home government, which felt that it could not abandon them. This prompted a Dutch member of parliament, Elout van Soeterwoude, to question why the state was not also compensating the enslaved: "Would not [also] the slave be entitled to some compensation from his master – and from us in the Netherlands who permitted this injustice – for the bitter suffering that was passed on from father to son for two centuries?"[44]

In July 1862, the government presented its abolition proposal to the Dutch Parliament as a package with four components: first, the lifting of slavery in Holland's West Indian colonies; second, compensation for the owners of slaves; third, state control over freed slaves for ten years; and fourth, assisted immigration of indentured labourers from British-controlled India for a decade.[45] The first proposal was tied to the last, and was mediated through the second and the third. The reason for presenting the abolition proposals as a package was the feeling that a general vote against each of the four components could delay the abolition of the trade.

Though some Dutch parliamentarians objected to the package and considered it an act of intimidation by the government, they eventually went along with the proposals because they argued that slavery had become a curse and a stain on the honour of the Dutch nation.[46] The Dutch government then set the date for the abolition of slavery in its Caribbean territories as 1 October 1863. But, as a result of the debate and amendments, the date was moved forward to 1 July 1863. Second, the government proposed compensation for the enslavers. The planters demanded compensation of 400 guilders for every enslaved person who would be granted "freedom" under the abolition proclamation of 1 July 1863. But in the end, the parliament and government agreed to set different rates of compensation for the various territories: 300 guilders for Suriname; 250 guilders for Curaçao, Bonaire, Aruba, and Sint Eustatius; 200 guilders for Saba; and 150 guilders for Sint Maarten.

The government then proposed state control (*staatstoezicht*) – a kind of apprenticeship of former enslaved people – for ten years. There were reasonable arguments against state control, but the majority voted in favour. The *staatstoezicht* constituted "progressive" control, namely, accepting change but without sharing power with the victims of oppression. Finally, the government proposed the immigration of indentured labourers for a period of ten years, which the majority of parliamentarians supported.

In the end, the abolition of slavery became a means to an end: to maintain Suriname as an agricultural colony. When the decision was taken in August 1862 to end slavery a year later, and the news reached Suriname, the mood of the enslaved awaiting their emancipation was communicated by a Dutch missionary, Jansa, to an American newspaper as follows:

> The intelligence of the speedy emancipation of the negroes naturally awakens in me, who have so long laboured in this Colony, the most heartfelt joy. Having been requested by several planters to make known to their slaves the Proclamation of the Governor and the Emancipation law, I [Jansa] did so. They assembled, neatly dressed, in the church, and I tried to explain everything to them, getting them to repeat aloud all that I said, so that there might be no misunderstanding.

The joy and the praise of the poor Negroes were touching. They had previously heard, but refused to believe the news, saying: "The whites have deceived us so often!" But now that I made known truth and told them, it is really so, our Saviour has influenced the King and his counsellors to set you free on the first of July 1863, – they doubted no longer. Big tears of joy rolled down their black cheeks, and with jubilee joy they exclaimed: Our dear teacher tells us; we believe it; we will be free! What our mothers heard of before we were born, that is now come to pass, that we will see! Thanks, thanks unto God.[47]

It should be noted that the official proclamation of the abolition of slavery contained information on compensation for the enslavers. However, this information was omitted in the Suriname-language version which was communicated to the enslaved.[48]

A day after the proclamation, the editorial of the Dutch newspaper *Utrechtsch Provinciaal en Stedelijke Dagblad* stated: "Only where a civilisation is founded upon natural principles of freedom and equality, can prosperity and flourishing be expected in the long run. May this prosperity and flourishing become the destiny of our West Indian colonies so that in the future one will always – with even more joy – remember the first of July 1863 as the happy day in Dutch history, as a fortunate moment during the reign of Willem III."[49]

Instead of remembrance and commemoration by the Dutch, there was silence and denial. It was only 130 years later that the issue of slavery was brought to Dutch public attention. In July 1993, black people of Surinamese and Antillean descent – predominantly women – publicly commemorated the abolition of Dutch slavery in Amsterdam. This was followed by a formal request to the government for the erection of a monument where slavery could be commemorated annually. This goal was achieved in July 2002, and the event has been observed annually ever since.[50]

Concluding Reflections

This chapter has shed some light on the role of the Dutch in the enslavement of Africans in the Caribbean from the sixteenth to the nineteenth century. I have placed Dutch slavery within the broader context of state formation in Europe after the voyages of Christopher Columbus and Vasco da Gama. The Dutch were directly or indirectly entangled in the colonial adventures of Spain while they remained under Iberian domination. Thus, by the time Holland gained recognition of its sovereignty through the Peace of Westphalia in 1648, its subjugation of people in the Americas and the Caribbean through colonisation and slavery had become deeply entrenched. Viewed within this context, the transatlantic slave trade was a constituent part of Holland's Eighty Years War with Spain. Several treaties were agreed after Dutch independence, such as the Treaty of Breda in 1667 for the acquisition of Suriname, culminating in the Treaty of Utrecht in 1713, which consolidated Dutch territorial sovereignty.

Holland was involved in the kidnapping and transporting of more than 500,000 Africans into slavery across the Americas, before being forced out of this trade in 1814 after the end of the Napoleonic occupation of the Netherlands. The number of slaves transported was more than that of those enslaved, but this was a function of Holland's inability to outcompete larger European nations such as England, France, and Spain in the trade. The enslaved resisted their position and condition in many ways in their new homeland (see Brereton, Aragón Falomir and Silva Jr in this volume), and in the Caribbean and the Americas they created and moulded distinctive cultures.[51]

When Britain abolished slavery in the 1830s and the French in 1848, the Dutch were obliged to follow suit in 1863.[52] But this abolition was predicated on Suriname remaining a Dutch agricultural colony.[53] Thus, slavery was not abolished in the name of the "humanity" of enslaved Africans, as is often sanctimoniously claimed, but rather to maintain Suriname's colonial status.

The impact of slavery – and the European colonisation that led to the development of the transatlantic slave system – is actually far broader than is commonly acknowledged by Western scholars and in the popular media. The sugar, coffee, cotton, tobacco, rice, salt, and other goods produced by the enslaved directly shaped the consumption patterns of nations across Europe and the globe. These products also influenced tastes, fashions, and lifestyles. Shipping routes, maritime trade, and shipbuilding all developed during this period and beyond. Factories, work routines, and infrastructure – especially in port cities – across Western Europe were established as part of this colonial global network. Furthermore, the legal abolition of slavery did not lead to the emancipation of the enslaved. They continued to perform exploitative labour long after formal abolition. Finally, the political domination and economic exploitation of Africans and their descendants under slavery was consolidated and expanded under imperialism. European nations massively extended their penetration and occupation of vast swathes of Africa, as a result of the Berlin Conference of 1884–1885, which effectively set the rules for the partition of the continent (see Introduction in this volume).[54]

In the end, the Atlantic world economy strengthened European nations and directly helped and facilitated their colonisation of Asia and Africa. That is why a full and accurate evaluation of European chattel slavery and its legacies must be a far more comprehensive undertaking than has been rendered so far.

Part Four

Slavery in the Americas

11

Slavery in Lusophone America

Carlos da Silva Jr

DISCUSSIONS OF REPARATIONS should involve an analysis of the pervasive effects of slavery on Brazilian society. The establishment of Brazil's colonial society and the rise of African slavery in the Americas are intimately linked. About 45 per cent of the enslaved Africans who crossed the Atlantic disembarked in Brazil between the mid-sixteenth and the mid-nineteenth century, and were employed in plantations, mining, and urban settings. The transatlantic slave trade supplied Brazil with a labour force for 300 years, and the region's dependence on the African workforce is reflected in the resistance of slave owners to giving up the trade in human beings with Africa. Slavery continued after the abolition of the transatlantic slave trade in 1850, and Brazil was the last country in the Americas to abolish the institution in 1888. This chapter seeks to investigate the impact of slavery on Brazilian society and specifically on its black population.

As early as the sixteenth century, Portugal began the extraction of the red wood known as brazilwood in the new colony. In order to fell and transport the trees, Portuguese traders relied on the labour of the Amerindians in exchange for European tools and trinkets. Later, indigenous groups were enslaved and forced to work on sugar plantations (see Brereton in this volume). However, as sugar plantations expanded in the coastal zones of the north-east, requiring long-term labour and work discipline, new sources of slave labour were necessary. Resistance proved to be a challenge for Portugal's attempts to implement a system based on the forced labour of native peoples.[1] The

Crown then decided to use African slaves, a move that was not completely new, for they had been used in both the Portuguese Atlantic islands – namely the Azores and Madeira – and in Portugal itself. The slave trade allowed Portugal to exercise greater control over the colonists' access to labour, and presented an opportunity for profiting from the commodification of the African population.[2] With the development of the transatlantic slave trade, indigenous slavery was prohibited, except for captives acquired as a result of a "*guerra justa*" (so-called just war). But this is not to say that the enslavement of indigenous groups was completely abandoned. Catholic missionaries and colonists continued to exploit Amerindians well into the eighteenth century and even beyond, particularly in regions with limited access to African labour, such as the colony's northern areas.[3]

African slavery in Brazil began in the 1530s with the first shipments to Pernambuco and later to Bahia.[4] For almost a century Pernambuco was the centre of Brazil's major sugar plantations. This position lasted until 1630, when the Dutch, eager to control sugar production, conquered the most productive plantation zone of the Atlantic world at the time (see Nimako and Allen in this volume). In order to supply Pernambuco with African captives, the Dutch also conquered Portuguese strongholds on the African coast.[5]

Enslaved Africans performed the most demanding tasks in the fields. The labour regime worsened during the harvest season, when the mills were also active. Moreover, "physical coercion, the whip, and the threat of worse punishment were an integral part of the field management".[6] As a consequence, African mortality was higher than that of other groups such as Brazilian-born captives and free workers.

These African captives were named *negros da Guiné* (literally, blacks of Guinea), a generic term for African peoples in the early transatlantic slave trade, when Senegambia and adjacent regions – so-called Upper Guinea – supplied Portuguese merchants with captives.[7] But as knowledge of African regions increased, new terminologies were incorporated into the repertoire of ethnicities reconstructed in the Americas: the so-called African nations.[8]

South Atlantic exchanges between Brazil and west-central Africa (Kongo and Angola) marked the history of the Atlantic slave trade in the seventeenth century (see Coquery-Vidrovitch in this volume). Angola became the single most important source of slaves throughout the era of commerce in human trafficking. Between 1601 and 1700, west-central Africa lost as many as 1,134,807 people to the traffic, or 60.5 per cent of those transported across the Atlantic. Of these, 80 per cent ended up in Brazil. Brazilian dependence on

Angolan captives can be summed up in this sentence of a Jesuit priest in 1646: "Without Angola there is no Brazil."[9] Geribita (Brazilian rum) was a leading trade commodity in that African region, and gave merchants from Brazil an advantage over others. But the Dutch seizure of Pernambuco and of Portuguese entrepôts in Africa (Elmina, São Tomé and Príncipe, and Luanda) temporarily disrupted communication and traffic between the two regions. Similarly, the Dutch also realised the importance of Angola for the supply of captives, and at the suggestion of the Governor of Dutch Brazil, Johannes Moritz von Nassau-Siegen, Luanda was occupied in 1641. The reconquest of Angola in 1648 by a Portuguese fleet led by Rio de Janeiro's Governor, Salvador Correia de Sá e Benevides, provides additional evidence of the ties between Angola and Brazil.[10]

In a religious perspective, Father Antônio Vieira argued that the enslavement, displacement, and transportation of Africans to Brazil provided a means of salvation from "paganism" in Africa.[11] Similarly, Catholic theologians found a justification for African slavery even after they were baptised. This religious justification thus underlay the intensification of the slaving operations in Atlantic Africa.[12]

Africans and their descendants did not passively accept the oppression of slavery. Resistance began as soon as they were captured and taken to slave ships, and this rebellious attitude crossed the Atlantic. Resistance occurred everywhere in Brazil and took different forms, from sabotage to open rebellion, from individual flight to the formation of runaway communities (*mocambos* or *quilombos*). These communities flourished throughout Portuguese America, as the communications between Portuguese authorities make clear. Planters were particularly worried about the impact of these settlements on sugar production and slavery itself. *Quilombolas* (maroons) settled both in isolated areas and near urban centres where there was limited access for colonial forces. They developed an economy based on the cultivation of food crops and the exchange of their surplus in neighbouring villages. They also disrupted trading networks, attacking caravans and individual travellers on the roads and confiscating their goods.[13]

Quilombos varied in the number of members, but some constituted sizeable settlements. The best known was that of Palmares in the Serra da Barriga (in the modern Brazilian state of Alagoas), which remains a symbol of slave resistance to this day. It is not exactly known when Palmares was founded, but there is evidence that it already existed in the early seventeenth century. Its inhabitants numbered as many as 10,000 people, who belonged to different groups in the Portuguese colony: Africans and Brazilian-born captives, Indians, and even a few poor or outcast whites. Palmares presented a serious challenge to colonists and colonial authorities, as more and more slaves left the plantations to join it. Several Portuguese and Dutch expeditions were dispatched to defeat the *quilombo*, but they were unsuccessful. After decades of failure, the Portuguese decided to negotiate a treaty with its leaders, partially recognising their autonomy. This was similar to the story of Jamaican maroons (see Introduction and Brereton in this volume). As part of the deal, Palmares agreed not to accept new residents (particularly fugitive slaves). A few scholars have argued that the diplomatic relations between Portuguese colonial authorities and the leaders of Palmares provide evidence that the settlement was recognised by the former as an African kingdom that had been recreated in Brazil. However, not all leaders accepted the agreement, particularly Zumbi, who led the resistance until the final years of the seventeenth century. After Zumbi's death in 1695 and the final destruction of Palmares two years later, some of the residents were killed while others were re-enslaved. But the end of Palmares did not represent the end of slave resistance in the area, as many fled repression and organised new runaway communities.[14]

Urban Slavery in Eighteenth-Century Brazil

The establishment of sugar plantations in the Dutch, English, and French Caribbean in the mid-seventeenth century changed Brazil's position in international markets.[15] Yet sugar plantations and slavery continued to form the colony's economic basis until the late seventeenth century. As the Jesuit priest André João Antonil noted in the early eighteenth century, "slaves are the hands and feet of the *senhores de engenho* [plantation owners]".[16]

However, this changed with the discovery of gold in the south-east of Brazil in the 1690s. It also intensified the enslavement, commodification, and displacement of Africans. Miners required large numbers of enslaved workers, and Luso-Brazilian transatlantic traders were eager to meet their demands. This coincided with the re-establishment of commercial links between Brazil and the Bight of Benin after half a century of Dutch prohibition. Luso-Brazilian slavers bought human beings with the third-grade tobacco produced in Bahia, which was highly appreciated by African consumers, thus giving Bahian – and, to a lesser degree, Pernambuco – traders an advantage over those of other nations.[17] This also coincided with the rise of Dahomey as a major supplier of captives to European and American traffickers after the Dahomean conquest of the two leading regional states: the kingdoms of Allada (1724) and

Heuda (1727). The latter controlled Ouidah (Whydah), the second-largest African enslaving port in the era of the slave trade.[18]

With the integration of new African zones into the Atlantic slave trade, new ethnicities were incorporated into the mosaic of African nations in Brazil. Although the majority of the ethnic designations were generic, sometimes they described existing ethnic groups within Africa.[19] Slave owners came to understand and classify different groups according to their facial marks and psychological features (their propensity to adapt, to work, and to rebel).[20] Enslaved Africans in Brazil were also classified according to their skills and temperament. The concentration of enslaved Africans from similar ethnicities and the consequent possibility of slave revolts provoked widespread fear among masters, even though they would not abandon slavery as a labour system. Mina slaves – a term that encompassed different Gbe-speaking peoples from the Bight of Benin – for example, were regarded as particularly prone to rebellion. In the early seventeenth century, a group of Mina captives rebelled on board a slave ship, and fled as soon as the vessel landed in Bahia.[21] Later, in 1719, Mina and Angolan slaves plotted an uprising in Minas Gerais, which failed because they disagreed about who would assume the movement's leadership. Around 1736, the Governor of Rio de Janeiro, Luís Vahia Monteiro, confirmed the reputation Mina slaves had for rebellion.[22]

In spite of attempts to mix African ethnicities to prevent insurrections, the routes of the transatlantic slave trade reinforced the ethnic and linguistic homogeneity of different groups of captives. Besides, slave masters were particularly keen to obtain Mina slaves due to their physical strength and skills. Governor Monteiro declared that miners preferred Mina slaves owing to their "magic" skills in finding gold. Brazilian merchants in the meantime procured captives able to speak the *língua geral*: a pidgin based on various languages of the Gbe-speaking area (present-day Benin). The search for *língua geral* slaves was closely related to economic performance. As the Brazilian scholar Luiz Felipe de Alencastro has stressed: "the slaving culture pre-existing in the community conditioned the search for fresh slaves".[23] This facilitated the "seasoning" of the newly arrived (*boçal*) captive by other Gbe speakers who had previously landed in Brazil (*ladino*). This is not to say that masters were unaware of the dangers involved in their ethnic concentration. In 1741, a list was compiled of words and expressions from the so-called *língua geral de mina* in Brazil's Minas Gerais to help masters and overseers prevent rebellions.[24]

Slavery expanded into the urban centres in eighteenth-century Portuguese America. A French traveller who visited Salvador in Bahia early in the century described it as "new Guinea".[25] In fact, slavery was so widespread in Brazil's social fabric that a large proportion of rich and poor colonists owned slaves. Both African freedmen and -women were slave owners, and even the enslaved possessed slaves. The latter situation was not widespread but it was also not rare, which shows the perverse nature of the institution of slavery in Brazil.

Urban life in colonial Brazil relied heavily on skilled and unskilled enslaved workers. Brazilian-born slaves (Creoles) performed activities within the households, as well as more skilled occupations as bricklayers, carpenters, blacksmiths, shoemakers, and tailors. African men worked as porters, carrying goods or people in sedan chairs, while women sold fresh and cooked food. These workers were known as *ganhadores/ganhadoras* (earners). They enjoyed some freedom of movement, sometimes living on their own, but they had to share their weekly income with their owners. After years of hard work and judicious savings, some were able to buy their freedom.[26] The ways the enslaved purchased their manumission varied. They could accumulate enough money to pay a lump sum, or they could pay it in instalments. Many manumissions were tied to certain conditions, one of the most common being that they had to keep on working for their former masters until the latter died.[27] Several studies have demonstrated that manumission rates in Brazil were higher than in other slave societies in the Americas.[28] Yet most captives remained in captivity for their entire lives.

Slavery in Nineteenth-Century Brazil

Brazilian slavery experienced profound transformations at the turn of the nineteenth century. With the fall of Saint-Domingue, the world's leading sugar producer, Brazilian production expanded rapidly along with the transatlantic slave trade to Brazil.[29] For example, the traffic between Bahia and the Bight of Benin increased dramatically in the 20 years immediately after the Haitian Revolution (1791–1804), to meet the demand for enslaved Africans.[30]

The reorientation of the world economy in the nineteenth century had repercussions for the transatlantic slave trade and for slavery in the Americas. England, which became the world's leading power after Napoleon's defeat, abolished the transatlantic slave trade and forced other countries to do the same. However, the African slave trade, in particular, continued to provide labour for the production of sugar and (from the 1830s) coffee in Brazil, as well as sugar in Cuba to supply European markets: a phenomenon that the American scholar Dale Tomich has referred to as "second slavery".[31] In 1815, a treaty between Portugal and Britain prohibited slaving operations north of the Equator.[32] This agreement did not, however, prevent traders from procuring captives in West Africa. For a period of 15 years between 1815 and 1830 – the first period of illegality – Brazilian traders based in the northern part of the region developed strategies to circumvent this prohibition.[33] During this interval, at least 100,000 captives from the Bight of Benin were illegally introduced into Bahia, most of them of Yoruba origin. Brazil's independence from Portugal in 1822 did not alter the situation, as traders became fundamental to state formation in the following period.

Brazil's independence did not bring any improvements for the enslaved population. The new 1824 constitution offered limited citizenship to the freed population born in Brazil. In other words, there was no place in post-independence Brazilian society for African freedmen and -women as well as for captives of all origins, whether born in Brazil or in Africa. Thus, the denial of citizenship in the 1824 constitution replicated the segregation and exclusion in colonial times of the non-slave black population.[34]

The new country also had to deal with the problem of the transatlantic slave trade. In 1826, Brazil and England signed a new treaty aimed at ending, by March 1830, the trade in slaves from any part of Africa. In 1831, the Brazilian Parliament passed legislation to put an end to slaving activities in Africa. This ban jeopardised the trade with Angola, the major supplier of free African labour to Brazil. The traffic slowed for a few years but soon returned to its previous high numbers. The expansion of coffee production in the Paraíba River Valley (Vale do Paraíba), coupled with the demand for enslaved labour, encouraged Brazilian merchants to defy the British government's efforts to clamp down on the trade.[35] Powerful planters claimed that the ending of the trade in slaves would ruin their plantations and the Brazilian economy. Accordingly, Brazilian authorities made no real efforts to suppress the transatlantic slave trade, colluding with and supporting the disembarkation of thousands of African captives illegally transported to Brazil.[36] According to the Brazilian scholar Beatriz Mamigonian, "slave traders and buyers had adapted to illegality as authorities responsible for the repression created a protocol of connivance with the traffic".[37] For the second period of illegality between 1831 and 1850, almost 750,000 enslaved Africans entered Brazil, mostly from West and Central Africa.[38]

The abundant supply of African captives to Brazilian ports in the years immediately prior to the 1831 ban – a result of the forthcoming cessation of the trade – increased the demand for slaves by small and big consumers. This was a period in which manumissions by substitution grew substantially in number.

Under this system, newly arrived slaves were bought and trained by seasoned African or Creole slaves, and offered to their masters in exchange for their own manumission. The system was advantageous for both parties. On the one hand, slaves were able to buy cheaper captives in the market; on the other, masters could obtain younger slaves, fully trained and capable of performing the same tasks as the manumitted captives. Manumission by substitution rarely involved more than 5 per cent of slaves in the overall system, however. Although most studies of this phenomenon are concentrated in eighteenth- and nineteenth-century Bahia, it has also been observed in other Brazilian regions, though less so in other slave societies in the Americas.[39]

Another specific feature of nineteenth-century Brazil was the presence of *africanos livres* (liberated Africans) recaptured from illegal slave ships. Their status was quite ambiguous. They were legally free but they performed tasks designated for captives. According to Brazilian legislation, *africanos livres* had to undergo an apprenticeship period of up to 14 years before regaining their freedom. In reality, they were exploited as if they were slaves in all but name. Some *africanos livres* were assigned to public services, while others worked for locals. The latter often neglected their obligations – to pay a modest wage, for example – and, in some cases, they falsely reported their deaths when, in fact, they had been sold as slaves to the plantations in the Paraíba Valley or elsewhere. There was no guarantee of their freedom after the period of apprenticeship. Some remained "in slavery" for 20 years or more, while others never regained their freedom. But *africanos livres* frequently complained about their condition, and records that survive reveal the precariousness of their freedom in Brazil, which was a point of permanent tension between Brazilian and British authorities.[40]

Slavery in Brazil must also be understood in the light of political and religious events in West Africa, whose repercussions were felt on the other side of the Atlantic. The 1804 Fulani *jihad* in the interior of the Bight of Benin – namely Hausaland and its neighbours – resulted in the enslavement of thousands of prisoners of war who were sold to Bahian slave traders; the latter practically dominated the commerce in human cargo in the region at this time. These captives – mostly of Hausa origin – were to lead the first wave of slave rebellions that took place in Bahia between 1807 and 1816.[41]

A second wave of slave rebellions shook Bahia from the early 1820s. These were led and waged mainly by the Nagô, as Yoruba-speaking peoples were known in Bahia. The influx of Yoruba slaves brought into Bahia was the result of the civil wars that led to the disintegration of the Oyo empire in West Africa in the nineteenth century. Many were *imale*, as Yoruba Muslims were known (Malê in Bahia). They launched a series of slave uprisings in Salvador and the Recôncavo. The most well-known – the 1835 Malê Rebellion – brought as many as 600 enslaved and freed Yoruba rebels onto the streets of Salvador. Yoruba Muslims, both enslaved and freed, were the leaders of the movement, but people of different ethnicities and non-Muslim Yoruba also participated in it. As the Brazilian scholar João José Reis has stressed: "the rebellion was a complex, multifaceted movement, conceived primarily by enslaved individuals, who sought freedom in the first place and faced a powerful enemy, against whom they had to mobilise people and groups committed to Islam in varying degrees, or even uncommitted to a religious purpose".[42] For a few hours, these Africans, armed with swords and other weapons, instilled terror in the Bahian population. The rebellion was soon suppressed, but it demonstrated the organisational potential of the African enslaved and freed populations.

Local authorities rapidly took control measures, such as the mass deportation to Africa of freed individuals suspected of involvement in the rebellion.[43] The settlement of former slaves in West Africa's coastal zones (Ouidah, Porto-Novo, and Lagos) was central to the formation of communities of African returnees in the Bight of Benin during the nineteenth century. Commercial and religious interests also responded to the return flow of freed Africans to their homeland.[44] South-east Brazil experienced further slave rebellions, such as the 1832 slave rebellion in Campinas and the Manuel Congo revolt of 1838 (which also had a religious dimension) on the coffee plantations of Rio de Janeiro.[45] Five years earlier, the slave uprising in Carrancas, Minas Gerais, had led to a debate about stricter punishment for slaves who threatened their owners. But the Malê uprising was key to the Brazilian Parliament's approval of the death penalty for slaves accused of conspiring against their masters.[46]

The religious affiliation of Africans was not restricted to Islam. They re-elaborated and reconstructed their native religions in the diaspora. For example, Calundu and later Candomblé, religious expressions brought from the Jeje (Gbe) and Nagô (Yoruba) nations, contributed significantly to the institutionalisation of Candomblé in Brazil.[47] And although each nation performed different religious rites, their specialists circulated among the various traditions. Some priests such as the *babalaô* Domingos Sodré, of Yoruba origin – Nagô, therefore – became famous in nineteenth-century Bahia, and there was a regular circulation of religious leaders between Bahia, Pernambuco, Rio de Janeiro, and West Africa.[48] Candomblé practitioners experienced intense persecution, for authorities believed in a connection between Candomblé and slave rebellions. In fact, the relationship between religion and slave resistance should not be ignored, but it must be understood as spiritual and cultural rather than a form of traditional resistance to slavery.[49]

With the definitive ending of the Brazilian slave trade in 1850, coffee planters began to import captives from sugar-growing north-eastern regions of Brazil. For slaves, this was a period of insecurity in which slave families could easily be separated. The internal slave trade lasted until the final decades of Brazilian slavery.[50] However, things changed from 1871. The *Lei do Ventre Livre* (Free Womb Law) ruled that individuals born after that date (*ingênuos*) should be free, although they remained under the control of their mothers' masters for a period of 21 years from birth.[51] In practice, these individuals stayed enslaved, and many only obtained their freedom close to the final date of abolition in 1888. The Free Womb Law also offered some protection for captives, preventing families from being broken up. Moreover, legal conditions were established that allowed slaves to purchase their manumission even against their masters' will. Many captives took their masters to courts of law in order to have their rights recognised, and as a result *ações de liberdade* (manumission cases) flooded courts across Brazil.[52]

A decade after the passing of the Free Womb Law, the abolition movement, which had abated in 1870, returned with full force in Rio de Janeiro, the Brazilian Empire's capital, and the provinces. Since the 1980s, Brazilian scholars have challenged the hitherto dominant interpretation of the role of white activists in Brazilian abolitionism. The work by black historians has also focused on the agency of the enslaved in pressing for the ending of slavery in different ways, including flight from plantations and rebellions. Popular participation was driven by labour organisations that fomented slave rebellions, and mutual aid societies formed by "people of colour" purchased the manumission of their members.[53] Abolitionist newspapers fought slavery, contributing to the dissemination of the cause of abolition, while abolitionist societies were created in different parts of Brazil. Black and white Brazilian writers such as Machado de Assis, Joaquim Manuel de Macedo, Bernardo Guimarães, and Maria Firmina dos Reis denounced racial discrimination within Brazilian society.[54] Other black activists such as José do Patrocínio, André Rebouças, and Luiz Gama launched fiery debates in the press in defence of freedom.[55] Luiz Gama, a famous unofficial lawyer, was himself a victim of the internal slave trade, and worked on several trials, including some related to the 1831 law. He contested the illegal enslavement of those who arrived after 1831 when the slave trade was already illegal, with some success.[56]

Concluding Reflections

The slave population across Brazil declined significantly in the 1880s, though the rate of decline differed from area to area. Discussion about the ending of Brazilian slavery was widespread in the provinces, and was debated in the parliament, in abolitionist newspapers, and on the streets of the country's largest cities. Aside from this, slave revolts in the expanding coffee areas of Campinas and São Paulo terrified slave masters and authorities.[57] But they were not willing to give up their captives. Slave masters attempted to delay abolition as long as possible. However, in May 1888, Princess Isabel signed the *Lei Áurea* (Golden Law) which ended slavery in Brazil. For many years, abolition was seen as Isabel's personal feat. In the last few decades, however, Brazilian historians such as Robert Daibert Jr and Renata Moraes have demonstrated that her signature was the result of decades of pressure for the ending of slavery in Brazil.[58] With abolition, the Brazilian Empire lost political support, especially from landowners and since it came without compensation. It is no coincidence that the imperial regime fell a year later following a military coup.

The abolition of slavery was celebrated in Brazilian cities and villages in the interior. However, it produced tensions between former masters and former enslaved men and women. As the Brazilian scholar Wlamyra Albuquerque has noted: "the ending of slavery did not only represent the loss of property [in human beings], but of fundamental references in the formation of the slaveowners' identity".[59] Former captives negotiated new and not always acceptable conditions with landowners in order to remain on the properties where they had served as slaves. These conditions included access to land to cultivate their own crops, and the establishment of a weekly routine in the plantations that would not include Sundays and Catholic holidays. Others decided to leave the plantations with their memories of punishment and oppression. They migrated to small and larger urban centres, often leaving the provinces where they had lived until then.[60] Former masters felt that their authority had eroded, and tried to re-establish it through violence, as some episodes of physical punishment of freed individuals demonstrated.[61]

But "scientific" racial theories – already in the making since the mid-nineteenth century – were incorporated into the discourses and practices of Brazilian society. At the same time, the immigration of North European workers from the mid-nineteenth century was seen as an instrument of civilisation and "whitening" of Brazilian society. The supposed inferiority of black people provided a justification for discrimination and the denial of full citizenship to blacks. Nineteenth-century racialisation was critical to the construction of racial hierarchies in Brazilian society, even before emancipation.[62] The effects of racism that pervaded imperial Brazil continued long after independence, and today, more than 130 years after abolition, Brazil's black people continue to fight for the recognition of their rights as full citizens.[63]

12

Slavery in the United States

Jeffrey R. Kerr-Ritchie

SLAVERY WAS FOUNDATIONAL to the United States. In 1789, 13 former English colonies – now states – ratified the US Constitution. Because these states both legalised and illegalised slaveholding, nationhood demanded several compromises.[1] Article I, section 2 apportioned popular representation and direct taxation among the states according to the population of each, which was determined by adding the numbers of free persons and "three fifths" of all other persons (i.e. slaves). It increased the representation of southern slave states in the US Congress, and decreased the population of slave states for taxation purposes. Article I, section 8 authorised the assembly of militias to "suppress insurrections". It provided federal power to stamp out popular revolts, including those fomented by slaves. Article I, section 9 declared that the importation of slaves would not be "prohibited" prior to 1808. This resulted in a temporary increase in slave imports. The Carolinas and Georgia imported more than 71,000 captive Africans between 1790 and 1810.[2] Article 4, section 2 required fugitive slaves crossing state borders to "be delivered", if claimed by slave owners. This illustrated federal cooperation in protecting property rights in humans, regardless of whether states allowed or disallowed slaves.

Slaveholders

Over the next several decades, slave states massively expanded their political power. Louisiana (1812), Mississippi (1817), Alabama (1819), Missouri (1821),

Arkansas (1836), Florida (1845), and Texas (1845), which all recognised chattel slavery, joined the Union.[3] At the same time, slaveholders dominated the executive branch of government. Five of the first seven US presidents between 1789 and 1832 were slaveholders. George Washington owned 123 slaves until his demise in 1799.[4] James Monroe owned 49 slaves.[5] Moreover, the highest court in the antebellum United States was dominated by jurists such as Chief Justice John Marshall, Associate Justice Joseph Story, and Chief Justice Roger Brooke Taney. All believed that US slavery should be left untouched, and that abolitionists threatened the nation's stability.[6] They brushed aside the idea that slaveholders threatened the Union.

American slaveholders also wielded unprecedented economic power. In 1790, American cotton output was a mere 3,000 bales.[7] By 1860, US production topped 3,841,000 bales. Cotton exports earned $192 billion – about four times the federal government's revenue. During the 1850s, slave-produced cotton exports accounted for more than half of all US exports.[8] When one South Carolina senator famously declared that "Cotton was King!", he was referring to the region's economic clout nationally. The result was the dramatic entry of the United States on the world's economic stage. At the heart of this production process were enslaved workers on plantations and farms in a region whose native peoples had been displaced by new seekers of the "white gold".

Owing to the Haitian Revolution (1791–1804),[9] France was forced to sell its Louisiana territories to the United States. Countless American schoolchildren have been taught about this "bargain". The reality, however, was that Napoleon's power in North America had been severely curtailed as the result of a successful slave rebellion. Moreover, the Spanish colony of Florida was invaded and successfully conquered by American forces led by General Andrew Jackson in 1819. Consequently, indigenous people were forcibly removed from their lands in the south-eastern Atlantic and Gulf territories. The Creek, Cherokee, Choctaw, and Seminole nations were militarily defeated or pressured into signing unequal treaties with the US government. The subsequent land annexations facilitated the expansion of America's cotton and slave empire across the Mississippi Valley.[10]

Along with the dispossession of native peoples, there was technological transformation. In 1786, planters in Georgia grew the first long-staple cotton. This silky yarn was in great demand by manufacturers in Britain. After the Haitian Revolution, cotton production for European factories largely ceased. French slaveholders emigrated to the American South, which increased cotton production. New varieties of the fibre were grown in upland regions, including short-staple cotton whose fibre is wrapped around the small black seeds. These seeds often jammed the gins, thus slowing the production process. The New England inventor Eli Whitney solved the problem with his new cotton gin, which removed these seeds, paving the way for the massive expansion of short-staple cotton production in the American South.[11]

After technological change and the dispossession of native people, the expropriation of unfree labour was the third dynamic in the making of America's cotton and slave empire. The decline of tobacco and wheat economies in the Upper South contrasted with the explosive expansion of cotton in the Lower South. Between the early 1800s and 1850s, an estimated one million enslaved men, women, and children were relocated across the American South. A third of them were marched overland as part of migratory planter households. In 1834, 44 slaves owned by Henry Tayloe were transported across the Appalachian Mountains from south-west Virginia into Tennessee and southward to Alabama to work on a new cotton plantation.[12] The majority of relocated captives, however, were sold and bought by professional slave traders in Baltimore, Richmond, Charleston, and New Orleans, before being transported in chained coffles overland. Some captive women experienced sexploitation during these forced marches. Hundreds of thousands of captives were forced to make new lives, adjust to new harsh realities, and survive this forced relocation to a new and hostile environment where profitability determined life itself.[13] Recent research on the antebellum American slave trade reveals that more than 50,000 captives were moved in hundreds of slave ships like the *Comet, Encomium, Enterprise, Hermosa*, and the *Creole* from Chesapeake Bay ports to coastal entrepôts in the Gulf Sea as part of this massive forced relocation of unfree labour.[14]

The cotton and slave empire could not have existed without external demand from Europe, especially Britain. Between 1770 and 1831, cotton manufacturing increased from more than 2 per cent to over 22 per cent of the value of the British economy. By 1831, one in six labourers worked in the cotton industry. Two decades later, 3.5 million Britons found employment in the country's cotton industry. King Cotton's retainers, then, stretched from factory workers in Britain to finance capitalists in New York and plantation owners in the American South.[15] The political economy of cotton and slaves reached its apogee in the 1850s.

Slaves

What was it like to have been enslaved during the antebellum era? Most respondents would probably echo the seventeenth-century English philosopher Thomas Hobbes, who spoke about life being nasty, brutish, and short. While European serfs, Asian indentured servants, and factory operatives were all embroiled in exploitative labour regimens, they were not enslaved.

Work was central to the slave experience, but it varied across time and space. Working in the sugar and cotton fields in the new south-western states was much harsher than working in the wheat and tobacco fields in the older states of Maryland and Virginia. A former slave, Frank Bell, recalled: "Growed mostly wheat on de plantation, an' de men would scythe and cradle while de women folks would rake and bind."[16] The tobacco regime of the slaves consisted of a long and tedious set of tasks – burning plant beds, sowing seeds, making hills, transplanting seeds to beds, topping, worming, cutting, curing, stripping, tying, and packaging for market.[17] In contrast, cotton was an even harder taskmaster, especially because it was so profitable. Its regime consisted of an endless routine of preparing and sowing beds, frequent hoeing, cotton picking, and sundry other tasks. A former slave, John Brown, who self-emancipated (ran away) and later wrote his life story, observed: "When the price [of cotton] rises in the English market, even but half a farthing a pound, the poor slaves immediately feel the effects, for they are harder driven, and the whip is kept more constantly going."[18]

Moreover, work in the plantations contrasted sharply with the labour of enslaved craftsmen and artisans. They included coopers, blacksmiths, shoemakers and clothmakers, builders, caulkers, and designers. Most skilled slaves were employed by their owners, while the rest were either hired out or apprenticed to free craftsmen. Their importance grew as southern cities expanded, with significant numbers of enslaved craftsmen working in Richmond, Charleston, Savannah, and New Orleans. The scarcity of white artisans – due to high wage expectations and rapid turnover because of high demand – made enslaved artisans possible.[19] Their expertise offered a quotidian refutation of the ideology of racial inferiority, according to which slaves could *only* work on plantations.

Similarly, slaves who were hired out to work in either tobacco factories in Richmond, Petersburg, and Baltimore or on board merchant ships had different work experiences from those on plantations and in workshops. Slaves in tobacco factories laboured long hours in hot, noisy, and dangerous conditions where injuries were common.[20] Hired slaves aboard ships faced hazardous weather conditions, poor diets, familial separation, and draconian control from the officer class.[21] But these workplaces permitted degrees of autonomy for slaves removed from the watchful eye of gang overseers in the cotton, tobacco, and wheat fields.

Despite these contrasting work experiences, there were some key commonalities among the enslaved. As only Africans were imported as slaves into the United States, slavery became a racialised system of economic exploitation. Because they were property, all slaves were taxable at local, state, and federal levels. These tax laws recognised slaves as chattel rather than colonial subjects or republican citizens. Indentured servants worked off several years of a contract, but slaves were the only labourers who were legally required to work for life: *durante vita*.

Most importantly, slaves laboured without compensation in contrast to free labour, which was rewarded with wages and the potential of success, fortune, and upward mobility. As the Reverend Garrison Frazier, a 67-year-old former slave and Baptist elder, succinctly put it: "Slavery is receiving by *irresistible power* the work of another man, and not by his *consent*. The freedom ... is taking us from under the yoke of bondage, and placing us where we could reap the fruit of our own labor."[22] His definition mixed biblical allusion with the theory of labour surplus value in interesting ways. The key point, though, is that uncompensated labour left a legacy of wealth for free European Americans that was denied to generations of enslaved African Americans, who neither accumulated nor passed on the fruits of their labour to their heirs.

Gender further complicated the picture. On the one hand, women and girls laboured in the plantation economies of the antebellum South. Women worked in the tobacco and wheat fields of Virginia, Maryland, and Kentucky,[23] while women and girls worked in the cotton and sugar fields of the Lower South. According to its manifest listing captives aboard, the slave ship *Creole* transported 74 male and 61 female captives intended for the cotton and sugar fields of the Lower South.[24] In short, there was a limited sexual division of slave labour in agricultural production. Every enslaved person experienced labour exploitation and was denied the fruits of their labour.

But it was enslaved women and girls who were primarily the victims of sexploitation. The abuse by white men of black female slaves took two major forms in the South. The first was extensive sexual violence in slaveholding households, in coffles, aboard ships transporting slaves southward, and elsewhere. Both slave narratives and subsequent interviews with former slaves testify to this ubiquitous maltreatment, although the more lurid and salacious details were often suppressed by older generations of African American narrators.

Enslaved women's bodies were also exploited for the reproduction of slave populations. Between 1810 and 1860, the slave population in the United States expanded from more than 1.1 million to over 3.9 million.[25] As a result of the ending of the American transatlantic slave trade in January 1808, demographic growth could not depend on continued imports of enslaved Africans into the United States. Rather, it was primarily due to enslaved women not being allowed to control their own bodies. For several decades, female slaves experienced high fertility rates. At the same time, birth rates exceeded mortality rates, as enslaved people lived for longer. Scholars often cite better nutrition, less harsh work regimes, and epidemiological resistance to pathogens through native birth as explanations for the longer lifespans and greater fertility rates of enslaved women in the American South. Their aim has been to try to understand why enslaved women in the United States experienced higher fertility rates and lower mortality rates than those of enslaved women in the Caribbean and in Brazilian slave societies.[26]

We should not, however, overlook the role of force in this reproductive process. Rose, enslaved in Texas, recalled how her new owner fed her well, housed her well, and did "not force 'em to work too hard". After a year, "De massa come to me and say 'You gwine live with Rufus in dat cabin over yonder'." Rufus tried to sleep with her, but Rose defended herself with a poker. Next day, Rose told the mistress, who replied: "De massa wants you-uns fer to bring forth portly chillen."[27] There is thus little doubt that innumerable enslaved women's progeny resulted from the carnal desires of slave owners. Moreover, Rufus was also a victim of sexual abuse, although clearly not to the same degree as Rose.[28]

The best sources for the range of experiences of slaves emanated from those formerly enslaved. More than 200 autobiographies were produced or co-written by former slaves. Their primary aim was to challenge paternalistic depictions of American slavery and to promote anti-slavery activities for the purpose of terminating the system. Many readers are familiar with Frederick Douglass's best-selling *Narrative of the Life of Frederick Douglass* (1845),[29] but there were many other powerful and eloquent ex-slave narratives. Questions have been raised about the authorship of some of this literature, as well as the propaganda content of others. But their voices are indispensable to any serious and measured understanding of the difficult-to-define experience of being enslaved. These works have been rightly characterised as classics of American literature.[30]

Moreover, African American scholars at Nashville's Fisk University and elsewhere revived interest in the lived experiences of slaves during the 1920s. This culminated in the remarkable efforts of the Federal Writers Project of the Works Project Administration, which interviewed more than 2,300 surviving former slaves in 17 US states between 1936 and 1938. Their recollections are fraught with all sorts of issues including memory loss, presentism, and childhood recollections that produced a more benign view of slavery. But like published slave narratives in the antebellum South, the testimonies of these survivors remain indispensable for understanding the complicated nature of slave experiences.[31]

In 1860, all those enslaved in the United States were of African descent, but not all African-descended people were enslaved. According to the US census returns, there were just under 262,000 free Negroes in 15 states and the District of Columbia. These southern African Americans were mostly concentrated in Maryland, Virginia, and North Carolina.[32] They often inhabited urban centres like Baltimore, Richmond, Charleston, Mobile, and New Orleans. They were both male and female, although the latter were numerically greater. They were both propertied and propertyless. Some black men at or over 21 years old exercised the suffrage. There were, for example, 300 African American voters in Halifax County and 150 in Hereford County, North Carolina, in 1835.[33] As a result of several factors – the expansion of southern slavery, the emergence of an organised abolitionist movement, and slave conspiracies and insurrections – the civic position of free blacks became increasingly undermined. African Americans in the South were prevented from entering other states, were barred from owning real estate, were not allowed to vote, and were precluded from testifying in court. This legal denial of civic rights was buttressed by local custom and prejudice. It was this decline in their civic status that provided demonstrable proof of the inaccuracy of Chief Justice Roger Taney's argument in his notorious 1857 Dred Scott decision that Negroes in the United States had no citizenship rights.

The precarious condition of liberty in a slave society encouraged many southern African Americans to emigrate. In 1816, the American Colonization Society (ACS) was formed. Its underlying premise was that the United States was for European Americans only and that African Americans could never achieve racial equality in their own country. In 1822, the ACS established the settlement of Liberia on the West African coast. The organisation attracted numerous African American settlers, especially from Maryland and Virginia, who ended up becoming a dominant Americo-Liberian class. They declared independence in 1847 and penned a constitution based on the 1789 US model. Its glaring difference from the latter was the illegality of slavery. Over the next several decades, some 20,000 settlers – including African Americans, manumitted slaves, and Africans liberated from US slave ships – populated Liberia.[34]

Greener pastures for Americans of African descent were also identified elsewhere. Mary Ann Shadd, born free in Wilmington, Delaware, emigrated to Canada in 1851.[35] The following year, she penned *A Plea for Emigration, or, Notes on Canada West* with the aim of attracting free African Americans and fugitive slaves across the border.[36] Martin R. Delany, born free in Pittsburgh, was accepted by and attended Harvard Medical School for several months before being dismissed for being black. In 1852, he penned and self-published *The Condition, Elevation, Emigration and Destiny of the Colored People of the United States*.[37] After castigating the nation's practice of racial inequality, he concluded with a call to young people to "take their position on the stage of Central and South America, where a brilliant engagement of certain and most triumphant success"[38] awaited them. The legal termination of American slavery in 1865 did not end these utopian schemes. However, post-emancipation struggles for racial equality and civic incorporation shifted efforts towards transforming American society.

Slave Rebellions

In *The Myth of the Negro Past* (1941), the American anthropologist Melville Herskovits pointed to the many contemporary accounts of slave revolts, noting that he found the idea of the docile slave "surprising".[39] Around the same time, the American Marxist historian Herbert Aptheker estimated that more than 250 slave revolts and conspiracies took place from seventeenth-century Virginia to the American Civil War.[40] Since then, historians have devoted individual book-length studies to many of these rebellions: Charles Deslondes's rebellion in 1811 Louisiana; Nat Turner's in 1831 Virginia; Madison Washington's in 1841 aboard the *Creole*, and so forth.[41] In addition, there are works on revolutionary attempts to overthrow American slavery by the radical abolitionist John Brown and his followers.[42] Moreover, studies have been made of plots and conspiracies that were either prematurely discovered or betrayed, such as slave artisan Gabriel's planned rebellion in 1800 Richmond and free carpenter Denmark

Vesey's in 1822 Charleston.[43] Winthrop Jordan's remarkable detective work in revealing a major slave conspiracy in Adams County, Mississippi, in 1861, which was covered up for fear of contagion, raises the question of how many other plots were silenced.[44] There is little doubt that future research will uncover more slave revolts, conspiracies, and rumours. In sum, there was a long tradition of slave revolts against American slavery.

Between 1789 and 1850, American politicians successfully compromised over the divisive issue of slavery. The election of Abraham Lincoln to the presidency in 1860, however, ended this pattern. Slaveholders rebelled against the new Republican administration. They viewed the president as the thin end of an abolitionist wedge which would overthrow their political and economic power. Although Lincoln was not an abolitionist, southern slaveholders succeeded in leading their states out of the Union. As one North Carolina lawyer reported in response to the president's call for volunteers to put down the insurrection: "Lincoln had done nothing wrong, nothing unconstitutional, nothing but what his oath of office constrained him to do." This "present war", he added, will "make the poor man poorer, and the rich man richer."[45]

The most significant political crisis in nineteenth-century American history provided a further opportunity for slaves to rebel. This view – what can be called the "Great American Slave Rebellion" – is best understood through three components: the mass desertion of slaves from farms, plantations, and urban areas during wartime; the employment of former slaves as federal workers; and their service in the US military.[46] In short, the 1860s witnessed less of an American Civil War than a slaveholders' rebellion against the United States in search of new nationhood and an uprising by enslaved people seeking liberty at an opportune moment. In May 1861, General Benjamin F. Butler wrote to US General-in-Chief, Winfield Scott, from Fort Monroe, south-east Virginia: "Up to this time I have had come within my lines men and women with their children – entire families – each family belonging to the same owner ... I am in the utmost doubt what to do with this species of property."[47] General Butler's "doubt" arose from his need to obey the 1850 Fugitive Slave Act, requiring federal support in returning slaves to their masters (slave states like Maryland and Kentucky stayed in the Union, thus requiring observance of the federal law), yet doing so would aid the slaveholders' rebellion. His devious solution was to confiscate slaves as "contraband" of war. By the war's end in 1865, some 750,000 self-emancipators had entered Union lines. Their wartime movements represented a barefoot plebiscite on US slavery.

Once in Union camps, they worked in support of the American war effort to defeat slaveholder rebels. By the spring of 1865, at least 474,000 former slaves and free African Americans were working for the federal government as urban labourers, agricultural workers, camp workers, and soldiers. Some women found employment as laundresses, cooks, seamstresses, and hospital attendants. They were now free and could transition towards liberty and even civic incorporation. At the same time, they encountered difficulties as federal workers. Old black people and children had less chance to earn a living. Some federal employees received their wages late or not at all. Some women experienced abuse and sexual violence. Some eventually fled these federal workplaces in the same way they had fled slavery originally.[48]

Finally, former slaves, together with free African Americans and Afro-Canadians, worked in a military capacity for the federal government. By 1865, nearly 180,000 men had served in the United States Colored Troops (USCT), and about 18,000 men and several dozen women had served in the Union navy.[49] Some recruits were free African Americans from southern and northern cities. Others came from across the border in Canada. William Clark, a 24-year-old waiter born in Canada, enlisted aboard the USS *Rachel Seaman*. Thomas Crafford, a 27-year-old labourer, enlisted in the 25th USCT, before deserting and returning to Canada. James Donnell, a 35-year-old labourer, also enlisted in the 25th USCT, but was to perish in July 1865.[50]

Most USCT members, however, were former slaves who had absconded from southern slavery. Some 32,671 enlisted from northern free states. About 41,719 enlisted from Union slave states, and 98,594 enlisted from Confederate slave states.[51] Moreover, far from "performing only garrison duty", as William Dobak's *Freedom by the Sword* erroneously argues, the military duties of black soldiers included "offensive and defensive battles, sieges, riverine and coastal expeditions, and cavalry raids".[52] About 36,000 black soldiers died serving to keep the Union together. This represented one in six of all enlistees. Most were former slaves, and most died from disease.[53]

The US military both trained and ordered former slaves and free African Americans to shoot and kill southern rebels – including former slave owners. What had once constituted legal grounds for execution was now the federal law of the land. Abolitionists hailed this glorious turnaround, while white southerners condemned these slave rebels. But serious issues emerged regarding federal recruitment. Black soldiers – who were originally paid the same wage as white soldiers – had their wages reduced from $16.50 to $6 a month, while the pay of white soldiers stayed at the original rate. They protested and refused to accept the inferior wage. Company D of the 55th

Massachusetts Infantry petitioned President Lincoln in July 1864: "We came to fight For Liberty justice & Equality. These are gifts we Prise more Highly than Gold For these We Left our Homes our Familys Friends & Relatives most Dear to take as it ware our Lives in our Hands To Do Battle for God & Liberty."[54] The wage scales were eventually returned to their original parity. Moreover, black troops faced numerous challenges, including racist contempt and well-meaning paternalism from white officers. They also experienced a greater number of disciplinary actions for mutiny, disobeying orders, and resisting unfair military practices.[55]

And then there was southern retribution for black enlistment. Testifying before a court at Camp Nelson, Kentucky, Patsey Leach reported: "When my husband was Killed my master whipped me severely saying my Husband had gone into the army to fight against white folks and he my master Would let me know that I was foolish to let my husband go, he would 'take it out of my back', he would 'Kill me by piecemeal' and he hoped that the last one of the nigger soldiers would be Killed."[56]

Nine months later, the 13th Amendment to the US Constitution was ratified in December 1865. It read: "Neither slavery nor involuntary servitude, except as a punishment for crime whereof the party shall have been duly convicted, shall exist within the United States, or any place subject to their jurisdiction." This had been preceded by abolition in Washington DC (1862) and Maryland (1864). In contrast, slavery died a slower death elsewhere. Isabella Boyd, a former slave in Texas who was interviewed during the 1930s, recollected: "When we all gits free, they's the long time letting us know."[57] But American slavery's legal termination ended the constitutional protection of property in humans, as well as its economic and political bases. The rebellion of slaves succeeded, but the slaveholders' rebellion failed. Moreover, the victory overthrew the largest slaveholding regime in the Americas. There is little doubt that the days of the unfree system in Spanish Cuba and Portuguese Brazil (see Ramirez and Silva Jr in this volume) were numbered after slavery's termination in the hemisphere's most powerful nation.

Concluding Reflections: Legacies of Slavery

Slavery has been taught quite benignly to generations of Americans. Textbooks have ignored its importance, cast it aside as incidental, or viewed it as an unfortunate legacy bequeathed by British colonialism. Fictional treatments like Margaret Mitchell's *Gone with the Wind* (1936)[58] depicted a moonlight-and-magnolias past replete with happy slaves. Its 1939 film adaptation remains one of the most watched movies in the United States. In 2024 streets, institutions, municipal buildings, federal buildings, and monuments throughout the nation still bore the names of former slaveholders.

This genial interpretation has been gradually undermined over the past several decades. Many contemporary high school and college textbooks on American history provide more critical, accurate, and nuanced depictions of slavery. These alternative views are buttressed by hundreds of journal articles, book chapters, and specialised monographs. Universities themselves are beginning to spotlight their own complicated pasts with slavery: the Lemon Project at the College of William & Mary in Virginia, the Roberson Project at Sewanee University in Tennessee, McGill University in Montreal, the University of Pennsylvania, and Georgetown University in Washington DC, as well as Harvard and Yale (see Maginn and Beckles in this volume). Some academic institutions have sought broader racial justice beyond the campus grounds.[59]

The last few decades have brought American slavery into the public sphere. Enslaved workers who helped construct the White House are now commemorated.[60] Slave rebel leaders Gabriel Prosser, Denmark Vesey, and Nat Turner all have statues or markers.[61] (In 2023, the *Creole* rebels had yet to be commemorated.) Plantation houses open for public tours used to downplay or ignore slavery, either because of the material disappearance of slave quarters on the property or because of concern over the potential impact such a controversial topic might have on ticket sales. This is now changing, as slave quarters are being reconstructed, tour guides discuss slavery, and employees of the US National Park Service (some trained at the historically black college Howard University) publicise past US crimes. The lower floors of the National Museum of African American History and Culture in Washington DC, opened in September 2016 by the first black US president, Barack Obama, reveal the harsh realities as well as staying power of formerly enslaved people over two centuries. Movies such as *Glory* (1989), *Amistad* (1997), *Beloved* (1998), *Twelve Years a Slave* (2013), and *The Birth of a Nation* (2016) offer more realistic and complicated views of American slavery. Monuments to America's slaveholders and contented slaves are being increasingly defaced, dismantled, and removed. Reparative history – repairing the past through more accurate depictions in the hope of contributing towards a more balanced society – is well under way. As the British historian Katie Donington eloquently put it, such efforts "represent the opening of a necessary dialogue in which the unpalatable parts of the past are silenced no longer".[62]

This positive historical redress has been met with pushback from conservative commentators and slavery deniers. According to American academic Jeffrey Sachs, 35 US states have introduced 137 bills seeking to restrict educating public schoolchildren in US history, gender identity, sexual orientation, and matters of race. With regard to slavery, teachers were prevented from discussing the politics and economics of slavery, and were instead encouraged to characterise slaveholders merely as "racist individuals".[63] As this chapter suggests, slavery was not only at the heart of the US political and economic system: the subsequent wartime bloodbath seems unfathomable if only individual racists had been involved. Moreover, efforts either to redress or to deny the past have often failed to tackle structural inequalities rooted in American slavery. African Americans continue to lag behind European Americans in property ownership, wealth accumulation, and educational qualifications, while experiencing disproportionate rates of poverty, poor health, inadequate education, imprisonment, and single-person households. The Covid-19 crisis has starkly revealed many of these ongoing inequalities (see Introduction in this volume). We are free to believe that such iniquities come from individuals with a pathological proclivity towards failure in America. Alternatively, one could attribute these sad realities to the devastation wrought by free market capitalism in the twentieth century and hyper-capitalism in the twenty-first century.[64] But to deny the foundational role of America's first century of coerced labour without wages, sexual reproduction without personal choice, denial of opportunities for generational wealth, and energy diverted to the simple wants of survival, would be foolish at best and perverse at worst. If we are at all interested in redressing contemporary racial inequalities, then we must understand their deep roots in past inequalities. Reparative justice for the American yoke of bondage remains unfinished business.

13

The Role of Women in North America's Liberation Struggle

Dann J. Broyld

BLACK WOMEN PLAYED A major role in emancipation from slavery in North America. Their involvement was crucial to the success of the abolitionist movement in the United States and Canada, and has recently received more attention from contemporary historians and scholars. These groundbreaking works – particularly those relating to black women intellectuals – challenge centuries of oppression along sexual and gender lines, to provide clearer depictions of the black freedom struggle. This move from marginalisation to mainstream offers representation, redress, and repair.[1] It allows historical voices to be counted, heard, and understood. These entry points of black women into the historical narrative awake and rearrange this history as a more accurate depiction of diversity and truth.[2] Like their male counterparts, black women were agitating, publishing, lecturing, and organising throughout this movement. The texture and complexities they added led directly to social and political outcomes.

This chapter underscores Harriet Tubman's transnationalism in the American–Canadian borderlands (she lived in St Catharines, Canada West, from 1851 to 1858) and her intersectionality, balancing the social inequalities of race, ethnicity, class, gender, age, and ability.[3] I will also highlight the contributions of lesser known women such as Mary Ellen Pleasant, Mary Bibb, and Caroline Elizabeth Loguen, whose actions were as important as those of men and help to inform the historical narrative of the dynamic role of women in North America's liberation struggles. The history of black women has to be popularised beyond the nineteenth-century's well-known figures such as Harriet Tubman, Sojourner Truth, Harriet Jacobs, Frances Ellen Watkins Harper, and Ellen Craft. Others worked in the trenches of black struggles. The names of these heroines have to be known, better acknowledged, reach a broader audience, and be subjected to a multiplicity of intellectual interpretations. These women help reshape conceptions of race and gender, and to debunk the popular mythology of the "Great Man in History".[4] They relieve history from what the Nigerian writer Chimamanda Ngozi Adichie called "the danger of a single story".[5] In this chapter, the inclusion of more black women voices will be underscored before I conclude with Tubman's contributions to the liberation struggles.

Middle-Class Entrepreneurs

I first examine the role of the entrepreneur and Underground Railroad supporter Mary Ellen Pleasant, whose story was brought to life for a broader audience by the African American historian Kellie Carter Jackson. Pleasant attended the African American activist John Brown's Chatham Convention in May 1858 and donated $30,000 to his cause. The white male "Secret Six" – Thomas Wentworth Higginson, Samuel G. Howe, Theodore Parker, Franklin Benjamin Sanborn, Gerrit Smith, and George Luther Stearns – have been credited with leading roles in supporting the 1859 Harpers Ferry raid, even though it was Pleasant who contributed more than her counterparts combined. Secondly, the chapter highlights Mary Bibb, wife of the abolitionist Henry Bibb, who – thanks to the work of the Jamaican-Canadian historian Afua Cooper – can now take her rightful place as an editor and producer of Canada's first successful black newspaper, *Voice of the Fugitive*. Although her husband's name appeared on the masthead of the paper, which started in 1851, the brainchild behind the endeavour was Mary. She was not the only editor of a black Canadian newspaper. In 1854, Mary Ann Shadd Cary started the *Provincial Freemen* and edited it alongside Samuel G. Ward and the Reverend Alexander McArthur. But much of the labour rested in her hands.

Finally, Caroline Elizabeth Loguen has also been cast in the background of her abolitionist husband, the Reverend Jermain Wesley Loguen. Operating out of Syracuse, New York, Jermain was hailed as the "Underground Railroad King".[6] However, it was Caroline who oversaw the day-to-day movement of fugitives to British Canada and the American North. Caroline also kept a travel record of all the fugitives who arrived at the Loguens' home in Syracuse. Jermain intended to publish it, believing that this log and journal had great value. However, it never saw the light of day and has since been lost.[7] Perhaps Caroline's log contained information as detailed as William Still's *The Underground Railroad* (1872) and Sydney Howard Gay and Louis Napoleon's *Record of Fugitives* (1855–1856).[8] The contribution of these three dynamic women – Pleasant, Bibb, and Loguen – to black liberation is beyond question.

Mary Ellen Pleasant amassed her wealth through several means. She inherited the fortune of her first husband, James Smith, who was a plantation owner and flour contractor. During her second marriage to John James Pleasant and her settling in California, she owned several restaurants and invested in a score of successful businesses, including the Bank of California.[9] Pleasant was disappointed that John Brown's raid was quickly defeated. After hearing the news, she made her way back to San Francisco using the alias of "Ellen Smith" so as to remain undetected. In 1904 she told the *People's Press*: "Before I pass away I wish to clear the identity of the party who furnished John Brown with most of his money to start the fight at Harpers Ferry." Pleasant then admitted: "I furnished the money."[10] She knew very well that if her involvement in the raid of 1859 had been discovered at the time, she would surely have been captured and killed with Brown. Pleasant lamented: "I wished that I had gone up on the scaffold with him, for I would at least have died in a good cause and in good company."[11]

In April 1858, John Brown had gone to St Catharines, Canada West, to visit Harriet Tubman in order to recruit black activists for his planned attack on Harpers Ferry, Virginia.[12] The two met in April 1858 at Tubman's rented residence in the heart of the city's "Colored Village".[13] By this time, Tubman had retired from her daring trips to the American South and refocused her energy on assisting local blacks in St Catharines.[14] Tubman and Brown shared a common belief in direct action against the "peculiar institution" of slavery, and he sought the advice of the woman he dubbed "General Tubman".[15] In August 1859, John Brown was almost ready to launch his attack. Tubman believed in Brown's cause, but when the Harpers Ferry raid occurred in October 1859, she was far from the action, in Massachusetts, stricken by sickness.[16] Like Mary Ellen Pleasant, Tubman was devastated by Brown's detention and death. Demonstrating her profound admiration and respect for Brown, Tubman later told a close acquaintance that he had "done more in dying, than 100 men would in living".[17]

Pleasant, Tubman, and Anna Murray Douglass – the wife of Frederick Douglass, who cared for Brown in Rochester, New York, where he drew up the preliminary constitution for his proposed rebel Appalachian state – were the "silent and silenced black partners of Harpers Ferry".[18] As Kellie Carter Jackson explains: "The greatest contribution was not the counsel and contributions of the Secret Six but those of a savvy black woman from California and the potential guidance of America's Moses [Tubman]."[19] Historians have long pontificated about the self-sacrificing white "Secret Six" social aristocrats, when the real secret artillery was black women who sponsored and strategised Brown's risky rebellion in Virginia.[20] Their participation, though documented, represented an inconvenient truth for the dominant narrative that sought to paint the liberation of blacks in white. Moreover, Pleasant and Tubman were not simply passive but employed controlled rage and violence to try to force black liberation.[21] Anger, aggression, and involvement in revolt and assault do not neatly fit the nineteenth-century narrative of Victorian-era black womanhood. But this was the harsh reality.[22]

Black women gave birth to the revolution, and were not going to orphan the creation they had actively joined in nurturing. The black poet Frances E.W. Harper wrote to John Brown prior to his execution and eulogised him in her poem "Bury Me in a Free Land". The last lines of the poem explicitly noted John Brown's dying request:

I ask no monument, proud and high
To arrest the gaze of the passers-by
All that my yeaning spirit craves
Is bury me not in a land of slaves.[23]

Black women activists also sent notes of sympathy and money in support to Brown's widow, Mary Ann Brown.[24] On the fiftieth anniversary of John Brown's raid, New York reporter Nathan K. Sebastian explained: "Harpers Ferry was to the Civil War what the Boston Massacre was to the American Revolution … It was the small skirmish which foretold and made unavoidable the momentous, devouring battle that was to follow."[25] Black women were directly connected to this remarkable moment and its memory. They stood at its core, and not on its periphery; they were not a branch but rather the trunk that was tied to its roots. Early books on the "Secret Sixers" scarcely mentioned Tubman and Mary Ellen Pleasant, who did not even appear in the indexes of much of this literature.[26] Their erasure and lack of recognition was not the result of their absence or failure to speak out, but because past scholars failed to see or hear black women conspirators in the same manner as they did white men.

The Voice of the Fugitive

Mary Bibb, a free-born New Englander who was raised by Quakers and became a schoolteacher, married Henry Bibb in 1848. The couple left for Canada after the 1850 Fugitive Slave Act. There they started the *Voice of the Fugitive*. As Afua Cooper explains: "If Henry Bibb is the father of African Canadian journalism, one could argue that Mary Bibb is the mother of the black press in Canada. She can be rightly credited as the first black newspaperwoman in Canada."[27] Cooper supports this claim by pointing out that "she was formally educated, but her husband was not". Mary Bibb attended Lexington Normal School in Massachusetts and taught in classrooms in that state as well as in New York and Ohio. Her formal schooling was certainly of great assistance to her husband and the *Voice of the Fugitive*. Cooper notes: "The elegant language of the paper, somewhat beyond the style of the self-taught Henry Bibb, suggests that she [Mary Bibb] was more involved in its production than she has been given credit for."[28] Mary also produced the newspaper when her husband was away on lecture tours during its first year. She wrote feature articles for it and solicited funds from people like the New York abolitionist and Brown's "Secret Sixer", Gerrit Smith, to keep it from folding.[29]

Reading the *Voice of the Fugitive*, one can clearly hear the language and the lexicon of Mary Bibb. Traces of her work are embedded in the words credited to her husband. His private everyday correspondence does not match the polished prose displayed in the *Voice of the Fugitive*.[30] Henry Bibb also helped to establish the Anti-Slavery Society and the Refugee Home Society, which was a fugitive settlement initiative. He was active in the Detroit frontier Underground Railroad, helping to welcome runaways to Canadian soil alongside his wife. Nonetheless, of all his contributions, Henry knew that the newspaper was paramount. In November 1850, the foundation for the *Voice of the Fugitive* was laid at the Sandwich Colored Convention, where he shared his vision to set up a paper, explaining: "We have no instrument that we can use with more effect than the public press ... we need a press."[31] Mary Bibb worked in the shadows of her husband, like many other famous men's wives. However, recent scholarship has brought about a new retrospective interpretation of her.

Caroline Elizabeth Loguen

Caroline Elizabeth Loguen's efforts were also eclipsed in public by those of her husband, the Reverend Jermain Wesley Loguen. While he was celebrated in the public sphere for his lectures and sermons, Caroline laboured to feed, clothe, and house runaways at their Syracuse home. "Born free", Caroline Storum grew up on a farm in Busti, New York, a small town in Chautauqua County. Her parents – William and Sarah Storum – were prosperous farmers who owned "one of the best farms of the county" and gained the respect of their neighbours.[32] Moreover, they were known abolitionists who aided fugitives. Jermain's *Narrative* explained: "Caroline was privileged with the best education country opportunities afforded."[33] In stark contrast, the Tennessee-born Jermain was enslaved but fled the American South and by 1834 was living in the greater St Catharines area in Canada West. In 1837, he moved to Rochester, New York, before settling in Syracuse.[34] In 1840, Caroline and Jermain's relationship "ripened into mutual attachment, and resulted in their marriage".[35] Throughout the 1850s, they assisted about 1,500 fugitives from slavery to reach Canada.[36]

Caroline Loguen, like Anna Murray Douglass, played a key role in the movement of people on the Underground Railroad. "Mrs Loguen, in the absence of her husband, is often aroused from her bed to attend to the pressing wants of those flying for Liberty and the blessings of those social ties of which their *native land* [America] deprives them." The letter in which this observation appeared was simply signed "a woman for a woman".[37] Mrs Douglass was similarly engaged. The American historian Carol Hunter notes that Caroline received runaways in a state of destitution. With their spouses on the road advocating abolition, it was the women who helped to preserve the freedom of fugitives in flight. These women were a vital source of information. When a "beautiful mulatto woman" and new bride from Maryland's Eastern Shore came to Syracuse in 1856 seeking the whereabouts of her husband, Mrs Loguen read the log of passengers that had stopped by the house, until the woman exclaimed: "That is the name of my husband."[38] Mrs and Mr Loguen remembered they had sent "Fred" to Auburn, New York, and they personally made the journey in the middle of December to reunite the couple.[39]

When Jermain took a firm stance against the 1850 Fugitive Slave Act and became involved in the October 1851 William "Jerry" Henry rescue, Caroline fully supported him.[40] Jerry was arrested by federal marshals in Syracuse. However, before his arraignment, a crowd broke into the jail and freed him, and then sent him to Canada. Jermain's involvement left him in danger of being arrested. Afraid for his safety, Caroline and others persuaded him to go to Canada, where he stayed with Hiram Wilson in St Catharines. In December 1851, Jermain's wife and four children joined him there.[41] After things settled by 1852, the Loguen couple and family returned to Syracuse to help more fugitives flee to British soil.[42] The Reverend Samuel May, in an obituary of this heroine, wrote in September 1867: "Could the history of American Slavery, its subversion and overthrow, be fully written, and the labors of those who conducted the underground railroad be adequately described, the name of Mrs Loguen would stand conspicuously among the friends of the oppressed."[43] In other words, the tireless role of Caroline Elizabeth Loguen cannot easily be forgotten if a genuine history of African Americans is to be narrated. Men did not have a monopoly on advocating for social change. Even when the historical voices of black women are muffled or silenced, their involvement needs to be excavated. They were the backbone in the struggle for freedom from slavery.

Harriet Tubman: The Moses of the Anti-Slavery Struggle

Harriet Tubman's role in the emancipation of black people is epic. Her contemporaries Mary Ellen Pleasant, Mary Bibb, and Caroline Elizabeth Loguen certainly agreed with this perspective. Tubman transcended nationality, sexuality, gender, and age. She challenged the roles assigned to women of her day, by hunting muskrat on Maryland's Eastern Shore and by returning to the American South to free enslaved blacks from captivity. She led the Union Army into battle at the Combahee Ferry raid, which liberated about 700 black slaves during the American Civil War (1861–1865). She fought for women's suffrage.[44] She took care of marginalised people whom society had washed its hands of: the disabled, orphans, and the elderly. In December 1858, in the midst of a cold Canadian winter, Tubman took a black child off the street, and then petitioned the St Catharines City Council to support her care. The Council approved her request, noting: "H. Tubman one dollar per week for four weeks: for keeping child found in street, carried."[45] In Auburn, New York, Tubman later adopted a daughter, Gertie Davis; she was also responsible for caring for "Blind Aunty" Sarah Parker, supported a full household of relatives, and started the Harriet Tubman Home for the Aged.[46] Tubman constantly grew as a person to meet the needs of her people. She had a soul of God, gold, and greatness. She was both human and hero, blood and blessed, the object of people's awe and their inspiration.

As a young woman, Tubman recognised her West African ancestral heritage. Her Ashanti blood and her membership of the African diaspora enabled her to think outside the conventional American framework. She grew to understand that the border between the United States and British Canada separated different political sovereignties but could not break social and cultural ties or deter a common cause to end black bondage. She lived in Canada for about seven years and became familiar with the British Empire and the Atlantic world.

Her gender awareness was expressed in 1850 when she said: "I wouldn't trust Uncle Sam with my people no longer", highlighting: "I brought 'em all clear off to Canada."[47] She realised that her dual objectives of racial and sexual liberation could only be achieved in Canada, where slavery had been abolished by an Imperial Act of 1834. Unfortunately, on the "Queen's soil", racism and sexism still existed. But moving to Canada demonstrated that Tubman thought deeply about race, sex, and gender, and their intersection. Always conscious of others' needs, Tubman lived with chronic and debilitating illness after suffering a blow to the head as a child, which left her struggling with epilepsy. She experienced pain, dizziness, and long spells of lack of sleep throughout her life. However, she learned to adapt and to empathise with those living with similar or worse conditions. During America's Civil War, at the Second Battle of Fort Wagner in July 1863, she cared for the wounded and comforted the dying.[48] In the 1890s, her childhood injury led to brain surgery at Massachusetts General Hospital in Boston.[49] However, Tubman still cared selflessly for the ill, even as she was ailing herself. Pain was an element she transferred into her passion to help her own people. She understood the multitude of ways in which black life was oppressed, neglected, and undervalued. Tubman wanted blacks to be fully incorporated in the human equation.

She embodied the finest qualities of humanity. In 2016, US Treasury Secretary, Jack Lew, announced that Harriet Tubman would be placed on the front of the $20 bill and former US president Andrew Jackson demoted to the back. Tubman is historically multifaceted, and cannot be reduced to a parochial nationalism. The $20 bill is an unlikely place for Tubman, the American-Canadian, militant, direct-action abolitionist, who struggled financially for most of her life. She was also a veteran who had to petition repeatedly for her compensation.[50] In 1899, nearly 80 years old, she received $12 per month for her service as a nurse and $8 monthly as a widow's pension for her deceased Union husband, Nelson C. Davis, the two ironically totalling $20.[51]

In 2017, a new photo of Tubman was discovered in an album in New York City. It was once owned by the schoolteacher and abolitionist Emily Howland. At the time Tubman was in her mid-forties, and was on the eve of marrying her second husband, Nelson Davis, who was considerably younger than her.[52] The portrait captures Tubman self-fashioning her image, in tune with modernity.

Tubman has been called the "Moses" of the freedom struggle and likened to a latter-day "Joan of Arc". But she needs no biblical comparison nor portrayal as a national symbol. Tubman stands alone – original and unmatched. She is worthy of the adulations of words, the depictions of artists, yet it was her deeds, in the times she performed them, that make her alluring and timeless. She worked to overturn the brutality of slavery, spied on the Confederacy, led an assault on the American South, and nursed the Union during America's bloodiest conflict. She survived the economic woes of the Gilded Age and remained true to her people. This Amazon of Ashanti descent was honoured by Queen Victoria, who read Tubman's narrative and was "pleased with it", sending her a silver medal that memorialised Victoria's Diamond Jubilee in 1897.[53]

Concluding Reflections

There is much to gain by approaching history with the aim of uncovering the real role of women. They are often not on the periphery but at the very core of liberation struggles. They were at the crossroads of intersectionality, where they were constantly oscillating and challenging the demarcations of race, sex, and gender. As more black women historians have entered the profession, their work has led to a revision of the mainstream historical narrative that recognises women's involvement and engagement in the black past. These efforts will affect the future interpretations of black women and empower them to recognise that their historical role has been vital and vivid, and left an indelible mark on the path to greater rights and liberties across North America. This work of repair is restorative. Moreover, it moves history closer to the reality of what happened. Can this restorative work that highlights black women serve as a kind of historical and literary reparation for the exclusions and silences of the past? At the very least, we need to recognise the contributions of women like Harriet Tubman, Mary Ellen Pleasant, Mary Bibb, and Caroline Elizabeth Loguen.

Part Five

Colonialism in Africa

14

Colonialism in British Africa

Samuel Igba

BRITAIN WAS A MAJOR player in European capitalist expansion into Africa, which
began with slavery from the fifteenth century, then imperialism from the early
eighteenth century, and subsequent colonisation occurring during the period
of the industrial revolution in the eighteenth century, which started in Britain
itself.[1] The British claimed territory in Africa as early as the sixteenth century,
and carried on acquiring real estate until the late nineteenth century. The
industrial revolution pushed capitalist expansion further, as the need for slaves
was replaced with the need for markets to consume the excess supply of goods
out of Europe. The African continent became fertile ground, not only as a
market to supply finished goods and services, but also as an extraction paradise
for raw materials such as palm products, groundnuts, cotton, and rubber.[2]

Britain was not the only European nation interested in capitalist expansion
in Africa. Other European nations including France, Portugal, and Germany
(see Yates, Sousa, and Blackler in this volume), competed for territory,
leading to the scramble for and ensuing partition of Africa in the late 1880s.
This gave European nations, including Britain, the international legal right
– as defined by the major international powers at the time – to plunder and
pillage the African continent. London sought a variety of ways to impose
its rule on African societies, implementing different approaches to colonial
administration, including indirect rule. This was practised in most British
colonies, especially where identifiable formal indigenous governance structures
existed in a system of colonial rule in which colonies were administered directly

by colonial rulers. This chapter examines Britain's role in the "Scramble for Africa" from the 1880s, commercialisation and capitalist expansion, civilisation and Christianisation missions, and administrative strategies. British colonial atrocities and African resistance and independence struggles are also discussed.

In many ways, this chapter highlights Nigerian writer Chinweizu Ibekwe's argument in his 1975 book, *The West and the Rest of Us*, that "White hordes have sallied forth from their Western homelands to assault, loot, occupy, rule, and exploit the world. Even now the fury of their expansionist assault on the rest of us has not abated."[3] The violent history of imperialism enabled Europe to subdue its African colonies. Britain's ambitious capitalist expansion was responsible for a range of atrocities related especially to land appropriation in East Africa and blatant racial segregation in southern Africa. Also present were the divide-and-rule policies which fostered ethnic divisions across British-administered colonies such as Kenya, Nigeria, and Sudan. The British further deposed and subverted African kings including Jaja of Opobo in the Niger Delta area in modern Nigeria and Lobengula of Matabeleland in modern Zimbabwe.

By the mid-twentieth century, liberated Africans across the continent gained a new spirit of national consciousness that led to struggles against colonialism and culminated in African independence from the 1950s. The scars of colonialism remain today, as former British colonies on the continent continue to interact with the world from a position of great disadvantage. This chapter traces the history of British colonialism in Africa by highlighting key political events that continue to shape the fate of the continent today.

The Scramble for Africa

Between the British arrival in Africa in the sixteenth century and the end of colonialism by 1980 with the liberation of Zimbabwe, the British practised imperialism through economic, political, and cultural domination of African indigenous groups and territories. In West Africa, British colonialism started in Sierra Leone in 1787 and involved populating the country with formerly enslaved Africans from Britain, as well as captives rescued from slavery and other enslaved Africans from parts of the African diaspora in the Americas.[4] British West Africa was first referred to as the Colony of Sierra Leone and its Dependencies, making the territory the capital of British West Africa.[5] In southern Africa, British settlers lived alongside the Dutch in the 1820s, while in eastern Africa, British penetration began in Zanzibar around the late nineteenth century. In 1888, the British East Africa Company claimed areas in what is now Kenya.[6]

The primary purpose of the European invasion of Africa was economic. Consequently, all European states involved were in competition to gain territory on the continent. The competition between European states culminated in what became known as the "Scramble for Africa" in the 1880s. This led to the partition of the continent in 1884–1885 following the convening of the Berlin Conference, which set the rules for African states to be divided among European powers.[7] As a result of this partitioning, Britain acquired parts of western, eastern, southern, and northern Africa and came to control Botswana, Egypt, Gambia, Ghana, Kenya, Malawi, Nigeria, north-western Somalia, Sierra Leone, South Africa, Sudan, Uganda, Zambia, and Zimbabwe. The signatories to the General Act of the Berlin Conference sanctioned the "civilizing mission of commerce and Christianity".[8] They also expressed concern for the moral well-being of indigenous people in the colonies. The partitioning represented the commercialisation, Christianisation, and civilisation missions, which were the three supposed purposes of European, and specifically British, colonialism in Africa.

Commercialisation: Economics and Capitalist Expansion

A fitting narrative of European capitalist expansion in Africa is provided by Guyanese historian Walter Rodney in his 1972 book, *How Europe Underdeveloped Africa*. Rodney recounts the story of European penetration of Africa from the 1400s through the 1800s and 1900s. He argues that development on both continents shared, and continues to share, an antithetical relationship: development in Europe brought underdevelopment to Africa. The rich and poor regions of the current global capitalist system have been in continuous contact with each other for over four centuries. Rodney argues that within this contact period, Africa contributed to developing Europe in the same proportion that Europe contributed to underdeveloping Africa.[9]

According to British philosopher John Stuart Mill in his 1848 book, *Principles of Political Economy*: "The trade of the world is hardly to be considered as external trade, but more resembles the traffic between town and country."[10] In the context of British colonialism, this means, for example, that trade between Africa, Britain, and the West Indies was more beneficial to Britain. London relegated Africa and the Caribbean to the peripheral role of providing raw materials and labour in a process that took two centuries of the transatlantic slave trade to develop (see Brereton and Beckles in this volume). Europe obtained economic and capitalist prosperity at the expense of untold suffering for Africans.[11] This signalled the dawn of the European imperial era of global capitalist production and expansion.[12] An example of early slavery and exploitation of Africa by the British can be traced back to English explorer John Hawkins's three expeditions to Africa in the 1560s, which earned him handsome profits and a knighthood, conferred by Queen Elizabeth I for the capture and sale of slaves from Africa.[13]

Initially, Europe was able to advance in international trade because it produced far more goods by using its resources and labour, while at the same time using Africa's resources and labour. Then, between 1760 and 1840, European imperial capitalists, led by Britain, started to develop machinery that tremendously boosted economic production, as opposed to human and land-based productions found in other parts of the world. As a result, what was merely a slight difference – between development in Europe and development in Africa in 1444 when the Portuguese arrived – improved greatly in the nineteenth century, enabling Europeans to consolidate their advantageous capitalist position.[14] The capitalist system had already been established within Europe, where some countries had become rich at the expense of others. Britain, France, and Germany were the most prosperous, while Ireland, Portugal, and Spain lagged far behind. Within each country, there was polarisation between capitalists, on the one hand, and workers and peasants on the other. Large capitalists expanded massively, while little ones were eliminated.

Monopolies developed in iron, steel, textiles, and banking. Monopoly firms further fought to control raw materials, markets, and means of communication outside Europe,[15] as the scope for expansion became limited within their own countries. As a result, European imperialists turned to the less developed economies of Africa. The capitalist penetration of foreign economies is what Walter Rodney refers to as "imperialism". Areas of immediate super-profit for Britain included southern African gold and diamond mines – exploited royally by Cecil Rhodes – as well as the invasion of Egypt and control of the Suez Canal from 1882 as a strategic trading route to the East. Other raw materials of great value to British capitalists included palm products, groundnuts, cotton, and rubber, especially from the late 1800s to the mid-1900s. This trade was grossly unbalanced vis-à-vis Africa, and remains so today.

Many changes inside Britain had transformed the slave trade into the nineteenth-century need to clear the remnants of slavery from Africa, so as to organise the local exploitation of land and labour. The British self-righteously worked to end slavery, as the institution was no longer useful in Africa and other parts of the world. London simultaneously deposed and subverted kings in order to control the trade of products such as palm oil, rubber, and, it was hoped, diamonds.

Colonialism was also facilitated by Africans who served as economic, political, and cultural agents of European imperialism.[16] Colonialism downgraded many African rulers into mere middlemen in commercial and other affairs, and raised some ordinary Africans to the same status.[17] Culturally, there was a push to learn the ways of the white man. The middleman status of African leaders meant that they needed to understand the customs and languages of the Europeans. This also meant that they absorbed European culture, and in pushing European trade further into the hinterland, Western culture also spread into the interior. This learning process resulted in values that further subjugated African cultures and propagated negative stereotypes about Africa. An example of this phenomenon is that Africans returning from slavery helped to establish British colonial rule in Sierra Leone. In Zanzibar, Arab Africans were also used to help establish British rule.[18]

Christianisation and "Civilisation" Missions into the "Dark Continent"

Africa was perceived by Europeans, including the British, as a "Dark Continent": an image held in the popular consciousness during the pre-colonial and colonial periods by people who had never been to the continent and based their narratives on negative stereotypes and assumptions.[19] They were exposed to second- and third-hand accounts of colourful tales of Africa, including "fables about noble savages degraded by muskets and gin, and infant races awaiting Gospel's dawn".[20] Moreover, John Stuart Mill – the lodestar of Victorian liberalism – defended colonial rule, listing, as justification, the reported improvements it had brought to the colonies. Some scholars have noted that this perception of Africa represented the beginnings of racism in geopolitics as a justification for the exploitation of Africa. Hannah Arendt, for example, argues that "imperialism would have necessitated the invention of racism as the only explanation for its deeds even if no race thinking had ever existed in the civilised world".[21]

This point is buttressed by the comments made by British imperial businessman and one-time prime minister of the Cape Colony, Cecil Rhodes, referring to the inhabitants of southern Africa:

Either you have to receive them on an equal footing as citizens, or to call them a subject race. Well, I have made up my mind that there must be class legislation ... and that we have got to treat natives, where they are in a state of barbarism, in a different way to ourselves. We are to be lords over them ... Treat the natives as a subject people as long as they continue in a state of barbarism and communal tenure.[22]

Rhodes, like other Victorians at the time, believed that Britain was a superior civilisation that bore the obligation to carry "civilisation", humanity, peace, good governance, and the knowledge of God to the ends of the earth.[23] British colonialists had as justification – for what Nigerian scholar Adekeye Adebajo terms "profit, plunder, and prestige"[24] – a mission to commercialise, Christianise, and civilise, resulting in depletion, dehumanisation, and disregard for the African continent and its people. Depletion, because resources from the continent became scarce to African people; dehumanisation, due to the inhumane manner of the plunder;[25] and disregard, because African problems remain at the bottom of the list of contemporary geopolitical issues.

The British colonial system also produced intricate patterns of knowledge about Africa that were designed to serve imperial interests.[26] These continue to shape the contemporary world today, even though British global dominance has largely diminished since the mid-twentieth century. The triple missions of commercialisation, Christianisation, and civilisation continue – both covertly and overtly – to find their way into Western and European relations with Africa even in the present day. The argument that Africa needed, and needs, civilising, or – in keeping with more recent terminology – "saving", continues to shape inter-subjectivity relations. In her 2022 book, *White Saviourism and Popular Culture*, South African cultural anthropologist Kathryn Mathers argues that "white saviourism" or the "white saviour industrial complex"[27] is a phenomenon in which a white person is seen as a liberator, rescuer, or uplifter of non-white people – particularly Africans in poor countries that are majority black – thus effectively denying them any agency. This colonial-era phenomenon reduces Africans to mere recipients of white benevolence.

British Administrative Strategies

The British adopted various administrative and governance strategies to achieve their goals. These strategies were tailored to meet the imperial needs of the colonies themselves, as well as the imperialist needs of the British Empire.

While a more direct form of rule was necessary to achieve these objectives in some colonies, indirect rule was more appropriate in most. These decisions were based on the pre-colonial administrative arrangements that existed before British control of the areas.[28] Entities with familiar and recognisable administrative structures – comparable to the imperial British system – were ruled indirectly through indigenous rulers, while those with unfamiliar pre-colonial arrangements different from the British were ruled directly, with Africans only participating at very low levels of governance.

Unlike the French, who implemented direct rule throughout their colonies across the continent – viewing the pre-colonial chiefs as subsidiary representatives following instructions of colonial agents, in the belief that Africans would be Europeanised[29] (see Yates in this volume) – the British were more preservationist, as they did not believe that Africans could be Europeanised. The British did not appear overtly committed to importing British culture into their non-settler territories.[30] This is not to suggest that there was no deliberate attempt at altering traditions and culture within other aspects of society. It is rather an acknowledgement that, in administration specifically, indirect rule was more suited for controlling local people. Indirect rule was introduced by British colonial administrator Frederick Lugard and spread to most British colonies. A famous example of the practice of indirect rule was Lugard's policy in Northern Nigeria in which he stressed the need for preserving local established traditional authorities and customary laws, but under British supervision.[31] This made it important for the British to identify, catalogue, and homogenise indigenous ethnic communities in order to establish who had legitimate authority over whom.[32]

In both direct and indirect rule, British colonial laws were designed to enforce the colonial presence. As such, there were dual laws in each colony: one aimed at maintaining the traditional authority, and the other at establishing a claim to colonial authority and upholding the colonial "peace", which essentially meant keeping opposition to colonial rule quiet through a Pax Britannica. This fed directly into approaches to policing in British colonies, which have been described as geared towards maintaining peace "against disturbance and unrest among primitive tribes that were less than open rebellion, and of a political rather than a criminal character".[33] In colonies such as what is now Nigeria, former Royal Irish constabulary officers and ex-members of the British armed forces were hired by colonial authorities to maintain militaristic approaches to policing. Such colonial police forces and constabularies would kill or maim – and burn the villages of – indigenous peoples and rulers who rejected collaboration with the British colonialists. The anti-tax protests in Nigeria's Warri Province (1927–1928), as well as the women's anti-tax protests in eastern Nigeria (1929–1930) where colonial police killed 55 women, are examples of British colonial police violence.[34]

To keep colonised Africans from forming a united front against British imperialism, a system of divide and rule was adopted across colonies to pit ethnic, clan, religious, and linguistic groups against each other. In Nigeria, for example, despite the amalgamation of the Northern and Southern protectorates by Lugard in 1914, both regions were governed as separate administrative and political entities, with their economies the only identifiable links fostered by the colonial administration. According to Nigerian political scientist Abdul Raufu Mustapha, these administrative strategies laid the foundations for divisive ethno-religious blocs in contemporary Nigeria.[35] In Sudan, British rule ensured that the South was isolated from the North in an attempt to prevent Islam from spreading to the South, thus resulting in marginalisation of the South.[36] In Sierra Leone, missionary work grew the country's modern education system, which earned the Krio elite many accolades in different fields: they thus became the privileged class compared with other ethnic groups and religions.[37] These three cases represent examples of how Europeanisation and colonisation led to the marginalisation of indigenous groups on the continent.

British Colonial Atrocities, African Resistance

Atrocities by the British colonial administration across Africa took the form of land expropriation, land grabbing, racial segregation, subversion of local kings, and the use of unethical military tactics such as "scorched earth" policies.

The Mau Mau Struggle in Kenya

British colonial policies in Kenya with regards to race and land were like those of Rhodesia and South Africa. The Mau Mau movement began long before it became identifiable and cohesive, but it reached its apogee in 1952.[38] It was a revolutionary and military reaction to aggressive British imperialism, land expropriation, and exploitation of natural resources. British settler attitudes towards Africans developed over time and informed racial atrocities.[39] As previously mentioned, not only did the British, from Victorian times, feel superior to the rest of the world, and particularly Africa, they also believed that Africans were bloodthirsty cannibals as well as treacherous, lecherous, and cruel beings.[40] These stereotypes developed in pre-colonial times and carried on throughout the colonial period, leading to racist policies and legislation in British colonies.[41] Since many Africans rejected British colonial advances, the first step was to conquer the "natives" through violence.

British settlers were invited to Kenya by the British Commissioner, Charles Eliot, in 1902. Eliot had no compunctions about airing his racist views, as well as implementing them. He often disagreed with his critics who could not see any British legal or moral mandate to dispossess Africans of their lands.[42] To buttress this point, Eliot noted: "There can be no doubt that the Maasai and many other tribes must go under ... It is a prospect that I view with equanimity and a clear conscience."[43]

British settlers soon populated Kenya, forming associations, and encouraging the British administration to enact laws and legislation that not only expropriated land from Africans but also forced them to work on this land. Examples of such legislation include[44] the East Africa Lands Ordinance in Council of 1901, which defined Crown land as all public land that was not private. Private land included land occupied by African villages. The Crown Lands Ordinance of 1902 stated that all unoccupied land could be sold at two rupees per 100 acres per annum to Europeans, but that the land must be developed or forfeited; while the Master and Servants Ordinance of 1906 (see Cobley in this volume) sought to retain labour on settler farms and decreed that employers could pay workers in kind. Under this ordinance, if a Kenyan employee broke his contract, he could be imprisoned.

In 1907, Alfred Claud Hollis was appointed as British Secretary of Native Affairs in Kenya. This did not meet the approval of the settlers, as Hollis produced a circular forbidding the forced recruitment of labour. The circular resulted in a demonstration by British settlers in 1908 demanding flogging to be legalised, pass laws be introduced, and taxation to be increased in order to force the "natives" to come to work. A poll tax was eventually added to the hut tax, and the need to find yet more money forced young men to offer their services to the settlers.

The Mau Mau movement grew out of land grievances arising from years of discriminatory regulations. White British settlers expropriated land and refused to share it with Africans, who were its rightful owners. The Mau Mau leaders questioned the legal rights and justification for land ownership, as well as the declaration of Kenya as a "white man's country" in 1915. This declaration was to last at least 999 years, within which period no economic or political changes could be made, especially with regard to the black people of Kenya.[45] The Mau Mau movement was able to galvanise the support of local farmers and peasants to resist British rule by creating political and economic awareness to challenge injustices.

The movement reached its zenith in 1956, when Senior Chief Waruhiu wa Kung'u, regarded as pro-British, was assassinated by the Mau Mau. This led to the British Governor, Evelyn Baring, declaring a state of emergency in Kenya.[46] The uprising was further exacerbated by the British arrest of prominent Mau Mau leaders such as Dedan Kimathi in 1953.[47] The Mau Mau rebels used different insurrectionary tactics to launch attacks, including assassinations, bombings, and ambushes against the British, as well as against their African collaborators. The rebels were known for terror tactics like mutilation and beheadings as a means of spreading fear across the country in order to enable them to gain control of territory.[48] The British reacted with military action of their own, including the Hola Massacre in January 1954, in which British guards tortured Mau Mau prisoners, killing 11 of them.[49] Another notable British reaction was the October 1956 incident in which the British attempted to flush out Mau Mau fighters hiding in the forests, triggering further conflict.[50] The Mau Mau rebellion officially ended in January 1960 after the remaining rebel groups surrendered. An estimated 11,500 deaths were recorded among the Mau Mau. On the British side, 1,800 African loyalists, 170 Africans in the official armed forces, 63 European combatants, and 32 British settlers were killed during the uprising.[51]

The Imperial Strongman: Cecil Rhodes and Southern Africa

Cecil Rhodes achieved success and fortune from his business ventures in southern Africa. His commercial empire began with the De Beers Mining Company, to which was added Gold Fields of South Africa, and led to the founding of the British South Africa Company, which had a royal charter. In 1870, when Rhodes came to Africa, the diamond rush had already begun in Kimberley, and gold was about to be discovered on the Witwatersrand.[52] Rhodes was determined to expand the British Empire. In her 2010 book, *Making a Killing: How and Why Corporations Use Armed Force to Do Business*, Canadian scholar Madelaine Drohan argues that there was more than one crime behind Rhodes's success.[53] I briefly discuss two atrocities committed by Cecil Rhodes: the disenfranchisement of black voters in the Cape Colony, and land expropriation.

In 1887, Rhodes made clear that he wanted to limit voting by black people.[54] The Cape Colony legislation that followed had far-reaching effects, as the

1887 Cape Parliamentary Registration Act reduced black voters by about 40 per cent in several districts. In 1891, there was a rise in the number of black voters. However, 1892 saw a 20 per cent reduction owing to the Cape Franchise and Ballot Act. By 1910, 15 per cent of Cape voters were black, albeit predominantly "Coloured" (mixed race), as opposed to black Africans, who made up 75 per cent of the general population.[55] In 1936, black Africans were effectively disenfranchised, losing their votes on the common voters' roll, while Coloureds lost theirs in 1956 during the early years of apartheid.[56]

At the height of Rhodes's political power, he led a war against the Ndebele in what is now Zimbabwe to suppress rebellion in 1896–1897. He was a strong supporter of British colonial efforts in the region, which included the use of "scorched earth" tactics: a military approach to suppress Ndebele resistance. After the war, the British South Africa Company, Rhodes's chartered company, looted on a large scale, and continued to pursue a scorched earth strategy, appropriating or destroying grain, livestock, and settlements across Zimbabwe.

Prior to this, Rhodes realised he would have to deal with the Ndebele king, Lobengula. A delegation led by Rhodes's lieutenant, Charles Rudd, was dispatched to reach an agreement with Lobengula in 1880. The Reverend Charles Helm of the London Missionary Society, who was present at the meeting as part of Lobengula's delegation, also belonged to Rhodes's camp – unbeknown to the Ndebele king. Helm worked to persuade Lobengula to accept a deal. Rudd's delegation also bribed Lotje, Lobengula's adviser, with gifts. A deal was finally brokered after several exaggerated promises by Rudd's delegation. The deal became known as the "Rudd Concession", and gave its British signatories a monopoly over mining and mineral rights in Lobengula's territory in exchange for £100 a month, 1,000 Martini-Henry rifles, and 100 rounds of ammunition, in addition to either a steamboat with guns or £500. Occupation rights were not mentioned in the deal. Thus, Lobengula, the Ndebele king and sovereign ruler of Matabeleland, was effectively duped by Rhodes's delegation.

Scorched Earth Tactics, and Divide and Rule Policies in Sudan

Sudan was under Egyptian rule when the British arrived in Egypt in 1873, and consequently Britain gained control over Sudan as an Egyptian territory.[57] During this period, the British committed several atrocities in Sudan, including the use of scorched earth tactics during the Mahdist War of the 1880s.[58]

General Charles Gordon, as Governor of Sudan, attempted to root out slave trading, an effort that was not well received by Sudan's Arab leaders. They were suspicious of British rule, viewing it as an attempt to subvert Muslim Arab dominance of Sudan.[59] After decades of dissatisfaction with Egyptian rule and with increasing resentment emerging towards British rule in Sudan, the self-proclaimed Mahdi – or "the Guided One" – Muhammad Ahmad, a Sudanese Islamic cleric, transformed what was initially a political movement into a religious-military one.[60] He formed an army and incited a jihad (holy war) against imperial Egypt and, by extension, the British. London collaborated with the Egyptian army in 1883, launching counter-attacks against the Mahdists in a war that lasted until January 1885. The British–Egyptian force defended Khartoum in a long siege that eventually saw the entire garrison killed.

It was during the British colonial administration in Sudan, and especially during the Mahdist War, that the British committed atrocities against the Sudanese population, including forced labour, land seizures, and torture. Another major atrocity was the use of scorched earth tactics to destroy entire villages, crops, and livestock in order to deprive Mahdist rebels of supplies and support.[61] These policies were deployed in Darfur, Kordofan, and the Blue Nile regions, and involved the intentional destruction of crops, the burning of villages, and the displacement of entire communities as a means of preventing resources from reaching the Mahdist rebels, thereby weakening their support base.

While the British unified Sudan, London also solidified conflicting racial, religious, and cultural identities by creating a North–South dualism based on racial, religious, and cultural differences. These identity issues were exacerbated by the adoption of a policy that ended up marginalising the South, while developing the North much more. The British justified this policy as a means of preserving the cultures of the South by keeping Islamic, Arabic, and northern Sudanese influences out. The policy included the prohibition on spreading Arabic in the South, the abolition of Arab names, the labelling of Northerners as slave dealers, as well as the privileging of Christian missionaries over Muslim preachers.[62] Overall, the effects of British colonialism in Sudan were catastrophic, with 11,000 Mahdists killed and another 16,000 wounded in the final battle alone, while British and Egyptian forces lost only 48 men.[63]

Jaja of Opobo

The final example of British colonial atrocities in Africa revolves around Jaja of Opobo, a successful businessman in the palm oil trade, who was also the first king of Opobo[64] in the Niger Delta area of what is now Nigeria. He acted as a middleman between European merchants and producers from the interior. Jaja's enterprise and monopoly soon made him an enemy of British capitalist firms, who believed that he was profiting unduly at their expense. In the 1880s, there was a trade depression in England, which led to British traders assuming that removing Jaja as a middleman would increase their profits. At the demand of the British consul, Edward Hyde Hewett, in 1884, Jaja signed a treaty giving control of his territory to the British under the conditions that access and trade would not be free for Europeans.[65] The British subsequently declared a protectorate over the territory of the Gulf of Guinea, ignoring Jaja's conditions.[66] Jaja rebelled against this decision, and rejected free trade in the area, leading to the British accusing him of engaging in terrorism, organising armed attacks, and obstructing trade and waterways. In 1887, Jaja was recommended for deportation by the British vice-consul, Harry Johnston, a step immediately approved by the British Foreign Office.[67] He was taken to Accra, tried, and sentenced to deportation for five years to the West Indies. Jaja appealed against the deportation and won his appeal with the help of a supportive British officer, Major Claude MacDonald. He died on the way home in July 1891. The British prime minister Lord Salisbury regretted the treatment of Jaja and insisted that in "civilised" lands, those who deported him would have been tried for kidnapping.[68]

The Road to African Independence

African citizens within the continent, and in the African diaspora in the Americas and the Caribbean, began to push back against European colonialism. The Pan-African movement started in the United States and soon spread across Europe and into Africa. Notable leaders of the fight for African independence in British colonies included Ghana's Kwame Nkrumah, Nigeria's Nnamdi Azikiwe, Kenya's Uhuru Kenyatta, Tanzania's Julius Nyerere, and later South Africa's Nelson Mandela. A wave of Pan-Africanism and African nationalism spread across the continent, and the 1950s and 1960s saw African colonies gain their independence from British colonial rule. Eastern and southern Africa included a large contingent of British settlers who were anxious to suppress independent movements, leading to violent reactions from African freedom fighters.

One event outside Britain which acted as a catalyst for African nationalism and pressure on the British was the Second World War (1939–1945) and the use of Africans as soldiers by the British. The West African Frontier Force was expanded from 8,000 to 146,000, and the East African contingent from 5,000 to 280,000, thus creating many disgruntled African ex-servicemen at the end of the war.[69] Within Britain, many citizens started to question why, and if, colonialism should exist, given the hardships that followed the war.[70] Many argued that colonialism should involve social and economic progress. Economic problems during and following the end of the Second World War encouraged vigorous exploitation of African resources, as the manpower demands of the war caused the colonial administrations to lose European men, which imposed new difficulties in economic production.[71] Internationally, colonialism became discredited in the eye of the international community, with the United States and the Soviet Union, as new superpowers in a bipolar system, calling for an end to European colonialism in Africa.[72]

Concluding Reflections

Today the legacy of British colonialism in Africa has contributed to shaping current realities on the continent. Both politically and economically, former British colonies in Africa continue to lag behind in trade and political stability. In politics, culture, and religion, the British colonial influence remains intact 60 years after the end of imperial rule. Relations created during the colonial era continue to shape Africa's interaction with the rest of the world.[73] The fact that Africa's problems are placed at the bottom of the global order of importance represents a continuation of the racism and superiority complexes developed during the colonial period. This point is buttressed by the continued "white saviour industrial complex" and developmental interventions from external donors, which seem to bear a striking resemblance to European colonial policies justified by the Christianisation, commercialisation, and "civilisation" of Africans. International trade today places Africa at a massive disadvantage with European and Western nations, which continue to see the continent as a raw material and natural resource honeypot. Socio-economic inequalities caused by the legacies of Cecil Rhodes remain a big challenge for post-independent southern Africa, while ethnic and inter-ethnic conflicts caused by British divide-and-rule policies continue to plague countries such as Kenya, Nigeria, Sierra Leone, and Sudan.

15

Colonialism in French Africa

Douglas Yates

WHEN DISCUSSING FRENCH colonialism, a distinction is generally made between the first colonial empire, which existed from the seventeenth century until 1814, and the second colonial empire, which began with the conquest of Algiers in 1830 and came to an end in 1977. The focus of this chapter will be on the second empire. But France had wide experience of imperialism before the "Scramble for Africa". It had already built and, then in 1815, lost an enormous empire, including India, Canada, and Louisiana. Only 15 years after the defeat of Napoleon – following a genocidal invasion of Algeria – did France again become involved in an overseas adventure of conquest and colonisation. The birth of France's latter black African empire can be dated to the appointment, in 1854, of Louis Faidherbe, who sought to expand and consolidate his base in Senegal along the coast, then open up trade routes into the interior and link the upper Niger with the Atlantic. Frustrated by its loss in the Franco-Prussian War of 1870, Paris continued African colonial expansion in the 1880s, with two quite independent thrusts into the interior: one up the Niger River, pursued by J.S. Gallieni, who conquered what would become French West Africa (FWA), and another up the Congo River, begun by Pierre Savorgnan de Brazza, which established the basis for French Equatorial Africa (FEA).[1]

At the Berlin Conference in 1884–1885, these new French conquests and territorial claims, in addition to their starting point in Senegambia, were recognised by the other major powers. These included Gabon (1839), French Somalia (1862), French Congo (1875), and French Sudan (1883). After the

Berlin Conference, France seized Niger (1890), Guinea (1891), Djibouti (1892), Dahomey (1892), Côte d'Ivoire (1893), Madagascar (1895), Upper Volta, or what is now Burkina Faso (1896), Chad (1900), Mauritania (1902), and Ubangi-Chari (1905). Once Britain had seized the mouth of the Niger River, thus frustrating French ambitions to connect its possessions with the Atlantic, the whole West African sub-region was partitioned between these two rivals in 1898 to avoid direct military conflict. After their stand-off in Fashoda the following year, France forswore territorial ambitions in the Anglo-Egyptian Sudan, thus setting the eastern limits of its new African empire. Outstanding Anglo-French differences in West Africa were eventually settled in 1904, forming the basis of what would become the Entente Cordiale. Finally, the First World War gave two former German colonies to victorious France: Togoland (1918) and Cameroon (1918). In this way, almost all of France's colonial empire, except Madagascar, Comoros, and Djibouti, consisted of one vast contiguous territory in West and Central Africa.

When the French scrambled for their second African empire in the late nineteenth and early twentieth century, they based their imperial policies on the ideology of nationalism centred around people. A hallmark of the French colonial project was its "civilising mission" (*mission civilisatrice*) by which colonial officials undertook a policy of cultural assimilation into the French Empire. So it came to pass that a small but important group of Africans devoted themselves to their own education and acculturation, to achieve French citizenship, and to gain their full political rights. These were individuals known as évolués because they accepted the French cultural logic of evolution into full citizens. They adopted the Christian religion, learned the French language, and adopted the codes of French culture, as well as the economic outlooks of their colonial masters. Prior to 1945, only a minority of local francophone Africans who entered school stayed long enough to achieve literacy or learn a skilled trade. Yet it was this small group who would enable the late-colonial institutions to function. Its members served as employees of the administration and commerce, or as teachers, pastors, priests, founding fathers and – in collaboration with their French teachers – national historians.

One of the problems with the historiography of francophone Africa is the preponderant role played by assimilated elites in the construction of dominant narratives about colonialism: what it was, what happened, and what it meant. Subalterns were silent. Other more critical French voices existed such as Albert Londres, André Gide, Denise Moran, Marcel Homet, and Emmanuel Dongala,[2] who gained an audience, thereby generating changes in colonial policy. Assimilation, for example, was a result of political reforms brought about by scandals that came to light through critical journalism. A complete account of all the battles and bloodshed culminating in colonial conquest is beyond the scope of this chapter. Instead, its focus will be on the struggle over establishing the historical record between defenders of colonialism and critical journalist-authors concerning the most emblematic colonial project of Central Africa: the Congo–Ocean Railway, which today links the Atlantic port of Pointe-Noire with Brazzaville. Bypassing the rapids on the lower Congo River, the railway allows river boats to ascend the Congo River and its major tributaries, including the Oubangui River to the Central African Republic (CAR) capital of Bangui. French colonial administrators contracted the Société de Construction des Batignolles to build this railway, using forced labour, at a heavy cost in human lives. Total deaths were estimated in excess of 17,000 workers, from a combination of both industrial accidents and diseases, including malaria.[3] All this, in turn, led to the Kongo-Wara rebellion between 1928 and 1931. How do we know all this?

Poking Our Pen into the Wound

In 1987, the French historian Didier Folléas, then a teacher at the Lycée Français de Casablanca, found an envelope in an old flea market at Derb Ghallef. Three decades after Moroccan independence, you could still find traces of the French colonial past for sale in dusty street markets. Book vendors there sold second-hand collections of used books too heavy for the fleeing French settlers to carry back to the metropole, with shoeboxes of black-and-white photographs and abandoned postcards, their antique stamps still affixed to them. These were placed aside handwritten messages from long-dead senders, addressed to recipients who were themselves long departed: "It was at one of these stalls selling rarities and songbirds that I found some small 6 x 10.5 format photos in an envelope upon which was written only, in Indian ink: 'ALBERT LONDRES'."[4]

Folléas bought the whole lot for a very modest sum and, later, when he returned to Paris, purchased a copy of Londres's *Terre d'ébène* (Land of Ebony). This book, which was first published in 1929, after Londres's return from four months in France's colonies south of the Sahara, was still on sale in bookstores, as it is today. It presents a vivid first-person narrative of the colonial era in France's two vast African federations of French West Africa and French Equatorial Africa. Londres was a newspaper journalist who had reported on the abuses of the French colonial system, especially the cruelty of concessionary capitalists, in a series of articles for the daily newspaper *Le Petit Parisien*. As Folléas read this book, he immediately recognised the characters described by Londres in the old black-and-white photographs that he had found in Casablanca. "But my intuitions were not solidly established certainties. I needed indisputable proof." He went to the Bibliothèque Nationale de France to consult the 1928 newspaper archives in which Londres had first published his articles with his photos: "I had been right. The photographs were there, at least some of them. As for the others, I came to classify them easily alongside those which were published thanks to serial numbers that were printed on their backs by the laboratory."[5]

Reading and re-reading *Terre d'ébène*, Folléas soon became convinced that this book had been a turning point in that journalist's career. The voyage to Central Africa had changed Londres's tone from a gentleman globetrotter to something else, someone harder and more direct. Folléas pored over published portraits of the man, like the memoir by his daughter Florise Londres,[6] the profile by Paul Mousset,[7] and what is still the main Londres biography by Pierre Assouline,[8] *Albert Londres: Vie et mort d'un grand reporter, 1884–1932*, to try to understand this writer whose name is associated with the most prestigious prize in French journalism.[9] He examined Londres's notebooks and correspondence preserved in the archives of the Albert Londres Prize headquarters in Paris. There, he discovered, as he had suspected, that *Terre d'ébène* had only revealed a small portion of what the journalist experienced in the colonies. Folléas did the work of the historian, examining the minutiae of the written record, exploring the archives, reading the secondary sources, comparing the old data with the new. After retracing the steps of his historical subject, Folléas then published Londres's long-lost photographs in paperback, thereby adding a few new pictures to history's always unfinished puzzle of the past.

It is difficult to know how many people still read *Terre d'ébène*. Originally published in 1929 by Albin Michel with the provocative subtitle *La traite des noirs* (The Slave Trade), its first edition must have been a bestseller, given its popularity, the large number of contemporaries who cited it in their own writings on French Equatorial Africa, and the reputation that his book has enjoyed ever since. There have been numerous paperback re-editions of this classic, published by Serpent à Plumes (1994), Arlea (1998, 2008), and Editions du Rocher (2011). However, only a few new editions have come out since 2011.

Whatever the exact numbers, one thing is certain: nobody reads the book in English anymore. The English translation came out in 1929 under the title *A Very Naked People*, and has never been reissued.[10] This author procured a vintage used hardcover copy in New York. The translation, by the American Sylvia Stuart, has the merit of capturing the zeitgeist, with vocabulary and figures of speech used by writers of the 1920s that give it a feel of authenticity, as if one is listening to someone back then recounting his exotic voyage to "deepest, darkest Africa". But this same style does not work when addressed to today's young readership: it sounds too old-fashioned. The late American publisher Horace Liveright announced on its dustjacket that Londres's journal would offer its readers "the romance and tragedy of French Africa", which Stuart's literary translation delivers. For while Londres had written a hard-hitting report of the abuses of colonialism and forced labour in Africa, his shock subtitle, "The Slave Trade", was removed from the English edition, along with his critical four last chapters in which he described the construction of the Congo–Ocean Railway as a form of modern slavery. Therefore, instead of a scandalous exposé by an investigative journalist, readers of the English translation were given a sort of aristocratic, gentleman-dandy's travel journal.

Yet, according to the book's most famous sentence, his apothegm, which was added by Londres in a preface to the first edition of the book in which he tried to defend himself and his newspaper from a barrage of virulent critiques by irate colonial authorities and concessionaires: "I remain convinced, for my part, that a journalist is not a choirboy, and that his role should not consist of running in front of processions scattering rose petals. Our job is neither to please, nor to harm, but to poke our pen into the wound."[11]

The Congo–Ocean Railroad

In a more recent collection of re-edited colonial-era texts, produced in 2006 by Harmattan, there is a long excerpt from *Terre d'ébène* (chapter 27 on the Congo–Ocean railroad) among other writings by colonial officers, engineers, travel writers, novelists, and journalists of the colonial press who published articles or books or chapters in books about the construction of the Congo–Ocean railroad (1921–1934). In this two-volume anthology, the Dutch academic Ieme van der Poel of the University of Amsterdam sets out "to show how the polemic about the Congo–Ocean contributed to the destruction of the myth of the grand colonial project in general, and that of the railroad in particular".[12]

Colonial discourse heralded the arrival of grand engineering projects like steam-powered railroads in mythical terms: in this case, as a triumph of industrial modernisation that would link the coast to the interior and thereby bring commerce, Christianity, and the "civilising mission" to Africans. The last chapters of Londres's *Terre d'ébène* exposed a lack of equipment (no boats, no roads, no food supplies, no blankets, no wheelbarrows, no jackhammers, only a hammer and bar to break the stone); the lack of medicine; the whippings, the skeletons along the side of the iron road; the cruel foremen – sick with tropical diseases – screaming orders while beating the bare-backed black locals, 200 of them strapped to ropes pulling giant tree trunks, their faces lacerated by whips, their fingers crushed or missing. Such images of forced labour drawn from personal eyewitness accounts by a reliable journalist helped to debunk the myth of the colonial train as an unbridled triumph of progress and civilisation.

Van der Poel's ample selections in her anthology from other authors writing about the topic show that Albert Londres was not alone. He was partly inspired by the success of René Maran, who had already published a series of articles in the left-wing *Journal du Peuple* in 1926 which brought to light the forced labour of the Congo–Ocean Railway. Londres was also inspired by the sensation in Parisian literary circles stirred by the publication of André Gide's *Voyage au Congo* (1927), which transformed newspaper reports into a controversial issue that captured a literary-salon public's attention and involved it in heated debate. This was when Londres persuaded his editors to send him to Africa to see for himself what these writers had reported. His example was followed by others and grew into a virtual drumbeat of criticism.

"What interests me in this debate," explains Van der Poel, "more than the shocking facts that it reveals, is the way that it functions as an indicator of the evolution of the discourse on colonialism."[13] While the colonial press was reproducing stereotyped imagery inherited from the nineteenth century, these critics of the railway endeavoured to subvert the received wisdom. This leads Van der Poel to wonder if these travel writings, because of their critical and often corrosive nature, prepared the way for the great post-war African independence writers, such as Léopold Senghor of Senegal[14] and Sekou Touré of Guinea,[15] many of whom made explicit reference to what was by then the established abuses of the Congo–Ocean railroad.

Take, for instance, the often repeated image that each railroad tie represented a human life (*"un mort par traverse"*). The first time this expression appears was in the French engineer Louis Delmer's 1899 book on railroads, in an otherwise triumphalist chapter about the remarkable feats of the railroad engineers who had to build without any maps or geological surveys to help them. In his chapter on "The Colonial Train", he writes that "one could say that each sleeper tie represents a man's life".[16] But Delmer presented this as an unfortunate consequence of the hard conditions, not an intentional act of cruelty. André Gide's concise formula – "*un traverse, un mort*" – was used by socialist parliamentarians in Paris to blame the Kongo-Wara revolt on its forced labour, "of which", they declared, "each tie crushed the corpse of a writhing black" – a polemic that was criticised by Henriette Roussel in his 1934 doctoral dissertation on the railroad.[17]

After the Kongo-Wara rebellion (1928–1931), this image was picked up by francophone poets such as the Haitian Jacques Roumain, whose poem "Bois d'ébène", published in Léopold Senghor's 1948 *Anthology of New Negro Poetry*, invoked the "silence of twenty-five thousand negro cadavers/ of twenty-five thousand ebony wood ties" (i.e. one cadaver per tie).[18] More recently, the Brazzaville-Congolese novelist Emmanuel Dongala, has a black railroad worker explain to a white passenger that "there is a dead man for each railroad tie".[19] This formula was also used to generalise European deaths. In his travel journal, the French writer Robert Poulaine repeated the expression, "One black per tie, one white per kilometre."[20]

Historical scholarship on the mortality rate of the construction of the Congo–Ocean railroad has examined this "*une traverse, un mort*" discourse by writers like Gide and Londres. At 1,500 ties per kilometre,[21] if the one-death-per-tie formula were accurate, then at 502 kilometres the death toll would have actually been around 753,000 men, rather than 17,000, the figure voiced with poetic licence in Paris by socialist parliamentarians in National Assembly debates.[22] The 17,000 death estimate first appeared in Gide's *Voyage au Congo* (1927). According to Gilles Sautter, based on the statistical data of Raymond Susset, the number of victims is estimated at between 15,000 and 18,000.[23] And in her much-cited classic, Catherine Coquery-Vidrovitch estimates around 20,000.[24] These estimates are drawn from recruitment figures and mortality rates. In 1924, around 8,000 local workers were recruited from throughout French Equatorial Africa, coming from as far away as what is today Chad. As they died, another 8,000 were recruited in 1925, and again 8,000 in 1926, thus totalling 24,000, of whom perhaps 4,000 survived.[25]

Even if we take the highest estimates, we arrive at a still unacceptable figure of one death per 37.65 ties. But the "one-death-per-tie" trope remains indelibly etched in the discourse of the Congo–Ocean railroad. Exact figures notwithstanding, this critique of the Congo–Ocean railroad by investigative journalists, novelists, and intellectuals – the established truth of the anti-colonial discourse – directly confronted the colonialist discourse that had "manufactured" French public opinion.[26] Before René Maran, André Gide, and Albert Londres exposed the abuses of the Congo–Ocean railroad, the main source of information about French Equatorial Africa (known with gentle reproach as the "Cinderella of French colonies") was the colonial press, which, despite its false reporting, Van der Poel champions as an "extremely rich but still seldom explored source of French colonial history and literature".[27]

La Revue Indigène, for example, was a bi-monthly review entirely devoted to what was euphemistically called "the great colonial work" (*la grande* œuvre *colonial*). In its issues from 1925 there are articles about the fine job being accomplished by the new French Governor-General, Raphael Antonetti (1872–1938), who is credited with commencing the construction of a railroad on the "French" side of the Congo River (note the nationalist discourse of colonialism) after years of neglect by the Ministry of the Colonies and overreliance on dubiously motivated concessionary companies. The French had depended on their rivals – the Belgian authorities – to export "French" goods down the "Belgian" side of the Congo River by using the Matadi–Léopoldville railroad.

The French politician Joseph Peyrat blamed the reliance on the Belgian railroad for the economic underdevelopment of the French Congo. This railroad, by the time he was writing in 1925, had been worn out by 26 years of heavy usage and was too small to handle the export potential of the Congo basin. "A railway", he extolled, "is itself a creator of movement and life", which "by its high salaries and distribution of better rations for a more regular employment can train the natives and bring them to a condition of greater resistance" to those tropical diseases which, he claimed, were decimating the population (the official explanation for the depopulation of French Equatorial Africa). Peyrat writes that sleeping sickness, poor hygiene, and lack of agriculture were the factors responsible for demographic decline, all of which would be ameliorated by Governor Antonetti's ambitious railroad project.[28]

Another writer for the colonial press, Louis Martel, praised the French colonial agents for paying high wages to workers, feeding them well, supplying them with good tools, and providing them with health care and housing, resulting in "few deaths, and few sick people".[29] It was not just the euphemistic language of "recruitment" as being "courageously accepted" by locals, nor the uncritical repetition of official proclamations that they were well paid, well fed, and well treated for tropical sickness; it was the bold-faced lies that corroded French public opinion. "Cases of desertion from worksites are rare," Martel writes. "Workers, thanks to the solicitude of the administration toward them, are happy with their rewards provided by the sites. They return to their villages with a little money, joyful and satisfied with their stay at the sites. Many return to work as volunteers."[30]

René Maran, a black writer from the French Antilles who made his career in the colonial administration of Oubangui-Chari (now the Central African Republic) but became one of its outspoken critics, was the first author to publish a condemnation of the construction of the Congo–Ocean railway. The Martinican had denounced its "tragic horror" in an article in the *Journal du People* in 1925 which explicitly described how Saras from Chad were being brought to replace Congolese workers who had been decimated by hunger, sickness, and cruelty. His article, "AEF, Red Colony", criticised André Gide for covering up the French "criminal administration" in *Voyage au Congo* because Gide personally knew these officers. Gide had blamed the concessionaires for the excesses. Maran compared the situation to the murderous era of conquest.

In another article, Maran wrote, "We are as cruel at the end of 1925 as we were in 1914 or 1902." For Governor-General Antonetti, he could find no better description of his project to build a railroad quickly than a "disordered and despotic tyranny". Maran described in vivid detail how barges full of starving workers were being deposited in Brazzaville two or three weeks before the arrival of their food and supplies. "One of these contingents of around 300 individuals, when they arrived in Brazzaville, after three months counted no more than 69. *All the others were dead.*"[31]

Citing in anecdotal form the random shooting of blacks, the 12-hour days, and the banal "crimes perpetrated by the Société de Construction des Batignolles",[32] Maran made the case that it was the impunity of the authors of these crimes, tolerated by Governor-General Antonetti and his subordinate colonial officers (what today we would call the failure of their "responsibility to protect"), which was ultimately responsible for "the largest roads and the smallest paths being paved with negroes, their bones, their putrid corpses".[33]

Maran was a famous author after he had won the Prix Goncourt (France's highest literary prize) for his novel *Batouala: Veritable roman nègre* in 1921, in which he cited the use of forced labour on colonial trains, challenging the colonial myth of the "civilising mission". *Batouala*, however, so scandalised his superiors that Maran was forced to resign from the colonial administration. So he turned to journalism to make his living. The influence of his newspaper articles was tied to his reputation as an author. Like André Gide, Maran had an impact on public opinion by, if not opposing colonialism itself, then reminding the colonisers of their moral duties towards the colonised: the beginning of black anti-colonial discourse by nationalists after the war.

Maran is today remembered as the first black writer to win the Goncourt Prize. This was a major achievement, especially in the 1920s. Yet it also reflected his white Parisian readership who awarded the Goncourt, a marketplace reality that eventually compromised his critique. For example, he later wrote for the right-wing Parisian paper *Je Suis Partout* from 1936 to 1937 in praise of the Congo–Ocean railroad, using the mythology and discourse of the colonial train. And in an article that appeared in *Journal du Peuple* on the day of the railroad's inauguration, Maran proclaimed it an "exemplary work" which represented the "honour of France" and increased France's "prestige in the eyes of the world".[34]

The Kongo-Wara Rebellion (1928–1931)

Robert Poulaine, another French journalist who travelled to French Equatorial Africa in 1928 and witnessed, with his own eyes, the deserted villages and countless victims of the outbreak of violence connected with the Kongo-Wara rebellion, drew the simplest and most evident conclusion from his eyewitness observations: that this local uprising had been caused by violent recruitment for the construction of the railroad. In a series of articles published in *L'Impartial Français* in 1929, Poulaine criticised the concessionaires, as Gide had done, but he also condemned the colonial administration, as Londres had done: "The way this large colony is governed", he wrote, "gives the appearance that the only policy of France is to decimate thousands of defenceless blacks."[35] He wanted to contradict the colonial press that mendaciously "sings the praises of an administration against whom we bring the most undeniable proofs".[36]

Poulaine provided as his evidence several verbatim extracts from an official government report by the Ministry of the Colonies which instructed its agents to use force when necessary to meet their recruitment quotas. "The governor's policy has provoked a revolt in the French Congo," wrote Poulaine.[37] Rebels had started taking European hostages and threatening the authorities with pillage and murder, "provoked by the intensive recruitment conducted in remote regions".[38] Poulaine published a book on this subject, *Etapes africaines*, in 1930, with the intention of exposing the administrators responsible for the tragedy. It described how the previous French Governor-General, Jean-Victor Augagneur, had provided supplies, housing, and medical support to workers, who were drawn by persuasion, not force, from the local populations. Local chiefs had at first volunteered men from their villages in lieu of paying cash for the hut tax. It was only in 1924, he noted, with the arrival of Governor-General

Antonetti, that the pace of recruitment was expedited beyond reason, and the mortality rate started decimating the workforce through dysentery (caused by insufficient and unsanitary food), pneumonia (caused by the humid climate and inadequate shelter), and exhaustion (caused by inhuman long-distance porterage of supplies across the road-less terrain). Despite losing almost the entire local workforce, wrote Poulaine, "We persisted in our errors and soon arrived on the border of Chad, on the banks of the Chari, on the edges of the Haute-Sangha, recruiting men like the devil."[39] The mortality rate had risen to such proportions that it became difficult to repatriate a fifth of the workers at the end of their contracts. Desertions to neighbouring colonies had multiplied. Recruitment had become more difficult.

This was when, in October 1928, a revolt broke out in the Haute-Sangha region of what is now the Central African Republic and in the neighbouring districts of Cameroon (a former German colony now under a French mandate). Armed militia were employed by district officers to repress rebels and to pacify the "natives". These military pacification operations did not end until 1931. Although they were soon forgotten in France, because of much deadlier events leading up to the Second World War (1939–1945), the Kongo-Wara rebellion was the largest inter-war insurrection in Cameroon and French Equatorial Africa. What little was known in France about the rebellion was due largely to the writings of Robert Poulaine, which led to calls for changes to the scandalous forced-labour practices of the colonial concessionary regime. The colonial government said that this rebellion had been caused by an African "native doctor" called "Karnou", who had used his magical fetishes to play on the superstition of locals. "We were there ourselves," wrote Poulaine. "Contrary to the affirmations of Governor-General Antonetti, this sedition was not due exclusively to a black sorcerer, but to abusive profit-seeking recruitment by the railroad."[40]

L'Humanité, the newspaper of the French Communist Party, picked up these critical reports and turned them into a weapon of class struggle. In 1929, it published a series of articles by the journalist Marcel Joubert, which moved the discourse from concerned humanitarianism (fingering corrupt concessionaires and colonial officials) to anti-imperialist rhetoric (parading the abuses of forced labour as inherent in the system of colonial capitalism, rebellion, and class warfare). In other words, they moved the discourse from a critique of immoral practices by colonial actors to a full-scale attack on the colonial system itself. "It is too simple to explain with a grotesque argument that sorcerers have excited the hatred of whites," wrote Joubert. "The insurrection has a deeper cause. Its origin lies in the oppression of French imperialism, the bloodiest domination that black Africa has ever known."[41]

French communists framed the Kongo-Wara rebellion as a Spartacus-type slave rebellion by exploited workers against the greedy capitalists, who were being protected by colonial officers. They thus portrayed the rebels as "negroes revolting against colonisation".[42] If their early twentieth-century communist rhetoric sounds antiquated today, as when they referred to socialists as "petit bourgeois" or when they described black workers as "negroes", their Marxian analysis of recruitment by colonial officers as an economic cause of this bloody uprising does not.

Joubert had apparently consulted Londres's *Terre d'ébène* but criticised him as a *"frondeur bourgeoise"*[43] (bourgeois curmudgeon). He cited some passages from Londres's book (which may suggest he actually read it) to support his argument that forced labour on the railroad was a form of modern slavery, which had resulted in more than 120 deaths per kilometre, "almost as many corpses as wooden ties". He repeated reports that black railworkers had been killed with impunity by concessionaires.[44] Joubert quoted a colonial officer interviewed by Londres who had declared that "killing a nigger isn't murder", concluding that, "a few rare exceptions aside, in black Africa every white-skinned man is a murderer".[45] Joubert criticised both concessionaires and the colonial administrators, seeing the latter – in classical Marxian analysis – as the handmaidens of the former. Article 4 of the railroad concession granted the Société de Construction des Batignolles a guaranteed supply of cheap black labour. Colonial authorities were required by that article to supply 8,000 men to work on the railroad, a system of forced labour that Joubert equated with the slave trade:

> A decree by a local or regional potentate decides that this region or that village must furnish a pre-determined number of workers for some enterprise. The teams of recruiters show up at the designated villages, "enrol" the able-bodied men with their cudgels and whips, and rape the women on the same occasion. If there is resistance, a punitive expedition is sent to pillage and burn down the village or region that resists.[46]

The Empire Strikes Back

Such charges of abusive colonial practices made their way in 1929–1930 to the League of Nations in Geneva, where France was accused of running a modern-day form of slavery. The League had been created in 1919 to resolve inter-state conflicts but had also adopted a reformist discourse on colonial labour, calling for a European-type labour regime to be implemented in the colonies. League members in Geneva now accused France of human rights abuses on the basis of evidence gleaned from the writings of journalists like Albert Londres who had exposed the crimes of the Congo–Ocean railroad. This train had become a case study in forced labour, something comparable to the modern "blood diamonds" antonomasia, which refers to the African resource curse in general by means of an exemplar.

To the "Congo–Ocean critique" – if I may call it that – came a reply from the colonial press. Paul Bourdarie, a member of the High Council on the Colonies, wrote a defence of the colonial labour regime in *La Revue Indigène* in which he argued that it would be impossible to institute a European-type labour regime. He regretted the initial errors of missing supplies at the beginning of the Congo–Ocean project but said that, compared with practices in other colonies – notably the British use of coolies in Asia – black African labour in Equatorial Africa was not so bad. "Maybe the League of Nations and the International Labour Office [ILO]", insisted Bourdarie, "should look at its other member states". He continued:

> There is, in the Orient, one of your signatory member state where slavery reigns openly, under the eyes of European consulates. Its slave markets are public; local officials collect a special tax of 250 francs per head for each transaction. The sales price is known. Old slaves cost 12,000 francs. Younger ones cost double … What has Geneva done over the last ten years to bring those things to an end?[47]

This kind of affirmative defence is a fallacy of argumentation known as "whataboutism", which justifies wrongful, immoral, or illegal conduct by pointing to others committing wrongful, immoral or illegal acts and asking rhetorically, "What about them?"[48] Two wrongs do not make a right. British coolies in China did not justify modern-day slavery in the Congo. But one of the defences of the system of forced labour in Equatorial Africa was to attack similar practices by other colonisers elsewhere, and ask: what about *them*?

Another defence was ideological. Critics of the French colonial system were labelled "Bolsheviks", with echoes of antisemitism. This anti-communist strategy was used by the Minister of the Colonies, Albert Lebrun, in his report to the Senate on the colonial budget. He lamented how "the least incident, true or false, peddled in the European press, gives rise to manifestly exaggerated and malicious articles".[49] Lebrun blamed early reports on the Kongo-Wara rebellion as hysterical rumours taking a minor incident of a "sorcerer who abused the credulity of blacks in an insufficiently administered region" and turning it into a *cause célèbre*.

He continued: "What are the origins and aims of such a campaign, which has gotten worse over the past few years, and which it would be dangerous to ignore? They are many. First and foremost, the action of Bolshevism, operating in our colonies, as in all the countries where it hopes to spread trouble and revolution."[50] Lebrun also accused those countries which had been "dispossessed of their colonies" (i.e. Germany) "of enviously spreading these false rumours".[51] But his trump card was to accuse his critics of being amateurs, "journal-keeping tourists" who had not lived in Africa long enough to really understand the colonial situation: "It is indispensable to stay a very long time and live entirely in the atmosphere of a country to allow oneself to judge it … How do you expect the traveller, be he a savant, a financier, a journalist, or a tourist, always insufficiently informed, passing through like a whirlwind, to be a fair and impartial judge?"[52] Lebrun suggested that the only way to respond to such false, envious, amateur judgements would be to present the positive works of French colonialism, its roads, its bridges, its hospitals, its schools, its water and power utilities, and its granting of some self-government to those more evolved "natives". He noted the forthcoming 1931 International Colonial Exposition in Paris, which would present the "trademark of French genius" in the administration of its colonies and defend its net results.[53]

In similar vein, Paul Bourdarie, French explorer and founder of the Académie des Sciences Colonials, described the efforts of the International Labour Organization (ILO) to suppress forced labour as "a political business led by the Workers' International and leading to the dictatorship of the proletariat".[54] He condemned the ILO director, Albert Thomas – a French socialist who ran that international organisation from its creation in 1919 until his death in 1932 – for placing the interests of international workers above French national interests. Bourdarie dismissed the ILO Convention Concerning Forced or Compulsory Labour of 1930 as a political vote by non-colonial states (the majority) against colonial states (the minority). This treaty had suppressed forced labour but left equivalent practices in anglophone colonies unaffected, since under indirect rule it was traditional rulers and not British colonial officers who delivered workers to the projects. "Mr Albert Thomas has participated, so to speak, in a plot against colonial

France,"[55] concluded Bourdarie, even comparing France to a martyred "Christ of the International".[56]

All Frenchmen who lobbied against forced labour in the colonies were branded "traitors". "We must recognise that several French writers whose talent is uncontestable", wrote an undersecretary of state for the merchant marines, Maurice Ajam, in *La Dépêche Coloniale et Maritime*, "have singularly excited against us the feelings of countries that have no colonies" (i.e. Germany), "who will never forgive us our black troops nor our foreign legion."[57] He continued: "Today the international conference in Geneva is allowing Germany to return to its war campaign indirectly ... but it is really the communist anti-colonial doctrine which had made its official appearance there."[58] Trade unionists who were present at this conference were not recognised by Maurice Ajam as having just passed one of the eight fundamental conventions of the ILO. Instead, Ajam saw them as denying "the great humanitarian principle that civilised nations must develop all of the planet's resources".[59]

Louis Proust, a deputy from the Loire, blamed the "drama" of the Congo–Ocean railroad on the Parisian press: "This drama does not unfold on construction sites of the French Congo, but in the editorial rooms of certain Parisian newspapers and in the hallways of the Palais Bourbon" (i.e. the National Assembly). "Mr Antonetti, I know, has one great fault: He's not Parisian enough."[60] Proust repeated testimony by one of his constituents who had just returned from Equatorial Africa and who "wanted to see for himself if what was being said about our Cinderella colony was still exact". This man had reported to him that the natives "ate well", "slept well", and were "perfectly cared for".[61] The mortality rate had fallen to 1.48 per cent (in February 1929) and desertions had also declined, from 35 per cent (1926) to 16 per cent (1927) to only 5 per cent in 1928.[62] Proust argued that the "violent press campaign of criticisms came from the metropole and not from the colonies", and from men "who were ignorant of the realities and difficulties of African life".[63] He ended by suggesting that much of this "fake news" was in reality being generated by German spies.

There was another, different kind of argument raised in the colonial press in defence of forced labour. It was the racist xenophobic thesis that "lazy natives" only worked when told to do so by a superior. The French journalist Pierre Mille, applying the theory of "primitive mentalities in inferior societies" – as developed by the ethnocentric French anthropologist Lucien Lévy-Bruhl in his *Les fonctions mentales dans les sociétés inférieures* (1910)[64] – pontificated about how ILO conference members had failed to understand that "the modalities of work vary with latitude and race" and said that they spoke about workers "as if they were all white men in Europe", but "a white worker was not a black worker, nor a black worker a yellow worker". "The native does not work, not even for himself, unless he receives an order from a chief or sorcerer-priest of his village or tribe ... Consequently, in black Africa, a great amount of labour appears to be forced, in our eyes, without looking so in the eyes of the native."[65]

Another tactic was to personalise the defence of Governor-General Antonetti, who was being attacked by Maran as a tyrant, and by Poulaine as personally responsible for the uprising. *La Presse Coloniale Illustrée* devoted a special issue to the Congo–Ocean Railway which painted a heroic portrait of both Antonetti and his project. Two years before the train's completion, this illustrated supplement tried to reverse polemical coverage of the man and his train. It argued that the latter was necessary to develop the hinterland, and the former had achieved a *grand* œuvre.

Georges Boussenot, director of the *La Presse Coloniale Illustrée* newspaper, wrote a long preface to this special issue (whose comic-book illustrations could be used to decorate a Banania box) which explained how Antonetti had arrived at the most difficult moment of the project. In 1925, when the two relatively flat sections – from Pointe-Noire on the Atlantic coast and from its other terminus at Brazzaville on Stanley Pool – had arrived at the Mayombe massif: "that tormented region, challenging, hostile to man, Europeans as well as natives, covered with forests, and constantly humid".[66] For the first 170 kilometres, the Société de Construction des Batignolles had constructed the line in relatively dry and flat terrain. Recruitment of labour from local populations around the two terminal points of Pointe-Noire and Brazzaville had been possible by working through local chiefs and traditional rulers who were eager to pay their taxes with human muscle. But when the engineers reached the sparsely populated mountain, which was in some spots uninhabitable, they realised that they would be unable to find enough workers locally, or even within the French Congo, to fill the construction sites. That was when the forced recruitment of populations in Ubangi-Chari and other parts of the hinterland began.

In this way, responsibility was shifted from the shoulders of Antonetti to Daladier, from the French Equatorial Africa Governor-General's office in Brazzaville to the Ministry of the Colonies in Paris. It was said that the modern slave trade criticised by Maran, Londres, and Joubert was not Antonetti's fault. He was just following orders. By telling the story of Antonetti's arrival this way, Boussenot transformed him from a modern-day slaver (Londres), a lackey of the imperialists (Joubert), and a handmaiden of concessionaires (Poulaine), into a hero. Antonetti, he said, arrived at the project when things had reached an insurmountable obstacle: the Mayombe massif. He had received his orders to build the railroad through those mountains. And he had done just that. As for his critics, like Londres, they were dismissed as mere "globetrotters" who indulged in painting picturesque fables, "whereas they should have been pronouncing facts and producing documents". To satisfy their public with "sensational stories", they were "giving despisers of French colonisation, not, alas, only those in our own country, arms against us".[67]

Boussenot's special issue – with its comic-book illustrations of the colonial train – proceeded to enumerate what he described as the achievements of the honourable Governor-General Antonetti, thereby rehabilitating the man who had personified the abuses and excesses of forced labour by French colonial authorities. So enthusiastic was the colonial press about the completion of the project that discussion now turned to the positive future instead of lingering on the negative past. Hopes were placed on new exports coming from the Belgian Congo, including minerals from Katanga (then being transported through Portuguese Angola and Mozambique). The Congo–Ocean railroad, they wrote, once completed, promised to leave behind an industrial, wage-earning workforce. Thus the hero's tale told by *La Presse Coloniale Illustrée* ended with a romantic shining path into the dark hinterland, with the old myth of the colonial train. This was the power of personalising the story around the heroic figure of Antonetti.

Concluding Reflections

This case study of the Congo–Ocean railroad is intended to illustrate how colonial exploitation in Central Africa by the French was cruel, unjust, violent, destructive, and racist. But another equally important lesson is to be drawn from the historiographical battles between defenders of the colonial project and their critics: the representations made of French colonialism range from a mythical *mission civilisatrice* to a capitalist imperialist nightmare. There has been something of a deficit of explicit methodological reflection on history. However, there now exists a widespread sense that this must change. There is no question that the "post-modern" debate has done a great deal to put serious reflection about historiography on the agenda of researchers, teachers, and students of history. The time has now come critically to re-examine documents produced during the colonial era for evidence of the dark underbelly of colonial rule, of which the story of the Congo-Ocean railroad is a supreme example.

16

Colonialism in Belgian Africa

Guy Vanthemsche

THIS CHAPTER WILL EXAMINE Belgium's colonial rule in the small Central African countries of Burundi and Rwanda between 1916 and 1962, before focusing in more detail on the case of the Democratic Republic of the Congo (DRC), which was ruled by King Leopold II and, subsequently, by the Belgian government between 1885 and 1960. As in the Congo, Belgian colonial rule left a profound legacy in Burundi and Rwanda that fundamentally influenced their fate in the six subsequent post-independence decades: both suffered episodes of genocide and mass atrocities, while parts of the Congo have remained anarchic and acephalous for two and a half decades.

The Tragic Twins: Burundi and Rwanda (1916–1962)

During the First World War (1914–1918), Belgian-led European and African troops in the Force Publique participated in the Allied struggle against German troops in East Africa. The Belgian colonial forces seized large parts of modern-day Tanzania and occupied one of its main inland cities, Tabora. At the 1919 Paris Peace Conference, the Germans were stripped of their colonial empire, and the Belgians rewarded. In 1923, the League of Nations granted Brussels a mandate over two previously German-controlled territories in the Great Lakes region: Ruanda and Urundi. After the Second World War (1939–1945), both territories became UN trusteeships.

Two ethnic groups – an 85 per cent Hutu majority and a 15 per cent Tutsi minority – lived in both small but densely populated kingdoms. Traditionally, royal authority – exercised by the *mwami* – was in the hands of the Tutsi. The Belgians introduced a system of indirect rule, maintaining these traditional authorities, but also turning them into subservient instruments of their own power. The originally fluid boundaries between the ethnic groups – and their economic activities – were gradually transformed under colonial rule into sharp and rigidified distinctions. The Belgians presented the pastoral Tutsi as "natural-born" rulers, a sort of *Herrenvolk* destined to dominate what they saw as the passive and subservient Hutu peasants. Under Brussels's administration, this hierarchical view of Ruandese and Urundese society was reinforced and disseminated through education and propaganda, and the ethnic origins of individuals from both groups were inscribed on legal identity documents.[1]

In the late 1950s, Belgian officials changed their minds, and overturned the traditional power relations in Ruanda (henceforth known as Rwanda), allowing the Hutu to take control of the country on becoming independent on 1 July 1962. In contrast, in Urundi (henceforth Burundi), which gained independence on the same day, Tutsi pre-eminence remained firmly in place. Belgian interference in Burundi on the eve of the end to colonial rule took another form: local officials incited the murder, in October 1961, of the popular and recently elected prime minister, Prince Louis Rwagasore, who was deemed "hostile" to Belgian interests.

The Congo Free State: A Unique Colonial Experiment (1885–1908)

On 1 July 1885, in the heart of Central Africa, around the Congo River basin, a strange state emerged that explicitly claimed to be "independent". Yet that political entity had all the characteristics of a classic nineteenth-century colony: a few thousand white soldiers and civil servants imposed their authority on the region's original inhabitants by force. The Congo Free State was thus a colony without a "motherland". Nevertheless, there was a clear link with Belgium. How can one explain this peculiar situation?

In the context of the period's imperialist expansion, the Congo Free State was a strange construct. All other colonies had been conquered by a Western European nation or by a Charter company, such as Cecil John Rhodes's British South Africa Company, acting as its instrument. Those conquests stemmed from a complex mixture of economic, diplomatic, and strategic motives impelling leading politicians and businessmen of the nations involved.

However, the events in Congo deviated from that standard model.[2]

In Belgium, the political and economic establishment was not enthusiastic about overseas expansion. There was also a lack of colonial ardour in broader sections of the population. However, the second king of the Belgians, Leopold II, saw things differently. His motives were manifold. According to him, tiny Belgium could and had to punch above its weight by being much more present globally, through trading companies, concession areas, or colonies. This would benefit Brussels's economic prosperity as well as Leopold's own personal wealth and prestige. In the royal mind, economic and political aspects, as well as public and private (even personal) dimensions, were always inextricably linked. Leopold's seemingly obsessive interest in overseas expansion – supported by a small group of collaborators, such as the diplomat Auguste Lambermont and the high-ranking mandarin Émile Banning – was reflected in numerous fruitless initiatives spread around the globe.[3]

The First Phases of King Leopold II's Congolese Initiative

A unique window of opportunity to establish themselves on the African continent emerged from the mid-1870s, when white adventurers, scientists, businessmen, and missionaries began to penetrate Central Africa. At the time, this region was still virtually unknown to Europeans. In the foreseeable future, several European powers – Britain, France, Germany, and Portugal – would eventually come to dominate the area. However, this political and economic process was also set within a particular cultural and ideological atmosphere. According to the dominant view expressed by British explorer David Livingstone, "Commerce, Christianity, and Civilisation" constituted the European *mission civilisatrice* of the epoch to overcome and destroy "barbarism" and "superstition" in black Africa. All over Europe, many individuals and groups (with varying degrees of idealism) committed themselves to this cause. Leopold began to fish in this pond in a strategic way. In 1876, he organised an International Geographic Conference in Brussels, attended by numerous European authorities from the scientific, religious, and diplomatic worlds.

The Belgian monarch suggested exploring the area around the Congo River for scientific and philanthropic reasons, especially to eliminate the endemic slave trade. Various private organisations were set up for this purpose: successively, the Association Internationale Africaine (AIA), the Comité d'Études du Haut-Congo, and the Association Internationale du Congo (AIC). Behind the scenes, the king was the driving force of these initiatives. The official, seemingly altruistic goals of these associations, however, obscured the true motives of the monarch: to trade first, then to acquire political sovereignty. After all, sovereignty soon proved indispensable to the realisation of trade across these territories. France and Portugal were on the verge of thwarting Leopold's commercial activities through the acquisition of administrative and military power in the African interior (see Yates and Sonsa in this volume).[4] As was widely noted during the "Scramble for Africa", trade followed the flag.

The Creation and Development of an Authoritarian State

The race for imperial supremacy in the Congo was eventually settled on the margins of, but not by, the 1884–1885 Berlin Conference. The 14 mostly European powers[5] sat around a horseshoe table in Berlin to determine the rules of the game that would govern the European penetration of Africa. Through separate declarations, the governments represented in Berlin successively recognised the AIC as a legitimate political force – which consequently was given the name of the Congo Free State. Leopold also received permission from the Belgian Parliament to become the sovereign of this new state. Contrary to what is often said and written, Congo was not Leopold's "private property". It was instead a full-fledged state, with its own legislation, administration, justice, army, customs, and tax authorities, just like any colonial entity. But the Congo certainly was, in the full sense of the word, an authoritarian state at the heart of Africa. Leopold, the head of state, had all powers over the vast territory and was accountable to no one. He administered this state from Brussels, with the help of his local High Representative, the Governor General, who himself headed the few hundred civil servants and officers in the Congo that exercised colonial authority.[6]

The Congolese colonial state was obviously not implemented overnight. The posts that the agents of the AIC had implanted in various places throughout the huge Congolese territory were in 1885 only the embryos of a state structure. Large parts of the territory which theoretically belonged to the Congo Free State, according to diplomatic treaties, were barely occupied or not at all. Thus, various expeditions had first to ensure the real establishment of state authority. That process took decades. The south-eastern region, Katanga, for example, did not come under effective control of the Congo Free State until around the turn of the twentieth century. There and elsewhere bloody wars were fought to subdue the native authorities. The so-called Arab campaigns (1892–1894), in the east of the Congo Free State, were then, and subsequently, presented as military expeditions against slave traders. In reality, they were campaigns against rulers who defied agreements "signed" between them and the evolving colonial government, or against local "big men" and merchants who had not yet been subdued.

Those campaigns and the development of the state apparatus itself were both very costly. Congo was not exactly the cornucopia that Leopold and his supporters had dreamed of. On the contrary, the adventure soon turned into a financial nightmare. Years before the foundation of the Congo Free State, Leopold had paid a large part of the costs out of his own pocket. These funds had been supplemented with loans. In 1885, he owed the Rothschild bank – only one of his creditors – some 2.7 million Belgian francs (the equivalent of £108,000 at the time).[7] After 1885, these financing methods continued because the budgetary revenues of the state (for example, export duties on ivory and other export products) were completely inadequate to cover the enormous expenses which had been incurred. On several occasions, the Belgian state provided funds to support Leopold's Congo, most notably 25 million and 6.8 million Belgian francs in 1890 and 1895 respectively, the equivalent of £1 million and £272,000 at the time.[8] Brussels also made the whole undertaking possible by offering Belgian officers and soldiers the opportunity to enter the service of the AIC, then of the Congo Free State, as seconded staff. Gradually, Leopold succeeded in gaining support for his colonial initiatives. Politicians started to help him, either to strengthen their own position on the Belgian political scene by winning the king's sympathy or out of newly found colonialist conviction. Belgian businessmen and financiers also began to perceive the opportunities for private profit in the Congo. In short, around the turn of the century, the "colonial party" in Belgium had the wind in its sails.

The Catholic Church and other religious groups also played a pivotal role in the emergence of the Congo Free State and in solidifying King Leopold II's rule. The Congolese saw not only soldiers and civil servants coming. In some regions, these newcomers were accompanied and sometimes even preceded by groups of missionaries who had their own agenda in spreading the Protestant and Catholic faiths. These proselytisers were usually British, Americans, Scandinavians, or French, and not only Belgians. In order to limit, and even reduce, foreign influences on "his" Congo as much as possible, Leopold sought support from the highest Catholic authorities in the country and even in Rome. At first, the Catholic Church was reluctant, but eventually a close collaboration – even a symbiosis – developed between the Congo Free State and the Catholic Church. Numerous Belgian Catholic groups sent missionaries to this new mission area. They could count on strong support from the government. The Protestant missions, however, did not enjoy such privileges.

The Brutalities of "Red Rubber"

Nonetheless, the further development of the Congo Free State depended on one essential condition: its financial viability. In the early 1890s, this was not certain. The Congo was on the brink of bankruptcy. According to the agreement reached between Leopold and the Belgian government following the 1890 loan, this situation could have led to the takeover of Congo by the Belgian state. However, two events resulted in the financial rescue – and thus (temporary) survival – of the Congo Free State.

First, Leopold broke with a fundamental commitment he had made to the international community in 1885: the guarantee that every foreign power would have free access to the country's economic resources, and that merchants of any nationality would enjoy the benefits of free trade in Congo. For Britain in particular, this had been the decisive argument for recognising the Congo Free State. In 1891–1892, Leopold reversed this firm commitment and decreed that all so-called vacant land in Congo belonged to the state. The public authorities thus owned the riches above and below the earth's surface. Anyone who exploited or traded those riches without their express permission was thus guilty of theft and faced detention. Moreover, local Congolese had their ancestral collective heritage taken away with one stroke of the pen.

The second event that resulted in the Congo's financial rescue occurred around 1895 when the demand for rubber soared, fuelled by new transport technologies, among other factors. The natural presence of rubber lianas in the Congolese forests thus provided an unexpected source of income. Certain parts of the Congo were directly allocated to and exploited by the state. Other extensive areas were given in concession to private companies in which Leopold was sometimes a co-shareholder. However, rubber extraction required an enormous amount of labour. Consequently, the Congolese population was put under great pressure to collect increasingly large quantities of rubber and hand it over to the concession companies or the Congo Free State, whether as "taxes" paid in kind or as rewards from labour. This system of exploitation was accompanied by the widespread use of various forms of violence: corporal punishment; taking hostages; burning villages; rape and the maltreatment of women and children; and individual or mass executions. These atrocities were committed by both state officials and agents of concession companies, with the help of their black troops.[9]

Even though these were not evenly distributed across the country, the acts of terror were not the result of accidental excesses by "deranged individuals". Instead, they were the logical consequence of a system imposed on the Congo by Leopold II and his closest associates, which prioritised profit maximisation above all else. Thus the sovereign himself was well aware of what was happening in the territory. At times, he expressed his "concern" about the Congolese population. But that did not change the inherently violent nature of the Congo Free State. The human death toll resulting from colonisation cannot be precisely quantified: owing to the lack of demographic sources, the exact population figure for pre-colonial Congo remains unknown. However, the population undoubtedly decreased considerably, either from 15 million in 1885 to 10.3 million in 1930 (highest estimate), or from 11.5 million to 10.3 million (lowest estimate).[10] This dramatic decline of the population was not only (and probably not mainly) the result of direct violence. It was also compounded by the spread of diseases, the disruption of families and communities, hunger and malnutrition caused by the neglect of agricultural production, and the decline of birth rates. Hence, the indirect violence of the colonial state was more devastating than direct exploitation and subjugation.

National and International Protests against Atrocities in the Congo

The relentless and bloody exploitation of the Congo and a significant part of its inhabitants did not go unnoticed. The atrocities of the Congo Free State were denounced both in Belgium and abroad. As early as the mid-1890s, Protestant missionaries played a key role in this protest. Since they mainly came from Britain and the United States, these criticisms found a particular echo in the Anglo-Saxon world. A British consul, Roger Casement, drew up a report in 1903 in which concrete evidence of atrocities was submitted to the British government in London. Another Briton, Edmund Morel, considered it his life's work to denounce the abuses of the Leopoldian regime in the Congo. Together, both founded the Congo Reform Association in 1904, an association that criticised the Congo Free State's cruel policies.[11]

Leopold and his associates initially responded with counter-propaganda, arguing that these allegations were just inventions and slander. However, in 1904 the sovereign tried once and for all to refute the criticisms by setting up a commission of inquiry to assess the state of affairs in the territory. The 1905 report confirmed the seriousness of the human rights abuses in the Congo, albeit in cautious terms. After two previous unsuccessful attempts by Brussels to take over the Congo from Leopold, these accusations presented a perfect opportunity. This action was necessary for Belgium to avoid losing all its Congolese investments to other European powers. Leopold continued to resist, but after long parliamentary debates the die was cast and, in 1908, the Congo Free State became a Belgian colony.

Belgian Congo (1908–1960): The Dark Side of a "Model Colony"

Colonialism from the Belgian Perspective

Belgium, therefore, became a colonial power in an unusual way. From the end of 1908, it headed an overseas empire that was not the result of a deliberately expansionist national project. Was Belgium a coloniser, therefore, "against its own will"? The original opposition of Belgian politicians to colonial adventures had gradually given way to an overtly pro-colonial attitude. When the fate of the Congo Free State was finally decided, a large majority of the Belgian Parliament supported the annexation of the Congo by the Belgian state, a move which was upheld by most Catholics and liberals. A handful of "progressive" liberals, Christian Democrats, and almost all socialists were against this development. Originally, Belgian colonialism could not count on unanimous political and public support. Yet the opposition and scepticism disappeared fairly quickly.

After a few years, the Belgian political community defended the legitimacy of its colonial authority in the Congo. In the inter-war period (1919–1939), only Belgium's tiny Communist Party remained fundamentally opposed to colonialism. In Flemish (Dutch-speaking) national circles, there was some criticism of the thoroughly francophone character of the colonial administration. The Belgian Catholic Church naturally remained a staunch supporter of the colony, as its mission there had grown into one of its largest endeavours. Colonialism also boosted Belgian nationalism. The colonial propaganda machine, soon running at full speed, proclaimed that the small nation could be proud of its overseas possessions and "civilising mission". The dynastic cult was also involved in the colonial enterprise. While alive, Leopold was quite unpopular. However, after giving up the Congo Free State in 1908 before his death the following year, he became the object of a "secular cult". Leopold was presented as the genius to whom Belgium owed its "beautiful colony" and, with this, its unexpectedly prominent international status.[12]

In the country's leading economic circles, the switch to and enthusiasm for colonialism had already started before Belgium took over the Congo Free State. By the early twentieth century, the leading Belgian banks, especially the Société Générale de Belgique, had abandoned their initial fears about the perils of colonial investment. Significant support and guarantees from the colonial government were not unimportant in winning over these investors.[13] Particularly in the 1920s, huge amounts of Belgian capital flowed to Congo to develop various infrastructural projects and to set up large mining and plantation companies. While the colony then absorbed 7.3 per cent of Belgium's total foreign direct investment, this figure rose to 29.8 per cent by 1939.[14] In 1938, an estimated total of £143 million had been invested in the Congo: the highest amount of all colonial territories in sub-Saharan Africa, with the exception of South Africa. In relative terms, measured per head of the population, the Congo also outranked all other colonies (£13 per inhabitant), except for South Africa and Rhodesia.[15] However, Belgium's status as a colonial power caused the government new problems.

Past events in the Congo, under Leopold, had tarnished Belgium's reputation. Even after 1908, the small European colonial power's capacity to manage this large African colony was openly questioned. Furthermore, before and after the First World War, the Congo was also the subject of political manoeuvres. In European diplomatic circles, politicians periodically considered a redrawing of the colonial borders in Central Africa to the detriment of Belgium. Brussels, therefore, developed a long-lasting and obsessive attitude towards the Congo. The new acquisition had to be defended at all costs against the "malicious intentions" of other European nations. The colony also had to remain Belgian through and through. Foreign influences had to be kept out as much as possible. Moreover, in order to remedy the reputational damage of Leopold's epoch, every effort was made to highlight Brussels's later, "exceptional" achievements in the heart of Africa, especially in the fields of primary education and health care. Particularly after the Second World War, Belgians talked about their "model colony". The Congo would and should become "exemplary". However, this propaganda sometimes led to self-delusion.[16]

The Harsh Realities of the Congo

A considerable gap existed between ideology and reality around Belgian colonisation of the Congo. In several ways the situation in the Belgian Congo differed from the regime of the Congo Free State. In other ways, there was more continuity than change. Leopold's autocratic rule had indeed been abolished. Henceforth, the national and democratic authorities mapped out Belgian colonial policy. However, in practice, a small group of "specialists", consisting of colonial civil servants, top businessmen, and missionaries, controlled the political process. In the colony itself there was no democratic rule at all. The constitutional rights that existed in Belgium did not apply in the Congo, such as freedom of association, freedom of the press, and free elections. The ten million Congolese subjects continued to suffer from an oppressive and exploitative regime.

Another break with the Congo Free State was that in the Belgian Congo the large-scale terror regime that had caused the "red rubber" scandal was no longer in place. Yet forced labour remained an essential part of colonial society.[17] Compulsion took many forms: adult men were required to work on major public infrastructure works. An impressive network of railways and roads was thus created in a relatively short period. The railroad network was extended from 1,100 kilometres in 1913 to 4,600 kilometres in 1939. At the same dates, the road network increased from 6,000 to 68,900 kilometres.[18] Congolese were forcibly removed from their villages and sent to work for the new Belgian enterprises such as the palm nut plantations and ore mining.[19] For example, in the south-eastern province of Katanga the focus was mainly on copper, while in the Province Orientale, in the north-eastern part of the country, it was gold. These enterprises were often located at great distances from their places of origin, and the working conditions were appalling, resulting in high rates of desertion and mortality (see Yates in this volume on the Congo–Ocean Railway). In this painful fashion, a Congolese wage-earning class gradually emerged. The population was often also requisitioned to carry the colonisers and their goods over very long distances in a practice known as *portage*. Moreover, Congolese farmers were obliged to grow certain export crops such as cotton and to sell them to Belgian companies, which unilaterally determined the often low purchase prices.[20] Those who did not comply with the established production quotas were subject to sanctions, including corporal punishment.

Violence and exploitation were thus two pillars on which the Belgian colonial regime was built, as was the case throughout the European colonial system. The third pillar was racism. There was a separate legal system for whites and blacks: guilt and punishment were determined by different criteria. There was also a de facto form of apartheid because the daily lives and human contacts of blacks and whites were kept separate as much as possible. Congolese were also confronted daily with discrimination, disdain, and insults, even though friendly and respectful relationships between whites and blacks also existed.

Belgium's Ambiguous "Civilising Mission"

The excesses of Belgian colonialism in the Congo were not spared from condemnation, as had been the case during the era of King Leopold II. A handful of Belgian politicians, civil servants, and clergy did denounce abusive practices, especially forced recruitment. But their condemnation of these oppressive acts was mainly done in private rooms and closed circles, rarely in the public glare. These mild criticisms were not necessarily anti-colonial but more "reformist", in favour of a more humane policy rather than for radical change.

There was some improvement in the working conditions of Congolese people, but this had little to do purely with humanitarianism. It was based instead on purely economic considerations. There was a dire and chronic shortage of labour, especially during the 1920s, as large Belgian companies increasingly focused on the mechanisation of business operations and on the better care of their black workers. The powerful company Union Minière du Haut-Katanga played a pioneering role in these efforts. Special workers' barracks, hospital wards, medical consultations, and leisure associations were the most visible manifestations of corporate paternalism, which was widely presented as the social face of colonial society. Such improvements in the lot of Congolese workers were significant. It was not until the 1950s that the purchasing power and consumption patterns of larger groups of wage-earners improved, particularly in the rapidly growing cities.

The period after the Second World War also contrasted with previous years in other respects. In 1949, the colonial government launched an ambitious Ten-Year Plan for the economic and social development of the Belgian Congo.[21] Thanks to extensive investments in all kinds of fields, the government started to "modernise" Congolese society. During this period, the educational and medical programmes for the Congolese population also improved significantly. In the inter-war years, the colonial state had "outsourced" primary education to the Catholic Church. In exchange for subsidies and other benefits, missionaries were charged with providing a rudimentary form of primary education to black children. Gradually, this system achieved remarkable results – at least by colonial standards. Many boys and girls in the Congolese countryside acquired basic maths, reading, and writing skills, mainly in their own language. Technical training was also provided for a select group of Congolese who could work as laboratory technicians, medical assistants, bookkeepers, lower clerks, and locomotive drivers. However, more advanced and general secondary education was deliberately retarded for fear of the creation of a highly educated anti-colonial Congolese elite.

Higher education only got off the ground in the very last phase of Belgian colonial rule with the establishment of the Catholic University Lovanium near Léopoldville (now Kinshasa) in 1954 and the official University of Élisabethville (now Lubumbashi) two years later. In 1960, only 29 Congolese men had obtained a university degree in the country. Two years earlier, a mere 13 Congolese were studying at Belgian universities.[22] After the Second World War, health care became another showpiece of the "model colony" that Belgian authorities were touting. However, the reality was somewhat more complicated. The intrusion of the white conquerors in the first phase of colonisation led to an enormous spread of disease and mortality among the Congolese population. The European medical system was also virtually non-existent at the time. The few doctors in the colony were mainly intended to care for the small white population of around 3,000 in 1908.[23] It was not until the inter-war years that the colony's medical and hygiene infrastructure also began to reach the local population, at first mainly through large-scale campaigns to combat endemic diseases. After 1945, the network of medical facilities expanded further, eventually covering almost the entire territory of the Congo.

The Abrupt and Tragic End of the Belgian Congo

The Belgian authorities gladly celebrated what they regarded as worthy achievements. They assumed the Congolese were satisfied with their "model colony". After 1945, in the eyes of the Belgian officials, it seemed the colonial regime could last for decades. However, this view was totally disconnected from reality as discontent was widespread among the black population. This often took individual forms of resistance such as insubordination, passivity, and sarcasm towards the white rulers. It eventually grew into violent and collective forms of resistance. Until 1939, there was endemic unrest in the Congolese countryside which regularly had to be suppressed by the *promenades militaires* (military tours) of the Force Publique, the Congolese army. Sometimes, even outright revolts erupted, like that of the Pende in 1931. In the industrial centres, black wage-earners sometimes revolted, especially during the Second World War, when the productive effort peaked. There was a bloody repression of a strike in Élisabethville in 1941, which left about 60 people dead.[24] This was just one of the many symptoms of the social malaise in the early 1940s. Congolese resistance to colonial rule was also expressed in local religious movements, which voiced open criticisms of the white regime. The frightened colonial government thus kept a close eye on them. For example, followers of the "prophet" Simon Kimbangu from the early 1920s, or the followers of the Kitawala, from the "Watch Tower" movement, introduced into the Congo from around 1925, were regularly punished with imprisonment or exile.

After 1945, expressions of resistance to colonial rule were less numerous, less pronounced, and less visible. The gradual improvements in the social situation of certain parts of the Congolese population may have played a part in this. It was precisely this relatively calm atmosphere that strengthened the colonial authorities' belief that they would rule the Congo for decades. However, another form of growing frustration had gone unnoticed by the Belgian authorities. A new group had gradually emerged within the Congolese population during the inter-war period, consisting of skilled workers who occupied subordinate positions in government administration and private companies. After 1945, these civil servants and technicians became more prominent. Not only did their numbers increase, but they were also encouraged by the colonial government to embrace a Western lifestyle. For example, the 900 male nurses in the Belgian Congo in 1950 increased to 8,000 by 1958; about 12,000 Congolese clerks worked in public employment in 1959; while an estimated 110,000 qualified or semi-qualified wage-earners were located in private enterprises.[25]

Based on special legislation, these so-called évolués were also made to believe that they had a special status that would give them more privileges than the ordinary non-Westernised Congolese.[26] However, in practice, upward social mobility and, above all, equal rights turned out to be a vain hope for the vast majority of Congolese. Only 2,325 of them obtained some measure of official recognition through a *carte du mérite civique* (civic merit card) or *immatriculation* (registration). The literate and empowered évolués thus turned out to be a breeding ground of frustration and even dissatisfaction with the rigid colonial regime, which did little to eliminate racial discrimination. One idea that took shape in leading colonial circles in 1955 – the creation of a "Belgian–Congolese community" in which white and black would live together on an equal footing – proved to be utopian and did not stem growing Congolese discontent.

In 1956, a group of Catholic évolués published a manifesto demanding – for the first time in Congolese history – a thorough political regime change. Immediately after these demands, other Congolese groups formulated more radical positions in which the word "independence" was mentioned. Congolese nationalism was thus born, metamorphosing into numerous political parties. Most of them had an ethnic or regional basis, and only a few had pan-Congolese ambitions and roots. In 1958, the Belgian government finally began to think about the colony's political future. On 13 January 1959, Brussels made a rather ambiguous statement which was further echoed in a speech by King Baudouin on the same day. This statement expressed Brussels's intention to grant Congo independence. Yet when and how this would happen was not specified. In the meantime, however, the flames had been ignited in the Congo itself.

A few days earlier, on 4 January 1959, bloody riots had erupted in Léopoldville, which were violently suppressed. These events finally shattered the illusion of the "colonial peace". Congolese protests and civil disobedience increased, not only in the capital, but also in other places such as the province of Bas-Congo and Stanleyville (now Kisangani). The colonial authorities began to lose their grip on the situation. Nevertheless, Belgian political parties ruled out any military intervention. Since Brussels rejected colonial war, dialogue with the numerous Congolese political parties was the only option. Discussions effectively started in the Belgian capital in January 1960. In barely a few weeks, this Round Table conference reached agreement: independence was to be granted on 30 June 1960. The future independent Congolese Republic had to be worked out hurriedly, and elections were held in May 1960. The pan-Congolese party Mouvement National Congolais emerged victorious. Its leader, Patrice Lumumba, consequently became the country's first prime minister. The leader of the Abako (Alliance des Bakongo), a regional party that dominated the Lower Congo, Joseph Kasavubu, became president of the new Republic.

Concluding Reflections

At first glance, the decolonisation of Congo had therefore gone smoothly. In little time, the Belgians and the Congolese had managed to put an end to 75 years of colonial rule without much bloodshed. However, the decolonisation process was fraught and fragile. Many important problems had been left unresolved, especially the financial and economic issues, as well as the role of the Congolese army in a new political dispensation. It was also clear at the time that Brussels's rigid colonial policy had created much Congolese resistance to alien rule. The "Africanisation" of the leading or even intermediary functions (in the army, administration, and companies) had made almost no headway at all, since colonial authorities had deliberately slowed down the creation of an educated Congolese elite. The Belgians were therefore convinced that the fledgling Congolese state could not possibly survive on its own. They firmly believed that interference from Brussels was inevitable and necessary. Belgian officials were therefore determined to steer the Congolese republic, mainly through the presence of white officials and advisers who would guide the young, inexperienced Congolese politicians. In this way, major Belgian economic interests would also be safeguarded. This state of mind played a decisive role in the Congo crisis that erupted barely a few days after the festive celebration of independence on 30 June 1960.

Four days later, a mutiny broke out in the Force Publique, led by Congolese soldiers dissatisfied with their conditions: one of the major problems that the January 1960 Round Table conference in Brussels had failed to resolve. Those incidents soon unleashed physical attacks on white civilians in Léopoldville, Thysville (now Mbanza Ngungu), Luluabourg (now Kananga), and Élisabethville (Lubumbashi), which triggered a panic reaction that eventually led to a massive flight of Belgians and Europeans from the Congo. A unilateral military intervention by Brussels made a flammable situation explosive, caused a major breach with the Congolese government, and resulted in United Nations intervention between 1960 and 1964.

In no time, the Congo had become a critical player in the proxy conflicts of the Cold War, and slipped into years of civil conflict. The mineral-rich province of Katanga unilaterally declared its independence on 11 July 1960, while Kasai province did the same a month later. Officially, Congolese politicians were the leaders of these separatist "states" (Moïse Tshombe and Albert Kalonji, respectively). However, these initiatives would have been impossible without the open support of Belgian politicians and businessmen, in particular the powerful Union Minière, who backed the secessionists. In the meantime, US and Belgian authorities planned the removal and even physical elimination of the lawful Congolese prime minister, Patrice Lumumba, whom they considered a dangerous communist demagogue opposed to Western interests. A *coup d'état* inspired by Western powers and carried out by Colonel Joseph Mobutu, the head of the Congolese armed forces and former protégé of Patrice Lumumba, led to the latter's dismissal and house arrest in September 1960.

After trying to flee, Lumumba was recaptured and handed over to the Katangese authorities, who murdered him on 14 January 1961. The Belgian authorities did nothing to stop the elimination of the first democratically elected Congolese prime minister.[27] Patrice Lumumba immediately became an icon and even a martyr of African nationalism, despite the fact that he was in office for just 76 days. The Congo's unity was finally restored in 1963, following a UN military intervention that put an end to the Katangese secession. However, the Congolese republic remained a fragile state, prone to civil war, dictatorship, and the plundering of its riches by both local elites and foreigners. Belgian colonialism ended in tragic failure: a legacy whose effects are still being felt six and a half decades later.

17

Colonialism in Portuguese Africa

Sandra Sousa

Everything is real apart from the war, which never existed. There were never any colonies, no Fascism, no Tarrafal prison camp, no PIDE [secret police], no Revolution, nothing, do you understand! The calendars of this country stopped moving so long ago that we have forgotten all about them. Luanda is an invented city of which I take my leave. The plane that brings us back to Lisbon is carrying a cargo of ghosts who slowly appear as officers and soldiers, yellow with malaria, who sit riveted to their seats, empty eyes staring out the window at the colourless, uterine space of the sky.
António Lobo Antunes, *Os cus de Judas* (2004)

THIS EPIGRAPH COMES FROM the Portuguese author António Lobo Antunes's 1979 novel, *Os cus de Judas* (*South of Nowhere* or *The Land at the End of the World*), in which he draws on his personal experiences after the end of Portugal's imperial epoch. Antunes served as an army doctor in Angola from 1971 to 1973, and witnessed a brutal and ultimately unpopular 15-year war, which had been initiated by the Portuguese to maintain control over its centuries-old colonies in Africa. The British scholar Charles Boxer noted that the Portuguese were the first to establish a colonial empire in the Atlantic, and the last to surrender it, between 1415 and 1999, when Portugal transferred its sovereignty over Macau to China.[1] As this demonstrates, the Portuguese empire was the most enduring of European empires, which perhaps makes it unique. However, just like all its counterparts, Lisbon was no different in "embrac[ing] and emphasis[ing] exceptionalism to serve its purposes".[2] Like all other colonial empires, as Lobo Antunes highlights, Portugal embarked on a period of amnesia after decolonisation in the 1970s, in an attempt to forget and erase its colonial past. This past has been described by the American scholars Daniel Silva and Lamonte Aidoo as "a fragmented process of power-building and extraction of resources and bodies across different locales"[3] in Africa.

The Beginnings of Pax Lusofonia

Portugal's first imperial focus of interest was North Africa, in the port town of Ceuta in Morocco around 1415. Thereafter, colonial expansion was centred on the exploration of the coasts of Atlantic Africa. Several expeditions led to the establishment of the first European settlements in West Africa as trading posts in places such as Arguin in Mauritania in 1445, or as forts such as Elmina in Ghana in 1482. As the Portuguese historian Miguel Bandeira Jerónimo states, the nature of Portuguese political, military, and economic settlement enabled the establishment of relatively safe areas for advancing its interests, and further provided access to slaves and gold (see Introduction in this volume).[4] The shift from raids to more stable and peaceable modes of exchange worked to the advantage of Portuguese interests. It became easier for Lisbon to explore waterways to the interior – on the "rivers of Guinea" in West Africa – thereby "adding momentum to the entire enterprise".[5] With Portugal safeguarded by the Treaty of Alcáçovas of 1479, trade flourished during the fifteenth and much of the sixteenth century. Nonetheless, "Portuguese colonial aspirations in Africa were limited to military outposts along the western and eastern coasts as a means of ensuring Portuguese domination over sea routes to, and in, the Indian Ocean."[6]

Change came during the late sixteenth and mid-seventeenth century, when the Portuguese and Spanish crowns were united between 1580 and 1640. This union gave rise to a new era in the transatlantic slave trade (see Silva Jr in this volume). Colonial authorities set in motion an unprecedented expansion of African slave trafficking – both in scale and in volume – to support the interests of large landowners. The founding of Luanda in 1575 and its subsequent development can be attributed to the growth of the slave trade during this era. This capital of the Portuguese colony of Angola and its hinterlands became increasingly important within the overall slave trade for exporting thousands of west-central Africans to the Americas. This phase constituted an effective colonisation of the Americas, in which Portugal's focus was mainly directed at exploiting and commercialising the riches of Brazil at the expense of territorial expansion in Africa (see Ramirez in this volume).

Africa's ruling elites also benefited from the proceeds of the slave trade because they facilitated the provision of Africans from the interior to the coast. The Portuguese presence on African soil was thus based on diplomatic relations with local power structures. Regional conflicts among groups and kingdoms were used by Lisbon as a weapon of control. Portugal also benefited from direct military attacks on local populations or other European powers. According to Silva and Aidoo: "This mode of Portuguese imperial enterprise, focused on the extraction of bodies as commodities, would characterise Portuguese imperialism in Africa until and even after the formal abolition of the slave trade in 1810, and also after the official prohibition of slave importation by the few slaveholding states left in the Americas."[7]

The independence of Brazil in 1822,[8] and the formal abolition of slavery a decade later, shifted the Portuguese focus from the Americas towards Africa. It was now necessary to restrategise Lisbon's imperial enterprise and its colonial policies in what it saw as the "Dark Continent". Jerónimo bluntly affirms: "The rebuilding of the Portuguese empire was the ultimate goal, Africa its destiny. The erection of *new Brazils* in Africa turned into a recurrent political and strategic theme, bolstered by the political activation of collective myths, particularly those connected to the so-called discoveries."[9] Echoing Jerónimo's assertion, the Portuguese scholar Valentim Alexandre adds that "at the political level, that new interest in African possessions translates itself, most imme-diately, into measures taken in the defence of their incorporation by Brazil (to which they were strictly connected by the slave trade), followed by a first attempt to develop their commercial activity with the metropolis".[10] At this time, colonial settlements increased, but slowly and sparsely, mainly in the island colonies of Cape Verde and São Tomé and Príncipe, both uninhabited prior to Portuguese claims over them. "Sustained Portuguese colonial settlement in Africa had become stagnant over the nineteenth century, even more so after the end of the slave trade and had become based on penal colonisation."[11] The aim was to populate African territories with the "unwanted": like French Guyana, Australia, and colonial Georgia, lusophone Africa would become a place for outcasts who had committed some form of crime.

The Weaknesses of an Empire

After the 1820 liberal revolution, apart from the "kingdoms" of Angola and Benguela and the region of Cabinda – three coastal territories subjected to a sovereignty or a political influence imprecisely defined and vaguely exercised – the Portuguese presence was limited beyond the unstable borders of its western empire. It was only in 1887 that "the colonial administration would undertake the topographic delimitation of its effective sovereignty. The political map, as well as the geographic, that guided the strategies of the Portuguese authorities was extremely imprecise, and did not include the successive internal transformations of the border societies, the *sobados*."[12] During this period, the colonial borders and the levels of control or political influence were, therefore, rather unstable and improvised. Thus, the range and limits of the informal Portuguese influence in Africa were determined by the capacity of the colonial authorities to create and maintain political and economic relations as well as intermediary networks with the African political entities that controlled the commercial flows. It was this that made the survival of the colonial administration possible. At the same time, there was considerable ignorance on the Portuguese side about the nature of the local societies they ruled.

The weakness and instability of colonial authorities and their dependence on local African political and economic structures were due to several factors. These included political unrest in the metropolis, the scarcity of economic resources, the indifference towards the African colonies on the part of the Portuguese financial sector and the general Portuguese population, and the weakness of the colonial administration. In 1836, Sá da Bandeira, Portugal's Minister of the Navy and Overseas, sent a report to the parliament in Lisbon in which he described the general state of the country's African overseas provinces: "these were 'decaying fragments' of a ruined empire and practically non-existent, 'invaded and conquered by black Africans' and marked by internal dissent".[13] Despite the neglected condition of the colonies, the 1830s saw increasing political rhetoric and debate about Portugal's African possessions as well as the colonial project in general. Several reasons were put forward as to why Portugal should maintain its African territories: historical legitimacy suggested by the pioneering role of the Portuguese in overseas expansion; the justification of a "civilising mission" based on the propagation of Christianity; the loss of the Luso-Brazilian empire; and the nationalistic fear of dependence in relation to France and Britain (see Yates and Igba in this volume), as well as the economic rationale that viewed colonial trade as fundamental in preserving Portugal's independence.

By the second half of the 1850s, the government faced difficulty in finding support among Portuguese capitalists for its colonial project. Plans to modernise and consolidate the imperial system faced opposition in the African colonies. Valentim Alexandre explains that these settlements were "peripheral zones of the empire centred in Brazil, which had inherited from the old regime an administrative apparatus where public powers and private powers were inextricably intertwined, meaning that public positions offered access to increased means of coercion that were systematically used in pursuit of private purposes".[14] It was thus imperative to change the colonial administrative machinery that rendered Portugal's control weak. The slave trade would thus become the main reason for the Portuguese to resist British opposition to Portugal's expansionism. Despite the prevalent lack of focus regarding programmes and expansionist movements, one subject was nevertheless frequently discussed: the role that should be assigned to missionary work to reinforce Portugal's colonial presence in Africa.

During the 1860s, Portuguese dominance in Africa suffered a reversal, particularly in Angola, due in large part to a financial crisis in the metropolis. However, by the end of the decade, there were transformations and economic development in some overseas territories such as Angola and Mozambique. In the 1870s, the Portuguese imperial project faced inevitable changes due to the increased interest in Africa of other European powers. "The national political elites became aware of that change around 1875–1876, spurred by the news of the travels by several explorers in Africa ... and also the creation of the International African Association by King Leopold of Belgium in that last year."[15] In reaction to the growing impact of rival imperial European regimes, in 1875 the Geographic Society of Lisbon was founded. It would play an important role in the definition of Portuguese colonial policy in the years that followed. There were also a number of Portuguese expeditions to Africa that occurred in 1877 almost immediately after the Society's establishment.

The current of Portuguese opinion that defended the development and modernisation of the empire gained strength. At a social level, it became important to eliminate slavery (by decree of 25 February 1869) and initiate the compulsory apprenticeship to which the *libertos*[16] (freed slaves) were subjected. The modernisation project continued to be strongly opposed by some factions within both Africa and the metropolis. At a political level, the traditional belief that African territories should be self-sustaining continued to hold sway, and hence the development of the metropolis should not be sacrificed to the development of the colonies. Yet, as Valentim Alexandre explains, the traditional view of the colonial question would be "increasingly difficult to sustain in the last quarter of the nineteenth century, due to a new ideological factor: the growth and spread of a current of radical nationalism that was markedly imperialist and capable of mobilising the urban popular strata of the main cities in the country (Lisbon and Porto) around colonial themes".[17]

An Empire at the Tail of Its European Counterparts

In Africa, the borders of contemporary nation-states were drawn largely by European powers with no regard for the wishes of African populations, who lacked any representation at the Berlin Conference (1884–1885).[18] The Conference, as the British scholar Matthew Craven notes, "has assumed a canonical place in historical accounts of late nineteenth-century imperialism".[19] The overall purpose of the conference was "to 'manage' the ongoing process of colonisation in Africa (the 'Scramble' as it was dubbed by a *Times* columnist) so as to avoid the outbreak of armed conflict between rival colonial powers".[20] The direct result was a General Act ratified by all the major colonial powers. Among other things, "The General Act set out the conditions under which territory might be acquired on the coast of Africa; it internationalised two rivers (the Congo and the Niger); it orchestrated a new campaign to abolish the overland trade in slaves; and it declared as 'neutral' a vast swathe of Central Africa delimited as the 'conventional basin of the Congo'."[21] According to the Australian scholar Antony Anghie, the Berlin Conference "transformed Africa into a conceptual *terra nullius*",[22] silencing native resistance through the subordination of their claims to sovereignty, and providing an effective ideology of colonial rule. Berlin did not initiate European colonisation of Africa, but it did legitimise and formalise the process.

Two outcomes of the 1884–1885 Berlin Conference were particularly devastating for Portugal: the award of the Congo – despite Portugal's historical claim to the Congo region – to King Leopold of Belgium; and the principle that, for a claim to African territory to be valid, the claimant had to demonstrate effective occupation, not just historical rights. By the late nineteenth century, Portugal's African empire was nothing but "relics" lingering in a state of "extreme economic stagnation". This led to its claims at the Berlin Conference being seen as "extravagant" and "pretentious", while Portuguese control was said to be "tenuous and circumscribed". Nonetheless, "once the European Scramble for Africa accelerated, it destroyed Lisbon's complacency".[23]

After the Berlin Conference, the Portuguese insisted on their right to exercise sovereignty in the interior between Mozambique and Angola. This had resulted from two treaties signed in 1886 that delimited the boundaries between the Portuguese territories and those of France and Germany. To validate this claim, the Portuguese published its *mapa cor-de-rosa* (rose-coloured map) and organised successive expeditions into the interior between Mozambique and Angola. Meanwhile, the British were also exploring Africa from south to north under the auspices of Cecil Rhodes, who had designs on the same territory for the construction of a railroad that would run from the Cape to Cairo (see the Introduction and Igba in this volume). The Portuguese protested, but the British refused to recognise the "rose-coloured map", claiming that the territory was not Portuguese because Portugal had not effectively occupied it, as required by the terms of the Berlin Conference. There followed a demand for the immediate removal of all Portuguese military in the area – which became known as the British Ultimatum of 1890. Faced with the possibility of armed conflict against a much larger military power, Portugal had no option but to comply and renounce the territories it was claiming between the borders of Angola and Mozambique.

Portuguese historians, such as Fernando Tavares Pimenta, agree that the year of the British Ultimatum of 1890 marked "the beginning of the Portuguese twentieth century".[24] This involved the building of a new Portuguese empire-state. The history of twentieth-century Portugal is thus the history of the Luso-African empire, since it is impossible to understand the political history of the metropolitan country without considering the history of its African colonial territories. Despite the sense of national humiliation triggered by the British Ultimatum, there remained a feeling of colonial euphoria that paved the way for an intensified commitment to more effective colonisation. Apart from the blatant failure of demographic colonisation during the preceding centuries, this brought about the interplay of the political, military, economic, and religious dimensions of Portuguese imperial expansionism. Several pacification campaigns followed to seek to make Portugal's presence in its territories more effective. These were violent military campaigns that aimed to control and subdue the African territories and their populations. They had multiple purposes and continued for a couple of decades (around 1890–1910) because of their ineffectiveness. In Miguel Bandeira Jerónimo's words:

> They were as much proof of muscle as they were a revelation of
> frailty in authority and influence, and the muscle was frequently
> provided by African auxiliaries. These military campaigns were also

connected to efforts to expand taxation in each colony geographically and to particular economic interests of "legitimate commerce" (e.g., textiles and wine), as well as to prove "effective occupation", deemed important after the Berlin Conference.[25]

The campaigns were, nonetheless, not successful in transforming the existing political, economic, and socio-cultural landscapes in Portugal's colonies.

Following the period of "pacification", the decade of the 1920s saw the introduction of civil administration across Portugal's colonies. The colonial occupation of Africa in this period was also, as Leonor Pires Martins states, "a symbolic occupation of space, through the attribution of Portuguese names to the villages, streets, avenues and squares, and the construction of statues allusive to figures of Portuguese history – initiatives, in short, that translate into an effort to nationalise the colonial territories".[26] These efforts, though, were much more than merely symbolic.

In 1920, Lisbon announced that high commissioners were to be created to replace the existing governors general. These high commissioners were to have financial autonomy, and local opinion was to be expressed through legislative councils. This step was seen as an important breakthrough since two prominent Portuguese politicians – Norton de Matos and Brito Camacho – were appointed to the posts in Angola and Mozambique respectively. In the colonies, these appointments were seen as hopeful signs that the long-overdue development of both territories was about to begin.

African populations in Portuguese territories were frequently viewed as having both a deficient work capacity and a reduced productive capacity: characteristics that reportedly resulted from the "rudimentary" nature of their basic needs. From the point of view of the Portuguese colonisers, it was their "mission" to counteract the supposed predisposition of the Africans to idleness through several processes that would allegedly lead them towards "civilisation". These processes included applying taxes, repressive "vagrancy laws", service provision contracts, forced labour, and slavery. Even though slavery had been formally abolished in 1836, new questions were being posed and new solutions demanded. As Jerónimo explains, "'slavery' seems to appear as a first, even if unacceptable, solution to the proclaimed native resistance to organised ways of work".[27] Labour – either forced or voluntary – became a mechanism of disciplining and, concomitantly, of "civilising" the supposedly "lazy natives". "Civilisation" was an obligation and, given the state of social evolution of the native populations, also inevitable. This was the "*lógica circular*" (circular logic)[28] that had governed colonial texts and speeches since the end of the 1800s. It suited the politico-economic demands of colonisation and the desire of colonialists to ward off external pressures, such as those required by the League of Nations. The system of compulsory work was another alternative for those who were not so bold as to propose the reimplementation of slavery. Logically, this approach had the same objective as enslavement: to guarantee, by coercion, an indigenous labour force needed for the colonising project. Armando Zuzarte Cortesão, a Portuguese colonial administrator, noted:

> The colonial policy of the countries that have colonies must inevitably be guided by these two great and basic principles: (a) the indigenous people of the colonies must be considered to be human beings and not simply as animals, constituting their education and well-being is a sacred mission that Civilisation delegates to the colonising peoples; (b) mankind lacks the untapped riches of vast colonial regions and demands from the peoples who possess them their rapid use.[29]

Another aspect of the "civilising" rhetoric was the education of the native peoples for, and through, work. School education was not part of the plan and, at this time, the education system in Portugal's colonies comprised few, if any, schools. As Jerónimo explains, the idea was that "education should have a rather practical and instrumental dimension, where the teaching of the Portuguese language should be the priority, alongside a training oriented to an art and a craft. It should equally be addressed to educate the native bodies for work."[30] What "advancement" was possible for indigenous populations was typically consigned to various missionary efforts, since the Portuguese colonisers were more interested in securing means for their "material improvements" through exploiting the mineral and agricultural potential of the soil, opening new markets for commerce, and developing industry with newly trained workers. Despite the measures taken to improve the colonies and the modernisation projects, by 1924–1925 these initiatives had already failed. As the American scholar Alan Smith observes:

> Largely due to the indifference which had surrounded colonial affairs, many observers agreed that the Portuguese colonies were the worst administered territories in Africa. Mismanagement of the colonial apparatus permeated all levels of its attendant bureaucracy, which

lacked continuity in leadership, was beset by corruption from top to bottom, and was manipulated by special interests. Despite the good intentions of many individuals, decentralisation only served to allow greater scope of these pernicious influences.[31]

With the de facto dictator António de Oliveira Salazar at the country's helm and with the introduction of the *Estado Novo* (the New State) in the early 1930s, there was a new push for developing the ideological and material infrastructure of the colonies as well as emigration to them, on a scale that was previously unknown. Even though Salazar only held the post of Minister of the Colonies for six months, his "internal performance would prove to have major consequences for the whole of Portuguese politics for many years".[32] The impact of the "New State" was felt not only in Portugal, but across its colonies. "With the confluence of concentrated state power, authoritarian orientation, a repressive state police and the organs of censorship, and effective propaganda mechanisms (under the direction of António Ferro) and backed by technologies of mass communication, the new regime managed to generate a highly successful national ideal of Portugal grounded both in the present (the regime itself) and in the past (the Discoveries)."[33]

Within this context, Salazar published the Colonial Act in July 1930. This constitutional document – the first promulgated by the "New State" – articulated some fundamental principles for overseas territorial administration. The Act's second article declared that it was "of organic essence for the Portuguese nation to possess and colonise overseas territories and to civilise indigenous populations there".[34] The colonial question became inseparable from the nationalisation of the colonial empire, thereby perfecting the centralisation of power. According to Fernando Martins, "the colonial question would increasingly and fatalistically become the essential element of Portuguese foreign policy".[35]

At the same time as the Colonial Act, an "imperial mystique" was formulated by the Minister of the Colonies, Armindo Monteiro, who was widely considered the great architect and proponent of the "modernised empire". Several initiatives were launched with the goal of instilling this "imperial mystique" in the hearts and minds of the Portuguese population: colloquiums, conferences, international and national exhibitions such as Porto's Colonial Exhibition in 1934, and the Exhibition of the Portuguese World in 1940, which marked the zenith of the "imperial mystique".

According to Jerónimo, "The 'historical mission' to colonise turned into a crucial constitutional principle, and a pervasive element in the propagandistic efforts of the regime."[36] He added that:

> The 1933 Organic Charter of the Portuguese Colonial Empire and the Overseas Administrative Reform strengthened the centralising tendency, which included a desire to control the influence of the white settler communities and an effort to professionalise the colonial civil service. Armchair bureaucrats were downplayed; active administrators who were able to engage with, and influence, local authorities were promoted, in a process that also mobilised the *chefes de posto* (the remotest administrative posts) and the *cipaios* (indigenous administrative guards). In both, a particular politics of difference was given firm legal ground: the distinction between *civilizados* (civilised) and *indígenas*, those with rights of citizenship similar to Portuguese citizens and the unprivileged rest.[37]

Metropolitan interests took priority, even though there was a plan to strengthen the political and economic integration of local powers in the colonies. The so-called traditional authorities would continue their roles as labour brokers and tax collectors, among other functions. There was an effort to turn local African communities into taxpayers and to have workers and producers depend on the *chefes de posto* and the *cipaios*.[38] At the same time, in 1937 a regime of mandatory crop cultivation – *culturas obrigatórias* – was instituted, which increased the production of sugar, coffee, maize, and cotton.[39] The government set quotas and established fixed prices for commodities, salaries, property, and the like.

The Portuguese scholar Cláudia Castelo, in a definitive study of Portuguese migration to the colonies of Angola and Mozambique, observes that "during the 1930s and 1940s there was no attempt officially to colonise Angola or Mozambique as a direct state initiative".[40] After the 1930s, the Portuguese state created obstacles to the settlement in the colonies of poor white metropolitans who did not possess the necessary educational and professional qualifications or could not show proof of a guaranteed job or means of subsistence. In the Portuguese colonial empire, indirect rule persisted alongside centralisation efforts.

Concluding Reflections: The End of an Empire Swimming against the Tide

After the Second World War, which would foreshadow significant changes in colonial systems globally, Portugal began to see "the clouds gathering in the horizon of its colonial empire".[41] General Salazar's dictatorship, nonetheless, did everything to avoid acknowledging these clouds. As other European countries began the process of decolonisation, as mandated by the 1945 UN Charter, the Portuguese imperial state set itself against the prevailing "winds of change". The assimilationist discourse that had characterised Portugal's colonial policy since the nineteenth century now began to take on new dimensions. As the German historian Alexander Keese notes, "the ideology of imperial generosity which accompanied the civilising mission was reinforced and remodelled in the 1950s and 1960s".[42] The "New State" began to embrace the work of Brazilian sociologist and anthropologist Gilberto Freyre in its public rhetoric to justify its presence and permanence in Africa. At the core of Freyre's works – which were later borrowed for political purposes by the Portuguese government and introduced into the official doctrine of the regime – was the assertion of a distinctive Portuguese character, benign, humanistic, and non-racist, that was best evidenced in the African tropics.

In a trip financed by the Lisbon government across its colonies, Freyre declared in a public speech that at the core of the Portuguese work in Brazil, as well as in other "Brasis" (the African colonies), was simply love.[43] The term Freyre crafted in the 1950s, "Luso-tropicalism", suggested that the Portuguese colonisers had a special ability to adapt to the tropics by easily intermingling, intermarrying, and exchanging cultural elements with diverse colonial peoples, given that they were themselves the result of multiple mixtures. As Cristiana Bastos says, "from that assumption followed the claims about empire not being an empire but a unique multiracial nation across the continents, and colonies not being colonies but parts of a singular nation that extended from Minho in Northern Portugal to distant Timor in Southeast Asia".[44]

Thus in 1951 a constitutional amendment made these claims official: "colonies" became "overseas provinces", and the expression "colonial empire" was entirely expunged from Portugal's governance vocabulary. Two years later, the *Lei Orgânica do Ultramar* (Organic Law of Overseas Territories) was enacted. This reinforced the unity between the metropolis and its overseas provinces, granting more power to local authorities and opening up the possibility of mutual development plans. The relationships between the authorities and African elites were about to be subjected to several changes, including the loss of power by the latter. This also marked a turning point in the European settler presence in the colonies, especially in Mozambique and Angola. Their numbers had grown exponentially between the 1940s and 1960s. As a result of the increased presence of Portuguese citizens from the metropole in the colonies,[45] "welfare colonialism" became a reality in the Portuguese empire. Nonetheless, it existed more in words than in deed, and was inspired more by political and security concerns than by a genuine commitment to the widespread provision of education or health to indigenous communities.

The exclusionary politics of difference – the *indigenato* – endured. According to Valentim Alexandre, the *indigenato* "in practice removed Portuguese citizenship from the overwhelming majority of the African population".[46] Despite its rhetoric of "imperial exceptionality" that applied to its proclaimed "multiracial and pluri-continental nation", political and socio-economic rights were not granted to the African "natives" in Portugal's colonies. Colonial rule continued to be governed by the legal imposition of racial criteria on all societal levels. There was no major transformation in the overall provision of political, economic, and socio-cultural rights across the empire despite the provisions of the law in the 1950s that legally prevented discrimination between "primitive natives", "evolving natives", and "detribalised natives".

Land, especially the most productive, was taken away from its original owners, particularly after ethnic colonisation became more intense, and given to European interests, who were allocated the best plots. Labour was forcefully extracted; this had a significant impact on women and family dynamics at various levels. It also generated regular international outcries and internal criticism, even though some international labour conventions were ratified by Portugal and international norms were gradually adopted. Education was barely provided and was mainly rudimentary, a function delegated to clergy and missionaries, as per the 1941 Missionary Agreement. Although secondary schools and universities were eventually introduced, this did not substantially change the overall picture. Despite relative expansion from the 1960s onwards, public health services were still inadequate. The European presence in Mozambique and Angola increased four times between 1940 and 1960 to about 97,000 and 170,000 respectively. In 1973, these figures increased to about 190,000 and 324,000 respectively.[47]

Contrary to what the reformist agendas and initiatives claimed to show, with the increase of the white population from the 1940s to the 1970s,[48] there was also a stronger demarcation along the colour line. Isabela Figueiredo, born in 1963 in Mozambique as the daughter of a Portuguese colonialist family, writes in her *Caderno de memórias coloniais* (Notebook of Colonial Memories), "the life of a black man was worth the price of his usefulness. The life of a white man was worth much more, even if it was not worth much."[49] It was only in 1961 that the *indigenato* and the *culturas obrigatórias* were abolished. Forced labour was formally outlawed in 1962. The idea of a multiracial society was merely an idea on paper, given that racialised identities persisted along with racist practices and prejudices. Jerónimo's statement that "reform was more cosmetic than effective, more planned than actually accomplished",[50] was true of this period, in which there was noticeable development but no real progress.

The year 1961 marked the outbreak of conflict in Angola, which led to an anti-colonial war that endured for the next 13 years in Portugal's three main African colonies of Angola, Mozambique, and Guinea-Bissau. It was through this "absurd", "imbecile" war that the collapse of Portuguese colonisation finally came, to quote António Lobo Antunes in *Os cus de Judas*: his book of memories from a time when a lost empire could no longer confront its tragic reality.

18

Colonialism in German Africa

Adam A. Blackler

IMPERIAL GERMANY FORGED one of Europe's largest colonial empires between 1884 and 1914. In Africa, its imperial presence stretched from the Cape Colony north to Niger and Togo, and east to present-day Kenya. A vast and multicultural mixture of regions, German Africa presented its enthusiasts with a stage upon which to manifest their most intimate desires and racist fantasies. Though individuals shared wildly disparate motivations for imperial conquest, as well as numerous judgements on the necessity of an overseas imperium, empire pressured both its supporters and detractors to scrutinise the colonial project on a personal level. Citizens thereby encountered German Africa regularly as a result, either by embarking overseas themselves or in correspondence with friends abroad, exposés in newspapers, or colonial fairs in Germany. As informational conduits, these formal and informal encounters linked Africa and Germany together in all aspects of everyday life, enabling citizens who never left the confines of Central Europe to establish connections with areas far beyond the familiar landscapes of Prussia, Hanover, and Württemberg.

Most significantly, however, German interactions with Africa exposed the civilisational logic that initially inspired Europe's imperial enterprise in the nineteenth and twentieth centuries. In their important introduction to the book *Tensions of Empire* (1997), American scholars Frederick Cooper and Ann Laura Stoler remind us that European empires "were neither monolithic nor omnipotent".[1] They balanced a myriad of political agendas, economic strategies, and systems of control to maintain power in their respective overseas domains.

Though diverse in scope, European colonialisms were inherently violent campaigns that pushed entire societies into slavery, indentured servitude, and cultural ruin.[2] The conduct, practice, and rationale for colonial conquest may have differed from empire to empire, but all imperial powers pursued their goals without the consent of indigenous populations and with the essential aid of systemic bloodshed and cultural malice (see Introduction, Igba, Yates, Vanthemsche, Sousa, Nerín and Tofiño, and Fuller in this volume).

Germany's occupation of present-day Namibia, Tanzania, Kenya, Burundi, Rwanda, Togo, and Cameroon was no exception, and characterises this argument in two principal ways. First, the appearance of administrators, merchants, and settlers did not immediately transform Germany's African colonies into arenas that reflexively favoured imperial rule.[3] Even after the first contingent of soldiers arrived in Southwest Africa and East Africa in 1889, most polities on the ground did not regard German occupiers as the principal authority figures, either locally or regionally. Second, when the façade of imperial fantasy gave way to colonial reality, settlers increasingly sought to fortify their presence in Africa with juridical and physical acts of violence. As a result, imperial officials and stakeholders used civil decrees and legislation, segregatory land policies, and eliminatory warfare to uphold their position in Africa after the turn of the twentieth century. This evolution in brutality was not the culmination of an instinctive genocidal character unique to an authoritarian German culture. Rather, it was a product of chauvinistic settler-colonial logic that matured in an atmosphere that favoured hyper-masculinity, nationalism, and hierarchical world views over ethnic and social inclusion. Such an argument should not dissuade us from interrogating Germany's brutal colonial history and the factors that made it possible. Colonial violence compels us to acknowledge the dangerous potential of exclusionary nationalism, biological racism, and "great power" politics that helped inspire Europe's colonial age in the first place.

In order to trace the violent evolution of Germany's colonial project in Africa, this chapter will concentrate on Southwest Africa (present-day Namibia) between 1884 and 1914. As the first overseas protectorate and only settlement colony of the *Kaiserreich* (German empire), Southwest Africa forced metropolitans most directly to confront the inherent cruelties of Germany's colonial occupation in Africa. This periodisation also enables us to analyse the significance of the 1884–1885 Berlin Conference, Southwest Africa's corporatists beginnings, and the impact of the 1904–1908 Herero–Nama genocide on German conceptions of citizenship and national belonging. "Race thinking", in particular, surfaced as the most consequential legacy of Germany's imperial programme. As an ideological principle that upheld ethnic purity as the historical driver of national politics, race thinking not only shifted the paradigms of the imperial state, but also elevated the exclusionary perspectives of those in the *Kaiserreich* who framed citizenship along an inflexible colour line. Racism begot violence, and annihilatory violence begot an apartheid state in Southwest Africa. While the same dangerous potential existed in every other European imperial project, black Africans in *Heimat* (homeland) *Südwest* saw colonial officials unleash violence in courtrooms, local elections, "native reservations", and, most callously, in the Omaheke desert. Once Africans had shattered the veneer of German colonial fantasy, eliminatory racism provided white settlers with a convenient solution to what they considered the most pressing issue in Southwest Africa: white domination.

The Berlin Conference and "Effective Rule"

In a speech before the Reichstag (parliament) in 1881, the German Chancellor, Otto von Bismarck, declared his opposition to overseas expansion in unequivocal terms. "As long as I am Chancellor," he asserted, "we will not pursue a colonial policy. We have a fleet that cannot sail ... and we should not possess any vulnerable parts of the world that would fall prey to the French just as soon as it gets going."[4] Later that same year, Bismarck quipped that African colonies were to Germans as "sable furs [are] to Polish families with no shirts".[5] Yet within three years of delivering these dismissive pronouncements, the Iron Chancellor had reversed his entire position on the German imperial project. Much to the satisfaction of German liberal nationalists and advocates of colonial expansion, Bismarck and his policy of realpolitik now looked upon overseas conquest as a necessary enterprise.

No event marked this transformation more clearly than Bismarck's invitation to host the West Africa Conference in Berlin in November 1884. Today, more commonly known as the Berlin Conference or the Congo Conference, this occasion brought together government representatives from across Europe and the United States to formalise what scholars now recognise as the "Scramble for Africa". Germany had entered the African Scramble three months earlier, when the Reichstag officially designated Southwest Africa a *Schutzgebiet* (protectorate) in August 1884.[6] In the wake of this development, therefore, Bismarck's invitation to host the West Africa Conference propelled colonialism to the forefront of German national politics. On the eve of the Berlin Conference's inauguration, for instance, the popular family magazine

Die Gartenlaube: Illustrirtes Familienblatt praised the event as the start of a new era in colonial policy. "There was a time, barely a few years behind us," the weekly claimed,

> when zealous patriots raised their voice to warn that a "living danger to German nationality" was the increasing colonial expansion of the English. [Against the wishes of] politicians of the old school, Germans today herd together all the nations to deliberate on a peaceful solution to pending colonial questions … most have come as friends, even the traditional Gallic enemy has appeared as an ally [and] the German community has taken the first steps at the conference.[7]

In this fashion, the 1884–1885 Berlin Conference afforded participants and observers an opportunity to crystallise their notions of patriotism, scientific discovery, and the defence of "civilisation" into a German national cause. Berlin thus emerged as a central player in global colonial affairs. Interested parties from across the social spectrum – including prominent members of society, major political parties, economic interest groups, nationalist associations, social clubs, patriotic clubs, and overseas German enclaves – regarded the Berlin Conference as a harbinger of future success. They maintained that colonial rivalries were now a thing of the past, that resource-rich trade outposts could fill German markets with fresh produce and consumer goods, and that missionaries, explorers, and settlers could finally "civilise disparate communities" in need of "enlightened reason".[8]

Commercial enterprises and merchants, in particular, took special care to promote colonial markets as a solution to economic depression and stagnation. Carl Peters, the leader of the Society for German Colonisation and eventual founder of the German East Africa Company, described Africa as a potential windfall for the entire nation. Peters had first articulated his colonial ambitions in *The Presence* in March 1884. As a means of stoking nationalist feelings, he peppered his arguments with geopolitical overtones, specifically in reference to Britain. "In short," he wrote, "English society, with its amazing colonial possessions, is capable of using those forces which it has produced, or to be more precise, of caring for its members in an adequate way."[9] He went on to mention that the young German nation, meanwhile, lacked the same prospects and could not reach its full potential. "The English state is like a tree," Peters wrote, "which gets light and air in order to develop its branches freely and luxuriantly in all directions; the German state is like an even more noble trunk which is confined in a gorge among rugged mountains, and is thus hindered on all sides from developing its boundless vitality."[10] Apart from merchants and the general public, the Berlin Conference also gave leaders a stage to resolve pressing issues in the name of global peace and cultural morality. Delegates primarily used this self-appointed authority to draft international principles that they could subsequently employ to determine the legality of all imperial projects in the future.

The most significant of these covenants was the General Act of the Berlin Conference. This agreement bound each of the Great Powers to conventions on trade rights, navigation, territorial acquisition, and occupation standards.[11] It also recognised universal safeguards for the protection of indigenous populations. The General Act mandated a common standard for colonial conquest, making it one of the first truly international agreements in modern history. Article 35 and the "principle of effective occupation" perhaps demonstrated this fact more than any other section in the General Act. Here, signatories agreed that colonial powers had "the obligation to ensure the establishment of authority in the regions occupied by them on the coasts of the African continent sufficient to protect existing rights and, as the case may be, freedom of trade and of transit under the conditions agreed upon".[12] In this fashion, Article 35 stipulated that imperial governments needed to demonstrate genuine control of a colony in order for rival powers to recognise the sovereign legality of the occupation. Treaties with local leaders, local acceptance of a colonial state's national flag, and the presence of an official administration and police force, all qualified as acceptable conditions of control. This rule also extended to the economic domain. If a colonial authority did not regulate or utilise a region's natural resources to their fullest potential, other powers could appeal against the legality of the occupation to signatory states.

Most consequentially, however, the "principle of effectivity" authorised imperial governments to use all means at their disposal to create and maintain regional stability. In other words, if indigenous populations failed to realise the supposed "benefit" of imperial rule, West Africa Conference delegates deemed it permissible to use systematic violence to show Africans its supposed virtue. Nineteen years after Europeans drafted the General Act, Nama and Ovaherero peoples in Southwest Africa discovered the genocidal prospect of "effective occupation" at the hands of German settlers and soldiers in the Omaheke desert. "Great national movements are not the result of single deeds, single years," proclaimed the German Colonial Association in 1882:

They are rather subject to the laws of a slow, unseen growth ... the question of the broadening of our overseas military and economic zones, in not merely the product of our own day. Since the end of the last century, such pleas have grown louder ... These suggestions gained a tangible form in the years after 1848. What the homeland does not offer, foreign lands shall provide.[13]

While the official slogan of the German Colonial Association did not represent the views of every German citizen, it certainly spoke for a majority of associations and citizens, who constituted a flexible imperial consensus in Germany. As a result, the West Africa Conference ushered in a new era of national possibilities.

"If German politics proudly and decisively employs its means of power in the world in the interests of our nation," Carl Peters exclaimed on the eve of the Berlin Conference, "then we will have found the safest way to maintain all our limbs which are spread across foreign lands."[14] Peters's message gave voice to colonial advocates at a time when the imperial consensus enjoyed significant influence in the public domain and the German Reichstag. Regardless of individual benefit or collective purpose, the Berlin Conference established the legitimacy of Germany's colonial ambitions in the eyes of the international community. In the words of *Die Gartenlaube*'s editorial board, this marked Germany's departure "from the old Brandenburg fort" in the direction of "new worlds of vitality".[15]

Corporatism, Conquest, and Resistance in German Südwest

"If something is ever to become our colony," the German tobacco merchant Adolf Lüderitz expressed in May 1883, "Germans must be able to live there."[16] In the same article praising the initiatives of the man who first arrived in Southwest Africa in 1882, the editors of the *Deutsche Kolonialzeitung* also published a romantic portrayal of the African landscape from Lüderitz's personal correspondence. "One mountain of sand came after another; ostriches, antelopes and zebras crossed the path and disappeared in the distance or in the dark of night. On the way [into the interior], one gets on the stretched ox wagons of the German [Rhenish] Missionary Bam from Bethanien, who was just brewing his evening coffee and hospitably serving his riders."[17] Lüderitz's passage talks wistfully of a forlorn landscape that was devoid of urban poverty and industrial development. It purposely cast the region in desolate terms so as to generate interest in its limitless potential, most especially among affluent German investors and politicians.

Though Adolf Lüderitz championed colonialism as a worthy enterprise in the pages of the *Deutsche Kolonialzeitung*, a personal search for wealth initially guided his own colonial ambitions. In the aftermath of his purchase of Angra Pequena in 1882, Adolf Lüderitz looked to augment his regional holdings further, primarily along the south-western coast adjoining the Atlantic Ocean. The following year, he concluded an agreement with Captain Josef Frederiks of the Bethanien Oorlam for all of the land south of Angra Pequena to the Orange River, stretching inland for 20 miles.[18] He envisaged these acquisitions as the start of a much-larger expansionist project in southern Africa. After Bismarck extended "German protection" over Southwest Africa in April 1884, Lüderitz obtained additional territory from Kamaherero, supreme chief of the Ovaherero, and Jan Jonker Afrikaner, chief of the Oorlam. He sought to establish a commercial empire based on mineral extraction and regional trade, as well as a protective outpost from which Germany could expand into Central Africa.

At the same time in the new metropole, sympathetic groups and organisations moved to underscore the importance of Southwest Africa to the German state. Carl Gotthilf Büttner, a former Rhenish missionary, for example, celebrated Lüderitz's land deals as a national victory. "The significance of the newly acquired territory", he wrote in July 1884, "will only become fully manifest if one does not take a narrow view of the situation, but looks upon it as a way of gaining access to Africa's interior."[19] The famous German geographer Alfred Kirchhoff, meanwhile, noted: "Suddenly everyone is talking about Angra Pequena ... It appears that we Germans are finally beginning to take a serious and practical interest in overseas countries in order to use them for our colonial endeavours."[20] In the same issue of the *Deutsche Kolonialzeitung*, an unnamed contributor proclaimed sharply: "It should and must be colonised. There is agreement in extensive circles in Germany."[21]

While jubilant headlines roused audiences in Europe, they could not diminish Adolf Lüderitz's personal financial problems. He had staked a majority of his fortune on land procurement in Southwest Africa in the early 1880s. When that venture did not yield the immediate financial returns that he had envisaged, Lüderitz funded several speculative gold expeditions along the south-western coast. After these plans also failed to generate any success, he went bankrupt in November 1884. To avoid a further crisis, Bismarck ordered

Lüderitz to sell all of his assets and territorial claims to several prominent investors in Germany.[22] The railroad entrepreneur Adolph von Hansemann, the investment banker Gerson von Bleichröder, and the industrialist Count Guido Henckel von Donnersmarck were among the most prominent figures to capitalise on Lüderitz's misfortunes.[23] In concert with representatives from Deutsche Bank and other conspicuous German financial institutions, these men founded the German Colonial Society for Southwest Africa in April 1885.[24] The company's board styled the Society as both a private trading organisation and a "non-profit patriotic society acting in the national interest".[25] In so doing, the organisation effectively embodied Bismarck's long-held assessment of the ideal imperial project: moneyed stakeholders assuming all of the financial risks and rewards of colonialism, while the German state claimed ownership with only a minimal presence in the colony.

German Africa's corporatist beginnings notwithstanding, imperial testimonials, political propaganda, and a general curiosity for the unknown also propelled colonialism into the national spotlight. Images of landscapes, photographs of animals and farmhouses, rich descriptions of star-lit skies and sandy savannahs, and harrowing portrayals of occupation, all acquainted Germans with the stark realities of imperial domination.[26] What many once considered strange and alien suddenly became common and memorable. Individuals did not have to visit Windhoek personally or wade in the frigid waters off Swakopmund's coast to experience a shared closeness with *their* empire. Even the designation "German Southwest Africa" contributed to this collective mindset. It simultaneously announced Germany's claim to the territory and invited citizens to see the colony as a rightful constituent of the metropole. These were informal encounters that provided Germans with the emotional capacity to view a foreign territory as an equal part of the nation.[27] When citizens referred to the colony as "our Südwest" after 1884, it was because they deemed Southwest Africa to be a cultural and geographical extension of Germandom, thereby expanding the *Heimat* ideal on a global scale.[28]

Though imperial officials aspired to capture what they regarded as Southwest Africa's natural order, they also continued to propagate colonial fantasies among the German public. Perhaps the most egregious was the myth of German imperial domination. In the years between 1884 and 1894, the German Emperor's colonial authority existed almost entirely on paper. Africans, not Germans, controlled land rights and access to cattle and regional trade markets, and enjoyed numerical superiority on the ground.

Only later upon their arrival did settlers discover that "their" African homeland was far from the oasis they had read about in colonial missives and newspapers. Among the most powerful polities were the Witbooi Nama (led by Hendrik Witbooi) in southern Namaland and the Ovaherero (led by Samuel Maharero) in north and central Damaraland. When calls to suppress their regional dominance grew louder in the imperial and national press, the German government expanded its colonial presence considerably, culminating in Chancellor Caprivi's declaration of Southwest Africa as a settlement colony in March 1893.[29]

In a span of less than a decade, what had started as a minor commercial enterprise in a far-flung African territory had grown into a juridical constituent of the German nation. As Hendrik Witbooi and Samuel Maharero unmasked the truths about colonial life to the settlers, officials grew more determined to neutralise non-compliant African populations. After more military equipment and soldiers arrived in the colony, the role of the imperial regime grew in size and scope. The financial commitment these efforts necessitated far surpassed what imperial enthusiasts had promised politicians and other delegations in Germany at the start of the colonial era. This fact, in addition to Southwest Africa's dismal economic situation, prompted colonial leaders to rely on the metropole for most of their regulatory and military needs.

Africans played a significant role in this transformation. Their refusal to accept German authority compelled colonial officers to confront their administrative limitations, as well as to question the purpose behind imperial rule in southern Africa. This is not to say that Africans made their own conditions worse through acts of resistance. On the contrary, focusing on Africans and their successful resistance movements counters the persistent narrative that misrepresents the Nama and Ovaherero as nothing more than passive victims in the face of German pacification. More than any other factor, African resistance shattered the illusions of German cultural superiority: a belief upon which colonial enthusiasts had formulated and justified their imperial–national convictions since the "liberal revolutions" of 1848. When the veneer of imperial fantasy gave way to colonial reality, imperial officers increasingly relied on the military to subdue the Nama and Ovaherero populations. In spite of their controversial reception in the metropole, armed aggression and racial malice emerged as the principal instruments that colonial authorities employed to conquer, defend, and stabilise *Heimat* Südwest after the turn of the twentieth century.

"Ultimate Source of Control Is Violence"

In September 1909, Carl Becker, a German cattle farmer living near Vaalgras in southern Southwest Africa, sent a petition to Bruno von Schuckmann, imperial governor of the colony.[30] Becker's letter conveyed his apprehension about a series of race laws the German colonial administration had passed earlier in the year, specifically Paragraph 17f of the Regulation of the Reich Chancellor Concerning Self-Government in German Southwest Africa.[31] This new declaration revoked Becker's right to participate in all future elections because his wife was a *Bastardfrau* (Reheboth Baster woman), belonging to a southern African ethnic group descended from "Cape Coloured" and Nama communities in the nineteenth century. It also called into question the legal status of the couple's five children, including two who were at the same time living in Germany.[32] Left with no alternative, Becker pleaded his family's case to Governor Schuckmann, condemning the directive as "an illegitimate act designed to deny him civil rights and marriage".[33] He also claimed that German authorities had no legal right to subject his marriage retroactively to such a law because his wife was "nearly white".[34]

Carl Becker's argumentative rationale was both contemporarily logical and overtly hypocritical. He upheld the implied collective belief of whiteness as an essential component of *Deutschtum*, and simultaneously attacked the restrictive nature of race thinking as it applied to his family's legal struggle. Becker asserted that "§17 is born of the following idea: Southwest Africa is white man's land".[35] Though he was himself a white man, the colonial government had thrust him into a precarious position: that of the colonial "Other". Becker made every effort to underscore his contempt for the new state of affairs in Southwest Africa. He did so, however, with a notable degree of caution. Near the conclusion of his petition, Becker conceded that the government "has all the power" and that its "ultimate source of control is violence".[36] This remark was likely a reference to Germany's victory in the Herero–Nama war two years earlier, a supposed "triumph" that had culminated in the genocide of approximately 90,000 Ovaherero and Nama people between 1904 and 1907.[37]

Carl Becker's plight symbolises how imperial race policy in Southwest Africa affected the lives of Africans and German settler-colonists in the aftermath of the Herero–Nama genocide. He and his wife's experiences also serve as a clear illustration of the dangerous capabilities of states in the modern era. In the aftermath of the first genocide of the twentieth century, the colonial government retained the exclusive capacity to decide Becker's political orientation in relation to its German polity. Systemic racism and state-condoned acts of physical and juridical violence thus evolved into twin cornerstones of post-genocide Southwest Africa. Three specific conditions guided this process: first, the imperial government's adoption of *Rassentrennung* (racial separation) as official policy, most notably through bans on "mixed marriages" and the construction of *Eingeborenenwerften* (native settlements); second, through an increase in metropolitan efforts to encourage white women to emigrate to Southwest Africa; and, third, through the electoral landscape in the metropole that culminated in the "Hottentot elections" of 1907.

Perhaps the most explicit example of this new reality occurred when the colonial administration adopted *Rassentrennung* as official state policy. The Commissioner for Settlement, Paul Rohrbach, articulated the intentions of *Rassentrennung* in clear terms shortly after his arrival in Southwest Africa in the 1890s. "Our task", he pronounced, "is to divest [the Herero and Nama] ... of their specific *völkisch* and national characteristics and gradually meld them with the other natives into a single coloured work force ... This is to be a society based on work."[38] In this effort, German leaders passed an exclusionary "anti-miscegenation" Act, as well as various other racist laws, and also authorised local officials to construct segregated "native reservations" throughout the colony. Hans von Tecklenburg, deputy governor of Southwest Africa, issued the initial legal restriction on "mixed marriages" in October 1905. "Mixed-blood children produced by a native woman become German citizens," he claimed, "and are thereby subject to the laws valid for Germans. The male mixed-bloods will be liable for military service, capable of holding public offices, and will assume the right to vote sometime in the future, as well as other rights tied to citizenship. Not only is the preservation of purity of the German race and German civilisation here substantially impaired because of them, but also the white man's position of power is altogether endangered."[39] The racial motives behind Tecklenburg's security measures were explicit. In his estimation, "race mixing" was the very antithesis of a prosperous colonial state.[40] Miscegenation was so dire a threat, he alleged, that it authorised the imperial government to outlaw not only future mixed marriages, but also existing ones retroactively as well.

Imperial officers further endeavoured to persuade more white women to seek new prospects in Africa. Their tactics, however, generally focused on the dangers of miscegenation and the threats to German cultural identity and national prestige. German officials such as Theodor Leutwein had long feared the consequences of what he deemed to be "improper relationships". Even after Kaiser Wilhelm II forced him to step down as imperial governor in

1905, Leutwein complained about the supposed "bad traits" of black African women, and how they were on the verge of turning Southwest Africa into a "bastard colony".[41]

The most influential activists on this issue, however, were white German women themselves. Clara Brockmann, a white settler and advocate of social equality, for example, championed racial purity as a means of advancing the position of white women in her 1910 book, *The German Woman in Southwest Africa: A Contribution to the Question of Women in Our Colonies*. As she noted: "I challenge my sisters in the homeland", she charged, "to help with the work [and] make our colonies purposeful and agreeable. Support our cultural tasks on Africa's soil in the homeland to build and establish a new Germany."[42] Brockmann claimed that women were essential figures in the colonial sphere, and that during an era when authorities concentrated on racial segregation, "the prevention of intermarriage, which signifies the spiritual and economic ruin of the settler, the achievement of a profitable farm cannot reach successful development without the participation of the housewife".[43] In this fashion, the *Frauenfrage* (women's question) provided white women with a forum to promote their own roles in the colonial empire, as well as a means to demand more social representation in the metropole.

The German federal elections of 1907 – contemporarily known as the "Hottentot elections" – evolved into nothing less than a referendum on Germany's colonial occupation of Southwest Africa. They represented a watershed moment in the history of German national politics. Indeed, these elections were not about women's suffrage, tax reform, or social mobility. Nor did they contrast Prussian Junkers or the industrial "new right" against the urban electorate of the Social Democratic Party. Instead, these elections revolved around Germany's honour overseas and the status of white-settler authority in Africa.[44] For members of Germany's "new right", which included industrialists, pan-German nationalists, and champions of the colonial project in Africa, these concerns were especially prominent. In an effort to galvanise support for the imperial empire, Chancellor Bernhard, Prince von Bülow's government, the German Colonial Office, and the political right attacked left and centrist politicians for their supposed betrayal of German soldiers in their fight against what they called "Herero and Nama savages".[45] The "Bülow bloc" – as their devotees called them — moved to orchestrate an electoral campaign that associated colonial conquest with German patriotism in contrast to the anti-imperial German opposition's cowardice, deviancy, and racial betrayal.

In the weeks before the election, the Bülow bloc distributed racist leaflets that emphasised Ovaherero and Nama acts of violence, and regularly referred to their opponents as the "Black–Red League for the Defense of Kaffirdom against Germans".[46] An article in Nuremberg's *Frankischer Kurier* decried what its disciples regarded as the fundamental short-sightedness of the anti-colonial opposition. "[They] deal quite thoroughly with the colonial scandals objected to by all parties, and with the costs of German colonial policy," the article charged, "but entirely conceal that the Centre and Social Democracy refuse the means necessary to maintain the military readiness of the German troops standing against the savage and cruel enemy."[47] Thanks in large part to racist messages like these in the colonial press, the "Hottentot elections" produced a decisive outcome. Though the Social Democratic Party received nearly a quarter of a million more votes than it had won in 1903, the party lost exactly half of its pre-election seats in the Reichstag.[48] The Social Democratic Party, the Centre, and Bülow bloc parties all experienced electoral defeat as a sign of the new influence of colonialism on German politics. A national consensus that enthusiasts built on race had successfully diffused the power of oppositional groups who had traditionally focused on issues of class and social mobility.

Perhaps even more importantly, the outcome of the 1907 elections signalled that colonial racism had moved into the political lexicon of Germany's national electorate. This development was only possible because the Herero–Nama war presented a legitimate challenge to the colonial project in Southwest Africa. In colonial and national politics, "the beast" – as the conservative parliamentarian Graf Ludwig zu Reventlow referred to the Ovaherero in January 1904 – replaced "the subject". Much like General Lothar von Trotha's "peace through the graveyard" in the Omaheke desert, the racist atmosphere that politicians like Reventlow promoted encouraged officials in Southwest Africa to pursue segregationist policies – a precursor of South Africa's 1948 apartheid policies – against the Ovaherero and Nama populations, which Germans now regarded as inherently dangerous and inferior to the white settler class.

Concluding Reflections

European colonialism was an inherently violent enterprise in all respects. In Germany, collective motivations for empire fluctuated, as costs rose and conditions grew more brutal. By the turn of the twentieth century, nationalism gradually evolved into a central factor in German colonial policies. As exclusionary politics and racial segregation became more important to Germany's imperial agenda, Africans found fewer outlets to enjoy their own cultural, religious, and political ways of life beyond the reach of the colonial government.[49] In response, the Ovaherero – and later the Witbooi Nama – eventually found themselves in another violent conflict in 1904, one that forever shaped their cultural and social ways of life. At the height of the "Herero–Nama Rebellion" in 1904, Witbooi sent the following lines to Leutwein:

> I have for ten years abided by your law, stood under your law, and behind your law – and not I alone, but all chiefs of Africa. For this reason, I fear God the Father. You accuse me of murdering helpless white people and say that eighty of my men are in your custody, but who shall pay for the white people? I beg you, when you read this letter, sit down and quietly reflect [on my words]. Count up the souls who have perished in this country since you arrived, and the weeks and days and hours and minutes since they died.[50]

With these words, Witbooi not only justified his decision to join Samuel Maharero in his fight against the *Schutztruppe*, but also altered once more the nature of German colonial affairs in Southwest Africa. Though he did not live to see the end of his renewed campaign against imperial occupation, Witbooi's impact on German imperial practices carried into the next violent phase of colonial rule. In particular, he pressed settlers overseas and citizens in the metropole to question the kind of colonial power that they wanted Germany to be in the twentieth century. After the start of the Herero–Nama war, imperial authorities provided the answer in genocidal terms.

19

Colonialism in Spanish Africa

Gustau Nerín and Iñaki Tofiño

In 1963, Admiral Carrero Blanco, Spanish dictator Francisco Franco's right-hand man, proudly proclaimed in the Madrid Parliament that there was no injustice to correct in Spanish-ruled Equatorial Guinea. It is true that the admiral represented the most intransigent elements of the regime, but it is also true that his statements were not much different from those of other European politicians of his time. It may also seem strange that in 2019 the head of state of a democracy, King Felipe VI of Spain, noted that the foundation of Panama City and the expedition of Magellan and Elcano were "essential highlights of our history about which we can feel very proud".[1] In Spain, the issue of reparations for the colonisation of Spanish Africa is far from being part of the public agenda, because the government in Madrid does not seem to have any intention of reviewing Spain's colonial past history, let alone officially apologising for the crimes of African colonisation.

An Old and Conflictual History

Only 14 kilometres separate Spain from North Africa. Relations between the Iberian Peninsula and the territories located south of the Strait of Gibraltar have been intense, and throughout history several political entities such as the Umayyad caliphate and the Almohad empire have had a presence on both sides of the Strait.

From the fourteenth century on, the kingdom of Castile was involved in military actions in North Africa, as it perceived Muslims from the Maghreb and Al-Andalus, the Muslim-ruled part of the Iberian Peninsula, as a threat. As part of their aggressive policy towards their southern Mediterranean neighbours, Castilians began a policy of occupying enclaves in different parts of North Africa such as Oran or Béjaïa (Bugia) in Algeria. Their goal was not to conquer large territories, but rather to establish militarised coastal points through which to pressure North African societies.

Some of these enclaves – the so-called African strongholds – have lasted until today: Ceuta, Melilla, Alhucemas, Vélez de la Gomera, Perejil Island, the Chafarinas Islands, and the island of Alboran. Ceuta – occupied by the Portuguese in 1415 and transferred to Spain in 1640 – as well as Melilla, occupied by the Castilians in 1497, were incorporated into Spain's sovereign territory in 1995 when they were proclaimed "autonomous cities". Morocco has never ceased to claim these territories, and considers the very existence of these Spanish cities on the southern shore of the Mediterranean an assault on its national integrity. The rest of the territories remain, in practice, under military control. The tiny islet of Perejil even caused a military incident between Spain and Morocco in 2002.

The Canary Islands archipelago was conquered by Castile in the fifteenth century. Over time and with the replacement of the native population with Spaniards from the Iberian Peninsula, its colonial characteristics would disappear. However, some Canarian nationalists have continued to define the islands' situation as colonial (for example, the group Hijos de Canarias, who maintain the website La Raíz).[2]

The possession of Ceuta and Melilla led to various conflicts between Spain and Morocco, such as the 1859 African War or the Margallo War of 1893–1894. From 1912, a Franco-Spanish protectorate was established over Morocco: while the French occupied the central part of the territory, the Spanish took possession of the far north and the southern end of the country. The occupation of the north was terribly difficult, and the armed conflict lasted until 1927. Seven years later, Spain took over a small territory on the Moroccan coast, Ifni, which would be managed as an independent colony, separate from the Moroccan protectorate. In 1956, when France abandoned Morocco, Spain was forced to decolonise its portion but retained control of the Southern Protectorate and Ifni. It would decolonise the protectorate after a brief war in 1957–1958 but retained control of Ifni until 1969, when the territory was returned to Morocco.

In 1900, by the Treaty of Paris, Spain took control of Western Sahara.

Morocco also claimed this territory as its own from 1956, but Spain refused to leave. In the end, in 1975, during the last moments of the Franco dictatorship, Spain ceded the administration of the territory to Morocco and Mauritania, without having carried out the self-determination referendum demanded by the United Nations.

The islands of Fernando Po and Annobón were ceded by Portugal to Spain in 1777 but would not be effectively occupied until 1858. In 1900, Spanish Guinea was established when Madrid added Río Muni to its Central African territories (although effective colonisation of the interior would be delayed until 1926). Spanish Guinea remained under the control of Madrid until 1968.

Morocco: An Uncomfortable Claim from an Unconvinced State

When discussions occur in Spain about responsibility for the Morocco campaigns (1909–1927), they do not usually focus on the imperial power's responsibility towards Moroccan victims of the colonial war, but rather on the inspection party that tried to investigate the responsibility of military commanders and of King Alfonso XIII himself for the death of some 9,500 metropolitan soldiers during the so-called Disaster or Battle of Annual between 1921 and 1923. Public opinion in Spain has always been more concerned about the fate of Spanish conscript soldiers than about the memory of Moroccan victims of Spanish colonialism. This is in spite of compelling evidence that in the war waged against North Africans by the Spanish army, chemical gas was used, prisoners and corpses were mutilated, villages and crops were destroyed, and hostages were taken.[3]

The main Moroccan demand, in this case, has been one of reparations for the use of chemical weapons in the Rif between 1921 and 1926, mainly by the Spanish, but also by the French. The issue of reparations escalated in 2002, after the Perejil Island crisis and the publication of several studies that revealed the widespread use of chemical weapons in Morocco, most notably the book *Deadly Embrace* (2002) by Sebastian Balfour.[4] The request for apologies and reparations became a cause shared by numerous Spanish, Moroccan, and international associations, many of them Amazigh, such as the Amazigh World Congress.[5] To lend more weight to these requests, it was even argued that there is still a strong incidence of carcinogenic disease in the Rif due to the use of chemical weapons in the past. However, this argument has not been scientifically proven.[6]

In 2007, the Catalan independence party, the Republican Left of Catalonia, presented a motion to the Spanish Congress asking for state apologies to be formulated, and reparations to be granted for the use of chemical weapons in the Rif. This would be either in the form of development cooperation in the affected areas or through direct compensation to the families of victims. The motion was rejected by the votes of the major Spanish political parties: the Spanish Socialist Workers' Party and the conservative Partido Popular (PP, or People's Party).[7] After this parliamentary setback, the issue was abandoned and faded into oblivion. However, reparations for the victims of the Moroccan campaigns came under the scope of the Historical Memory Act, passed at the end of 2007, in which Madrid recognised the victims of its past actions.

Nevertheless, it seems that there are enough reasons to claim at least a state apology from Spain. Although chemical weapons were not banned in Spain during the Rif War between 1921 and 1926, because Madrid would not ratify the Geneva protocol until 1928, gases from Germany were used, something which the 1919 Treaty of Versailles had forbidden. Although the actions of the Spanish army cannot be called a "genocide", they could fall into the category of war crimes, which are imprescriptible.[8]

However, the Moroccan state has not openly called for reparations in the case of the Rif War. Many authors have noted that the Moroccan monarchy identifies strongly with the claim, which has also been capitalised upon by the Amazigh groups, who are opposed to the central government. They have noted too that Rabat itself launched a fierce wave of repression in the Rif shortly after independence in 1959 and later in 1984.[9] In fact, it is questionable whether the Moroccan monarchy can benefit from compensation, because the *Makhzen* – the Moroccan state – was an accomplice in the Hispano–French repression conducted against Riffians.[10]

Other scholars such as Nizar Messari, from Ifrane University in Morocco, allege that relations between the Moroccan monarchy and the Riffian population significantly improved with the rise to power of Mohammed VI in 1999. They even argue that the issue was closed in 2004 with the establishment of the Commission of Equity and Reconciliation, aimed at healing the wounds caused by King Hassan II's reign between 1961 and 1999.[11] But the Riffian conflict is far from over, as demonstrated by the outbreak of the Hirak revolutionary movement in 2016. The fact that Hirak defended Riffian and Berber identity, and that it considers Abd el-Krim and the Rif Republic of the 1920s as its referents, undoubtedly reinforced Rabat's reluctance towards Riffian claims, although, officially, Abd el-Krim is considered a hero of Moroccan nationalism.[12]

In the Rif, there remain very active grassroots movements with plenty of international connections which have made numerous demands based on historical arguments against Spain, France, and Morocco.[13] A contemporary Moroccan historian, Mimoun Aziza, notes that there is "an excess of memory but very little history and few good historians".[14] The demands for reparations for Morocco's campaigns that have been put forward by Riffian civil society – and Amazigh groups everywhere – have not received Rabat's support.

Even more complicated is the question of compensation to Moroccan soldiers who fought alongside the rebel forces during the Spanish Civil War between 1936 and 1939, and to whom General Franco promised "the best flowers" when the victory came. For decades, there was a protest movement of former Moroccan soldiers who demanded to be compensated in the same way as Spanish soldiers.[15] This petition was supported by the Centre of Shared Memory for Democracy and Peace, a Moroccan grassroots association.[16] This claim, unlike that of French askaris who fought alongside the Free French during the Second World War (1939–1945), has generated a conflict of historical memories. It is widely rejected in Spain because the Moroccans fought against a legally elected democratic government, and many political groups consider it an insult to reward those who fought against democracy. This claim has become less vocal with the death of the potential beneficiaries of reparations.

From time to time the claim has also arisen for Spanish citizenship for the descendants of the Moriscos (Muslims) expelled from Spain in 1609–1614.[17] The granting of Spanish citizenship to Sephardic Jews in 2015 triggered demands based on what was perceived to be the unfair treatment of Morisco descendants. However, the claim, led by the Memory of Andalusians Foundation, a grassroots association which involves Moroccans who consider themselves descendants of Andalusians, did not go far.

Morocco has not been very involved in the demand for various colonial reparations from Spain, probably because relations between Madrid and Rabat are extremely conflictual and depend on several elements: Moroccan multilateral negotiations with the European Union; migration flows; the Western Sahara question; sovereignty over Ceuta and Melilla; and anti-terrorist cooperation against radical Islam.[18] Reparations cannot be dissociated from other important policy issues in bilateral relations between Spain and Morocco.

Ifni: Complicated Claims

In addition to the demands of soldiers in the Spanish Civil War, there are some requests related to Ifni, occupied by Spain from 1934 to 1969, and currently part of Morocco. Many North African soldiers fought alongside the Spanish army during the Ifni War (1957–1958) against the Saharan Liberation Army (supported by Morocco). Spain has granted pensions to conscripted soldiers from Ifni and their widows. However, it has not offered them to soldiers – or their widows – who fought as volunteers or who were recruited in the Southern Protectorate – a territory which Spain should have returned to Morocco in 1956 because it was part of its overall protectorate. Madrid, however, retained the territory until 1958, after the end of the Ifni War. Those excluded from pensions continue to claim the right to be considered for all intents and purposes as conscripted fighters from Ifni.

In contrast, Ifni, the Sahara, Río Muni and Fernando Po were turned into Spanish provinces in 1959 in an attempt by Madrid to block the decolonisation process. Their locals were thus provided with Spanish identity cards. One of the persistent demands of the inhabitants of these colonies has been the granting of Spanish citizenship to them and their descendants. However, a ruling of the Spanish Supreme Court in 2020 established that being born in the African provinces of Spain and having an identity card did not automatically entitle one to Spanish citizenship.

Ifni's inhabitants have also repeatedly requested the opening of a Spanish Moroccan cultural centre in the area which could boost cultural activities and contribute to keeping the Spanish language alive in the region. This request was never considered by Spain, which does not even have a consulate in the city. In 2016, a group of Ifni youth occupied the emblematic colonial building of the former military paymaster's office, located in the centre of the city, to ask that Madrid heed their demands. They asked for the restoration of Spanish citizenship (something which they had already requested in 2007, 2008, and 2012), to which they considered themselves legally entitled. Eight activists were arrested and spent eight months in prison in Morocco for this action. The association Memory and Rights, which articulated these demands, was subsequently closed down by the Moroccan government.[19]

All things considered, the Moroccan state is the party most interested in silencing the protests of Ifni's colonised population, as Rabat feels that these civil society demands may threaten Morocco's national unity.

Western Sahara

Some of the inhabitants of Western Sahara, like others in Ifni and Spanish Guinea, have repeatedly claimed a right to Spanish citizenship, but this route was closed to them, definitively it seems, with the 2020 ruling of the Spanish Supreme Court.

Another case that has provoked a demand for an official apology is the disappearance of Mohamed Sidi Brahim Basir, founder of the nationalist Advance Organisation for the Liberation of Sahara, in 1970. It was officially announced that he had been deported to Morocco by the Spanish colonial authorities, but all evidence points to his execution in the Sahara by Spanish soldiers. Since 2008, the activist's relatives have demanded to know the truth about his disappearance. At that time, the Catalan pro-independence party, the Republican Left, passed a motion, based on the Historical Memory Act in the Spanish Congress, insisting that Madrid clarify Basir's fate. The motion was rejected by the votes of the major Spanish parties, which continue to highlight what they see as the positive benefits of Spanish colonialism.

The Moroccan government, despite presenting Basir as a pro-Moroccan national hero, has never called for an official investigation of his case, probably because this would discredit Rabat's official version about the Saharawi activist. There is no real desire by the Spanish government to investigate, in part because the Basir inquiry could cause new friction in what are always complex Spanish–Moroccan relations.[20] At the same time, the Polisario Front, the Saharan pro-independence guerrilla movement, is also not particularly interested in this issue. Firstly, its priority is to fight Morocco and to uncover the brutalities of the Moroccan state rather than those of Spain. In addition, the Polisario Front does not want to have a conflictual relationship with Spain, where it has important bases of support.

In 2022, the Spanish prime minister, Pedro Sánchez, completely changed his Moroccan policy, renouncing support for self-determination in Western Sahara and offering his support instead for Morocco's plan to grant autonomy to the territory, contrary to UN resolutions, which call for a referendum. Sánchez claimed that he was doing this so as to put a stop to Moroccan claims over the Spanish autonomous cities of Ceuta and Melilla.[21]

Equatorial Guinea

During the colonisation of Spanish Guinea there was no lack of violent episodes that could generate demands for reparations, such as the death of Sas Ebuera, leader of the Bubi;[22] military operations against the Fang chief Rokobongo during the First World War (1914–1918);[23] Lieutenant Ayala's repression of the Fang Ossumu clan in 1926;[24] and the "disappearance" of the nationalist leaders Enrique Nvo and Acacio Mañé in 1959. Between 1968 and 1979, the dictator Macías Nguema of Equatorial Guinea often highlighted the brutalities of Spanish colonialism and centred his discourse around historical memory.[25]

However, since 1979, the regime of Obiang Nguema Mbasogo, a former colonial military officer, has maintained a more ambiguous position. It has criticised Spanish colonialism, but not with the virulence of Macías.[26] In an interview in 2012, Obiang declared: "Do not forget that we were created and educated as Spaniards ... We have a deep feeling towards Spain and everything Spanish."[27] At first, when facing the economic problems triggered by Macías's dictatorship in 1979, Obiang proclaimed himself a follower of Hispanidad theories and demanded Spanish cooperation.[28] Massive cooperation assistance came, but no progress was made towards socio-economic development. Then Obiang moved away from a pro-Spanish position and initiated a policy of periodic confrontation with Madrid. However, so far he has not claimed reparations, preferring to ask Spain to maintain a better relationship with its former colony and, above all, to cease calls for democratisation and stop its alleged support for the regime's opposition. In 2016, the autocrat stated: "What has to improve is the atmosphere of trust between the two countries."[29]

In recent years, Bubi nationalist movements have called for Bubis – the native population of Bioko island – to be considered "indigenous people". They have sought to base their rights on the Declaration of the Rights of Indigenous Peoples, approved by the UN General Assembly in 2007. But this claim is directed at the Equatorial Guinean state, since the Bubi nationalist movement, even if it criticises past Spanish domination, considers Equatorial Guinea "one of the so-called artificial countries because they were created by the colonisers uniting scattered territories of different peoples with different languages and customs".[30] In 2013, before the Geneva Expert Mechanism on the Rights of Indigenous Peoples, Bubis filed a statement claiming: "We suffer a systematic extermination" and "We are a millenary people on the verge of extinction".[31] Therefore, Bubi demands, even if they fall within the discourse of the defence of indigenous peoples' rights, are not so much aimed at claiming reparations from the colonial power – even if Madrid acted against "indigenous" populations – but rather at altering the territorial structure of the Equatorial Guinean state.[32] Nevertheless, so far, the Bubi claim has had little impact in Spain.

Africans and Their Afro-descendants in Contemporary Spain

There have been a small number of Africans and Afro-descendants present in the Iberian Peninsula since the fifteenth century. However, in most cases, they did not establish any permanent clusters, except in towns such as Gibraleón in the province of Huelva, where a minority of descendants of black slaves can trace their origins back to the fifteenth century. They were discriminated against and prevented from receiving any education, and usually treated as part of the Roma people, who also arrived in the Peninsula during the fifteenth century and have suffered much discrimination and persecution ever since. Even if there was some discussion about the eventual abolition of slavery during the drafting of the 1812 Spanish constitution,[33] the idea was dismissed, and slavery was legal in metropolitan Spain until 1837. Unlike Britain, which passed the Slave Compensation Act in 1837 to compensate slave owners for their financial losses after the abolition of slavery (see Cobley, and Frith and Xosei in this volume), Spain did not establish a compensation scheme. Instead, it promoted the idea of slaves buying their freedom by paying their owners or continuing to work for them in indentured servitude.

During the nineteenth- and twentieth-century Spanish occupation of parts of Africa, some North and West Africans were allowed into the Peninsula, usually as students. Their numbers increased in the 1960s, when Spanish Guinea, Sidi Ifni, and the Spanish Sahara were nominally transformed into Spanish "provinces" and their inhabitants issued with Spanish identification cards. This theoretical equality between European and African Spaniards was used by the Franco dictatorship as an argument against decolonisation, claiming that, in fact, Madrid did not have any colonies but rather overseas provinces. However, this was but a legal fiction because Africans were not Spanish citizens but "Spanish subjects who benefited from Spanish nationality".[34]

By the end of Franco's dictatorship in 1975, Spain officially had no colonies. The 1978 Spanish constitution imposed a political and social pact of silence about the 1936–1939 Civil War and the Franco dictatorship. This meant that, for years, discussing the recent past – not to mention the Spanish role in Africa – was simply out of the question. Only during the twenty-first century has part of Spanish society begun to demand a public debate about the memory of the past and its implications for truth, justice, and reparations.

In 2007, the Spanish Socialist government approved law 52/2007 – the so-called Historical Memory Act – in support of those who had suffered persecution or violence during the Civil War and the Franco dictatorship.

This law has been contested by right, ultra-right, and fascist parties alike, thereby demonstrating the difficulty of implementing the politics of memory in contemporary Spain. In September 2020, the draft of a new Democratic Memory Act was presented in parliament, and finally passed into law in October 2022. Historical memory and the discussion about possible reparations in Spain are linked to the Civil War and the subsequent four-decade dictatorship. Neither in the 2007 nor the 2022 law can one find any reference to Spain's colonialism and its consequences in the Americas, Africa, or Asia.

The Case of Former Colonisers

After 1968, some white Spaniards remained in newly independent Equatorial Guinea. The growing tensions between Madrid and Malabo prompted the repatriation of most Spaniards in 1969. Ever since, groups of former colonists have tried to lobby both the Spanish and the Equatorial Guinean governments for reparations to compensate them for the goods and properties they left behind in the former colony after independence. In 1970, a commission was formed to study this matter, but the subject remains unresolved.[35] In subsequent years, various civil society associations have been created by former colonists to lobby the Spanish government: the Community of Spaniards with Interests in Africa in 1971, and the Association of Former Residents in Equatorial Guinea in 1980. Their cases have been discussed on several occasions in the Spanish Parliament, more often than the claims of former colonised peoples, but no reparations have ever been granted.

The Case of the Former Colonised

In 1994, the Annobonese writer Francisco Zamora published a book, *Cómo ser negro y no morir en Aravaca* (How to Be Black and Not to Die in Aravaca).[36] Today, people of colour are still reflecting on their role in Spanish society through books such as *Y tú, ¿por qué eres negro?* (And You, Why Are You Black?)[37] by Rubén H. Bermúdez; *Ser mujer negra en España* (To Be a Black Woman in Spain)[38] by Desirée Bela-Lobedde; and *¿Qué hace un negro como tú en un sitio como este?* (What Is a Nigger like You Doing in a Place like This?)[39] by Moha Gerehou. Since it is not common practice in Spain to enquire about ethnicity for statistical purposes, it is impossible to know how many African and Afro-descendant people of colour live in the country. The estimates about their numbers vary greatly: some authors cite figures as low as 2.66 per cent

(Toasijé) and others as high as 13 per cent (Barbosa) of the Spanish population.[40] Spaniards have an image of themselves as open-minded regarding questions of race and ethnicity – a stereotype based on the theoretical equality between colonisers and the colonised in the Americas and Africa. This idea is also based on the widespread existence of *mestizaje* (miscegenation) in Spanish colonies.

This idealised image was shattered in November 1992 when a newly arrived Dominican immigrant in Spain, Lucrecia Pérez Matos, was murdered by a policeman and three under-age accomplices in Aravaca, near Madrid. Her murder was recognised as the first recorded racially motivated crime in Spain. A day later, the Moroccan immigrant Hassan Al Yahami was murdered by a racist skinhead in Madrid as well. These crimes demonstrated the extent of racism in Spain and were a turning point in discussions about ethnicity and nationality. In 2000, the murder of three white Spaniards by Moroccan immigrants in El Ejido (in Almería) provoked a wave of racial riots, which only confirmed the pervasiveness of racial discrimination and hatred in Spain. Meanwhile, the country was undergoing a process of de-Africanisation in order to promote its entry into the European Union in January 1986. This involved the negation of its African legacy, growing persecution of migrants and racialised people, and stronger surveillance and control of its southern border, especially since the establishment of Frontex, the European Border and Coast Guard Agency, in 2004.

The work of pioneering grassroots organisations of people of colour, such as the Association of African Women E'waiso Ipola, the Black Africa Work Team in Teaching, Black Panthers Organised Front of African Youth, and the Pan-Africanist Federation, has been continued by groups such as the Life Foundation Green Ecological Group, the High Council of Spain's Black Communities, the Pan-African Centre, and the Pan-African Studies Centre. In a context of growing discrimination, some black Spaniards attended the 2001 World Conference Against Racism in Durban (see Introduction in this volume). From that moment on, several conferences and congresses have been organised to study the situation of people of colour in Spain, and to demand social and political improvements. In 2001, a Conference of Students and Young Guineans took place in Barcelona; in 2003, a Conference on Immigration and Black Communities in Spain was convened in Madrid; and in 2005, another Pan-Africanist Conference was held, and included discussions about possible reparations for Spanish colonialism and exploitation of Africa.

In 2014, the right-wing Partido Popular presented a motion in the Spanish Parliament, on the Memory of Slavery, Recognition and Support for the Black,

African and Afro-descendant Community, which "paid tribute to the millions of people who, collectively and individually, had the courage and moral conviction to fight for the abolition of slavery throughout the world" and "condemn[ed] the slavery suffered by African people".[41] The document urged the Spanish government to fight racism, xenophobia, and all other forms of discrimination "in order to achieve a more equitable world",[42] by working with associations of people of colour, collecting data on anti-discrimination regulations, promoting cooperation with Africa, and supporting Afro-descendant issues in international forums. The debates in the Spanish Parliament were not about actual content, but about party politics: a similar text had been presented by the Socialist Workers' Party four years earlier. It is easy to see why such a motion was promoted by the Partido Popular: it projected a modern, anti-racist image, but without any actual political engagement. Conversely, the Socialists were not very keen on the initiative because they wanted to move away from their image as a migration-friendly party. In any case, more than a decade has passed, and nothing has changed: Afro-descendants continue calling for reparations in order to fight racism and to improve the situation of people of colour and immigrants in Spain.

The traditional bipartisanship of the Spanish legislature vanished when a series of new left- and right-wing parties were able to obtain enough votes to enter parliament during the 2010s. Among them is Vox, a new party whose tenets include fighting against immigration and espousing a racial definition of Spain as white and Catholic – a definition which rendered black or Muslim Spaniards non-existent. Today, people of colour are very active on social media, some have been able to get elected as members of parliament or local councillors, and a new generation of activists of African descent, such as Guillermo Akapo and Jeffrey Abé, are challenging racism and stereotyping. Abé published *Cuando somos el enemigo: Activismo negro en España* (When We Are the Enemy: Black Activism in Spain)[43] in 2019: a collection of essays by black activists who spoke about their struggles around feminism, politics, journalism, and academia. Akapo is part of the Black African and Afro-descendant Community of Spain, whose goals include eliminating racism and guaranteeing the civil, political, economic, social, and cultural rights of black Africans and their Afro-descendants in Spain. This grassroots movement fights discriminatory immigration laws and promotes historical memory from an anti-colonial and anti-slavery perspective, working for truth, justice, and reparations for colonialism. Its members advocate the end of neo-colonial relations between Spain and Africa by demanding recognition, reparations, and the end to the exploitation by Spanish companies in different parts of Africa and other territories with Afro-descendant communities. Even if there have been some small victories, such as the removal of slave trader Antonio López's statue from its location in the centre of Barcelona in March 2018, and the fact that people of colour's claims are now more visible thanks to public demonstrations and works of art, the multiplicity of voices within the African and Afro-descendant communities makes it difficult to form a united front against racism and in favour of reparations.

A first step towards the effective inclusion of people of colour in the body politic should be to identify their actual situation in Spain, as well as that of the African and Afro-descendant population. We do not know, for instance, what has been the health and economic impact of the Covid-19 pandemic of 2020–2021 among these groups in Spain. Working from this knowledge, an intersectional perspective of identity should be part of any public policy, especially in areas such as education, crime prevention, and the fight against racism and discrimination. Reparations as acts of public redress for injustices such as slavery, colonialism, wars, and genocide in Africa or the Americas are unlikely to happen anytime soon. Spain is still coming to terms with its convoluted recent past and, unfortunately, the lives and struggles of people of colour are not part of the mainstream political agenda. Demanding reparations for colonialism and slavery is part of a larger fight against institutional racism.

Concluding Reflections

The issue of reparations for Spanish colonisation of Morocco, Western Sahara, and Equatorial Guinea has always been a secondary issue in Spain. None of the affected governments have directly asked for reparations, nor have they officially demanded any official state apology. Reparations and apologies must be requested by groups proving their links to the affected groups, and governments are often the most valid interlocutors. However, for various reasons, the governments affected by Spanish colonialism in Africa have not filed serious claims so far. The request for historical reparations has been carried out by Afro-descendant associations in Spain which seek to protest against racism in that country.

Madrid is clearly opposed to colonial reparations, mainly because colonialism – especially colonialism in the Americas (see Ramirez in this volume) – is a structural part of Spanish nationalism, which is on the rise in response to Catalan independence demands linked to the 2017 self-determination referendum. Spanish democratic thought has been unable to revisit Francoist colonialist thinking and the colonial experience in the Americas, which is often presented as a basic tenet of "Spanish pride" by right-wing and left-wing parties alike.

When in 2020 the Mexican president Andrés Manuel López Obrador demanded an official apology from Spain for the colonisation of his country, this generated a wave of outrage across Spain, which has often demonstrated a supremacist view of Spanish and Western "civilisation". In Spain, many still believe that there is no injustice to redress for its sordid five centuries-long history.

20

Colonialism in Italian Africa

Mia Fuller

MODERN ITALIAN COLONIALISM (1869–1947) was unusual in some ways, making it appear to many as significantly different from that of other European countries. Deemed by historians to have been "the least of the great powers" in the era of the "Scramble for Africa" (see Introduction in this volume), Italy arrived late to the continent's cannibalisation, having only achieved its own unification in 1861.[1] Even while it was still embroiled in shaking off both foreign oppression and papal hegemony, the new Italian state rushed to grab parts of the Horn of Africa (Eritrea and Somalia) from the late nineteenth century, thanks to Britain's help, which was reciprocated to support London's own rivalry with France.[2] As the Ottoman Empire crumbled, Italy began acquiring Mediterranean territories (Libya and the Dodecanese Islands).[3] Under Fascism (1922–1943), Benito Mussolini's extreme bellicosity came to the fore in Rome's war on Ethiopia – the Abyssinian Empire, at that time a member of the League of Nations. Italy's sixth and final acquisition was Albania, annexed in 1939. Defeated in the Second World War (1939–1945), the country was forced to surrender all of its colonial claims when it agreed to the 1947 Paris peace treaties. Rome was nevertheless charged with the trusteeship of Somalia, its former colony, from 1950 to 1960.

Colonialism on a Shoestring

France and Britain developed their African empires most importantly as motors of wealth extraction and only in some instances, such as Algeria and South Africa, as spaces for settler colonialism (see Yates and Igba in this volume). In Italy's case, these priorities were inverted: the distinguishing trait of Rome's modern colonial era was its strong emphasis on "demographic colonisation" (*colonizzazione demografica*): the idea that some of the country's most pressing problems could be solved by settling large groups of Italian farmer-colonists in fertile regions of North and East Africa. Italy had an abundant "surplus" population, most of it living on the edge of subsistence and prey to endemic rural diseases such as malaria, as well as to periodic urban epidemics such as cholera. By the outbreak of the First World War in 1914, Italy had seen the emigration of about 13 million citizens fleeing these conditions. Their exodus was lamented by some politicians and social scientists for economic reasons, as it represented a very sizeable loss of the workforce. Others decried the phenomenon as an embarrassment, claiming that it exposed the lack of patriotic sentiment among Italians. Various settlement schemes were pitched as remedies to all of these problems: moving Italians who were leaving the country for the sake of opportunity to a colonial territory would, it was hoped, boost the economy, stop the demographic bleeding, and enhance Italy's international prestige.

This is not to say that Rome did not aspire to extractive colonialism on the British and French models. Indeed, throughout the colonial era the state financed numerous exploratory missions, regardless of whether the government was "Liberal" (1861–1922) or Fascist. These efforts did not yield much, though, and the Italian state spent far more than it ever gained from any of its colonial projects. Owing to unsystematic and non-centralised record-keeping as well as changes in administration – such as the creation of a new Ministry of Italian Africa in 1937, which began its own archival system without coordinating it with the one already in use in the Ministry of the Colonies, created in 1912 – a thorough evaluation of Italy's colonial costs and profits is not feasible. Nonetheless, it is clear that not one of its six African territories turned a profit.[4]

Italy's most extensive investments were made in agriculture, with wheat as the main crop, as well as cotton, grapes, bananas, and tobacco. Over decades, Rome experimented with various formulas to create plantations and high-yield crops, almost always in tandem with a complementary state-sponsored settlement programme. Investments that did thrive, meanwhile, were privately owned, such as construction and manufacturing firms. Another sector that grew apace was the state bureaucracy.[5]

Quite unlike the majority of Italian colonials, who were city-dwelling bureaucrats and individual investors, it was the image of large Italian farming families that dominated the country's colonial pursuits. These propagandistic figures, cast as developing hitherto neglected land to its full potential, sustained a distinctly Italian desire to resurrect a long-lost glory, overcoming its own late-modern "backwardness" in order to achieve equal, or even greater, status among European nations. Rome was thus seeking its own place in the African sun. Parliamentary debates and propaganda placed enormous emphasis on the ancient Roman Empire, as if Italy owed it to its own past to colonise and rule others again. Anything recalling Roman colonisation, such as the classical antiquities found in Libya, inspired great enthusiasm, giving Italian pro-expansionists the sense that their armed forces were facilitating a destined "return" to the region and, with that, to Italy's place in history and the world.[6]

Settler-farmers were essential to this fantasy of historical return, as the Roman Empire had two millennia earlier expanded its territories by building encampments and settlements throughout the regions into which it advanced. This was typically done by providing parcels of appropriated lands to military veterans. Modern-day Italian farmers imagined themselves to be restoring some African lands to their illusory long-lost function as the "breadbasket of the Roman Empire", feeding the metropole as well as the colonists themselves (see Palumbo in this volume).[7] This was the aim for Libya especially, and it was in part realised, with close to 30 settlement villages built for Italians in the 1930s. The vision was intended for Ethiopia as well.[8] Eritrea saw a handful of attempts at sponsored agricultural settlements, which all failed. Instead, Italians there invested their private capital in large landholdings and factories.[9] In Somalia, large numbers of Italian workers were not settled by the state, and the single most important attempt at a government-supported plantation was serviced by mostly African labour.[10]

In respect of these particular needs – agricultural production, the stemming of emigration by redirecting it to colonial territories, and even the burden of the imperial past – the Italian case stands somewhat apart from the major types of European colonial rule in nineteenth- and twentieth-century Africa. But Italy's exceptionalism ends there. Belying views of Italian colonialism as historically negligible and benign compared with that of other European nations, Italy exercised familiar mechanisms of violence and terror without restraint.

From the early days of Italy's colonial enterprises, its forces created detention camps – notably, Nokra in Eritrea and Danane in Somalia – to isolate those who resisted colonial rule from the rest of society. Internment and other impediments to the movement of locals continued to develop from there. In the 1910s, Libyan civilians were deported to open-air camps in Italy, where many died of diseases that thrived on malnutrition and extreme temperatures. Internal exile – known as *confino* – in geographically isolated parts of Italy (many of them islands) had been used to incarcerate Italians since after unification in the early 1860s, and the practice was only abolished after 1945. Libyans and East Africans brought to Italy for *confino* were held along with Italians (Libyans were interned with the Marxist philosopher Antonio Gramsci at the Ustica *confino* barracks, for example), but the former were nonetheless isolated from the latter. Records of deaths were not kept, and no information is available about survivors, but between 5,000 and 10,000 people were probably deported to Italian *confino* in the initial phase of Italy's occupation of Libya.[11]

By the end of the 1920s, multiple camps had been created in Libya itself, into which Italian forces drove the Bedouin population of Cyrenaica, in order to "liberate" the land they inhabited for the use of Italian settlers, who began arriving by the early 1930s. Estimates of how many died in the Libyan camps and in the course of the forced marches vary from 100,000 to a million, but we can reasonably take 100,000 as a minimum number.[12] The war waged by Italian forces against resisters included the use of chemical weapons in the late 1920s, but it was the willingness of the Italian command – and, on the part of some, their intent – to exterminate the Bedouin, in combination with the gruelling marches to the camps, followed by the miserable life lived there, in which public executions and disease further ravaged the interned population, that allows us to talk of a "genocide".[13]

Ethiopia was the subsequent setting for even more widespread attempts to eradicate all obstacles to Italian rule, no matter how many civilians were killed in the process. The Italian Air Force notoriously bombarded civilian areas with mustard ("yperite") and other gases in the 1930s, while land forces perpetrated multiple massacres of unarmed civilians and clerics.[14] It is also in Ethiopia that Rome's social violence in its African colonies became most pronounced. As well as seeing East Africans as uncivilised and inferior, Italians exploited them as an inexhaustible, inexpensive means of labour, whether in the building sector or sexually. The erotic labour of East African women was always essential to the Italian military's recruiting efforts, which overtly promised men uninhibited libidinal adventure. This was systematised through the practice of *madamato* (also called *madamismo*), an accepted economic exchange in which Italian men enjoyed stable domestic situations with women who provided sexual, sometimes emotional, and usually home-type "comforts" for whatever length of time suited the Italian men.[15]

These arrangements, as well as most other forms of sexual transaction, naturally led to the births of many Afro-Italian children, which – in contrast to their mothers' sexual labour – represented a problem to the government.[16] In 1937, Rome instituted anti-miscegenation laws aimed at preventing the growth of a "mixed-race" population, at the same time that planners and government officials began to orchestrate state-driven segregation in colonial cities.[17]

Slavery and Forced Labour

Slavery was not exactly an integral mechanism of modern Italian colonialism, but Italy does have a history of enslaving Africans, and slavery did play a role – at least, a rhetorical one – in support of Italian conquest and colonisation in Africa. First, the purchase of sub-Saharan enslaved individuals (who arrived through Portuguese traders) was a symbol of the most rarefied prestige in fifteenth-century Florence, at the height of the Renaissance (see Coquery-Vidrovitch in this volume).[18] Several Italian cities still had instances of enslaved people as late as the early nineteenth century.[19] Second, Italian expansionists ironically invoked the Abyssinian Empire's institution of slaveholding in the build-up to attacking Ethiopia in 1935, as a pretext for Italy eradicating such "primitive" practices and bringing "freedom" and "civilisation" in their place. This was somewhat perverse, in the light of Italy's very recent cases of slavery.

The most straightforward use of forced African labour in the service of Italian colonisers occurred in Italian Somalia, the one African setting where Italians imagined a plantation economy of a standard imperial "indirect" type that would not rely primarily on back-breaking labour by Italians. Just barely skirting enslavement practices, Italians conscripted lower-ranked locals, members of a recently freed class of formerly enslaved people who were already considered suitable for the low-prestige work of agriculture and construction.[20]

In Eritrea, Ethiopia, and Libya, land concessions were developed with private investment, using local paid labour and some better-paid Italian workers as well. In the eyes of many non-Italian Europeans, an unwelcome "racial" ambiguity characterised such work sites, in that Italian whites were routinely seen working alongside Africans. While foreigners noted this with consternation,[21] it was cause for profound anxiety on the part of the upper echelons of Italian society, who were invested in a rigid class and racial hierarchy in which their compatriots were seen nowhere near the bottom rungs. But lower-class Italians (*petits blancs*) migrated to the colonies to seek economic opportunities, just as Italian expansionists had hoped they would – at least until they were repatriated by Italian authorities after 1937 – the year of the anti-miscegenation laws and new segregation regulations, as an added method for solidifying racial differences by simply removing low-ranking whites from the fields.[22]

In sum, less costly indigenous labour, much of it unacknowledged, was crucial to all of Italy's colonial enterprises in Africa, from the domestic and sexual, to construction and farming, and the military too. Without "native" soldiers from Eritrea, Somalia, and Libya, it is unlikely that Italy's "empire" would have grown beyond its first acquisition of Eritrea.[23] It also bears stressing that violence against the colonised was not unrelated to the creation of labour pools, as when male survivors of the Cyrenaican concentration camps were drafted to work for low wages on Libya's east–west great highway: the *Litoranea libica*.[24] Finally, many contributions made by the colonised to the lives and work of the colonisers are only discernible between the lines of the archival record, such as the reliance of Italian farmer-settlers on Arab neighbours in Libya for assistance, marriage partners, and even protection.[25] The use by Italian technocrats of local indigenous knowledge relating to Ethiopian crops also often went unacknowledged.[26]

Reparations

Italy has not paid reparations to any of the populations who lost civilians or wealth in any form as a result of Italian aggression in its African colonies. Rome has, however, made three restitutions that served political ends at a symbolic level. After decades of foot-dragging, in 2005 Italy finally returned the *stele* – often referred to as an obelisk – it had stolen from Ethiopia's sacred site at Axum in 1937 and planted at the top of the ancient Circus Maximus, adding it to the numerous Egyptian granite obelisks already dotting the Italian capital. These represented visible demonstrations, in propaganda terms, of Italy's resumption of the ancient Roman Empire.[27] A statue of the Lion of Judah was also stolen from Ethiopia in 1937, and returned in 1966 as part of a much-publicised restoration of diplomatic relations with Ethiopian Emperor Haile Selassie. Finally, in 2008 Italy at long last restored a classical sculpture stolen from eastern Libya in 1913, the "Venus of Cyrene", to Tripoli.

Italian attention to reparations, to the extent that it exists, has concerned former Italian settlers who lost everything they acquired in Libya, although no reparations were actually paid. Demands made by those who had to repatriate in the course of the Second World War have been countered with the argument that those Italians were part of the war-mongering Axis powers and are therefore not eligible for reparations. This is supported by the fact that, as of 1939, the coastal provinces of Libya had already been annexed as part of Italian territory, but it also excludes Libyans from receiving potential reparations. Italians who later had to leave everything behind when they were permanently expelled from Libya in 1970 under Colonel Muammar Qaddafi's new regime have equally been denied any reparations by Tripoli.[28]

Concluding Reflections

The amnesia of Italians regarding the damage and suffering their country inflicted on Africans in the colonial era (and elsewhere, in the course of the Second World War) is the subject of extensive discussion, if not in the public domain, then among scholars and critics.[29] Above all, the forgetfulness of Italians in general was initially facilitated by the fact that no equivalent of the Nuremberg trials of defeated Nazis in 1945–1946 was ever held in Italy. War crimes and colonial atrocities were rapidly forgotten, especially given the immediate pressures of Italy's post-war reconstruction and the sense of victimhood triggered by the high numbers of repatriating Italians and stateless people flowing into and through Italy.[30]

Lack of awareness among Italians persisted as a result of successive Italian governments failing to educate their citizens, through evasiveness and even the suppression of information. The long-term result is an ongoing "culture war" between Italians who regard their colonial past as no less harmful than France's or Britain's, at least in terms of violence, if not in numbers of civilians exploited and killed, and those Italians who vehemently deny any crimes were committed, even generations later.[31]

Post-colonial studies made a relatively late appearance in Italy,[32] and current discussions about decolonising Italy's colonial past are at least as likely to be published in English as in Italian. This is also true of theoretically oriented essays on the "returns" of Italian colonialism, such as the contemporary use in Libya of Italian-built camps for migrants attempting to reach the Mediterranean and, beyond it, Italian and European Union shores.[33] Contemporary debates continue to rage over monuments erected in honour of Italian imperialism, along with other ubiquitous but ignored historical legacies that still litter the Italian landscape.[34] Occasional scholarship is published regarding how Italian colonial rule is remembered in its former African colonies.[35]

Scholars have recurrently articulated what makes Italy's colonial era in Africa distinctive rather than a mere mimicry of the more extensive, better-known cases of late-modern European colonialism. Nevertheless, with respect to many aspects of colonial violence, Italy did not deviate from the patterns of other European colonisers. Italian expansionists aspired to catch up with France and Britain and, in many ways, they succeeded.

Part Six

Colonialism in the Caribbean and
the Americas

21

Colonialism in the British Caribbean

Scott Timcke and Shelene Gomes

The colonial condition is not just a matter of constitutional status.
Control by external powers is exercised in a variety of other ways.
Notable among these are ideological co-optation, finance, trade and
security arrangements.
Norman Girvan, "Colonialism and Neo-colonialism in the
Caribbean" (2012)

IN APRIL 1595, THE ENGLISH explorer Walter Raleigh landed at Puerto de
España in Trinidad, overran the small Spanish garrison, then moved inland to
San José de Oruña with the express objective of capturing Governor Antonio
de Berrio. Employing hostages as bargaining chips, Raleigh used the next few
days to fortify the town. Once satisfied, he left troops and embarked on an
exploration of the Orinoco River basin to try to find the fabled El Dorado.
Initially shadowed by Spanish forces, themselves based at nearby Margarita
Island, Raleigh travelled about 600 kilometres up the Caroni River. As
chronicled in his inflated 1596 account, *The Discovery of Guiana*, Raleigh was
unable to find El Dorado. So, in the shadow of Mount Roraima, he decided to
return to San José, whereupon he continued with his larger expedition. With
Raleigh gone, Berrio resumed his duties of warding off British, French, and
Dutch corsairs and pirates. While the Spanish were having difficulty securing
Trinidad, the English had set their sights on Tobago, an island that was much
sought after by several European powers. From 1632, the Dutch had held the

island, though the bays and hillsides became sites of naval and land skirmishes with the English and the French. Ultimately, however, it was stiff indigenous resistance that led to the island being designated no man's land in 1684. This was later formalised by the Treaty of Aix-la-Chapelle in 1748.[1]

Conquest and Colonialism

Despite the English having been in Barbados since 1627, Tobago was so remote in the British imagination that it inspired the setting for Daniel Defoe's 1719 novel, *Robinson Crusoe*. The novel's protagonist is at various times a planter and a slaver, then later subordinates Friday before converting him to Christianity. "He is the true prototype of the British colonist", James Joyce wrote of the character, while Friday "is the symbol of the subject races". Joyce concluded: "The whole Anglo-Saxon spirit is in Crusoe: the manly independence; the unconscious cruelty; the persistence; the slow yet efficient intelligence; the sexual apathy; the practical, well-balanced religiousness; the calculating taciturnity."[2] Writing after centuries of direct experience, an Irishman like Joyce was familiar with the attitudes and economy of British colonial subjugation, the kind that would later encompass the West Indies.

Crusoe initially lamented being cast by shipwreck in an "uninhabited wilderness", where he experienced disorientation. Still, this liminal condition brought about "new thoughts" and set in motion a metamorphosis that united predation and settlement. In much the same way that *Robinson Crusoe* guided an English readership to comprehend their form of colonialism, so the Caribbean islands – being among the first British colonies outside the British Isles – supplied proving grounds for methods of rule, economy, and habituation. The most useful of these techniques were later applied and reproduced in other territories worldwide. It is not an exaggeration to say that the dominions created by the 1926 Imperial Conference, like Canada, Australia, New Zealand, and South Africa, bear the genealogy of the West Indies.

We provide these vignettes of Raleigh and Defoe, emblematic of the military and imaginative components of colonialism, to build a bridge between slavery and post-emancipation in the West Indies. We also deal in this chapter with the entanglement of colonialism and settlement with the waxing and waning of imperial objectives. These themes are themselves predicated on opportunistic conditions and converging interests in the ever-shifting power struggle in the Atlantic that began in the 1500s.

With the reassertion of decolonisation discourse in Britain and elsewhere in the present, it is helpful to underscore not only the extent to which places like the Caribbean were the first incubators of colonial expansion, but also how this history is frequently overlooked in scholarship. On this note, it is perhaps telling that the Caribbean is absent from the index of the renowned British historian Eric Hobsbawm's *Industry and Empire* (1977), an economic history of Britain subtitled "from 1750 to the present day". This book covers a period that spans the intense extraction from the West Indies, as well as the call upon West Indians to become a "replacement population" in Britain after the Second World War.[3] However, to avoid repeating Hobsbawm's error, we maintain that there is little value in stipulating hard boundaries to the processes we have identified. This is because – to repurpose a phrase from Haitian-born scholar Michel-Rolph Trouillot – the influence of empire is "so slippery at the edges that one wonders when and where it started and whether it will ever end".[4]

Politics, Economics, and Colonial Rule

Within the Caribbean, the English initially colonised Bermuda (1609), Barbados (1625), the Bahamas (1648), Jamaica (1655), and the Leeward Islands (1671). Other territories were later added: Dominica (1805), Grenada (1763), St Vincent (1763), and Tobago (1763). Trinidad (1797) and British Guiana (1814) were seized from Spain and the Netherlands respectively.[5] During the Napoleonic Wars (1803–1815), Dutch colonies came under British rule, with only a few like the Dutch East Indies, Suriname, and the Antillean islands returned to Dutch authority after the signing of the Anglo-Dutch Treaty of 1814 (see Allen in this volume). Even though the West Indian colonies were mostly small territories with small numbers of people, there is good cause to describe them as "ports of globalisation, places of creolisation".[6] This legacy can still be seen in the demographics of the region. Of the 37 million people in the Caribbean, a quarter speak English.

In the view of the Trinidadian scholar-politician Eric Williams, the European mercantile trade wars of the seventeenth century made evident what was at stake in the competition among imperial states: gaining control over India and North America.[7] Through private interests and royal chartered companies, Britain invested heavily in colonial agriculture and domestic production, reducing their purchase of goods from the Dutch. On the ground in the West Indian and Antillean colonies, institutions were formed on the basis of the kinds of crops cultivated as well as land markets and labour demands.[8] For example, sugar production was particularly labour-intensive, and so planters initially sought to enslave indigenous populations. But when this finite labour pool was depleted owing to the genocide of the indigenous people by European colonialists, planters drew on the English poor and convicts through servitude and indentureship. When this also turned out to be insufficient, planters began importing African slaves (see Brereton in this volume).

By the early nineteenth century, irrespective of how "well-equipped and well-managed" sugar estates might have been – and many were not – planters "lacked the basic permissives of calculability of success or failure in their businesses. They seldom had any realistic idea of how the enterprise stood financially, or what its prospects were."[9] British merchants were aware of these circumstances and took advantage of the planters' financial illiteracy to create debts, mortgages, and interest. As the Jamaican-born scholar Douglas Hall wrote, "industrial expansion required finances", and in the eighteenth century, planters of large estates and slave traders were best positioned to invest capital. This wealth allowed them to exert considerable influence and even purchase political office, which in turn shaped the triangular trade system. The wealth generated by the Atlantic trade provided a demand for goods, which in turn fostered economic activity in Britain.

Portions of the West Indies were so central to the British Empire that as the American Revolution of 1776 loomed, the British chose to secure the Caribbean over those 13 colonies.[10] While Jamaica itself was not rich, its white population was among the richest in the British Empire owing to the local concentration of wealth, and had considerable influence at King George III's court. With loyalist rather than republican sympathies, these planters had little cause for independence. Indeed, Jamaica was a primary destination in the English component of the transatlantic slave trade and, correspondingly, its exports altered British consumption habits.[11] Effectively, the dividends of enslavement affected the lives of almost all Britons: few things in that country were disconnected from the small islands in the Caribbean. Jamaica was central not only to British merchants during this epoch, but also made the state richer through customs revenues. Accordingly, as a source of great wealth, the territory was indispensable to London. It was the one colony the British could not afford to lose to the French as the American War of Independence erupted. Therefore, when the French aided the American insurgency, the British desire to protect its position in Jamaica meant that London deliberately under-committed resources to the American conflict, lest it leave portions of the West Indies unduly exposed to Paris.

It was this dynamic that Eric Williams drew on to argue that slavery and colonialism spurred "the development of British capitalism" by providing "the capital which financed the Industrial Revolution in England".[12] For present purposes, we need not engage in debates over the precise amount of wealth transferred from the West Indies.[13] What is more important is the institutional forms and social relations that emerged because of these transfers of surpluses. In effect, sugar cultivation in the West Indies provided solutions for various economic crises in Europe: the "periphery" was thus at the centre of European capitalist development.

Still, the American Revolution of 1776 marked a change in British orientation to its West Indian colonies, signalling the demise of the plantation system and ending the prominence of the West Indies in the empire. Between fighting the American War of Independence and then using the British army to try to put down the slave revolt in Saint-Domingue in 1793, which inspired insurrections across Caribbean colonies, these military commitments were extremely costly. This led the British state to reassess what it had previously considered the high value of the West Indian colonies. One important conclusion was the need to make colonialism self-sustaining by reducing administrative overheads. For example, for at least a century, the British sought to create consolidated federal territories like the Windward Islands Federation from 1879 to 1885 and the Leeward Islands Federation from 1871 to 1958. These entities did not bring any noticeable changes to constitutional conditions. Rather, each territory had its own local institutions and local governmental habits, and developed at its own pace. There was hardly a modern colonial policy until 1854, when the British Colonial Office was established. In contrast to Dutch rule in the Caribbean, which has been described as "careless colonialism" (see Allen in this volume), British colonial policy was drawn from the metropole.[14] This involved a system of governors appointed by the Crown and legislative councils with property qualifications required for voting. It was hardly a democratic space where colonial subjects had any say over how their lives were governed.

Culture, Family, and Kinship

Following the emancipation of slaves in 1833, colonial officials in British Guiana, Trinidad and Tobago, Jamaica, Grenada, St Lucia, St Kitts, and St Vincent organised the introduction of indentured labourers from British India to aid plantation agriculture. This created conditions for ethnic plurality, with far-reaching consequences during decolonisation. There have been several notable attempts to understand the ramifications of indentureship. Set within "precocious modernity",[15] the creolisation model has been one of the most influential. This model sought to analyse culture contact following centuries of forced, free, and coerced movements to the Caribbean that produced a correspondingly complex value system.[16] The Barbadian scholar Kamau Brathwaite describes creolisation as "an unplanned, unstructured, but osmotic relationship, proceeding from this yoke" of colonialism, predicated upon plantation economies.[17] This system involved tacit codes based upon the intersections of gender, class, occupation, race, colour, and age.[18] Additionally, codes could be specific to place or circumstances. Nevertheless, the lynchpin in this system was "respectability".

Conversely, the groups that could not be respectable – often of low status and poor – turned to "reputation". In addition to class aspirations, "respectability" had a gendered component, shaped by – and articulated through – capitalist, racial, and hetero-patriarchal logics. Women were typically responsible for governing respectability and interpersonal conduct. In attempting to achieve respectability, women especially aimed to uphold British mores such as sexual chastity, state-sanctioned monogamous marriage, modest dress, and the like. However, poor women, mostly but not entirely black and brown, often could not fulfil these ideals. Poor men typically acquired reputation through public acts of strength and popularity. These behaviours included drinking, sexual relationships with women, siring children, and wittiness – practices that signified capability and dominance, given circumstances in which it was difficult to support families financially.

Notwithstanding the role of respectability and reputation, colonialism produced a set of paradoxical attitudes and behaviours with regard to biological and social reproduction. Judith Blake's surveys in mid-twentieth-century Jamaica found that black parents hardly prepared their daughters for sexual relations, or conveyed to them knowledge about birth control.[19] As Sidney Greenfield notes, repeated admonitions about staying away from boys never included a discussion of "what to stay away from [meant]".[20] Conversely, boy-child sexual aggression was not punished. Rather, in Jamaica "the proof of a man's maleness is the impregnation of a woman",[21] while in Martinique it was part of the "expectations of masculinity".[22] This double standard led to high rates of unplanned teenage pregnancies. Indeed, many daughters were "angry at their mother for not preparing them for motherhood".[23] Whereas daughters felt anger at falling pregnant, their mothers ritualised the performance of their anger. The Jamaican scholar Edith Clarke notes that on her island:

The discovery is greeted with noisy upbraiding, the girl is severely beaten, and in many cases turned out of the house. In the second stage the girl takes refuge with a neighbour or kinswoman. After a period, which may be quite short, the kinsfolk and neighbours intercede with the mother on her behalf, and the girl is taken back into her mother's home for the birth of her child.[24]

Marriage with the prospective father was not generally a condition of re-entry into the household. The mother's performative ejection and acceptance of the pregnant child points to the logic underlying unequal treatment between sons and daughters, which created conditions conducive to pregnancy. A mother's physical violence and reconciliation was her way of asserting control over the household which her grandchild would join and contribute her or his labour towards.

Afro-Caribbean household production was a legacy of the plantation society and formed what the American scholar Sidney Mintz describes as a "slave proto-peasantry".[25] In the post-emancipation Caribbean economy, household production became a means of safeguarding the family against turbulence in the labour market and starvation more generally, while also supplementing the minuscule incomes that came from plantation labour. Mintz characterises household production as concurrently a "mode of response" as well as a "mode of resistance".[26] Subsistence crops were planted, and small animals raised and taken to market if there were surpluses. This pattern of reproduction differed from that of Indo-Caribbean families and households.[27] When predominantly Hindu Indian indentured workers arrived in the British West Indies, they sought to continue their cultural and religious practices, adapting and altering them to suit place and circumstance.[28]

Following emancipation in 1833, men's wage migration became a key feature of British Caribbean social life, as this provided more income than local plantation work.[29] In the nineteenth century, many of these men worked on the Panama Canal, on American fruit plantations in Central America, or in the cane fields of Trinidad and Guiana. Decades later, the Trinidadian oil sector and British factories required labour, and males sought opportunities there. Men were thus encouraged to undertake foreign wage-labour and to remit money to their families at home. Male wage migration may have financed the construction of homes, but it was women who were the managers of this sphere. The physical absence of men meant that other sources of labour were required for household production. This is where new children entered the picture.[30] Children were not deemed material burdens, but were instead seen as contributing to keep starvation at bay in a wider context in which the market and the racial biases of planters led to low wages. More broadly, child labour was condoned by colonial officials. The Trinidadian scholar Jerome Teelucksingh notes that, while the British Parliament began banning child labour from the 1840s in Britain, these regulations only arrived in the West Indies in 1927.[31] Moreover, colonial authorities had little appetite for consistent enforcement because it was "part of the legacy of colonial rule during the centuries of slavery, apprenticeship and indentureship".[32] In short, within the political economy of the post-emancipation plantation, daughters were preferred to sons because they produced labourers and were a dependable source of assistance to the family. Reproducing the family in this manner was a livelihood strategy in a capitalist polity that had little regard for the welfare of black subjects, leaving them to fend for themselves.

Historiography and Decolonisation Struggles

Midway through his seminal *Capitalism and Slavery*, Eric Williams turns to the history of the Codrington Library at All Souls College, University of Oxford. The library's construction was funded from a £16,000 bequest by Christopher Codrington, who was a British-descended Barbadian slaver and planter. Sitting at the nexus of epistemology and ruling-class formation, the library can be read as part of the material culture produced by violent dispossession and extraction in the West Indies. The descendants of those subjugated still face considerable racial, class, and geographical barriers even to enter the premises. Like All Souls, many British institutions bear the imprint of colonial oppression. Even after emancipation in 1833, the wealth from slavery funded English institutions in the Victorian period. For example, fundraisers for King's College London included Anglican donors such as the Society for the Propagation of the Gospel in Foreign Parts, which had owned the Codrington estates in Barbados. Among the 50 slave owners were John Gladstone, a slaver in British Guiana, and the British parliamentarians John Bolton and John Atkin, as well as Charles Nicholas Pallmer, who was once chairman of the Standing Committee of the West India Planters and Merchants group, which owned hundreds of enslaved people in Jamaica.[33]

Notwithstanding the exceptional quality of scholarship in and from the West Indies; the region has not received fair and adequate coverage relative to the studies of other places in the Atlantic world, as the result of demographics, underdevelopment, and Western bias. Although this prejudice has been eroded through the exceptional work of Trinidadians such as Claudia Jones, C.L.R. James and Eric Williams, there remains a lingering assumption that the British West Indies were peripheral to British economic development, that while these places added something to the total share, this contribution was meagre. Typically, a good portion of the British public and academy do not recognise the connections between enslavement, colonialism, and the historical foundations of their own lives. This belief is aided by geographical distance, the passage of time, and the gentle sway of ideologies that do not encourage closer scrutiny (see Small, and Frith and Xosei in this volume). As the Jamaican scholar Charles Mills explains, this is the very basis of "white ignorance".[34]

There is a righteous anger that animates Eric Williams's critique of empire. This anger was directed, first and foremost, at the unrelenting complacency, indeed celebration, of almost all British society, converting cruel and violent pasts into tales of enlightened benevolence in which colonialists were deemed agents and adherents of progressive reason, which the formerly enslaved ought to exemplify. This attitude can be seen in the self-congratulatory tone and pageantry around the centenary of the Emancipation Act in 1933. As Jessica Moody wrote: "Nationally, this centenary was used by the Anti-Slavery and Aborigines Protection Society to celebrate white abolition heroes and promote contemporary campaigns against 'modern-day slavery'."[35] By contrast, Eric Williams rejected the interpretation that emancipation was best understood as an imperial triumph that had been bequeathed to humanity.

The ideology behind the centenary of the abolition of slavery lacked any recognition of what has been described as the sustained, coordinated resistance by indigenous and enslaved persons to their colonisers.[36] This spirit of active resistance continued even after emancipation. From the 1816 Bussa Rebellion in Barbados to texts like Eric Williams's *Capitalism and Slavery*, resistance to imperial rule was ever present. It is with this in mind that decolonisation can best be understood as a two-centuries-long struggle against empire. In view of the Morant Bay rebellion of 1865 and similar protests, British colonial administrators initiated some reforms, but within a few decades there was retrogression as colonial governors became more autocratic.[37] Indeed, this constant dissent provided the British with little hope that circumstances could be altered. Consequently, London treated the Caribbean colonies with some ambivalence. Elsewhere in Europe, no such compunction existed. Denmark sold the West Indian islands it had seized to the United States, giving rise to the US Virgin Islands by 1917. From at least the end of the 1860s, concurrent with the Dutch emancipation law of 1863, segments of the Dutch Parliament pointed to the treasury balance sheets to highlight that the Caribbean colonies had become a fiscal liability (see Nimako in this volume).

The British Decline

After the First World War, the economic profile of several West Indian colonies changed, as did the colonial relationship between the islands and the metropole. For example, Suriname moved from plantations to small-scale agriculture, while US firms sought to develop a bauxite industry. Britain was also under pressure and consequently relied on its "white dominions" – Canada, Australia, and New Zealand – to help rebuild the metropole. Under the guise of voluntary cooperation involving independent countries, the Commonwealth of Nations was established in 1931 to achieve this goal. By contrast, the dependent colonies were left to fend for themselves. This was not unexpected since in the early 1920s British colonial policy was articulated through tropes of progress, development, and technical assistance. This understanding was encoded in law with the Colonial Development Act of 1929. The Act allocated £1 million annually (worth about £65 million in 2021), which was intended to improve medical and scientific staffing in the colonies to promote colonial development. But before these initiatives could fully begin, the Great Depression of the 1930s severely hit the region's economies. The effects of the depression led to an increase in intra-Caribbean migration, as well as emigration from the West Indies to English cities such as Birmingham, Leeds, London, and Manchester. The economic crisis also fostered unrest, strikes, and demonstrations throughout the Caribbean. Subsequently, the Colonial Development and Welfare Act of 1940 was passed to provide some services to the colonies to temper rebellion and to discourage white settlers from seeking greater local political authority.[38] The implementation of the plan was, however, interrupted by the Second World War.

Severely weakened by two major wars and superseded in power by the United States and the Soviet Union in the post-war era, Britain sought to re-engineer the empire, in what has been called the "second colonial occupation" of sub-Saharan Africa – involving the establishment of the Central African Federation (Northern and Southern Rhodesia and Nyasaland) and the suppression of the Mau Mau uprising in Kenya in the 1950s (see Igba in this volume). London also sought to constrain and contain decolonisation sentiments in the Caribbean by attempting to form the West

Indian Federation at the Montego Bay Conference in Jamaica in 1947. In this climate, technical assistance and overseas intervention acted as strategic continuations rather than disruptions of colonial approaches. Even the British Ministry of Overseas Development, which was established in 1964, and the Department for International Development (DFID), which was established in 1997 (and merged into the Foreign and Commonwealth Office in 2020), tended to reflect a colonial approach in which, like the celebratory attitudes during the centenary of slave emancipation, Britain was portrayed as the provider of aid and as a benevolent host of transnational humanitarian organisations.

Concluding Reflections

It is important to underscore that decolonisation is not, and was not, one process. Aside from a "huge and marked unevenness within the post-colonial world" more broadly, the post-imperial predicament included ambivalence towards the imposed structures, institutions, and ideas that governed newly independent states.[39] Advocates of decolonisation weighed principle, pragmatism, and priority, and drew different conclusions, based on each specific local situation. Whereas in other parts of the world, decolonisation was "a calculated process of military engagement and diplomatic negotiation between the two contending parties: colonial and anticolonial",[40] in the British West Indies there was a marked absence of military engagement in the post-war era. This has given rise to the notion that British Caribbean decolonisation was negotiated and voluntarist.[41] But this kind of analysis does not account for how unprepared Britain and other European powers were for this moment. "The colonial order fell to pieces," as the British historian John Darwin wrote.[42] This disintegration came about because Britain had been weakened and exhausted by war, and was unable fully to impose its rule. "Nearly everywhere in the non-European world … the coming of the white man brought forth some sort of resistance", as Edward Said wrote. "The response to Western domination", he added, "culminated in the great movement of decolonisation across the Third World."[43]

Building on prior rebellions and revolts, decolonisation movements in the British Caribbean gathered momentum during the inter-war period (1919–1939). As captured in pamphlets like C.L.R. James's *The Case for West-Indian Self Government* (1933), these movements were informed by experiences in the early post-emancipation period when a change had occurred in legal status from slavery to limited freedom. However, this change did not radically alter social relations and its associated class, race, and gender inequalities.[44] There persisted a continued "pattern of exploitation" of Afro-Caribbean peoples.[45] Certainly, a post-emancipation black middle class gradually emerged from the 1960s, and this class formation did permit some changes in status. But changes in class composition did not bring about macro-institutional changes. Society still constituted a stratified system within a capitalist political economy. The composition of elites changed, but this class maintained control over land and benefited from the rise of new economic sectors. At the time, this new post-colonial middle class of merchants and professionals largely neglected issues to do with the exploitation of the working class.

At a degree of abstraction, British colonialism in the Caribbean involved conquest, exploitation, and subjugation as well as the imposition of a hetero-patriarchal, socio-cultural political economy that included associated gender and sexuality constructs. As with that of other European powers, British colonial policy used enslavement, then exploitation, as an element of trade and economic policy. But this was also a way temporarily to address the contradictions of capitalism by using surpluses from the colonies to stave off working-class rebellion in the metropolis. This situation generated considerable misery and trauma in the Caribbean.

There is value in summary statements like these, much as there is value in the theory of the plantation society that the New World group produced. But we need to ensure that abstractions do not lose sight of the nuanced history of the place and its own contradictions and politics. Otherwise, one-dimensional theorising inadvertently becomes a method to silence the past.[46] From the standpoint of the British Caribbean, our approach in this chapter has been to map these contradictions and entanglements in order to demonstrate that the history of the West Indies is also the history of Britain.

22

Colonialism in the Dutch Caribbean

Rose Mary Allen

THIS CHAPTER IS ABOUT colonialism and its joint institution of slavery in the Dutch Caribbean. Colonialism can be defined as a complex of socio-political structures with specific narratives, scales of power, legitimacy, and violence, which are manifested in material, spatial, territorial (geopolitical), epistemological, and existential (biopolitical) forms.[1] Any approach to studying colonialism must therefore necessarily take into account the various and multiple forms that it encompasses, to which the Dutch territories in the Caribbean have also made their own contribution.

I use the term "Dutch Caribbean" to denote the places in and around the Caribbean that have or had been under Dutch rule for centuries. The term refers to six islands, together with the mainland country of Suriname. These places are not all located geographically near each other and have very different natural environments. The islands of Aruba, Bonaire, and Curaçao – also called the Dutch Leeward Islands or the ABC Islands – are semi-arid and are situated near the South American country of Venezuela. The Dutch Windward Islands, which include Saba, Sint Eustatius ("Statia"), and Sint Maarten (the Dutch spelling distinguishes it from French Saint-Martin),[2] are located near the Greater Antilles and have heavier rainfall than the ABC Islands. Suriname is located in South America, north of Brazil, and consists of an extensive rainforest. The physical and natural conditions have contributed to the way in which colonisation took place in these societies and have also determined their importance for the coloniser. The experience of colonisation and decolonisation is different among the seven territories of the Dutch Caribbean.

The islands were all conquered by the Netherlands between 1631 and 1648. Suriname became a Dutch colony in 1667. As Dutch possessions in the Caribbean, they have been grouped together in one way or another for the convenience of The Hague in ruling them. The impact of colonial rule in the Dutch Caribbean and the different forms of decolonialisation have become subjects of heated debate. In Holland, current discussions on the decolonisation of institutions reveals an awakening sense of injustice in the former mother country, thanks to the large group of diaspora citizens from Suriname and the islands. But Suriname and the Dutch Caribbean islands still play a relatively minor role in these decolonial debates compared with Indonesia, even though the decolonisation processes in the Dutch Caribbean are more recent.[3] Meanwhile, local debates on decolonisation, particularly on the Caribbean islands, have unsettled conventional ways of thinking about sovereignty and non-sovereignty, and offer different ideas about the possibilities of non-sovereignty in the post-colonial era.

This chapter has two key aims. First, it provides an overview of the Dutch Caribbean experiences of colonialism and its persistence through institutions such as economic models, trade linkages, the educational system, culture, and language. Second, it provides an overview of some of the ways in which these territories have "talked back" to colonial rule. The analysis is conducted from a Dutch Caribbean perspective and covers, firstly, an exposition of the concept of colonialism; secondly, a brief description of the colonisation and enslavement processes in the Dutch Caribbean (see Nimako in this volume); and, thirdly, several ways of dealing with colonialism and coloniality.

Colonisation during Slavery

Economic factors determined where and how European colonisers established themselves and remained in the Caribbean. For the Spaniards, gold was the strategic product of the time, and in the Caribbean it was found in Hispaniola, Puerto Rico, and Cuba. The absence of gold on the Dutch Caribbean islands reduced their economic importance for Spanish imperialists, who dismissed them as "useless islands". In 1513, the Spaniards transported almost the entire indigenous Amerindian population of the islands of Aruba, Bonaire, and Curaçao to work as enslaved persons, mainly in the copper mines on Hispaniola. After remaining practically uninhabited for a number of years, the ABC Islands were used primarily to keep large herds of cattle, until they ceased being Spanish property at the beginning of the seventeenth century. In Suriname, there is still an indigenous presence, while on the islands the Amerindian heritage remains present only in some words of the vernacular languages and, to some extent, in the physical appearance of segments of the population.

The Dutch, whose principal interest was trade and property acquisition, were mainly attracted by the salt pans along the coast of South America and on some of the Caribbean islands. From the seventeenth century, the seven Dutch Caribbean territories became Dutch colonial possessions in the western hemisphere.[4] Owing to a growing need for labour on the plantations in America and also in the Caribbean, a new industry emerged in the seventeenth century which turned out to be profitable for the Dutch: slavery. The Dutch slave trade, originally organised by the controversial and highly profitable public entity called the Dutch West India Company, transformed the islands – especially Curaçao and Sint Eustatius, until the latter was ravaged by the British in 1781 – into important official trade bases in the seventeenth and eighteenth centuries. This trade network saw hundreds of thousands of enslaved people – mainly from West Africa – transit through the Dutch Caribbean to the surrounding European colonies in the Caribbean and the coastal regions of South America.

During the eighteenth century, this rapidly expanding transatlantic slave trade became the largest forced migration in history, transporting enslaved people to different parts of the Americas. After 1713, the Dutch slave trade declined owing to British competition, and the Dutch West India Company's monopoly was abolished in 1737, allowing other entities and individuals to trade in slaves. The proceeds of this human trafficking have been the subject of contentious discussions in Holland in the course of time. New studies show, however, that in the eighteenth century, before the Dutch prohibited the slave trade under pressure from the British, 5.2 per cent of its gross domestic product (GDP) was based on slavery.[5]

There was no large plantation economy in the Dutch Caribbean, except for Suriname, where sugar and coffee were produced in large quantities as commodities for export to Europe.[6] On the islands, plantations were mostly small in size, with tiny concentrations of enslaved people. Colonial rule in these territories recognised slavery in its laws, and normalised and legalised unequal power relationships by constructing ethnic and racial divisions that have permeated social, political, and economic relations across these societies.

351

Resistance against Colonialism during Slavery

Dutch slavery-based societies were extremely unequal and also very violent, and slave owners consistently had the law on their side. Slavery determined the social fabric and shaped the lives of whites, enslaved Africans, and the liberated who were descendants of enslaved people. In the social hierarchy, people of African descent were at the bottom, either as enslaved or as freed persons. In Curaçao, the Dutch and other Europeans such as the Swiss and French were the ruling class, and below them were the Sephardic Jews, who, after arriving in the seventeenth century, devoted themselves mostly to commerce.[7] Miscegenation led to a significant number of people of mixed race. In all the Dutch Caribbean islands, people of mixed heritage added to the complexity of these societies. With the increase in the numbers of free "Coloured" people, colourism became a determinant factor for social mobility, especially on the island of Curaçao, where the white population that settled in the territory itself was proportionally larger than that in Suriname. There was also less mixing between the races in Suriname, and the proportion of free Coloureds was smaller than on the islands.[8] Only one per cent of the enslaved in Suriname were on average freed annually, the lowest rate in the region.[9] Scholars long held that the situation of the enslaved in Suriname was much worse than that on the islands. However, a 2019 study of excavated bones of enslaved people on the islands shows that, even here, the transatlantic crossing and subsequent heavy physical labour had a negative impact on the physical health of the enslaved.[10]

In adapting to their life in slavery, the people of African heritage contributed richly to the cultural tapestry of the Dutch Caribbean, for example in the realm of music, dance, oral traditions, religion, and technology. Some of these expressions have survived even though they were prohibited by law, and those practising them were persecuted. The *tambú*[11] of Curaçao and *barí* of Bonaire were actively suppressed by both the government and the Roman Catholic Church,[12] while the same fate befell the Afro-Surinamese religious philosophy called *Winti*. Resistance and persistence are also visible in the survival of the local Creole languages: Papiamentu on the three ABC Islands and Creole English on the three Windward Islands. Papiamentu flourished already in the seventeenth century, as documents show. It has since become part of the Creole identity, of which people are extremely proud.[13] In contrast to the islands, in Suriname people speak more Dutch than the local Creole called Sranan Tongo. Creole languages have also endured in oral traditions, such as in the West African-derived trickster stories called *Kuenta di Nanzi* (Anansi stories) on the

Leeward Islands; *Anansi Tori* in Suriname; and Brer Rabbit narratives on the Windward Islands. These stories go back a long way in history, and have been transmitted orally. They are multi-genred, as the storytellers make use of sign languages, modulations, and songs.

The British-born Jamaican scholar F.S.J. Ledgister's 2016 essay "Caribbean Anti-Colonialism"[14] is useful for understanding the link between anti-colonialism and slave resistance in the context of intellectual challenges to colonial rule as articulated by journalists, scholars, activists, domestic politicians, and armed rebels. Enslaved people resisted slavery in active and passive forms. They ran away, and sometimes tried to leave the islands permanently. The violent, inhumane institution of slavery led to acts of resistance, particularly in Curaçao and Suriname. Curaçao experienced its largest slave revolt in 1795,[15] inspired in part by the 1789 French Revolution and the 1791 slave revolt in Saint-Domingue (Haiti). In Suriname, large numbers of enslaved people continually fled into the rainforest, where they established new maroon societies, and engaged in attacks on the Dutch.

Abolition of Slavery: A Breakthrough in Equal Citizenship?

Slavery was abolished in the Dutch colonies in 1863, which was much later than in the British and the French Caribbean colonies, where abolition took place in 1834 and 1848 respectively. The abolition of slavery in French Saint-Martin in 1848 led to strikes on the Dutch side of the island, claims of freedom by the enslaved in that part of the island, and a large number of escapes by the enslaved on the Dutch side of the island of Sint Maarten to the French side. This forced the Dutch to promulgate measures through which the enslaved on the islands came to be treated essentially as free workers with employment contracts.[16]

The abolition of slavery did not bring about much change in the social position of the formerly enslaved. While the slave owners were financially compensated for the loss of their so-called property, freed people did not receive anything in return for having experienced dehumanisation, ill-treatment, and misuse of their labour for centuries. In Suriname, slave owners were given 300 guilders per enslaved person by way of compensation, while on the islands the amount was 200 guilders, with the exception of Sint Maarten where slave owners received 100 guilders since the colonial government had regarded the enslaved there as free people since 1848. People who, during the pre-abolition era, had already gained their freedom and managed to obtain certain material resources – primarily land – could continue to live under fairly reasonable conditions. But the majority – both those who gained freedom in July 1863 and those who had previously been freed but lacked resources – remained socially marginalised.

The abolition of slavery involved legal changes which affected the various ethnic groups in these societies in different ways. Legally, there was no longer a large group of people objectified as property and considered non-human under the authority of an owner. However, a large group of people found themselves in a difficult starting position as new citizens in these societies, where the political, social, and economic power structure of the old slave society remained firmly in place (see Cobley, Brereton, and Mtombeni in this volume). When slavery ended, there were no organised programmes to assist mainly freed populations. Budgets prioritised not social and educational improvement, but rather law enforcement and judicial matters. In Suriname, the freed people were required to continue working on the plantations on a contract basis until 1873. Afterwards, indentured workers were imported from China, India, and the Dutch East Indies. Many of these became small-scale farmers after their terms of plantation employment were completed, eventually transforming agricultural patterns of production and making rice the major crop. Colonial population movements have constructed ethnic, racial, and insular divisions that permeate social, political, and economic relations.

Colonialism and Resistance in the Early Twentieth Century

Post-abolition economic stagnation on the Dutch islands in the Caribbean took a dramatic turn when Royal Dutch Shell established an oil refinery in Curaçao in 1917, while Lago Oil and Transport Company established one in Aruba in 1924.[17] Both refineries soon began refining Venezuelan oil. The resulting relative prosperity of Curaçao and Aruba attracted thousands of migrant workers, including people from the other Dutch Caribbean islands and Suriname. Surinamese people came to Curaçao to work not only on the oil refinery, but also as teachers, doctors, pharmacists, nurses, police officers, and customs officers.[18]

In Curaçao and Aruba, the changes brought about by industrialisation also stimulated political awareness. Until 1948, a substantial number of people had been excluded from the general suffrage on the grounds of income, education, and gender restrictions. Governance was in the hands of an appointed Governor, who exercised executive, legislative, and judicial powers, and was assisted by the members of a Colonial Council consisting of plantation owners and merchants.

Increased political consciousness was attached to the struggle and movement for universal suffrage. Key political activists included figures such as the Curaçaoan Moises Frumencio da Costa Gomez (1907–1966), known simply as "Dòktor", and Henry Pieters Kwiers, who worked towards combating the "culture of fear" among the black working class, particularly those in the countryside who were still burdened by a past defined by racial hierarchies.[19] The work of Da Costa Gomez and his followers was similar to Brazilian scholar Paulo Freire's method of "conscientisation", in strengthening people's assertiveness by teaching them to problematise their situation, to face, analyse, and tackle the obstacles to a better life, and take concrete actions to change their lives.[20] However, Da Costa Gomez's call for self-governance and his intense involvement in bringing about constitutional autonomy through the *Statuut* (Charter) of 1954 did not produce the desired effects.

The twentieth-century movement towards greater self-affirmation and self-realisation in the rest of the Caribbean was evident also on the Dutch Caribbean islands. Aruba and Sint Maarten were increasingly opposed to the political dominance of Curaçao, the largest of the six islands and the centre of Dutch colonial rule. In Aruba, this movement resulted in 1942 in the founding of a political party under the leadership of Henny Eman, which came to play an important role in Aruba's struggle to achieve *status aparte*: a new constitutional status, separate from the other five Dutch Caribbean islands and with a direct link to the Netherlands. In Suriname, the resistance fighter and anti-colonial activist Cornelis Gerard Anton de Kom (1898–1945) was arrested in 1932, and exiled to the Netherlands, where he wrote the classic anti-colonial book, *Wij slaven van Suriname* (We Slaves of Suriname), first published in 1934 and republished several times thereafter. The same fate befell the Curaçaoan anti-colonial activist Pedro Pablo Medardo de Marchena, who was jailed by the Dutch authorities in Bonaire during the Second World War (1939–1945).[21] In Sint Maarten, Joseph (José) H. Lake Sr (1925–1976) founded the newspaper *Windward Islands Opinion* and the People's Printery in 1959, in order to problematise the subordinate and neglected position of the island relative to Curaçao, as well as to seek to improve the social, economic, educational, and political situation of the Windward Islands. His son, the well-known poet Lasana M. Sekou , the pen name of Harold Hermano Lake – one of the authors of the 1990 essay "Slavery and Independence" – became a leading advocate of independence for Sint Maarten.[22]

Colonialism and Resistance after the Second World War

After the Second World War, the Dutch colonies in the Caribbean gained internal self-governance from the Netherlands through the 1954 *Statuut* (charter) of the Kingdom of the Netherlands. The *Statuut* defined the kingdom as consisting of three autonomous partners: the Netherlands, Suriname, and the Dutch Antilles, which was a federation of the six Caribbean Islands.

In Curaçao, young intellectuals who returned from tertiary education in the Netherlands with new ideas and visions of society became a driving force in the growing protest against the hierarchies, divisions, and contradictions on the island. The uprising of May 1969 – known locally as *Trinta di Mei* – rocked the very foundations of Curaçaoan society. The deployment of Dutch marines to stop the rioting and looting, as well as to re-establish law and order, only reinforced the perception of heavy-handed political interference and colonial intervention. A study of *Trinta di Mei* by the American scholars William Anderson and Russell Dynes shows that the uprising was not only a labour strike demanding higher wages, but also a social movement protesting against class and racial oppression.[23] They conclude that ethnicity, colour, and race continued to determine many aspects of life in Curaçao, a situation that caused profound dissatisfaction at the lack of self-determination and of civil and political rights among Curaçaoan citizens, notwithstanding the autonomy obtained by the Netherlands Antilles in 1954.[24]

May 1969 proved to be an important turning point in Curaçao's history. The late 1960s and the 1970s saw the rise of several organisations on the island that pursued the recognition and equitable inclusion of black Curaçaoans within all sectors of social life, and sought to craft a new, post-colonial identity for this group. The 1970s also saw the formalisation of important nation-building processes on the island. Nevertheless, *Trinta di Mei* sought societal change without necessarily obtaining full independence. Within the Dutch Caribbean, only Suriname had gained its full independence by 1975, and a significant portion of its population who wished to maintain their Dutch nationality migrated to the Netherlands. Aruba left the constellation of the Dutch Antilles in 1986, acquiring a direct constitutional relationship with Hollard, while the Antilles continued as a five-island federation, comprising Curaçao, Bonaire, Sint Maarten, Sint Eustatius, and Saba.

In the economic sphere, from the 1960s tourism and international banking emerged as important sectors on the islands, primarily on Curaçao, Aruba, and Sint Maarten, where tourism attracted substantial new streams of migrant workers from elsewhere in the Caribbean region, with the largest group coming from Jamaica, Haiti, and the Dominican Republic. Bauxite mining has also since become the largest contributor to Surinamese GDP. Throughout the Dutch Caribbean, government employment and international (primarily Dutch) economic assistance helped to support local economies, in the process highlighting the absence of a diverse, sustainable economic foundation.

The End and Turn of the Twentieth Century

At the end of the twentieth and start of the twenty-first century, while most Caribbean countries had long left their colonial past behind, and some were already celebrating 50 years of independence, Curaçao and the other Dutch Caribbean islands were grappling with constitutional reforms. The issue was not independence, but whether the islands should remain together or whether each should have a more direct link with the mother country. Through a series of referenda held during the first decade of the twenty-first century, the five islands except for Sint Eustatius voted to change the constitutional status that had defined the federation of the Dutch Antilles since 1954 and the reforms of 1986.

The 2009 referendum in Curaçao led to heated discussions with The Hague on the advantages and disadvantages of the newly negotiated agreements. The outcome of the referendum was that 52 per cent of voters approved the agreements, while 48 per cent disapproved. This reflected sharp divisions on the island, in particular about the desirability of increased Dutch influence in local affairs. The referendum was a clear reflection of how ethnic differences defined in the past still model present social life. Hidden behind the main theme of constitutional reform were sub-discourses on the less tangible and often more emotionally laden issues of national belonging, cultural diversity, and difference, mixed with race and ethnicity, as well as feelings of rootedness, togetherness, loyalty, and trust.

The Dutch Antilles federation was dismantled and ceased to exist in October 2010. The two largest islands – Curaçao and Sint Maarten – each became internally self-governing entities with direct ties to The Hague, while the three smallest islands – Bonaire, Sint Eustatius, and Saba – each became an overseas municipality and integral part of the Netherlands.[25] This meant that all of these islands, along with Aruba, remain part of the Kingdom of the Netherlands in one form or another. Inter-island cooperation of varying intensity continues in the judicial and administrative fields.[26]

In Curaçao, in particular, debates have raged on matters of autonomy and independence to this very day. Those who are in favour of maintaining ties with Holland point to the social benefits and facilities that flow from them, and often use Suriname as a negative example of how independence can result in greater social and economic problems. This group seems to be very large. According to the results of the 2005 Curaçao referendum, the proportion of people who want the island to remain part of the Netherlands was 95 per cent. This confirmed the results of opinion polls carried out in 1997–1998, as reported in the study *Ki sorto di reino?* (What Kind of Kingdom?).[27] Furthermore, more recent studies in 2016 show that only 14.4 per cent of the population would like the island to become fully independent, while the great majority wish to remain part of the Netherlands.[28]

Yet, the de facto unequal power relationship with Holland, which has grown historically and tends to be reinforced by current global power hierarchies, greatly affects the ways in which Curaçao can chart its own route towards nation-building and national belonging. Particularly during the negotiations with The Hague on constitutional reforms, as well as after the October 2010 disintegration of the Dutch Antilles federation, there were intense discussions on issues such as political autonomy, governance, citizenship, and nation-building. Subsequently, the discussion in Curaçao has been more focused on how precisely the ties to the Netherlands are to be maintained. It matters to people whether the relative autonomy which the island has known since 1954 increases, remains the same, or decreases. A significant section of the population sees the negotiated constitutional transition of 2010 as a process of subordination to the Netherlands, which involves not only sovereignty and administrative authority, but also indigenous economic control, local resource ownership, and the preservation of cultural traditions.[29] Some locals regard Holland as a decadent Western society and fear its influence on local culture. For example, it is feared that The Hague will seek to impose on Curaçao the liberal laws that exist in that country on issues such as same-sex marriage, euthanasia, and abortion. These concerns are not always made explicit in local discussions, but clearly they exist beneath the surface. Furthermore, the situation in Bonaire since 2010, where the new constitutional status has meant a significant influx of new Dutch immigrants from the metropolis, and where the indigenous culture and identity are expected to become marginal if this influx continues, has alarmed the local population in Curaçao. In Bonaire, the movement *Nos ke Boneiru bek* (We Want Bonaire Back) actively campaigns against this new status.

Of significance were the debates about the requests by Curaçao, Aruba, and Sint Maarten for financial assistance from the Netherlands to alleviate the social and economic problems caused by the 2020–2021 Covid-19 pandemic. They clearly demonstrated the realities on these small islands that feed this ambivalent attitude towards the mother country. The significance of 10 October 2010 has become more confused in the sense that the economic muscle of the Netherlands is increasingly felt now that the island economies are struggling and the islands have requested financial help from The Hague. The Dutch mantra *"Wie betaalt bepaalt"* (He who pays the piper calls the tune) is widely quoted, and has led to many debates on the islands. The Puerto Rican scholar Rocío Zambrana's book on colonial debts – even though it deals with the colonial relationship between Puerto Rico and the United States – helps explain the situation of indebtedness and the ways this can lead to a form of coloniality in which race, gender, and class divisions are intensified and could reinforce a colonial relationship.[30]

The decolonial protests that result from such situations are evident especially in Curaçao and Sint Maarten. In 2021, parliamentary factions on these islands accused the Dutch of "persistent acts of racial discrimination and violations of international human-rights law"[31] because of the conditions that Holland imposed on financial aid in the context of Covid-19. A heated debate has resurfaced on these islands about renegotiating the relationship with The Hague and requesting the support of the United Nations Special Committee on Decolonisation to place these two islands back on the list of non-self-governing territories, from which they were removed when the *Statuut* entered into force in 1954.

Concluding Reflections

The Dutch Caribbean islands are non-sovereign, albeit in ways different from, for example, the French and American Caribbean (see Aragón Falomir and Ramirez in this volume). On the Dutch Caribbean islands, constitutional reform has remained an issue on the political agenda. It seems that in these societies, the majority of the population wants to maintain constitutional ties with the metropolitan government, although there are those who are opposed to this and describe the arrangement as "colonisation by consent".

Political autonomy, which implies the possibility (both the ability and the authority) of managing one's own internal affairs, contributes much to national consciousness and is important for national identity. However, it is precisely this ability to deal with one's own affairs that is questioned by those who favour greater Dutch influence in Curaçaoan society. The local discussions on constitutional reform are also complicated by the presence of large numbers of Dutch Caribbean immigrants in the Netherlands, who have moved there in search of improved opportunities and who maintain diasporic ties with their country of birth.

There is thus a constant wavering between colonialism and decolonialisation. These discussions represent expressions as well as concerns about national identity and citizenship, which are now fuelled more clearly by various aspects of the evolving relationship with the mother country, in particular constitutional reform, financial supervision, legislation on ethical issues, and migration. The Dutch scholars Lammert de Jong and Dirk Kruijt refer to this as "extended statehood" given that people have chosen to remain under the dominion of a mother country. Consequently, one cannot speak of colonies or colonisation, which presumes forced dominion.[32] However, the concept of "extended statehood" fails to take into account the unequal power relationship that has often continued since colonial times and that is sometimes reinforced by the contemporary global order. This relationship is often presented as one of equality within a system that, from the outset, has always been unequal. The Dutch scholars Wouter P. Veenendaal and Gert Jan Oostindie describe this process as a struggle between head and heart: the people in the Dutch Caribbean may express a desire to remain part of the Netherlands from a financial point of view, whereas their heart may crave independence from Holland.[33] However, the continuing discourse suggests that one is dealing with much more than an issue of head versus heart, and that it also involves people's vision of self-identity in a globalised world, a shared sense of vulnerability, estrangement within societies that navigate constantly between economic security and financial dependence, and the creation of cultural symbols of nationhood in a context of historical discontent.[34]

This "double perspective complex", a term which the American scholar H. Adlai Murdoch coined in the context of the French Caribbean, as a "symbiosis of contentious subordination" or "the game play of sovereignty",[35] demonstrates that the relationship between the Dutch Caribbean islands and the motherland is not as clear-cut as that between politically independent Suriname and the Netherlands.[36] Legally, Aruba, Curaçao, and Sint Maarten are equal partners with Holland. They have control over their own domestic affairs and send a representative to the Council of Ministers in The Hague. However, in reality, Holland always makes the final decision on key issues.

Why people remain – whether by choice or not – in situations like this that challenge conventional notions of freedom, equality, and belonging is a pertinent question.[37] The Dutch Caribbean experience can thus help enrich global discussions about constitutional reforms and the ongoing process of constructing, negotiating, claiming, and reclaiming Caribbean identities.

23

Colonialism in South America

Susan Elizabeth Ramírez

THE ORIGINS OF IBERIAN colonialism in the Americas can be traced back to the desire to trade, not to settle. Both Spanish and Portuguese explorers and monarchs dreamed of the lucrative spices that could be obtained in the Orient. In their quest, the Portuguese, having consolidated their state in the middle of the thirteenth century, began sailing along the coasts of Africa. Italian explorer Christopher Columbus, sponsored by the Catholic Spanish monarchs Ferdinand and Isabella, sailed west into largely unknown waters to reach the eastern Spice Islands at the end of the fifteenth century. This chapter assesses the efforts, first of the Spanish, and then the Portuguese, to create the structures that established Iberian power in the western hemisphere. Madrid and Lisbon siphoned off their surplus from trade, mining, and agriculture to finance their colonial expansions. These stories cover colonialism from first encounters to independence.

Spain in the Americas

The agreement, or *capitulacion*, between Christopher Columbus and the Spanish monarchs established a maritime trading company, the Enterprise of the Indies, to sail to Asian islands in order to trade for what was thought to be their profitable spices, silks, and porcelain. The company was owned by the Crown, and Columbus was a partner, sharing in its profits. There was no mention of settlement in this 1492 document nor was there provision for a colony with rights to settle, hold land, or engage in private trade. The agreement said nothing about the status of the indigenous people and their governments. Columbus's voyage was a failure if judged by his original aim of reaching Asia.[1] Instead, he sailed into the waters of an unexpected continent. Over the next 12 years, he made a total of four round trips between Europe and America. He sacrificed his governorship and his status to pursue his main objective of finding a passage to the East. In the process, he contended with pressures from his sponsors to find valuable commodities to export to Europe. He found some gold, but never enough. He initially thought that the indigenous people would make good vassals but ran into resistance when he demanded gold as tribute. The *encomienda* (grants to Spaniards who had served the Crown of local people who gave their labour in return for protection and conversion) became a reality in 1503 in order to satisfy calls for labour from sailors from Spain.[2] Eventually, during his second visit (September 1493 – June 1496), Columbus enslaved hundreds of indigenous people who challenged his rule. They were exported to Spain along with some brazilwood and a few pearls found off the coast of Venezuela: all were sold for profit. The Spanish Crown collected up to 20 per cent of the auction price for the slaves.[3]

The early encounters with hitherto unknown peoples confused many Europeans. Intellectuals and jurists energetically discussed and debated such questions as where the Indians came from, and where they fitted into the European world view or cosmology, especially since Christians believed that everything that existed had already been revealed in the Bible.[4] Perceptions changed constantly and differed markedly with each interpreter and his or her experience. Crown policy, therefore, vacillated. Queen Isabella insisted that the indigenous people were free, with the exception of the alleged cannibalistic Caribes: she thought they would benefit from close contact with Europeans, who could convert them, thus ending their "paganism" and the alleged habit of eating their own species. After her death in 1506, King Ferdinand was less concerned with native well-being, but promoted good treatment and the provision of wages for indigenous labour.[5]

With news of the abuses of the indigenous people in the Americas still ringing in the ears of Spanish authorities, two documents were promulgated. The first was the Laws of Burgos of 1512, a comprehensive law code, which provided for the humane treatment of indigenous people. "Natives" were to be compelled to spend nine months a year in service to the Spanish, and the remaining three months working on their own farms or as wage labourers.[6] The second law was the *Requerimiento* (or Requirement), published in 1513. This relatively short document was required to be read aloud to indigenous people.

It briefly explained the history of Christianity, and informed those who heard it that if they resisted conversion, they would be enslaved and their goods confiscated. What was unstated was the practical aspects of communicating this to indigenous people, who initially could not understand Spanish, and who might not hear the recitation from across a battlefield, for example.[7] The problem with these documents, as with many law codes, was one of enforcement. Royal officials had no real power. They were at the mercy of the *encomenderos* (the holders of *encomiendas*). Thus these first attempts at Spanish control were frustrated, and the laws and decrees proved ineffectual.

In 1542, the New Laws were announced with another plea for humanitarian consideration of the natives. These laws prohibited Indian slavery, even as a punishment, and forbade granting new *encomiendas*. The reaction was swift. In New Spain, the *encomenderos* protested. Those of New Castile (Peru) revolted, and eventually captured and beheaded the Viceroy (Blasco Núñez Vela), who had been sent to announce and enforce the new laws.[8]

These royal decrees embodied an ideal view of the relationships between indigenous people and Spanish occupiers. The reality was far different. Forced labour was employed to search for gold, which imposed a severe toll on the indigenous people. Sickness and heavy work obligations caused thousands to die. Spanish authorities often used violence, first as reprisals for resistance, and then as preventive acts against the threat of revolt. Segregation of "native" and Spanish living spaces in *pueblos* and villas, respectively, proved ineffectual in mitigating harsh treatment. The unintended consequence of the encounters between "natives" and Spaniards was a sharply diminished indigenous population as a result of disease, hard labour, starvation, and flight.[9]

While the explorers were still seeking cinnamon and nutmeg and gradually establishing the physical outlines of the "other world" that Columbus had found, and even while Francisco Pizarro and Diego de Almagro were sailing into uncharted waters along the west coast of the southern hemisphere, the Spanish Crown was establishing, re-evaluating and reforming policy to secure its rights in what came to be called the "New World" and America. It was also building a bureaucracy to execute its dictates, guarantee its rights, and collect what it regarded as its dues. The monarchy and its advisers realised that they needed effective governing institutions to control the indigenous peoples that the Europeans were encountering. They wanted to break the threat of the strong *encomendero* elite and prevent the encroachment of their rivals, the Portuguese, Dutch, and English.

The direct administration of the Indies began when the Crown appointed royal representatives, Governors Francisco de Bobadilla (1499–1502) and Nicolas de Ovando (1502–1509), to bring order to the people on Hispaniola in the wake of Columbus's predilection for exploring and his consequent disregard for the quotidian administration of the island. In this first phase of governance, the Spanish founded cities and established fortresses, especially near goldfields.[10]

In Spain, the Crown created the House of Trade (Casa de Contratación) in 1503, which supervised commerce, issued licences to travel to America, controlled shipping and exports and imports, and collected taxes on these. It also received consignments of goods and bullion. The Casa's power as a royal treasury and revenue office increased as the empire expanded. A special judicial department studied and arbitrated civil and criminal cases relating to trade and navigation. Officials of the Casa also trained pilots for the Atlantic crossing, regulated their activities, recorded the progress of geographical discoveries, and maintained the master map.[11] An advisory board to the king – the Council of the Indies – was created in 1524. It served as a clearing house for information coming from the Indies. Based on this knowledge, the council drafted and issued decrees which the king signed as "*Yo el Rey*" (I, the King).[12]

To administer the affairs of America on site and to counter, in part, the rising power of the *encomenderos*, the Spanish king appointed Viceroys to represent his person and interests. The power of these high-ranking royal servants extended to all inhabitants subject to the king, be they Spanish, native, black, or some combination of the three (the *castas*). The Viceroy, a king's man and his deputy in the Americas, ruled at the pleasure of the Crown from Mexico City or Lima. Almost all were Spaniards who came from the established nobility, serving usually for five or six years. The first Viceroy, Antonio de Mendoza, was appointed in 1535 for New Spain. In 1542, King Charles appointed the ill-fated Blasco Núñez Vela as the Viceroy of Peru. He set out for the Andes in 1544 and, once there, proved so intransigent in implementing the New Laws of 1542 that a group of incensed *encomenderos* captured and beheaded him. A civil war ensued, thus preventing the establishment of a stable viceregal administration in Peru for at least three years.

With time and the weakening influence of the *encomenderos*, however, the Viceroy proved a reasonably effective institution to uphold the Crown's power. As the embodiment of the monarch, surrounded by ritual and numerous retinues and a court, he represented the pinnacle of prestige and authority. The Viceroy was first and foremost an executive officer required to implement the will of the king. But he could issue edicts and thus had some legislative power. The Viceroy was also charged with maintaining civil order and therefore had some military responsibilities, although these tended to be more illusory than real in early colonial times. He was also vice-patron of the Church, with influence in the nomination and appointment of high ecclesiastical officials. The great distance from the metropolis of Madrid tended to increase the Viceroy's authority, but there was a limit to what one man could do in the vast expanse of the American viceroyalties.

Another important institution was the *audiencia*, or supreme tribunal. The main role of the judges (*oidores* – literally, listeners) who sat on the various high courts that were gradually established in the Americas was to settle disputes between residents under their jurisdictions. Most *oidores* were Spaniards, but towards the end of Habsburg rule in 1700 and into the first decades of the Bourbon administration in the eighteenth century, the number of Creoles (offspring of European parents born in the Americas) increased. Their colonial Spanish American rulings established precedents with the force of law. In addition to their judicial and legislative roles, the *audiencias* could, under certain circumstances, assume an executive role. If both the Viceroy and the Archbishop (who succeeded him) died in office, the chief judge (president) of the *audiencia* served as interim Viceroy until another could be sent from Spain.[13]

Supporting these institutions were the officials of the Real Hacienda (Treasury) who controlled fiscal and monetary affairs. They received tax revenues and paid the expenses of government administration. The Casa de la Moneda – the mint – struck the coinage, including the world-famous Spanish pieces of eight (*peso de ocho reales*), from the silver and gold bullion brought from the mines.[14]

At the local level, the Crown representative was akin to a local governor, called a *corregidor* or *alcalde mayor*. He lived in the area so that he could better "protect" indigenous people, administer justice, and collect tribute. He was also charged with maintaining order and morality and managing the town or city. Peninsular regulation established checks over the *corregidor*'s power. The *corregidor* was not supposed to be a local person, although there were exceptions. Even when a non-local man assumed control, he often became involved with and beholden to the local elite – often through marriage or godparentage ties – both of which made him less effective as a Crown agent. The Crown also required the *corregidor* to submit an inventory of his property and post bond because he controlled the collection of certain tax and tribute revenues. A substantial bond assured the central government that he would be available for a judicial review (*residencia*) after his term expired, to answer to any charges of corruption and abuses of power. The fact that the salary was low, and the position was sold (in the seventeenth century) encouraged the *corregidor* to benefit illegally and exploit the office for personal gain. One way he did this was by distributing goods to the Indians, forcing them to buy items (such as mules, stockings, and mirrors) that they did not always need or want at high mark-ups. A second way was reminiscent of the putting-out system in Europe. The *corregidor* thus provided the locals with cotton or wool and required them to spin and weave it into a garment which he then sold for up to ten times what he paid the indigenes.[15]

A second locus of local power rested in the town council, or *cabildo*, made up of citizens chosen as aldermen or councillors (*regidores*) and magistrates (*alcaldes*), with jurisdiction over the urban-dwelling settlers (*vecinos*). Town councils passed laws for the municipality, decided issues such as who got what building site (*solar*), and screened applicants for citizen status. *Alcaldes* also served as judges of minor crimes. Aldermen administered the water supply and public lands around the town, maintained the sanitation system, and guaranteed public order. In addition, they set prices for basic foodstuffs and regulated certain kinds of artisanal production. Councillors were appointed at first, but later these positions were sold. Over time, seats on the council came to be seen as private possessions that could be renounced and sold or inherited by a male family member.[16]

Built into these governing institutions was a latent centralisation of power. Jurisdictions, which were huge given the state of communications of the day, were designed to be overlapping, so that conflicts between institutions and persons that could not be resolved on a local level were appealed up the bureaucratic hierarchy. The king, as the embodiment of natural and divine law, was the ultimate authority. He had the right, as the supreme leader, to interpret God's law on earth. Viewed over the long run, the system was a superb mechanism for asserting royal power. This regime of nebulous and loosely defined jurisdictions built centralisation into a system in which the king was the ultimate judge and arbiter of issues deemed important enough to merit his attention.[17]

A fortune in silver and gold, sent back to the Casa de Contratación, came from the system of collecting tribute from the indigenous people, of using their forced labour,[18] of selling political offices, and of taxing mining, commerce, and other productive activities. Exact numbers are hard to establish, but credible estimates have come from treasury registers. From 1503 to 1660, the official accounts show that public remittances totalled 117,386,086.5 pesos, while private remittances totalled 330,434,845.8 pesos, giving a combined total of 447,820,932.3 pesos. Silver accounted for 98.9 per cent of these imports.[19] Remittances to Spain from 1650 to 1699 equalled 665.2 million pesos. As less than 10 per cent was registered and taxed,[20] smuggling accounted for an unknown but significant amount of bullion flowing into the metropolis.[21]

By the end of the seventeenth century the Viceroys and the *audiencias* ruled over a multiracial society. The well-entrenched Spanish bureaucracy was by this time fully formed. It functioned from the cities, slowly adjudicating the issues pending before it. The Creoles, who had long before replaced the *encomenderos* in the upper class, controlled large tracts of land, thousands of grazing animals, textile workshops, tanning facilities, and the mines, generating sometimes great wealth, a portion of which was paid to Spain as taxes. Political power was purchased. The wealthy bought seats on the *cabildos* and positions as *corregidores*, which generated prestige but little power outside the locality. They also bought the rights to tax farming, collecting taxes such as the *alcabala* (sales tax) and the ecclesiastical tithes. The Creoles, furthermore, monopolised the top positions in the local militias, which participated in ceremonials but never in war. Distance gave the local elites autonomy. They had the advantages of education, travel, networks, and understanding, which they used to manipulate the system for their own parochial benefit.

In 1700, the Bourbons inherited the Spanish throne. After a war to settle succession from 1700 to 1713, Philip V assumed the throne and ruled without contestation until 1746. He had been raised outside the Peninsula, so upon arrival he viewed Spain with the eyes of a newcomer. He found a country that was beset with internal decay and corruption. The quality of leadership had declined. Pressing matters were neglected or relegated to a slow and ponderous bureaucracy. Spain's economy had been ruined by the inflation caused by bullion imports. The Bourbons realised that the kingdoms in the Americas were unwieldly and unprofitable. In consequence, the Crown began a programme of reforming policy initiatives, first in Spain, and later in the Americas.

The Bourbon reforms, sponsored by Philip V and his successors, were the product of the ideal of the eighteenth-century enlightened despot – a monarch who used his power to reform or change society for the common good. Gone were the days when the king's right to rule was based on divine right or revealed truth. Now the king's rule had to be justified by his achievements or expertise, his ability to accomplish things better than anyone else. It was the results of a king's rule, rather than tradition, that gave him legitimacy. He had become the first servant of the state.[22]

These innovations were designed to make the system more rational and orderly. The underlying motivations for the reforms were to centralise power and increase the revenues flowing into Spanish coffers. To this end, the Bourbons improved the efficiency of administration by simplifying and streamlining the bureaucracy and decision-making apparatus. Unlike the Habsburgs, who purposely designed jurisdictions to overlap, the Bourbon state set about clarifying the duties of officials, so that the overall system lost the flexibility of the Habsburg design that had lasted for about three centuries.

Among their most important reforms was the extension of the viceregal system. Viceroyalties were large and unwieldy jurisdictions, so large that one man (the Viceroy) could not effectively govern the entire area. Distances were great and roads poor, making communication slow. Even when communication was possible, the central government had no real way to enforce orders. The Creoles controlled local power. The Viceroy and his officials depended on them for execution. To end non-compliance, the Crown established two new viceroyalties: one in New Granada with a capital in Bogotá, and the other in La Plata with a capital in Buenos Aires. The latter was created from the southern part of the Peruvian viceroyalty to protect it from European invaders and stop the smuggling of Potosi silver down the river system to Buenos Aires, where it bought contraband goods. Tax collection consequently rose and smuggling moved elsewhere. In addition, the number of *audiencias* increased and, concomitantly, Creole judges were replaced with Peninsular-born ones.[23]

To complement these reforms, the Bourbons replaced *corregimientos* and *corregidores* with *indendants*, mostly well-educated, meritorious, and well-paid Peninsular-born men. A few intendancies replaced scores of *corregimientos*. Furthermore, jurisdiction over justice, administration, finance, and war gave the *intendants* a wider scope of action than their predecessors. What is more, responsibilities for bettering the roads and bridges, introducing new crops, teaching new technologies, and spreading useful knowledge expanded an *intendant*'s power.[24]

To protect Spain's American colonies against the encroachment of other European powers, Madrid strengthened the defensive system. The government had tried to maintain a monopolistic trading system, but, militarily and administratively, it was unable to do so. Spain's failure to supply the colonies with ample goods at reasonable prices invited French, English, and Dutch traders to engage in contraband commerce, thus harming Spanish merchant houses and Crown revenues. In order to stop smuggling and keep foreign interlopers out, the Bourbons turned the militia into a more traditional army. They sent Peninsular military men to the Americas to train the troops and opened the ranks to the entire male population. A large number of *castas* or mixed-bloods joined the army to earn a salary and gain access to the military courts.[25]

These military reforms were part of the king's wider plan to strengthen colonial institutions. But the Church – the Habsburg's long-time partner in governing – was not one of them. The Jesuit order became the Crown's most visible target. The Jesuits had earned a good reputation by running the most prestigious private schools for the Creole elite's sons. The order had also amassed valuable rural and urban real estate either from donations of the faithful or through outright purchase. Their emphasis on "useful knowledge" enabled them to turn these properties into productive and profitable possessions. Their cash surpluses financed elite investments and lifestyles. In the interior, the Jesuits ran missions called *reducciones*, which developed into profitable production centres. Yet, in 1767, all Jesuits were summarily escorted to ships and expelled from Spanish America under secret orders from the Crown, which accused them of spreading seditious ideas: reading banned books such as those by John Locke, Jean-Jacques Rousseau, and other philosophers of the Enlightenment; and presenting their ideas to their pupils. Furthermore, the Jesuits had taken an additional vow to obey the Pope,[26] and passed on their ultramontane beliefs to the faithful. These notions threatened a jealous king's desire to centralise power.[27]

To increase revenues, the Bourbons took other actions. They raised tax rates and created wholly new charges, with one exception. They decreased the taxes on the mining sector from 20 per cent to 10 per cent to encourage and bolster production. The Crown also moved to monopolise the production and sale of non-essentials such as tobacco, playing cards, and alcohol. Tobacco cultivation, for example, was restricted and the leaf could only be sold to the government for processing into cigarettes, cigars, snuff, and the like. Tobacco thus became the second most important source of revenue after silver.[28]

Related to these efforts was the liberalisation of trade in 1778. The Decree of Free Trade allowed Spanish American ports to trade directly with one another and with most ports in Spain. Commerce would thus no longer be restricted to four colonial ports: Veracruz, Cartagena, Lima/Callao, and Panama. The volume of trade rose and, with it, the revenues from duties collected on imports and exports. Freer commerce also undercut trade in contraband.[29]

Urban areas were not exempt from change either. The Bourbons proposed ideas to inculcate a modern morality and work ethic among the local people.

Educational initiatives aimed at local boys and girls were designed to instil ideas of cleanliness, industry, virtue, and punctuality in students. In the capitals of New Spain and Peru, authorities reorganised urban space, creating delineated districts and hiring policing units to monitor behaviour and curb the vices of the working class. Their aim was to transform what they saw as the lazy and slothful into productive, tax-paying citizens. In Mexico City, to improve hygiene and eliminate the filth of the city, officials created garbage collection services. Markets were moved and reorganised. Street vendors were licensed. Authorities removed dogs, cows, and pigs from the Central Plaza and palace courtyard. A new sewer system and public toilets were built. To end drunkenness and prevent absenteeism from work, authorities regulated taverns. In Lima, zealous reformers installed street lighting and regulated *chicherias* (corn-beer dispensing bars) to decrease drinking, gambling, and vagrancy.[30]

The overall effects of the Bourbon efforts were mixed. In general, revenues increased at first, and royal officials were reasonably honest. But the hierarchy of Crown officials ultimately expanded, given the increased accounting necessary to follow the revenue flows, and the cost of administration rose. Over time, the interests of provincial officials became compromised as they intermarried with the daughters of the Creole elite, purchased property, and became part of the comfortable class. The expulsion of the Jesuits checked but did not eliminate debates over "subversive" ideas.[31]

These reforms were disruptive. Diverse sectors of colonial society were alienated by the replacement of Creole bureaucrats with Peninsular-born and educated Spaniards (*peninsulares*), the free trade decrees that hurt local industries and bankrupted merchant houses, the expansion of the military, the new taxes, the expulsion of the Jesuits, and the increased control of the populace. Creoles resented the loss of the judgeships, corregidorships, and other government positions to the *peninsulares* as well as the loss of Jesuit educational tutelage for their sons. They disliked rubbing elbows with the *castas* in the military. The opening of the ports to wider trade opportunities reoriented overland transport routes and hurt some inland commercial centres. The Jesuit expulsion upset the other missionary orders, who wondered collectively which order would be expelled next. New taxes on alcohol, tobacco, and playing cards, and increasing sales tax and import and export duties, alienated consumers. Locals – most notably in the Andean South under the leadership of Túpac Amaru II – revolted because of increasing tribute, taxes, and other abuses.[32]

Thus, the Bourbons' top-down reforms changed the structure of government and affected the colonial balance of power. Creoles lost control at the same time that there was a change in the political culture. The paradox was that these reforms – designed to streamline the centralisation of the monarchy's power and improve Spain's overall position vis-à-vis other European nations – coupled with the consequent tensions that erupted, so destabilised society that they ironically contributed to the nineteenth-century struggles for independence.

Portugal: The Colonisation of Brazil

After its "discovery" by Europeans in 1500, the eastern coast of South America fell under the authority of the Portuguese according to the 1494 Treaty of Tordesillas. It was first called Ilha de Vera Cruz (Island of the True Cross) or Terra or Provincia de Santa Cruz (Land or Province of the Holy Cross). The area became valuable as a source of the brazilwood tree, highly prized for its use as a red dye. Thus, over time, the land became known as Terra do Brasil (Land of the Brazilwood Tree).[33]

Brazil was different from Spanish America in two ways. First, there were no great indigenous empires and civilisations. The semi-nomadic locals represented tropical forest cultures, dependent primarily on slash-and-burn agriculture and fishing. Because there was no centralised power structure, there was no "conquest" of "natives". Exploration was gradual. Some Portuguese scholars, such as Capistrano de Abreu and Prado Junior, thus write of Portugal "taking" Brazil, rather than conquering it. The second difference was that there was no source of quick or easy wealth. No mines were discovered early in the settlement efforts. The Crown established a monopoly over the only item of value, brazilwood, whose lucrative exploitation was sold to eager Portuguese and other European merchants. Foreign interlopers, especially the French, soon followed.[34]

The fear of foreign competition induced the Portuguese to settle Brazil. The Crown sent Martim Afonso de Sousa and other colonists to establish São Vicente (near Santos) in 1532. Sousa parcelled out land, appointed municipal officers, and ordered the colonists to plant wheat, grape vines, and sugar cane, and to raise cattle. At Piratininga (now São Paulo) a second settlement and mission were established. Land was distributed as individual holdings in units called *sesmarias* that were so large they were measured in leagues. The emphasis thus shifted from exchanging at trading posts to agriculture as the basis of the economy and wealth. Mining took off later.

To attract and persuade the Portuguese to emigrate, the Crown allowed individuals to colonise by implementing the captaincy or donatory system. King John III divided Brazil into 15 captaincies, or *donatorios* – private settlement enterprises – in the mid-1530s. The *donees* were granted the power to tax, administer law and justice, make appointments, and distribute lands. They were expected to use their own funds and defend the land for the king. These jurisdictions could be inherited by the eldest son. The *donees* expected a return on their investment, but few rose to the challenges of colonising Brazil. Most had inadequate resources for the expenses involved, and the majority of the private captaincies failed.[35]

Two private captaincies, however, did prosper: Pernambuco and São Vicente. The first was close to Portugal, had lots of brazilwood, and good soil for sugar cane. The *donee*, Duarte de Coelho, introduced commercial crops such as cotton and tobacco, in addition to sugar cane. By the mid-sixteenth century, it had become a thriving agricultural colony. By 1570, 23 *engenhos* (sugar mills) produced sugar; 13 years later, the number had jumped to 66 in Pernambuco alone. The total number of mills was 60 in 1570, and 115 in 1583. By 1600, the *engenhos* produced 600,000 *arrobas* or between 8,000 and 9,000 metric tonnes a year, enough sugar to export and fill scores of ships annually.[36]

The difficulties experienced in most captaincies and increasing foreign encroachment led the Portuguese king to reconsider the situation. He decided to impose centralised administration to coordinate further settlement, provide effective protection, unify the justice system, collect taxes, and prevent French contraband trade. He also wanted to reduce the autonomy of the *donees*. Therefore, in 1548, the Crown bought back the captaincy of Bahia and made it the seat of government. He then appointed Tomé de Sousa as governor general with civil and military jurisdiction. This official had two assistants: the *provedor-mor*, or chief treasurer, and the *ouvidor-geral*, the chief justice. They jointly established central government and stimulated economic activities by distributing *sesmarias*, thus encouraging agriculture. The locals reluctantly provided the labour force. This is thus an example of "defensive colonisation", whereby a colonial power establishes a government and encourages settlement to keep usurpers at bay.[37]

The chief problem with developing Brazil was the perennial shortage of labour. Pernambuco and São Vicente needed a workforce, and each year more locals either died or fled into the interior. There was not yet a large African slave trade in the mid-sixteenth century. Therefore, enterprising individuals organised expeditions into the interior to engage locals in wars, capture them, and bring them back to the coast for sale as slaves. While seeking locals, the Portuguese also explored the interior and expanded Brazilian territory way beyond the line of demarcation set by the Treaty of Tordesillas. In order to "save" the locals, the Jesuits gathered them together into *aldeias*, or villages (equivalent to the *reducciones* of Spanish America) – later called missions – where they could be easily instructed in the Christian faith and "protected". The missions produced a surplus that was invested for the benefit of both the missions and the order.[38]

Settlements were scattered along the coast. Many catered to traders. Land-owning families lived on their farms or on sugar plantations, but a few also kept a townhouse. Thus, the degree of urbanisation was less than in Spanish America. However, each urban centre had a *senado da câmara*, or town council, akin to the *cabildos* of Spanish America. Its members gained power early and never lost it, using it as an effective tool against Crown officials.

Brazil's economy was diverse and is best thought of as a series of regionally based boom-and-bust cycles. The first economic cycle was that of the exploitation of brazilwood, which was collected and shipped out of coastal trading posts. Since there were no mines, there was less demand for labour, numerically speaking, than in Spanish America. Because the natives tended not to be sedentary but semi-nomadic and less densely settled than in Spanish America, the institution of the *encomienda* was not used. The Portuguese Crown had no policy towards the locals, who were never separated and segregated as an unequal group. The one institution that both Spaniards and Portuguese used was the "just war" to rationalise enslaving indigenous people whom they needed to work.

The next product of significance was sugar cane, especially in Pernambuco and São Vicente. In a few years, sugar cane became the dominant commercial crop in the north-east. A landed elite arose from among those colonists who had been given *sesmarias* and had planted sugar cane. Because local labour was scarce, the Portuguese turned to Africa for exploitative free labour as early as 1550, which did not end, at least on paper, until 1888 (see Silva Jr in this volume). Lisbon established the "triangular trade" in which European manufactured goods were shipped from Portugal to Africa, to be exchanged there for slaves. These were transported across the Atlantic to be sold, with the payment in sugar and cash used to begin another round.[39]

Sugar was so profitable that other European countries were attracted to the industry. The Dutch started the industry on Caribbean islands, where the latest and most efficient technology enabled them to outcompete Brazilian producers and capture the North American market (see Nimako and Allen in this volume). This competition brought about a decline of the Brazilian sugar industry, and a decline of the economic power of the planting class by the late seventeenth century.[40]

Another economic sector was the cattle industry, which developed in the interior of the north-east and around São Vicente. Cattle ranches supplied meat and draught animals to the plantations. Later, ranchers exported hides to Europe. The rural society that appeared in cattle-producing areas was not as hierarchical as in the sugarcane-growing regions. Ranches were less profitable than cane fields and needed fewer labourers. So in lieu of scores of expensive slaves, labour was provided by mixed-blood *caboclos* (either Indians who became Europeanised or Brazilians of European and indigenous parentage).

The mining industry began as a result of the explorations into the interior by slave hunters. While in the interior in 1695 these expeditions discovered gold in an area now called Minas Gerais (General Mines). The gold rush that followed depopulated the sugar-producing areas of the north-east, which were already in decline, as men moved south to seek their fortune. The slave trade shifted following the appearance of the gold prospectors. Diamonds were discovered in 1729. Such lucrative finds motivated the Crown to regulate production closely in order to collect its share of taxes.[41]

The machinations of Napoleon on the Iberian Peninsula also affected Brazil. The invasion of Spain and the assumption of the throne by Joseph, Napoleon's brother, in 1808,[42] triggered a crisis of legitimacy in Portugal. Rather than submit to rule from Paris, the Portuguese court boarded British ships and sailed to Brazil. Upon landing in Bahia, a city of 130,000 people, the regent Dom João recognised that Brazil had been neglected. Subsequently, partly for security reasons, he transferred the seat of his government from Bahia to Rio de Janeiro. He also opened Brazil to foreign trade, abrogated the royal monopolies, opened certain industries to Brazilians, and reduced tariff duties on imported goods. Dom João further founded schools of military and naval studies, law, and medicine. In 1815, Brazil became a kingdom, equal in theory to Portugal. A year later, Dom João became King John VI of Portugal and Brazil.[43]

But trouble was brewing. The residents of Rio de Janeiro were proud that their city had become the capital of the Portuguese Empire. But Brazilians resented the Portuguese newcomers, who treated them as lesser subjects of the Crown and seized some of their finest homes. A revolt broke out in Pernambuco in 1817, which was quickly put down. Almost simultaneously, the Portuguese on the Iberian Peninsula began complaining about their absent king amidst rumblings of revolt.

So, in 1821, John reluctantly returned to the mother country, leaving his son Dom Pedro as regent, and counselling him to take the lead of any potential independence movement in order to keep Brazil under the sway of the House of Braganza. Dom Pedro was young, strong, an excellent horseman, and handsome. But he proved to be controversial. The conservative elites of the north-east disliked him, while he won the favour of the more liberal population of the central regions. As Grand Master of the Masonic Order, he could communicate easily with liberal and revolutionary-minded citizens.

Events in Portugal soon contributed to heightened demands for change. A constituent assembly, the Cortes, began to draw up a constitution. Brazilians were invited to attend the deliberations. But, before they could arrive in Lisbon, the Cortes had already dissolved recently formed juntas and replaced them with governing bodies responsible to themselves. Besides, the Brazilians – like the Creoles of Spanish America – were treated with contempt, and their proposals were not seriously considered. Such news angered people back home. Finally, the resulting constitution demoted Brazil in status and, in many ways, reduced it to what it had been before becoming a kingdom. Brazil was to be governed by a junta responsible to the Cortes. The old colonial captaincies were to be revived, and some reserved for the benefit of the metropolis. Laws and treaties had to be approved by Portugal before they could take effect. Freedom of trade was abrogated, and old, highly restrictive government trade monopolies were reintroduced.

Brazilians were incensed. The proverbial last straw was when the Cortes demanded that Dom Pedro return. He resisted these entreaties from abroad and declared that he would stay in Brazil. Pedro then assumed the title of Perpetual Defender and Protector of Brazil and convoked an assembly to work on a constitution. He sent delegates to Lisbon with proposals for continued cooperation and alliance that were summarily rejected. Renewed demands that he return were sent back to Brazil. This information reached him in September 1822 while he was riding along the banks of a stream called the Ypiranga in the state of São Paulo. There he made the *Grito de Ipiranga* (independence or death) pledge. A month later in Rio de Janeiro, Dom Pedro was recognised as Brazil's constitutional "emperor". Portuguese troops in Bahia mounted some resistance, but Dom Pedro's land forces, aided by the British, forced the Portuguese to surrender. Commanders in Maranhão and Pará also surrendered. Portugal finally recognised Brazil's independence in 1826.

The fact that a son of the king had declared independence prevented Brazil from fragmenting along regional lines like the Spanish American viceroyalties. The Crown provided a common identity, and there was no crisis of legitimacy in Lisbon. Instead there was continuity, and no massive physical destruction as a result of wars.

Concluding Reflections

The words "colonial" and "colonialism" are ubiquitous in the history of Latin America. But the words were not generally applied to the Americas until they were codified in the eighteenth century by the administration of the Bourbon kings. The Habsburgs had referred to their overseas American jurisdictions as kingdoms, theoretically equal to the kingdom of Spain, all united through the person of the king. "Colonial" and "colonialism" denoted a subservient category. Thus, both the Habsburgs and the Bourbons and the Portuguese Crown viewed the Americas as "possessions", regarding them as beholden to the monarchies and existing for the benefit of the mother country. And therein lies the essence of the relationship between Latin America and the Iberian Peninsula. The administration of American subjects should, it was thought, primarily benefit the metropolis.

In both Spanish and Portuguese America, the metropolis quickly abandoned its original trading plans and moved to establish colonial regimes in which jurisdiction over the Americas yielded surpluses for its advantage. The Crowns constructed governing institutions effectively to secure royal rights. Court luxuries and foreign wars were paid for by American silver from the mines of Potosi, northern Mexico, and elsewhere; by trading tariffs and concessions; and by other royal revenues. In Spain, the introduction of bullion caused inflation that ruined some industries, which were unable to compete with other European producers. Consequently, their manufacturers filled the need for goods in the Americas and still shipped them across the Atlantic on Spanish boats. Thus, exported American silver subsidised the industrialisation of rival European powers.

Creoles born in the Americas and some Brazilian elites resented their subordination and second-class status, which became more evident in the late eighteenth and nineteenth centuries. Discontent was heightened by the Bourbon reforms in Spanish America, which systematically made the empire more centralised and increased tax revenues, and the royal court's presence in Brazil. This frustration motivated them to support local rule and eventually declare independence. In Spanish America, this movement caused widespread destruction and deaths on the battlefields, while a son and heir to the Portuguese king ushered in a future of imperial rule in Brazil with little bloodshed.

Part Seven

The Global Struggle for Reparations

24

The Struggle for Reparations
in the Caribbean

Hilary Beckles

IT HAS BEEN TWO decades since African governments, and diaspora nations and communities across the Americas, divided and travelled in opposite directions at the United Nations (UN) Conference Against Racism, Racial Discrimination, Xenophobia and Related Intolerance in Durban in August–September 2001 on the matter of reparations for the transatlantic slave trade.[1] Caribbean governments, in particular, were adamant that the chattel slavery system, spawned by trafficking in enchained African bodies, was a crime against humanity that should ethically, legally, and politically attract reparations in multiple forms. African governments did not agree, and rejected diaspora claims while siding with Europe and the West in shutting down the reparations campaigners (see Adebajo in this volume for another perspective).

Since then, the movement for reparations has greatly advanced globally, reflecting my plenary statement in Durban in 2001 that reparatory justice will become the greatest political campaign of the twenty-first century.[2] Everywhere that descendants of enslaved Africans are to be found, civil society campaigns – sometimes with government backing, as is the case in the Caribbean – are actively demanding reparations as a civil and human right, and as a critical part of post-colonial economic development paradigms. Indeed, the entire post-colonial world, with and without a legacy of African enslavement, has found a voice within the movement and is calling for justice and compensation for colonial economic exploitation as well as for racial and cultural denigration under white supremacy's imperial hegemony.

The Caricom Example

The Caribbean Community (Caricom) found good cause formally to declare a regional policy demanding reparations from European states for three centuries of exploitative slavery and unpaid labour in the region.[3] In 2013, governments finally joined with civil society in declaring that the regional good would best be served by a dialogue in the form of an international reparations summit. To give effect to this policy position, a Caricom Reparations Commission was established to provide strategic advocacy and official advice, to which I was appointed chair.

The Caricom approach now serves as a global model and has attracted the attention of states and civil societies. One consequence has been the setting up of reparations commissions and committees across the Americas and Europe. The Caricom initiative rekindled the century-old movement in the United States, where an African American reparations commission has taken shape (see Maginn in this volume) and energised the national campaign, thus providing commendable global leadership in the process. In addition, similar organisations have sprung up in Canada, Colombia, the European Union (EU), and Britain (see Frith and Xosei, and Small in this volume). These effectively networked institutions have had considerable domestic impact and constitute a discursive infrastructure that is shaping community comprehension and national dialogue at the highest political levels.

Globally, this movement has ushered in what are best described as "regimes of regrets". Everywhere that the campaign has counted on civil society groups to advocate the cause, governments have responded by issuing "statements of regret". Famously, the British prime minister Tony Blair joined with US president George W. Bush Jr in travelling to Africa – not the Caribbean – to inform hosting governments that their nations "regret" the atrocities that defined the transatlantic slave trade. "Sorry" has become the storyline that now shapes official responses to the reparations movement. Inscribed in legal language, the "regretting" narrative constitutes a legally skilful but politically sloppy engagement.

The "sorry-regret" refrain from Western capitals has emerged from an incipient fear of litigation, which a sincere "apology" it is thought might provoke. An apology, as an invitation to discuss restitution, is far from the intention of the "West", hence the avoidance strategy, which falls short of policy sincerity. At the top of the Caricom Ten Point reparations document is a "sincere apology", which is intended to lay the path for a reparations conversation.[4]

Western Universities

This is where the dialogue begins, and there is no escaping it. Critically, it includes an admission that slave trading and chattel enslavement were "crimes against humanity".[5] The West has consistently argued before and since the Durban Conference in 2001 that slavery "should" have been crimes but were not, hence there is nothing for which to apologise. This remains the narrative of the British and other European nations. Slavery was legalised by national parliaments and, therefore, did not constitute crimes. Reparationists have responded that the Nazi regime of Adolf Hitler also "legalised" its genocide of six million European Jews.

Where the movement has gained the greatest visible traction is within the Western university sector. One by one, the most prestigious universities – Harvard, Yale, Oxford, Cambridge – have traced their rise and development to the slave-based enterprise. They received substantial capital injections and other forms of endowment from the slaveocracy, and could not imagine their sustainability without a deep attachment to African chattelisation. Colleges needed black chattel to prosper and were historically not ashamed to reflect this on their financial statements and balance sheets. It was simply an indication of a "sound and legitimate business practice".

The relationship was mutually existential. The slave system and the university could not survive without each other. From the outset, the concept of African biological inferiority – central to the design and practice of slavery – was formulated and propagated by professors who provided enslavers with the rationale to justify and sustain their crime. The law professor, for example, went to work illustrating how enchained Africans could be reduced within institutions and commercial practices to property, chattel, and real estate. He showed how the economic system could treat humans as non-humans, with all the attendant values of property. He explained how the enslaved could be bought, sold, leased, mortgaged, rented, and bequeathed; how they could be used as cash and as collateral. The precision of these legally enforced practices required the technical and intellectual skill of trained and experienced professors of law.

Then the Christian theologians got in on the business as professors of divinity, by promoting the judgements of popes, who assured the enslavers that Africans had no mortal souls, and were beasts to be kept to labour in the field. Theology colleges campaigned for the chattelisation enterprise and might have been as valuable to Western slavery as the economists who demonstrated how the profitability of enslavement was in the national interest and, therefore, to be upheld. In all faculties – from the Humanities and the Economic Sciences, to Law and Divinity – academia provided the theoretical and practical infrastructure to develop and sustain slavery.

Chief financial officers of colleges could not ignore the revenue inflows from slavery investments, especially as institutions became increasingly competitive for cash, students, and popular professors. They received support from the plantations, and also participated as investors and owners of enslaved persons. They were not simply passive recipients of endowments. They were owners, managers, and speculators in black chattel as capital assets. Campus balance sheets tell the story of the slavery lifeline. Today, the regretting and repenting is repetitious. One by one, they have been owning up to their criminal involvements.

On both sides of the Atlantic, the best and finest of them have issued statements of regret for their centuries of commodifying Africans for the advancement of white academia. They are caught within a dilemma that reflects the depth of the racism of white supremacy. As they collect the data on their drinking from the slavery well, the shame and guilt cycle stands in the way of an impulse to repair and drives them into a strategic urge to hide and minimise the exposure. The norm, then, is for the Western university to "research and run" rather than "research and repair". Typically, the University of Hull, built around the imagery of the legendary William Wilberforce, abolitionist extraordinaire, established the Wilberforce Institute for the Study of Slavery and Emancipation.[6] The acronym WISE stands as a rejection of the proposed word "reparations" in the institution's name, which should have been represented as WISER. Racism, deep and unyielding, could not accept the "R" word. WISE, in the process, in yielding to "research and run", missed a historic, seminal opportunity to be relevant.

From the University of Glasgow to Harvard, Cambridge, and Georgetown, these prestigious universities opted for a minimalist response that reflects the perception of black people as marginal to the future of "Western civilisation". But the moral question remains, though hidden and buried beneath liberal notions of tokenism in response to these historical crimes against humanity.

The award of a small number of student scholarships and, in the case of Bristol University, the hiring of a black professor, are meant to calm the appetite for structural and meaningful reparations. How, then, can such universities be considered "excellent" when their past and present actions consolidate unethical practices. The generally accepted methodologies of quality assurance in academia suggest the unacceptability of excellence within the context of conduct considered unethical. This is now the predicament the Western university faces.

Other Western institutions, primarily in the financial sector, have been dabbling in the shallow end of the reparations pool. Tentatively tip-toeing into the waters of truth and compensations, all the brand-name high-street financial institutions have come forward with "regret" statements and the offer of embarrassing little gestures to unresponsive, targeted black communities.

Western Finance, the Church, and the Monarchy

Lloyd's of London, the global insurer, admitted to knowing of its past as the grand insurer of slave ships and their shackled cargo.[7] They have offered student scholarships; so too have the big banks such as JP Morgan Chase and the Royal Bank of Scotland. The Bank of England, established in 1694, served as chief regulator of the loot from slavery, and admitted to slave-owning and keeping black chattel on its balance sheet. Provincial banks have also come forward seeking redemption in order to "move on". The global public, unaware of the popular economic culture they represented, was more surprised when the Church of England in January 2023 admitted to being a significant enslaver, with billions of pounds of reserves resulting from its involvement. The Archbishop of Canterbury, Justin Welby, has offered regrets to its congregations and black communities, and in January 2023 established a £100 million investment fund for communities affected by slavery.[8]

While the established Church has now bowed before the altar of reparations, the British monarchy has entered an era of playing "hide and seek", as popular opinion in the country and the wider Commonwealth of former colonies calls for a definitive stance from Buckingham Palace. For 400 years, the British monarchy was a chief architect, investor, and policy participant in the development of the slavery enterprise.[9] The enrichment of the throne threw Africans deeper into the pit of plantation slavery and the dungeons of slave ships. Kings and queens defined slavery as serving the "national interest" and used their naval might to protect slave ships, also providing political solidarity to enslavers in the British Parliament.[10]

The June 2022 Commonwealth meeting in the Rwandan capital of Kigali witnessed considerable pressure being placed upon the monarchy to engage in reparations conversations with Global Africa. Prince Charles – now King Charles III – responded to the demands for a statement, and announced that the time had come for a dialogue. On becoming king in September 2022, the questions continue to mount. Will there be an apology and reparations payment from Buckingham Palace?

The burden is particularly heavy on the shoulders of Charles III. After all, it was Charles I who endorsed the 1636 Barbados enslavers' policy that Africans were not human but property, and should therefore serve their owners for life.[11] Charles II was the lead corporate designer of "Royal African" slave-trading companies whose business model was the kidnapping of thousands of Africans for Caribbean enslavement.[12]

King Willem-Alexander of the Netherlands broke the royal silence in January 2023 when, from the Dam Square Palace in Amsterdam, he announced, on behalf of his kingdom, an apology for his country's participation in the slave trade and slavery. He acknowledged that the Dutch state and society had been pioneers in the slave enterprise and inflicted immeasurable pain and suffering upon the African people (see Nimako and Allen in this volume). The royal apology was supported by a similar statement, in December 2022, from the prime minister Mark Rutte, who alluded to a reparations strategy in the near future and announced a fund of €200 million to raise awareness and find means of restitution for Dutch slavery and colonialism. The Dutch declaration places considerable political pressure upon King Charles III and his country.

The Caricom response to the Dutch apology and promise of a reparatory justice programme was cautiously optimistic. The Dutch were commended for making the apology but criticised for their unilateral approach, which excluded the victim communities from the dialogue. It was noted that this strategy reflected the white supremacy stance long embedded in communications with black communities. In Suriname and Guyana, the outrage was palpable. The persistence of the Dutch colonisers in the Caribbean served to inflame attitudes that "game-playing" is a feature of Dutch colonial policy and is well known in the colonial islands of Aruba, Bonaire, and Curaçao.

Western Parliaments

These developments nevertheless suggest a continuous rise in the current tide of global reparations, especially as the US Congress has prepared reparations legislation that could eventually go to the Senate in the shape of an endorsement of HR 40, named after the historic bill to prepare a national reparations strategy.[13] Floundering for decades in the corridors of Congress, HR 40 has now reached a moment of solidarity within the Democratic Party's control of the Senate, though there is an expectation of filibustering by the Republicans. The Congressional Black Caucus seems more ready than ever to push the cause of reparations.

Another critical development in Western party politics occurred when the British Labour Party contested the December 2019 general election with a manifesto that promised the opening of reparations talks with Caricom in the event of victory. This was a seminal development. The Conservative Party, however, won the polls and returned the country's politics to the status quo. In opposition, however, the Labour Party has continued its call for a national dialogue and engagement with Caricom. In March 2023, Labour MP Clive Lewis raised the political temperature by calling on the British prime minister Rishi Sunak to "enter negotiations with Caribbean leaders on paying reparations for Britain's role in slavery". Lewis described London's relationship with members of Caricom as "400 years of the most hideous abuse", and indicated that reparations involved "not charity but restitution".[14]

The Westminster sitting of parliamentarians found consensus on the need to support Caribbean development within the context of reparatory justice but was divided on the methods to be used in securing a capital injection for Caricom. The case of fiscal and financial support in the form of Caricom market access to Britain was made by Conservative MPs, which represents a significant move away from the traditional non-supportive position. British politics, then, can now be described as pro-reparationist in principle.

In the United States, on the other hand, the system of governance that allows the 50 states to implement policies within their own boundaries gave Democrat-governed states opportunities to provide the country with a reparations momentum. In recent years, state legislatures in California, New York, and New Jersey and cities such as Evanston, Detroit, and San Francisco have addressed the matter and resolved that slavery was a crime against humanity, with legacies to be repaired.[15] Many US states have recently passed laws allowing state executives to implement reparatory policies in housing and education, and, in some instances, to provide families with restorative access to their stolen assets. State legislatures, then, have not waited on the US Congress to act, and have adopted reparations policies across the country. Again, it is reasonable to say that the United States is, in effect, preparing to become a country of reparations.

Caricom: Building Bridges with Africa

Within Caricom, meanwhile, there has been a patient call for Africa to change its Durban position and come on board in support of a Global Africa reparations strategy.[16] It has been a common refrain that the "West" would keep Caricom at bay, owing to its small size, despite its loud voice on the global stage. Caricom has thus focused on an outreach to the African Union (AU) in order to build a development bridge that would allow for conversations on all aspects of post-colonial bonding and policy coordination. At the heart of this development discourse has been the need to heal the wound opened at Durban, which I have described elsewhere as the "great betrayal".[17]

Prime Minister Mia Mottley of Barbados led the charge. In her role as chair of the Regional Prime Ministerial Sub-committee with oversight responsibility for the Reparations Commission, she was well positioned to launch the Africa outreach initiative. She began with an intense diplomatic dialogue in 2019 with President Uhuru Kenyatta of Kenya and then with President Nana Akufo-Addo of Ghana. Both presidents visited Caricom and, while in Barbados, spoke in a manner that illustrated the need of the moment. They declared solidarity with Caricom on the reparations agenda and pledged to promote it within the African Union (see Adebajo in this volume).

President Akufo-Addo showed a deeper understanding of the Caribbean agenda. Ghana was a leading exporter of people to the Caribbean: Barbados had a majority Akan community as early as the 1660s. The Mottley diplomacy has been particularly effective, and when in November 2019 she addressed the Ghanaian Parliament in Accra, it was evident that Ghana was fully supportive of the Caricom reparations agenda. This constituted a grand reversal of the country's 2001 position, which had then been outlined by President John Kufuor.

In August 2022, at a reparations conference in Accra, President Akufo-Addo reaffirmed Ghana's position in a powerful speech in which he said that Africa and Caricom would henceforth speak with one voice on reparations. The time had come, he declared, and the African Union would now be a force to be reckoned with.[18] Within Caricom, then, the feeling is that the ghost of Durban has finally been exorcised, and that Global Africa is now at one, at peace, in pursuing reparations with the multiple strategies available. In effect, this is seen as an ending of the Mbeki–Kufuor–Obasanjo–Wade alliance that shut the door in Caricom's face in favour of the company of the West at the 2001 UN Durban Conference.

Caricom's Global Outreach

Meanwhile, Caricom has continued to devise innovative strategies to advance the movement globally. Conversations with enslaving institutions and families in Britain, in particular, have provided advocates with focus, while inter-state dialogue seems dormant. The Drax family has been a primary focus, now visibly and ethically exposed. They were leading pioneers of the slave plantations in Barbados in the 1640s and Jamaica in the 1650s. They were legislators who defined Africans as non-human and proceeded to enslave them as chattel for nearly 200 years. Today, they still own the sugar plantation in Barbados, Drax Hall, which was established in the 1640s. In Barbados, slavery was genocidal. Around 600,000 enslaved Africans were imported by the English, led by the Drax family at the beginning. At the time of emancipation in 1834, only 83,000 remained, a genocidal experience that in some regards transcends, legally and ethically, the process of enslavement.[19] The Drax family, then, is charged with the crime of enslavement as well as genocide.

There is now a global campaign, led by the Barbados government and civil society, to bring the Draxes to the reparations table. The principal demand is that their 300-acre sugar plantation be handed over to the people of the island as a reparatory action. The British press, and members of Richard Drax's Conservative constituency, have called on Drax to comply with the Barbados request. The Labour Party members of his constituency have held several demonstrations outside his home in support of Barbados. He has remained adamantly opposed.

Meanwhile, another elite slave-owning British family, the Trevelyans, have come forward, in the most revolutionary fashion, to rally reparations advocates to the centre of the global conversations. The Trevelyans were the leading enslavers on the island of Grenada. At the time of emancipation they received a handsome sum of £26,989 for their 1,004 enslaved Africans (the equivalent of £4 million in 2023), whom they owned under British colonial law. The Trevelyans have remained a very visible British family, with high-level representation in most sections of society. Their economic empowerment from slavery was the salvation of this upwardly mobile family.[20]

Led by Laura Trevelyan, a well-known BBC producer, the family agreed to meet with the leadership of the Caricom Reparations Commission, which I have chaired since its creation in 2013. The purpose of the meeting was to enable the family to make an apology to the people of Grenada and the

Caribbean, and to roll out the core of a reparations plan. This was an online town hall meeting, involving near 50 members of the family. After several negotiations, the family agreed to the Caricom position that chattel slavery was "a crime against humanity". They agreed formally to apologise to the people of the Caribbean. They announced plans to travel to Grenada to make the apology in a public forum and present a reparations project to the public. This was a truly historic event. About ten members of the Trevelyan family met in a town hall format under the auspices of the University of the West Indies and the Grenada National Reparations Committee. The prime minister of Grenada, Dickon Mitchell, and several of his cabinet ministers attended the event in February 2023.

This was the first occasion that an enslaving family or institution admitted publicly that slavery was not just cruel and an atrocity, but a "crime against humanity" which must, therefore, be repaired. The family broke ranks with the official British state position that slavery "should" have been declared a crime but had not been. Subsequently, the family called on the royal family and government to follow in its footsteps. King Charles III was told to do the right thing, and the Rishi Sunak government was urged to open a reparations dialogue with Caricom and Africa.

The Trevelyans were hailed as twenty-first-century trailblazers when they presented the £100,000 student learning Reparations Fund for the children of Grenada in February 2023. This, they said, was a seed investment, part of a larger fund to which they would commit over the next five years. Laura Trevelyan had visited the island before, exploring the legacy of slave-owning and meeting descendants of the enslaved. Her credibility as spokesperson for the family thus guaranteed the success of the event.

Prime Minister Mitchell accepted the apology on behalf of his nation and Caricom, and called for redemption and forgiveness. It was a pivotal moment in post-Durban history. It was the penultimate project intended to bring down the curtains on the twenty-first year of the Durban Declaration. The Trevelyans had rejected the "should" of the Declaration on slavery as "a crime against humanity" and joined forces with the new Caricom–African reparations axis.

Concluding Reflections

The week after the "Grenada apology", the University of the West Indies, of which I am the vice-chancellor, and the Caricom Reparations Commission

THE STRUGGLE FOR REPARATIONS IN THE CARIBBEAN

hosted a delegation of traditional African kings and queens, who were invited to participate in an academic conference entitled "Reparations and Royalty: Africa and Europe; Exploding Myths, Empowering Truths". The event was held at the regional headquarters of the University of the West Indies on the Mona campus in Jamaica. About 15 African monarchs attended and spoke about the impact of the slave trade in Africa and the multiple experiences of their ancestors. They rejected the Eurocentric narrative that monarchs had, in general, been partners of European slave traders. They declared their support for the Caricom–African reparations initiative and committed to being African advocates for the cause. The group was led by Paul Jones Eganda, head of the Africa Diaspora Royal Kingdoms Alliance (AIDO), based in Britain. The delegation positioned itself as the royal voice of the Global Africa reparations movement. This political position was celebrated by delegates who had travelled from Africa, Europe, and the Americas to devise strategies to advance the Global Africa position.

Before and after Durban, then, the reparations movement has not been ad hoc in its development. Rather, it has evolved on the basis of multiple layered events, intertwined with a diversity of conceptual and ideological interventions from several pedagogical directions. In the Caribbean context, the present upsurge of the movement represents the seventh peak since the emancipation discourse of the 1820s. There has been nothing linear about its trajectory: it has experienced ebbs and flows, and disappointments have been interspersed with strategic and sustainable advances and successes. The 2001 Durban Declaration, and the politics that gave life to it, are now dead, awaiting burial on the continent that birthed it.

25

The Struggle for Reparations in the United States

Andrew Maginn

THE NARRATIVE OF THE reparations movement in the United States is filled with many sprints and breaks. There are moments when those of African descent gained mobility and believed there would be a shared reconciliation for the sins of slavery (and later that of Jim Crow), only to be disappointed. The reparations movement takes place over four periods: the early US reparations (1783–1915), the re-emergence of the reparations movement (1950–1989), the era of reparations discourse (1989–2014) and the contemporary reparations attempts in the US (2014 to the present). This chapter explores each of these periods, marking the incremental growth and the setbacks of the reparations movement, as well as the debates over its implementation in the United States.

Early US Reparations, 1783–1915

During the American Revolution (1776–1783), several suits were brought for freedom from enslavement in Massachusetts.[1] However, African American activist Belinda Sutton took a step further during the New Republic period (1783–1820). In a 1783 suit, she petitioned the Massachusetts General Court for a pension from her enslaver Isaac Royall Jr's estate. The Massachusetts General Court approved Sutton's petition, and she received an annual pension of 15 pounds and 12 shillings.[2] While many historians have repeated this narrative, they omit to say that while Sutton won her suit, she did not receive the full restitution. Payments to Sutton stopped after two years.[3] This was the start of a trend of unfulfilled promises to previously enslaved people and their descendants in the United States.

As the nineteenth century became the Age of Emancipation, the governments of the United States, Britain, and France undertook "compensated emancipation". The goal of this practice was to end the debate on emancipation, since the enslavers would receive funds from their governments to compensate them for the loss of their free labour. While men and women who held black people in bondage were paid by way of compensation, the formerly enslaved did not have access to resources and typically remained geographically close to their former enslavers, working for meagre rewards on tasks reminiscent of those during their servitude. Compensated emancipation was discussed in President Abraham Lincoln's administration as a path towards peace during the early days of the American Civil War (1861–1865).[4] In 1861, it was proposed that it be tested in Delaware. If approved by the Delaware General Assembly, the plan would reward enslavers who agreed to the gradual emancipation of their enslaved with a "payment of an average of $500 per person with funds … [provided] by the Republican-majority Congress".[5] If this version of compensated emancipation proved successful, it would be applied to other slaveholding states within the United States.

The Delaware General Assembly struck down the proposed measure, but it was later tested in the District of Columbia in April 1862, with the approval of the United States Congress. The District of Columbia Compensated Emancipation Act of 1862 provided enslavers in the district with a "maximum [payment] of $300 per enslaved" individual, and resulted in the emancipation of 3,185 persons.[6] By the end of the process, the US Congress had paid around $1 million to former enslavers. Emboldened by the success within the District of Columbia, President Lincoln attempted to expand his "compensated emancipation" programme, offering it to slaveholding states in the Union (Kentucky, Maryland, Delaware, and Missouri) as well as to the Vice-President of the Confederacy, Alexander H. Stephens. However, enslavers in the Union and the Confederacy were uninterested, refusing upwards of $400 million (over $7 billion today) in exchange for emancipation.[7]

Remarkably, compensation for the emancipated also emerged during the American Civil War. This included the "Port Royal experiment", in which 8,000 formerly enslaved individuals worked in cotton production for the Union in exchange for low wages that could be used to purchase former plantation land at $1.25 an acre between 1862 and 1863.[8] While Northern investors bought most of the property, the United States government set aside certain lots for purchase by the formerly enslaved.[9] Similarly, in January 1865, General William Sherman issued Special Field Order no. 15, which set aside 400 acres of land recently confiscated from Confederate supporters for newly emancipated families. It was parcelled out in plots "of not more than forty acres of tillable ground".[10] In addition, General Sherman assisted the formerly enslaved to work on their land by loaning them mules owned by the army. Sherman's actions led to the expression "forty acres and a mule" being tied to the idea of reparations. In the early days of Reconstruction after 1865, US congressman Thaddeus Stevens proposed that the model followed by General Sherman and the Port Royal experiment could be extrapolated to the broader South. The Union had confiscated 394 million acres of property, and Congressman Stevens moved that this land be divided and redistributed to formerly enslaved family groups.[11] However, this and other efforts proved unsuccessful as the reunification of the United States was prioritised over reparations.[12] Like the former slave Belinda Sutton, those who received land from General Sherman and the Port Royal experiment were only allowed a two-year taste of compensation before the Federal Government returned the land to ex-Confederates.

Following emancipation, calls for compensation by the formerly enslaved continued but were ignored. Even the expression "forty acres and a mule" – once a rallying cry – became a myth and a symbol of lost hope.[13] Prominent African Americans such as Sojourner Truth pushed for restitution in the form of land or funds from the Federal Government for those formerly enslaved. Nevertheless, these attempts fell upon deaf ears, even with the endorsement of African American abolition activist Frederick Douglass.[14] When appeals to the government failed, a grassroots effort was begun in Nashville, Tennessee, in 1894 through the Ex-Slave Mutual Relief, Bounty, and Pension Association. While the organisation gained the support of 600,000 formerly enslaved, there was a focused effort by the Federal Government to shut down this movement, and the group's organisers were arrested on trumped-up mail fraud charges.[15]

The legal route to obtain reparations was followed in a 1915 lawsuit against the United States Treasury by Callie House, a formerly enslaved woman, who was represented by Cornelius J. Jones. In the suit, Jones asserted that $68 million was owed to the formerly enslaved from the taxes on cotton collected by the Federal Government before the American Civil War.[16] However, even with this reasoning, many American whites believed the bill for slavery had been paid through the blood sacrificed on the battlefield for black emancipation. They also argued that the Civil War was about state rights, rather than the institution of slavery or emancipation, which was an unintended result of the conflict. These justifications are unfounded and neglect the role that slavery played in the causes of the American Civil War as well as the role that hundreds of thousands of black soldiers played in bringing about the conclusion of this conflict. Nevertheless, these have remained the standard replies for those who are opposed to reparations. It was in this milieu that inequity continued during post-emancipation, which, for many advocates of reparations, only compounds the moral debt of the United States. These inequities include the sins of Jim Crow, the destruction of black wealth, the lynching of blacks, the wealth gap between blacks and whites, the lack of social mobility, limited access to fair and equal housing (red-lining), medical experimentation, and racialised issues in the health-care industry (including access to physicians, medicine, and recurring myths and biases regarding black bodies that have led to misdiagnosis and mistreatment). Many of these issues were supported by various states, if not by the Federal Government.[17]

The Re-emergence of the US Reparations Movement, 1950–1989

While the discussion of reparations was muted in public discourse, compensation remained on the minds of people of colour during the Reconstruction era.[18] Rumblings of reparations were heard again in the American public arena following the Second World War (1939–1945) as the American Civil Rights Movement renewed discussions about the legacies of slavery. In 1950, Ewart Guinier, a prominent black Jamaican-American educator, activist, and legal scholar, called for the creation of a $50 billion federal works programme to assist the black community. This was echoed in 1963 by African American civil rights leader Whitney Young, who called for a "domestic Marshall plan".[19] Within the Civil Rights Movement, many considered the call for reparations too extreme, as its advocates were part of the black radical tradition, including Marcus Garvey and Malcolm X, who "demanded land and cash payments".[20] However, even Martin Luther King Jr sought to shift Congressional spending from "destruction and military containment" to compensation for the black community in "education, housing, employment, and health care" within what he called a "Bill of Rights for the disadvantaged".[21]

While reparations were considered important, the issue was overshadowed by the fact that people of colour still did not have civil rights enshrined in the United States Constitution. These included the Thirteenth, Fourteenth and Fifteenth Amendments, which were a product of Radical Reconstruction (1865–1877) at a time when progressive racial policies were implemented following the American Civil War. But they were never truly enforced. However, following the support for these rights provided by the American Civil Rights Act (1964) and the Voting Rights Act (1965), the discussion of compensation for slavery and its legacies came to the forefront. In 1966, the Black Panther party promoted reparations, stating that the "racist government" of the United States "has robbed us and now we are demanding our overdue debt of forty acres and two mules ... We will accept payment in currency which will be distributed to our many communities."[22] While the majority of Americans largely ignored this demand, the topic was thrust into the public sphere by James Forman, a former member of the Student Non-Violent Coordinating Committee (SNCC) and participant in the 1960 National Black Economic Development Conference. Forman interrupted a service at Riverside Church in New York in May 1969 and read "The Black Manifesto" (1969) to the congregation.[23]

The manifesto called for $500 million in reparations to be raised by white religious institutions (Jewish and Christian) that were "part and parcel of the [capitalist] system", which had been supported by slavery.[24] The calculations were based on $15 per enslaved person. To assuage fears that reparations would be given to individuals, the manifesto provided an itemised plan for how the funds would be implemented to uplift the black community. This would be accomplished through the establishment of black banks, media companies, educational institutions, research initiatives, a welfare organisation, a legal defence fund, and trade initiatives throughout the African diaspora.[25] For any unused funds, an Inter-religious Foundation for Community Organization (IFCO) would be created to support the mission outlined in the manifesto.[26] This proposal for reparations was not immediately dismissed, and several religious groups answered the call, raising around $1 million. Nonetheless, support eventually declined, and the National Black Economic Development Conference retained around $300,000 to support this mission.[27]

Similarly, the Republic of New Africa Movement (RNA), a group founded in 1968, proposed an "Anti-Depression programme" to the Federal Government in 1972.[28] The programme would allow African Americans to vote for the creation of a homeland within the United States that would be called the Republic of New Africa. The RNA demanded $300 billion in reparations to finance this new community, and the distribution of funds would be decided through negotiations between the Federal Government and the organisation's leadership. This proposal was rejected outright, but requests for compensation from the Federal Government persisted. The same year, the National Black Political Convention, at its annual meeting, also called for black reparations.[29] These requests resulted in no legislative change, but instead drew ridicule, police surveillance, and even coordinated violence against these groups.

The multiple calls for restitution in the late 1960s and early 1970s led Boris Bittker, a white American legal scholar, to write *The Case for Black Reparations* (1973).[30] This book took the discussion of reparations into the realm of the activist-scholar. The importance of this watershed moment – the publication of the first major scholarly work in America to discuss this topic – was not lost on Bittker, who stated his intention to make reparations a national debate.[31] However, within his legal examination of reparations, Bittker focused on the problems that citizens of African descent had faced during post-emancipation rather than during slavery. The justification for this, according to Bittker, was that present-day injustices were more recognisable in that period.[32] Bittker continued to simplify the complexities of the debate by stating that, owing to the administrative difficulty of providing individual reparations, compensation for groups of African Americans would be the best solution.[33] Interestingly, the model of group reparations began to be adopted by state and federal governments around this time. A year after the publication of *The Case for Black Reparations* in 1974, a $10 million out-of-court settlement was awarded by the Federal Government to the victims of the "Tuskegee experiments": black men who had been unwittingly subjected to experiments for treating syphilis.[34]

Bittker's point about group reparations was that the United States had a tradition of providing this kind of restitution since the 1920s, primarily through providing funds to Native American groups for lands taken by the Federal Government. This first began with the Pueblo Lands Act of 1924, by which the US Congress authorised the establishment of the Pueblo Lands Board and a payment of $1.3 million to the Pueblo. The demand for the US government to act in reparation for its transgressions against Native Americans continued to grow until the 1932 Indian Reorganization Act, which allowed Congress to pay $2 million a year in reparations for land acquisition. While these yearly payments ended in 1941, the US Congress continued to pay individual Native American groups as a result of lawsuits brought by several legal aid organisations. By 1987, the Federal Government had paid varying amounts to Native American groups throughout the United States, totalling around $2.2

billion.[35] Similarly, in 1987, the US government introduced bill H.R. 442, the Civil Liberties Act, which provided reparations for 82,250 Japanese Americans forced into internment camps during the Second World War by the Franklin D. Roosevelt administration. The bill was years in the making, and was brought before the Federal Government by community activists, legal advocates, and political leaders. The bill was signed into law by President Ronald Reagan in 1988, and provided all surviving internees with a total of $1.2 billion ($20,000 per person) in compensation.[36]

While the Federal Government was debating restitution to Japanese Americans, many advocates of reparations for African Americans saw the possibility of finally receiving restitution for them. In 1987, an advocacy group was formed to see this mission through: the National Coalition of Blacks for Reparations in America, known as N'COBRA.[37] It put pressure on the Federal Government with the assistance of the Republic of New Africa, which had circulated a proposed reparations bill to each member of Congress the same year.[38] This combined pressure paid off, as African American Democratic congressman John Conyers introduced bill H.R. 3745 on 20 November 1989 to create a commission to "address the fundamental injustice, cruelty, brutality, and inhumanity of slavery ... its subsequent *de jure* and *de facto* racial and economic discrimination against African Americans, and the impact of these forces on contemporary African Americans".[39]

Conyers to Coates: The Era of US Reparations Discourse, 1989–2014

Conyers's 1989 bill provided the first official legislative guide for the Federal Government to address the harm done to people of African descent. This would be accomplished by appropriating $8 million to establish the Commission to Study Reparation Proposals for African Americans. The commission would study slavery and its legacies, and consider a national apology and other remedies for the descendants of enslaved people, including reparations. While this seemed like a simple first step, each time the bill has been presented to Congress, it has remained in legislative limbo. All the same, the bill, now retitled H.R. 40, has been a rallying cry for advocates. Yet many politicians of the 1990s and 2000s have ignored the push for H.R. 40. They have instead attempted to sidestep the topic of reparations altogether by providing half-hearted apologies and implementing limited social policies. This can be seen in the actions of President Bill Clinton, who in 1997 created the President's Initiative on Race, also known as the One America Initiative – through Executive Order 13050 – which encouraged community dialogue on the topic of race.[40] In addition, while not apologising directly to African Americans for the institution of slavery, Clinton apologised in 1998 for the damage that slavery had caused to the African continent in an impromptu speech while visiting Uganda.[41] Similarly, President George W. Bush (2003) and President Joe Biden (2022) apologised to Africans, not African Americans, for the transatlantic slave trade.[42] At the time of writing this chapter, no sitting US president has yet apologised to the African American people for slavery and the slave trade.

While the United States Congress – led mostly by the Democrats – has apologised for slavery and Jim Crow in 2008, the Federal Government is still at an impasse regarding reparations, thus leaving American states and private organisations to lead the way in providing restitution to citizens of African descent. This began in 1994 when the state of Florida committed $2.1 million to the living survivors of the Rosewood Massacre, a harrowing event in 1923 in which 29 blacks and 2 whites lost their lives owing to racialised violence.[43] The promise of local authorities providing reparations for past attacks on African Americans has led several advocacy groups to push their local governments to act. The most prominent are the descendants of the Tulsa Massacre, an attack by a white mob on a prominent black neighbourhood and "economic hub" called Greenwood in 1921, which resulted in the death of "as many as 300 people".[44] While Tulsa created a commission to review the racial injustice in 1997, it decided that restitution would not be provided. This decision is still being appealed by survivors and their descendants.[45] For many advocates of reparations, the monetary restitution provided to those of Rosewood, Florida, remains the model they would like local, state, and federal governments to emulate.

Like the current debates on critical race theory and the future of African American Studies, the battleground for reparations debates has been located within higher education. This began with two key events, the publication of the late African American activist Randall Robinson's *The Debt: What America Owes to Blacks* (2000), and the response to it in an advertisement, placed in 70 college newspapers, by David Horowitz entitled "Ten Reasons Why Reparations for Blacks Is a Bad Idea for Blacks – and Racist Too" (2001).[46] While Robinson's *The Debt* provides a moving and strongly structured defence of reparations, Horwitz's advertisement led to a more vigorous response, as it was a direct challenge to the academic community. He employed old arguments that are still standard fare for opponents of reparations: slavery was not an American invention; the institution of slavery happened so long ago; no one person benefited exclusively from slavery; those that did benefit were a minority of white Americans; the legal claimants of reparations have long since died and their descendants do not include all African Americans; the bill was paid through the American Civil War; and, finally, reparations would be divisive and not uplift those of African descent.[47] These arguments have led to a wave of publications by people from diverse academic backgrounds.[48]

While academics within higher education have been reviewing the case for reparations in the United States, their home institutions have also begun to examine their legacies of slavery. This started in 2003 when the president of Brown University, Ruth J. Simmons, appointed a steering committee of faculty, students, and administrators to study the institution's historical ties to the transatlantic slave trade.[49] The result was the *Report of the Brown University Steering Committee on Slavery and Justice*, which "detailed how several Brown founders and benefactors participated in, and benefited from, the slave trade. The report then concluded with a list of recommended actions that the University could take to confront its history."[50] This sparked a trend of similar examinations of institutions, and the states that housed them, into their ties to slavery and Jim Crow. Many multi-year commissions began to review the legacies of institutions with ties to slavery in higher education following the Slavery and the University Conference in 2011.[51] Inter-institutional research flourished after the establishment at the University of Virginia of the President's Commission on Slavery and the University. Besides undertaking a research project to understand the role of slavery in the creation and success of various universities, these institutions established the Universities Studying Slavery Consortium. The roster of this organisation includes institutions from the United States, Canada, Colombia, Scotland, Ireland, and England.[52] However, before 2014, none of these institutions had provided reparations. Many of these efforts seemed to be aimed at making these universities appear progressive in the public eye, as well as a recruitment tool for a growing multi-ethnic student population.

What forced many of these institutions into action was the increasing number of publicised deaths of unarmed people of colour and the 2014 *Atlantic* article "The Case for Reparations" by the African American journalist Ta-Nehisi Coates. In February 2012, a white neighbourhood vigilante, George Zimmerman, assaulted and killed Trayvon Martin, a young black man whom Zimmerman suspected of break-ins within his Florida housing community. Despite following and attacking Martin while having a police dispatcher on the line, Zimmerman claimed self-defence. Zimmerman was acquitted of this atrocity. There was widespread protest in reaction and the creation of the social media hashtag #BlackLivesMatter.[53] This hashtag led to the formation of the global organisation Black Lives Matter in 2013, to "eradicate white supremacy and build local power to intervene in violence inflicted on Black communities by the state and vigilantes".[54] The following year, Ta-Nehisi Coates published his article "The Case for Reparations", which made clear that the horrors of slavery persisted in continuing inequity, particularly in housing. All of this was a part of America's debt to those of African descent, Coates explained. He further argued that this was similar to someone running up "a credit-card bill and, having pledged to charge no more, [they] remain befuddled that the balance does not disappear ... [as the] interest accrues ... daily".[55] Coates's article spread like wildfire, leading institutions, including universities, as well as state and local governments to begin working towards tangible reparations for African American descendants of slavery.

These tangible reparations took two forms: symbolic and monetary. Symbolic reparations were usually made by creating memorials to formerly enslaved or modern prominent black citizens, or by removing memorials or the names of known Confederates and white supremacists from public spaces. The movement towards symbolic reparations coincided with the first wave of growing interest by students in exploring the legacies of slavery. The Unsung Founders Memorial, which commemorates people of colour who worked at the University of North Carolina, Chapel Hill, was a gift by the 2002 senior class. While it was not initially embraced by the institution, it was dedicated and unveiled in 2005 as a counter-memorial to Silent Sam, a monument to the Confederacy.[56] Similarly, Brown University in 2012 approved the creation by African American artist Martin Puryear of a "Slavery Memorial", which was installed in 2014.[57] The movement for symbolic reparations only grew following Ta-Nehisi Coates's article. This was evident at Georgetown University, which was one of the first institutions to remove the names of slave owners from campus buildings following its 2016 announcement of a memory project.[58] Likewise, in 2017 Yale University renamed its Calhoun College, which memorialised nineteenth-century politician John C. Calhoun of South Carolina,[59] who had steadfastly supported the institution of slavery and thereby helped lay the foundations of the American Civil War. The trend of renaming spaces or moving controversial monuments of historical actors on campuses has continued to grow. Typically, these problematic spaces have been changed, but influential donors and alumni have often tried to retard the process.

Say Their Names: The Contemporary Reparations Attempts in the US, 2014 to the Present

The call to move beyond symbolic reparations to monetary reparations has continued to increase as reports of deaths of African Americans at the hands of mostly white police officers have flooded the public sphere. Through social media, those that oppose reparations cannot hide behind the statement that inequality is a matter of history. It is a present issue. In 2014, a month after Coates's "The Case for Reparations" was published, New York police stopped a Caribbean-American man, Eric Garner, on suspicion of illegally selling cigarettes. The altercation ended when he was placed in an illegal chokehold and repeated that he could not breathe 11 times before dying. The incident was filmed and widely shared on social media.[60] A month later, the African American youth Michael Brown was killed by a white police officer who stopped him on suspicion of having stolen cigars in Ferguson, Missouri.[61] Both of these deaths led to protests and civil unrest, and Black Lives Matter continued to gain support for its campaign against police abuse. This only continued as the Covid-19 pandemic from early 2020 saw most people stay at home and glued to their television screens. Many were devastated by the tragic deaths of African American Breonna Taylor, killed during a mistaken police raid on her apartment, and of another African American, George Floyd, killed by a white police officer kneeling on his neck for over nine minutes. Both deaths sparked global outrage, especially after the video of Floyd's death was widely shared on social media.[62] These repeated offences against citizens of African descent in the United States have forced many institutions and individuals to recognise that there are devastating inequities in the society, for which monetary reparations are needed to bring about any hope of reconciliation.

Police brutality led the City of Chicago to sign into law approval for 57 victims of police torture to receive reparations in 2015. The allotted budget, earmarked as reparations, was $5.5 million and took the form of cash payments, free college tuition, and a "range of social services" accompanied by an apology.[63] Likewise, Georgetown University rolled out its own version of monetary reparations by providing tuition as reparation for the descendants of the 272 enslaved individuals sold by the Jesuits in 1838 to keep the university afloat. The student body, however, believed that free tuition was not enough, and voted in 2019 to create a reparations fund. This was accomplished by adding $27.20 to each student's tuition fees to be given to the 4,000 known descendants of the 272 enslaved. It should be noted that this student-led effort has been held up by an administration that claims it will instead raise funds through benefactors and other campaigns but has left the cause to wither within administrative committees. The current most impactful programme for monetary reparations can be found in the efforts of Virginia Theological Seminary, which in 2019 announced a programme to provide direct cash payments to the descendants of campus enslaved and workers from the Jim Crow era from a $1.7 million fund. The programme also offers free tuition, and has sought to build relationships with descendants as well as community stakeholders.[64]

Religious organisations, while initially having a head start in apologising for their connections to the institution of slavery, have only recently joined the reparations movement. This was a result of the legacies of slavery appearing on their parishioners' social media feeds and their use of their moral authority to activate their more conservative congregants. These faith-based organisations have taken their cue from Christian institutions of higher education such as the Jesuits at Georgetown University, the Presbyterians at Princeton Theological Seminary (who created a $27 million reparations fund in 2019), and the Episcopalians at Virginia Theological Seminary.[65] Over the last few years, funds have been set aside for reparations programmes in several dioceses of the Episcopal Church, including New York ($1.1 million), Texas ($13 million), Maryland ($1 million), and Virginia ($10 million).[66] Discussion of restitution was the focus of the 2022 General Convention of the Episcopal Church, but no definitive announcement of a reparations programme has been made.[67] However, the format could be similar to that of the Jesuit Conference of Priests, which pledged in 2021 to raise $100 million for the descendants of enslaved people. The worldwide Catholic Church seems to be gearing up to assist in global reparations, as the Vatican hosted several American activists at a five-day conference for reparations in July 2022.[68]

Beginning in 2019, certain states, cities, and towns began to provide what they call "monetary reparations". The majority of these "reparations programmes" did not include direct cash payouts, but investments in the black community and equal housing initiatives. The first was the City Council of Evanston, Illinois, which voted in 2019 to use the first $10 million of tax revenue from the sale of recreational marijuana to create a restorative housing programme for people of African descent. In 2021, the first payouts from this programme of $25,000 were sent to Evanston community stakeholders.[69] In Asheville, North Carolina, a programme was approved to provide reparations through investing in black businesses and communities.[70] Likewise, Amherst,

Massachusetts, has set aside $210,000 for a reparations fund, but it still needs to create as well as implement a reparations plan.[71] Owing to the difficult subject matter, commissions usually take two to three years to complete these plans and present them to their local governing bodies.

Two examples of this kind of commission are the Task Force to Study and Develop Reparation Proposals for African Americans for the state of California and San Francisco's African American Reparations Advisory Council. These are different from their predecessors because they include direct cash payouts within their proposed reparations plans. The Task Force, the first committee sponsored by a state government in the United States, submitted its final plan, entitled "The California Reparations Report", on 29 June 2023.[72] The report includes recommendations for the state of California to issue a formal apology, provide compensation and restitution for multiple harms to African American residents, and implement policies that address former and current racial injustices. Monetary compensation is calculated on the basis of the lived experiences of qualifying African American Californians, but the maximum amount of reparations was estimated by the committee to be a $1.2 million down payment per person.[73] The final report recommends a "substantial initial down payment" to be decided by the state legislature after "further data collection and research".[74] The city of San Francisco's African American Reparations Advisory Council released a 398-page plan, shortly after the California Task Force, on 7 July 2023. Its hope is that its recommendations will serve as a template for other municipalities to follow, involving a formal apology from the city and its agencies, multiple economic empowerment initiatives to close the racial wealth gap, and other initiatives in education, health, and civic policy. San Francisco's Reparations Advisory Council was in advance of its colleagues at the state level and suggested an initial $5 million "lump sum payment" to the qualified black population of San Franciscans "for the decades of harms that they have experienced", including "economic and opportunity losses" as well as "intentional decisions and unintended harms" by the city of San Francisco.[75] While the state of California and the city of San Francisco are at the forefront of the movement for monetary reparations at the local level, other American cities and states are moving more slowly as they work on reparations programme that will meet the needs of their constituents.[76] Still other local governing bodies that support the cause believe that the responsibility of reparations lies not at the city or the state level, but that of the Federal Government, and have passed resolutions that call on these bodies to intervene and provide monetary reparations for its citizens.[77]

Concluding Reflections

As of the time of writing, there is no plan by the US government to provide reparations. While H.R. 40 has been approved by a House Judiciary Committee and has been advanced, there has not yet been a vote in the chamber. H.R. 40 was reintroduced to the House of Representatives by the late Sheila Jackson Lee in January 2023, but it remains in limbo.[78] The reasons for this can be found in the Judiciary Committee hearings on reparations that occurred on 19 July 2019. On the holiday that celebrates the end of slavery in the United States following the enforcement of the Emancipation Proclamation in Texas by Major General Gordon Granger, those that supported reparations brought in experts and activists who contributed to nuanced discussions, supported by the latest data on the wealth gap between white and black Americans. However, they were rebuked by lawmakers who opposed reparations, reciting the arguments of David Horowitz that slavery was a matter of the past; that those that benefited from slavery were only a few; that reparations would be divisive; and that slavery and Jim Crow had been overcome as a result of the Civil War and the Civil Rights Movement. These lawmakers also added the racist comment that reparations would be just another government handout to the black community.[79] After the Donald Trump presidency (2016–2020), politicians who continue to oppose reparations use the Horowitz playbook, dismissing reparations as part of "woke" politics to garner support in more conservative regions of the United States.[80] The politicising of reparations and the refusal to acknowledge the moral, social, and historical obligations of the Federal Government only help delay what can be accomplished by the United States Congress.

There has been much momentum in America within the four periods of the reparations movement, which began with Belinda Sutton's 1783 suit against her enslaver. As fierce debates over reparations continue, the path for their implementation within the US seems clear. As with compensation provided to enslavers in exchange for emancipation in the United States (see Kerr-Ritchie and Broyld in this volume), Britain (see Small, and Frith and Xosei), and France (see Aragón Falomir), the lead needs to come from the US Federal Government. The frustration that many groups and institutions have expressed about the inaction of the US government is palpable. It is for this reason that many cities and states, colleges and universities, and faith-based organisations have attempted to begin their own reparations programmes, whether symbolic or monetary. However, these efforts can only represent attempts to absolve individual guilt and serve as another unfilled promise to descendants of the enslaved and those who suffered under Jim Crow. As history has shown, slavery and its legacies are part of a collective national guilt. While current organisational movements for reparations are important to keep the debate alive within the public discourse, if the United States wants to achieve any sort of reconciliation for its "original sin", restitution is the answer.

26

The Struggle for Reparations in Britain

Nicola Frith and Esther Xosei

THE STRUGGLE FOR REPARATIONS and reparative and transitional justice for the trafficking, enslavement, and colonisation of African peoples – with all their attendant legacies of national and racial oppression – has a long and varied history that dates from the beginnings of chattel enslavement itself. In this chapter, we will focus on the history of grassroots activism in Britain, showing it to be a struggle that dates back to the eighteenth century. While acknowledging the longevity of this unmet claim, our contribution will concentrate primarily on the important groundwork undertaken by reparations activists following the 1993 Abuja Declaration (see Adebajo in this volume). This will cover the years that led up to the 2007 bicentenary of the Abolition of the Slave Trade Act of 1807 and beyond, into contemporary calls for reparations.

We examine some of the longer-term goals of this activism, including the importance of self-determination and the creation of an All-Party Parliamentary Commission of Inquiry for Truth and Reparatory Justice. We will also highlight the centrality of "Planet Repairs" to reparations campaigns, and its links to Extinction Rebellion, a movement that began in 2018 and exists in over 60 countries,[1] and most recently to the Green Party of England and Wales (GPEW). The term "Planet Repairs" refers to the need to proceed from a standpoint of pluriversality that highlights the nexus between reparatory, environmental, and cognitive justice in articulating the need to repair holistically the relationship of humans with the earth, the environment, and the pluriverse. This means giving due recognition to indigenous knowledges in contrast with Western-centric Enlightenment ideals that separated humanity from nature and devalorised indigenous systems of knowledge in order to justify exploitation for capital accumulation.

Our aim in this chapter is not just to showcase the different strategies and ideologies that have been adopted, used, and transformed by British-based activists, but also to identify and address two key concerns. First, the legalistic concept of reparation often tends to be misunderstood as monetary compensation to individual claimants; and, second, the central role played by grassroots activism is frequently overlooked in the production of historical and conceptual knowledge about reparations. To challenge these misunderstandings and oversights, we will foreground the concept of "holistic repairs", which is central to reparations activists and practitioners, by exploring some of the most pioneering ideas that have emerged from the British-based reparations movement. This exploration will note their persistent commitment to Pan-Africanism, internationalist solidarity, intergenerational knowledge transfer, and intersectionality.[2] For Britain is and always has been "a vibrant site of successive waves of resurgence of the reparatory justice endeavours of Black peoples from various parts of the continent and diaspora of Africa".[3]

Forgetting Enslavement, Remembering Abolition

Before we look in further detail at this history of reparations activism, it is worth sketching Britain's role in the enslavement of African peoples. It is well documented that Britain played a leading role in the transoceanic trafficking of enslaved Africans and its system of chattel enslavement. British involvement began in 1562 with the voyages of the cousins and enslavers John Hawkins and Francis Drake, and ended officially with the 1833 Slavery Abolition Act. According to statistics based on the surviving archives, Britain was responsible for outfitting the second highest number of voyages conducted by European powers (30.9 per cent) and for capturing and enslaving the second-highest number of Africans (3,259,900 people), after the Portuguese (see Cobley, Brereton, Silva Jr, Sousa, and Ramirez in this volume).

In the interceding years, Britain accrued wealth vast enough to fund its own industrial revolution and develop the modern system of capitalism that survives today.[4] As the Barbadian historian and scholar Hilary Beckles writes, the West Indies was the base from which "the British exported the financially successful model of African enslavement to the rest of its colonized world", making "global the ideas and methods that were critical to colonial modes of capital accumulation".[5] And yet the practice of enslavement remained illegal, in principle rather than in practice, on Britain's shores.[6]

Although the 1833 Abolition Act ended this illegal system of enslavement, it did not end the system of capitalism and all its associated harms. Britain both continued to profit from enslaved labour, for example by importing countless tonnes of raw cotton produced by the enslaved populations of America, and created "new" names and rules for human exploitation, such as the forced apprenticeship system and indentured labour.[7]

Four years after the Abolition Act, the 1837 Slave Compensation Act led to the enslavers receiving £20 million (approximately £2.4 billion in today's money) as compensation for the loss of their "property". Equivalent to around 40 per cent of the British Treasury's annual income at the time, this represents a bond debt that British taxpayers only fully repaid to their creditors in 2015.[8] As the British scholar Marcus Wood notes, the payment of this compensation not only put "a very precise economic value on human life and human freedom", but also created a "paradoxical phenomenon" by perverting the logic of the "gift-exchange nexus".[9] The implied "contract" cut the proper recipients – the formerly enslaved populations – out of the equation. Instead, "the powerful gave to the powerful": what was bought "was an infinite sense of British moral superiority" that simultaneously required the formerly enslaved to "remain forever in the British people's debt".[10]

The facts of this perverse compensation can be more fully explored by looking at the remarkable database of records of the Slave Compensation Commission produced by University College London.[11] It dispels the myth that the ownership of enslaved persons was limited to a small, wealthy elite by revealing how widespread it was among the British middle classes. These "bit players", as the Nigerian-British scholar David Olusoga calls them, "were home county vicars, iron manufacturers from the Midlands and lots and lots of widows" who owned no land in the Caribbean but "rented their slaves out to landowners, in work gangs".[12]

Facts such as these were carefully avoided throughout the 2007 commemoration in which, as Hilary Beckles notes, every "effort was made to divert attention from the truth and legal implications of British slavery".[13] The official commemoration itself represented little more than a "Wilberfest" (after the slavery abolitionist William Wilberforce) by focusing predominantly on Britain's anti-slavery heritage.[14] Activists had long campaigned for the

2007 bicentenary to go much further. For example, in 2004, Rendezvous of Victory (ROV) – an initiative aimed at educating people about the history and legacies of African enslavement as well as reparations – called for "the Queen to issue a formal apology on behalf of Britain in 2007".[15] As ROV's joint coordinator, the Ghanaian Pan-Afrikanist Kofi Mawuli Klu, stated, this needed to be "an apology of substance, accompanied by educational and other reforms". He called for "a change in the rules that govern the global economy to bring about a different global order", noting that "the true prize is self-determination, and the African diaspora integrated into a global system where they can have self-identity".[16]

Despite pressure from activists, the bicentenary did not result in an apology from the Queen or from Prime Minister Tony Blair, who offered only a statement of regret.[17] However, the commemoration did result in the inauguration of key cultural and educational sites, not least of which is Liverpool's International Slavery Museum. Overall, the official events served to obscure less palatable truths, such as the fact that the Act that "Wilberforce worked so hard to pass did nothing to end the system of British slavery", since slavery "was not abolished until 1834 and was followed by a three-year 'apprenticeship', which was essentially an extension of enslavement".[18]

For the Jamaican-British scholar Kehinde Andrews, this process of deliberate forgetting is part of a broader "psychosis of Whiteness" that constantly serves to distance Britain from "the horrors of African enslavement".[19] The myth works by imagining that "slavery happened elsewhere and is not part of Britain's legacy, whose role in slavery was to abolish it".[20] This abolitionist mythology serves multiple functions. It not only denies the existence of ongoing damage, but also defers Britain's responsibility. Championing the success of British abolitionism, therefore, becomes a useful political tool for rejecting the rationale underpinning calls for reparative justice.

Conceptualising the British–Based Reparations Movement

In recent years, media attention has been drawn towards calls for the British government to engage with reparations through the Caricom (the Caribbean Community) Reparations Commission's ten-point programme of reparative justice (see Beckles in this volume).[21] However, the media's focus on Caricom downplays the existence of a long-standing grassroots, British-based reparations movement. This oversight, in turn, points to a key issue that this chapter wishes to address: the failure of scholarship properly to acknowledge the important work of British-based activists within the International Social Movement for Afrikan Reparations (ISMAR). We can see this as part of a more general process of power inherent in the production of knowledge and historiography. As the Haitian scholar Michel-Rolph Trouillot has argued, history produces "truths", while at the same time silencing unwanted or unimaginable alternatives to hegemonic narratives.[22] The history of Britain's ISMAR might be viewed as one such alternative whose exclusion obscures the diversity of histories, narratives, and spatial geographies that are at play in these debates.

Within Britain, reparations campaigns have been led by community activists, movements, and networks, most recently involving the Pan-Afrikan Reparations Coalition in Europe (PARCOE), the Stop the Maangamizi: We Charge Genocide/Ecocide Campaign, the Global Afrikan People's Parliament (GAPP), the Afrikan Emancipation Day Reparations March Committee, and the International Network of Scholars and Activists for Afrikan Reparations (INOSAAR). These movements are not just interconnected within Britain, but also look to leadership from Africa. For example, the Maatubuntumitawo-Global Afrikan Family Reunion International Council (GAFRIC) is an organisation that promotes indigenous African community leadership and seeks to secure African sovereignty through the reunification of the Global African Family. It is a structure that enables Africans living in the diaspora to reconnect with those on the continent through a process of "rematriation". The emphasis here is not just on the physical return to Africa (as in repatriation), but on engaging in spiritual and cultural forms of reconnection that offer an alternative path to the reclamation of African indigeneity and citizenship.[23]

It is also important to acknowledge that these groups are following a reparations path that has been charted by their predecessors. As will be shown in more detail below, this long history is defined by its ongoing commitment to Pan-African internationalisation, intergenerational knowledge transfer, and intersectionality. The different constituents that make up this movement are part of what is termed the International Social Movement for Afrikan Reparations and the People's Reparations International Movement (PRIM). These are struggles that are interwoven with the histories of African-led resistance to enslavement in both the former colonies and on the African continent. It should be noted, however, that despite this longevity and lobbying from both internal and external parties, the British government has yet to take concrete steps to engage with any reparative justice process.

To begin with, we must see the struggle for reparation, reparative justice, and other forms of transitional justice as being intimately connected to the long history of Pan-Africanism and the struggle for black liberation.[24] While many people view Pan-Africanism as a counter-response to European colonialism, we see it here as part of the initiatives taken by African people in recognising and charting their own developmental needs.[25] There are both earlier forms of Pan-Africanism that emerged on the African continent and across its diaspora, which called for unity and liberation as a result of transatlantic enslavement, and later forms that were part of the anti-colonial struggle. As Kofi Mawuli Klu states, Pan-Africanism represents "an anti-imperialist decolonisational movement rallying together a broad array of All-Africa-loving forces".[26] It operates locally and globally in pursuit of an "independent, worldwide, politico-ideological, cultural, and organisational framework of Struggle for the total liberation, unification and self-determined progression of Africans and their kith and kin worldwide".[27] As such, Pan-Africanism represents the epistemological and ideological framework in which reparations are set (see Introduction in this volume).

One of the earliest known attempts to find alternatives to the system of African enslavement is the 1726 letter written by the Dahomean De (traditional king) Fiaga Agaja Trudo Audati, addressed to King George I. The letter did not reach England until 1731, by which time George II was on the throne. It was delivered by a specially designated Dahomey ambassador named Adomo Tomo, as well as by a British merchant and former employee of the Royal African Company, Bulfinch Lambe. The original letter demanded an end to chattel enslavement and trafficking, and its repair through an alternative "Scheme of Trade" by means of setting up "local plantation agriculture" within Ouidah, one of the foremost Atlantic ports through which enslaved Africans were trafficked, situated in the former kingdom of Dahomey (modern Benin) in West Africa.[28] According to an account written at the time of the letter, this scheme would not only ensure that captives were no longer "carried off" and enslaved, but was also deemed to be "quite foreign to the former Slave Trade".[29] The desire to find an alternative represents an important historical initiative taken in Africa and addressed to the British monarch by a key abolitionist and freedom-fighting leader.

In Britain, the earliest known examples of calls for reparation can be traced to the Sons of Africa, including one of its key protagonists, Attobah Kwodjo Enu aka Ottobah Cugoano. Ottobah Cugoano was an enslaved African originally from the Fante village of Ajumako in present-day Ghana. The Sons of Africa movement was started in London in 1797 by Ottobah Cugoano and the Nigerian writer Olaudah Equiano as a "political group led by African abolitionists who campaigned to end slavery".[30] But these men were not just abolitionists; they were also reparationists. With Equiano's help, Cugoano published a book entitled *Thoughts and Sentiments on the Evil and Wicked Traffic of the Slavery and Commerce of the Human Species* (1787).[31] In the postscript to the 1791 version, Cugoano raises "the issue of 'adequate reparation' and 'restitution for the injuries' enslaved persons received", making him the first published African author in English to denounce the so-called trade and "to pronounce the African human right to resistance against enslavement, as well as to advocate in writing the demand for reparations including restitution".[32]

By the beginning of the twentieth century, shared grievances among colonised and oppressed peoples led to the establishment of the first transnational efforts to unite diasporic and continental Africans through the Pan-African Conferences. These were held in 1900 (London), 1921 (London, Paris, and Brussels), 1923 (London and Lisbon), 1927 (New York) and, most importantly, 1945 (Manchester) (see Introduction in this volume). These events – especially the one in Manchester – consolidated a growing Pan-African social movement out of which more recent movements for reparations emerged both globally and in Britain.[33]

Importantly, the current British movements both acknowledge this previous work and build transgenerationally from the knowledge and solidarity that it generated. The First International Conference on Reparations, held in Lagos in December 1990, resulted in the creation of the Group of Eminent Persons (GEP), set up by the Organisation of African Unity (OAU). Its remit was "to pursue the goal of reparations to Africa", with precedents being offered by the "reparations to Jews for the Holocaust, and the movement in the United States for reparations to African-Americans".[34] In 1993, a second conference was held in Abuja, sponsored by the GEP, which led to the issuing of the Abuja Proclamation. This conference and the resulting proclamation represent the first transnational effort to call "upon the international community to recognize that there is a unique and unprecedented moral debt owed to the Afrikan peoples which has yet to be paid".[35] Its lasting significance lies in its having established "the legitimacy of a transnational movement for reparations" (see Adebajo in this volume).[36]

In response, other groups were formed at a national level. In Britain, the African Reparations Movement (ARM) was created in 1993, led by the late Guyanese-born British MP Bernie Grant. His early-day motion called attention to the Abuja Proclamation (he attended the 1993 OAU Reparations Conference at which this was agreed), and was signed by 46 Labour MPs.[37] Its objectives – set out in the Birmingham Declaration of 1993 – were to "support the movement for reparations and join forces with a view to forming a strong united front capable of exposing, confronting and overcoming the psychological, economic and cultural harm inflicted upon us by peoples of European origin".[38] The ARM succeeded in organising a series of awareness-raising events about reparations and demanded the return of stolen African artefacts from the British government, but its operations ceased in April 2000 with the death of its founder, Bernie Grant (see Small in this volume).[39]

The work of ARM laid the groundwork for the emergence of new reparations organisations such as the Afrikan Liberation Support Campaign (ALISC), the Pan-Afrikan Grassroots Educational Network (PAGEN), the Afrikan United Action Front, and the Black Quest for Justice Campaign. However, it was the Pan-Afrikan Reparations Coalition in Europe (PARCOE), formed in 2001 and spearheaded by Caribbean-British scholar-activist Esther Xosei and Kofi Mawuli Klu, that became the dominant structure which sought to carry on the legacy of the ARM. Over the course of its lifetime, PARCOE has been at the forefront of developing multiple reparative initiatives that are both British-based and internationally focused. Their approach is encapsulated in the idea of "Sankofa". As an Adinkra symbol, Sankofa is often depicted as a bird with its head turned backwards, reaching for the egg that it carries on its back. This symbolises the importance of taking the best from the past and bringing it into the present in order to inform positive progress towards the future. For the British contingent of the International Social Movement for Afrikan Reparations, this means acknowledging the learnings of previous struggles to inform the continuation of the struggle.

Complementing these internationalist and intergenerational approaches is the centrality of intersectionality and cognitive justice, or the equity of all knowledges. For members of Britain's International Social Movement for Afrikan Reparations, the scope of reparation is never narrowly defined and is always informed by the need for holistic repair, as outlined by the United Nations' "Basic Principles and Guidelines on a Right to Remedy and Reparation".[40] Indeed, the need for a holistic and intersectional approach – one that understands how the interconnections between race, class, and gender create overlapping and interdependent forms of discrimination which need repair – arises directly from the multidimensional nature and longevity of the harm inflicted. A multifaceted approach is therefore required, which cannot simply be reduced to economic compensation or a "paycheque".[41]

Among some British reparations activists, the word used to define this harm is Maangamizi. This is a Kiswahili term that refers to the Holocaust of chattel, colonial, and neo-colonial forms of enslavement. As the African American scholar Maulana Karenga notes, it is derived from the verb *angamiza*, which means to cause destruction, to destroy utterly, and thus carries with it a sense of intentionality. The prefix "a" suggests an amplified destruction and thus speaks to the enormity of these crimes against humanity.[42] In response, reparations are not just concerned with crimes committed in the past. Rather, they are needed to address the continuing persistence of harm that links chattel enslavement, colonialism, and neo-colonialism, including the devastating effects that this historical exploitation has had on planet Earth. The call to "Stop the Maangamizi" is therefore one that seeks to recognise the origins of these crimes, link them to contemporary manifestations, and find practical solutions.

Envisioning this repair means imagining a new equitable, multipolar, and pluriversal world order which the Pan-Afrikan Reparations Coalition in Europe refers to as Ubuntudunia.[43] In this new world order, African peoples will no longer be subject to dehumanisation, Afrophobia, and discrimination within white supremacist structures. The use of the term "white supremacy" here does not simply refer to the extremist belief in the superiority of "white" people, but its structures are understood – in critical race theory – as contributing to a social system in which people racialised as white continue to enjoy structural advantages and privileges over other ethnicities despite the existence of formal legal equality. In response, systemic global change is required to redistribute ill-gotten wealth and resources, as well as cultural capital, and end extractivism by placing the need for Planet Repairs at the very heart of the reparative process. The restoration of African sovereignty is also required to address the destructive effects that chattel enslavement, colonisation, and recolonisation have had on African people. For PARCOE, this means creating a Pan-African Government of People's Power, known as Maatubuntumandla. This government aims to act as the sovereign authority over a Pan-African Union of Communities, which will ultimately integrate African people of the continent and in the diaspora in their own polity of Maatubuntuman as a global superpower.[44] This Pan-Africanist, internationalist, transgenerational, and intersectional vision is what guides the British contingent of the International Social Movement for Afrikan Reparations.

Key Actions towards Reparations

Having outlined the conceptual thinking and future visioning that underpins the reparations movement in Britain, we turn to the key actions that have moved the reparations agenda forward in recent years. The years 2004–2007 mark a key period within this history. At the start, 2004 saw the bicentenary of the Haitian Revolution, which coincided with the UN General Assembly's call to recognise 2004 as the International Year to Commemorate the Struggle against Slavery and its Abolition. The year 2007 was the bicentenary of the Abolition of the Slave Trade Act in Britain. These anniversaries provided a window of opportunity for reparations activists to collaborate strategically with institutional players by ensuring that reparations were an important part of the commemorations.

In the build-up to this period, PARCOE set about advancing the Pan-African radical tradition that had previously influenced the African Reparations Movement by charting a strategic organisational direction for the International Social Movement for Afrikan Reparations. For example, from 2004 to 2007, these groups led the conceptualisation and organisation of an educational initiative called "Rendezvous of Victory", named after the poem by Martinique's Aimé Césaire. This included conducting a series of cross-community forums in association with Anti-Slavery International and the World Development Movement (now called Global Justice Now). These events brought different stakeholders into dialogue around themes related to slavery and reparations. They included state and non-state actors, people from diverse heritage communities, representatives from educational institutions, museums, galleries, and archives, and researchers and historians invested in the history and memory of chattel enslavement. As educational initiatives, they aimed to assist discussions and alliance-building on issues arising from the legacies of African enslavement, such as awareness of the continuation of harms (Maangamizi), Afrophobia, reparations, ongoing global injustices, and contemporary forms of enslavement.[45]

Rendezvous of Victory also collaborated with the Greenwich Maritime Museum to commemorate the Haitian Revolution and worked as advisors to Anti-Slavery International on UNESCO's Associated Schools Project, for which it created educational materials.[46] On the initiative of PARCOE, driven by the International Social Movement for Afrikan Reparations, Rendezvous of Victory succeeded in opening dialogue with the British government through the Home Office Minister for Race and Communities, Fiona Mactaggart. This resulted in the 2004 Bicentenary Programme to commemorate 23 August as the UN International Day for the Remembrance of the Slave Trade and its Abolition. The programme, launched by Fiona Mactaggart and organised in association with Anti-Slavery International, was entitled "Commemorations 2004–2007: Time to Resolve the Big Question of Reparations".[47] It included a debate in the House of Commons in October 2004, during Britain's Black History Month, "to demonstrate Britain's support for the United Nations international year to commemorate the struggle against slavery and its abolition".[48]

In parallel with these commemorative initiatives, British reparationists from one of the co-founding groups of PARCOE, the Forum of Africans and African Descendants Against Racism (FAADAR), were also involved in planning the Barbados Conference in October 2002. This was a follow-up to the 2001 Durban UN World Conference Against Racism, Racial Discrimination, Xenophobia and Related Intolerance (see Introduction in this volume), and led to agreement that "reparationists in key centres connected with the enslavement of African people would target European nations for legal action in pursuit of reparations".[49] In Britain, this inspired the Black Quest for Justice Campaign, which initiated a "Pan-African legal challenge to British justice" by "taking steps of class action in law to secure their right to reparations".[50] To do this, the Black Quest for Justice Campaign, with PARCOE, the former Black United Front, Global Afrikan Congress United Kingdom, and the US-initiated International Front for African Reparations (IFAR) called on Britain's Attorney General, Lord Goldsmith, "to trigger the power to investigate and prosecute the appropriate persons associated with the 'British Crown, its agencies and corporations' under the 2001 International Criminal Court Act".[51] The grounds for this were that the British Crown continues "to perpetrate crimes against humanity from the era of chattel enslavement through colonialism to the present era of neo-colonialism against Africa and people of African descent worldwide".[52]

While the lawsuit was not successful, it articulated the "legal case for Africans as a Pan-African case", as opposed to "arguing that reparations should be for Black people in Britain in isolation from the wider case that people of African heritage have been making for centuries".[53] This provides a clear example of the international focus of the British-based reparations movements, which at the same time tested the capacity of the country's legal system for dealing with crimes against humanity, and found it wanting. In the end, the Black Quest for Justice case could not be carried any further because it came up against the stipulation in British law that the monarch is considered sovereign for legal purposes and, as such, is immune to prosecution as head of the British state.[54] So, as Kofi Mawuli Klu argues, "the only use of law, including international law, that will meaningfully serve the cause of our African struggle for Reparations is that which conceptualises and effects *Law as Resistance*".[55] This means utilising the stipulations within existing law to fight for justice in such a way that will enable people to break those unjust stipulations and operations, and thereby advance towards new framings and operations of law that will deliver more substantive justice.

Linked to this legal case has been the push to create an All-Party Parliamentary Commission of Inquiry for Truth and Reparatory Justice.[56] Over the past four decades, there have been as many as a hundred truth commission bodies in over 40 countries as a response to historical and contemporary injustices.[57] The proposal to create a commission of inquiry linked to African enslavement in Britain emerged from the campaigning efforts of what is now termed the Stop the Maangamizi campaign and its associated petition, which has been steadily building support since the early 2000s.[58] This was modelled on the original "We Charge Genocide Petition" of 1951, which was repopularised by the Black United Front in the United States. The call for this commission was formulated first in 2003 as the "We Charge Genocide Petition", then in 2014 as the "We Charge Genocide/Ecocide Petition", and finally in 2015 as the "Stop the Maangamizi: We Charge Genocide/Ecocide Petition". The movement thereby built on the American framing of the reparations case in the language of genocide through the key addition of the words "Maangamizi" and "ecocide". PARCOE took this petition to the British Black United Front from 2002 to 2007, and subsequently the Interim National Afrikan Peoples Parliament (2012–2015). Since 2015, the associated petition has been submitted to the British Houses of Parliament every 1 August as part of the Afrikan Emancipation Day Reparations March.[59]

The proposed All–Party Parliamentary Commission is envisaged as having truth commission functions, while also acting as a specialised form of public inquiry. Its purposes are twofold. First, it will inform the public of the nature of colonialism and slavery, as well as its long-term consequences, including present-day impacts upon both individuals and communities. Second, the commission will act as a suitable forum for a conversation in which different constituencies and communities of reparatory justice interest can all be heard.

Primarily, it will allow affected communities and individuals to voice their own self-determined solutions and identify their participation in any reparatory process going forward.

There are now signs that this campaign is gaining ground. In July 2020, London's Lambeth Council – home to the largest Afro-Caribbean population in Britain – became the first local authority to pass a successful motion calling for the commission, shortly followed by Islington and then Bristol in March 2021.[60] Building on this success, on 11 October 2020 the Green Party, working in collaboration with PARCOE and INOSAAR, became the first major national party in Britain to commit to seeking reparatory justice for African enslavement. Members voted by a 94 per cent majority in favour, which means that reparations are now enshrined in Green Party policy. This commits elected Green Party councillors and MPs to campaign for the motion at local council level and lobby at national government level.

In the meantime, a proposal to create an All-Party Parliamentary Group on African Reparations (APPGAR) was put forward by the Stop the Maangamizi campaign.[61] It resulted in the historic launching of Britain's first ever All-Party Parliamentary Group on African Reparations in the British Houses of Parliament in October 2021. This represents a continuation of the work of Bernie Grant, and was chaired by Streatham's Labour MP, Bell Ribeiro-Addy, with Marsha de Cordova (Labour MP for Battersea) and Caroline Lucas (Green Party MP for Brighton) as vice-chairs, and Peter Bottomley (Conservative MP for Worthing West) as assistant secretary.[62]

A key part of the success of these campaigns has been the drive of activists to contest narrow definitions of reparation and demonstrate how reparative justice for the crimes of slavery, colonialism, and neo-colonialism has real meaning for multiple constituencies. Often this means bringing into dialogue movements and peoples that are perceived as separate or even antagonistic. For example, Hilary Beckles has noted the attempt to push the global reparations movement aside in favour of the climate change agenda in order to create separate and competing movements.[63] To counter this in Britain, PARCOE and the Stop the Maangamizi: We Charge Genocide/Ecocide campaigns have been working with environmentalists – notably Extinction Rebellion – to create the Extinction Rebellion Internationalist Solidarity Network (XRISN) in 2018.[64]

The significance of these dialogues and their resultant joint-action programmes with Extinction Rebellion and the Green Party is that they are driven by African heritage community formations. This work does not limit itself to a British base, but is always seeking to broaden the dialogue and action by linking with a wide range of indigenous African and other majority world communities of resistance. Key examples of a global Pan-African, internationalist network in Africa are the Maatubuntumitawo-Global Afrikan Family Reunion International Council and the VAZOBA Afrikan and Friends Networking Open Forum. Guided by PARCOE, these formations are now working with XRISN through the XR Affinity All-Afrikan Network (XRAAAN).

To bring these different constituents together within and across national borders has meant placing the concept of Planet Repairs at the centre of the dialogue between environmentalists and reparationists. Planet Repairs is a cognitive justice concept that enables members to participate in the conversation on an equal footing. It has meant developing a shared understanding that the people, societies, and nations affected by the legacies of enslavement and colonialism are the very same people, societies, and nations bearing the brunt of the global climate and ecological emergency. Indeed, the genocide and ecocide started as part of the Maangamizi hundreds of years ago.[65]

Concluding Reflections

From these selected examples, we can see that there are number of key strengths to the British-based International Social Movement for Afrikan Reparations. First, reparations are not narrowly defined by legacy issues that impact only on people within the borders of the British Isles. Unlike movements that have tended to focus on the case of African people within national borders, this movement has always articulated a reparations case for *all* people of African ancestry and heritage, wherever they may live. It has done this by connecting internationally, while building on and adapting the work of predecessors, such as expanding the "reparations as genocide" concept to include ecocide.

Second, the movement has links to the grassroots. Building from the bottom up and anchoring within African heritage communities has proved to be a far more enduring and successful approach than top-down, state-led initiatives such as the Group of Eminent Persons, which resulted in the collapse of the African Reparations Movement.

Third, British-based reparations activists are able to address tensions through dialogue and find points of agreement between different stakeholders, while promoting an intersectional and holistic approach to reparations. Importantly, the process of bringing together these different constituents requires engaging with, and educating others about, cognitive justice concepts like Planet Repairs, as well as rematriation – or the cultural and spiritual return to African indigeneity that underpins any physical return to the African continent – and the building of Maatubuntuman in Ubuntudunia.

There is no doubt that PARCOE has been at the forefront of initiating these kinds of multifaced engagements with a wide diversity of forces, thus creating initiatives that have made possible a broadening of dialogues and the creation of joint-action programmes. It is only by bringing these different constituents into conversation with each other that the cause of Pan-African reparations has become one, galvanising not only the International Social Movement for Afrikan Reparations and the People's Reparations International Movement, but also change-making forces far beyond movements for reparatory justice. It is in this sense that the idea of building Maatubuntuman in Ubuntudunia is becoming a material force that is gripping many beyond African heritage communities across the world.

27

The Struggle for Reparations in Africa

Adekeye Adebajo

ONLY 13 KILOMETRES SEPARATE Africa from Europe across the Strait of Gibraltar. That proximity has, however, not historically yielded a policy of "good neighbourliness" but rather four and a half centuries of European exploitation of Africa through slavery and imperialism. This chapter argues that Pan-Africanism was the ideology of primary resistance used in fighting these twin scourges. The concept can be defined simply as the efforts to promote the political, socio-economic, and cultural unity; emancipation; and self-reliance of Africa and its diaspora in the Americas, the Caribbean, and Europe. Pan-Africanists in the Caribbean and the Americas felt physically and culturally dispossessed by slavery, while those on the continent felt economically and mentally dislocated through colonialism.[1]

Both groups were therefore seeking to affirm their sense of self-worth and dignity by resisting European slavery and imperialism, and restoring Africa to itself. Reparations have a long history of struggle, from the eighteenth century, when early Pan-Africanists in the diaspora demanded restitution for European slavery and imperialism (see Introduction in this volume). More contemporary struggles in Africa have, curiously, not enjoyed much public and civil society attention or spawned as many grassroots movements in the post-colonial era as would have been expected. However, this issue has, more recently in the post-Cold War era, seen inter-governmental efforts such as the Abuja Proclamation of 1993, the Accra Declaration of 1999, the Durban Declaration of 2001, and the Accra Proclamation of 2023: efforts which this chapter will examine in detail.

I will also assess the thinking of leading African intellectuals such as Nigeria's Jacob Ade Ajayi and Wole Soyinka, Kenya's Ali Mazrui, and South Africa's Thabo Mbeki on the issue of reparations. The chapter then examines contemporary initiatives by African and Caribbean actors – led on behalf of the African Union (AU) by Ghanaian president Nana Akufo-Addo, and engaging leaders of the Caribbean Community (Caricom) – to coordinate efforts more closely in the global struggle for reparations. These initiatives and ideas have sought to respond to four and a half centuries of European slavery and imperial rule which have left Africa geographically divided, economically fragmented, and militarily vulnerable to external intervention.[2]

Restitution and Reparations: A Tale of Four African Prophets

Four African prophets have been at the forefront of intellectual thinking and activist struggles for reparations to heal the damaging impacts of European slavery and imperialism in Africa: Nigerian historian Ade Ajayi, Kenyan political scientist Ali Mazrui, Nigerian Nobel literature laureate Wole Soyinka, and former South African president Thabo Mbeki. Also worthy of mention is Nigerian businessman-politician Moshood Abiola, who funded several continental reparations efforts in the early 1990s.

Jacob Ade Ajayi

The late Nigerian historian Ade Ajayi argued for a central focus in the reparations struggle on the transatlantic slave trade due to its links with colonialism and neo-colonialism. Ajayi was a member of the Organisation of African Unity's (OAU's) Group of Eminent Persons (GEP) on Reparations in 1992–1993, which – through the 1993 Abuja Declaration – demanded that the West recognise its moral debt to Africa and its diaspora for slavery and colonialism, and pay these populations full monetary compensation. Ajayi was among the most eloquent continental advocates of reparations. As he noted in 1993: "The Crusade for Reparation is ... to seek to understand the African condition in depth, to educate the African and the non-African about it, to seek an acknowledgment of wrongs which have impaired the political and socio-economic fabric of Africa and, through restitution or reparation, to attempt to give Africa and Africans a fresh start."[3]

Ajayi noted that discussions about the contribution of the slave trade to the West's industrialisation have been neglected, and criticised the ambiguous or indifferent attitude of many African scholars towards this issue. He noted that European imperialists had used the justification of ending the transatlantic slave trade to penetrate into the African "interior" in order to annex territories. He further observed that a major motive of European colonial rule was to keep African labour in a cheap state akin to slavery, using methods perfected during two centuries of imperial slavery in the Caribbean and South America. A landless African proletariat was thus created as a limitless source of cheap labour.[4] As Ajayi explained: "The nature of colonial rule in Africa, and the oppression of black people in the Americas, even after emancipation, cannot be understood unless it is emphasised that both grew out of the capitalist slave system."[5]

Ajayi further observed that about one million Africans had died in Africa, Europe, Burma, and Indo-China defending their European colonial masters during two world wars (1914–1918 and 1939–1945). He thus called for four key measures to achieve reparations: domestic education and mobilisation of African societies to see what, why, and how to bring about restitution; second, documentation and research (through national documentation centres gathering local knowledge) on the costs of slavery and colonialism; third, using examples such as the Jewish campaign against the Nazi Holocaust (which killed six million European Jews) to make a cogent case to influential groups for African reparations; and, finally, making detailed calculations of the costs of reparations, after agreeing on the strategy, manner, and mode of restitution, before placing the issue on the agenda of the United Nations.[6]

Ali Mazrui

Our second prophet, the Kenyan scholar Ali Mazrui, was one of the most active proponents of reparations for European slavery and colonialism until his death in October 2014. He linked the damaging impacts of colonialism to more contemporary developments in post-Cold War Africa such as civil wars in Liberia, Angola, and Somalia. Mazrui further noted the failures of colonial economies in transforming African states, and the disruption of socio-economic ties between Africa and its diaspora. As he put it: "The struggle for black reparations is not based on Western guilt but on Western *responsibility*. While guilt need not be inherited from generation to generation, rights and responsibilities are."[7]

Mazrui thus proposed four concrete acts of restitution: first, Western material and moral support for democracy in Africa and reduction of support to tyrants; second, Western decrease or elimination of economic impediments to Africa's development by, for example, annulling Africa's external debt (which stood at $1.1 trillion in 2023[8]); third, assisting Africa to overcome socio-cultural impediments to democratisation by, for example, supporting women empowerment programmes and their greater involvement in governance and development initiatives; fourth, making capital transfers from the West to Africa – which Mazrui dubbed "the Middle Passage Plan" – similar to the Marshall Plan through which the United States transferred $12 billion for European reconstruction between 1948 and 1952. This Middle Passage Plan would also involve massive capacity-building and skills transfers from the West to Africa and its diaspora. Finally, Mazrui urged greater power-sharing with Africa at the international level by reforming institutions of global governance such as the World Bank and the International Monetary Fund (IMF) in order to make them more democratic, with Africa also granted veto power on the 15-member UN Security Council.[9]

Mazrui further noted that it was Africa that had shifted the focus of restitution from a diaspora demand to a global movement for reparations for the Black World. He was part of the OAU Group of Eminent Persons established in Dakar in June 1992, along with fellow academics, Nigeria's Ade Ajayi, Burkina Faso's Joseph Ki-Zerbo, and Egypt's Samir Amin. The group also included Mozambique's Graça Machel, South Africa's Miriam Makeba, Jamaica's Dudley Thompson, and American congressman Ron Dellums. Members pushed forcefully for reparations for the damage done to Africa and its diaspora by slavery, colonialism, and neo-colonialism. The group was co-chaired by Nigerian multi-millionaire philanthropist Moshood Abiola, who had sponsored the First Reparations Conference in Lagos in December 1990. He regarded the payment of reparations as similar to the annulment of Africa's external debt. As Abiola noted: "It is international law that compels Nigeria to pay her debts to western banks and financial institutions: it is international law which must now demand that the western nations pay us what they owed us for nearly six centuries."[10]

The other co-chair of the group was the Senegalese intellectual and former director general of UNESCO, Amadou-Mahtar M'Bow. The Eminent Persons met again in Abuja in September 1992 to address substantive issues of reparations for European slavery and colonisation but, sadly, the group was discontinued after Nigeria ended its chairing of the OAU in 1993, and the movement's main financier, Moshood Abiola – the presumed winner of the June 1993 presidential elections in Nigeria – was jailed by military ruler General Sani Abacha in June 1994 while trying to reclaim his mandate, and died four years later on the eve of his release.

Mazrui was clearly instrumental in drafting the Abuja Proclamation during the First Pan-African Conference on Reparations in Abuja in April 1993, organised by the OAU under its Nigerian chair. The proclamation noted that "the damage sustained by the African peoples is not a 'thing of the past' but is painfully manifest in the damaged lives of contemporary Africans from Harlem to Harare, in the damaged economies of the black world from Guinea to Guyana, from Somalia to Surinam (*sic*)".[11] The proclamation went on to note, in Mazruian terms, that Africans were "the most humiliated and exploited people of the last four centuries of modern history",[12] and that other groups like Jewish victims of the Nazi Holocaust and Japanese-American victims of US internment during the Second World War had received reparations. The document further argued that such compensation need not be made in capital transfers, but could involve mutually agreed restitution between perpetrators and victims. Abuja stressed that Western countries that had benefited from nearly five centuries of free slave labour and colonial exploitation must repair this damage. It advocated cash transfers and debt annulment not just for African countries, but also for diaspora states and communities in the Caribbean and the Americas. The document further called for greater African representation in institutions of global governance and a permanent seat on the UN Security Council. These were all ideas that Mazrui has consistently championed.

The Abuja Proclamation was visionary in calling for the return of looted African artefacts to their rightful owners, which the French, German, British, and Belgian governments started to do by the 2010s. Clearly influenced by Ajayi, the proclamation called on African governments to establish national committees to study the damage of slavery and colonialism, disseminate information on these issues, and initiate educational courses. Abuja further called on the OAU to grant observer status to diaspora groups working on restitution in order for them to be able to engage with the continental body. The document, finally, requested African states to accede to the "right of return" of all diaspora citizens wanting to settle in their ancestral homelands.[13]

Wole Soyinka

The African World Reparations and Repatriation Truth Commission was held in the Ghanaian capital of Accra in August 1999. The meeting made similar demands to those of Abuja, and was attended by civil society representatives of 15 African and Caribbean states, as well as diaspora delegates from the United States and Britain. Accra called specifically for compensation of $777 trillion as reparations from the West for slavery and colonialism, and for African traditional leaders to make land available for diaspora returnees.[14]

Though not a delegate in Accra, Nigerian Nobel literature laureate Wole Soyinka published his book, *The Burden of Memory, the Muse of Forgiveness* in the same year as the conference, and tackled similar issues. In the book, Soyinka, our third prophet, stresses the importance of truth in rebuilding nations, and notes that truth commissions in Africa are similar to the reparations movement in demanding restitution to exorcise the past in order to achieve cathartic healing.[15] He notes that the crimes of the post-colonial African elite against African populations have echoes of colonial crimes, and that such human rights violations had weakened the OAU's crusade for reparations for Western slavery and colonialism. Citing the case of post-apartheid South Africa and jihadist Sudan in Darfur, Soyinka remarks that, in some ways, contemporary crimes demand more urgent reparations, as the victims and perpetrators are still identifiable.[16] He further insisted that the looted wealth of African autocrats, such as Zaire's Mobutu Sese Seko and Nigeria's Generals Ibrahim Babangida and Sani Abacha, must be returned to the continent as a form of "internal moral cleansing", so as to strengthen Africa's case for global reparations.[17]

For Soyinka, "the Atlantic slave trade remains an inescapable critique of European humanism".[18] Like Ade Ajayi, Soyinka argues that the slave trade dislocated a great part of Africa's organic economic systems, resulting in many of the continent's present-day economic challenges. He thus supports reparations as "a necessity for the credibility of Eurocentric historicism, and a corrective for its exclusionist worldview".[19] For the Nobel laureate, reparations should serve as a form of atonement and a critique of history to prevent evil from recurring. Like Ali Mazrui, Soyinka calls for the annulment of Africa's debt in exchange for the continent annulling Europe's historical injustices perpetrated against Africa over four and a half centuries. He also calls for the return of looted African artistic treasures, describing these as expressions of Africa's very humanity.[20]

Thabo Mbeki

August 2021 marked the 20th anniversary of the UN World Conference Against Racism, Racial Discrimination, Xenophobia and Related Intolerance, which took place in South Africa's port city of Durban in August–September 2001. The Durban Declaration and Programme of Action were its key outcomes. Civil society groups from Africa, the Caribbean, the Americas, Canada, and Europe actively sought to shape the conference's agenda through the African and African Descendants Caucus (AADC), insisting that slavery and colonialism be declared crimes against humanity for which reparations should be paid. This position appeared to have been endorsed by the preparatory meeting of African governments convened in the Senegalese capital of Dakar seven months before the UN summit.[21]

The Durban Conference was hosted by our fourth prophet of reparations, then South African president Thabo Mbeki (1999–2008), the apostle of the "African Renaissance". More than any other contemporary African leader, Mbeki had a deep engagement with the Black World. As a young student, he had imbibed the activism of Martin Luther King Jr, the scholarship of Frantz Fanon, and the poetry of Langston Hughes. As president, he preached black solidarity from Atlanta to Bahia, Havana, and Haiti.[22] Like Ali Mazrui, Mbeki consistently urged the reform of institutions of global governance such as the UN, the World Bank, the IMF, and the World Trade Organization (WTO), in order to give Africa a greater voice in them.

In a stirring opening speech to the UN World Conference Against Racism in Durban, Mbeki championed cultural equality, and unequivocally condemned racism while noting: "We meet here because we are determined to ensure that nobody anywhere should be subjected to the insult and offence of being despised by another or others because of his or her race, colour, nationality or origin ... There are many in our common world who suffer indignity and humiliation because they are not white. Their cultures and traditions are despised as savage and primitive and their identities denied."[23] Mbeki then went on to demonstrate diasporic solidarity in musical tones: "To those who have to bear the pain of this real world, it seems the blues singers were right when they decried the world in which it was said – if you're white you're alright; if you are brown, stick around; if you are black, oh brother! Get back, get back, get back!"[24]

But, despite these stinging words, Caribbean delegates such as the Barbadian historian Hilary Beckles later criticised Mbeki and other African leaders such as Nigeria's Olusegun Obasanjo, Senegal's Abdoulaye Wade, and Ghana's John Kufuor for having betrayed the continent and the diaspora by allowing Western delegates to exclude strong clauses in the final conference resolution condemning slavery and colonialism, and for failing to hold these countries accountable for their crimes against humanity.[25] As Beckles lamented: "Africa broke with its own diaspora, joined with the former enslavers and colonisers … One by one, African leaders told the West that it had nothing to fear from the diaspora, now cast in the diplomatic dungeon as disruptors of the Durban peace."[26]

African leaders, however, felt that the conference, by its very nature, involved multilateral negotiations between governments, and that what was agreed reflected how much the political traffic could bear. They pragmatically decided to live to fight another day. These were nine days of arduous negotiations in which the withdrawal of the American and Israeli delegations – as a result of perceived anti-Israel bias – nearly scuttled the whole process. Japan and India also vigorously resisted any references to discriminatory caste systems. The Ethiopian-American scholar Adom Getachew's depiction of Nigeria and South Africa as having acted as Western "client states" in Durban thus smacks of crude caricature.[27]

An important achievement in Durban was to have declared slavery and the slave trade "crimes against humanity". The transatlantic slave trade was described as an "appalling tragedy" of "abhorrent barbarism" that "should always have been" a crime against humanity. Durban also argued that colonialism had resulted in racism and suffering that have endured into the present age. Many of the conference's recommendations were, however, quixotic, with little chance of implementation due to the international economic system of "global apartheid",[28] which has kept much of the global South poor and dependent. Nebulous national action plans and stronger legislation were advocated, alongside strengthening "national institutions to combat racial discrimination". More concrete were Durban's calls for education, research, and awareness-raising initiatives to tackle racism – echoing Ade Ajayi's ideas – including sensible calls for religious groups to help fight the scourge.

But Durban was, in some ways, also subversive. The Declaration pushed for the inclusion of the history and contributions of Africans in educational curricula, as well as for fully integrating into public services, and increasing social services to, "communities of primarily African descent": issues of particular sensitivity to Brazil and the United States. Durban also noted disapprovingly that colonial-era theories of racial superiority were still prevalent and easily spread through social media, thus anticipating Donald Trump's nativist, hate-spewing presidency by 15 years. Furthermore, Durban was bold in bemoaning the plight of Palestinians and calling for their right to an independent state. The Declaration further condemned the ubiquitous negative stereotyping of vulnerable groups in parts of the global media, as well as the resurgence of neo-fascist ideologies, anticipating the continued rise of Islamophobic and Afrophobic European parties demonising black and brown migrants.[29]

While Durban did not change the world, it helped lay the foundation for contemporary Black Lives Matter-led racial struggles involving anti-racism protests around the globe, particularly in the United States, Brazil, France, England, Belgium, and Canada, following the death in Minnesota, in May 2020, of unarmed African American George Floyd under the knee of a white police officer. These demonstrations were more effective than at any other time in living memory. Unlike the OAU, the African Union (AU) – born in Durban in July 2002, a year after the UN racism conference – has only since 2022 taken concrete initiatives to revive the OAU's work on reparations of three decades ago. The AU's designation of the African diaspora as the continent's sixth sub-region has been largely devoid of substance.

Rebuilding Afro-Caribbean Bridges for the Global Reparations Struggle

As noted earlier, Caribbean delegates felt aggrieved at the 2001 Durban summit by what they perceived as the failure of African leaders to push further for an unequivocal condemnation of the transatlantic slave trade, and to demand concrete reparations from Western governments.[30] More recently, the Ghanaian government of President Nana Akufo-Addo sought to rebuild African bridges with the Caribbean through an active diplomatic outreach. Taking advantage of the 400th anniversary of the arrival of the first African slaves in the United States, the Ghanaian president promoted the "Year of Return", urging Caribbeans and African Americans to relocate to Ghana, while seeking to promote increased trade during a tour of the Caribbean in June 2019.

Akufo-Addo became the first incumbent Ghanaian president to visit Guyana, where he laid a wreath at the Georgetown Non-Aligned Movement monument, which includes a bust of the first Ghanaian leader, Kwame Nkrumah. Akufo-Addo also laid a wreath at Georgetown's Square of the

Revolution, which includes a statue of the Ghanaian-descended Guyanese national hero Kofi, who led slave rebellions in Guiana and Suriname. In St Vincent and the Grenadines, Akufo-Addo addressed the island's parliament. He became his country's first leader to visit Barbados, where he addressed a joint sitting of parliament; signed bilateral agreements in education and health with premier Mia Mottley; advocated strengthened links between the AU, the Economic Community of West African States (ECOWAS), and the Caribbean Community; and expressed delight at being in the country of his childhood cricket hero, Garfield Sobers.[31] In Jamaica, the Ghanaian president met the prime minister, Andrew Holness; toured Seville Great House and Heritage Park; and laid a wreath at the Marcus Garvey monument in National Heroes Park.[32]

In August 2022, the government of Ghana and the African Union co-hosted the Summit on Reparations and Healing in Accra, in a further effort to craft a common trans-regional reparations plan.[33] A year later, a high-level AU delegation embarked on a study tour to Barbados to develop stronger AU–Caricom cooperation, and to coordinate a common strategy between both regional bodies in order to advance their common reparations agenda. In November 2023, the AU Reparations Conference was convened in Accra. This resulted from AU support of a request, made by the Ghanaian government nine months earlier, to co-host a reparations conference with the continental body. The conference was attended by five African leaders, the prime minister of Barbados, policymakers, scholars, and civil society activists from the African diaspora in the Americas, the Caribbean, and Europe.

In his opening address to the meeting, President Akufo-Addo noted: "The entire period of slavery meant that our progress, economically, culturally, and psychologically, was stifled … [The] entire continent of Africa deserves a formal apology from the European nations involved in the slave trade. No amount of money can restore the damage caused by the transatlantic slave trade and its consequences. But, surely, this is a matter that the world must confront and can no longer ignore."[34]

Carla Barnett, Caricom's secretary general, similarly noted in Accra: "We are at an important inflection point in the global movement for reparatory justice." She went on to urge that the movement "speak with one voice to advance the call for reparations".[35] Barnett further encouraged a multifaceted approach to reparations involving the adoption of socio-economic, legal, and mass mobilisation strategies. She stressed the transformative influence of the creative arts in popularising the cause of reparations, while advocating the promotion of sub-regional conferences to recognise the diverse experiences of different regions.[36]

Debates at the conference centred around issues such as historical contexts that have shaped contemporary inequalities; ethical requirements for reparatory justice; the socio-economic consequences of reparations; using reparations to remove structural barriers that continue to perpetuate inequality; strengthening grassroots networks and organisations; and recognising Haiti's special role in the African Atlantic.[37]

Suggestions adopted in Accra included setting up an African committee of experts on reparations to develop a common African position on reparations and healing, and incorporating this common position into an Afro-Caribbean programme of action; establishing a global reparations fund with the support of the UN and other multilateral institutions that are supportive of reparatory justice; the AU co-convening an international conference on reparations with the UN Permanent Forum on People of African Descent, involving former European colonial powers; increasing the role of African regional economic communities such as ECOWAS, the East African Community (EAC), and the Southern African Development Community (SADC) in promoting reparations; setting up a trans-continental partnership framework between the AU, Caricom, Latin American states, and the African diaspora in Europe and other regions; creating a global expert committee to bolster the economic case for reparations; employing international law to hold to account perpetrators of historical injustices; enacting anti-racism legislation; creating budgeted programmes; involving more women, youth activists, and faith-based groups in the reparations crusade; creating an AU special envoy on reparations for Africa; and identifying legislative champions to pursue restitution.[38]

Surprisingly, there was no reference in the Accra 2023 Proclamation to the 1993 OAU Reparations Conference in Abuja, the 1999 Accra Reparations Conference, or the 2001 UN Durban Anti-Racism Conference. Several of the ideas at the 2023 Accra summit had already been made in Abuja and Accra in the 1990s, and at Durban in 2001: these included mass mobilisation and education for reparations; the AU to work more closely with diaspora groups; pushing for reform of multilateral bodies like the UN Security Council, the World Bank, and the IMF; transforming educational curricula; and calling for the return of looted African cultural artefacts from Europe. This suggests a worrying lack of institutional memory within the AU, as well as limited historical grounding among African and diaspora civil society delegates in Accra in 2023: a gap that this book seeks to fill.

Concluding Reflections

In concluding this chapter, it is important to note a burning issue that has still not been adequately responded to by former European imperial powers and beneficiaries of enslavement in the Caribbean and the Americas: reparations for the victims of the two European-led scourges of slavery and colonialism in Africa, Europe, the Americas, and the Caribbean. How can European nations who enslaved and colonised African people for nearly five centuries repair this pernicious damage that has left Africa, the Caribbean, and black people in the Americas with the triple burdens of a lack of development and crippling debt, diseases, and deadly conflicts? This remains a festering wound that must be urgently healed, despite some looted African art having been returned to their countries of origin by European governments from the 2010s. The movement to abolish slavery took generations to succeed, and so also will the contemporary movement for restitution for African slavery and colonialism. Awareness is, however, growing: the African Union declared 2025 to be the year of "Justice for Africans and People of African Descent through Reparations;"[39] Caricom continues to push reparations forcefully; while grassroots diaspora groups across Europe and the Americas continue persistently to demand reparatory justice.

One of the most important recent developments in the area of reparations is the agreement by the German government, in June 2021, to pay €1.1 billion in compensation for the genocide in its then colony of Southwest Africa (Namibia) between 1904 and 1908 (see Introduction and Blackler in this volume). On the centenary of the start of these massacres, Berlin offered an apology to the Herero and Nama for these crimes. After 108 years of denial and equivocation, Germany finally conceded, in 2015, that these acts constituted "a war crime and a genocide". The governments of Namibia and Germany thereafter took six years to negotiate a joint agreement. Berlin agreed to pay €1.1 billion in aid over 30 years in the critical areas of land reform, rural infrastructure, health care, energy, education, and vocational training. The crimes were, however, described as genocide "from today's perspective", suggesting that international law did not apply to their African victims. Berlin further stressed that the accord should not open the door to any "legal request for compensation", as it feared similar claims from Poland, Greece, and Italy for Nazi war crimes committed during the Second World War (1939–1945).[40]

Germany further refused to include the word "reparations" in the June 2021 joint declaration. Windhoek was widely seen to have been outmanoeuvred in these negotiations of unequals between the government and its largest aid donor. The main challenge in implementing this historic accord remains how to persuade Herero and Nama leaders to accept it. Several of them have complained that they were not represented at the negotiation table, and voiced strong hostility to the deal. The distrust of indigenous groups relates largely to what many see as their continuing marginalisation within Namibian society, as well as their criticisms of what they regard as a corrupt elite in Windhoek that cannot be relied on to spend aid money honestly and equitably.

Under its prime minister, Mark Rutte, the Netherlands government also apologised for the Dutch role in the transatlantic slave trade in December 2022, establishing a €200 million fund to address its impact. As Rutte – himself a trained historian – noted: "On behalf of the Dutch government, I apologise for the past actions of the Dutch state; to enslaved people in the past, everywhere in the world, who suffered as a consequence of these actions, as well as to their daughters and sons, and to all their descendants, up to the present day."[41] On the 160th anniversary of the abolition of slavery in Holland's territories across the globe, the King of the Netherlands, Willem-Alexander, similarly offered an apology to victims of the slave trade at the country's national slavery monument in Amsterdam's Oosterpark, noting: "On this day that we remember the Dutch history of slavery, I ask forgiveness for this crime against humanity."[42] The king went on to note that racism remained a challenge in present-day Dutch society. It was also revealed in June 2023 that the House of Orange – the Dutch royal family – had profited from the slave trade through the Dutch East India Company, between 1675 and 1770, to the tune of $600 million (in 2023 monetary terms).[43]

The governments of Germany and the Netherlands have started to atone for their crimes from the colonial and slave trade eras. Former European colonial powers like France, Britain, Belgium, Portugal, Spain, and Italy (see Yates, Igba, Vanthemsche, Sousa, Nerín and Tofiño, Fuller, and Palumbo in this volume) have, however, yet to come to terms with the atrocities that their governments, citizens, and companies committed in Africa: an estimated one million Algerians died in the savage Gallic war of 1954–1962; about 90,000 Malagasies were killed by French forces during the Malagasy uprising of 1947–1949;[44] mercenaries of Cecil Rhodes's British South Africa Company slaughtered thousands of Ndebele and Shona during rebellions in the 1890s in what is now Zimbabwe, also stealing their herds of cattle; while British troops killed about 25,000 Kenyans, and detained another 100,000 without trial in torture-filled concentration camps during the Mau Mau liberation struggle of the 1950s.[45] Belgium stands accused of the death of half of the Congolese population of 20 million people during King Leopold's brutal reign of murder and mayhem between 1885 and 1908.[46]

Portugal engaged in widespread slavery and forced labour across Africa from the fifteenth century (see also Sousa in this volume).[47] Italian soldiers used chemical weapons to engage in massacres in which at least 100,000 Libyan Bedouins perished, while its soldiers raped countless Ethiopian, Eritrean, and Somali women (see also Fuller in this volume).[48] Spain occupied large areas of North Africa from the fifteenth century as well as Equatorial Guinea, and used chemical weapons in the Moroccan Rif mountains between 1921 and 1926 (see also Nerín and Tofiño in this volume).[49] Two and a half centuries of brutal American slavery destroyed the lives of millions of disenfranchised black populations (see Kerr-Ritchie and Broyld in this volume), as did Portuguese and Spanish reigns of terror across the Americas (see Silva Jr, Ramirez, and Soomer in this volume). Will these European and European-descended powers follow Berlin's and The Hague's lead in offering full apologies for their colonial crimes, and make amends to repair this enduring damage?

The West's relationship with Africa will require such a restitutive approach, and must be understood in a much longer and wider perspective. Relations between an Africa Caliban and a European Prospero continue to be shaped by the historical trauma of nearly five centuries of slavery and colonialism, and the shadows of empire still stalk these ties.[50] Despite the European Union's talk of "partnership" and the provision of development aid, non-reciprocal trade access (since revoked), and security assistance, the African side still often feels that an unequal, paternalistic relationship has continued with Europe, similar to the exploitative patterns of the past. African migrants continue to be scapegoated; the French military continues to act like a pyromaniac fireman on the continent; and the European Union's trade experts continue to negotiate with their African counterparts like an Italian Mafia don with a loaded gun.

28

The Struggle for Reparations in Latin America

June Soomer

COLONIALISM HAS LEFT structural barriers that remain an obstacle to the upliftment of indigenous persons and descendants of trafficked and enslaved Africans who have been excluded from full participation in the social, political, and economic life of Latin America. Built on an ideology of racism, these inequalities have been perpetuated and driven by two associated fallacies: the myth that enslavement in Brazil and Spanish America was milder than in North America and the Caribbean; and – based on the whitening of these countries – that class rather than racial origin was responsible for these continuing socio-economic disparities. Widespread acquiescence in the ideology of multicultural societies and miscegenation – advanced by academics and elites – as well as the perception of more benevolent societies, has also hindered the development of more active reparations movements. Nevertheless, these struggles have survived and transcended centuries of genocide, invisibility, and entrenched racism.

These issues have also been complicated by the establishment of Truth and Reconciliation Commissions from the 1990s, in countries such as Peru, Argentina, Chile, and Colombia, set up to examine human rights abuses under military rule and during civil wars in Central and Latin America. These platforms, which gave to victims of these crimes the opportunity to provide evidence, seek redress, and pursue social justice, were limited. They addressed violations which happened in recent years, thereby silencing the grievances of the four centuries of slavery from the fifteenth to the nineteenth centuries. To a large extent, these new violations were perpetrated against indigenous populations and other marginalised groups whose families hesitated to lodge grievances, especially as there was "still the powerful presence of those responsible for the violations".[1] In most cases, only a small number of victims were compensated. However, in Chile in 1992, the Truth Commission created the National Corporation for Reparations and Reconciliation, which "established a monthly pension for the families named in the report, medical benefits for the families, and a subsidy for the high school, and college education of the victims".[2] Many commissions in Latin America prioritised preventing new abuses and thus not only limited redress for the past, but also ensured continued abuses, as structural and cultural discrimination remained deeply entrenched across all states in the region.

The limitations placed on these truth commissions, the crimes they investigated, the few victims that were compensated, the presence of violators at the highest levels of society, and the inability to investigate each atrocity, all continue negatively to affect the issue of reparations in these countries. However, all the commissions across the region agreed on the "importance of justice as well as truth in dealing with the past".[3] This gives hope to the reparations movement across Latin America, which has reached out to the Caribbean, as it engages with Europe in the search for justice and redress for indigenous peoples, and atonement for the enslavement of black Africans in its quest for global dominance.

The First People

The philosophy of racism which accompanied the Europeans across the Atlantic resulted in three key outcomes that form the basis of the case for reparations in Latin America. The first is the "extinction project", which ensured a dramatic decline in indigenous populations on the islands as well as the mainland. Perhaps an example will bring more clarity to the extent of this genocidal European project. While there is no clear indication of the exact population of Tainos people, it is estimated that in Hispaniola more than 250,000 were killed by the time of Christopher Columbus's death in 1506. The "[remaining] Tainos were rounded up, and worked to death at a furious pace, to the point that by 1515 records indicate the indigenous population on the island of less than 50,000 survived. By 1555, 40 years later, there were 500."[4] Once these numbers had declined, attention shifted to subduing those who resisted confinement and who fought for the restoration of their land. This included the Kalinago and the Garifuna, or the Black Caribs, who were a product of African and indigenous miscegenation.

The second outcome was Europe's subordination of "lesser peoples". From 1503, the enslavement of Amerindians was authorised by various European royal decrees. This commenced with the attempt to subjugate the Kalinago through their demonisation as warlike, savage cannibals. The citizenship of indigenous peoples in the Americas can thus not be restored without a conscious effort to remove damaging European-imposed language and images. The resistance of the Kalinago people to enslavement and colonisation can no longer be depicted as belligerent savagery. There must be redress for the image of the "cannibal", as this was widely used to justify the European extinction ideology.

We should recall that the Spaniards who first arrived in the Bahamas, Cuba, and Hispaniola in 1492, and in Puerto Rico a year later, did not bring women on the first expeditions. They instead raped Taino women, resulting in *mestizo* children. Sexual violence in Hispaniola was therefore widespread. Numerous scholars, such as the Native American writer Sarah Deer,[5] write of widespread rape and violence, resulting in racial and cultural mixing in Cuba as well as in several communities surviving into the nineteenth century. It is important that we debunk the myth that these were consensual relationships (see Brereton in this volume). There must be reparations for this injustice.

The struggle for reparations for the "First People" has been hindered by the discussion centred around their "extinction". Yet there are today about 40 million indigenous people across Latin America and the Caribbean. They continue to fight to ensure that their struggle does not remain invisible in national statistics and that ancestral lands are returned to them. Their invisibility and powerlessness make it almost impossible for them to seek justice, and continue to relegate them to the ranks of purveyors of cultural trinkets for visiting tourists. Being invisible in plain sight speaks to an invalidation, a conscious inhumanity, that demands rectification.

The UN Declaration on the Rights of Indigenous Peoples of 2007 outlines the injustices faced by first citizens, recommending: "States shall provide redress through effective mechanisms, which may include restitution, developed in conjunction with indigenous peoples, with respect to their cultural, intellectual, religious and spiritual property taken without their free, prior and informed consent or in violation of their laws, traditions and customs."[6] Nearly

16 years after the United Nations Declaration was unanimously adopted,[7] Galina Angarova, the executive director of Cultural Survival, noted that "while several countries have made steps towards aligning their policies with the standards enshrined in the Declaration, however, an implementation gap remains".[8] In 2007, the rights of indigenous persons were recognised in Belize; in 2007 and 2012, in Suriname; and in 2012, in Ecuador. In all these cases, legal action preceded the recognition of rights to land and cultural heritage. In general, however, conversations on redress remain muted across the region, while in Brazil's Amazon rainforest actions against indigenous claims have resulted in their further displacement and even some deaths.[9] American historian Paul Ramirez reminds us that "Indigenous people remain invisible and uncentred because we continue to view them in the past tense, snapshots on time". He continues: "Little value is placed on the lives or knowledge of modern Indigenous people by outsiders. And these devaluations fit into the languages and practice of continued genocide against Indigenous peoples."[10] Reparations for indigenous people thus need a global voice (see Beckles, Maginn, Adebajo, Small, and Frith and Xosei in this volume). Otherwise, the struggle for reparations will continue to be ignored, even by the 144 countries that adopted the 2007 UN Declaration on the Rights of Indigenous Peoples.

Exiled: The Case of the Garifuna

From early in their history the Black Caribs (Garifuna) have found themselves in a struggle for reparations and the right to land tenure. The alliance they formed with the French against the British during the French Revolution in 1789 was centred around redress and for control of their lands in St Vincent and the Grenadines.[11] The Garifuna effectively fought the Spanish, French, and English in what has been described as 300 years against warfare, disease, and marginalisation (see Silva Jr, Aragón Falomir, and Brereton in this volume).

The Garifuna began as a mixed-race group of Kalinago and enslaved Africans who survived a shipwreck off the coast of St Vincent around 1635. Their numbers were replenished by similar groups from the mountainous regions of islands such as St Lucia, Grenada, Martinique, Dominica, and Guadeloupe. This group, therefore, recalled both an African and an Amerindian past,[12] after living for 200 years as free and independent people.

In 1763, St Vincent was ceded to the English under a treaty between London and Paris. The result was a war between the Garifuna and the British between 1763 and 1796, which resulted in the surrender of 5,080 Black Caribs to the English. Most of the Caribs were then sent to Balliceaux and later to Bequia, the northernmost of the St Vincent and Grenadine islands.

In February 1797, the Caribs were loaded onto HMS *Experiment* and transported to the coast of Honduras, and thus stripped of their homeland.[13] By the time of their surrender to the British in 1797, much of the Black Carib nation had been annihilated. As British journalist Christopher Taylor describes the process: "the desperate, and famished survivors of the war were interned on a waterless islet where half their number died. Finally, in March 1797 the remnants of the Black Carib nation – barely two thousand men, women, and children – were transported in British ships 1,700 miles away to the northwest where they were deposited on the Spanish-controlled island of Roatán off the coast of Honduras."[14] In exchange for the theft of 27,078 acres of Carib lands in St Vincent, the Garifuna were exiled on a dry land with six months' supply of food. The exile of Caribs to reservations in Trinidad and later Dominica would become part of an English policy to strip indigenous people of their lands throughout Latin America, North America, and the Caribbean. Regaining land remains at the heart of their calls for justice.

The story of the Garifuna continued with their expansion on the coasts of Central America. They were at the centre of the liberation and independence movements in Latin and Central America and helped to shape this history. Living across national boundaries, they have never lost their cultural identity, remaining until this day a distinct group. More importantly, they survived, and their numbers, now estimated at 300,000 today,[15] are a testimony of their enduring resilience. Garifuna are also to be found in Nicaragua, Costa Rica, Guatemala, Belize, and Honduras. They have an extensive diaspora in the United States and Britain. In 1992 the Garifuna were admitted to the World Council of Indigenous Peoples after overcoming resistance in that body to accepting black-skinned people in the Americas as authentically indigenous.[16] The descendants of Garifuna have recently joined the Caribbean Community (Caricom) reparations movement (see Beckles in this volume) after the acknowledgement of their indigenous status by the government of St Vincent and the Grenadines. They remain fighters for liberation and the right to self-determination.

The Culture of Whitening and Mestizaje

Whitening and *mestizaje* (miscegenation) occurred concurrently in Brazil and Latin America and have assisted in perpetuating the myth of multicultural societies that embrace all cultures. The reality of conquest, domination, and enslavement was that white women did not accompany white men on these journeys of exploration, and indigenous and enslaved women would thus become integral to both the reproductive and productive systems. At the same time, the dominant presence of Africans on plantations (5.5 million slaves were transported from Africa) and in the mines meant that African ancestry would remain dominant in contemporary Brazil. Yet the whitening process and the government systems have pushed Africans to self-identify as either brown (*parda*) or black (*preta*) in the federal census – which has five categories, white (*branca*), yellow (*amarela*), indigenous, brown, and black.[17]

This "colourism" has been designed to provide legitimacy to the open racism that sustains hierarchies and exclusion on the basis of culture. It is for this reason that the Peruvian scholar Marisol de la Cadena talks about the "discriminatory potential of 'culture' and its historical embeddedness in racial thought".[18] These bigoted practices are based on cultural differences and not on biological markers such as skin colour. As the African American scholar Henry Louis Gates Jr notes, "each of these countries had (and continues to have) many categories of colour and skin tone, ranging from as few as 12 in the Dominican Republic, and 16 in Mexico to 134 in Brazil".[19]

There was a formal effort to whiten Brazil towards the end of slavery in 1888. Between 1884 and 1939, nearly four million Europeans and 185,000 Japanese were brought to Brazil on a subsidised basis to work as indentured servants. The process, a formal government programme, was called *branqueamento* – which literally means "whitening". Obviously, the country's largely Portuguese-descended white elite hoped to increase the number of whites to lighten the national complexion. These whitening campaigns were aimed at eradicating vestiges of African culture and embracing "multiculturalism". The white elite declared itself unique precisely because of the extent of racial admixture among its citizens.[20]

Furthermore, as Paul Ramirez notes, "The myth of *mestizaje* (miscegenation) and the co-option of indigenous heritages have rendered indigenous people invisible in plain sight. Not only are identities trivialised and diminished, but the stigmas and negative impacts that are placed on 'indios' remain, regardless of dominant society's acceptance of them as being 'real' indios or not."[21] Anadelia A. Romo, a Hispanic American scholar, contends that the concept of multiculturalism ensured that "the role ascribed to African culture was still bound by the same concepts of superiority and inferiority. Blacks, now relabelled as 'Africans', retained an inferior position in a hierarchy of cultural influence and worth."[22] While whitening hindered the development of a civil rights movement in Brazil, white migration in the twentieth century was not open to blacks: "the goal was to eliminate African miscegenation".[23] In the end, these whitening agendas did not eliminate race and class stratification.

There is much statistical evidence showing that Brazil's racial inequality is due partly to ongoing discrimination, despite the historical absence of race-based laws or Brazil's apparently milder form of racism. It should be emphasised that Brazilian enslavement was harsh, and that it was easy to replace the term "Africans" with "brown" or "mixed race". The 2000 Brazilian census revealed that about 40 per cent of the national population considered itself brown or mixed race, while 5 per cent considered itself black and 54 per cent white. Less than one per cent was Asian or indigenous. These statistics are largely based on self-identity and on race or colour, which in Brazil is generally determined by appearance.[24] "Brazil is home to more people of African heritage than any country outside Africa. But it is rarely identified as a Black nation."[25] This is because people in the country are simply referred to as Brazilian and not by their race.

In Mexico, the number of people who self-identify as Afro-Mexican has increased in recent years. The 2020 census cited a figure for Afro-Mexicans of 2.5 million people, or 2 per cent of the total population: a significant increase from five years earlier.[26] This growing awareness will certainly – to paraphrase Henry Louis Gates Jr – remove the black grandma from the closet and bring more visibility to the fact that many have ancestors of African descent in their lineage. Even self-recognition has been distorted by the well-planned colourism of whitening schemes and government policy, which has rendered black people invisible. In 2021, the son of the legendary civil rights leader Martin Luther King Jr visited Mexico, and called for an acknowledgement of race dynamics and the establishment of a truth and reconciliation commission to give people the opportunity to apologise for past crimes in order to wipe the slate clean. He argued that discussions about reparations for slavery should also flow from such a process.[27]

Affirmative Action Programmes and Reparations

Most Latin American countries made the decision to pursue affirmative action programmes to address the issues raised by the small but dynamic reparations movements. Some of these countries also opted for public apologies and the erection of monuments to victims of historical crimes. Historically, "former slave societies such as Brazil, Cuba, and Colombia did not witness collective movements demanding reparations for slavery."[28] However, following payments to Jewish Holocaust victims by Germany of about $98 billion, there were "renewed calls for financial, material, and symbolic reparations for more than three centuries of slavery".[29]

The issue of reparations has been a conversation among Brazilian leaders since the end of enslavement in 1888. Abolitionists defended the payment of reparations to freed slaves. It was at this time that the work of Manuel Querino, the Afro-Brazilian writer and artist, became prominent: he wrote about African contributions to the development of Brazil and in this way established the basis for reparations. The Nigerian academic Niyi Afolabi has argued that the work of this cultural activist has been minimised in order to "re-historicize Brazilian history from a miscegenation prism".[30] As a result the myth of the racial democracy gained ground, as can be seen in the work of Gilberto Freyre, the Brazilian academic, writer, painter, journalist, and legislator, and Fernando Ortiz, the Cuban historian and anthropologist, which diminished the role of race as a construct in identity formation.

The argument against reparations has centred on what are seen as the technical difficulties in tracing human rights violations over the centuries and paying compensation to identified individuals. At least, this was the decision of the National Commission of Truth on Black Slavery, which noted that Brazil had been home to about 5.5 million enslaved Africans – the largest number of enslaved in the Americas – between 1530 and 1888. The commission acknowledged that enslavement was a state crime and that the government owed a debt to its black population. The Brazilian government has acknowledged its complicity in this sordid trade, and signed on to the 2001 UN Durban Declaration and Programme of Action (see Adebajo and Beckles in this volume), while President Luiz Inácio Lula da Silva apologised to African countries for slavery during a visit to the Senegalese capital of Dakar in April 2005. Lula argued that reparations would occur through Brazil's deepening of its relationships with the African continent. But by not calling for monetary reparations, the secretary of Brazil's Truth Commission, Humberto Adami, has prevented the body "from questioning more harshly the responsibility of the Brazilian government in slavery."[31] The suppression of the reparations movement in Brazil has clearly been orchestrated by government policy, and the genuineness of some reforms have been contradicted by the muting of growing calls for justice for these crimes against humanity.

Following its 1959 revolution, Cuba enacted land reform and redistributed some land to its black citizens. This set the stage for more Latin American countries to follow suit, and constitutional changes increasingly addressed "the right of land ownership for their black communities".[32] The affirmative action agenda began in the 1990s and accelerated after the 2001 UN Durban Conference and Programme of Action. In Brazil, the process started with an emphasis on land reform; between 1988 and 2013, the country's National Institute of Colonisation and Agrarian Reform (INCRA) transferred nearly 77 million hectares of land to nearly one million black families.[33] This was not insubstantial. Between 1930 and 2000 Brazil came sixth within Latin America in terms of land redistributed to displaced groups, after Bolivia, Chile, Colombia, Cuba, and Mexico.[34] But between 1988 and 2013, Brazil came second in Latin America in terms of land reform.[35] As agrarian reforms became more prevalent, and reparations movements advocated more land ownership for black communities, other Latin American countries such as Colombia, Venezuela, and Ecuador undertook constitutional changes to adopt land redistribution programmes. This also provided them with the opportunity to address agitation for such reform from indigenous people and rural peasants who campaigned against inequality in land ownership and started to take over vast tracts of land from large landowners.

Brazil named 21 March 2003 as the "Day for the Elimination of All Forms of Segregation" and also established a Secretariat for the Promotion of Racial Equality in order to target *quilombos*[36] (African communities). Once certified, these communities were given access to education and health services provided by the government. Many Latin American countries such as Argentina, Brazil, Mexico, and Colombia also commenced affirmative action in institutions of higher education and universities. This move met with fierce resistance from predominantly white populations throughout Latin America. Regional governments were accused of using affirmative action and diversity programmes to provide access to these groups without proper justification. According to American sociologist Edward E. Telles, affirmative action detractors "include much of the media, private school students, their parents and the schools themselves, scholars and artists who value the racial democracy ideal and even black students who believe in meritocracy".[37] Even some indigenous and African people have not accepted that they should be given special treatment, as it makes them stand out in these contexts.

The difficulty with many of these reforms stemmed from the lack of commitment by successive governments, as they are often associated with certain political leaders. Several reforms were introduced by President Lula da Silva (2003–2011) but were not continued by his successor, Dilma Rousseff, who was in office between 2011 and 2016. Many of Lula's policies were also reversed under the populist rule of Jair Bolsonaro (2019–2022). Citizens of African descent continue to wage a battle for rights in Brazil. While they have a chance of achieving self-determination in the *quilombos*, miscegenation programmes are diminishing the survival of these communities.

At the same time, since the initial reforms of the 1990s, most Latin American countries are reversing or dismantling programmes and institutions that monitored these programmes. This means that indigenous persons and peasants are losing lives and livelihoods to new neo-liberal policies. The revocation of Article 27 of the Mexican Constitution in 1991 and the Deregulation Decree in Argentina of the same year are two examples of such reversals. The struggle for rights continues, and new groups of peasants, indigenous people, and social actors are emerging to respond to these new challenges across the world (see Brereton in this volume).[38]

The Caribbean Community Reparations Movement and the Latin American Struggle

We next move to a discussion of the struggle for reparations in Latin America, rooted in the decision by the 20 Caribbean Community (Caricom) countries to inaugurate a regional Reparations Commission to pursue and "establish the moral, ethical, and legal case of all the former colonial powers, and the relevant institutions of those countries, to the nations and people of the Caribbean Community for the crimes against humanity of Native Genocide, the Trans-Atlantic Slave Trade, and a racialised system of chattel slavery".[39] Since its establishment in 2014, Caricom's well-organised advocacy (see Beckles in this volume) has re-energised debates spanning centuries of discussions and demands for justice and redress by enslaved persons, abolitionists, freed persons, and independent nations.

The basis of Caricom's determination was contained in the Barbadian historian Hilary Beckles's 2013 book, *Britain's Black Debt: Reparations for*

Caribbean Slavery and Native Genocide. This centred on the case for reparations against Britain, but it nonetheless provided a blueprint for the pursuit of reparations from all other former colonial powers. In the book, Beckles argued that "slave trading, and slavery were understood as crimes then, as they are now, and as such are subject to reparatory justice".[40] He further noted that European development and colonialism were dependent on African slavery, observations that had been made by the Trinidadian scholar-politician Eric Williams in his 1944 classic, *Capitalism and Slavery*, which made multi-layered connections between the growth of industrialisation in Europe and the enslavement of Africans.[41] Williams concluded that his work should not be limited to Britain as "the commercial capitalism of the eighteenth century developed the wealth of Europe by means of slavery and monopoly".[42] This is why the reparations movement in the English-speaking Caribbean has expanded to include other former European colonies in the region, for decolonisation projects cannot be limited by the colonial barriers of sea, land, and language.

Consequently, Caricom's decision has found resonance in the Association of Caribbean States (ACS), a Greater Caribbean construction which encompasses all the English, French, and Spanish-speaking countries that border the Caribbean Sea. This organisation consists of 25 independent states and 10 associate members.[43] It also involves observer states from the rest of Latin America, including Brazil.[44] Consequently, when the Declaration of Havana was issued at the end of the ministerial council meeting of the Association of Caribbean States in June 2016, it acknowledged Caricom's reparations movement. The document also ensured that the call for reparatory justice reverberated not just in English-speaking countries, but in all French, Spanish, and Dutch-speaking countries. The 2016 Havana Declaration

> recognises that slavery and the slave trade were atrocious crimes against humanity, reaffirms the Durban Declaration, in particular, the importance of establishing compensatory and reparatory effective resources and measures, among others, at the national, regional and international levels in order to cope with the persistent effects of slavery and the transatlantic slave trade; and welcomes Caricom's initiative for the creation of the Reparations Commission of the Caribbean Community, and praises the efforts of said commission to correct such injustices.[45]

Support for the Caribbean Community's reparations movement was again provided in 2019 by the same body. At its Managua meeting, the Association of Caribbean States supported "the 10-point Action Plan of the Reparations Commission of the Caribbean Community", and applauded the efforts to "correct injustices resulting from the genocide of the native peoples and the Transatlantic trafficking of enslaved Africans, and slavery".[46] This rhetorical support, however, did not mean that these governments also committed their own countries to advancing this process.

While these two declarations inextricably linked reparations in Latin America to the progress of Caricom's institutions, this was not the beginning of the Latin American and Brazilian experiences. As earlier noted, the displaced Black Caribs/Garifuna had originated from St Vincent and the Grenadines before being transplanted to Honduras, Nicaragua, Belize, and Guatemala. These groups have been making the case for reparations since their banishment to Central America in 1797. With the launch of the Caricom Commission, they again raised their voices for redress: their annual pilgrimages to St Vincent and the Grenadines reinforce the fact that repatriation remains a major part of the conversation about reparations in Latin America and the Caribbean. This group transcends national borders and is a good example of a movement that never lost its identity, remaining to this day a distinct group driven by an ideology that includes justice for all its ancestors.

The African contribution to the development of Brazil was explored and established by Manuel Querino, the Afro-Brazilian artist and ethnographer, during the late nineteenth and early twentieth centuries. Querino established the basis for reparations in his exploration of the contributions of Africans to the development of Brazilian civilisation: "the work of the Negro for centuries sustained the grandeur and prosperity of Brazil".[47] Querino's writings were also the basis of the work of both Eric Williams and Hilary Beckles, and continue to serve as a pillar of the reparations movement across Latin America and the Caribbean. More work must be done to document the contributions of both indigenous peoples and enslaved Africans to the socio-economic, cultural, and political development of Latin America.

Concluding Reflections

The struggle for reparations in Latin America has been affected by a series of factors that all stem from pervasive racism. This has fostered the inhumanity of millions of both indigenous peoples and the descendants of enslaved Africans. Authors such as Manuel Querino and Henry Gates Jr, as well as organisations like the United Nations, have written on the exclusion, discrimination, and domination affecting people who have lived through a historically embedded hierarchy in Latin America based on the colour of their skin. Under a new rhetoric that recognises culture and not race as the basis for their deprivation, these people have been made to embrace a colour grading system in a society in which visible discriminatory practices coexist with the denial of racism. Gates noted that, in Latin America, he "encountered a social and economic reality that is deeply troubled, deeply conflicted, by race, a reality in which race codes for class".[48] This pervasive racism has resulted in brutality, which has stripped these groups of their identity and has rendered them invisible in the face of continued visible discrimination. This chapter has demonstrated that the systematic invisibility of indigenous people and the denial of the contributions of Africans to the development of Latin America have undermined the very basis of claims for reparations. Being hidden in plain sight has ensured that these groups have been hindered in their struggles for justice, for equal access to schools, health care, and land. Apologies cannot be enough when injustices remain persistent across the region.

The image of miscegenation as purifying and changing has also contributed substantially to this invisibility of these marginalised groups, and to reinforcing the notion of white superiority and black inferiority. The myth of racial democracy in Latin America has perpetuated this racism. Ivone Caetano, the first black woman sworn in as a Court of Appeals judge in Brazil's state of Rio de Janeiro, declared that "all social problems in Brazil are remnants of slavery. Blacks do not know their history, so much so that many are against racial quotas. The extermination of young blacks responds to an old desire for whitening of the population."[49] Her words ring true for the whole of Latin America, and the call to open up the conversation on racism and genuine reparations must be pursued by all descendants of indigenous people. There should be a conscious effort to obliterate the stereotypical images of "savages" who have to be civilised by white people, and of the inferiority of Africans. This must be undertaken through mass education about black history, in alliance with other social movements.

The only reparations movement that places emphasis on both indigenous people and people of African descent is the Caricom Reparations Commission, whose ten-point action plan has been gaining global momentum (see Beckles in this volume). As the commission noted, the struggle for reparations has "ebbed and flowed over the decades of the 19th and 20th centuries but has always been consistent in the demands for restitution, and recompense for the crimes of chattel slavery in the Western Hemisphere".[50] This has certainly been the case in Brazil and across Latin America. The globalisation of the Caricom movement provides us with an opportunity to consolidate a movement in the region that can effectively confront not only Europe with one voice, but also Latin America, which developed economically on the back of the oppression and free labour of these groups. The images of the killing of indigenous and black activists defending their land in countries like Colombia and Brazil, and of black bodies killed in *favelas* – Latin American ghettos – are the only visible signs that these institutions still exist and have survived four centuries of sustained oppression. Being hidden in plain sight cannot continue to dominate Latin America's reparations movement.

Notes

Chapter 1. The Black Atlantic's Triple Tragedies: Slavery, Colonialism, and Reparations

1   I thank Stephen Small for his extremely useful comments on an earlier version of this chapter. I am also grateful to Kweku Ampiah, Hilary Beckles, and Selwyn Cudjoe for comments on an earlier version of sections of this chapter.

2   See, for example, Adekeye Adebajo, "Thabo Mbeki: The Pan-African Philosopher-King", in Adekeye Adebajo (ed.), *The Pan-African Pantheon: Prophets, Poets, and Philosophers* (Johannesburg: Jacana, 2020; Manchester: Manchester University Press, 2021), pp. 162–181.

3   United Nations, "World Conference Against Racism, Racial Discrimination, Xenophobia and Related Intolerance Declaration and Programme of Action", UN Department of Public Information, 2002, chrome-extension://efaidnbmnnnib pcajpcglclefindmkaj/https://www.ohchr.org/sites/default/files/Documents/ Publications/Durban_text_en.pdf.

4   African Union, "Concept Note on the African Union Theme of the Year for 2025", 45th Ordinary Session of the Executive Council, EX.CL/1528 (XLV) Rev.1, 19 June – 19 July 2024, Accra, Ghana.

5   Cited in, and summarised from, Helen Pidd, "Justin Welby Defends £100m Fund to Address C of E's Past Links to Slavery", *The Guardian* (London), 9 April 2023, www. the guardian.com.

6   Sam Gruet, "Lloyd's of London 'Deeply Sorry' over Slavery Links", BBC, 8 November 2023, www.bbc.com.

7   For broader studies on reparations, see, for example, Jacqueline Bhabha, Margareta Matache, and Caroline Elkins (eds.), *Time for Reparations: A Global Perspective* (Philadelphia: University of Pennsylvania Press, 2021); and Ana Lucia Araujo, *Reparations for Slavery and the Slave Trade: A Transnational and Comparative History* (London: Bloomsbury, 2017).

8   Adebajo, *The Pan-African Pantheon*.

9   Pew Research Center, "Key Facts about the Nation's 47.9 Million Black Americans", www.pewresearch.org; Statistics Canada, "Black History Month 2023 ... by the Numbers", www.statcan.gc.ca; *Project on Ethnicity and Race in Latin America*, Princeton University, 4 May 2022, https://web.archive.org/web/20220504001627/ https://perla.princeton.edu/; and Worldometer, Population in Africa, 2024, www.

worldometers.info.

10   This section draws from Adekeye Adebajo, *Global Africa: Profiles in Courage, Creativity, and Cruelty* (Johannesburg: Jacana, 2023; London and New York: Routledge, 2024).

11   Ali A. Mazrui, "The Black Atlantic from Othello to Obama: In Search of a Post-racial Society", in Adekeye Adebajo and Kaye Whiteman (eds.), *The EU and Africa: From Eurafrique to Afro-Europa* (New York: Columbia University Press; London: Hurst; and Johannesburg: Witwatersrand University Press, 2012), p. 420.

12   Paul Gilroy, *The Black Atlantic: Modernity and Double-Consciousness* (Cambridge: Harvard University Press, 1993), p. 4.

13   Mazrui, "The Black Atlantic from Othello to Obama", p. 420.

14   See, for example, Hilary McD. Beckles, *Britain's Black Debt* (Jamaica, Barbados, and Trinidad and Tobago: University of the West Indies Press, 2013).

15   Adebajo, *Global Africa*, p. 60.

16   Ali A. Mazrui, *The Africans: A Triple Heritage* (London: BBC Publications, 1986), pp. 109–113.

17   See, for example, Hakim Adi, *Pan-Africanism: A History* (London: Bloomsbury, 2018); and Elliot P. Skinner, *African Americans and US Policy toward Africa, 1850–1924: In Defense of Black Nationality* (Washington DC: Howard University Press, 1992).

18   See, for example, Pearl T. Robinson, "Randall Robinson: Pan-African Foreign Policy Virtuoso", in Adebajo, *The Pan-African Pantheon*, pp. 277–296.

19   Amiri Baraka (previously LeRoi Jones), *Blues People: Negro Music in White America* (New York and London: Harper, 1963), p. 17.

20   Baraka, *Blues People*, pp. 17–31.

21   Maya Angelou, *I Know Why the Caged Bird Sings* (New York: Random House, 1969).

22   This section draws from Adekeye Adebajo, "Pan-Africanism: From the Twin Plagues of European Locusts to Africa's Triple Quest for Emancipation", in Adebajo, *The Pan-African Pantheon*, pp. 3–57.

23   Ole J. Benedictow, "The Black Death: The Greatest Catastrophe Ever", *History Today*, vol. 3, March 2005, www.historytoday.com; and BBC History Extra, "Black Death Facts: Your Guide to the 'Worst Catastrophe in Recorded History'", 23 March 2020, www.historyextra.com.

24   I thank Stephen Small for this observation.

25   Office of the Historian, US Department of State, "Louisiana Purchase, 1803" and "The Spanish-American War, 1898", https://history.state.gov.

26   See Linda M. Heywood, *Njinga of Angola: Africa's Warrior Queen* (Cambridge: Harvard University Press, 2017).

27   J.F. Ade Ajayi, "The Atlantic Slave Trade and Africa", in Toyin Falola (ed.), *Tradition and Change in Africa: The Essays of J.F. Ade Ajayi* (Trenton and Asmara: Africa World Press, 2000), p. 289.

28   Ajayi, "The Atlantic Slave Trade and Africa", p. 290.

29   Horace Campbell, *Rasta and Resistance: From Marcus Garvey to Walter Rodney* (Trenton: Africa World Press, 1987), pp. 12, 15.

30   See, for example, Jennifer L. Morgan, *Reckoning with Slavery: Gender, Kinship and Capitalism in the Early Black Atlantic* (Durham: Duke University Press, 2021).

31   Campbell, *Rasta and Resistance*, p. 15.

32   I have relied for this analysis on Walter Rodney, *How Europe Underdeveloped Africa*

(Washington DC: Howard University Press, 1982 [1972]), pp. 98–100.

33   See Rodney, *How Europe Underdeveloped Africa*; and Maxine Berg and Pat Hudson, *Slavery, Capitalism and the Industrial Revolution* (Cambridge: Polity Press, 2023).

34   This paragraph and the next have drawn from Eric Williams, *Capitalism and Slavery* (Chapel Hill: University of North Carolina Press, 1944), pp. 30–50.

35   Williams, *Capitalism and Slavery*, p. 39.

36   Ajayi, "The Atlantic Slave Trade and Africa", p. 288.

37   See, for example, Emmanuel Akyeampong, "History, Memory, Slave-Trade and Slavery in Anlo", *Slavery and Abolition*, vol. 22, no. 3, December 2001, pp. 1–24.

38   Beckles, *Britain's Black Debt*, p. 168.

39   Rodney, *How Europe Underdeveloped Africa*, p. 102.

40   Campbell, *Rasta and Resistance*, p. 13.

41   Ajayi, "The Atlantic Slave Trade and Africa", pp. 291–292.

42   I have summarised much of the information in this paragraph and the following two from Campbell, *Rasta and Resistance*, pp. 19–30.

43   C.L.R. James, *The Black Jacobins: Toussaint L'Ouverture and the San Domingo Revolution* (New York: Vintage Books, 1989 [1938]).

44   This information is gleaned from the 2013 Public Broadcasting Service (PBS) documentary by Henry Louis Gates Jr, *The African Americans: Many Rivers to Cross*, Episode 2: "The Age of Slavery (1780–1860)" and Episode 3: "Into the Fire (1861–1896)".

45   See, for example, Dann J. Broyld, "Harriet Tubman: Transnationalism and the Land of a Queen in the Late Antebellum", *The Meridians: Feminism, Race, and Transnationalism*, special issue: "Harriet Tubman: A Legacy of Resistance", vol. 12, no. 2, November 2014, pp. 78–98; Erica Armstrong Dunbar, *She Came to Slay: The Life and Times of Harriet Tubman* (New York: Simon and Schuster, 2019); Kate Clifford Larson, *Bound for the Promised Land: Harriet Tubman; Portrait of an American Hero* (London: One World, 2004); and Clarence Lusane, *Twenty Dollars and Change: Harriet Tubman and the Ongoing Fight for Racial Justice and Democracy* (San Francisco: City Lights Books, 2022).

46   Micere Mugo, "Art, Artists and the Flowering of Pan-Africana Liberated Zones", in Issa Shivji (ed.), *Reimagining Pan-Africanism: Distinguished Mwalimu Nyerere Lecture Series, 2009–2013* (Dar es Salaam: Mkuki Na Nyota, 2015), p. 178.

47   W.E.B. Du Bois, *The Souls of Black Folk* (New York: Penguin, 1996 [1903]).

48   See Abiola Irele, "Black Utopia I: Slavery and Providence", in Abiola Irele, *The African Scholar and Other Essays* (Ibadan: Bookcraft, 2019), pp. 137–139.

49   See, for example, Campbell, *Rasta and Resistance*.

50   I thank Stephen Small for nuancing this point.

51   Cited in Theresa Singleton and Marcos André Torres de Souza, "Archaeologies of the African Diaspora: Brazil, Cuba, and the United States", in Teresita Majewski and David Gaimster (eds.), *International Handbook of Historical Archaeology* (New York: Springer, 2009), p. 450; and Ana Lucia Araújo, "Slavery and the Atlantic Slave Trade in Brazil and Cuba from an Afro-Atlantic Perspective", *Almanack*, vol. 12, January–April 2016, p. 1.

52   Araújo, "Slavery and the Atlantic Slave Trade", pp. 1–5.

53   Singleton and Souza, "Archaeologies of the African Diaspora", p. 457.

54   I thank Stephen Small for nuancing this point.

55   See Jacob U. Gordon, "Yoruba Cosmology and Culture in Brazil: A Study of African Survivals in the New World", *Journal of Black Studies*, vol. 10, no. 2, December 1979, pp. 231–244; and Henry Louis Gates's PBS documentary *Black in Latin America*, "Brazil: A Racial Paradise?", 2011.

56   See Shubi L. Ishemo, "From Africa to Cuba: An Historical Analysis of the Sociedad Secreta Abakuá (Ñañiguismo)", *Review of African Political Economy*, vol. 29, no. 92, June 2002, pp. 253–272.

57   See Henry Louis Gates's PBS documentary *Black in Latin America*, "Cuba: The Next Revolution", 2011.

58   I am grateful for this summary to Adi, *Pan-Africanism*, pp. 202–203.

59   Garry Steckles, *Bob Marley* (Oxford: Macmillan Education, 2008), p. 219. See also Stephen Davis, *Bob Marley: Conquering Lion of Reggae* (London: Arthur Barker, 1983); Vivien Goldman, *The Book of Exodus: The Making and Meaning of Bob Marley and the Wailers' Album of the Century* (London: Aurum Press, 2006); and Clinton Hutton, "Bob Marley: Revolutionary Prophet of African Unity", in Adebajo, *The Pan-African Pantheon*, pp. 543–554.

60   This section draws from Adekeye Adebajo, "Introduction: Bismarck's Sorcery and Africa's Three Magic Kingdoms", in Adekeye Adebajo, *The Curse of Berlin: Africa after the Cold War* (New York: Oxford University Press, 2013 [2010]; Hurst: London, 2010; and Scottsville: University of KwaZulu-Natal Press, 2010), pp. 1–27.

61   Ajayi, "The Atlantic Slave Trade and Africa", pp. 295–296.

62   See Adebajo, *The Curse of Berlin*.

63   Rodney, *How Europe Underdeveloped Africa*.

64   Ali A. Mazrui, "Black Berlin and the Curse of Fragmentation: From Bismarck to Obama", Preface in Adebajo, *The Curse of Berlin*, pp. ix–xxviii.

65   See A. Adu Boahen, "Africa and the Colonial Challenge", in A. Adu Boahen (ed.), *General History of Africa*, vol. 7, *Africa under Colonial Domination, 1880–1935* (Berkeley: University of California Press, 1985), pp. 1–18.

66   Ali A. Mazrui, *The African Condition: A Political Diagnosis* (Cambridge: Cambridge University Press, 1980), p. 95.

67   My summary of the Berlin Conference in this section relies largely on the narratives in Thomas Pakenham, *The Scramble for Africa: White Man's Conquest of the Dark Continent from 1876 to 1912* (New York: Avon, 1991), pp. 239–255; Wm Roger Louis, "The Berlin Congo Conference and the (Non-) Partition of Africa, 1884–1885", in Wm Roger Louis, *Ends of British Imperialism: The Scramble for Empire, Suez, and Decolonization* (London: Tauris, 2006), pp. 75–126; and G.N. Uzoigwe, "The Results of the Berlin West Africa Conference: An Assessment", in Stig Förster, Wolfgang J. Mommsen, and Ronald Robinson (eds.), *Bismarck, Europe, and Africa: The British Africa Conference, 1884–1885, and the Onset of Partition* (Oxford: Oxford University Press, 1988), pp. 543–544.

68   See Adam Hochschild, *King Leopold's Ghost: A Story of Greed, Terror, and Heroism in Colonial Africa* (London: Pan Macmillan, 1998).

69   Quoted in David Olusoga, "Germany Comes to Terms with Its Forgotten Namibian Death Camps", *The Guardian* (London), 15 January 2017.

70   See, for example, Eric Ames (ed.), *Germany's Colonial Pasts* (Lincoln: University of Nebraska Press, 2005); and Horst Drechsler, *"Let Us Die Fighting": The Struggle of the Herero and Nama against German Imperialism (1884–1915)* (London: Zed Press,

1980).

71   See, for example, Shelley Baranowski, *Nazi Empire: German Colonialism and Imperialism from Bismarck to Hitler* (Cambridge: Cambridge University Press, 2011); and Casper Erichsen and David Olusoga, *The Kaiser's Holocaust: Germany's Forgotten Genocide and the Colonial Roots of Nazism* (London: Faber and Faber, 2011).

72   See, for example, Kwame Nkrumah, *Neo-Colonialism: The Last Stage of Imperialism* (London: Thomas Nelson and Sons, 1965).

73   These figures are cited in Stephen Small, *20 Questions and Answers on Black Europe* (The Hague: Amrit Publishers, 2018), p. 37.

74   This section builds on my past work, such as Adekeye Adebajo, "Folie de Grandeur", *World Today*, vol. 53, no. 6, 1997, pp. 147–150; and Adekeye Adebajo, "*Pax Nigeriana* Versus *Pax Gallica*: ECOWAS and UN Peacekeeping in Mali", in Tony Karbo and Kudrat Virk (eds.), *The Palgrave Handbook of Peacebuilding in Africa* (New York: Palgrave Macmillan, 2018), pp. 209–231.

75   Quoted in Christopher M. Andrew, "France: Adjustment to Change", in Hedley Bull (ed.), *The Expansion of International Society* (Oxford: Clarendon, 1984), p. 337.

76   See John Chipman, *French Power in Africa* (Oxford: Blackwell, 1989); Paul Gifford and W.R. Lewis (eds.), *The Transfer of Power in Africa: Decolonization, 1940–1960* (New Haven: Yale University Press, 1982); Guy Martin, *Africa in World Politics: A Pan-African Perspective* (Asmara: Africa World Press, 2002); and Victor T. Le Vine, *Politics in Francophone Africa* (Boulder: Lynne Rienner, 2007).

77   Guy Martin, "Continuity and Change in Franco-African Relations", *Journal of Modern African Studies*, vol. 33, no.1, March 1995, pp. 9–10.

78   For two recent detailed studies on French complicity in Rwanda's genocide, see Daniela Kroslak, *The Role of France in the Rwandan Genocide* (London: Hurst, 2007); and Andrew Wallis, *Silent Accomplice: The Untold Story of France's Role in the Rwandan Genocide* (London: Tauris, 2006).

79   Kaye Whiteman, "Côte d'Ivoire: The Three Deaths of Houphouet-Boigny", in African Centre for Development and Strategic Studies, Ijebu-Ode, Nigeria, *African Conflict, Peace, and Governance Monitor* (Ibadan: Dokun, 2005), pp. 43–59.

80   See François Soudain, "La cooperation dans le sang", *Jeune Afrique*, 8–14 January 1997, p. 7.

81   See Guy Martin, "France's African Policy in Transition: Disengagement and Redeployment", in Chris Alden and Guy Martin (eds.), *France and South Africa: Towards a New Engagement with Africa* (Pretoria: Protea Book House, 2003), p. 105.

82   See, for example, Adekeye Adebajo, "The Return of West Africa's 'Men on Horseback'", *Horizons*, no. 25, Winter 2024, pp. 116–125.

83   For a rich background, see Trica Keaton, *#You Know You're Black in France When ...: The Fact of Everyday Antiblackness* (Cambridge: MIT Press, 2023).

84   Cited in Jon Henley, "French Policing Called into Question Again after Brutal Arrest at Peaceful March", *The Guardian* (London), 9 July 2023.

85   "Billion-Euro Bill for Business as France Hopes Riots Over", France 24, 4 July 2023, www.france24.com/en/live-news/20230704-billion-euro-bill-for-business-as-france-hopes-riots-over.

86   Cited in Esther Addley, "Tuesday Briefing: How the Killing of a Teenager Sparked Fierce Unrest on the Streets of France", *The Guardian* (London), 4 July 2023.

87   Angelique Christafis, "Emmanuel Macron's Uphill Battle to Achieve 'Lasting Order'

in Deeply Divided France", *The Guardian* (London), 5 July 2023.

88 Cited in Jon Henley, "French Police Tendency to Violence Questioned after Latest Killing", *The Guardian* (London), 30 June 2023.

89 Cited in Addley, "Tuesday Briefing".

90 Cited in Pauline Bock, "Of Course Macron Won't Tackle Police Violence: He Knows His Power Depends on It", *The Guardian* (London), 4 July 2023.

91 Cited in Angelique Christafis, "French Authorities Ban March for Black Man Who Died in Police Custody", *The Guardian* (London), 7 July 2023.

92 Jonathan Yerushalmy, "France Protests: More than 1,300 Arrested as Riots Surge in Marseille and Lyon", *The Guardian* (London), 1 July 2023.

93 Alexander Parker, "Sarkozy's Balancing Act", *The Weekender*, 28–29 April 2007, p. 7.

94 Quoted in Yerushalmy, "France Protests".

95 Quoted in Bock, "Of Course Macron Won't Tackle Police Violence".

96 Quoted in Kim Willsher, "Macron Accused of Authoritarianism after Threat to Cut Off Social Media", *The Guardian* (London), 5 July 2023.

97 Angelique Christafis, "A Monument to French Rage: Buses Torched in Riots over Police Killings", *The Guardian* (London), 30 June 2023.

98 See, for example, Frantz Fanon, *The Wretched of the Earth* (New York: Grove Press, 1963 [1961]); and Alistair Horne, *A Savage War of Peace: Algeria, 1954–1962* (London: Macmillan, 1977).

99 Cited in Henley, "French Police Tendency to Violence Questioned after Latest Killing".

100 Rokhaya Diallo, "France Has Ignored Racist Police Violence for Decades: This Uprising Is the Price of That Denial", *The Guardian* (London), 30 June 2023.

101 Diallo, "France Has Ignored Racist Police Violence for Decades".

102 See, for example, Theodore Zeldin, *The French* (New York: Kodansha International, 1996); and Nicholas Atkin, *The Fifth French Republic* (Hampshire: Palgrave Macmillan, 2005).

103 Williams, *Capitalism and Slavery*.

104 Adekeye Adebajo, *The Trial of Cecil John Rhodes* (Johannesburg: Jacana, 2021).

105 Nigel Biggar, "Rhodes, Race and the Abuse of History", *Standpoint*, March 2016, https://www.mcdonaldcentre.org.uk/sites/default/files/content/events/standpoint_rhodes_published_march_16.pdf.

106 Biggar, "Rhodes, Race and the Abuse of History", p. 40.

107 Biggar, "Rhodes, Race and the Abuse of History", pp. 40–42.

108 Biggar, "Rhodes, Race and the Abuse of History", p. 42.

109 Biggar, "Rhodes, Race and the Abuse of History", p. 43.

110 Paul Maylam, *The Cult of Rhodes: Remembering an Imperialist in Africa* (Cape Town: David Philip, 2005), p. 9.

111 Biggar, "Rhodes, Race and the Abuse of History", p. 42.

112 Biggar, "Rhodes, Race and the Abuse of History", p. 42.

113 Adekeye Adebajo, "Worse than the Rest", *Times Literary Supplement*, 28 July 2006, www.thetls.co.uk.

114 See Maylam, *The Cult of Rhodes*, p. 14; Antony Thomas, *Rhodes: The Race for Africa* (Johannesburg: Jonathan Ball, 1996), p. 14; and Felix Gross, *Rhodes of Africa* (London: Cassell and Co., 1956), p. 242.

115 Nigel Biggar, "Decolonising Activists Are Pillaging Britain's Past for Political

Advantage", *Sunday Telegraph*, 2 May 2021.

116   Maylam, *The Cult of Rhodes*, p. 14; and Stanlake Samkange, *What Rhodes Really Said about Africans* (Harare: Harare Publishing House, 1982), p. 10.

117   "The Glen Grey Speech: A transcription of Cecil John Rhodes' Speech on the Second Rereading of the Glen Grey Act to the Cape House Parliament on July 30 1894", https://www.sahistory.org.za/sites/default/files/glen_grey_speech.pdf.

118   Maylam, *The Cult of Rhodes*, p. 108.

119   Caroline Elkins, *Legacy of Violence: A History of the British Empire* (New York: Alfred A. Knopf, 2022).

120   This analysis is based largely on the rich life-stories in Colin Grant, *Homecoming: Voices of the Windrush Generation* (London: Jonathan Cape, 2019).

121   Grant, *Homecoming*.

122   This phrase is from Charles Dickens, *Little Dorrit* (Toronto: Penguin Random House, 2002 [1857]).

123   Government UK, "Ethnicity Facts and Figures: Population of England and Wales", 22 December 2022, https://www.ethnicity-facts-figures.service.gov.uk/uk-population-by-ethnicity/national-and-regional-populations/population-of-england-and-wales/latest/.

124   John Grace, "Selective Spectator", *The Guardian* (London), 21 October 2004.

125   This section draws from Adebajo, "Pan-Africanism".

126   This point is made in Bernard Makhosezwe Magubane, *The Ties That Bind: African-American Consciousness of Africa* (Trenton: Africa World Press, 1987), p. 135.

127   See John C. Shields (ed.), *The Collected Works of Phillis Wheatley* (New York: Oxford University Press, 1988).

128   Quoted in Irele, *The African Scholar*, p. 137.

129   Adi, *Pan-Africanism*, p. 217.

130   This paragraph draws from Adi, *Pan-Africanism*, pp. 6–7.

131   Hollis R. Lynch, *Edward Wilmot Blyden: Pan-Negro Patriot, 1832–1912* (Oxford and New York: Oxford University Press, 1967), p. 3.

132   Quoted in V.Y. Mudimbe, "E.W. Blyden's Legacy and Questions", in *The Invention of Africa: Gnosis, Philosophy, and the Order of Knowledge* (Bloomington: Indiana University Press, 1988), p. 133.

133   Adi, *Pan-Africanism*, p. 25.

134   Adi, *Pan-Africanism*, pp. 21–22.

135   Quoted in Geoffrey Barraclough, "The Revolt against the West", in Prasenjit Duara (ed.), *Decolonization: Perspectives from Now and Then* (London: Routledge, 2004), p. 118.

136   See Tajudeen Abdul-Raheem, "Introduction: Reclaiming Africa for Africans; Pan-Africanism, 1900–1994", in Tajudeen Abdul-Raheem (ed.), *Pan-Africanism: Politics, Economy, and Social Change in the Twenty-First Century* (London: Pluto, 1996), pp. 1–30.

137   Magubane, *The Ties That Bind*, p. 125.

138   Colin Legum, *Pan-Africanism* (London: Pall Mall Press, 1962), pp. 28–29.

139   See, for example, Adekeye Adebajo, "Facing Up to Woodrow Wilson's True Legacy", *Times Literary Supplement*, 6 August 2020.

140   See Colin Grant, "Marcus Garvey: 'Africa for the Africans'", pp. 104–117; and Rhoda Reddock, "Amy Ashwood Garvey: Global Pan-African Feminist", pp. 131–143; both

in Adebajo, *The Pan-African Pantheon*.

141   Adi, *Pan-Africanism*, p. 217.

142   I am grateful for this summary to Adi, *Pan-Africanism*, pp. 31–33. See also Alaine Locke (ed.), *The New Negro: Voices of the Harlem Renaissance* (New York: Touchstone, 1999 [1925]).

143   See, for example, W.E.B. Du Bois, "Manifesto of the Second Pan-African Congress", in Eric J. Sundquist (ed.), *The Oxford W.E.B. Du Bois Reader* (New York and Oxford: Oxford University Press, 1996), pp. 640–644.

144   Legum, "Pan-Africanism", pp. 29–30.

145   Kwame Nkrumah, *Ghana: The Autobiography of Kwame Nkrumah* (London: Panaf, 1957), p. 53.

146   Legum, "Pan-Africanism", pp. 31–32.

147   Adi, *Pan-Africanism*, p. 217.

148   This paragraph is summarised from Adi, *Pan-Africanism*, pp. 217–219. See also Robert J. Cottrol, *The Long Lingering Shadow: Slavery, Race, and Law in the American Hemisphere* (Athens: University of Georgia Press, 2013); and Petra R. Rivera-Rideau, Jennifer Jones, and Tianna S. Paschel (eds.), *Afro-Latin@s in Movement: Critical Approaches to Blackness and Transnationalism in the Americas* (London and New York: Palgrave Macmillan, 2016).

149   The summary in this section has drawn from Adi, *Pan-Africanism*, pp. 89–105, 186 and 193–195.

150   Cited in Kris Manjapra, "When Will Britain Face Up to Its Crimes against Humanity?", *The Guardian* (London), 29 March 2018, www.thegurdian.com.

151   Toni Morrison, "The Slavebody and the Blackbody", in *The Source of Self-Regard: Selected Essays, Speeches, and Meditations* (New York: Alfred A. Knopf, 2019), p. 74.

152   Randall Robinson, *The Debt: What America Owes to Blacks* (New York and London: Penguin Books, 2000), pp. 199–216.

153   Robinson, *The Debt*, pp. 199–234.

154   "Many Black Americans Aren't Rushing to Get the COVID-19 Vaccine: A Long History of Medical Abuse Suggests Why", Associated Press Television News, 25 February 2021, https://www.republicworld.com/world-news/us-news/many-black-americans-arent-rushing-to-get-the-covid-19-vaccine-a-long-history-of-medical-abuse-suggests-why.html.

155   Tom Flanagan, "Canadian Taxpayers Not Consulted About Massive Reparations to First Nations People", *Western Standard* (Canada), 26 May 2023, https://www.fraserinstitute.org/article/canadian-taxpayers-not-consulted-about-massive-reparations-to-first-nations-people.

156   Beckles, *Britain's Black Debt*, p. 2.

157   Cited in Verene A. Shepherd, "Reparation and Diversity: Building an Inclusive Moment in the Caribbean", in Verene A. Shepherd, Henderson D. Carter, and Ahmed N. Reid (eds.), *Interrogating Injustices: Essays in Honour of Hilary McD. Beckles* (Kingston and Miami: Ian Randle Publishers, 2023), p. 1034.

158   Beckles, *Britain's Black Debt*, pp. 163–171.

159   Caricom, "Ten Point Plan for Reparatory Justice", 11 March 2014, https://caricom.org/caricom-ten-point-plan-for-reparatory-justice/.

160   This paragraph and the one above are summarised from Shepherd, "Reparation and Diversity", pp. 1025–1031.

161 See "Portugal Should Apologise for Role in Slave Trade, Says Its President", *The Guardian* (London), 25 April 2023; and Imani Tafari-Ama, "Recharging Reparations Responsibilities", *The Gleaner* (Jamaica), 5 May 2024, https://jamaica-gleaner.com.

162 Both the St Maarten and Colombia cases are cited in African Union, "Building a United Front to Promote the Cause of Justice and Payment of Reparations to Africans", Executive Council 44th Ordinary Session, 15 January – 15 February 2024, Addis Ababa, Ethiopia, EX.CL/1501 (XLIV), p. 4.

163 Quoted in Jermain Ostiana, "Why the Dutch Apology for Slavery Leaves a Bitter Taste in My Mouth", *The Guardian* (London), 14 January 2023.

164 Quoted in Donna Ferguson, "Dutch King Apologises for Country's Historical Involvement in Slavery", *The Guardian* (London), 1 July 2023.

165 Cited in Ferguson, "Dutch King Apologises for Country's Historical Involvement in Slavery".

166 See African Union, "Building a United Front".

167 Amelia Gentleman, "Africa and Caribbean Nations Agree Move to Seek Reparations for Slavery", *The Guardian* (London), 17 November 2023.

168 Cited in Gentleman, "Africa and Caribbean Nations".

169 Hedley Bull, "The Revolt against the West", in Hedley Bull and Adam Watson (eds.), *The Expansion of International Society* (Oxford: Clarendon Press, 1984), p. 217.

170 This section benefited from Piers Brendon, "The Kaiser's Holocaust by David Olusoga and Casper W. Erichsen: Review", *The Guardian* (London), 4 December 2010; Olusoga, "Germany Comes to Terms with Its Forgotten Namibian Death Camps"; Norimitsu Onishi and Melissa Eddy, "A Forgotten Genocide: What Germany Did in Namibia, and What It's Saying", *New York Times*, 28 May 2021; European Centre for Constitutional and Human Rights, "The 'Reconciliation Agreement': A Lost Opportunity", June 2021; and Joint Declaration by the Federal Republic of Germany and the Republic of Namibia, "United in Remembrance of Our Colonial Past, United in Our Will to Reconcile, United in Our Vision of the Future", June 2021.

171 "How Not to Repair America" and "The Tide Goes Out", *The Economist* (London), 10 June 2023, www.economist.com.

172 See "How Not to Repair America" and "The Tide Goes Out".

173 Zeeshan Aleem, "New CDC Data Shows Covid-19 Is Affecting African Americans at Exceptionally High Rates", *Vox*, 18 April 2020, https://www.vox.com/coronavirus-covid19/2020/4/18/21226225/coronavirus-black-cdc-infection.

174 Angela Davis, *The Prison Industrial Complex* (Chico, CA: AK Press, 2001).

175 National Center for Education Statistics, "Status and Trends in the Education of Racial and Ethnic Groups", https://nces.ed.gov/programs/raceindicators/indicator_rads.asp (accessed 14 February 2024).

176 Stockholm International Peace Research Institute, "The Top 15 Military Spenders, 2022", https://www.sipri.org/visualizations/2023/top-15-military-spenders-2022.

177 "How Not to Repair America" and "The Tide Goes Out".

178 Taryn Luna, "Is California Giving Slavery Reparations? What You Need to Know", *Los Angeles Times*, 6 May 2023, www.latimes.com.

179 Kurtis Lee, "California Panel Sizes Up Reparations for Black Citizens", *New York Times*, 1 December 2022, https://www.nytimes.com/2022/12/01/business/economy/california-black-reparations.html.

180   Greg Grandin, "'The Economist' Has a Slavery Problem", *The Nation*, 9 September
2014   (https://www.thenation.com/article/archive/economist-has-slavery-
problem/); and Chris Taylor, "The Economist Has a Slavery Problem," *Africa Is a
Country*, 9 November 2014 (https://africasacountry.com/2014/09/the-economist-
magazine-has-had-a-slavery-problem-since-1843).

181   See David Horowitz, *Uncivil Wars: The Controversy over Reparations for Slavery* (San
Francisco: Encounter Books, 2002).

182   International Organization for Migration (IOM), "World Migration Report 2020",
Geneva, p. 4.

183   IOM, "World Migration Report 2020", p. 4.

184   See, for example, Small, *20 Questions and Answers on Black Europe.*

185   See, for example, Adekeye Adebajo, "Africa's 'Boat People' Encounter 'Fortress
Europe': Conflict and Migration in Africa–EU Relations", in Adeoye O. Akinola
and Jesper Bjarnesen (eds.), *Worlds Apart? Perspectives on Africa–EU Migration*
(Johannesburg: Jacana, 2022), pp. 47–72; and Clare Castillejo, "The EU Migration
Partnership Framework: Time for a Rethink?", ECONSTOR Discussion Paper no.
28, 2017, Deutsches Institut für Entwicklungspolitik, Bonn.

186   These figures are all derived from reports of the International Organization for
Migration, notably "Flow Monitoring".

187   "32 Million Africans Forcibly Displaced by Conflict and Repression", Reliefweb, 17
June 2021, www.reliefweb.int.

188   "The Other African-Americans", *The Economist*, 19 October 2019, pp. 38–39. See also
Nemata Amelia Ibitayo Blyden, *African Americans and Africa: A New History* (New
Haven and London: Yale University Press, 2019).

189   Quoted in Adi, *Pan-Africanism*, p. 222.

190   See, for example, Pierre Barrot (ed.), *Nollywood: The Video Phenomenon in Nigeria*
(Oxford: Currey, 2008); Jonathan Haynes, *Nollywood: The Creation of Nigerian Film
Genres* (Chicago: University of Chicago Press, 2016; Ibadan: Bookcraft, 2017); John
C. McCall, "Nollywood Confidential: The Unlikely Rise of Nigeria's Video Film",
Transition, vol. 13, no. 1, 2004, pp. 98–109; and Odia Ofeimun, "In Defence of the
Films We Have Made", *Chimurenga*, vol. 8, 2006, pp. 44–54.

191   Frederick Douglass, "West India Emancipation", speech delivered at Canandaigua, New
York, 3 August 1857 (https://www.blackpast.org/african-american-history/1857-
frederick-douglass-if-there-no-struggle-there-no-progress/).

**Chapter 2. Masters and Servants in Barbados and South Africa: From Enslaved Labour
to Coerced "Free" Labour in the British Empire**

1   Douglas Hay and Paul Craven, *Masters, Servants, and Magistrates in Britain and the
Empire, 1562–1955* (Chapel Hill: University of North Carolina Press, 2004). p.iii.

2   Ravi Ahuja, "Review Essay: Making the Empire a Thinkable Whole: Master and
Servant Law in Transterritorial Perspective", *International Review of Social History*,
vol. 52, 2007, pp. 287–294.

3   One example of such unrest was the so-called Federation Riots in Barbados in 1876.
Ironically, a judge from the South African colony of Natal, Henry Lushington, was
appointed as a special commissioner to investigate and report on the causes of the
disturbances.

4   Hilary Beckles, *A History of Barbados: From Amerindian Settlement to Caribbean Single*

Market (2nd edn, Cambridge: Cambridge University Press, 2006), pp. 129–135.

5   Jackie Loos, *Echoes of Slavery: Voices from South Africa's Past* (Cape Town: David Philip, 2004), p. 125.

6   For amelioration in Barbados, see Woodville Marshall, "Amelioration and Emancipation in Barbados", in Alvin Thompson (ed.), *Emancipation I: A Series of Lectures to Commemorate the 150th Anniversary of Emancipation* (Bridgetown: National Cultural Foundation and History Department, the University of the West Indies, 1984); for amelioration at the Cape, see John Edwin Mason, *Social Death and Resurrection: Slavery and Emancipation in South Africa* (Charlottesville: University of Virginia Press, 2003), pp. 46–58.

7   In both Barbados and the Cape Colony, provisions were made for eight stipendiary magistrates, despite the much-smaller number of apprentices at the Cape. This was justified due to the much larger area of the Cape Colony.

8   William A. Green, *British Slave Emancipation: The Sugar Colonies and the Great Experiment, 1830–1865* (Oxford: Clarendon Press, 1976), pp. 136–144; and Nigel Worden, "Between Slavery and Freedom: The Apprenticeship Period, 1834–8", in Nigel Worden and Clifton Crais (eds.), *Breaking the Chains: Slavery and Its Legacy in the Nineteenth-Century Cape Colony* (Johannesburg: Witwatersrand University Press, 1994).

9   Marshall, "Amelioration and Emancipation", p. 76.

10   Green, *British Slave Emancipation*, p. 134.

11   Green, *British Slave Emancipation*, pp. 134–135.

12   Beckles, *A History of Barbados*, p. 130.

13   Worden, "Between Slavery and Freedom", pp. 136–140.

14   Kate Boehme, Peter Mitchell, and Alan Lester, "Reforming Everywhere and All at Once: Transitioning to Free Labor across the British Empire, 1837–1838", *Comparative Studies in Society and History*, vol. 60, no. 3, 2018, pp. 688–718.

15   Green, *British Slave Emancipation*, p. 157.

16   Quoted in Worden, "Between Slavery and Freedom", p. 135.

17   Worden, "Between Slavery and Freedom", p. 135.

18   Peter Delius and Stanley Trapido, "Inboekselings and Oorlams: The Creation and Transformation of a Servile Class", *Journal of Southern African Studies*, vol. 8, no. 2, 1982, pp. 214–242.

19   On the celebration of Emancipation Day at the Cape, see Nigel Worden, "The Changing Politics of Slave Heritage in the Western Cape", *Journal of African History*, vol. 50, no. 1, 2009, pp. 23–40.

20   Quoted in Mandy Banton, "The Colonial Office, 1820–1955: Constantly the Subject of Small Struggles", in Hay and Craven, *Masters, Servants, and Magistrate*, p. 251.

21   Banton, "The Colonial Office, 1820–1955", p. 260.

22   Banton, "The Colonial Office, 1820–1955", p. 260.

23   Beckles, *A History of Barbados*, pp. 148–149.

24   The key feature of a "house of correction", as opposed to a common gaol, was that the inmates were put to hard labour. This ranged from working in chain gangs on public works such as road-mending and building, to the use of the treadmill. An 1837 investigation of the prison system in the British West Indies by Captain J.W. Pringle found widespread abuses, including poorly constructed treadmills that were, in effect,

instruments of torture. See, for example, Thomas Holt, *The Problem of Freedom: Race, Labor, and Politics in Jamaica and Britain, 1832–1938* (Baltimore: Johns Hopkins University Press, 1991), pp. 106–107.

25   Act No. 165 and Act No. 166, 7 January 1840: *Laws of Barbados*, vol. 1 (London: William Clowes and Son, 1855), https://www.google.com/books/edition/Laws_of_Barbados/JmFGAAAAYAAJ?hl=en.

26   Beckles, *A History of Barbados*, p. 149.

27   Quoted in Bentley Gibbs, "The Establishment of the Tenantry System", in Woodville Marshall (ed.), *Emancipation II: Aspects of the Post-slavery Experience in Barbados; A Series of Lectures to Commemorate the 150th Anniversary of Emancipation* (Bridgetown: National Cultural Foundation and the History Department, the University of the West Indies, 1974), p. 31.

28   Gibbs, "The Establishment of the Tenantry System", p. 33.

29   Act No. 165, 7 January 1840: *Laws of Barbados*.

30   Quoted in Gibbs, "The Establishment of the Tenantry System", p. 35.

31   This definition is contained in the preamble to the Act: Act No. 166, 7 January 1838, in *Laws of Barbados*.

32   Act No.166, 7 January 1838, in *Laws of Barbados*, clause 3.

33   Quoted in Mason, *Social Death and Resurrection*, p. 273.

34   Robert Shell, *Children of Bondage: A Social History of the Slave Society at the Cape of Good Hope, 1652–1838* (Hanover and London: Wesleyan University Press, 1994), p. 34.

35   Quoted in Mason, *Social Death and Resurrection*, p. 272.

36   Quoted in Mason, *Social Death and Resurrection*, p. 272.

37   Robert Ross, "'Rather Mental than Physical': Emancipations and the Cape Economy", in Worden and Crais, *Breaking the Chains*, pp. 162–163; and Mason, *Social Death and Resurrection*, p. 274.

38   Quoted in Banton, "The Colonial Office, 1820–1955", p. 260.

39   Banton, "The Colonial Office, 1820–1955", p. 260.

40   Elizabeth Elbourne, "Freedom at Issue: Vagrancy Legislation and the Meaning of Freedom in Britain and the Cape Colony, 1799 to 1842", in Paul Lovejoy and Nicholas Rogers (eds.), *Unfree Labour in the Development of the Atlantic World* (London: Routledge, 1993), p. 143.

41   Mason, *Social Death and Resurrection*, pp. 275–276.

42   Mason, *Social Death and Resurrection*, pp. 275–276.

43   Banton, "The Colonial Office, 1820–1955", p. 264.

44   Banton, "The Colonial Office, 1820–1955", p. 264; and Pamela Scully, "Private and Public Worlds of Emancipation in the Rural Western Cape, c.1830–47", in Worden and Crais, *Breaking the Chains*, p. 221.

45   Douglas Hay, "England, 1562–1875: The Law and its Uses", in Hay and Craven, *Masters, Servants, and Magistrates*, p. 116.

46   Gavin Williams, "Slaves, Workers, and Wine: The 'Dop System' in the History of the Cape Wine Industry, 1658–1894", *Journal of Southern African Studies*, vol. 42, no. 5, 2016, pp. 893–909.

47   Act No. 59 of 2003, The Liquor Act, *Government Gazette* 466, no. 26294, Cape Town, 26 April 2004.

48   Richard Ligon, *A True and Exact History of the Island of Barbados* (London: Humphrey Moseley, 1657), p. 129.

49   See Henderson Carter, "History of the Rum Enterprise in Barbados, 1640–1815" (MPhil thesis, University of the West Indies, Cave Hill Campus, 1993).

50   An Act to Amend the Laws Relating to Marriage in this Island, Act No. 158, 6 March 1839, *Laws of Barbados*. On the implementation of the Marriage Act at the Cape, see Pamela Scully, *Liberating the Family? Gender and British Slave Emancipation in the Rural Western Cape, South Africa, 1823–1853* (New Hampshire, Oxford, and Cape Town: Heinemann, James Currey and David Philip, 1997), pp. 110–125.

51   Quoted in Banton, "The Colonial Office, 1820–1955", p. 283.

52   For a detailed discussion of this seminal period in the social and political history of Barbados, and of other Caribbean islands, see O. Nigel Bolland, *On the March: Labour Rebellions in the British Caribbean, 1934–39* (London: James Currey, 1995).

53   Banton, "The Colonial Office, 1820–1955", p. 295.

54   Banton, "The Colonial Office, 1820–1955", pp. 296–299.

Chapter 3. Colonialism: Mamma Italia and Her Imperial Orphans

1   This chapter is adapted from my previously published chapter, "Orphans for the Empire: Colonial Propaganda and Children's Literature during the Imperial Era", in Patrizia Palumbo (ed.), *A Place in the Sun: Africa in Italian Colonial Culture from Post-unification to the Present* (Berkeley and Los Angeles: University of California Press, 2003), pp. 199–225.

2   The most exhaustive history of Italian colonialism in Africa is provided by Angelo Del Boca, *Gli Italiani in Africa orientale* (Milan: Mondadori, 1992).

3   Tracy Koon, *Believe, Obey, Fight: Political Socialization of Youth in Fascist Italy, 1922–1943* (Chapel Hill: North Carolina, 1985).

4   Edward Tannenbaum, *The Fascist Experience: Italian Society and Culture, 1922–1945* (New York: Basic Books, 1972), pp. 172–173.

5   Koon, *Believe, Obey, Fight*, p. 82.

6   Tannnenbaum, *The Fascist Experience*, p. 161.

7   Adolfo Mignemi, *Immagine coordinata per un impero: Editori, biblioteche e libri per ragazzi durante il Fascismo* (Turin: Gruppo Editoriale Forma, 1992), p. 56.

8   Adolfo Scotto Di Luzio, *Appropriazone imperfetta* (Bologna: Il Mulino,1996), pp. 202–203.

9   Arnaldo Cipolla, *Balilla regale* (Milano: EST, 1935).

10   Antonio Lugli, *Libri e figure: Storia della letteratura per l'infanzia e per la gioventù* (Bologna: Cappelli, 1982), p. 174.

11   Tannenbaum, *The Fascist Experience*, p. 167.

12   Duilio Gasparini, *Olga Visentini* (Florence: Le Monnier, 1968).

13   Olga Visentini, *Africanelle: Fiabe* (Turin: S.E.I., 1937).

14   Visentini, "The Goblin on the Roof", in *Africanelle*, pp. 157–165.

15   Judith K. Proud, *Children and Propaganda: Il Était une Fois … Fiction and Fairy Tale in Vichy France* (Oxford: Intellect Books, 1995), pp. 134–169.

16   Tenente Anonimo, *Volontario in Africa: Racconti di guerra per ragazzi* (Milan: La Prora, 1935); Slavator Gotta, *Piccolo legionario in Africa orientale* (Milan: Baldini and Castoldi, 1938); Nonno Ebe, *Genietti e sirenelle in Africa orientale* (Milan: Carroccio, 1938); and Cipolla, *Balilla regale*.

17   Maurizio Cesari, *La censura nel periodo fascista* (Naples: Liguori, 1978).

18   Deniz Kandiyoti, "Identity and its Discontents: Women and the Nation", in Patrick Williams and Laura Chrisman (eds.), *Colonial Discourse and Post-colonial Theory: A Reader* (New York: Columbia University Press, 1994), p. 376.

19   Elleke Boehmer, "Stories of Women and Mothers: Gender and Nationalism in the Early Fiction of Flora Nwapa", in Sysheuka Basta (ed.), *Motherlands: Black Women's Writing from Africa, the Caribbean and South Asia* (London: Women's Press, 1991).

20   Michael Adas, *Machine as the Measure of Men: Science, Technology, and Ideologies of Western Dominance* (Ithaca: Cornell University Press, 1989).

21   Tannenbaum, *The Fascist Experience*, p. 82.

22   Koon, *Believe, Obey, Fight*, pp. 96–98.

23   Cicely Hamilton, *Modern Italy as Seen by an Englishwoman* (London: J.M. Dent and Sons, 1932), pp. 35–40.

24   Visentini, "Reginetta Imperiale", in *Africanelle*, p. 102.

25   Scotto Di Luzio, *Appropriazone imperfetta*, pp. 146–147.

26   Lugli, *Libri e figure*, p. 174.

27   Gian Piero Brunetta, *L'ora d'Africa del cinema italiano: 1911–1989* (Rome: Materiali di Lavoro, 1990).

28   Visentini, "The Olive Grove in the Sands", in *Africanelle*, p. 4.

29   Barbara Sorgoni, "La zona grigia", in Barbara Sorgoni (ed.), *Parole e corpi: Antropologia, discorso giuridico e politiche sessuali interrazziali nella colonia Eritrea (1890–1941)* (Naples: Liguori, 1998), pp. 203–228.

30   On the kingdom of Ghera being immortalised by Italian explorers, see Augusto Franzoj, *Continente nero* (Novara: Istituto Geografico De Agostini, 1961).

31   Scotto Di Luzio, *Appropriazone imperfetta*, pp. 208–209.

32   Cipolla, *Balilla regale*, p. 72.

33   Piero Meldini, *Donna, sposa e madre* (Turin: Elle Di Ci, 1995), pp. 126–127.

34   Tannenbaum, *The Fascist Experience*, p. 125.

Chapter 4. Reparations for Imperialism: Legacies beyond Slavery in the British Empire

1   Tony Lane, *Liverpool: Gateway of Empire* (London: Lawrence and Wishart, 1987); Jessica Moody, *The Persistence of Memory: Remembering Slavery in Liverpool, "Slaving Capital of the World"* (Liverpool: Liverpool University Press, 2020).

2   Kwame Nimako and Glenn Willemsen, *The Dutch Atlantic: Slavery, Abolition and Emancipation* (London: Pluto Press, 2011).

3   Nicolas Draper, *The Price of Emancipation: Slave-Ownership, Compensation and British Society at the End of Slavery* (Cambridge: Cambridge University Press, 2010).

4   W.L. Burn, *Emancipation and Apprenticeship in the British West Indies* (London: Cape, 1937).

5   John Darwin, *The Empire Project: The Rise and Fall of the British World-System, 1830–1970* (Cambridge: Cambridge University Press, 2009).

6   Marika Sherwood, *After Abolition: Britain and the Slave Trade after 1807* (London: I.B. Tauris, 2007), p. 88.

7   Geoffrey Jones, *Merchants to Multinationals: British Trade Companies in the Nineteenth and Twentieth Centuries* (London: Oxford University Press, 2002).

8   Sherwood, *After Abolition*, p. 47.

9   Adu A. Boahen, *African Perspectives on Colonialism* (Baltimore: Johns Hopkins University Press, 1987).

10 Sven Beckert, *Empire of Cotton: A Global History* (New York: Vintage Books, 2015), p. 358.

11 Chris Evans and Göran Rydén, *Baltic Iron and the Atlantic World in the Eighteenth Century* (Leiden: Brill, 2007); Jason W. Moore, "'Amsterdam Is Standing on Norway', Part II: The Global North Atlantic in the Ecological Revolution of the Long Seventeenth Century", *Journal of Agrarian Change*, vol. 10, no. 2, April 2010, pp. 188–227.

12 Michael Flinn, "Scandinavian Iron Ore Mining and the British Steel Industry, 1870–1914", *Scandinavian Economic History Review*, vol. 2, no. 1, 1954, pp. 31–46; and Niels Buus Kristensen, "Industrial Growth in Denmark, 1872–1913, in Relation to the Debate on an Industrial Break-Through", *Scandinavian Economic History Review*, vol. 37, no. 1, 1989, pp. 3–22.

13 See, for example, Adekeye Adebajo, *The Curse of Berlin: Africa after the Cold War* (New York: Columbia University Press; London: Hurst; and Scottsville: University of KwaZulu-Natal Press, 2010).

14 Boahen, *African Perspectives on Colonialism*.

15 Kenneth Morgan, "Liverpool's Dominance in the British Slave Trade, 1740–1807", in David Richardson, Suzanne Schwarz, and Anthony Tibbles, *Liverpool and Transatlantic Slavery* (Liverpool: Liverpool University Press, 2017), pp. 14–42.

16 Folarin Shyllon, *Black People in Britain, 1555–1833* (London: Oxford University Press, 1977).

17 Hakim Adi, *West Africans in Britain, 1900–1960: Nationalism, Pan-Africanism and Communism* (London: Lawrence and Wishart, 1998); and Graeme Milne, *People, Place and Power on the Nineteenth Century Waterfront* (London: Palgrave Macmillan, 2016).

18 Stephen Small and John Solomos, "Race, Immigration and Politics in Britain: Changing Policy Agendas and Conceptual Paradigms, 1940s–2000s", *International Journal of Comparative Sociology*, 2006, pp. 235–257.

19 Stephen Small, "Black Expressive Culture in England and Europe", in Pawlet Brookes (ed.), *Reflections: Cultural Voices of Black British Irrepressible Resistance* (Leicester: Serendipity Institute for Black Arts and Heritage, 2020).

20 Ellen Craft and William Craft, *Running a Thousand Miles for Freedom: The Escape of William and Ellen Craft from Slavery* (Athens: University of Georgia Press, 1999); Anna Julia Cooper, *A Voice from the South by a Black Woman of the South* (New York: Dover Publications, 2016); and Hollis Lynch, *Edward Wilmot Blyden: Pan-Negro Patriot* (London: Oxford University Press, 1967).

21 Ray Jenkins, "Gold Coasters Overseas, 1880–1919: With Specific Reference to Their Activities in Britain", *Immigrants and Minorities*, vol. 4, 1985, pp. 5–52.

22 Adi, *West Africans in Britain*.

23 David Killingray, "Africans in the United Kingdom: An Introduction", in David Killingray, *Africans in Britain* (London: Frank Cass, 1994), pp. 2–27; and George Padmore, *Pan-Africanism or Communism? The Coming Struggle for Africa* (London: Dennis Dobson, 1956).

24 Milne, *People, Place and Power*.

25 Morgan, "Liverpool's Dominance in the British Slave Trade". See also David Pope, "The Wealth and Social Aspirations of Liverpool's Slave Merchants of the Second Half of the Eighteenth Century", in Richardson, Schwarz, and Tibbles, *Liverpool and*

Transatlantic Slavery, pp. 164–226.

26   Draper, *The Price of Emancipation*.

27   Anthony Tibbles, *Liverpool and the Slave Trade* (Liverpool: Liverpool University Press, 2018), p. 93.

28   Katie Donington, Ryan Hanley, and Jessica Moody (eds.), *Britain's History and Memory of Transatlantic Slavery: Local Nuances of a "National Sin"* (Liverpool: Liverpool University Press, 2016).

29   Roland Quinault, "Gladstone and Slavery", *Historical Journal*, vol. 52, no. 2, June 2009, pp. 363–383.

30   Beckert, *Empire of Cotton*, p. 208.

31   Beckert, *Empire of Cotton*, p. 200.

32   Beckert, *Empire of Cotton,* p. 200.

33   Reuben Loffman and Benoît Henriet, "'We Are Left with Barely Anything': Colonial Rule, Dependency, and the Lever Brothers in the Belgian Congo, 1911–1960", *Journal of Imperial and Commonwealth History*, vol. 48, no. 1, 2020, pp. 71–100.

34   Martin Lynn, *Commerce and Economic Change in West Africa: The Palm Oil Trade in the Nineteenth Century* (Cambridge: Cambridge University Press, 1997); Loffman and Henriet, "'We Are Left with Barely Anything'".

35   P.N. Davis, *The Trade Makers: Elder Dempster in West Africa, 1852–1972* (London: George Allen and Unwin, 1973).

36   Francis E. Hyde and J.R. Harris, *Blue Funnel: A History of Alfred Holt and Company of Liverpool, from 1865–1914* (Liverpool: Liverpool University Press, 1956).

37   John Farley, *Bilharzia: A History of Tropical Medicine* (Cambridge: Cambridge University Press, 1991).

38   Phillip Curtin, "The End of the 'White Man's Grave'? Nineteenth-Century Mortality in West Africa", *Journal of Interdisciplinary History*, vol. 21, no. 1, 1990, p. 69.

39   Curtin, "The End of the 'White Man's Grave'?", pp. 63–70.

40   Douglas M. Haynes, *Imperial Medicine: Patrick Manson and the Conquest of Tropical Disease* (Philadelphia: University of Pennsylvania Press, 2011).

41   Davis, *The Trade Makers*.

42   Farley, *Bilharzia*, p. 3.

43   Farley, *Bilharzia*, p. 4.

44   David M. Williams, "Merchanting in the First Half of the Nineteenth Century: The Liverpool Timber Trade", *Business History*, vol. 8, no. 2, 1966, pp. 103–121; and Sheila Marriner, *The Economic and Social Development of Merseyside* (London: Croom Helm, 1982).

45   Priya Satia, *Empire of Guns: The Violent Making of the Industrial Revolution* (Palo Alto: Stanford University Press, 2018).

46   Lane, *Liverpool*, p. 34.

47   Jeremy Black, *The British Seaborne Empire* (New Haven and London: Yale University Press, 2004).

48   Ian Law and June Henfrey, *A History of Race and Racism in Liverpool, 1660–1950* (Liverpool: Whitechapel Press, 1981); Ray Costello, *Black Liverpool: The Early History of Britain's Oldest Black Community, 1730–1918* (Liverpool: Liverpool University Press, 2001); and Mike Boye, Tony Walley, and Madeline Heneghan, *From Pitt Street to Granby Street* (Liverpool: Writing on the Wall, 2018).

49   Costello, *Black Liverpool*.

50   John Belchem, *Before the Windrush: Race Relations in 20th-Century Liverpool* (Liverpool: Liverpool University Press, 2017).

51   Belchem, *Before the Windrush*.

52   Belchem, *Before the Windrush*.

53   Diane Frost, *Work and Community among West African Migrant Workers* (Liverpool: Liverpool University Press, 1999).

54   Frost, *Work and Community*.

55   Laura Tabili, "The Construction of Racial Difference in Twentieth-Century Britain: The Special Restriction (Coloured Alien Seamen) Order 1925", *Journal of British Studies*, vol. 33, no. 1, January 1994, pp. 54–98.

56   Milne, *People, Place and Power*.

57   Jacqueline Jenkinson, *Black 1919: Riots, Racism and Resistance in Imperial Britain* (Liverpool: Liverpool University Press, 2009); and Tabili, *The Construction of Racial Difference*.

58   Stephen Borne, *Black Poppies: Britain's Black Community and the Great War* (Stroud: History Press, 2014).

59   Marika Sherwood, *Pastor Daniels Ekarte and the African Churches Mission, 1931–1964* (London: Savannah Press, 1994).

60   See Stephen Small, "Following in Father's Footsteps: Slavery, Imperialism and the William Ewart Gladstone Memorial Statue in Liverpool City Centre", in Juliee Decker (ed.), *Fallen Monuments and Contested Memorials* (London and New York: Routledge, 2023), pp. 12–27.

61   Small, "Black Expressive Culture"; Stephen Small and Kwame Nimako, "Collective Memory of Slavery in Great Britain and the Netherlands", in Marten Schalkwijk and Stephen Small (eds.), *New Perspectives on Slavery and Colonialism in the Caribbean* (The Hague: Amrit Publishers, 2012), pp. 92–115.

62   Alex Renton, "My Ancestors Profited from Slavery: Here's How I Am Starting to Atone for That", *The Guardian* (London), 24 April 2023; and Paul Lashmar and Jonathan Smith, "My Forefathers Did Something Horribly Wrong: British Slave Owners' Family to Apologise and Pay Reparations", *The Observer*, 4 February 2023.

63   Ramsey Muir, *The Character of the British Empire* (London: Constable, 1917), p. 12

64   Annie Coombes, *Reinventing Africa: Museums, Material Culture and Popular Imagination in Late Victorian and Edwardian England* (New Haven and London: Yale University Press, 1994).

65   Annette Joseph-Gabriel, *Reimagining Liberation: How Black Women Transformed Citizenship in the French Empire* (Champaign: University of Illinois Press, 2020); Cooper, *A Voice from the South*; Mary Church Terrell, *A Colored Woman in a White World* (Blue Ridge Summit: Rowman and Littlefield Publishers, 2020); and Lynch, *Edward Wilmot Blyden*.

66   Ernest Marke, *In Troubled Waters: Memoirs of My Seventy Years in England* (London: Karia Press, 1986).

67   Killingray, *Africans in Britain*.

68   Adekeye Adebajo (ed.), *The Pan-African Pantheon: Prophets, Poets, and Philosophers* (Johannesburg: Jacana, 2020; and Manchester: Manchester University Press, 2021), p. 17.

69   Stephen Small, *20 Questions and Answers on Black Europe* (The Hague: Amrit Publishers, 2018).

Chapter 5. Slavery in Central and Eastern Africa

1 Jan Vansina, *Paths in the Rainforest: Toward a History of Political Tradition in Equatorian Africa* (Madison: Wisconsin University Press, 1990); and W.-G.-L. Randles, *L'ancien royaume du Congo, des origines à la fin du XIXe siècle* (Paris and La Haye: Mouton, 1968).

2 Alvise Ca' da Mosto, *The Voyages of Cadamosto and Other Documents on Western Africa in the Second Half of the Fifteenth Century*, translated and edited by G.R. Crone (London: Hakluyt Society, 1937).

3 Alexander Popovic, *The Revolt of African Slaves in Iraq in the 3rd–9th Century* (Princeton: Markus Wiener Publishers, 1999; French edition, 1976).

4 Henri Médard and Shane Doyle (eds.), *Slavery in the Great Lakes Region of East Africa* (Oxford: James Currey; Kampala: Fountain Publisher; Nairobi: East African Educational Publishers; Athens: Ohio University Press, 2007).

5 White Fathers Archives, Rome.

6 See Médard and Doyle, *Slavery in the Great Lakes Region of East Africa*.

7 Médard and Doyle, *Slavery in the Great Lakes Region of East Africa*, pp. 9–10.

8 Randles, *L'ancien royaume du Congo*.

9 Louis Jadin and Mireille Dicorato, *Correspondance de Dom Afonso, roi du Congo, 1506–1543* (Brussels: Académie Royale des Sciences d'Outre-Mer, 1974): *Écrit en notre ville de Congo, le 18 Octobre 1526 par João Teixeira. [signed] Le roi Dom A. Addressee*: Très haut et très puissant prince, roi du Portugal, notre frère. *Sender*: Le roi de Manicongo.

10 John K. Thornton, *The Kingdom of Kongo: Civil War and Transition, 1641–1718* (Madison: University of Wisconsin Press, 1983).

11 Elias Alexandre da Silva Corrêa, *História de Angola*, vol. 2 (Lisbon: Editorial Africa, 1937); and David Birmingham, *Trade and Conflict in Angola* (Oxford: Oxford University Press, 1966).

12 Pope Paul III, in *Veritas ipsa* (June 1537) and *Sublimis Deus* (June 1537), condemned the enslavement of American Indians, and confirmed their rights as human beings to freedom, thanks to the action of the Dominican missionary Las Casas in Valladolid.

13 Ángel Losada, "Controversy between Sepúlveda and Las Casas", in Juan Friede and Benjamin Keen (eds.), *Bartolomé de las Casas in History: Toward an Understanding of the Man and His Work* (Dekalb: Northern Illinois University Press, 1971); and J. Minahane, "The Controversy at Valladolid, 1550–1551", *Church and State*, no. 116, 2014, pp. 279–309, which discusses whether American Indians have a soul or not.

14 Joseph C. Miller, *Way of Death: Merchant Capitalism, and the Angolan Slave Trade, 1730–1830* (Madison: University of Wisconsin Press, 1988).

15 John K. Thornton, *A History of West Central Africa to 1850* (Cambridge: Cambridge University Press, 2020), pp. 217–237.

16 Miller, *Way of Death*.

17 See, for example, C.L.R. James, *The Black Jacobins: Toussaint L'Ouverture and the San Domingo Revolution* (London: Secker and Warburg, 1938).

18 Catherine Coquery-Vidrovitch, *Les routes de l'esclavage: Histoire des traites africaines, VIe-XXe siècle* (Paris : Albin Michel, 2018).

19 Marcia Wright, *Strategies of Slaves and Women Life-Stories from East/Central Africa* (New York: Lillian Barber, 1993).

20 Jan Vansina, *The Children of Woot: A History of the Kuba Peoples* (Madison: University of Wisconsin Press, 1978).

21 See Coquery-Vidrovitch, *Les routes de l'esclavage*.

22 "Slavery in Africa: Past, Legacies and Present", conference in Nairobi, Kenya, 27–29 October 2014.

Chapter 6. Slavery in West Africa

1 An earlier version of this chapter was published as Martin A. Klein, "Urban Slavery in West and West Central Africa during the Transatlantic Slave Trade", *Journal of African Diaspora Archaeology and Heritage*, vol. 10, nos. 1–2, 2021, pp. 46–67. It profited from a year spent at the Institut für Arbeit und Lebenslauf in Global-geschichtliche Perspektiv at Humboldt University in Berlin, as well as from two conferences comparing the history of Saint-Louis-du-Sénégal and New Orleans, Louisiana. I also want to thank Lindsay Gish, a former graduate student at Michigan State University, for sharing her research on the history of Saint-Louis. I further owe a special debt to Ann McDougall, who has stimulated me over many years to think about the Senegal River valley and the arid lands north of it.

2 Suzanne Miers and Igor Kopytoff (eds.), *Slavery in Africa* (Madison: University of Wisconsin Press, 1977).

3 Frederick Cooper, *Plantation Slavery on the East Coast of Africa* (New Haven: Yale University Press, 1977).

4 Paul E. Lovejoy, "Plantations in the Economy of the Sokoto Caliphate", *Journal of African History*, vol. 19, no. 3, 1978, pp. 341–368.

5 Mohammed Bashir Salau, *Plantation Slavery in the Sokoto Caliphate: A Historical and Comparative Study* (Rochester: University of Rochester Press, 2018).

6 For examples outside the geographic scope of this chapter, see Cooper, *Plantation Slavery on the East Coast of Africa*, pp. 182–195; Janet Ewald, "Crossers of the Seas: Slaves, Freedmen and Other Migrants in the Northwestern Indian Ocean, c.1750–1914", *American Historical Review*, vol. 105, 2000, pp. 69–91; Mark Horton and John Middleton, *The Swahili: The Social Landscape of a Mercantile Society* (Oxford: Oxford University Press, 2000), pp. 134–136; John Edwin Mason, *Social Death and Resurrection: Slavery and Emancipation in South Africa* (Charlotesville: University of Virginia Press, 2003); Stephen Rockel, "Between Pori, Pwani and Kisiwani: Overlapping Labour Cultures in the Caravans, Ports and Dhows of the Western Indian Ocean", in Abdul Sheriff and Enseng Ho (eds.), *Indian Ocean: Oceanic Connections and the Creation of New Societies* (London: Hurst, 2014), pp. 95–122; Abdul Sheriff, *Dhow Cultures of the Indian Ocean: Cosmopolitanism, Commerce and Islam* (New York: Columbia University Press, 2010); and Nigel Worden, *Slavery in Dutch South Africa* (Cambridge: Cambridge University Press, 1985).

7 Martin A. Klein, "The Role of Slavery in the Economic and Social History of Saint-Louis, Senegal", in Emily Clark, Ibrahima Thioub, and Cécile Vidal (eds.), *New Orleans, Louisiana and Saint-Louis, Senegal: Mirror Cities in the Atlantic World, 1659–2000s* (Baton Rouge: Louisiana State University Press, 2019), pp. 35–54.

8 Toby Green, *The Rise of the Trans-atlantic Slave Trade in Western Africa, 1300–1589* (Cambridge: Cambridge University Press, 2011).

9 Philip Curtin, *Economic Change in Precolonial Africa: Senegambia in the Era of the Slave Trade* (Madison: University of Wisconsin Press, 1975); and James Searing, *West African Slavery and Atlantic Commerce: The Senegal River Valley, 1700–1860* (Cambridge: Cambridge University Press, 1993), pp. 103–104.

10 Karen Amanda Sackur, "The Development of Creole Society and Culture in Saint-

Louis and Gorée, 1719–1867" (PhD dissertation, School of Oriental and African Studies, University of London, 1999, pp. 55–57); and Michael David Marcson, "European–African Interaction in the Precolonial Period, Saint Louis, Senegal, 1758–1854" (PhD dissertation, Princeton University, 1976, pp. 47–50).

11 George E. Brooks, *Eurafricans in Western Africa: Commerce, Social Status, Gender, and Religious Observance from the Sixteenth to the Eighteenth Century* (Athens: University of Ohio Press, 2003), p. 126.

12 Marcson, "European–African Interaction", p. 46.

13 Marcson, "European–African Interaction", pp. 38–46.

14 Norman Bennet and George Brooks, "Samuel Swan's Journal of a Voyage along the West Coast of Africa, 1815–18", in Norman Bennet and George Brooks (eds.), *New England Merchants in Africa: A History through Documents, 1802–1865* (Boston: Boston University Press, 1965), p. 65.

15 Malcolm J. Thompson, "In Dubious Service: The Recruitment and Stabilization of West African Marine Labor by the French Colonial Military, 1659–1900" (PhD dissertation, University of Minnesota, 1989).

16 Curtin, *Economic Change in Precolonial Africa*, pp. 117–121.

17 François Manchuelle, *Willing Migrants: Soninke Labor Diasporas, 1848–1960* (Athens: University of Ohio Press, 1997).

18 Marcson, "European–African Interaction", pp. 22–24.

19 Malcolm, "In Dubious Service".

20 Charles Becker, Martin Vincent, Jean Schmitz, Monique Chastanet, Jean-François Maurel, and Saliou Mbaye, *Les premiers recensements au Sénégal et l'évolution démographique: Présentation de documents* (Dakar: ORSTOM, 1983).

21 Brooks, *Eurafricans in Western Africa*, p. 217.

22 Archives of the Republic of Senegal, Dakar, 13 G 1/124. Piece 2, 1847. We do not have a similar census for Saint-Louis, but the figures should be similar.

23 Marcson, "European–African Interaction", pp. 25–31.

24 Marcson, "European–African Interaction", p. 28.

25 I did research in rural areas of the Sine-Saloum region of Senegal in 1963, 1968, and 1975, and in the Wasulu region of Mali in 1988. Informants often spoke in passing of slaves buying slaves or enslaved men marrying a second wife.

26 Mbaye Guèye, "La fin de l'esclavage à Saint-Louis et à Gorée en 1848", *Bulletin de l'Institut Français d'Afrique Noire*, vol. 28, 1965, pp. 641–645; and Mbaye Guèye, "L'esclavage au Sénégal du XVIIe au XVIIIe siècle", Thèse du 3e cycle, Université de Nantes, 1969.

27 Guèye, "La fin de l'esclavage", pp. 641–645; Guèye, "L'esclavage au Sénégal"; Roger Pasquier, "À propos de l'émancipation des esclaves au Sénégal en 1848", *Revue Française de l'Histoire d'Outre-Mer*, no. 47, 1967, pp. 387–426; and Mamadou Kane, "L'esclavage à Saint-Louis et à Gorée à travers les archives notariées, 1817–1848" (Master's thesis, Université de Dakar, 1984).

28 Brooks, *Eurafricans in Western Africa*, p. 214.

29 Martin A. Klein, "Women and Slavery in the Western Soudan", in Claire C. Robertson and Martin A. Klein (eds.), *Women and Slavery in Africa* (Madison: University of Wisconsin, 1983), pp. 67–92; Martin A. Klein, "The Demography of Slavery in the Western Soudan in the Late 19th Century", in Dennis D. Cordell and Joel W. Gregory (eds.), *African Population and Capitalism: Historical*

Perspectives (2nd edn, Madison: University of Wisconsin Press, 1987), pp. 50–61; and Martin A. Klein, "La traite transatlantique des esclaves et le développement de l'esclavage en Afrique occidentale", in Myriam Cottias, Alessandro Stella, and Bernard Vincent (eds.), *L'esclavage et dépendances serviles* (Paris: Harmattan, 2006), pp. 35–54.

30   James Searing, *West African Slavery and Atlantic Commerce: The Senegal River Valley, 1700–1860* (Cambridge: Cambridge University Press, 1993).

31   Searing, *West African Slavery and Atlantic Commerce*, p. 185.

32   Rebecca Shumway, *The Fante and the Slave Trade* (Rochester: University of Rochester Press, 2011).

33   Larry Yarak, "Elmina and Greater Asante in the Nineteenth Century", *Africa*, vol. 56, no. 1, 1986, pp. 33–52; Larry Yarak, "Creative and Expedient Misunderstandings: Elmina–Dutch Relations in the 19th Century", in John Kwadwo Osie-Tutu (ed.), *Forts, Castles and Societies in West Africa* (Leiden: Brill, 2018), pp. 72–92.

34   Larry Yarak, "West African Coastal Slavery in the Nineteenth Century: The Case of Afro-European Slaveowners of Elmina", *Ethnohistory*, no. 36, 1989, pp. 47–51.

35   Susan Kaplow, "Primitive Accumulation and Traditional Social Relations in the 19th Century Gold Coast", *Canadian Journal of African Studies*, no. 12, 1978, pp. 19–36.

36   Larry Yarak, "West African Coastal Slavery in the Nineteenth Century", pp. 47–51.

37   National Archief, Ministerie van Koophandel en Kolonien West-Indie, 2.01, 51E. I thank Larry Yarak for sending this document to me.

38   Johannes Postma, *The Dutch in the Atlantic Slave Trade, 1600–1815* (Cambridge: Cambridge University Press, 1990), pp. 71–73; and Christopher DeCorse, *An Archeology of Elmina: Africans and Europeans on the Gold Coast, 1400–1900* (Washington, DC: Smithsonian Institution Press, 2001).

39   Robin Law, *Ouidah: The Social History of a Slaving "Port", 1727–1892* (Athens: University of Ohio Press, 2004), p. 78.

40   Law, *Ouidah*, pp. 73–74.

41   Law, *Ouidah*, pp. 84–85.

42   Kristin Mann, *Slavery and the Birth of an African City: Lagos, 1760–1900* (Bloomington: Indiana University Press, 2007), pp. 3–7.

43   Mann, *Slavery and the Birth of an African City*, p. 76.

44   Mann, *Slavery and the Birth of an African City*, p. 16.

45   Ugo G. Nwokeji, *The Slave Trade and Culture in the Bight of Biafra: An African Society in the Atlantic World* (Cambridge: Cambridge University Press, 2010).

46   E.J. Alagoa, "The Niger Delta States and Their Neighbours, 1600–1800", in J.F.A. Ajayi and Michael Crowder (eds.), *History of West Africa* (New York: Columbia University Press, 1972), pp. 269–303; and G.I. Jones, *The Trading States of the Oil Rivers: A Study of Political Development in Eastern Nigeria* (Oxford: Oxford University Press, 1963).

47   Ralph A. Austen and Jonathan Derrick, *Middlemen of the Cameroons Rivers: The Duala and the Hinterland, c.1600 – c.1960* (Cambridge: Cambridge University Press, 1999); and A.J.H. Latham, *Old Calabar, 1600–1891: The Impact of the International Economy upon a Traditional Society* (Oxford: Oxford University Press, 1973).

Chapter 7. Slavery in Southern Africa

1   Igor Martins, *Collateral Effect: Slavery and Wealth in the Cape Colony* (Lund: Media-Tryck, Lund University, 2020), p. 1.

2   Markus Vink, "The World's Oldest Trade: Dutch Slavery in the Indian Ocean in the Seventeenth Century", *Journal of World History*, vol. 14, no. 2, 2003, pp. 131–177.

3   Vink, "The World's Oldest Trade", pp. 131–177.

4   See Herman Nieboer, *Slavery as an Industrial System: Ethnological Researchers* (The Hague: Martinus Nijhoff, 1900); and Evsey Domar, "The Causes of Slavery or Serfdom: A Hypothesis", *Journal of Economic History*, vol. 30, 1970, pp. 18–32.

5   Erik Green, "The Economics of Slavery in the Eighteenth-Century Cape Colony: Revising the Nieboer–Domar Hypothesis", *International Review of Social History*, vol. 59, no. 1, 2014, p. 39.

6   See Charles Feinstein, *An Economic History of South Africa: Conquest, Discrimination and Development* (Cambridge: Cambridge University Press, 2005), p. 23; and Robert Shell, *Children of Bondage: A Social History of the Slave Society at the Cape of Good Hope, 1652–1838* (Johannesburg: Witwatersrand University Press, 1995), p. 2.

7   Green, "The Economics of Slavery in the Eighteenth-Century Cape Colony" , p. 46.

8   Martins, *Collateral Effect*, p. 2.

9   Nigel Worden, "Indian Ocean Slaves in Cape Town, 1695–1807", *Journal of Southern African Studies*, vol. 42, no. 3, 2016, pp. 389–408.

10   Worden, "Indian Ocean Slaves in Cape Town", p. 289.

11   Worden, "Indian Ocean Slaves in Cape Town", p. 292.

12   Worden, "Indian Ocean Slaves in Cape Town", p. 292.

13   Martins, *Collateral Effect*, p. 3.

14   Sophia du Plessis, Ada Jansen, and Dieter von Fintel, "Slave Prices and Productivity at the Cape of Good Hope from 1700 to 1725: Did Everyone Win from the Trade?", *Cliometrica*, vol. 9, no. 3, 2015, p.10.

15   Johan Fourie, Ellen Hillbom, and Patrick Svensson, "Slaves as Capital Investment in the Dutch Cape Colony, 1652–1795", Stellenbosch University and Bureau for Economic Research (BER) Working Paper Series, no. 21, 2011, p. 13.

16   James C. Armstrong and Nigel A. Worden, "The Slaves, 1652–1834", in Richard Elphick and Hermann Giliomee (eds.), *The Shaping of South African Society, 1652–1840* (Middletown: Wesleyan University Press, 1989 [1979]), p. 137.

17   Kate Ekama, Johan Fourie, Hans Heese, and Lisa Martin, "When Cape Slavery Ended: Evidence from a New Slave Emancipation Dataset", African Economic History Working Paper Series, vol. 53, 2020, p. 9, www.aehnetwork.org/working-papers/when-cape-slavery-ended-evidence-from-anew-slave-emancipation-dataset/.

18   Robert C. Shell, "Between Christ and Mohammed: Conversion, Slavery and Gender in the Urban Western Cape", in Richard Elphick and Rodney Davenport (eds.), *Christianity in South Africa: A Political, Social and Cultural History* (Cape Town: David Philip, 1997), p. 268.

19   Shell, "Between Christ and Mohammed", p. 268.

20   John Edwin Mason, *Social Death and Resurrection: Slavery and Emancipation in South Africa* (Charlottesville: University of Virginia Press, 2003), p. 178.

21   Shell, "Between Christ and Mohammed", p. 268.

22   Mason, *Social Death and Resurrection*, p. 181.

23   Mason, *Social Death and Resurrection*, p. 181.

24   Shell, "Between Christ and Mohammed", p. 271.

25   Shell, "Between Christ and Mohammed", p. 172.

26   Shell, "Between Christ and Mohammed", p. 273.

27   Karel Schoeman, *The Early Mission in South Africa* (Pretoria: Protea Book House, 2005), p. 132.

28   Mason, *Social Death and Resurrection*, p. 181.

29   Shell, "Between Christ and Mohammed", p. 269.

30   Bernard Lewis, *Race and Slavery in the Middle East: An Historical Inquiry* (New York: Oxford University Press, 1990), p. 6.

31   Mason, *Social Death and Resurrection*, p. 187.

32   Jackie Loos, *Echoes of Slavery: Voices from South Africa Past* (Claremont: David Phillip Publishers, 2004), p. 48.

33   Mason, *Social Death and Resurrection*, p. 178.

34   Shell, "Between Christ and Mohammed", p. 271.

35   Vink, "The World's Oldest Trade", p. 23.

36   See, for example, James C. Scott, *Weapons of the Weak: Everyday Forms of Peasant Resistance* (New Haven: Yale University Press, 1987).

37   Vink, "The World's Oldest Trade", p. 23.

38   Vink, "The World's Oldest Trade", p. 23.

39   Nigel Worden, "Armed with Swords and Ostrich Feathers: Militarism and Cultural Revolution in the Cape Slave Uprising of 1808", in Richard Bessel, Nicholas Guyatt, and Jane Rendall (eds.), *War, Empire and Slavery, 1770–1830* (London: Palgrave, 2010), p. 134.

40   Nicole Ulrich, "Abolition from Below: The 1808 Revolt in the Cape Colony", in Marcel van der Linden (ed.), *Humanitarian Intervention and Changing Labour Relations: Long-Term Consequences of the British Act on the Abolition of the Slave Trade, 1807* (Leiden and Boston: Brill, 2010), p. 195.

41   Ulrich, "Abolition from Below", p. 193.

42   Ekama, Fourie, Hesse, and Martin, "When Cape Slavery Ended", p. 2.

43   See Ekama, Fourie, Hesse, and Martin, "When Cape Slavery Ended"; and Nigel Worden, "Between Slavery and Freedom: The Apprenticeship Period, 1834–1838", in Nigel Worden and Clifton Crais (eds.), *Breaking the Chains* (Johannesburg: Witwatersrand University Press, 1994).

44   Ekama, Fourie, Hesse, and Martin, "When Cape Slavery Ended".

45   Ekama, Fourie, Hesse, and Martin, "When Cape Slavery Ended", pp. 6–7.

46   Ekama, Fourie, Hesse, and Martin, "When Cape Slavery Ended", p. 8.

47   Ekama, Fourie, Hesse, and Martin, "When Cape Slavery Ended", p. 4.

48   Ekama, Fourie, Hesse, and Martin, "When Cape Slavery Ended", p. 3.

Chapter 8. Slavery in the British Caribbean

1   Elsa V. Goveia, "Introduction", *Savacou*, vol. 1, no. 1, 1970, p. 7.

2   Elsa V. Goveia, *Slave Society in the British Leeward Islands at the End of the Eighteenth Century* (New Haven, CT: Yale University Press, 1965), p. vii. See also Barry W. Higman, "The Invention of Slave Society", in Brian L. Moore, B.W. Higman, Cari Campbell, and Patrick Bryan (eds.), *Slavery, Freedom and Gender: The Dynamics of Caribbean Society* (Kingston: University of the West Indies Press, 2001), pp. 57–75.

3   I will use "English" for the period before 1707, when Scotland was united to England to form the United Kingdom, and "British" for the subsequent period.

4   Federico Mayor, "Preface", in Franklin K. Knight (ed.), *General History of the*

Caribbean, vol. III, *The Slave Societies of the Caribbean* (London: UNESCO and Macmillan, 1997), p. vi.

5   A succinct account can be found in Hilary M. Beckles, "The 'Hub of Empire': The Caribbean and Britain in the Seventeenth Century", in Nicholas Canny (ed.), *The Oxford History of the British Empire*, vol. 1, *The Origins of Empire: British Overseas Enterprise to the Close of the Seventeenth Century* (Oxford: Oxford University Press, 1998), pp. 218–240.

6   Beckles, "The 'Hub of Empire'", p. 227

7   Beckles, "The "Hub of Empire"", p. 232.

8   A good account of these developments can be found in J.R. Ward, "The British West Indies in the Age of Abolition, 1748–1815", in Peter James Marshall (ed.), *The Oxford History of the British Empire*, vol. II, *The Eighteenth Century* (Oxford: Oxford University Press, 1998), pp. 415–439.

9   For slaves on coffee estates, Kathleen Monteith, *Plantation Coffee in Jamaica, 1790–1848* (Kingston: University of the West Indies Press, 2020); for slaves on Jamaican "pens", see Verene A. Shepherd, *Livestock, Sugar and Slavery* (Kingston: Ian Randle, 2009); for urban slaves, see Pedro L. Welch, *Slave Society in the City: Bridgetown, Barbados, 1680–1834* (Kingston: Ian Randle, 2003); for jobbing slaves, see Nigel O. Bolland, "Proto-Proletarians? Slave Wages in the Americas", in Mary Turner (ed.), *From Chattel Slaves to Wage Slaves* (London: James Currey, 1995), pp. 123–147; for slavery in the Bahamas, see Michael Craton and Gail Saunders, *Islanders in the Stream: A History of the Bahamian People*, vol. 1 (Athens: University of Georgia Press, 1992); and Howard Johnson, *The Bahamas from Slavery to Servitude, 1783–1933* (Gainesville, FL: University Press of Florida, 1996).

10   Slave Voyages: The Trans-Atlantic Slave Trade Database, 2008.

11   David Eltis, Stephen D. Behrendt, David Richardson, and Herbert S. Klein, *The Trans-Atlantic Slave Trade: A Database on CD-ROM* (Cambridge: Cambridge University Press, 1999). For the *Zong*, see James Walvin, *The Zong: A Massacre, the Law and the End of Slavery* (New Haven, CT: Yale University Press, 2011).

12   This and the preceding three paragraphs are based on Barry W. Higman's massive study, *Slave Populations of the British Caribbean, 1807–1834* (Baltimore, MD: Johns Hopkins University Press, 1985). Its "Statistical Supplement" alone is over 300 pages.

13   Karl Watson, *The Civilised Island Barbados: A Social History 1750–1816* (Barbados: self-published, 1979), p. 100.

14   The account of enslaved life in this and the preceding three paragraphs is based on a large body of published research. For two recent examples, see Richard S. Dunn, *A Tale of Two Plantations: Slave Life and Labour in Jamaica and Virginia* (Cambridge, MA: Harvard University Press, 2014); and Randy M. Browne, *Surviving Slavery in the British Caribbean* (Philadelphia, PA: University of Pennsylvania Press, 2017). On the Newton plantation women, see Karl Watson, "Escaping Bondage: The Odyssey of a Barbadian Slave Family", paper presented to the 16th Annual Conference of Caribbean Historians, Barbados, 1984.

15   Welch, *Slave Society in the City*.

16   On Thomas Thistlewood, see Douglas Hall, *In Miserable Slavery* (London: Macmillan, 1989); and Trevor Burnard, *Mastery, Tyranny and Desire* (Kingston: University of the West Indies Press, 2004). For Higman's Jamaican study, see his *Slave Population and Economy in Jamaica, 1807–1834* (Cambridge: Cambridge University Press, 1976).

17   There has been an explosion of published research on the topics covered in this and the preceding three paragraphs. The foundational texts are Lucille Mathurin Mair, *A Historical Study of Women in Jamaica, 1655–1844* (Kingston: University of the West Indies Press, 2006); Barbara Bush, *Slave Women in Caribbean Society* (London: James Currey, 1990); Marietta Morrissey, *Slave Women in the New World: Gender Stratification in the Caribbean* (Lawrence, KS: University Press of Kansas, 1989); and Hilary Beckles, *Centering Women: Gender Discourses in Caribbean Slave Society* (Kingston: Ian Randle, 1999). A more recent work is Sasha Turner, *Contested Bodies: Pregnancy, Childrearing, and Slavery in Jamaica* (Philadelphia, PA: University of Pennsylvania Press, 2017). On "gynaecological resistance", see Bush, *Slave Women in Caribbean Society*; Turner, *Contested Bodies*; and Matthew Lewis, *Journal of a West India Proprietor, Kept during a Residence in the Island of Jamaica* (London: John Murray, 1834).

18   The literature on these topics is vast. A good summary is Mary Turner, "Religious Beliefs", in Knight, *General History of the Caribbean*, pp. 287–321; also see Mary Turner, *Slaves and Missionaries: The Disintegration of Jamaican Slave Society, 1788–1834* (Urbana, IL: University of Illinois Press, 1982). A recent and original interpretation of Caribbean slave culture can be found in Peter A. Roberts, *A Response to Enslavement: Playing Their Way to Virtue* (Kingston: University of the West Indies Press, 2018).

19   See, for example, C.L.R. James, *The Black Jacobins: Toussaint L'Ouverture and the San Domingo Revolution* (London: Secker and Warburg, 1938).

20   For an excellent overview, see Michael Craton, *Testing the Chains: Resistance to Slavery in the British West Indies* (Ithaca, NY: Cornell University Press, 1982).

21   There was a major African-led rebellion in Berbice in 1763; it subsequently became a British colony but was part of the Dutch Caribbean in 1763. On Antigua in 1736, see David Barry Gaspar, *Bondmen and Rebels: A Study of Master–Slave Relations in Antigua* (Baltimore, ML: Johns Hopkins University Press, 1985); on Jamaica in 1760, see Vincent Brown, *Tacky's Revolt: The Story of an Atlantic Slave War* (Cambridge, MA: Belknap Press, 2020).

22   On Barbados in 1816, see Hilary Beckles, *A History of Barbados* (Cambridge: Cambridge University Press, 1990), pp. 75–102; on Demerara in 1823, see Emilia Viotti da Costa, *Crowns of Glory, Tears of Blood: The Demerara Slave Rebellion of 1823* (Oxford: Oxford University Press, 1994); on Jamaica in 1831, see Tom Zoellner, *Island on Fire: The Revolt That Ended Slavery in the British Empire* (Cambridge, MA: Harvard University Press, 2020). On the impact of enslaved resistance on Britain, see Gelien Matthews, *Caribbean Slave Revolts and the British Abolitionist Movement* (Baton Rouge, LA: Louisiana State University Press, 2006).

23   Higman, *Slave Populations*, pp. 386–393.

24   There is a large literature on the Jamaican Maroons. For a succinct summary, see Craton, *Testing the Chains*, pp. 67–96; and Kenneth Bilby, *True Born Maroons* (Kingston: Ian Randle, 2006).

25   On slave bargaining see Turner, "Chattel Slaves into Wage Slaves: A Jamaican Case Study", in Turner, *From Chattel Slaves*, pp. 33–47. On the Amelioration period, see Browne, *Surviving Slavery*; on Berbice and Trinidad, see Claudius K. Fergus, *Revolutionary Emancipation* (Baton Rouge, LA: Louisiana State University Press, 2013).

26 Craton, *Testing the Chains*, pp. 31–57.
27 See James C. Scott, *Weapons of the Weak: Everyday Forms of Peasant Resistance* (New Haven, CT: Yale University Press, 1987).
28 The foundational texts are Mair, *A Historical Study of Women in Jamaica, 1655–1844*; Bush, *Slave Women in Caribbean Society*; Morrissey, *Slave Women in the New World: Gender Stratification in the Caribbean*; and Beckles, *Centering Women*.
29 Eric Williams, *Capitalism and Slavery* (Chapel Hill, NC: University of North Carolina Press, 1994 [1944]). For a succinct summary which takes in the whole Caribbean, see Franklin W. Knight, "The Disintegration of the Caribbean Slave Systems, 1772–1886", in Knight, *General History*, pp. 322–345. For the British Caribbean specifically, see Andrew Porter, "Trusteeship, Anti-Slavery and Humanitarianism" and Gad Heuman, "The British West Indies", both in Andrew Porter (ed.), *The Oxford History of the British Empire*, vol. III, *The Nineteenth Century* (Oxford: Oxford University Press, 1999), pp. 198–221 and 470–493.
30 See, for example, James, *The Black Jacobins*.
31 These registration returns form the basis for Higman's massive *Slave Populations*. Also see Meredith A. John, *The Plantation Slaves of Trinidad, 1783–1816* (Cambridge: Cambridge University Press, 1998).
32 On Amelioration, see Browne, *Surviving Slavery* (Berbice), and Fergus, *Revolutionary Emancipation* (Trinidad).
33 See Nicholas Draper, *The Price of Emancipation: Slave-Ownership, Compensation and British Society at the End of Slavery* (Cambridge: Cambridge University Press, 2009); and University College London, "Legacies of British Slave-Ownership" online database.
34 William G. Sewell, *The Ordeal of Free Labour in the British West Indies* (London: Frank Cass, 1968 [1861]).

Chapter 9. Slavery in the French Caribbean
1 Jaime Aragón Falomir, "Les Apaches face à la colonisation et globalisation du réel et de l'imaginaire", *Amerika Journal*, no. 22, 2021, https://doi.org/10.4000/amerika.13693. This chapter is a modified version of my article "Uma análise da história da escravatura através das teorias contemporâneas do poder nas Antilhas francesas", *Revista Islenha* (Madeira, Portugal), vol. 71, July–December 2022, pp. 24–35.
2 Darcy Ribeiro, *As Americas e a civilizaçao* (Petropolis: Editora Vozes, 1977), p. 87.
3 Ribeiro, *As Americas e a civilizaçao*, p. 88.
4 Ribeiro, *As Americas e a civilizaçao*, p. 88.
5 Elena Esposito, "Side Effects of Immunities: The African Slave Trade", Working Paper, European University Institute, Max Weber Programme, no. 2015/09, 2015.
6 Eric Williams, "Capitalism and Slavery", in Verene Shepherd and Hilary McD. Beckles (eds.), *Caribbean Slavery in the Atlantic World* (Kingston and London: Ian Randle Publishers, 2000); C.L.R James, "French Capitalism and Caribbean Slavery", in Shepherd and Beckles, *Caribbean Slavery*, pp. 466–471; Robert Stein, "The French West Indian Sugar Business", in Shepherd and Beckles, *Caribbean Slavery*, pp. 335–342; and Rosamunde A. Renard, "Labour Relations in Martinique and Guadeloupe, 1848–1870", in Hilary McD. Beckles and Verene Shepherd (eds.), *Caribbean Freedom: Economy and Society from Emancipation to the Present* (Princeton: Markus Weiner Publishers, 1996), pp. 80–93.

7   Esposito, "Side Effects of Immunities", p. 7.

8   Stanley L. Engerman and Kenneth L. Sokoloff, "Factor Endowments, Inequality, and Paths of Development among New World Economics", *Latin American and Caribbean Economic Association*, vol. 3, no. 1, 2002, pp. 41–109; Daron Acemoglu, Garcia-Jimeno Camilo, and James A. Robinson, "Finding Eldorado: Slavery and Long-Run Development in Colombia", *Journal of Comparative Economics*, vol. 40, 2012, pp. 534–564; and Rodrigo R. Soares, Juliano J. Assunção, and Tomás F. Goulart, "A Note on Slavery and the Roots of Inequality", *Journal of Comparative Economics*, vol. 40, 2012, pp. 565–580. See also Miriam Bruhn and Francisco A. Gallego, "Good, Bad, and Ugly Colonial Activities: Do They Matter for Economic Development?", *Review of Economics and Statistics*, vol. 94, no. 2, 2012, pp. 433–461.

9   John Scott, "Modes of Power and the Re-conceptualization of Elites", *Sociological Review*, vol. 56, 2008, pp. 25–43, https://doi.org/10.1111/j.1467-954X.2008.00760.x; see also Jaime Aragón Falomir and Julián Cárdenas, "Análisis de redes empresariales y puertas giratorias en México: Cartografía de una clase dominante público-privada", *Temas y Debates Journal*, no. 39, 2020, pp. 81–103, https://doi.org/10.35305/tyd.v0i39.458.

10 Pierre Bourdieu, "Symbolic Power", *Critique of Anthropology*, vol. 4, 1979, pp. 77–85.

11 Although Laura Morales defines them as "settler elites", she does not develop this reflection. Laura Morales, "Literatura y cultura: Letras y artes", in Ana Crespo Solana and Maria Dolores González-Ripoll (eds.), *Historia de las Antillas* (Madrid: Doce Calles, 2011), p. 106.

12 Scott, "Modes of Power", p. 29.

13 Luc Boltanski, *De la critique: Précis de sociologie de l'*émancipation (Paris: Gallimard, 2009), pp. 176 and 213.

14 David Held, *Political Theory and the Modern State: Essays on State, Power, and Democracy* (Stanford: Stanford University Press, 1989), p. 102.

15 David Beetham, *The Legitimation of Power* (Basingstoke: Palgrave Macmillan, 1991), pp. 10–12.

16 Scott, "Modes of Power", p. 32.

17 Scott, "Modes of Power", p. 31.

18 Boltanski, *De la critique*, p. 217.

19 Philip Boucher, "The French and Dutch Caribbean, 1600–1800", in Stephan Palmié and Francisco Scarano (eds.), *The Caribbean: A History of the Region and Its Peoples* (Chicago and London: University of Chicago Press, 2011); Trevor Burnard and John Garrigus, *The Plantation Machine* (Philadelphia: University of Pennsylvania Press, 2016); Trevor Burnard, "Planter Class", in Trevor Burnard and Gad Heuman (eds.), *The Routledge History of Slavery* (London: Routledge, 2011); and Frederic Régent, *La France et ses esclaves: De la colonisation aux abolitions 1620–1848* (Paris: Grasset and Fasquelle, 2007).

20 Jean Cavignac, "Jean Pellet, commerçant de gros (1694–1772): Contribution à l'étude du négoce bordelais au XVIII siècle (Paris, S.E.V.P.E.N, 1967), p. 170; and Régent, *La France et ses esclaves*, p. 90.

21 Soares, Assunção, and Goulart, "A Note on Slavery", p. 566.

22 Stein, "The French West Indian Sugar Business", p. 335.

23 See Régent, *La France et ses esclaves*, p. 91.

24 Rene Bélénus, *L'esclave en Guadeloupe et en Martinique du XVII au XIX siècle* (Pointe-

à-Pitre, Guadeloupe: Jasor, 1998), p. 59.

25 Boucher, "The French and Dutch Caribbean, 1600–1800", pp. 228–229.

26 Roger Toumson, *Mythologie du métissage* (Paris: Presses Universitaires de France, 1998), p. 85.

27 James Carnegie and Patricia Patterson, *The People Who Came*, Book 2 (Singapore: Longman Singapore Publishers, 1996), p. 75.

28 Kenneth F. Kiple and Kriemhild C. Ornelas, "After the Encounter: Disease and Demographics in the Lesser Antilles", in Robert L. Paquette and Stanley L. Engerman (eds.), *The Lesser Antilles in the Age of European Expansion* (Florida: University Press of Florida, 1996), p. 54.

29 Ana Crespo Solana and Maria Dolores González–Ripoll, "Población y sociedad", in Ana Crespo Solana and Maria Dolores González-Ripoll (eds.), *Historia de las Antillas no hispanas* (Madrid: Doce Calles, 2011).

30 Boucher, "The French and Dutch Caribbean, 1600–1800".

31 George Lamming, *The Pleasures of Exile* (London: Pluto Press, [1960], 2005).

32 Laura Muñoz and Johanna von Grafenstein, "Economia colonial", in Solana and González-Ripoll, *Historia de las Antillas no hispanas*, p. 35.

33 Bélénus, *L'esclave en Guadeloupe et en Martinique du XVII au XIX siècle*, p. 8.

34 Régent, *La France et ses esclaves*, p. 40.

35 Muñoz and Grafenstein, "Economia colonial", p. 54; and Boucher, "The French and Dutch Caribbean, 1600–1800", pp. 53-55.

36 Régent, *La France et ses esclaves*, pp. 94–95.

37 Boucher, "The French and Dutch Caribbean, 1600–1800", p. 224.

38 James Pritchard, *In Search of Empire: The French in the Americas, 1670–1730* (Cambridge: Cambridge University Press, 2004), p. 424.

39 Régent, *La France et ses esclaves*, pp. 55–67.

40 Régent, *La France et ses esclaves*, p. 51.

41 Both within the popular classes – see Natacha Coquery, "Préface", in Maud Villeret (ed.), *Le goût de l'or blanc: Le sucre en France au XVIIIe siècle* (Rennes: Presses Universitaires de Rennes, 2017), p. 23 – and bourgeois classes, who used it to sweeten other colonial products such as tea, coffee, and chocolate – see Maurice Burac, "La plantation dans la mondialisation", in Maurice Burac and Danielle Bégot (eds.), *L'habitation–plantation: Héritages et mutations, Caraïbe-Amérique* (Paris: Karthala, 2011), p. 143.

42 Wagley Charles, *Race and Class in Rural Brazil* (New York: Columbia University Press, 1963), p. 12.

43 Roger Bastide, *Les Amériques noires: Les civilisations Africaines dans le nouveau monde* (3rd edn, Paris: Editions L'Harmattan, 1968), p. 21.

44 Esposito, "Side Effects of Immunities", p. 13.

45 Letter from Étienne-François de Choiseul to the Governor of Saint-Domingue in 1766, in Régent, *La France et ses esclaves*, p. 67.

46 Boltanski, *De la critique*, p. 176.

47 Régent, *La France et ses esclaves*, pp. 60 and 64.

48 Confiant, *Commandeur du sucre*, p. 9.

49 Magali M. Carrera, *Imagining Identity in New Spain: Race, Lineage, and the Colonial Body in Portraiture and Casta Paintings* (Austin: University of Texas Press, 2003); and Laura Catelli, "Pintores criollos, pintura de castas y colonialismo interno", *Cuadernos*

del CILHA (Interdisciplinary Center for Spanish-American Literature), vol. 13, no. 2, 1 December 2012, pp. 147–175.

50   Charles Frostin, *Les révoltes blanches à Saint-Domingue aux XVIIe et XVIIIe siècles (Haïti avant 1789)* (Paris: L'École, 1975). See also Muñoz and Grafenstein, "Población y sociedad", p. 27.

51   Muñoz and Grafenstein, "Economia colonial", p. 27.

52   See, for example, C.L.R. James, *The Black Jacobins: Toussaint L'Ouverture and the San Domingo Revolution* (London: Secker and Warburg, 1938).

53   Kamau Brathwaite, "Caliban, Ariel, and Unprospero in the Conflict of Creolization: A Study of the Slave Revolt in Jamaica in 1831–32", in Shepherd and Beckles, *Caribbean Slavery in the Atlantic World*, p. 880.

54   Jaime Aragón Falomir, "Women, Violence and Tourism: Modes of Domination in the Mexican Caribbean", *Canadian Journal of Latin American and Caribbean Studies*, vol. 47, no. 3, 2022, pp. 499–520, https://doi.org/10.1080/08263663.2022.2110784.

55   Richard D.E. Burton, "The French West Indies à l'heure de l'Europe: An Overview", in Richard D.E. Burton and Fred Reno (eds.), *French and West Indian: Martinique, Guadeloupe and French Guiana Today* (Hong Kong: Macmillan Press, 1995), p. 11.

56   Michel Giraud, "Dialectics of Descent and Phenotypes in Racial Classification in Martinique", in Burton and Reno, *French and West Indian*, p. 77.

57   Gerry L'Etang, "Créolisation et créolité à la Martinique: Essai de périodisation", in Burac and Bégot, *L'habitation–plantation*, pp. 187–188.

58   Régent, *La France et ses esclaves*, p. 10.

59   Toumson, *Mythologie du métissage*, pp. 111–115.

60   Giraud, "Dialectics of Descent and Phenotypes in Racial Classification in Martinique", p. 80.

61   Giraud, "Dialectics of Descent and Phenotypes in Racial Classification in Martinique", p. 82.

62   Confiant, *Commandeur du sucre*, p. 96.

63   Roger Toumson, "Vieux-Habitants: L'habituée", in Burac and Bégot, *L'habitation–plantation*, p. 115.

64   Dale Tomich, "Slavery in the French Martinique", in Shepherd and Beckles, *Caribbean Slavery in the Atlantic World*, pp. 428–429.

65   They were in charge of carrying "the whip and an iron-tipped cane". See Tomich, "Slavery in the French Martinique", pp. 428-429.

66   Bélénus, *L'esclave en Gaudeloupe et en Martinique*, p. 15; Tomich, "Slavery in the French Martinique", p. 428; and Régent, *La France et ses esclaves*, p. 140.

67   Tomich, "Slavery in the French Martinique", p. 415.

68   Pierre Bourdieu, *La distinction: Critique sociale du jugement* (Paris: Les Éditions de Minuit, 1979), p. 191.

69   The fact of imposing or accepting domination is, therefore, influenced by a group of dispositions inherited or learned within that *habitus*, which may be part of a "symbolic imposition effect", see Bourdieu, *La distinction*, pp. 24–25.

70   Bourdieu, *La distinction*, p. 139.

71   Burac and Bégot, *L'habitation–plantation*, p. 1; Carnegie and Patterson, *The People Who Came*, pp. 75 and 102.

72   Danielle Bégot, "Maisons de maître et grand'cases aux Antilles françaises (XVII–XIX siècles)", in Burac and Bégot, *L'habitation–plantation*, p. 15.

73   L'Etang, "Créolisation et créolité à la Martinique", p. 187.

74   Toumson, *Vieux-Habitants*, p. 230.

75   Toumson, *Vieux-Habitants*, p. 229; and Bourdieu, "Social Space and Symbolic Power", *Sociological Theory*, vol. 7, no. 1, 1989, p. 78.

76   Toumson, *Vieux-Habitants*, pp. 230–231.

77   Burac and Bégot, *L'habitation–plantation*, p. 9.

78   L'Etang, "Créolisation et créolité à la Martinique", p. 186.

79   Cécile Bertin-Elizabeth, "L'espace de la plantation", in Burac and Bégot, *L'habitation–plantation*, p. 364.

80   Burac, "La plantation dans la mondialisation", p. 145.

81   Stéphanie Grousset-Charrière, *La face cachée de Havard: Observatoire national de la vie étudiante* (Paris: La Documentation Française, 2012), p. 162. See also Jaime Aragón Falomir, "Review: Grousset-Charrière, *La face cachée de Havard: Observatoire national de la vie étudiante*", *Ideas*, vol. 3, 2012.

82   Boltanski, *De la critique*, p. 176.

83   Their identity is reinforced by a high endogamy, a recalcitrant patriarchy, and the religion of Catholicism. See L'Etang, "Créolisation et créolité à la Martinique", p. 187.

84   See Acemoglu, Garcia-Jimeno, and Robinson, "Finding Eldorado", pp. 534–564; Engerman and Sokoloff, "Factor Endowments, Inequality, and Paths of Development among New World Economics", pp. 41–109; Soares, Assunção, and Goulart, "A Note on Slavery and the Roots of Inequality", pp. 565–580; Bruhn and Gallego, "Good, Bad, and Ugly Colonial Activities", pp. 433–461; and Graziella Bertocchi and Arcangelo Dimico, "The Racial Gap in Education and the Legacy of Slavery", *Journal of Comparative Economics*, vol. 40, no. 4, 2012, pp. 581–595.

Chapter 10. Slavery in the Dutch Caribbean

1   Kwame Nimako, "Lost and Found: Sovereignties and State Formations in Africa and Asia", in Pedro Miguel Amakasu Raposo de Medeiros Carvalho, David Asare, and Scarlett Cornelissen (eds.), *Routledge Handbook of Africa–Asia Relations* (Oxford: Routledge, 2017), pp. 46–59.

2   Nimako, "Lost and Found".

3   Pieter Geyl, *The Revolt of the Netherlands, 1555–1609* (London: Williams and Norgate, 1932), p. 208.

4   Geyl, *The Revolt of the Netherlands*.

5   Nimako, "Lost and Found".

6   Kwame Nimako and Stephen Small, "Collective Memory of Slavery in Great Britain and the Netherlands", in Marten Schalkwijk and Stephen Small (eds.), *New Perspectives on Slavery and Colonialism in the Caribbean* (The Hague: Amrit, 2012), pp. 92–115.

7   Nimako, "Lost and Found".

8   Walter Rodney, *How Europe Underdeveloped Africa* (London: Verso, 2018 [1972]).

9   Kwame Nimako, "Conceptual Clarity, Please! On the Uses and Abuses of the Concepts of 'Slave' and 'Trade' in the Study of the Transatlantic Slave Trade and Slavery", in Marta Araujo and Silvia Rodriguez Maeso (eds.), *Eurocentrism, Racism and Knowledge* (London: Palgrave Macmillan, 2015), pp. 178–191.

10   C.L.R. James, *The Black Jacobins: Toussaint L'Ouverture and the San Domingo Revolution* (London: Alison and Busby, 1980 [1938]).

11   Antoin Boi and Luckhardt Cees, *Bonaire, zout en koloniale geschidenis* (The Hague: Amrit, 2012).

12   Geyl, *The Revolt of the Netherlands, 1555–1609*, p. 234.

13   Geyl, *The Revolt of the Netherlands, 1555–1609*, p. 135.

14   Andre Gunder Frank, *ReOrient: Global Economy in the Asian Age* (Berkeley: University of California Press, 1998).

15   Karel Davids, *The Rise and Decline of Dutch Technological Leadership: Technology, Economy and Culture in the Netherlands, 1350–1800*, vols. 1 and 2 (Leiden: Brill, 2008), p. 146.

16   Frank, *ReOrient: Global Economy in the Asian Age*, p. 135.

17   Frank, *ReOrient: Global Economy in the Asian Age*, pp. 139–140.

18   Frank, *ReOrient: Global Economy in the Asian Age*, pp. 177–178.

19   Eric Williams, *Capitalism and Slavery* (Chapel Hill: University of North Carolina Press, 1944).

20   Lowell Joseph Ragatz, *The Fall of the Planter Class in the British Caribbean, 1763–1833* (New York: Century Company, 1928).

21   Glenn Willemsen and Kwame Nimako, *The Dutch Atlantic: Slavery, Abolition and Emancipation*, translated by Eric Mielants (London: Pluto Press, 2011).

22   Nimako and Small, "Collective Memory of Slavery in Great Britain and the Netherlands".

23   Willemsen and Nimako, *The Dutch Atlantic*.

24   Several authors have referred to how sugar was the product mainly associated with Atlantic slavery including James, *The Black Jacobin*; and Williams, *Capitalism and Slavery*. See also Ragatz, *The Fall of the Planter Class in the British Caribbean*; and Hilary Beckles, *A History of Barbados: From Amerindian Settlement to Nation-State* (Cambridge: Cambridge University Press, 1990).

25   Beckles, *A History of Barbados*.

26   Willemsen and Nimako, *The Dutch Atlantic*.

27   Willemsen and Nimako, *The Dutch Atlantic*.

28   Armand Zunder, *Herstellbetalingen: de "wiedergutmachung" voor de schade die Suriname en haar bevolking hebben geleden onder het Nederlands colonialisme* (The Hague: Amrit, 2010); and Alex van Stipriaan, *Surinaams contrast: Roofbouw en overleven in een Caraïbische plantagekolonie, 1750–1863* (Leiden: Brill, 1993).

29   Willemsen and Nimako, *The Dutch Atlantic*.

30   Willemsen and Nimako, *The Dutch Atlantic*.

31   Wim Klooster, *Illicit Riches: Dutch Trade in the Caribbean, 1648–1795* (Leiden: Brill, 1998).

32   Willemsen and Nimako, *The Dutch Atlantic*.

33   Rose Mary Allen, *Di ki Manera? A Social History of Afro-Curaçaoans, 1863–1917* (Amsterdam: SWP, 2007).

34   Boi and Cees, *Bonaire, zout en koloniale geschidenis*.

35   See Philomena Essed and Kwame Nimako, "Designs and (Co-)Incidents: Cultures of Scholarship and Public Policy on Immigrants/Minorities in the Netherlands", *International Journal of Comparative Sociology*, vol. 47, nos. 3–4, 2006, pp. 281–312. See also Nimako and Small, "Collective Memory of Slavery in Great Britain and the Netherlands".

36   Willemsen and Nimako, *The Dutch Atlantic*.

37   Willemsen and Nimako, *The Dutch Atlantic*.

38 Kwame Nimako, Mano Delea, and Mitchell Esajas, *Waarom vrijheid niet kon wachten: Het parlementair debat rondom de afschaffing van de slavernij: Een rapport met betrekking het onderzoeksproject over de periode voor de afschaffing van de slavernij (1853–1863) in Nederland* (Amsterdam: NiNsee, 2020).

39 Willemsen and Nimako, *The Dutch Atlantic.*

40 Nimako Delea, and M. Esajas, *Waarom vrijheid niet kon wachten.*

41 Willemsen and Nimako, *The Dutch Atlantic.*

42 Beckles, *A History of Barbados.*

43 Nimako, Delea, and Esajas, *Waarom vrijheid niet kon wachten.*

44 Nimako, Delea, and Esajas, *Waarom vrijheid niet kon wachten*, pp. 124–125.

45 Nimako, Delea, and Esajas, *Waarom vrijheid niet kon wachten*, pp. 124–125.

46 Nimako, Delea, and Esajas, *Waarom vrijheid niet kon wachten*, pp. 124–125.

47 Willemsen and Nimako, *The Dutch Atlantic*, p. 160.

48 Willemsen and Nimako, *The Dutch Atlantic*, p. 160.

49 *Utrechtsch Provinciaal en Stedelijke Dagblad*, no. 155, 2 July 1863, quoted in Willemsen and Nimako, *The Dutch Atlantic.*

50 Kwame Nimako, Amy Abdou, and Glenn Willemsen, "Chattel Slavery and Racism: A Reflection on the Dutch Experience", in Philomena Essed and Isabel Hoving (eds.), *Dutch Racism* (Amsterdam: Thamyris, 2014), pp. 31–51.

51 Kwame Nimako, "Location and Social Thought in the Black: A Testimony to Africana Intellectual Tradition", in Sabine Broeck and Carsten Junker (eds.), *Post-coloniality–Decoloniality–Black Critique: Joints and Fissures* (Frankfurt: Campus Verlag, 2014), pp. 53–62.

52 Nimako and Small, "Collective Memory of Slavery in Great Britain and the Netherlands".

53 Kwame Nimako and Glenn Willemsen, *Suriname en de banvloek van haar naturlijke hulpbronen* (Suriname and the Curse of Natural Resources), in H.W. Campbell and F.E.R. Derveld (eds.), "Wegen van verandering: Indicaties en effecten van politieke, economische en sociale ontwikkelingen in Suriname" (Roads of Change: Indications and Effects of Political, Economic and Social Development in Suriname) (Beuningen: Studia Interetnica, 2004).

54 See Kwame Nimako, "Nkrumah, African Awakening and Neo-colonialism: How Black America Awakened Nkrumah and Nkrumah Awakened Black America", *Black Scholar*, vol. 40, no. 2, 2010, pp. 54–70. See also Nimako, "Location and Social Thought in the Black".

Chapter 11. Slavery in Lusophone America

1 Stuart B. Schwartz, *Sugar Plantations in the Formation of Brazilian Society: Bahia, 1550–1750* (New York: Cambridge University Press, 1985); Ronaldo Vainfas, *A heresia dos índios: Catolicismo e rebeldia no Brasil colonial* (São Paulo: Companhia das Letras, 1995); Pedro Puntoni, *A guerra dos Bárbaros: Povos indígenas e a colonização do sertão nordeste do Brasil, 1650–1720* (São Paulo: Hucitec, 1720); Alida C. Metcalf, *Go-betweens and the Colonisation of Brazil, 1500–1600* (Austin: University of Texas Press, 2005); Alida Metcalf, "The Entradas of Bahia of the Sixteenth Century", *The Americas*, vol. 61, no. 3, 2005, pp, 373–400; and Maria Hilda Baqueiro Paraíso, "Revoltas indígenas, a criação do governo geral e o regimento de 1548", *Clio: Revista de Pesquisa Histórica*, no. 29, vol. 1, 2011, pp. 1–21.

2 Fernando A. Novais, *Portugal e Brasil na crise do antigo sistema colonial (1777–*

1808) (São Paulo: Editora 34, 2019 [1979]); and Luiz Felipe de Alencastro, *O trato dos viventes: Formação do Brasil no Atlântico Sul, séculos XVI e XVII* (São Paulo: Companhia das Letras, 2000), pp. 11–43.

3   John Hemming, *Red Gold: The Conquest of Brazilian Indians, 1500–1760* (Cambridge, MA: Harvard University Press, 1978); John Monteiro, *Negros da terra: Índios e bandeirantes nas origens de São Paulo* (São Paulo: Companhia das Letras, 1994); Beatriz Perrone-Moisés, "Índios livres e índios escravos: Os princípios da legislação indigenista do período colonial (séculos XVI a XVIII)", in Manuela Carneiro da Cunha (ed.), *História dos índios no Brasil* (São Paulo: Companhia das Letras; Secretaria Municipal de Cultura; FAPESP, 1992); Barbara Sommer, "Colony of the Sertão: Amazonian Expeditions and the Indian Slave Trade", *The Americas*, vol. 61, no. 3, 2005, pp. 401–428; and Rafael Chambouleyron and Fernanda Bombardi, "Descimentos privados de índios na Amazônia colonial (séculos XVII e XVIII)", *Varia Historia*, vol. 27, no. 46, 2011, pp. 601–623.

4   Alexandre Vieira Ribeiro, "The Transatlantic Slave Trade to Bahia, 1582–1851", in David Eltis and David Richardson (eds.), *Extending the Frontiers: Essays on the New Transatlantic Slave Trade Database* (New Haven and London: Yale University Press, 2008), pp. 130–154.

5   Evaldo Cabral de Mello, *Olinda restaurada: Guerra e açúcar no Nordeste, 1630–1654* (São Paulo: Editora 34, 2007 [1975]).

6   Schwartz, *Sugar Plantations in the Formation of Brazilian Society*, p. 154.

7   Maria Inês Cortes de Oliveira, "Quem eram os 'negros da Guiné'? A origem dos Africanos na Bahia", in João José Reis and Carlos da Silva Jr (eds.), *Atlântico de dor: Faces do tráfico de escravos* (Belo Horizonte: Fino Traço, 2017), pp. 565–605.

8   See, for example, João José Reis, *Rebelião escrava no Brasil: A história do Levante dos Malês em 1835* (São Paulo: Companhia das Letras, 2003); Luis Nicolau Parés, *The Formation of Candomblé: Vodun History and Ritual in Brazil* (Chapel Hill: University of North Carolina Press, 2013); and Mariza de Carvalho Soares, *People of Faith: Slavery and African Catholics in Eighteenth-Century Rio de Janeiro* (Durham, NC: Duke University Press, 2012).

9   Alencastro, *O trato dos viventes*, p. 226.

10   Evaldo Cabral de Mello, *O negócio do Brasil: Portugal, os Países Baixos e o Nordeste, 1641–1669* (São Paulo: Companhia das Letras, 2011), pp. 154–156; Alencastro, *O trato dos viventes*, pp. 228–238; and Charles R. Boxer, *Salvador de Sá and the Struggle for Brazil and Angola (1602–1686)* (London: Athlone Press, 1952).

11   Ronaldo Vainfas, *Antônio Vieira, Jesuíta do rei* (São Paulo: Companhia das Letras, 2011), pp. 52–61; and Alfredo Bosi (ed.), *Essencial: Padre Antônio Vieira* (São Paulo: Penguin Classics Companhia das Letras, 2011), pp. 532–571.

12   Alencastro, *O trato dos viventes*, pp. 155–187; Carlos Alberto M.R. Zeron, *Linha de fé: A Companhia de Jesus e a escravidão no processo de formação da sociedade colonial (Brasil, séculos XVI e XVII)* (São Paulo: Edusp, 2011); and Giuseppe Marcocci, *A consciência de um império: Portugal e o seu mundo (sécs. XV–XVIII)* (Coimbra: Imprensa da Universidade de Coimbra, 2012).

13   Flávio dos Santos Gomes, *Histórias de quilombolas: Mocambos e comunidades de senzalas no Rio de Janeiro, século XIX* (São Pulo: Companhia das Letras, 2006); Flávio dos Santos Gomes, *A hidra e os pântanos: Mocambos, quilombos e comunidades de fugitivos no Brasil, séculos XVII–XIX* (São Paulo: Editora da UNESP, 2005); Eurípedes Funes,

Nasci nas matas, nunca tive senhor: História e memória dos mocambos do baixo Amazonas (Fotaleza: Plebeu Gabinete de Leitura, 2022); and José Maia Bezerra Neto, *Fugindo, sempre fugindo: Escravidão, fugas escravas e fugitivos na Amazônia brasileira (1840–1888)* (Teresina: Cancioneiro, 2023).

14   Raymond K. Kent, "Palmares: An African State in Brazil", *Journal of African History*, vol. 6, no. 2, 1965, pp. 161–75; Silvia Hunold Lara, "Marronnage et pouvoir colonial: Palmares, Cucaú et les frontières de la liberté au Pernambouc à la fin du XVIIe siècle", *Annales*, vol. 67, no. 3, 2007, pp. 639–662; Silvia Hunold Lara, "Depois da batalha de Pungo Andongo (1671): O destino atlântico dos príncipes do Ndongo", *Revista de História*, no. 175, 2016, pp. 205–225; Stuart B. Schwartz, "Rethinking Palmares: Slave Resistance in Colonial Brazil", in Stuart B. Schwartz, *Slaves, Peasants, and Rebels* (Urbana: University of Illinois Press, 1992), pp. 103–136; and John K. Thornton, "Les états de l'Angola et la formation de Palmares (Brésil)", *Annales*, vol. 63, 2008, pp. 769–797. See also several articles in João José Reis and Flávio dos Santos Gomes (eds.), *Liberdade por um fio: História dos quilombos no Brasil* (São Paulo: Companhia das Letras, 1996); Flávio Gomes (ed.), *Mocambos de Palmares: Histórias e fontes (séculos XVI–XIX)* (Rio de Janeiro: 7Letras, 2010); Silvia Hunold Lara and Phablo Roberto Machis Fachin (eds.), *Guerra contra Palmares: O manuscrito de 1678* (São Paulo: Chão Editora, 2021); and Silvia Hunold Lara, *Palmares & Cucaú: O aprendizado da dominação* (São Paulo: Edusp, 2021).

15   Barry W. Higman, "The Sugar Revolution", *Economic History Review*, vol. 53, no. 2, 2000, pp. 213–236; and Joseph Calder Miller, "O Atlântico escravista: Açúcar, engenhos e escravos", in João José Reis and Carlos da Silva Jr (eds.), *Atlântico de dor: Faces do tráfico de escravos* (Belo Horizonte: Fino Traço, 2017), pp. 39–67.

16   André João Antonil, *Cultura e opulência no Brasil por suas drogas e minas* (São Paulo: Edusp, 2007), p. 97.

17   Pierre Verger, *Fluxo e refluxo: Do tráfico de escravos entre o golfo do Benin e a Bahia de Todos os Santos, dos séculos XVII a XIX* (Salvador: Corrupio, 2002 [1967]); Robin Law, *The Slave Coast of West Africa, 1550–1750: The Impact of the Atlantic Slave Trade on an African Society* (Oxford: Clarendon Press, 1991); Jean Baptiste Nardi, *O fumo brasileiro no período colonial* (São Paulo: Brasiliense, 1991); and Gustavo Aciolli Lopes, *A fênix e o Atlântico: A capitania de Pernambuco e a economia-mundo europeia (1654–1750)* (São Paulo: Alameda, 2018).

18   Robin Law, *The Kingdom of Allada* (Leiden: Centre of Non-Western Studies, 1997); and Robin Law, *Ouidah: The Social History of a West African Enslaving "Port", 1727–1892* (Athens: Ohio University Press, 2004).

19   Maria Inês Cortes de Oliveira, "Viver e Mmorrer no meio dos seus: Nações e comunidades africanas na Bahia do século XIX", *Revista USP*, no. 28, 1995–1996, pp. 174–193; and Carlos da Silva Jr., "Identidades afro-atlânticas: Salvador, século XVIII (1700–1750)" (Master's thesis, Universidade Federal da Bahia, 2011).

20   Carlos da Silva Jr, "Ardras, minas e jejes, ou escravos de 'primeira reputação': Políticas africanas, tráfico negreiro e identidade étnica na Bahia do século XVIII", *Almanack*, no. 12, 2016, pp. 6–33; Carlos da Silva Jr, "Identidades afro-atlânticas", especially Chapters 3 and 5; Aldair Rodrigues, "African Body Marks, Stereotypes and Racialisation in Eighteenth-Century Brazil", *Slavery and Abolition*, 2020, pp. 1–30; and Aldair Rodrigues, "'Com duas gejas em cada uma das fontes': Escarificações e o processo de tradução visual da diáspora Jeje em Minas Gerais durante o século XVIII", *Afro-Ásia*, 63, 2021, pp. 128–180.

21 *Documentos Históricos*, XL (1938), pp. 195–196.

22 Silvia H. Lara, *Fragmentos setecentistas: Escravidão, cultura e poder na América portuguesa* (São Paulo: Companhia das Letras, 2007).

23 Alencastro, *O trato dos viventes*, p. 150.

24 Antônio da Costa Peixoto, *Obra nova de língua geral de Mina*, edited by Luís Silveira and Edmundo Correia Lopes (Lisboa: Agência Geral das Colónias, 1945 [1741]); Olabiyi Yai, "Texts of Enslavement: Fon and Yoruba Vocabularies from Eighteenth- and Nineteenth-Century Brazil", in Paul E. Lovejoy (ed.), *Identity in the Shadow of Slavery* (London: Continuum, 2000), pp. 102–112; Yeda Pessoa de Castro, *A língua mina-jeje no Brasil: Um falar africano em Ouro Preto do século XVIII* (Belo Horizonte: Fundação João Pinheiro and Secretaria da Cultura do Estado de Minas Gerais, 2002); Silvia H. Lara, "Linguagem, domínio senhorial e identidade étnica nas Minas Gerais de meados do século XVIII", in Cristiana Bastos, Miguel Vale de Almeida, and Bela Feldman-Bianco (eds.), *Trânsitos coloniais: Diálogos críticos luso-brasileiros* (Campinas: Editora da Unicamp, 2007), pp. 221–241; and Ivana Stolze Lima, "O conceito de língua geral de Mina: Apontamentos para a compreensão de seu significado histórico", *Revista do Gel*, vol. 18, no. 3, 2021, pp. 143–168.

25 Amédée François Frézier, *Relation d'un voyage de la mer de Sud, detroit de Magellan, Brésil, Cayenne et les isles Antilles* (Amsterdam: Honoré et Chatelain, 1715), p. 275.

26 João José Reis, *Rebelião escrava no Brasil*; Maria Inês Cortes de Oliveira, *O liberto: O seu mundo e os outros (Salvador, 1790–1890)* (Salvador: Corrupio, 1988); Daniele dos Santos Souza, "Entre o 'serviço de casa' e o 'ganho': Escravidão em Salvador na primeira metade do século XVIII (Master's dissertation, Universidade Federal da Bahia, 2010); and João José Reis, *Ganhadores: A greve negra de 1857 na Bahia* (São Paulo: Companhia das Letras, 2019).

27 Katia Maria de Queirós Mattoso, "A propósito das cartas de alforria: Bahia, 1779–1850", *Anais de História*, no. 4, 1972, pp. 23–52; Stuart B. Schwartz, "The Manumission of Slaves in Colonial Brazil: Bahia, 1684–1745", *Hispanic American Historical Review*, vol. 54, no. 4, 1974, pp. 603–635; Ligia Bellini, "Por amor e por interesse: A relação senhor-escravo em cartas de alforria", in João José Reis (ed.), *Escravidão e invenção da liberdade: Estudos sobre o negro no Brasil* (São Paulo: Brasiliense, 1988); Mieko Nishida, "Manumission and Ethnicity in Urban Slavery: Salvador, Brazil, 1808–1888", *Hispanic American Historical Review*, vol. 73, no. 3, 1993, pp. 361–391; Roberto Guedes, *Egressos do cativeiro: Trabalho, família, aliança e mobilidade social (Porto Feliz, São Paulo, c.1798 – c.1850)* (Rio de Janeiro: MauadX, 2008); Marcio de Souza Soares, *A remissão do cativeiro: A dádiva da alforria e o governo dos escravos nos Campos dos Goitacases, c.1750 – c.1830* (Rio de Janeiro: Apicuri, 2009); and Katia Lorena Novais Almeida, *Alforrias em Rio de Contas: Bahia, século XIX* (Salvador: EDUFBA, 2012).

28 Rafael de Bivar Marquese, "A dinâmica da escravidão no Brasil: Resistência, tráfico negreiro e alforrias, séculos XVII–XIX", *Novos Estudos CEBRAP*, no. 74, 2006, pp. 107–123; Robert W. Slenes, "Brazil", in Robert L. Paquette and Mark M. Smith (eds.), *The Oxford Handbook of Slavery in the Americas* (New York: Oxford University Press, 2010), p. 120; and Sidney Chalhoub, The Precariousness of Freedom in a Slave Society: Brazil in the Nineteenth Century", *International Review of Social History*, vol. 56, no. 3, 2011, pp. 405–439.

29 Bert B. Barickman, *A Bahian Counterpoint: Sugar, Tobacco, Cassava, and Slavery in the Recôncavo, 1780–1860* (Stanford: Stanford University Press, 1998).

30 "Trans-atlantic Slave Trade: Estimates", *Slave Voyages*, http://www.slavevoyages.
org/estimates/iPB0gpUU (accessed 10 June 2021); and Philip D. Curtin, *The Atlantic
Slave Trade: A Census* (Madison: University of Wisconsin Press, 1969).

31 Dale Tomich, *Through the Prism of Slavery: Labour, Capital, and World Economy*
(Boulder: Rowman and Littlefield, 2004), pp. 56–71.

32 Leslie Bethell, *The Abolition of the Brazilian Slave Trade: Britain, Brazil and the Slave
Trade Question, 1807–1869* (Cambridge: Cambridge University Press, 1970); Jaime
Rodrigues, *O infame comércio: Propostas e experiências no final do tráfico de africanos para
o Brasil (1808–1850)* (Campinas: Editora da Unicamp, 2000); Guilherme de Paula
Costa Santos, "A convenção de 1817: Debate político e diplomático sobre o tráfico
de escravos durante o governo de D. João no Rio de Janeiro" (Master's dissertation,
Universidade de São Paulo, 2007); and Paulo Cesar Oliveira de Jesus, "Mantendo
o curso: Restrições, subterfúgios e comércio da escravatura na Bahia (1810–1817)"
(PhD thesis, Universidade Federal da Bahia, 2017).

33 João José Reis and Carlos da Silva Jr, "Decompondo o tráfico", in João José Reis and
Carlos da Silva Jr (eds.), *Atlântico de dor: Faces do tráfico de escravos* (Belo Horizonte:
Fino Traço, 2017), pp. 15–37; João José Reis, "'Por sua liberdade me oferece uma
escrava': Alforrias por substituição na Bahia, 1800–1850", *Afro-Ásia*, no. 63, 2021, pp.
232–290; and Carlos da Silva Jr, "A Bahia e a Costa da Mina no alvorecer da Segunda
Escravidão (c.1810–1831)", *Afro-Ásia*, no. 65, 2022, pp. 91–147.

34 Manuel Carneiro da Cunha, *Negros, estrangeiros: Os escravos libertos e sua volta à África*
(São Paulo: Companhia das Letras, 2012); and Beatriz Mamigonian, "Os direitos
dos africanos libertos no Brasil oitocentista: Entre razões de direito e considerações
políticas", *História*, vol. 34, no. 2, 2015, pp. 181–205.

35 Rafael Marquese and Dale Tomich, "O Vale do Paraíba escravista e a formação do
mercado mundial do café no século XIX" in Mariana Muaze and Ricardo Salles (eds.),
O Vale do Paraíba e o Império do Brasil nos quadros da Segunda Escravidão (Rio de
Janeiro: 7Letras, 2015), pp. 21-56.

36 Tâmis Parron, *A política da escravidão no Império do Brasil, 1826–1865* (Rio de Janeiro:
Civilização Brasileira, 2011); Sidney Chalhoub, *A força da escravidão: Ilegalidade e
costume no Brasil oitocentista* (São Paulo: Companhia das Letras, 2012); and Alain El
Youssef, *Imprensa e escravidão: Política e tráfico negreiro no Império do Brasil* (São
Paulo: Intermeios; Fapesb, 2016).

37 Beatriz Mamigonian, *Africanos livres: A abolição do tráfico de escravos no Brasil* (São
Paulo: Companhia das Letras, 2017), p. 63. See also Jake Cristopher Richards, "Anti-
Slave-Trade Law, 'Liberated Africans' and the State in the South Atlantic World,
c.1839–1852", *Past and Present*, vol. 241, no. 1, 2018, pp. 179–219.

38 "Trans-atlantic Slave Trade: Estimates", *Slave Voyages*.

39 João José Reis, "Slaves Who Owned Slaves in Nineteenth-Century Bahia, Brazil",
Mecila Working Paper Series, vol. 36, 2021, pp. 1–23; and Reis, "Por sua liberdade me
oferece uma escrava', pp. 232–290.

40 Mamigonian, *Africanos livres*.

41 Reis, *Rebelião escrava no Brasil*; Paul E. Lovejoy, *Jihad in West Africa during the Age
of Revolutions* (Athens: Ohio University Press, 2016); Manuel Barcia, *West African
Warfare in Bahia and Cuba: Soldier Slaves in the Atlantic World, 1807–1844* (Oxford:
Oxford University Press, 2014); João José Reis, "Há duzentos anos: A revolta escrava
de 1814 na Bahia", *Topoi*, vol. 15, 2014, pp. 68–115; João José Reis, "Resistência e

controle de escravos na Bahia: A conspiração haussá de 1807", in João Fragoso and Maria de Fátima Gouvêa (eds.), *Na trama das redes: Política e negócios no império português, século XVI–XVIII* (Rio de Janeiro: Civilização Brasileira, 2010), pp. 549–599; and João José Reis, "A revolta haussá de 1809 na Bahia", in João José Reis and Flávio Gomes (eds.), *Revoltas escravas no Brasil* (São Paulo: Companhia das Letras, 2021), pp. 177–226.

42   Reis, *Rebelião escrava no Brasil*, p. 282.

43   Luciana da Cruz Brito, *Temores da África: Segurança, legislação e população africana na Bahia oitocentista* (Salvador: EDUFBA, 2015).

44   Cunha, *Negros, estrangeiros*; Milton Guran, *Agudás: Os "brasileiros" do Benim* (Rio de Janeiro: Nova Fronteira, 2000); Mônica Lima, "Entre margens: O retorno à África de libertos do Brasil, 1830–1870" (PhD dissertation, Universidade Federal Fluminense, 2008); Lisa Earl Castillo, "The Exodus of 1835: Aguda Life Stories and Social Networks", in Tunde Babawale, Akin Alao, and Tony Onwumah (eds.), *Pan-Africanism and the Integration of Continental Africa and Diaspora Africa* (Lagos: Centre for Black Arts and Civilisation, 2011), vol. 2, pp. 27–51; Lisa Earl Castillo, "Mapping the Nineteenth-Century Brazilian Returnee Movement: Demographics, Life Stories and the Question of Slavery", *Atlantic Studies*, vol. 13, no. 1, 2016, pp. 25–52; Elaine S. Falheiros, "Luis e Antonio Xavier de Jesus: Mobilidade social de africanos na Bahia oitocentista" (Master's thesis, Universidade Federal da Bahia, 2015); Luis Nicolau Parés, "Afro-Catholic Baptism and the Articulation of a Merchant Community, Agoué, 1840–1860", *History in Africa*, vol. 42, 2015, pp. 165–201; and Luis Nicolau Parés, "Entre a Bahia e a Costa da Mina, africanos libertos no tráfico ilegal", in Giuseppina Raggi, João Figuerôa-Rego, and Roberta Stumpf (eds.), *Salvador da Bahia: Interações entre América e África (séculos XVI–XIX)* (Salvador and Lisbon: EDUFBA and CHAM, 2017), pp. 13–49.

45   On Campinas, see Ricardo Pirola, *Senzala insurgente: Malungos, parentes e rebeldes nas fazendas de Campinas (1832)* (Campinas: Editora da Unicamp, 2011); and Gomes, *Histórias de quilombolas*.

46   Marcos Ferreira de Andrade, "'Nós somos os caramurus e vamos arrasar tudo': A história da revolta dos escravos de Carrancas, Minas Gerais (1833)", in João José Reis and Flávio Gomes, *Revoltas escravas no Brasil*, pp. 262–324; and Ricardo Figueiredo Pirola, *Escravos e rebeldes nos tribunais do império: Uma história social da lei de 10 de junho de 1835* (Rio de Janeiro: Arquivo Nacional, 2015).

47   Parés, *The Formation of Candomblé*.

48   João José Reis, *Divining Slavery and Freedom: The Story of Domingos Sodré, an African Priest in Nineteenth-Century Brazil* (New York: Cambridge University Press, 2015); Lisa Earl Castillo, "Between Memory, Myth and History: Transatlantic Voyagers of the Casa Branca Temple", in Ana Lucia Araújo (ed.), *Paths of the Atlantic Slave Trade: Interactions, Identities and Images* (Amherst, NY: Cambria Press, 2011), pp. 203–238; Lisa Earl Castillo, "Bamboxê Obitikô and the Nineteenth-Century Expansion of Orisha Worship in Brazil", *Tempo*, vol. 22, no. 39, 2016, pp. 126–153; Lisa Earl Castillo and Luis Nicolau Parés, "Marcelina da Silva: A Nineteenth-Century Candomblé Priestess in Bahia", *Slavery and Abolition*, vol. 31, 2010, pp. 1–27; Luis Nicolau Parés and Lisa Earl Castillo, "José Pedro Autran e o retorno de Xangô", *Religião e Sociedade*, vol. 35, no. 1, 2015, pp. 13–43; and Luis Nicolau Parés, "Libertos africanos, comércio atlântico e candomblé: A história de uma carta que não chegou ao destino", *Revista de*

História, no. 178, 2019, pp. 1–34.

49   João José Reis, "Candomblé and Slave Resistance in Nineteenth-Century Bahia", in Luis Nicolau Parés and Roger Sansi (eds.), *Sorcery in the Black Atlantic* (Chicago: University of Chicago Press, 2011), pp. 55–74.

50   Richard Graham, "Another Middle Passage? The Internal Slave Trade in Brazil"; Robert Wayne Slenes, "The Brazilian Internal Slave Trade, 1850–1888: Regional Economies, Slave Experience, and the Politics of a Peculiar Market", in Walter Johnson (ed.), *The Chattel Principle: Internal Slave Trades in the Americas* (New Haven and London: Yale University Press, 2004), pp. 291–324, 325–372; José Flávio Motta, *Escravos daqui, dali e de mais além: O tráfico interno de cativos na expansão cafeeira paulista (Areias, Guaratinguetá, Constituição/Piracicaba e Casa Branca, 1861–1887)* (São Paulo: Alameda, 2012); Maria de Fátima Noves Pires, *Fios da vida: Tráfico interprovincial e alforrias nos Sertoins de Sima – Ba (1860–1920)* (São Paulo: Annablume, 2010); and Luiz Carlos Laurindo Jr, "Rios de escravidão: Tráfico interno e o mercado de escravos do vale do Amazonas (1840–1888)" (PhD thesis, Universidade de São Paulo, 2021).

51   Katia Maria de Queirós Mattoso, "O filho da escrava (em torno da Lei do Ventre Livre)", *Revista Brasileira de História*, vol. 8, no. 16, 1988, pp. 37–55; Eduardo Spiller Pena, *O jogo da face: A astúcia escrava frente aos senhores e à lei na Curitiba provincial* (Curitiba: Quatro Ventos, 1999); Sidney Chalhoub, *Visões da liberdade: Uma história das ultimas décadas da escravidão na corte* (São Paulo: Companhia das Letras, 1990); Sidney Chalhoub, *Machado de Assis, historiador* (São Paulo: Companhia das Letras, 2005); and Maria Helena Pereira Toledo Machado, Luciana da Cruz Brito, Iamara da Silva Viana, and Flávio dos Santos Gomes (eds.), *Ventres livres? Gênero, maternidade e legislação* (São Paulo: Editora UNESP, 2021).

52   Ricardo Tadeu Caíres Silva, "Caminhos e descaminhos da abolição: Escravos, senhores e direitos nas ultimas décadas da escravidão (Bahia, 1850–1888)" (PhD thesis, Universidade Federal do Paraná, 2007); Ricardo Tadeu Caíres Silva, "Memórias do tráfico ilegal de escravos nas ações de liberdade (Bahia, 1885–1888)", *Afro-Ásia*, no. 35, 2007, pp. 37–82; and Camillia Cowling, *Conceiving Freedom: Women of Color, Gender, and the Abolition of Slavery in Havana and Rio de Janeiro* (Chapel Hill: University of North Carolina Press, 2013).

53   See the several chapters in Maria Helena Pereira Toledo Machado and Celso Castilho (eds.), *Tornando-se livre: Agentes históricos e lutas sociais no processo de abolição* (São Paulo: Edusp, 2015); and Celso Thomas Castilho, *Slave Emancipation and Transformations in Brazilian Political Citizenship* (Pittsburgh: University of Pittsburgh Press, 2016).

54   Chalhoub, *Machado de Assis*; Maria Firmina dos Reis, *Úrsula* (São Paulo: Penguin-Companhia, 2018); F.C. Duarte Badaró, *Fantina: Cenas da escravidão*, edited by Sidney Chalhoub (São Paulo: Chão Editora, 2019 [1881]); Bernardo Guimarães, *A escrava Isaura* (São Paulo: Ática, 2019 [1885]; and Joaquim Manoel de Macedo, *As vítimas-algozes: Quadros da escravidão* (São Paulo: Difusão Cultural do Livro, 2006 [1869]).

55   Humberto Fernandes Machado, *Palavras e brados: José do Patrocínio e a imprensa abolicionista no Rio de Janeiro* (Niterói: EDUFF, 2014); André Rebouças, *Cartas da África: Registro de correspondência, 1891–1893*; Ligia Fonseca Ferreira (ed.), *Lições de resistência: Artigos de Luiz Gama na imprensa de São Paulo e do Rio de Janeiro* (São

Paulo: Edições SESC, 2020); and Ana Flávia Magalhães Pinto, *Escritos de liberdade: Literatos Negrors, Racismo e cidadania no Brasil oitocentista* (Campinas: Editora da Unicamp, 2018).

56   Angela Alonso, *Flores, votos e lalas: O movimento abolicionista brasileiro (1868–1888)* (São Paulo: Companhia das Letras, 2015); Jeffrey D. Needell, *The Sacred Cause: The Abolitionist Movement, Afro-Brazilian Mobilisation, and Imperial Politics in Rio de Janeiro* (Stanford: Stanford University Press, 2020); Elciene Azevedo, *Orfeu de Carapinha: A trajetória de Luiz Gama na imperial cidade de São Paulo* (Campinas: Editora da Unicamp, 1999); and Elciene Azevedo, *O direito dos escravos: Lutas jurídicas e abolicionismo na província de São Paulo* (Campinas: Editora da Unicamp, 2010).

57   Maria Helena Pereira Toledo Machado, *O plano e o pânico: Os movimentos sociais na década da abolição* (São Paulo: Edusp, 1994); Célia Marinho de Azevedo, *Onda negra, medo branco: O negro no imaginário das elites* (Rio de Janeiro: Paz e Terra, 1987); and Emília Viotti da Costa, *Da monarquia à república: Momentos decisivos* (São Paulo: Editora da UNESP, 1999).

58   Robert Daibert Jr, *Isabel, a "redentora" dos escravos: Uma história da princesa entre olhares negros e brancos (1846–1988)* (Bauru, SP: UDESC, 2004); Roderick J. Barman, *Princesa Isabel do Brasil: Gênero e poder no século XIX* (São Paulo: Editora da UNESP, 2005); and Renata Figueiredo Moraes, *As festas da abolião no Rio de Janeiro (1888–1908)* (Rio de Janeiro: FGV, 2023).

59   Wlamyra R. de Albuquerque, *O jogo da dissimulação: Abolição e cidadania negra no Brasil* (São Paulo: Companhia das Letras, 2009), p. 125.

60   Peter Eisenberg, *Modernização sem mudança: A indústria açucareira em Pernambuco, 1840–1910* (Rio de Janeiro: Paz e Terra, 1977); Walter Fraga, *Crossroads of Freedom: Slaves and Freed People in Bahia, Brazil, 1870–1910* (Durham: Duke University Press, 2016); and Maria Emília Vasconcelos dos Santos, "Os significados do 13 de maio: A abolição e o imediato pós-abolição para os trabalhadores dos engenhos da Zona da Mata Sul de Pernambuco (1884–1893)" (PhD thesis, Universidade Estadual de Campinas, 2014).

61   Iacy Maia Mata, "'Libertos de 13 de maio' e ex-senhores na Bahia: Conflitos no pós-abolição", *Afro-Ásia*, no. 35, 2007, pp. 163–198.

62   Lilia Moritz Schwarcz, *O espetáculo das raças: Cientistas, instituições e questão racial no Brasil* (São Paulo: Companhia das Letras, 1993); Mariza Corrêa, *As ilusões da liberdade: A escola Nina Rodrigues e a antropologia no Brasil* (Rio de Janeiro: Fiocruz, 2014); and Maria Helena Pereira Toledo Machado, *Raça, ciência e viagem no século XIX* (São Paulo: Intermeios, 2018).

63   Lilia Schwarcz, "Race and Inequality in Brazil: A Deep Shadow", in Francisco Bethencourt (ed.), *Inequality in the Portuguese-Speaking World: Global and Historical Perspectives* (Brighton: Sussex Academic Press, 2018), pp. 21–38.

Chapter 12. Slavery in the United States

1   The Constitution of the United States of America (Archives.gov).

2   Slave Voyages Database, https://www.slavevoyages.org/ (accessed 1 November 2021).

3   John Mack Faragher, Mari Jo Buhle, Daniel Czitrom, and Susan H. Armitage (eds.), *Out of Many: A History of the American People*, vol. 1 (4th edn, Upper Saddle River, NJ: Prentice Hall, 2005), Appendix 16.

4   Henry Wiencek, *An Imperfect God: George Washington, His Slaves, and the Creation of America* (New York: Farrar, Straus and Giroux, 2003), pp. 45–46.

5   Matthew Costello, "The Enslaved Households of President James Monroe", White House Historical Association, https://www.whitehousehistory.org/the-enslaved-households-of-president-james-monroe#:~:text=The%201810%20census%20records%20show,the%20county's%20largest%20slave%20owners (accessed 1 August 2022).

6   Paul Finkleman, *Supreme Injustice: Slavery in the Nation's Highest Court* (Cambridge, MA: Harvard University Press, 2018).

7   One bale weighed between 480 to 500 (British) pounds.

8   Jonathan Hughes and Louis P. Cain, *American Economic History* (5th edn, New York: Addison-Wesley, 1998), pp. 169–170.

9   See, for example, C.L.R. James, *The Black Jacobins: Toussaint L'Ouverture and the San Domingo Revolution* (London: Secker and Warburg, 1938).

10   Jeffrey R. Kerr-Ritchie, *Freedom's Seekers: Essays in Comparative Emancipation* (Baton Rouge: Louisiana State University Press, 2013), pp. 23, 35–36; and Steven Hahn, *A Nation without Borders: The United States and Its World in an Age of Civil Wars, 1830–1910* (New York: Viking, 2016), pp. 29–37.

11   Sven Beckert, *Empire of Cotton: A Global History* (New York: Alfred A. Knopf, 2014), pp. 101–102.

12   Richard S. Dunn, *A Tale of Two Plantations: Slave Life and Labor in Jamaica and Virginia* (Cambridge, MA: Harvard University Press, 2014), p. 279.

13   Frederic Bancroft, *Slave-Trading in the Old South* (Baltimore: J.H. Furst, 1931); Walter Johnson, *Soul by Soul: Life inside the Antebellum Slave Market* (Cambridge, MA: Harvard University Press, 1999); and Damian Alan Pargas, *Slavery and Forced Migration in the Antebellum South* (New York: Cambridge University Press, 2015). Whether directly or indirectly, all these important studies make the same point: slavery was most harsh where it was most profitable.

14   Calvin Schermerhorn, *The Business of Slavery and the Rise of American Capitalism, 1815–1860* (New Haven: Yale University Press, 2015); and Jeffrey R. Kerr-Ritchie, *Rebellious Passage: The Creole Revolt and America's Coastal Slave Trade* (New York: Cambridge University Press, 2019).

15   Beckert, *Empire of Cotton*, pp. 73, 121.

16   Jeffrey R. Kerr-Ritchie, *Freedpeople in the Tobacco South, Virginia, 1860–1900* (Chapel Hill: University of North Carolina Press, 1999), p. 24.

17   Kerr-Ritchie, *Freedpeople in the Tobacco South*, pp. 26–27.

18   Solomon Northrup, *Twelve Years a Slave* (New York: Norton, 2017 [1853]), pp. 94–101; John Brown, *Slave Life in Georgia: A Narrative of the Life, Suffering, and Escape of John Brown, a Fugitive Slave, Now in England*, edited by L.A. Chamerovzow (London: L.A. Chamerovzow, 1855).

19   James E. Newton and Ronald L. Lewis (eds.), *The Other Slaves: Mechanics, Artisans, and Craftsmen* (Boston: G.K. Hall, 1978).

20   Lynda J. Morgan, *Emancipation in Virginia's Tobacco Belt, 1850–1870* (Athens: University of Georgia Press, 1992).

21   W. Jeffrey Bolster, *Black Jacks: African American Seamen in the Age of Sail* (Cambridge, MA: Harvard University Press, 1997).

22   Cited in Ira Berlin, Joseph P. Reidy, and Leslie S. Rowland (eds.), *Freedom's Soldiers: The Black Military Experience in the Civil War* (New York: Cambridge University

Press, 1998), p. 149. Italics in original.

23   Kerr-Ritchie, *Freedpeople in the Tobacco South*, pp. 23–25.

24   Kerr-Ritchie, *Rebellious Passage*, p. 92.

25   Ira Berlin, *Generations of Captivity: A History of African-American Slaves* (Cambridge, MA: Harvard University Press, 2003), Table 1.

26   Laird W. Bergad, *The Comparative Histories of Slavery in Brazil, Cuba, and the United States* (New York: Cambridge University Press, 2007), pp. 96–131; and Stanley L. Engerman, *Slavery, Emancipation, and Freedom: Comparative Perspectives* (Baton Rouge: Louisiana State University Press, 2007), pp. 33–36.

27   Rose's testimony from Texas Slave Narratives, Part 4, pp. 174–178, reproduced in Willie Lee Rose (ed.), *A Documentary History of Slavery in North America* (Athens: University of Georgia Press, 1999), pp. 434–437.

28   Thomas A. Foster, *Rethinking Rufus: Sexual Violations of Enslaved Men* (Athens: University of Georgia Press, 2019).

29   *Narrative of the Life of Frederick Douglass* (Boston: Anti-Slavery Office, 1845).

30   North American Slave Narratives, Documenting the American South, https:// docsouth.unc.edu/browse/collections.html; and William L. Andrews (ed.), *North American Slave Narratives: The Lives of Moses Roper, Lunsford Lane, Moses Grandy, and Thomas Jones* (Chapel Hill: University of North Carolina Press, 2003).

31   For the published interviews, see George Rawick (ed.), *The American Slave: A Composite Autobiography*, Smithsonian Libraries and Archives, 19 vols. (1972), 12 vols. (1977), 10 vols. (1979). For an excellent collection which is easily accessible, see Charles L. Perdue, Jr, Thomas E. Barden, and Robert K. Phillips (eds.), *Weevils in the Wheat: Interviews with Virginia Ex-slaves* (Charlottesville: University of Virginia, 1992). For audio recordings, listen to Library of Congress, "Voices Remembering Slavery: Freed People Tell Their Stories", https://www.loc.gov/collections/voices-remembering-slavery/about-this-collection/.

32   Berlin, *Generations of Captivity*, Table 3.

33   John Hope Franklin, *The Free Negro in North Carolina, 1790–1860* (Chapel Hill: University of North Carolina Press, 1995), pp. 105–107.

34   Virginia Emigrants to Liberia, http://www.vcdh.virginia.edu/liberia/index. php?page=Virginia%20Emigrants%20To%20Liberia; and C. Patrick Burrowes, *Liberia and the Quest for Freedom: The Half That Has Never Been Told* (Liberia: self-published, 2019).

35   See Mary A. Shadd, *A Plea for Emigration, or, Notes of Canada West, in its Moral, Social and Political Aspect, with Suggestions Respecting Mexico, West Indies, and Vancouver's Island, for the Information of Colored Emigrants* (Detroit: George W. Pattison, 1852).

36   Jeffrey R. Kerr-Ritchie, *Rites of August First: Emancipation Day in the Black Atlantic World* (Baton Rouge: Louisiana State University Press, 2007), p. 140.

37   Martin R. Delany, *The Condition, Elevation, Emigration and Destiny of the Colored People of the United States* (Philadelphia: self-published, 1852), in Robert S. Levine (ed.), *Martin R. Delany: A Documentary Reader* (Chapel Hill: University of North Carolina Press, 2003).

38   Delany, *The Condition, Elevation, Emigration and Destiny of the Colored People of the United States*, p. 216.

39   Melville J. Herskovits, *The Myth of the Negro Past* (Boston: Beacon Press, 1958), p. 87.

40   Herbert Aptheker, *American Negro Slave Revolts* (New York: International Publishers,

1970), p. 162.

41   Daniel Rasmussen, *American Uprising: The Untold Story of America's Largest Slave Revolt* (New York: Harper Press, 2011); and Kenneth Greenberg (ed.), *The Confessions of Nat Turner and Related Documents* (Boston: Bedford and St. Martin's, 1996).

42   Louis A. DeCaro, Jr, *"Fire from the Midst of You": A Religious Life of John Brown* (New York: New York University Press, 2002); and Steven Lupet, *The "Colored Hero" of Harper's Ferry: John Anthony Copeland and the War against Slavery* (New York: Cambridge University Press, 2015).

43   Douglas R. Egerton, *Gabriel's Rebellion: The Virginia Slave Conspiracies of 1800 and 1802* (Chapel Hill: University of North Carolina Press, 1993); and Douglass R. Egerton, *He Shall Go Out Free: The Lives of Denmark Vesey* (Lanham: Rowman and Littlefield, 2004).

44   Winthrop D. Jordan, *Tumult and Silence at Second Creek: An Inquiry into a Civil War Slave Conspiracy* (Baton Rouge: Louisiana State University Press, 1993).

45   W.A. Littlejohn to North Carolina governor H.T. Clark, 16 August 1861, in W. Buck Yearns and Mark L. Bradley (eds.), *North Carolina Civil War Documentary* (Chapel Hill: University of North Carolina Press, 2002 [1980]), p. 27.

46   Professor Robert F. Engs, my former advisor at the University of Pennsylvania, first coined the term in an unpublished paper in 1987, which gracefully recognised the longevity of the interpretation.

47   General Benjamin F. Butler to US General-in-Chief Winfield Scott, 27 May 1861, in Ira Berlin, Barbara J. Fields, Steven F. Miller, Joseph P. Reidy, and Leslie S. Rowland (eds.), *Free at Last: A Documentary History of Slavery, Freedom, and the Civil War* (New York: New Press, 1992), pp. 9–10.

48   Ira Berlin, Barbara J. Fields, Steven F. Miller, Joseph P. Reidy, and Leslie S. Rowland (eds.), *Slaves No More: Three Essays in Emancipation and the Civil War* (New York: Cambridge University Press, 1992), pp. 45, 178.

49   Berlin, Reidy, and Rowland, *Freedom's Soldiers*, p. 20.

50   Dr Adam Arenson, "Black Canadians in U.S.C.T.", open-source database (accessed 1 November 2021).

51   Berlin, Reidy, and Rowland, *Freedom's Soldiers*, Table 1, pp. 16–17.

52   William A. Dobak, *Freedom by the Sword: The U.S. Colored Troops, 1862–1867* (Washington DC: Center of Military History, US Army, 2011), pp. 22–23.

53   Berlin, Reidy, and Rowland, *Freedom's Soldiers*, p. 126.

54   Berlin, Reidy, and Rowland, *Freedom's Soldiers*, p. 125.

55   Berlin, Reidy, and Rowland, *Freedom's Soldiers*, p. 32; and Dobak, *Freedom by the Sword*, pp. 113–115.

56   Patsey Leach, Camp Nelson, Union encampment, Kentucky, March 25, 1865, in Berlin, Fields, Miller, Reidy, and Rowland, *Free at Last*, pp. 400–401.

57   Randolph B. Campbell, *An Empire for Slavery: The Peculiar Institution in Texas* (Baton Rouge: Louisiana State University Press, 1989), p. 249.

58   Margaret Mitchell, *Gone with the Wind* (New York: Macmillan, 1936).

59   New England Board of Higher Education, "Reparative Justice", https://nebhe.org/reparative-justice/ (accessed 1 November 2021).

60   Joe Heim, "New Lafayette Square Marker Highlights Role of Slavery in Building White House", https://www.washingtonpost.com/local/slave-labor-white-house-lafayette-square/2021/07/28/c64a8f9c-efd6-11eb-bf80-e3877d9c5f06_story.html

(accessed 17 November 2021).

61   US National Park Service, https://www.nps.gov/people/denmark-vesey.htm (accessed 1 November 2021).

62   Katie Donington, *The Bonds of Family: Slavery, Commerce and Culture in the British Atlantic World* (Manchester: Manchester University Press, 2020), p. 290.

63   Terry Gross, "From Slavery to Socialism, New Legislation Restricts What Teachers Can Discuss", 3 February 2022, National Public Radio (NPR), https://www.npr.org/2022/02/03/1077878538/legislation-restricts-what-teachers-can-discuss (accessed August 2022).

64   Thomas Picketty, *Time for Socialism: Dispatches from a World on Fire, 2016–2021* (New Haven: Yale University Press, 2021).

Chapter 13. The Role of Women in North America's Liberation Struggle

1   See Bell Hooks, *Feminist Theory: From Margin to Center* (New York: Routledge, 1984); and Bell Hooks, *Black Looks: Race and Representation* (New York: Routledge, 2014).

2   See Paula J. Giddings, *When and Where I Enter* (New York: W. Morrow, 1984).

3   Dann J. Broyld, "Harriet Tubman: Transnationalism and the Land of a Queen in the Late Antebellum", *The Meridians: Feminism, Race, and Transnationalism*, special issue: "Harriet Tubman: A Legacy of Resistance", vol. 12, no. 2, November 2014, pp. 78–98; Jennifer C. Nash, *Black Feminism Reimagined: After Intersectionality* (Chapel Hill: Duke University Press, 2019); Patricia Hill Collins, *Intersectionality* (Medford: Polity Press, 2020); Patricia Hill Collins, *Intersectionality as Critical Social Theory* (Chapel Hill: Duke University Press, 2019); and Peggy Bristow (ed.), *We're Rooted Here and They Can't Pull Us Up: Essays in the African Canadian Women's History* (Toronto: University of Toronto Press, 1994).

4   See, for example, Thomas Carlyle, *On Heroes, Hero-Worship, and the Heroic in History* (London: James Fraser, 1841).

5   Chimamanda Ngozi Adichie, "The Danger of a Single Story", TED Talk, July 2009; and Janell Hobson, "Chimamanda Ngozi Adichie: Storyteller", *Ms.*, 6 March 2015, pp. 26–29.

6   *Weekly Anglo-African*, 24 November 1860.

7   *Syracuse Standard*, 20 June 1856, and Carol Hunter, *To Set the Captives Free: Reverend Jermain Wesley Loguen and the Struggle for Freedom in Central New York, 1835–1872* (CreateSpace Independent Publishing Platform, 2013), p. 143.

8   William Still, *The Underground Railroad* (Edinburgh: Benediction Books, 2009 [1872]); and *Record of Fugitives* held at Columbia University, New York. Also see the books that highlight the *Record of Fugitives*: Eric Foner, *Gateway to Freedom: The Hidden History of the Underground Railroad* (New York: W.W. Norton 2015); and Don Papson and Tom Calarco, *Secret Lives of the Underground Railroad in New York City: Sydney Howard Gay, Louis Napoleon and the Record of Fugitives* (Jefferson: McFarland, 2015).

9   Kellie Carter Jackson, *Force and Freedom: Black Abolitionists and the Politics of Violence* (Philadelphia: University of Pennsylvania Press, 2019), p. 113; and Lynn M. Hudson, *The Making of "Mammy Pleasant": A Black Entrepreneur in Nineteenth-Century San Francisco* (Champaign: University of Illinois Press, 2008).

10   Mary Ellen Pleasant, Interview by Sam P. Davis, "How a Colored Woman Aided John Brown: A Piece of Unwritten History Disclosing the Identity of the Mysterious Backer of the Hero of Harpers Ferry", *People's Press*, 5 January 1904.

11   *People's Press*, 5 January 1904.
12   See St Catharines Assessment Roll (St Paul Ward), 1858; and Broyld, "Harriet Tubman". See also Erica Armstrong Dunbar, *She Came to Slay: The Life and Times of Harriet Tubman* (New York: Simon and Schuster, 2019).
13   Dann J. Broyld, *Borderland Blacks: Two Cities in the Niagara Region during the Final Decades of Slavery* (Baton Rouge: Louisiana State University Press, 2022), pp. 133–137; Rosemary Sadlier, *Harriet Tubman: Freedom Seeker, Freedom Leader* (Toronto: Dundurn, 2012), pp. 92–93; and Kate Clifford Larson, *Bound for the Promised Land: Harriet Tubman, Portrait of an American Hero* (New York, Ballantine Books, 2004), pp. 159 and 151–152.
14   Larson, *Bound for the Promised Land*, p. 162.
15   Milton C. Sernett, *Harriet Tubman: Myth, Memory, and History* (Chapel Hill: Duke University Press, 2007), pp. 77–82.
16   Sernett, *Harriet Tubman*, pp. 79–81; and Jackson, *Force and Freedom*, pp. 120–126.
17   Martha Coffin Wright to William Lloyd Garrison II, 10 January 1869, Garrison Family Papers, Sophia Smith Collection, Smith College, Northampton, Massachusetts.
18   Jackson, *Force and Freedom*, pp. 111–120, quote on p. 116.
19   Jackson, *Force and Freedom*, p. 116.
20   Edward J. Renehan, Jr, *The Secret Six: The True Tale of the Men Who Conspired with John Brown* (Columbia: University of South Carolina Press, 1997).
21   See Brittney C. Cooper, *Eloquent Rage: A Black Feminist Discovers Her Superpower* (New York: St. Martin's Press, 2018); Myisha Cherry, *The Case for Rage: Why Anger Is Essential to Anti-Racist Struggle* (New York: Oxford University Press, 2021); and Bell Hooks, *Killing Rage: Ending Racism* (New York: Henry Holt and Company, 1995).
22   See Vanessa D. Dickerson, *Dark Victorians* (Urbana: University of Illinois Press, 2008); and Gretchen Holbrook Gerzina (ed.), *Black Victorians, Black Victoriana* (New Brunswick: Rutgers University Press, 2003).
23   *The Liberator*, 14 January 1864.
24   Utz McKnight, *Frances E.W. Harper: A Call to Conscience* (Medford: Polity Press, 2020), pp. vii, 29, 36–37; Ellen Carol DuBois and Lynn Dumenil, *Through Women's Eyes: An American History with Documents* (3rd edn, Boston: Bedford and St. Martin's, 2012), p. 282; and Jackson, *Force and Freedom*, p. 116.
25   Nathan K. Sebastian, "Fifty Years after Harpers Ferry", *New York Tribune*, 16 October 1909.
26   See Renehan, Jr, *The Secret Six*; and Otto J. Scott, *The Secret Six: John Brown and the Abolitionist Movement* (New York: New York Times Books, 1979).
27   Aufa Cooper, "*The Voice of the Fugitive*: A Transnational Abolitionist Organ", in Karolyn Smardz Frost and Veta Smith Tucker (eds.), *A Fluid Frontier: Slavery, Resistance, and the Underground Railroad in the Detroit River Borderland* (Detroit, Michigan: Wayne State University Press, 2016), p.143.
28   Cooper, "*The Voice of the Fugitive*", p.138.
29   Cited in Cooper, "*The Voice of the Fugitive*", pp. 143 and 137.
30   C. Peter Ripley, Paul A. Cimbala, Michael F. Hembree, Mary Alice Herrle, and Debra Susie (eds.), *The Black Abolitionist Papers*, vol. 2: *Canada, 1830–1865* (Chapel Hill: University of North Carolina Press, 1987), p. 108.
31   *Voice of the Fugitive*, 1 January 1851.
32   Jermain Wesley Loguen, *The Rev. J.W. Loguen, as a Slave and as a Freeman: A Narrative of Real Life* (Syracuse: J.G.K. Truair & Co., 1859), p. 355.

33   Loguen, *The Rev. J.W. Loguen*, p. 355.

34   Broyld, *Borderland Blacks*, pp. 22–26.

35   Loguen, *The Rev. J.W. Loguen*, pp. 354–355.

36   Fergus F. Bordewich, *The Epic Story of the Underground Railroad: America's First Civil Rights Movement* (New York: Amistad, 2006), pp. 410–411.

37   *Syracuse Daily Standard*, 3 January 1855.

38   *Syracuse Daily Standard*, 13 December 1856.

39   *Syracuse Daily Standard*, 13 December 1856.

40   Loguen, *The Rev. J.W. Loguen*, pp. 341–345 and 393–394. See Jayme A. Sokolow, "The Jerry McHenry Rescue and the Growth of Northern Antislavery Sentiment during the 1850s", *Journal of American Studies*, vol. 16, no. 3, December 1982, pp. 427–445; Monique Patenaude Roach, "The Rescue of William 'Jerry' Henry: Antislavery and Racism in the Burned-Over District", *New York History*, vol. 82, no. 2, Spring 2001, pp. 135–154; and Angela F. Murphy, *The Jerry Rescue: The Fugitive Slave Law, Northern Rights, and the American Sectional Crisis* (New York: Oxford University Press, 2014).

41   Hiram Wilson to George Whipple, 5 November 1851 and 17 December 1851, AMA Archives, Tulane University.

42   Loguen, *The Rev. J.W. Loguen*, pp. 208–209; and Rev. Jermain Wesley Loguen to Henry Bibb, 13 August 1852, *Voice of the Fugitive*, 9 September 1852. Also see *Syracuse Daily Standard*, 2 October 1851.

43   *Syracuse Daily Standard*, 7 September 1867.

44   See Jeff W. Grigg, *The Combahee River Raid: Harriet Tubman and Lowcountry Liberation* (Charleston: History Press, 2014); and Alexis Pauline Gumbs, "Prophecy in the Present Tense: Harriet Tubman, the Combahee Pilgrimage, and Dreams Coming True", *The Meridians*, vol. 12, no. 2, 2014, pp. 142–144.

45   St Catharines Municipal Minutes, 20 December 1858 and 30 December 1858. See also "Christmas", *St Catharines Journal*, 23 December 1858.

46   Larson, *Bound for the Promised Land*, p. 260.

47   Sarah H. Bradford, *Harriet Tubman, the Moses of Her People* (Mineola: Dover Publications, 1995 [1886]), p. 22.

48   Larson, *Bound for the Promised Land*, pp. 201–221; and *National Anti-Slavery Standard*, 8 August 1863.

49   Larson, *Bound for the Promised Land*, pp. 42–43 and 282.

50   Dann J. Broyld and Matthew Warshauer, "Harriet Tubman and Andrew Jackson: A Match Made in the US Treasury Department", Blogpost, *Borealia* and *The Republic*, June 2016.

51   Larson, *Bound for the Promised Land*, pp. 10, 225–226, 252, 279. Also see Clarence Lusane, *Twenty Dollars and Change: Harriet Tubman and the Ongoing Fight for Racial Justice and Democracy* (San Francisco: City Lights Books, 2022); and Kate Clifford Larson, *Harriet Tubman: A Reference Guide to Her Life and Works* (New York: Rowman and Littlefield, 2022).

52   Larson, *Bound for the Promised Land*, pp. 239, 261 and 264.

53   Broyld, "Harriet Tubman", pp. 90–91.

Chapter 14. Colonialism in British Africa

1   Isaac Land and Andrew Schocket, "New Approaches to the Founding of the Sierra Leone Colony, 1786–1808", *Journal of Colonialism and Colonial History*, vol. 9, no. 3,

2008, p. 1; and Walter Rodney, *How Europe Underdeveloped Africa* (London: Bogle-L'Ouverture Publications, 1972), p. 135.

2   Rodney, *How Europe Underdeveloped Africa*, p. 135.

3   Chinweizu, *The West and the Rest of Us: White Predators Black Slavers and the African Elite* (New York: Random House, 1975), p. 520.

4   Land and Schocket, "New Approaches to the Founding of the Sierra Leone Colony", p. 1.

5   John Joseph Crooks, *A History of the Colony of Sierra Leone, Western Africa: With Maps and Appendices* (Dublin: Browne and Nolan Limited, 1903), p. 1.

6   Thomas Pakenham, *The Scramble for Africa, 1876–1912* (London: Phoenix, 2001), p. 318.

7   Ali Mazrui, *The African Condition: A Political Diagnosis* (Cambridge: Cambridge University Press, 1980), p. 1.

8   Kevin Grant, "Human Rights and Sovereign Abolitions of Slavery, c.1885–1956", in Kevin Grant, Philippa Levine, and Frank Trentmann (eds.), *Beyond Sovereignty: Britain, Empire and Transnationalism, c.1880–1950* (London: Palgrave Macmillan, 2007), pp. 80–102.

9   Rodney, *How Europe Underdeveloped Africa*, p. 75.

10   John Stuart Mill, *Principles of Political Economy* (London: John W. Parker, 1848).

11   Festus Iyayi, "The Primitive Accumulation of Capital in a Neo-Colony: The Nigerian Case", *Review of African Political Economy*, vol. 13, no. 35, 1986, pp. 27–39.

12   Ali Mazrui, "From Slave Ship to Spaceship: Africa between Marginalization and Globalization", *African Studies Quarterly*, vol. 2, no. 4, 1999, pp. 5–11.

13   Rodney, *How Europe Underdeveloped Africa*, p. 135.

14   Rodney, *How Europe Underdeveloped Africa*, p. 135.

15   Joseph Inikori, *Africans and the Industrial Revolution in England* (Cambridge: Cambridge University Press, 2002), pp. 215–219.

16   Benjamin Lawrance, Emily Lynn Osborn, and Richard Roberts, (eds.), *Intermediaries, Interpreters, and Clerks: African Employees in the Making of Colonial Africa* (Madison: University of Wisconsin Pres, 2006).

17   Rodney, *How Europe Underdeveloped Africa*, p. 142.

18   Jonathon Glassman, *War of Words, War of Stones: Racial Thought and Violence in Colonial Zanzibar* (Indiana: Indiana University Press, 2011).

19   Ronald Robinson and John Gallagher, *Africa and the Victorians: The Official Mind of Imperialism* (London: Macmillan, 1963), p. 21.

20   Robinson and Gallagher, *Africa and the Victorians*, p. 27.

21   Hannah Arendt, *The Origins of Totalitarianism* (Ohio: World Publishing Company, 1958), p. 184.

22   William Beinart, "Cecil Rhodes: Racial Segregation in the Cape Colony and Violence in Zimbabwe", *Journal of Southern African Studies*, vol. 48, no. 3, 2022, p. 583.

23   Beinart, "Cecil Rhodes", p. 583.

24   Adekeye Adebajo, "Introduction: The Roots and Routes of Pan-Africanism", in Adekeye Adebajo (ed.), *The Pan-African Pantheon: Prophets, Poets, and Philosophers* (Johannesburg: Jacana, 2020; Manchester: Manchester University Press, 2021), p. 17.

25   Adebajo, "Introduction: The Roots and Routes of Pan-Africanism", p. 17.

26   Noah Bassil, "The Roots of Afro-Pessimism: The British Invention of the 'Dark Continent'", *Critical Arts*, vol. 25, no. 3, 2011, pp. 377–396.

27 Kathryn Mathers, *White Saviorism and Popular Culture: Imagined Africa as a Space for American Salvation* (New York: Taylor and Francis, 2023).

28 Mahmood Mamdani, "Historicizing Power and Responses to Power: Indirect Rule and Its Reform", *Social Research*, vol. 66, no. 3, 1999, pp. 859–886.

29 Natalie Wenzell Letsa and Martha Wilfahrt, "The Mechanisms of Direct and Indirect Rule: Colonialism and Economic Development in Africa", *Quarterly Journal of Political Science*, vol. 15, no. 4, 2020, p. 4.

30 Letsa and Wilfahrt, "The Mechanisms of Direct and Indirect Rule", p. 4.

31 Taiwo Olufemi, *How Colonialism Preempted Modernity in Africa* (Bloomington: Indiana University Press, 2010), p. 147.

32 Letsa and Wilfahrt, "The Mechanisms of Direct and Indirect Rule", p. 5.

33 Letsa and Wilfahrt, "The Mechanisms of Direct and Indirect Rule", p. 5.

34 Etannibi Alemika, "Colonialism, State and Policing in Nigeria", *Crime, Law and Social Change*, no. 20, 1993, p. 204.

35 Abdul Raufu Mustapha, "The Three Faces of Nigeria's Foreign Policy: Nationhood, Identity and External Relations", in Adekeye Adebajo and Abdul Raufu Mustapha (eds.), *Gulliver's Troubles: Nigeria's Foreign Policy after the Cold War* (Scottsville: University of KwaZulu-Natal Press, 2008), p. 42.

36 Dani Fatiha, "Colonial Sudan: The Separate Administration of the South (1920–1933)", *Traduction et Langues*, vol. 15, no. 2, 2016, p. 195.

37 Gibril Raschid Cole, *The Krio of West Africa: Islam, Culture, Creolization, and Colonialism in the Nineteenth Century* (Ohio: Ohio University Press, 2013), p. 20.

38 Mwangi Wa-Githumo, "The Truth about the Mau Mau Movement: The Most Popular Uprising in Kenya", *Transafrican Journal of History*, vol. 20, no. 1, 1991, p. 2.

39 William Ochieng, "Moralism and Expropriation in a British Colony: The Search for a White Dominion in Kenya, 1895–1923", *Présence Africaine*, no. 1, 1985, p. 231.

40 Ochieng, "Moralism and Expropriation in a British Colony", p. 220.

41 Ochieng, "Moralism and Expropriation in a British Colony", pp. 214–232.

42 Moses Onyango, "Postcolonial Politics in Kenya", in Keneth Omeje (ed.), *The Crises of Postcoloniality in Africa* (Dakar: Council for the Development of Social Science Research in Africa, 2015), p. 186.

43 Ochieng, "Moralism and Expropriation in a British Colony", p. 225.

44 Ochieng, "Moralism and Expropriation in a British Colony", p. 225.

45 Wa-Githumo, "The Truth about the Mau Mau Movement", p. 2.

46 Melissa Tully, "Newspaper Coverage of the Mau Mau Movement, 1952–56", in Toyin Falola and Hetty ter Haar (eds.), *Narrating War and Peace in Africa* (Rochester: University of Rochester Press, 2010), p. 60.

47 Myles Osborne, "'The Rooting Out of Mau Mau from the Minds of the Kikuyu Is a Formidable Task': Propaganda and the Mau Mau War", *Journal of African History*, vol. 56, no. 1, 2015, pp. 77–97.

48 Trahair Esme, "Newspaper Coverage of the Mau Mau Movement: A Constructivist Argument", *Inquiries Journal*, vol. 10, no. 3, 2018, pp. 1–13.

49 David Anderson, "Mau Mau in the High Court and the 'Lost' British Empire Archives: Colonial Conspiracy or Bureaucratic Bungle?", *Journal of Imperial and Commonwealth History*, vol. 39, no. 5, 2011, pp. 699–716.

50 Huw Bennett, *Fighting the Mau Mau: The British Army and Counter-insurgency in the Kenya Emergency* (Cambridge: Cambridge University Press, 2013), p. 29.

51   John Lonsdale, "Mau Mau through the Looking Glass", *Index on Censorship*, vol. 15, no. 2, 1986, p. 21.

52   Beinart, "Cecil Rhodes", p. 582; and Joanna Lewis, "Nasty, Brutish and in Shorts? British Colonial Rule, Violence and the Historians of Mau Mau", *Round Table*, vol. 96, no. 389, 2007, p. 205.

53   Madelaine Drohan, *Making a Killing: How and Why Corporations Use Armed Force to Do Business* (Ontario: Vintage Canada, 2010).

54   Mordechai Tamarkin, *Cecil Rhodes and the Cape Afrikaners: The Imperial Colossus and the Colonial Parish Pump* (London: Frank Cass, 1996), p. 175; and Pakenham, *The Scramble for Africa*, p. 318.

55   Beinart, "Cecil Rhodes", p. 583

56   Beinart, "Cecil Rhodes", p. 583.

57   Pakenham, *The Scramble for Africa*, pp. 77–85; and Rami Ginat, *Egypt and the Struggle for Power in Sudan: From World War II to Nasserism* (Cambridge: Cambridge University Press, 2017).

58   Pakenham, *The Scramble for Africa*, pp. 77–85.

59   Alice Moore-Harell, *Egypt's African Empire: Samuel Baker, Charles Gordon and the Creation of Equatoria* (Chicago: Sussex Academic Press, 2014), p. 17.

60   Koçyiğit Ömer, "The Ottoman State's Perception about the Sudanese Mahdi Uprising", *International Journal of Turcologia*, vol. 9, no. 18, 2014, p. 101.

61   Michelle Gordon, "British Colonial Violence in Perak, Sierra Leone and the Sudan" (PhD dissertation, Royal Holloway, University of London, 2017), p. 113.

62   Fatiha, "Colonial Sudan", p. 195.

63   Michelle Gordon, "Viewing Violence in the British Empire: Images of Atrocity from the Battle of Omdurman, 1898", *Journal of Perpetrator Research*, vol. 2, no. 2, 2019, pp. 65–100.

64   Ebiegberi Alagoa, *Jaja of Opobo: The Slave Who Became a King* (London: Longman Publishing Group, 1970), p. 36.

65   Sylvanus Cookey, *King Jaja of the Niger Delta* (Lagos: NOK Publishers, 1984), p. 110.

66   Cookey, *King Jaja of the Niger Delta*, p. 120.

67   Kemi Rotimi and Olukoya Ogen, "Jaja and Nana in the Niger Delta Region of Nigeria: Proto-nationalists or Emergent Capitalists", *Journal of Pan African Studies*, vol. 2, no. 7, 2008, p. 51.

68   Rotimi and Ogen, "Jaja and Nana in the Niger Delta", p. 51.

69   Emmanuel Nwafor Mordi, "What If the Huns Come? Imperial Britain's Attitude towards Nigerians' Enthusiasm for Military Service during the Second World War, 1939–1942", *Journal of Asian and African Studies*, vol. 54, no. 6, 2019, p. 839.

70   Crawford Young and Brown Howard, "The African Colonial State in Comparative Perspective", *History: Reviews of New Books*, vol. 24, no. 1, 1995, p. 185.

71   Young and Brown, "The African Colonial State in Comparative Perspectives", p. 182.

72   Young and Brown, "The African Colonial State in Comparative Perspectives", p. 186.

73   Joy Asongazoh Alemazung, "Post-colonial Colonialism: An Analysis of International Factors and Actors Marring African Socio-economic and Political Development", *Journal of Pan African Studies*, vol. 3, no. 10, 2010, pp. 62–84.

Chapter 15. Colonialism in French Africa

1   Scholarly works written in the English language on French colonialism in black Africa include the following: Virginia Thompson and Richard Adloff, *French West Africa*

(Stanford: Stanford University Press, 1957); Stephen H. Roberts, *The History of French Colonial Policy: 1870–1925* (Oxford: Taylor and Francis, 1963); Patrick Manning, *Francophone Sub-Saharan Africa: 1880–1985* (Cambridge: Cambridge University Press, 1984); Francis Terry McNamara, *France in Black Africa* (Washington DC: National Defence University, 1989); and Robert Aldrich, *Greater France: A History of French Overseas Expansion* (New York: Macmillan: 1996).

2   Albert Londres, *Terre d'ébène: La traite des noirs* (Paris: Albin Michel, 1929); André Gide, *Voyage au Congo* (Paris: Gallimard, 1927); Denise Moran, *Tchad* (Paris: Gallimard, 1934); Marcel Homet, *Congo, terre de souffrance* (Paris: Fernand Aubier, 1934); and Emmanuel Dongala, *Le feu des origines* (Paris: Albin Michel, 1987).

3   Marcel Joubert, "L'esclavage aboli par la loi s'appelle aujourd'hui travail forcé et portage", *L'Humanité*, 24 January 1929, reporting figures cited in French National Assembly debates.

4   Didier Folléas, *Albert Londres en Terre d'ébène* (Paris: Arléa, 2009), pp. 14–15.

5   Folléas, *Albert Londres en Terre d'ébène*, p. 16.

6   Florise Londres, *Albert Londres, mon père* (Paris: Albin Michel, 1934).

7   Paul Mousset, *L'aventure du grand reportage* (Paris: Grasset, 1972).

8   Pierre Assouline, *Albert Londres, Vie et mort d'un grand reporter, 1884–1932* (Paris: Gallimard, 1990).

9   Created in 1932, the Prix Albert Londres is considered the French equivalent of America's prestigious Pulitzer Prize.

10   Albert Londres, *A Very Naked People*, translated by Sylvia Stuart (New York: Horace Liveright, 1929).

11   Albert Londres, *Terre d'ébène: La traite des noirs* (Paris: Editions du Rocher, 2011), p. 10

12   Ieme van der Poel, *Congo-Océan: Un chemin de fer colonial controversé*, vol. 1 (Paris: Harmattan, 2006), p. xiii.

13   Van der Poel, *Congo–Océan*, p. xiii.

14   See Christian Valantin, *Trente ans de vie politique avec Léopold Sédar Senghor*, with preface by Souleymane Bachir Diagne (Paris: Belin, 2016).

15   See Sidiki Kobélé-Keita, *Touré à Raymonde Jonvaux, militante anticolonialiste française (1948–1954)* (Paris: L'Harmattan, 2016).

16   Louis Delmer, *Les chemins de fer* (Paris: Schleicher Frères, 1899); and Van der Poel, *Congo–Océan*, vol. 1, p. 5.

17   Henri Roussel, *Le chemin de fer Congo–Océan: Grande oeuvre coloniale* (Bordeaux : Imprimerie-Librairie de l'Univeristé, 1934).

18   Cited in Léopold Sédar Senghor, *Anthologie de la nouvelle poésie nègre et malagache* (Paris: Presses Universitaires de France, 2001 [1948]); and Van der Poel, *Congo–Océan*, p. 115.

19   Emmanuel Dongala, *Le feu des origines* (Paris: Le Serpent à Plumes, 2001 [1987]); Van der Poel, *Congo–Océan*, vol. 1, p. 132.

20   Robert Poulaine, *Etapes africaines: Voyage autour du Congo* (Paris: Nouvelle Revue Critique, 1930); and Van der Poel, *Congo–Océan*, vol. 1, p. 164.

21   C. Camus, *L'utilisation de traverses en bois de chemin de fer en pays tropicaux* (Brussels: Académie Royale des Sciences d'Outre-Mer, 1965), p. 8.

22   Michel R.O. Manot, who worked for the railroad company, estimated 500,000 ties in his memoir *L'aventure de l'or et du Congo–Océan: Le Congo–Océan et la ruée vers l'or*

au Moyen-Congo et au Gabon (Paris: Libraire Seretan, 1950); and Van der Poel, *Congo–Océan*, vol. 2, p. 181.

23   Raymond Susset, "Chemin de Fer Congo-Océan (Notes sur la construction du) 1921–1934", *Cahiers d'Études Africaines*, vol. 7, 1967, p. 269.

24   Catherine Coquery-Vidrovitch, *Le Congo au temps des grandes compagnies concessionnaires, 1898–1930* (Paris and La Haye: Mouton, 1972), p. 195.

25   Robert Poulaine, "Le drame de l'AEF", *L'Impartial Français*, 20 January 1929; and Van der Poel, *Congo–Océan*, vol. 1, p. 126.

26   Noam Chomsky and Edward Herman, *Manufacturing Consent: The Political Economy of the Mass Media* (New York :Pantheon Books, 1988).

27   Van der Poel, *Congo–Océan*, vol. 1, p. xlv.

28   Joseph Peyrat, "Propos de politique coloniale", *La Revue Indigène*, nos. 193–194, January–February 1925, pp. 19–25.

29   Louis Martel, "En Afrique equatoriale: Le chemin de fer de Brazzaville–Océan et les populations indigènes – Le problème de la main-d'œuvre", *La Revue Indigène*, nos. 197–198, May–June 1925; and Van der Poel, *Congo–Océan*, vol. 1, pp. 49–60

30   Martel, "En Afrique equatoriale", p. 52.

31   René Maran, "Colonies et coloniaux", *Journal du Peuple*, November 1925. See also Van der Poel, *Congo–Océan*, vol. 2, pp. 66–68; "L'AEF, ou la colonie rouge: L'administration criminelle", *Journal du Peuple*, 17 April 1926; Van der Poel, *Congo–Océan*, vol. 2, pp. 70–73; "L'AEF, ou la colonie rouge: La macchabéisation d'une race", *Journal du Peuple*, 24 April 1926; and Van der Poel, *Congo–Océan*, vol. 2, pp. 74–79 (quote from p. 76).

32   Maran, "Colonies et coloniaux", p. 78.

33   Maran, "Colonies et coloniaux", p. 79.

34   René Maran, "Le Congo–Océan, inauguré aujourd'hui, couronne treize ans d'efforts et de lutte contre la brousse et la forêt vierge", *Journal du Peuple*, 10 July 1934; and Van der Poel, *Congo–Océan*, vol. 1, pp. 91–92.

35   Robert Poulaine, "Le drame de l'AEF", *L'impartial Français*, 13 January 1929; and Van der Poel, *Congo–Océan*, vol. 1, p. 118.

36   Poulaine, "Le drame de l'AEF", p. 121.

37   Robert Poulaine, "Les evénements donnent raison à notre campagne sur le drame de l'AEF", *L'Impartial Français*, 24 January 1929; and Van der Poel, *Congo–Océan*, vol. 1, p. 126.

38   Poulaine, "Le Drame de l'AEF", p. 126.

39   Poulaine, *Etapes africaines*; and Van der Poel, *Congo–Océan*, vol. 1, p. 157.

40   Poulaine, *Etapes africaines,* p. 169.

41   Marcel Joubert, "Le Gouverneur Antonetti et le Général Théry organisent la répression", *L'Humanité*, 23 January 1929; and Van der Poel, *Congo–Océan*, vol. 2, p. 8.

42   Joubert, "Le Gouverneur Antonetti et le Général Théry organisent la répression", p. 7.

43   The Fronde was a series of civil wars in seventeenth-century France where nobility (*frondeurs*) opposed the monarch. The suggestion is that Londres was an aristocratic critic and not a true revolutionary when it came to imperialism and the colonial question.

44   Marcel Joubert, "La révolte des noirs de la 'grande forêt': 'Ce n'est pas assassiner que

tuer du nègre' déclare un administrateur colonial", *L'Humanité*, 25 January 1929; and Van der Poel, *Congo–Océan*, vol. 2, pp. 14–17.

45   Joubert, "La révolte des noirs de la 'grande forêt'", p. 15.

46   Marcel Joubert, "L'esclavage aboli part la loi s'appelle aujourd'hui travail force et portage", *L'Humanité*, 24 January1929; andVan der Poel, *Congo–Océan*, vol. 2, p. 11.

47   Paul Bourdarie, "La vie coloniale: Le travail aux colonies devant Genève", *La Revue Indigène*, nos. 244–245, May–June 1929; andVan der Poel, *Congo–Océan*, vol. 2, p. 27.

48   "Whataboutism" is a variety of the "tu quoque" logical fallacy that attempts to discredit an opponent's position by charging them *ad hominem* as hypocrites without directly refuting or disproving their argument: a famous propaganda technique.

49   Albert Lebrun, "La France colonial devant le monde", *La Revue Indigène*, nos. 254–255, March–April 1930; and Van der Poel, *Congo–Océan*, vol. 2, p. 28.

50   Lebrun, "La France colonial devant le monde", p. 29.

51   Lebrun, "La France colonial devant le monde", p. 30.

52   Lebrun, "La France colonial devant le monde", p. 31.

53   Lebrun, "La France colonial devant le monde", p. 35.

54   Paul Bourdarie, "Le complot de Genève contre la France coloniale", *La Revue Indigène*, nos. 256–257, May–June 1930; andVan der Poel, *Congo–Océan*, vol. 2, p. 40.

55   Bourdarie, "Le complot de Genève contre la France coloniale", p. 43.

56   Bourdarie, "Le complot de Genève contre la France coloniale", p. 56.

57   Maurice Ajam, "Les conditions du travail indigène", *La Dépêche Coloniale*, 1 July 1929; and Van der Poel, *Congo–Océan*, vol. 2, p. 57.

58   Ajam, "Les conditions du travail indigène", p. 58.

59   Ajam, "Les conditions du travail indigène", p. 59.

60   Louis Proust, "La vérité sur le Brazzaville–Océan", *La Dépêche Coloniale et Maritime*, 3 July 1929; and Van der Poel, *Congo–Océan*, vol. 2, p. 61.

61   Proust, "La vérité sur le Brazzaville–Océan", p. 62.

62   Proust, "La vérité sur le Brazzaville–Océan", p. 64.

63   Proust, "La vérité sur le Brazzaville–Océan", p. 66.

64   Translated into English by Lilian A. Clare as *How Natives Think* (New York: Alfred Knopf, 1926).

65   Pierre Mille, "Le travail force dans les colonies", *La Dépêche Coloniale et Maritime*, 20 November 1929; andVan der Poel, *Congo–Océan*, vol. 2, p. 67.

66   Georges Boussenot, "La construction du Congo–Océan", *La Presse Coloniale Illustrée*, March 1930; and Van der Poel, *Congo–Océan*, vol. 2, p. 77.

67   Boussenot, "La construction du Congo–Océan", p. 74.

Chapter 16. Colonialism in Belgian Africa

1   René Lemarchand, *Rwanda and Burundi* (London: Pall Mall Press, 1970); Joseph Gahama, *Le Burundi sous administration belge* (Paris: Karthala, 1983); Filip Reyntjens, *Pouvoir et droit au Rwanda: Droit public et évolution politique, 1916–1973* (Tervuren: Musée royal de l'Afrique centrale, 1985); and Jean-Pierre Chrétien, *L'Afrique des Grands Lacs: Deux mille ans d'histoire* (Paris: Flammarion, 2011).

2   General reference works and handbooks: Jean-Luc Vellut, Florence Loriaux, and Françoise Morimont, *Bibliographie historique du Zaïre à l'époque coloniale (1880–1960): Travaux publiés en 1960–1996* (Tervuren: MRAC, 1996); Pierre-Alain Tallier, Marie Van Eeckenrode, and Patricia Van Schuylenbergh (eds.), *Guide des sources de l'histoire coloniale belge (Congo, Ruanda, Urundi), 19e–20e siècle* (Begijnhof: Brepols,

2021); Isidore Ndaywel è Nziem, *Nouvelle histoire du Congo: Des origines à la République démocratique* (Brussels: Le Cri, 2009); Georges Nzongola-Ntalaja, *The Congo from Leopold to Kabila: A People's History* (London and New York: Zed Books, 2003); and Charles Didier Gondola, *The History of Congo* (New York: Greenwood Press, 2002).

3   Jan Vandersmissen, *Koningen van de wereld: Léopold II en de aardrijkskundige beweging* (Leuven: Acco, 2009).

4   Jan Vansina and Jean Stengers, "King Léopold's Congo, 1885–1908", in John D. Fage and Roland Oliver (eds.), *Cambridge History of Africa*, vol. 6: *From 1870 to 1905* (Cambridge: Cambridge University Press, 1985), pp. 315–358.

5   Germany, France, Britain, Portugal, Belgium, Spain, Italy, Russia, Austria-Hungary, the United States, Denmark, Sweden/Norway, the Netherlands, and Turkey.

6   Pierre-Luc Plasman, *Léopold II, potentat congolais: L'action royale face à la violence coloniale* (Brussels: Racine, 2017), pp. 69–100.

7   Jean Stengers, *Congo, mythes et réalités* (Brussels: Racine, 1988), p. 47.

8   Jean Stengers, *Combien le Congo a-t-il coûté à la Belgique?* (Brussels: Académie Royale des Sciences Coloniales, 1957), pp. 31–33.

9   Aldwin Roes, "Towards a History of Mass Violence in the État Indépendant du Congo, 1885–1908", *South African Historical Journal*, vol. 62, no. 4, 2010, pp. 634–670.

10 Jean-Paul Sanderson, "Du reflux à la croissance démographique: Comment la démographie congolaise a-t-elle été influencée par la colonisation?", in Idesbald Goddeeris, Amandine Lauro, and Guy Vanthemsche (eds.), *Le Congo colonial: Une histoire en questions* (Brussels: La Renaissance du Livre, 2020), pp. 115–125.

11 Dean Pavlakis, *British Humanitarianism and the Congo Reform Movement, 1896–1913* (Aldershot: Ashgate, 2015).

12 Guy Vanthemsche, *Belgium and the Congo, 1885–1980* (Cambridge: Cambridge University Press, 2012), pp. 26–27.

13 Jean-Luc Vellut, *Congo: Ambitions et désenchantements, 1880–1960* (Paris: Karthala, 2017), pp. 95–113.

14 Vanthemsche, *Belgium and the Congo*, pp. 167–168.

15 S. Herbert Frankel, *Capital Investment in Africa: Its Course and Effects* (London: Oxford University Press, 1938), p. 170. Portugese colonies: £9.8; French colonies: £3.3; Kenya, Uganda, Tanganyika, and Nyassaland: £8.1; Nigeria: £3.9; British West Africa: £4.8; Northern and Southern Rhodesia: £38.4; South Africa: £55.8.

16 Matthew Stanard, *Selling the Congo: A History of European Pro-empire Propaganda and the Making of Belgian Imperialism* (Lincoln: University of Nebraska Press, 2012).

17 Julia Seibert, "More Continuity Than Change? New Forms of Unfree Labor in the Belgian Congo, 1908–1930", in Marcel van der Linden (ed.), *Humanitarian Intervention and Changing Labor Relations: The Long-Term Consequences of the Abolition of the Slave Trade* (Leiden: Brill, 2011), pp. 370–386.

18 Jean-Philippe Peemans, *Le Congo-Zaïre au gré du XXe siècle* (Paris: L'Harmattan, 1997), p. 41.

19 Areas where local people were forced to go and work included the south-eastern province of Katanga: mainly copper; and in the north-east of the colony: gold.

20 Osumaka Likaka, *Rural Society and Cotton in Colonial Zaire* (Madison: University of Wisconsin Press, 1997).

21 Guy Vanthemsche, *Genèse et portée du "Plan décennal" du Congo Belge (1949–1959)*

(Brussels: Académie Royale des Sciences d'Outre-Mer, 1994).

22 Marc De Paepe and Lies Van Rompaey, *In het teken van de bevoogding: De educatieve actie in Belgisch-Kongo (1908–1960)* (Leuven: Garant, 1995), p. 214.

23 Vanthemsche, *Belgium and the Congo*, p. 279.

24 Pierre Joye and Rosine Lewin, *Les trusts au Congo* (Brussels: Société Populaire d'Editions, 1961), pp. 52–53.

25 Michel Merlier, *Le Congo de la colonisation belge à l'indépendance* (Paris: Maspero, 1962), p. 191.

26 Daniel Tödt, *Elitenbildung und Dekolonisierung: Die Évolués in Belgisch-Kongo, 1944–1960* (Göttingen: Vandenhoeck and Ruprecht, 2018).

27 Ludo De Witte, *The Assassination of Patrice Lumumba* (London: Verso, 2001); and Emmanuel Gerard and Bruce Kuklick, *Death in the Congo: Murdering Patrice Lumumba* (Cambridge: Harvard University Press, 2015).

Chapter 17. Colonialism in Potuguese Africa

1   Charles R. Boxer, *The Portuguese Seaborne Empire, 1415–1825* (Manchester: Carcanet, 1991).

2   Ronald J. Granieri, "Exceptionalism, Empire, and the Dark Side of National Greatness", Foreign Policy Research Institute, 3 October 2016, www.fpri.org/article/2016/10/exceptionalism-empire-dark-side-national-greatness/.

3   Daniel F. Silva and Lamonte Aidoo (eds.), *Lusophone African Short Stories and Poetry after Independence: Decolonial Destinies* (London: Anthem Press, 2021), p. 8.

4   Miguel Bandeira Jerónimo, "Portuguese Colonialism in Africa", *Oxford Research Encyclopedia of African History* (Oxford: Oxford University Press, 2018).

5   See Jerónimo, "Portuguese Colonialism in Africa".

6   Silva and Aidoo, *Lusophone African Short Stories*, p. 9.

7   Silva and Aidoo, *Lusophone African Short Stories*, p. 10.

8   Brazil won its independence in 1822, but Portugal only recognised it in 1825 because it did not want to give up the benefits that were generated from the slave trade in the Americas.

9   See Jerónimo, "Portuguese Colonialism in Africa".

10 Valentim Alexandre, "O império português (1825–1890): Ideologia e economia", *Análise Social*, 2004, pp. 959–979 (author's translation).

11 Silva and Aidoo, *Lusophone African Short Stories*, p. 12.

12 Jerónimo, *Portuguese Colonialism in Africa*, p. 23 (author's translation).

13 Jerónimo, *Portuguese Colonialism in Africa*, p. 34 (author's translation).

14 See Alexandre, "O império português" (author's translation).

15 Alexandre, "O império português" (author's translation).

16 The *libertos* was a social category that included former slaves and Africans who were still being bought in the interior of the continent.

17 Alexandre, "O império português", p. 972 (author's translation).

18 See, for example, Adekeye Adebajo, *The Curse of Berlin: Africa after the Cold War* (London: Hurst; and Scottsville: University of KwaZulu-Natal Press, 2010).

19 Matthew Craven, "Between Law and History", *London Review of International Law*, vol. 3, no. 1, 2015, pp. 31–59.

20 Craven, "Between Law and History", pp. 31–32.

21 Craven, "Between Law and History", p. 32.

22 Antony Anghie, "Between Law and History: The Berlin Conference of 1884–1885

and the Logic of Free Trade", *London Review of International Law*, vol. 3, no. 1, 2015, p. 33.

23   Thomas Henriksen, "Portugal in Africa: A Non-economic Interpretation", *African Studies Review*, vol. 16, no. 3, 1973, p. 407.

24   Fernando Tavares Pimenta, *Portugal e o século XX: Estado-império e descolonização (1890–1975)* (Porto: Edições Afrontamento, 2010).

25   See Jerónimo, "Portuguese Colonialism in Africa".

26   Leonor Pires Martins, *Um império de papel: Imagens do colonialismo português na imprensa periódica ilustrada (1875–1940)* (Lisbon: Edições 70, 2012), pp. 223–249 (author's translation).

27   Miguel Bandeira Jerónimo, *Livros brancos, almas negras: A missão "civilizadora" do colonialismo português, 1870–1930* (Lisbon: Imprensa de Ciências Sociais, 2009), p. 155 (author's translation).

28   Jerónimo, *Livros brancos, almas negras*, p. 156 (author's translation).

29   *Boletim Geral das Colónias*, July 1925, p. 3 (author's translation).

30   Jerónimo, *Livros brancos, almas negras*, p. 166 (author's translation).

31   Alan K. Smith, "António Salazar and the Reversal of Portuguese Colonial Policy", *Journal of African History*, vol. 15, no. 4, 1974, p. 658.

32   Yves Leonárd, "O império colonial salazarista", in Francisco Bethencourt and Kirti Chaudhuri (eds.), *História da Expansão Portuguesa*, vol. V (Lisbon: Círculo dos Leitores, 1999), p. 14.

33   Paulo S. Polanah, "'The Zenith of Our National History!': National Identity, Colonial Empire, and the Promotion of the Portuguese Discoveries; Portugal 1930s", *e-JPH*, vol. 9, no. 1, 2011, p. 43.

34   Alexandre, *O império português*, p. 24.

35   Fernando Martins, "A questão colonial na política externa portuguesa: 1926–1975", in Valentim Alexandre (ed.), *O império africano: Séculos XIX e XX* (Lisbon: Edições Colibri, 2000), p. 144 (author's translation).

36   See Jerónimo, *Portuguese Colonialism in Africa*.

37   See Jerónimo, *Portuguese Colonialism in Africa*.

38   See Jerónimo, *Portuguese Colonialism in Africa*.

39   For more information, see Mary Anne Pitcher, *Politics in the Portuguese Empire: The State, Industry, and Cotton, 1926–1974* (Oxford: Clarendon Press, 1993); and Allen F. Isaacman, *Cotton Is the Mother of Poverty: Peasants, Work, and Rural Struggle in Colonial Mozambique, 1938–1961* (Portsmouth: Heinemann, 1996).

40   Cláudia Castelo, *Passagens para África: O povoamento de Angola e Moçambique com naturais da metrópole (1920–1974)* (Porto: Edições Afrontamento, 2007), p. 87 (author's translation).

41   Y. Leonárd, "O ultramar português", p. 31 (author's translation).

42   Alexander Keese, "Bloqueios no sistema: Elites africanas, o fenómeno do trabalho forçado e os limites de integração no Estado colonial português, 1945–1974", in Miguel Bandeira Jerónimo (ed.), *O império colonial em questão: Poderes, saberes e instituições* (Lisbon: Edições 70, 2012), p. 227 (author's translation).

43   "Dr Gilberto Freyre", *Boletim Geral do Ultramar*, January 1952, pp. 242–244.

44   Cristiana Bastos, "Luso-Tropicalism Debunked, Again: Race, Racism, and Racialism in Three Portuguese-Speaking Societies", in Warwick Anderson, Ricardo Roque, and Ricardo Ventura Santos (eds.), *Luso-Tropicalism and Its Discontents* (Oxford and New

York: Berghahn Books, 2019), p. 243.

45 See, for example, Castelo, *Passagens para África*.

46 Valentim Alexandre, *Velho Brasil, novas Áfricas: Portugal e o Império (1808–1975)* (Porto: Edições Afrontamento, 2000), p. 195 (author's translation).

47 Jerónimo, *Portuguese Colonialism in Africa*, pp. 17–18.

48 Cited in Jerónimo, *Portuguese Colonialism in Africa*, p. 17.

49 Isabela Figueiredo, *Caderno de memórias coloniais* (6th edn, Alfragide: Caminho, 2015), p. 109 (author's translation).

50 Jerónimo, *Portuguese Colonialism in Africa*, p. 17.

Chapter 18. Colonialism in German Africa

1 Frederick Cooper and Ann Laura Stoler (eds.), *Tensions of Empire: Colonial Cultures in a Bourgeois World* (Berkeley: University of California Press, 1997), p. 6.

2 Patrick Wolfe, "Settler Colonialism and the Elimination of the Native", *Journal of Genocide Research*, vol. 8, no. 4, 2008, pp. 387–409.

3 Jan-Bart Gewald, *Towards Redemption: A Socio-Political History of the Herero of Namibia between 1890 and 1923* (Leiden: Research School of Asian, African, and Amerindian Studies [*CNWS*], 1996), p. 38.

4 Otto von Bismarck, "Rede im Deutschen Reichstag", quoted in Heinrich von Poschinger, *Bismarck und die Parlamentarier*, vol. III (Breslau: Trewendt, 1894), p. 54.

5 Otto von Bismarck, quoted in Matthew Fitzpatrick, *Liberal Imperialism in Germany: Expansionism and Nationalism, 1848–1884* (New York: Berghahn, 2008), p. 116.

6 Konrad Canis, *Bismarcks Außenpolitik 1870 bis 1890: Aufstieg und Gefährdung* (Paderborn: Ferdinand Schöningh, 2004), pp. 85–108.

7 "Die neue Aera der Kolonialpolitik", *Die Gartenlaube: Illustrirtes Familienblatt*, vol. 49, 1884, p. 805.

8 Shelley Baranowski, *Nazi Empire: German Colonialism and Imperialism from Bismarck to Hitler* (Cambridge: Cambridge University Press, 2011), pp. 29–30.

9 Carl Peters, "Deutsche Kolonialpolitik aus Englischer Perspektive", in Arne Perras (ed.), *Carl Peters and German Imperialism, 1856–1918: A Political Biography* (Oxford: Clarendon Press, 2004), p. 36.

10 Peters, "Deutsche Kolonialpolitik aus Englischer Perspektive".

11 "General Act of the Conference of Berlin Concerning the Congo", *American Journal of International Law*, vol. 3, no. 1, Supplement: Official Documents January 1909, pp. 7–25.

12 Article 35, "General Act", p. 25.

13 Official slogan of the German Colonial Association, quoted in Fitzpatrick, *Liberal Imperialism*, p. 109.

14 Carl Peters, "Deutschtum in London", *Die Gegenwart*, 13 October 1884.

15 "Deutschlands Colonialbestrebung", *Die Gartenlaube*, quoted in Fitzpatrick, *Liberal Imperialism*, p. 193.

16 "Fünfundzwanzig Jahre Deutsch-Südwestafrika: Zum Gedenken an den 1 Mai 1883", *Deutsche Kolonialzeitung*, vol. 18, 2 May 1908, pp. 315–316.

17 *Fünfundzwanzig Jahre Deutsch-Südwestafrika: Zum Gedenken an den 1 Mai 1883*, p. 315.

18 Horst Drechsler, *"Let Us Die Fighting": The Struggle of the Herero and Nama against German Imperialism (1884–1915)* (London: Zed Press, 1980), pp. 33–34.

19 Carl Gotthilf Büttner, "Deutschland und Angra Pequena", *Deutsche Kolonialzeitung*,

vol. 1, no. 15, 1884, p. 303.

20   Alfred Kirchhoff, "Deutsch-Afrika", *Deutsche Kolonialzeitung*, vol. 1, no. 17, 1884, p. 333.

21   "Wie soll man Kolonisieren? Von einem alten Praktiker", *Deutsche Kolonialzeitung*, vol. 1, no. 17, 1884, p. 337.

22   Bundesarchiv-Berlin (hereafter BArchB) R 1001/1532, Bismarck, "Bericht des Kaisers und Königs Majestät", 12 April 1885, pp. 16–20.

23   Drechsler, "Let Us Die Fighting", p. 30.

24   BArchB Reichskolonialamt (hereafter R) 1001/1532, "G. von Bleichröder an die Reichskanzler Fürsten von Bismarck", 30 April 1885, pp. 3–6.

25   BArchB R 1001/1524, "Deutsche Kolonialgesellschaft für Südwestafrika an den Bundesrat", 6 July 1885, p. 105.

26   Jens Jaeger, "Colony as *Heimat*? The Formation of Colonial Identity in Germany around 1900", *German History*, vol. 27, no. 4, 2009, p. 468.

27   Bradley Naranch, "Inventing the *Auslandsdeutsche*: Immigration, Colonial Fantasy, and German Identity, 1848–1871", in Eric Ames (ed.), *Germany's Colonial Pasts* (Lincoln: University of Nebraska Press, 2005), pp. 21–40.

28   Eric D. Weitz, *A World Divided: The Global Struggle for Human Rights in the Age of Nation-States* (Princeton: Princeton University Press, 2019).

29   Adam A. Blackler, "From Boondoggle to Settlement Colony: Hendrik Witbooi and the Evolution of Germany's Imperial Project in Southwest Africa, 1884–1894", *Central European History*, vol. 50, 2017, pp. 449–470.

30   BArchB R 1001/2058, Carl Becker, "Eingabe: Annullierung Seiner Ehe mit Einer Rehebother", 1 September 1909, pp. 193–194.

31   BArchB R 1001/2058, *Verordnung des Reichskanzlers, betreff die Selbstverwaltung in Deutsch-Südwestafrika*, 28 January 1909, pp. 1–9.

32   *Verordnung des Reichskanzlers, betreff die Selbstverwaltung in Deutsch-Südwestafrika.*

33   BArchB R 1001/2058, Becker, "Eingabe", 1 September 1909, p. 194.

34   Becker, "Eingabe", p. 194.

35   Becker, "Eingabe", p. 194.

36   BArchB R 1001/2058, Wilhelm Külz, *Die Selbstverwaltung für Deutsch-Südwestafrika* (Bückeburg: 1909), p. 52.

37   Jürgen Zimmerer and Joachim Zeller (eds.), *Völkermord in Deutsch-Südwestafrika: Der Kolonialkrieg (1904–1908) in Namibia und seine Folgen* (Berlin: C.H. Links, 2003).

38   Paul Rohrbach, *Deutsche Kolonialwirtschaft, Kulturpolitische Grundsatze für die Rassen und Missionsfragen* (Berlin: Buchverlag der "Hilfe", 1909), p. 21.

39   Jonathan Hyslop, "White Working-Class Women and the Invention of Apartheid: 'Purified' Afrikaner Nationalist Agitation for Legislation against 'Mixed' Marriages, 1934–9", *Journal of African History*, vol. 36, no. 1, 1995, p. 65.

40   Robbie Aitken, *Exclusion and Inclusion: Gradations of Whiteness and Socio-Economic Engineering in German Southwest Africa, 1881–1914* (Bern: Peter Lang, 2007), pp. 109–117.

41   Theodor Leutwein, *Elf Jahre Gouverneur in Deutsch Südwestafrika* (Berlin: Siegfried Mittler und Sohn, 1907), pp. 232–234.

42   Clara Brockmann, *Die deutsche Frau in Südwestafrikaka: Ein Beitrag zur Frauenfrage in Unseren Kolonien* (Berlin: Ernst Siegfried Mittler und Sohn Königliche

Hofbuchhandlung, 1910), p. iv.

43   Brockmann, *Die deutsche Frau in Südwestafrika*, p. 2.

44   Frank Oliver Sobich, *"Schwarze Bestien, rote Gefahr": Rassismus und Antisozialismus im deutschen Kaiserreich* (Frankfurt am Main: Campus, 2006).

45   John Phillip Short, *Magic Lantern Empire: Colonialism and Society in Germany* (Ithaca: Cornell University Press, 2012), pp. 134–135.

46   Short, *Magic Lantern Empire*, p. 138.

47   Short, *Magic Lantern Empire*, p. 138.

48   Jonathan Sperber, *The Kaiser's Voters: Electors and Elections in Imperial Germany* (Cambridge: Cambridge University Press, 1997), pp. 248–249.

49   BArchB R 151-F, "Die Rechtlichen Verhältnisse der Eingeborenen, Abgesehen von der Gerichtsbarkeit", W.III.A1, Reichskolonialamt 3. Verordnungsentwürfe, 8 January 1907.

50   Hendrik Witbooi, "152. Witbooi an Leutwein", 14 November 1904, in Annemarie Heywood and Eben Maasdor (eds.), *The Hendrik Witbooi Papers* (Windhoek: Springwell Books, 1990), pp. 158–159.

Chapter 19. Colonialism in Spanish Africa

1   Casa Real, *Palabras de su Majestad el Rey en el acto conmemorativo del V centenario de la fundación de la ciudad de Panamá* (2019), www.casareal.es/ES/Actividades/Paginas/actividades_discursos_detalle.aspx?data=6125.

2   www.hijosdecanarias.com.

3   Gustau Nerín, *La guerra que vino de África* (Barcelona: Crítica, 2005), pp. 27–41.

4   Sebastian Balfour, *Deadly Embrace: Morocco and the Road to the Spanish Civil War* (Oxford: Oxford University Press, 2002).

5   Pablo La Porte, "La práctica internacional de las disculpas de estado: España, Marruecos y el Rif en el centenario del Protectorado (1912–2012)", *Revista electrónica de estudios internacionales*, vol. 13, no. 24, 2012, pp. 1–18.

6   La Porte, "La práctica internacional de las disculpas de estado", p. 16.

7   La Porte, "La práctica internacional de las disculpas de estado", p. 11.

8   La Porte, "La práctica internacional de las disculpas de estado", pp. 12–13.

9   See Yolanda Aixelà-Cabré, "Colonial Memories and Contemporary Narratives from the Rif: Spanishness, Amazighness, and Moroccaness Seen from Al-Hoceima and Spain", *Interventions: International Journal of Postcolonial Studies*, vol. 21, no. 6, 2018, pp. 856–873, https://doi.org/10.1080/1369801X.2018.1558093; see also Aziza Mimoun, "Memoria e historia en el Marruecos independiente: El caso del Rif", in José González Alcantud (ed.), *Culturas de frontera: Andalucía y Marruecos en el debate de la modernidad* (Barcelona: Anthropos, 2019), pp. 104–120; José Sánchez-García and Rachid Touhtou, "De la Hogra al Hirak: Neocolonialismo, memoria y disidencia política juvenil en el Rif", *Revista latinoamericana de estudios sociales: niñez y juventud*, vol. 19, no. 1, 2021, pp. 1–20; and Pablo La Porte, "Víctimas del Rif (1921–1926): Memoria, acción humanitaria y lecciones para nuestro tiempo", *Revista de estudios internacionales mediterráneos*, vol. 10, 2011, pp. 116–133.

10   La Porte, "La práctica internacional de las disculpas de estado", p. 15.

11   Nizar Messari, "L'utilisation des armes chimiques pendant la guerre du Rif (1921–1926) ou de l'ambiguïté des frontières et des séparations en politique", *Cultures & Conflits*, online forum, 25 April 2014, https://doi.org/10.4000/conflits.18827.

12   See Aixelà-Cabré, "Colonial Memories and Contemporary Narratives from the Rif";

and Sánchez-García and Touhtou, "De la Hogra al Hirak". See also Velasco Rocío de Castro, "La lucha anti-colonial en el Protectorado español según la historiografía marroquí: Raisuni y Abdelkrim", *Revista universitaria de historia militar*, vol. 8, no. 16, 2019, pp. 41–60.

13 Aixelà-Cabré, "Colonial Memories and Contemporary Narratives from the Rif", p. 13.

14 Aziza, "Memoria e historia en el Marruecos independiente", p. 118.

15 Adnan Mechbal, "Los moros de la Guerra Civil española: Entre memoria e historia", *Amnis*, vol. 2, 2011, pp. 66–73, http://journals.openedition.org/amnis/1487.

16 Aziza, "Memoria e historia en el Marruecos independiente", p. 116.

17 Aziza, "Memoria e historia en el Marruecos independiente", p. 105.

18 La Porte, "La práctica internacional de las disculpas de estado", p. 6.

19 Khalid El-Mansouri, "Després dels espanyols", in Eloy Martín, Alberto López, and Khalid El-Mansouri, *Ifni, la mili africana dels catalans* (Barcelona: Museu de les cultures del món – Ajuntament de Barcelona, 2019), pp. 127–138.

20 Ana Camacho, "El 'caso Bassiri', trabas a la investigación de un desaparecido del franquismo en el Sáhara espanyol", *Historia del presente*, vol. 16, no. 1, 2016, pp. 75–90.

21 Ángel Llorente, "Autonomía y 'realpolitik' para el Sáhara", *Política exterior*, vol. 36, no. 207, 2022, pp. 126–136.

22 José Fernando Siale Djangany, "Ësáasi Eweera: En el laberinto del estado dual", *Éndoxa: Series filosóficas*, vol. 37, 2016, pp. 169–198.

23 Ángel Barrera (ed.), *Operación Rokobongo, 1913* (Vic: Ceiba Ediciones, 2001).

24 Gustau Nerín, *La última selva de España: Antropófagos, misioneros y guardias civiles* (Madrid: Los Libros de la Catarata, 2010).

25 Gustau Nerín, "Francisco Macías: Nuevo estado, nuevo ritual", *Endoxa: Series filosóficas*, vol. 37, 2016, pp. 149–168.

26 Teodoro Nguema Mbasogo Obiang, *Guinea Ecuatorial, país joven* (Malabo: Editorial Guinea, 1985), pp. 19–31.

27 Alfonso Merlos, *Crónica de un desencuentro: Obiang responde* (Madrid: Fragua, 2012), p. 199.

28 Merlos, *Crónica de un desencuentro*, p. 34.

29 Merlos, *Crónica de un desencuentro*, p. 200.

30 Pueblo indígena bubi de la isla de Bioko, "Escrito dirigido al grupo de trabajo de UPR", *Universal Periodic Review*, 2013, https://www.uprinfo.org/sites/default/files/documents/2014-04/epibib_upr19_gnq_s_main.pdf.

31 Pueblo indígena bubi de la isla de Bioko, "Escrito dirigido al grupo de trabajo de UPR".

32 Coro Juanena, "Por qué en África no se reconoce la existencia de poblaciones indígenas: Un estudio de caso; los bubis de la isla de bioko", *Revista de antropología social*, vol. 25, no. 2, 2016, pp. 389–420, www.redalyc.org/articulo.oa?id=83848505007.

33 Enriqueta Vila Vilar, "La gran omisión en la Constitución de 1812: La esclavitud africana", *Boletín de la Real academia Sevillana de Buenas Letras*, vol. 39, 2011, pp. 107–120.

34 Paoloni Castelucci and Beatriz Olga, "Comentario a la sentencia del Tribunal Supremo de 20 de julio de 2020: Denegación de nacionalidad española a los nacidos en la antigua Guinea Ecuatorial", *Cuadernos de derecho transnacional*, vol. 13, no. 1,

2021, pp. 799–810.

35   Eduard Gargallo Sariol and Jordi Sant Gisbert, *El petit imperi: Catalans en la colonització de la Guinea espanyola* (Barcelona: Angle editorial, 2021), p. 271.

36   Francisco Zamora Loboch, *Cómo ser negro y no morir en Aravaca* (Barcelona: Ediciones B, 1994).

37   Rubén H. Bermúdez, *Y tú, ¿por qué eres negro?* (Madrid: Koln Studio, 2018).

38   Desirée Bela-Lobedde, *Ser mujer negra en España* (Madrid: Ediciones B, 2018).

39   Moha Gerehou, *¿Qué hace un negro como tú en un sitio como este* (Barcelona: Península, 2021).

40   Fernando Barbosa Rodrigues, *Estudio para el conocimiento y caracterización de la comunidad africana y afro-descendiente* (Madrid: Observatorio español del racismo y la xenofobia, 2021), p. 46, www.inclusion.gob.es/oberaxe/ficheros/documentos/ PDF-16-Estudio-para-el-conocimiento-de-la-C-Africana.-ACC_ARN_13.11.20. pdf. See also Andumi Toasijé, "Los desafíos de las comunidades africanas y africano-descendientes en España", in Elsa Aimé González and Itxaso Domínguez de Olazábal (eds.), *Informe África 2020: Transformaciones, movilidad y continuidad* (Madrid: Fundación Alternativas, 2020), p. 53, https://fundacionalternativas.org/ publicaciones/informe-africa-2020-transformaciones-movilizacion-y-continuidad.

41   Comisión de Igualdad, "Proposición no de ley presentada por el Grupo parlamentario popular en el Congreso, sobre la memoria de la esclavitud, reconocimiento y apoyo a la comunidad negra, africana y de afro-descendientes en España", *Boletín oficial de las Cortes generales*, 27 January 2014, pp. 29–31.

42   Comisión de Igualdad, "Proposición no de ley presentada por el Grupo parlamentario popular en el Congreso, sobre la memoria de la esclavitud, reconocimiento y apoyo a la comunidad negra, africana y de afro-descendientes en España".

43   Jeffrey Abé Pans, *Cuando somos el enemigo* (Barcelona: Editorial Mey, 2019).

Chapter 20. Colonialism in Italian Africa

1   Richard J.B. Bosworth, *Italy, the Least of the Great Powers: Italian Foreign Policy before the First World War* (Cambridge: Cambridge University Press, 1979).

2   Eritrea did not pre-exist as a state; it was brought into official existence in 1890 by treaty between Italy and Ethiopia, and it took two more decades to establish its borders. See Federica Guazzini, "Storie di confine: Percezioni identitarie della frontiera coloniale tra Etiopia e Eritrea (1897–1908)", *Quaderni Storici*, vol. 37, no. 1, 2002, pp. 221–258.

3   Libya is also a legacy of Italian colonialism, both in its name and its geographic contours. State and nation formation had, however, been emerging prior to the arrival of Italian imperialists. See Ali Abdullatif Ahmida, *The Making of Modern Libya: State Formation, Colonization, and Resistance, 1830–1932* (Albany: State University of New York Press, 1994); and Anna Baldinetti, *The Origins of the Libyan Nation: Colonial Legacy, Exile, and the Emergence of a New Nation-State* (London and New York: Routledge, 2010).

4   For detailed reasoning and some samples of the costs of Italian colonialism, see Nicola Labanca, *Oltremare: Storia dell'espansione coloniale italiana* (Bologna: Il Mulino, 2002), pp. 280–301. Labanca summarises as follows: "Italy tried every possible [financial] model in all the colonies … and ended up feeble in every one of them" (p. 280).

5   A useful overview of the sectors of Italian enterprise can be found in Gian Luca Podestà, "Eurafrica: Vital Space, Demographic Planning and the Division of Labour

in the Italian Empire; The Legacy of Fascist Autarky", *Journal of European Economic History*, vol. 50, 2021, pp. 17–50, especially pp. 29–30 and 33.

6   This was succinctly articulated by the poet Giovanni Pascoli in 1911, as follows: "We left signs that not even the Berbers, the Bedouins or the Turks have succeeded in destroying, the signs of our humanity and civilization, signs precisely that we are not Berbers, Bedouins or Turks. We are returning." Adriana M. Baranello, "Giovanni Pascoli's 'La grande proletaria si è mossa': A Translation and Critical Introduction", *California Italian Studies*, vol. 2, no. 1, 2011, p. 11, https://escholarship.org/uc/item/6jh07474.

7   In practice, Italy was following – and trying to catch up with – approaches already taken by France in Algeria. See Diana K. Davis, *Resurrecting the Granary of Rome: Environmental History and French Colonial Expansion in North Africa* (Columbus: Ohio University Press, 2007).

8   Key works on Italy's Libyan agricultural and settlement programmes include Claudio G. Segrè, *Fourth Shore: Italy's Colonization of Libya* (Chicago: University of Chicago Press, 1975); Federico Cresti, *Oasi di italianità: La Libia della colonizzazione agraria tra fascismo, guerra e indipendenza 1935–1956* (Turin: Internazionale, 1996); and Federico Cresti, *Non desiderare la terra d'altri: La colonizzazione italiana in Libia* (Rome: Carocci, 2011). Regarding Ethiopia, see Haile M. Larebo, *The Building of an Empire: Italian Land Policy and Practice in Ethiopia 1935–1941* (Oxford: Clarendon Press, 1994).

9   See Irma Taddia, *L'Eritrea: Colonia, 1890–1952; Paesaggi, strutture, uomini del colonialismo* (Milan: Franco Angeli, 1986); Tekeste Negash, *Italian Colonialism in Eritrea, 1882–1941: Policies, Praxis and Impact* (Stockholm: Uppsala University, 1987); and Yemane Mesghenna, *Italian Colonialism: A Case Study of Eritrea, 1869–1934; Motive, Praxis and Result* (Lund: University of Lund, 1988).

10   Namely, the SAIS (Società Agricola Italo Somala). Robert L. Hess, *Italian Colonialism in Somalia* (Chicago: University of Chicago Press, 1966); Annamaria Belli, *Lavoro e sperimentazione agricola in Somalia: La Società agricola italo somala e la canna da zucchero in Somalia* (Florence: Fiorentino, 2000); Marco Zoppi, "'Il cotone non è cosa che si possa mangiare': Politiche coloniali italiane in Somalia e sicurezza alimentare, 1900–1945", *Studi Storici*, vol. 4, 2020, pp. 1009–1033; and Nuredin Hagi Scikei and Maria Spina, "La Società Agricola Italo-Somala (SAIS), uno dei più importanti complessi agro-industriali di tutta l'Africa coloniale", in Susanna Bortolotto, Nelly Cattaneo, and Renzo Riboldazzi (eds.), *Infrastrutture e colonizzazione: Il caso africano tra heritage e sviluppo* (Florence: Altralinea, 2020), pp. 123–135.

11   Essential works on deportations to Italian camps include Mohamed Al-Jefa'iri, *The Libyan Deportees in the Prisons of the Italian Islands: Documents, Statistics, Names, Illustrations* (Tripoli: Libyan Studies Centre, 1989); Eliana Calandra, "Prigionieri arabi a ustica: Un episodio della guerra italo-turca attraverso le fonti archivistiche", in Carla Ghezzi (ed.), *Fonti e problemi della politica italiana: Atti del convegno Taormina–Messina, 23–29 ottobre 1989* (Rome: Ministero per i beni culturali e ambientali, 1996), pp. 1150–1167; Simone Bernini, "Documenti sulla repressione italiana in Libia agli inizi della colonizzazione (1911–1918)", in Nicola Labanca (ed.), *Un nodo: Immagini e documenti sulla repressione coloniale in Libia* (Lacaita: Manduria, 2002), pp. 117–122; Francesco Sulpizi and Salaheddin Hasan Sury, *Gli esiliati libici nel periodo coloniale* (Rome: Istituto Italiano per l'Africa e l'Oriente, 2002); Paolo Borruso, *L'Africa al confine: La deportazione etiopica in Italia (1937–39)* (Lacaita: Manduria, 2003);

Marco Lenci, *All'inferno e ritorno: Storie di deportati tra Italia ed Eritrea in epoca coloniale* (Pisa: Serantini, 2004); Francesca Di Pasquale, "I deportati libici in Sicilia (1911–1933)", in Carla Ghezzi and Salaheddin Hasan Sury (eds.), *Terzo convegno sugli esiliati libici nel periodo coloniale* (Rome: Istituto Italiano per l'Africa e l'Oriente e Centro Libico per gli Studi Storici, 2005), pp. 137–147; and Francesca Di Pasquale, "The 'Other' at Home: Deportation and Transportation of Libyans to Italy during the Colonial Era (1911–1943)", *International Review of Social History*, vol. 63, 2018, special issue: "Transportation, Deportation, and Exile: Perspectives from the Colonies in the Nineteenth and Twentieth Centuries", pp. 211–231.

12   For a detailed analysis of the stages of Italian atrocities perpetrated in Libya combined with judicious appraisals of all the sources at our disposal, see Nicola Labanca, *La guerra italiana per la Libia, 1911–1931* (Bologna: Il Mulino, 2012). An overview of the African camps built by Italians is provided by Gustavo Ottolenghi, *Gli Italiani e il colonialismo: I campi di detenzione italiani in Africa* (Milan: Sugarco, 1997).

13   The earliest call to recognise Italy's atrocities in Cyrenaica as a genocide was based on Italian military archives and published in Giorgio Rochat, "La repressione della resistenza araba in Cirenaica nel 1930–31 nei documenti dell'archivio Graziani", *Il Movimento di Liberazione in Italia*, vol. 110, 1973, pp. 3–39. The most recent work draws on invaluable Libyan materials: Ali Abdullatif Ahmida, *Genocide in Libya: Shar, a Hidden Colonial History* (London and New York: Routledge, 2021). A unique eyewitness account is provided in Knud Holmboe, *Desert Encounter: An Adventurous Journey through Italian Africa* (New York: Putnam's Sons, 1937).

14   An essential overview of how Italian occupation fits into the larger history of Ethiopia's modernisation is provided in Bahru Zewde, *A History of Modern Ethiopia, 1855–1974* (Addis Ababa: Addis Ababa University Press, 1991). On atrocities ranging from slaughter to rapes and mutilations committed in the capital, see Ian Campbell, *The Addis Ababa Massacre: Italy's National Shame* (Oxford: Oxford University Press, 2017). The uses of mustard gas and civilian massacres are treated in Matteo Dominioni, *Lo sfascio dell'impero: Gli Italiani in Etiopia, 1936–1941* (Rome and Bari: Laterza, 2008). The targeting of clerics, with the collaboration of the Vatican, is documented in Ian Campbell, *Holy War: The Untold Story of Catholic Italy's Crusade against the Ethiopian Orthodox Church* (London: Hurst, 2021).

15   This type of arrangement took hold from the early Italian days in Eritrea during the 1890s, and endured into the Ethiopian occupation. See Giulia Barrera, "Dangerous Liaisons: Colonial Concubinage in Eritrea, 1890–1941", Northwestern University, Programme of African Studies, Working Papers 1, 1996; Barbara Sòrgoni, *Parole e corpi: Antropologia, discorso giuridico e politiche sessuali interrazziali nella colonia Eritrea (1890–1941)* (Naples: Liguori, 1998); and Giovanna Trento, "*Madamato* and Colonial Concubinage in Ethiopia: A Comparative Perspective", *Aethiopica*, vol. 14, 2011, pp. 184–205.

16   On the evolution over time of Italian approaches to "mixed" sexual relations, from seeming tolerance to harsh attempts to stem the emergence of Italo-African offspring altogether, see Giulia Barrera, "Colonial Affairs: Italian Men, Eritrean Women, and the Construction of Racial Hierarchies in Colonial Eritrea (1885–1941)" (PhD dissertation, Northwestern University, 2002).

17   These Italian laws targeted at race in East Africa were followed up the very next year with the antisemitic laws of 1938, which began Italy's implementation of the Shoah. On the rise of official colonial segregation, see Mia Fuller, *Moderns Abroad:*

Architecture, Cities, and Italian Imperialism (London and New York: Routledge, 2007), pp. 137–147.

18 Sergio Tognetti, "The Trade in Black African Slaves in Fifteenth-Century Florence", in Thomas F. Earle and Kate J.P. Lowe (eds.), *Black Africans in Renaissance Europe* (Cambridge: Cambridge University Press, 2005), pp. 213–224.

19 Giulia Bonazza, *Abolitionism and the Persistence of Slavery in Italian States, 1750–1850* (Cham: Palgrave, 2019), pp. 103–165.

20 This previously enslaved group was typically described as being of "African" or Bantu descent, as opposed to "superior" Arabian heritage. On the Italian exacerbation of locally exercised social differences in the aftermath of slavery's abolition, see Lee V. Cassanelli, "The End of Slavery and the 'Problem' of Farm Labor in Colonial Somalia", in Annarita Puglielli and Francesco Antinucci (eds.), *Proceedings of the Third International Congress of Somali Studies: History, Anthropology and Archeology* (Rome: Pensiero scientifico, 1988), pp. 269–282; Catherine Besteman, "The Invention of Gosha: Slavery, Colonialism, and Stigma in Somali History", in Ali Jimale Ahmed (ed.), *The Invention of Somalia* (Lawrenceville, NJ: Red Sea Press, 1995), pp. 43–62; Omar A. Eno, "The Abolition of Slavery and the Aftermath Stigma: The Case of the *Bantu/Jareer* People on the Benadir Coast of Southern Somalia", in Gwyn Campbell (ed.), *Abolition and Its Aftermath in Indian Ocean Africa and Asia* (London and New York: Routledge, 2005), pp. 83–93; and Annalisa Urbano, "A 'Grandiose Future for Italian Somalia': Colonial Developmentalist Discourse, Agricultural Planning, and Forced Labor (1900–1940)", *International Labor and Working-Class History*, vol. 92, 2017, pp. 69–88.

21 See Fuller, *Moderns Abroad*, pp. 58–61.

22 Emanuele Ertola, "'White Slaves': Labor, Whiteness, and Italian Colonialism in Italian East Africa (1935–1941)", *Labor History*, vol. 61, nos. 5–6, 2020, pp. 551–567. Also see Emanuele Ertola, "'Terra promessa': Migration and Settler Colonialism in Libya, 1911–1970", *Settler Colonial Studies*, vol. 7, no. 3, 2017, pp. 340–353. On the multifaceted lives of lower-class Italians in African colonies, see Nicola Labanca, *Posti al sole: Diari e memorie di vita e di lavoro dalle colonie d'Africa* (Rovereto: Museo Storico Italiano della Guerra, 2001).

23 Marco Scardigli, *Il braccio indigeno: Ascari, irregolari e bande nella conquista dell'Eritrea, 1885–1911* (Milan: Franco Angeli, 1996); Alessandro Volterra, *Sudditi coloniali: Ascari eritrei, 1935–1941* (Milan: Franco Angeli, 2005); Luigi Goglia, "Popolazioni, eserciti africani e truppe indigene nella dottrina italiana della guerra coloniale", *Mondo Contemporaneo*, vol. 2, 2006, pp. 5–54; Uoldelul Chelati Dirar, "Truppe coloniali e l'individuazione dell'African agency: Il caso degli ascari eritrei", *Afriche e Orienti*, vol. 1, 2007, pp. 41–56; Uoldelul Chelati Dirar, "Fedeli servitori della bandiera? Gli ascari eritrei tra colonialismo, anticolonialismo e nazionalismo, 1935–1941", in Riccardo Bottoni (ed.), *L'impero fascista: Italia ed Etiopia (1935–1941)* (Bologna: Il Mulino, 2008), pp. 441–470; Massimo Zaccaria, *Anch'io per la tua bandiera: Il V Battaglione Ascari in missione sul fronte libico (1912)* (Ravenna: Giorgio Pozzi, 2012); Stephen C. Bruner, "'At Least So Long as We Are Talking about Marching, the Inferior Is Not the Black, It's the White': Italian Debate over the Use of Indigenous Troops in the Scramble for Africa", *European History Quarterly*, vol. 44, no. 1, 2014, pp. 33–54; Nir Arielli, "Colonial Soldiers in Italian Counter-Insurgency Operations in Libya, 1922–32", *British Journal for Military History*, vol. 1, no. 2, 2015, pp. 47–66.

24 Giorgio Rochat, "Il genocidio cirenaico e la storiografia coloniale", *Belfagor*, vol. 35, no. 4, 1980, p. 454.

25 Cresti, *Oasi*.

26 Michele Sollai, "How to Feed an Empire? Agrarian Science, Indigenous Farming, and Wheat Autarky in Italian-Occupied Ethiopia", *Agricultural History*, vol. 96, no. 3, 2022, pp. 379–416.

27 Eloi Ficquet, "La stèle éthiopienne de Rome: Objet d'un conflit de mémoires", *Cahiers d'Études Africaines*, nos. 173–174, 2004, pp. 369–385.

28 On the complex situation of Italians who remained after the Second World War, see Pamela Ballinger, "Colonial Twilight: Italian Settlers and the Long Decolonization of Libya", *Journal of Contemporary History*, vol. 5, no. 4, 2016, pp. 813–838.

29 Daniela Baratieri, *Memories and Silences Haunted by Fascism: Italian Colonialism MCMXXX–MCMLV* (Bern: Peter Lang, 2010); Giovanni Leone, Laurent Licata, Alessia Mastropietro, Stefano Migliorisi, and Isora Sessa, "Material Traces of a Cumbersome Past: The Case of Italian Colonial History", in Francesca Comunello, Fabrizio Martire, and Lorenzo Sabetta (eds.), *What People Leave Behind: Marks, Traces, Footprints, and Their Relevance to Knowledge Society* (Cham: Springer, 2022), pp. 205–220.

30 See Michele Battini, *The Missing Italian Nuremberg: Cultural Amnesia and Postwar Politics* (New York: Palgrave Macmillan, 2007); and Pamela Ballinger, *The World Refugees Made: Decolonization and the Foundation of Postwar Italy* (Ithaca: Cornell University Press, 2020).

31 We owe it to two historians in particular, Angelo Del Boca and Giorgio Rochat, that we know as much as we do. Starting in the 1960s they both unearthed evidence that had been well hidden regarding mustard gases, the deliberate attempt to exterminate the Cyrenaican population, and Italian dictator Benito Mussolini's explicit support of both. Their works are too numerous to cite here but as overviews, see Angelo Del Boca, *Italiani, brava gente?* (Vicenza: Neri Pozza, 2005); and Giorgio Rochat, *Il colonialismo italiano: La prima guerra d'Africa, la guerra di Libia, la riconquista della Libia, la guerra d'Etiopia, l'impero* (Turin: Loescher, 1973).

32 See Alessandro Triulzi, "Displacing the Colonial Event: Hybrid Memories of Postcolonial Italy", *Interventions: International Journal of Postcolonial Studies*, vol. 8, no. 3, 2006, pp. 430–443; Gaia Giuliani, "La sottile linea bianca: Intersezioni di razza, genere e classe nell'Italia postcoloniale", *Studi Culturali*, vol. 2, 2013, pp. 253–344; and Cristina Lombardi-Diop and Caterina Romeo (eds.), *Postcolonial Italy: Challenging National Homogeneity* (New York: Palgrave Macmillan, 2012). This last book was later updated and published in Italian: *L'Italia postcoloniale* (Florence: Le Monnier Università, 2014).

33 Stephanie Malia Hom, *Empire's Mobius Strip: Historical Echoes in Italy's Crisis of Migration and Detention* (Ithaca: Cornell University Press, 2019).

34 See Krystyna von Henneberg, "Monuments, Public Space, and the Memory of Empire in Modern Italy", *History and Memory*, vol. 16, no. 1, 2004, pp. 37–85; Rino Bianchi and Igiaba Scego, *Roma negata: Percorsi postcoloniali nella città* (Rome: Ediesse, 2014); and Elisabetta Campagni, "Looking for a Space to Breathe: Decolonising Italian Cities", *Anthropological Journal of European Cultures*, vol. 30, no. 2, 2021, pp. 86–94.

35 Mia Fuller, "Italy's Colonial Futures: Colonial Inertia and Postcolonial Capital in Asmara", *California Italian Studies*, vol. 2, no. 1, 2011, http://escholarship.org/

uc/item/4mb1z7f8; and Iman Mohamed, "Colonial Amnesia and the Material Remains of Italian Colonialism in Mogadishu", *Interventions: International Journal of Postcolonial Studies*, 2023, DOI: 10.1080/1369801X.2023.2222107.

Chapter 21. Colonialism in the British Caribbean

1   Only in 1763 with the Treaty of Paris did the English gain Tobago, subsequently establishing a settlement near present-day Mount St George, guarded closely by Fort Granby. English and Scottish settlers arrived from other parts of the Caribbean to develop sugar, cotton, and indigo estates. The British colonisation of Tobago was only disrupted by French occupation from 1781 to 1793 and again from 1801 to 1802. Meanwhile, in Trinidad, the Spanish pivoted from gold fever to agriculture, accepting French settlers to establish plantations, provided they were Roman Catholic. The French came from Haiti, Martinique, and St Lucia to cultivate sugar and cocoa. By the turn of the nineteenth century, Trinidad was a wealthy West Indian island with approximately 450 plantations cultivating 86,268 acres. It was this wealth that attracted English interest, and in February 1779 a British fleet, tasked with attacking Puerto Rico, invaded and captured Trinidad. The British now controlled both Trinidad and Tobago and would hold on to these islands until 1962.

2   James Joyce, "Daniel Defoe", in Michael Shinagel (ed.), *A Norton Critical Edition: Daniel Defoe: Robinson Crusoe* (New York: W.W. Norton & Co., 1994), p. 323.

3   Eric Hobsbawm, *Industry and Empire: From 1750 to the Present Day* (Harmondsworth: Penguin Books, 1977). See also G.C.K. Peach, "West Indians as a Replacement Population in England and Wales", *Social and Economic Studies*, vol. 16, no. 3, 1967, pp. 289–294.

4   Michel-Rolph Trouillot, *Silencing the Past: Power and the Production of History* (Boston: Beacon Press, 1995), p. 1.

5   Given the complex histories of incursions into and agreements and imperial conflicts over these territories, the dates cited indicate extended rule.

6   This is taken from the title of Weiss's edited volume. Holger Weiss (ed.), *Ports of Globalisation, Places of Creolisation: Nordic Possessions in the Atlantic World during the Era of the Slave Trade* (Leiden: Brill, 2006).

7   Eric Williams, *Capitalism and Slavery* (Chapel Hill: University of North Carolina Press, 1994 [1944]).

8   Also see Appendix II in George Beckford, *Persistent Poverty: Underdevelopment in Plantation Economies of the Third World* (Kingston: University of the West Indies Press, 1972).

9   Douglas Hall, "Incalculability as a Feature of Sugar Production during the Eighteenth Century", *Social and Economic Studies*, vol. 10, no. 3, 1961, pp. 340–352.

10   Trevor Burnard, *Jamaica in the Age of Revolution* (Philadelphia: University of Pennsylvania Press, 2020).

11   See Sidney W. Mintz, *Sweetness and Power: The Place of Sugar in Modern History* (New York: Viking, 1985); and Richard Dunn, *Sugar and Slaves: The Rise of the Planter Class in the English West Indies, 1624–1713* (Chapel Hill: University of North Carolina Press, 2012).

12   Williams, *Capitalism and Slavery*, p. vii.

13   Readers interested in this debate can consult Hilary Beckles, *Britain's Black Debt: Reparations for Caribbean Slavery and Native Genocide* (Kingston: University of West Indies Press, 2013).

14   By contrast to the British, Dutch colonies in the Caribbean were smaller, less populated, and had less economic potential. For these reasons, the Dutch state gave this land little thought, preferring instead to use a mixed system where, for example, Suriname was administered by the Chartered Society of Suriname while the Antillean islands were directly administered by the West India Company. Gert Oostindie and Inge Klinkers, *Decolonising the Caribbean: Dutch Policies in a Comparative Perspective* (Amsterdam: Amsterdam University Press, 2003), p. 57.

15   Sidney W. Mintz, "Enduring Substances, Trying Theories: The Caribbean Region as Oikoumene", *Journal of the Royal Anthropological Institute*, vol. 2, no. 2, 1996, pp. 289–311.

16   Sidney W. Mintz, *Caribbean Transformations* (Chicago: Aldine, 1974). With historical meanings of creole, criollo, Kreyol, and crioulo to refer to persons, animals, and plants born in the New World of the Old, the overarching meaning became that which was "local". See Edward Kamau Brathwaite, *The Development of Creole Society in Jamaica, 1770–1820* (Oxford: Clarendon Press, 1971); Chandra Jayawardena, *Conflict and Solidarity in a Guianese Plantation* (New York: Humanities Press, 1963); Mintz, "Enduring Substances, Trying Theories". In the nationalist meta-narrative of post-colonial Caribbean states, creole came to mean mixtures of African and European people, things, practices, and beliefs to the exclusion of other cultural and ethnic groups such as East Indians, descendants of Indian indentured workers, Chinese, and Javanese. Viranjini Munasinghe therefore questions the applicability of creolisation to indicate inclusivity, external to the Caribbean and in the "global village" when it has come to be narrowly defined in its original Caribbean context. See Viranjini Munasinghe, *Callaloo or Tossed Salad? East Indians and the Cultural Politics of Identity in Trinidad* (Ithaca: Cornell University Press, 2001).

17   Edward Kamau Brathwaite, *Contradictory Omens: Cultural Diversity and Integration in the Caribbean* (Mona, Jamaica: Savacou, 1974), p. 6.

18   Peter Wilson, *Crab Antics: The Social Anthropology of English-Speaking Negro Societies of the Caribbean* (New Haven: Yale University Press, 1973).

19   Judith Blake, *Family Structure in Jamaica: The Social Context of Reproduction* (New York: Free Press of Glencoe, 1961).

20   Sidney M. Greenfield, "Socio-economic Factors and Family Form: A Barbadian Case Study", *Social and Economic Studies*, vol. 10, no. 1, 1961, pp. 72–85.

21   Edith Clarke, *My Mother Who Fathered Me: A Study of the Family in Three Selected Communities in Jamaica* (London: George Allen and Unwin, 1966).

22   Michael Horowitz, *Morne-Paysan: Peasant Village in Martinique* (New York: Holt, Rinehart and Winston, 1967).

23   Greenfield, "Socio-economic Factors and Family Form: A Barbadian Case Study", p. 109.

24   Clarke, *My Mother Who Fathered Me*, p. 96.

25   Mintz, *Caribbean Transformations*.

26   Mintz, *Caribbean Transformations*.

27   See Arthur Niehoff and Juanita Niehoff, *East Indians in the West Indies* (Milwaukee: Milwaukee Public Museum, 1960), and Morton Klass, *East Indians in Trinidad: A Study of Cultural Persistence* (New York: Columbia University Press, 1960).

28   While there were and are debates regarding the degree of adaptation and persistence of Indo-Caribbeans outside debates on creolisation that were largely applied to

African and European cultural contacts, it is clear that cultural changes occurred. See Patricia Mohammed, *Gender Negotiations among Indians in Trinidad, 1917–1947* (New York: Palgrave Macmillan; and The Hague: Institute of Social Studies, 2002); Rhoda Reddock, "Indian Women and Indentureship in Trinidad and Tobago, 1845–1917: Freedom Denied", *Caribbean Quarterly*, vol. 32, nos. 3–4, 1986, pp. 27–49; and Verene Shepherd, *Transients to Settlers: The Experience of Indians in Jamaica, 1845–1950* (Leeds: Peepal Tree Press, 1993).

29   Nancie L. Gonzalez, *Black Carib Household Structure: A Study of Migration and Modernization* (Seattle: University of Washington Press, 1969).

30   For more detail, see M.G. Smith, "Kinship and Household in Carriacou", *Social and Economic Studies*, vol. 10, no. 1, 1961, pp. 455–477.

31   Jerome Teelucksingh, *Labour and the Decolonization Struggle in Trinidad and Tobago* (New York: Palgrave Macmillan, 2015).

32   Teelucksingh, *Labour and the Decolonization Struggle in Trinidad and Tobago*, p. 89.

33   While there have always been strands within British society that have critiqued the empire and its various legacies, such as J.A. Hobson and Arnold Toynbee, recently the South African originating movement #RhodesMustFall has charted the ties between imperialists like Cecil Rhodes, key British institutions, British nationalism and British supremacy, and extraction in British colonies. See, for example, Nicholas Draper, "British Universities and Caribbean Slavery", in Jill Pellew and Lawrence Goldman (eds.), *Dethroning Historical Reputations: Universities, Museums and the Commemoration of Benefactors* (London: University of London, 2018), pp. 93–106.

34   Charles W. Mills, *The Racial Contract* (Ithaca: Cornell University Press, 1988).

35   Jessica Moody, "Remembering the Imperial Context of Emancipation Commemoration in the Former British Slave-Port Cities of Bristol and Liverpool, 1933–1934", *Slavery and Abolition*, vol. 39, no. 1, 2018, pp. 169–189.

36   Hilary Beckles, "Kalinago (Carib) Resistance to European Colonisation of the Caribbean", *Caribbean Quarterly*, vol. 54, no. 4, 2008, pp. 77–94; and Gerald Horne, *The Counter-Revolution of 1776: Slave Resistance and the Origins of the United States of America* (New York: New York University Press, 2016).

37   Gad Heuman, *"The Killing Time": The Morant Bay Rebellion in Jamaica* (London: Macmillan Caribbean, 1994); and Horace Campbell, *Rasta and Resistance: From Marcus Garvey to Walter Rodney* (London: Hansib Publications, 2007).

38   Charlotte Lydia Riley, "'The Winds of Change Are Blowing Economically': The Labour Party and British Overseas Development, 1940s–1960s", in Andrew W.M. Smith and Chris Jeppesen (eds.), *Britain, France and the Decolonization of Africa: Future Imperfect?* (London: University College London Press, 2017).

39   Ranabir Samaddar, *Karl Marx and the Postcolonial Age* (New York: Palgrave Macmillan, 2018), p. viii.

40   Raymond Betts, "Decolonization: A Brief History of the Word", in Els Bogaerts and Remco Raben (eds.), *Beyond Empire and Nation* (Leiden: KITLV Press, 2012), pp. 23–38.

41   See Oostindie and Klinkers, *Decolonising the Caribbean*, p. 57.

42   John Darwin, *Britain and Decolonisation: The Retreat from Empire in the Post-war World* (London: Macmillan, 1988), p. 4.

43   Edward Said, *Culture and Imperialism* (New York: Vintage, 1993), p. xii.

44   C.L.R. James, *The Life of Captain Cipriani with the Pamphlet, The Case for West-Indian*

Self-Government (Durham: Duke University Press, 2014 [1933]).

45   Orme Wheelock Phelps, "Rise of the Labour Movement in Jamaica", *Social and Economic Studies*, vol. 9, no. 4, 1960, pp. 417–468.

46   Trouillot, *Silencing the Past*.

Chapter 22. Colonialism in the Dutch Caribbean

1   Jose Atiles-Osoria, "Colonial State Terror in Puerto Rico: A Research Agenda", *State Crime Journal*, vol. 5, no. 2, 2016, pp. 220–241.

2   Sint Maarten and Saint-Martin form a single island that is split into two parts by a border that runs from west to east. Between 1648 and 1816, the Dutch section became British three times and French four times. It was not until 1817 that the island fell permanently under Dutch and French administration. See Johan Hartog, *De Bovenwindse eilanden St Maarten, Saba, St Eustatius: Eens gouden rots, nu zilveren dollars* (Aruba: De Wit, 1964), pp. 706–711.

3   Miel Groten, interview with the historian Elizabeth Buettner, entitled "Activisme rond het koloniale verleden dwingt de erkenning van een nieuwe realiteit af", *Jonge Historici*, 3 November 2020.

4   The six Dutch Caribbean Islands were run by the New West India Company (NWIC, between 1674 and 1791) while Suriname was run by the Chartered Society of Suriname from 1683 to 1795. By 1750, Dutch power in the Caribbean was overturned by the British and then the French. In that period, the United Provinces (later the Netherlands) did not govern their Caribbean territories directly, but through private corporations.

5   Pepijn Brandon and Matthias van Rossum, *Nederland en de slavernij: Een wereldgeschiedenis* (Amsterdam: Spectrum Uitgeverij, 2020).

6   Not just the ABC Islands, but also Sint Maarten, Sint Eustatius and Saba were not a "typical" Caribbean plantation economy. Saba did have one sugar cane plantation, but most of the small number of enslaved on this island worked in households. In Sint Maarten and Sint Eustatius, cash crops such as tobacco and, later on, sugar cane, cotton, and indigo were produced. Both Sint Maarten and Bonaire used enslaved persons in the salt industry too. See Alex van Stipriaan, "The Suriname Rat Race: Labour and Technology on Sugar Plantations, 1750–1900", *Nieuwe West-Indische Gids / New West Indian Guide*, vol. 63, nos. ½, 1989, pp. 94–117. The island of Bonaire as a whole was a plantation of the Dutch West India Company; the small numbers of enslaved worked in the salt and the dyewood industries. See Luc Alofs, Greta Carolina, and Nel Casimiri, *Geschiedenis van de Antillen: Aruba, Bonaire, Curaçao, Saba, Sint Eustatius, Sint Maarten* (Zutphen: Walburg Pers, 1997).

7   Alan F. Benjamin, *Jews of the Dutch Caribbean: Exploring Ethnic Identity on Curaçao* (London and New York: Routledge, 2002).

8   Gert Jan Oostindie, *Paradise Overseas: The Dutch Caribbean; Colonialism and Its Transatlantic Legacies* (Oxford: Macmillan Caribbean, 1997).

9   Karwan Fatah-Black, *White Lies and Black Markets: Evading Metropolitan Authority in Colonial Suriname, 1650–1800* (Leiden: Brill, 2015).

10   Felicia Jantina Fricke, "The Lifeways of Enslaved People in Curaçao, St Eustatius, and St Maarten/St Martin: A Thematic Analysis of Archaeological, Osteological and Oral Historical Data" (PhD thesis, University of Kent, 2019).

11   These names refer to the social event in which African-derived drumming occurs, as well as to the music, singing, and dancing. In fact, the *tambú* and the *bari* have

continued until the present as an outlet for protest.

12   Dutch opposition to the incorporation of enslaved Africans in their religious practice, for example, left the conversion of the black population to the Roman Catholic Church on the ABC Islands, the Methodist Church and the Seventh Day Adventists on the Windward Islands, and the Moravians in Suriname. On the three ABC Islands, the Catholic Church came to play a very important role in the dynamics within which the cultural encounter between enslaved, freed, and free people took place and an important machinery of cultural control during the nineteenth century. See Rose Mary Allen, *Di ki manera? A Social History of Afro-Curaçaoans, 1863–1917* (Amsterdam: SWP Publishers, 2007); and Armando Lampe, "Yo te nombro libertad: Iglesia y Estado en la sociedad esclavista de Curazao 1816 to 1863" (PhD thesis, Free University of Amsterdam, 1988).

13   Unlike the Creole languages of most other (formerly) colonised societies, Papiamentu is not derived primarily from the language of the mother country. Quite early on, it was the lingua franca used both within and between the different social groups and through which these groups interrelated in complex ways.

14   F.S.J. Ledgister, "Caribbean Anti-Colonialism", *The Encyclopedia of Post-colonial Studies*, 2016, pp. 1–7, https://www.academia.edu/44928945/Caribbean_Anti_Colonialism.

15   In 1984, the date of the slave revolt of 1795, the day being 17 August, was recognised and officially designated *Dia di lucha pa libertat* (Day of the Struggle for Freedom). The annual day commemorates slavery, slave resistance, and the main leader of the slave revolt in 1795, Tula, who was proclaimed a national hero in 2010.

16   Alejandro F. Paula, "Van slaaf tot quasi-slaaf: Een sociaal-historische studie over de dubbelzinnige slavenemancipatie op Nederlands Sint Maarten, 1816–1863" (Thesis, University of the Netherlands Antilles, 1992).

17   The Lago Oil and Transport Company owned and operated a refinery in Aruba. Lago Oil was a subsidiary of Standard Oil Company, United States, US, later known as Exxon Corporation, https://legacy.lib.utexas.edu/taro/utcah/03179/cah-03179.html.

18   Barry Heiligers, *Samen leven Curaçao in de twintigste eeuw* (Willemstad: Amigoe, 2001).

19   Valdemar Marcha and Paul Verweel, *The Culture of Fear in Curaçao: The Shackles of Fear and Silence; A Cultural Paradox* (Victor, BC: Trafford, 2008).

20   Rose Mary Allen, *Kas di pueblo: Kas ku un mishon / House with a Mission* (Curaçao: Fundashon Maria Liberia-Peters, 2019).

21   Margo Groenewoud, "Decolonisation, Otherness, and the Neglect of the Dutch Caribbean in Caribbean Studies", *Small Axe: A Caribbean Journal of Criticism*, vol. 25, no. 1, 2021, pp. 102–115.

22   Lasana M. Sekou, Oswald Francis, and Napolina Gumbs (eds.), *The Independence Papers*, vol. I. *Readings on a New Political Status for St Maarten/St Martin* (Philipsburg, St Martin: House of Nehesi, 1990).

23   William Anderson and Dynes Russell, "The Organizational and Political Transformation of a Social Movement: A Study of the 30th of May Movement in Curaçao", Working Paper 39, Disaster Research Centre, Ohio State University, 1973.

24   Alejandro F. Paula had already addressed some of these identity-related issues, arguing that slavery had left many Afro-Curaçaoans with internalised standards of self-denial,

rootlessness, and a conflicted sense of identity. See Alejandro Felipe Paula, *From Objective to Subjective Social Barriers: A Historico-Philosophical Analysis of Certain Negative Attitudes among the Negroid Population of Curaçao* (De Curaçaosche Courant NV, 1968), pp. 31–32. Angela Roe's study shows the persistent habit of ranking people based on ethnicity and colour/race. See Angela Roe, "The Sound of Silence: Ideology of National Identity and Racial Inequality in Contemporary Curaçao" (PhD dissertation, Florida International University, 2016).

25   St Eustatius was the only island of the Dutch Antilles federation that voted, in its 2005 referendum, to maintain the federation. As all the other islands chose to leave the federation, subsequent negotiations led to the federation's dismantling and St Eustatius ended up as an overseas municipality of the Netherlands, even though its people had never chosen this option in a referendum.

26   Michael Orlando Sharpe, "Extending Post-colonial Sovereignty Games: The Multilevel Negotiation of Autonomy and Integration in the 2010 Dissolution of the Netherlands Antilles and Dutch Kingdom Relations", *Ethnopolitics*, vol. 21, no. 3, 2020, pp. 299–324.

27   Gert Jan Oostindie and Peter Verton, *Ki sorto di Reino? Visies en verwachtingen van Antillianen en Arubanen omtrent het Koninkrijk (What Kind of Kingdom?)* (The Hague: Sdu Uitgevers, 1998).

28   Wouter P. Veenendaal, *Eindrapport CCC-opinieonderzoek: Aruba, Bonaire, Curaçao, Saba and St. Eustatius* (Leiden: Royal Netherlands Institute of Southeast Asian and Caribbean Studies, 2016).

29   See the cultural policy paper approved by the government of Curaçao in 2001 titled *Rumbo pa Independensia Mental: "Konosé bo Historia i Kultura pa bo Konosé bo Mes", Plan di Maneho i Akshon di Kultura pa Kòrsou* [Toward Mental Independence: 'Know Your History and Culture So as to Know Yourself', Cultural Policy and Action Plan for Curaçao]. It was drafted by René Rosalia, one of the vocal intellectuals promoting Afro-Curaçaoan culture, and a passionate advocate of political sovereignty and independence.

30   Groenewoud, "Decolonisation, Otherness, and the Neglect of the Dutch Caribbean in Caribbean Studies".

31   Anthony Faiola and Ana Vanessa Herrero, "Racial Reckoning in the Caribbean: Former Colony Confronts the Netherlands over Coronavirus Aid Conditions", *Washington Post*, https://www.washingtonpost.com/world/the_americas/coronavirus-sint-maarten-netherlands/2021/03/10/d2f58bea-80e9-11eb-81db-b02f0398f49a_story. html; and "Two Caribbean Islands Wrestle with Their Colonial Powers", *The Economist*, https://www.economist.com/the-americas/2021/05/20/two-caribbean-islands-wrestle-with-their-colonial-powers.

32   Lammert de Jong and Dirk Kruijt (eds.), *Extended Statehood in the Caribbean: Paradoxes of Quasi Colonialism, Local Autonomy, and Extended Statehood in the USA, French, Dutch, and British Caribbean* (Amsterdam: Rozenberg Publishers, 2005).

33   Wouter P. Veenendaal and Gert Jan Oostindie, "Head versus Heart: The Ambiguities of Non-Sovereignty in the Dutch Caribbean", *Regional and Federal Studies*, vol. 28, no. 1, 2018, pp. 25–45.

34   Rose Mary Allen, "The Complexity of National Identity Construction in Curaçao, Dutch Caribbean", *European Review of Latin American and Caribbean Studies / Revista Europea de Estudios Latinoamericanos y del Caribe*, vol. 89, 2010, pp. 117–125;

and Margo Groenewoud, "Daar ligt mijn navelstreng: Cultuur tussen insularisme en transnationalisme", in Maxime van Haeren, Jack van der Leden, and André Nuchelmans (eds.), *Cultuur in het Caribisch deel van het Koninkrijk*, special issue of *Boekman*, vol. 128, no. 33, 2021, pp. 4–9.

35   Sharpe, "Extending Post-colonial Sovereignty Games".

36   H. Adlai Murdock, "Creole Counter Discourses and French Departmental Hegemony", in Jerome Branche (ed.), *Race, Colonialism, and Social Transformation in Latin America and the Caribbean* (Gainesville: University Press of Florida, 2008), p. 258.

37   Yarimar Bonilla, *Non-sovereign Futures: French Caribbean Politics in the Wake of Disenchantment* (Chicago: University of Chicago Press, 2015); and Branche, *Race, Colonialism, and Social Transformation in Latin America and the Caribbean*.

Chapter 23. Colonialism in South America

1   Horst Pietechmann, "Estado y conquistadores, las capitulaciones", *Historia*, vol. 22, 1987, pp. 249–262.

2   José de la Puente Brunke, *Encomienda y encomenderos en el Perú* (Sevilla: Diputación Provincial de Sevilla, 1992); and Robert Himmerich y Valencia, *The Encomenderos of New Spain, 1521–1555* (Austin: University of Texas Press, 1991).

3   Hans Koning and Bill Bigelow, *Columbus: His Enterprise; Exploding the Myth* (New York: New York University and Monthly Review Press, 1991); J.J. Barry, *Life of Christopher Columbus* (Fitzwilliam, NH: Loreto Publications, 1917); and Björn Landström, *Columbus: The Story of Don Cristóbal Colón* (New York: Macmillan, 1967), especially pp. 44–45.

4   Bernabé Cobo, *A History of the Inca Empire* (Austin: University of Texas Press, 1979 [1653]), pp. 47–48.

5   Carl Sauer, *The Early Spanish Main* (Berkeley: University of California Press, 1966), pp. 96, 102, 150, 161, 170, and 193.

6   Ronald D. Hussey, "Text of the Laws of Burgos (1512–13) Concerning the Treatment of the Indians", *Hispanic American Historical Review*, vol. 12, no. 3, 1932, pp. 301–326.

7   Patricia Seed, *Ceremonies of Possession in Europe's Conquest of the New World, 1492–1640* (Cambridge: Cambridge University Press, 1995), pp. 69–71.

8   Henry Stevens (ed.), *The New Laws of the Indies* (London: The Chisiwick Press, 1893).

9   John F. Richards, *Unending Frontier: An Environmental History of the Early Modern World* (Los Angeles: University of California Press, 2006), pp. 334–376; and Noble David Cook, *Demographic Collapse: Indian Peru, 1520–1620* (Cambridge: Cambridge University Press, 1982).

10   Sauer, *The Early Spanish Main*.

11   See Charles Gibson, *Spain in America* (New York: Harper and Row, 1966), pp. 100–101; and Clarence H. Haring, *Spanish Empire in America* (New York: Oxford University Press, 1947). The "master map" (*Padrón Real* or Royal Register and general sailing chart) was the official and secret Spanish master map that, after 1527, was used as a template for the maps present on all Spanish ships during the sixteenth century. Pilots could contribute to the map as exploration continued. The *Casa de Contratación* was responsible for revisions to the map.

12   On the administrative hierarchy in the Americas, see Susan E. Ramirez, "Institutions

of the Spanish American Empire in the Hapsburg Era", in Thomas H. Holloway (ed.), *A Companion to Latin American History* (Oxford: Blackwell Publishing, 2008), pp. 106–123; Charles Gibson, *Spain in America* (New York: Harper Torchbooks, 1966); Haring, *Spanish Empire in America*; and Mark Burkholder and D.S. Chandler, *From Impotence to Authority: The Spanish Crown and the American Audiencias, 1687–1808* (Colombia: University of Missouri Press, 1977). On viceroys specifically, see Lewis Hanke and Celso Rodríguez, *Los virreyes españoles en América durante el gobierno de la Casa de Austria: México*, 5 vols., and *Perú*, 7 vols., Biblioteca de Autores Españoles (Madrid: Ediciones Atlas, 1976–1980).

13   J.H. Parry, *The Audiencia of New Galicia in the Sixteenth Century: A Study in Spanish Colonial Government* (Cambridge: Cambridge University Press, 1948).

14   Herbert S. Klein, *American Finances of the Spanish Empire: Royal Income and Expenditures in Colonial Mexico, Peru, and Bolivia, 1680–1809* (Albuquerque: University of New Mexico Press, 1998).

15   On the relationship between the *encomienda* and the *corregimiento*, see Robert G. Keith, "Encomienda, Hacienda and Corregimiento", *Hispanic American Historical Review*, vol. 51, no. 3, 1971, pp. 431–446.

16   Julio Alemparte, *El cabildo en Chile colonial: Origenes municipales de la repúblicas hispanoamericanas* (Santiago: Ediciones de la Universidad de Chile, 1940); and Fredrick B. Pike, "The Municipality and the Systems of Checks and Balances in Spanish American Colonial Administration", *The Americas*, vol. 15, no. 2, 1958, pp. 139–158.

17   Ramirez, "Institutions of the Spanish American Empire in the Hapsburg Era"; and John Leddy Phelan, "Authority and Flexibility in the Spanish Imperial Bureaucracy", *Administrative Science Quarterly*, vol. 5, no. 1, 1960, pp. 47–65.

18   Peter Bakewell, *Miners of the Red Mountain* (Albuquerque: University of New Mexico Press, 1984).

19   Earl J. Hamilton, *American Treasure and the Price Revolution in Spain, 1501–1650* (Cambridge: Harvard University Press, 1934), pp. 34, 38, and 42.

20   Peter Bakewell, *A History of Latin America* (Massachusetts: Blackwell Publishing, 2004), pp. 187–188, 231 and 234–235.

21   Christoph Rosenmüller, *Corruption and Justice in Colonial Mexico, 1650–1756* (Cambridge: Cambridge University Press, 2019); Clarence H. Haring, *Trade and Navigation between Spain and the Indies in the Time of the Hapsburgs* (Cambridge: Harvard University Press, 1918); and Gervasio Artíñano y de Galácano, *Historia del comercio con las Indias durante el dominio de los Austurias* (Barcelona: Talleres de Oliva de Vilanova, 1917).

22   Peter H. Smith, "Political Legitimacy in Spanish America", in Richard Graham and Peter H. Smith (eds.), *New Approaches to Latin American History* (Austin: University of Texas Press, 1974), pp. 225–256.

23   Jacques A. Barbier, "The Culmination of the Bourbon Reforms, 1787–1792", *Hispanic American Historical Review*, vol. 57, 1977, pp. 51–68.

24   John Lynch, *Spanish Colonial Administration, 1782–1814: The Intendant System in the Viceroyalty of the Rio de la Plata* (London: University of London Press, 1958); John R. Fisher, *Government and Society in Colonial Peru: The Intendant System, 1784–1814* (London: Athlone Press, 1970); and Mark A. Burkholder, *Politics of a Colonial Career: José Baquíjano and the Audiencia of Lima* (Albuquerque: University of New Mexico

Press, 1980).

25 Ben Vinson III, *Bearing Arms for His Majesty* (Palo Alto: Stanford University Press, 2001); and Christon I. Archer, *The Army in Bourbon Mexico, 1760–1810* (Albuquerque: University of New *Mexico* Press, *1977).*

26 The first Pope to institutionalise the vow was Paul III in 1539.

27 James Seager, *The Chaco Mission Frontier* (Tucson: University of Arizona Press, 2000).

28 Catalina Vizcarra, "Markets and Hierarchies in Late Colonial Spanish America: Royal Tobacco Monopoly in the Viceroyalty of Peru, 1752–1813", *Journal of Economic History*, vol. 63, no. 2, 2003, pp. 541–545.

29 John R. Fisher, *Commercial Relations between Spain and Spanish America in the Era of Free Trade, 1778–1796* (Liverpool: University of Liverpool, 1985); John R. Fisher, "The Effects of Comercio Libre on the Economies of New Granada and Peru", in John R. Fisher, Allan Kuethe, and Anthony McFarlane (eds.), *Reform and Insurrection in Bourbon New Granada and Peru* (Baton Rouge: Louisiana State University Press, 1990), pp. 147–163; and John R. Fisher, "Imperial 'Free Trade' and the Hispanic Economy, 1778–96", *Journal of Latin American Studies*, vol. 13, 1981, pp. 21–56.

30 William Cohoon, "Information Empire: Communication Infrastructure and the State in Bourbon Peru, 1718–1821" (PhD dissertation, Texas Christian University, Fort Worth, Texas, 2020).

31 Klein, *American Finances of the Spanish Empire.*

32 Sergio Serulnikov, *Revolution in the Andes: The Age of Tupac Amaru* (Durham: Duke University Press, 2013); and Charles Walker, *The Tupac Amaru Rebellion* (Cambridge, MA: Belknap Press, 2014).

33 Leslie Bethell, *Colonial Brazil* (London: University of London Press, 1987); and Caio Prado Junior, *Colonial Background of Modern Brazil* (Berkeley: University of California Press, 1967).

34 Capistrano de Abreu, *Chapters of Brazil's Colonial History* (New York: Oxford University Press, 1997), p. 25.

35 Boris Fausto, *A Concise History of Brazil* (2nd edn, New York: Cambridge University Press, 2014), pp. 11–13.

36 Francis A. Dutra, "Duarte Coelho Pereira, First Lord-Proprietor of Pernambuco: The Beginnings of a Dynasty", *The Americas*, vol. 29, no. 4, April 1973, pp. 416–441; Peter Bakewell, *A History of Latin America* (Malden: Blackwell Publishers, 1997), pp. 306–307; and Stuart B. Schwartz, *Sugar Plantations in the Formation of Brazilian Society: Bahia, 1550–1835* (New York: Cambridge University Press, 1985), especially pp. 161, 165, and 189.

37 Stuart B. Schwartz, *Sovereignty and Society in Colonial Brazil: The High Court of Bahia and its Judges, 1609–1751* (Berkeley: University of California Press, 1973).

38 John Hemming, *Red Gold: The Conquest of the Brazilian Indians* (Cambridge: Harvard University Press, 1978). On the concept of "just wars", see Paul Ramsey, *The Just War, Force and Political Responsibility* (New York: Scribner, 1968).

39 Phyllis Emert, "Colonial Triangular Trade: An Economy Based on Human Misery", *Business History*, vol. 3, no. 1, pp. 1–7.

40 Matthew Edel, "The Brazilian Sugar Cycle of the Seventeenth Century and the Rise of West Indian Competition", *Caribbean Studies*, vol. 9, no. 1, April 1969, pp. 24–44.

41 Bailey W. Diffie, *A History of Colonial Brazil, 1500–1792* (Malabar: Robert E. Krieger

Publishing Company, 1987), p. 263.

42   He was in power from June 1808 to December 1813.

43   Judy Bieber Freitas, "Imperial Brazil: 1822–1889", in Thomas H. Holloway (ed.), *A Companion to Latin American History* (New Jersey: Wiley-Blackwell, 2010), pp. 230–246.

Chapter 24. The Struggle for Reparations in the Caribbean

1   See, for example, Hilary Beckles, "The Great Durban Betrayal: Global Africa, Reparations, and the End of Pan-Africanism", in Adekeye Adebajo (ed.), *The Pan-African Pantheon: Prophets, Poets, and Philosophers* (Johannesburg: Jacana, 2020), pp. 58–69.

2   Beckles, "The Great Durban Betrayal", pp. 58–69.

3   See, for example, Hilary Beckles, *Britain's Black Debt: Reparations for Caribbean Slavery and Native Genocide* (Kingston: University of the West Indies Press, 2013).

4   See *Caricom Ten Point Plan for Reparatory Justice*, www.caricom.org.

5   See, for example, John Torpey, *Making Whole What Has Been Smashed: On Reparations Politics* (Cambridge: Harvard University Press, 2006).

6   See, for example, Christopher Brown, *Moral Capital: Foundations of British Abolitionism* (Chapel Hill: University of North Carolina Press, 2006).

7   Sam Gruet, "Lloyd's of London 'Deeply Sorry' over Slavery Links", BBC, 8 November 2023, www.bbc.com.

8   Cited in Helen Pidd, "Justin Welby Defends £100m Fund to Address C of E's Past Links to Slavery", *The Guardian* (London), 9 April 2023, www.theguardian.com.

9   See Hilary Beckles, *How Britain Underdeveloped the Caribbean: A Reparation Response to Europe's Legacy of Plunder and Poverty* (Kingston: University of the West Indies Press, 2021).

10 See, for example, Ahmed N. Reid, "Royalty and Reparations: The British Royal Family and the Trade in Enslaved Africans", in Verene A. Shepherd, Henderson D. Carter, and Ahmed N. Reid (eds.), *Interrogating Injustices: Essays in Honour of Hilary McD. Beckles* (Kingston and Miami: Ian Randle Publishers, 2023), pp. 45–64.

11 Beckles, *How Britain Underdeveloped the Caribbean*.

12 Beckles, *How Britain Underdeveloped the Caribbean*.

13 For background, see Michael Martin and Marilyn Yaquinto (eds.), *Redress for Historical Injustices in the United States: On Reparations for Slavery, Jim Crow and Their Legacies* (Durham: Duke University Press, 2007).

14 Cited in Aamna Mohdin, "Clive Lewis Calls for UK to Negotiate Caribbean Slavery Reparations", *The Guardian* (London), 8 March 2023, www.theguardian.com.

15 For background, see Boris Bittker, *The Case for Black Reparations* (Boston: Beacon Press, 2003).

16 See, for example, Verene A. Shepherd, "Reparation and Diversity: Building an Inclusive Moment in the Caribbean", in Shepherd, Carter, and Reid, *Interrogating Injustices*, pp. 1024–1042.

17 Beckles, "The Great Durban Betrayal", pp. 58–69.

18 See "Time for Africa to Get Reparations – Ghana's President", *Africanews*, 2 August 2022, https://www.africanews.com/2022/08/02/time-for-africa-to-get-reparations-ghanas-president/.

19 See, for example, Nicholas Draper, *The Price of Emancipation: Slave Ownership,*

Compensation and British Society at the End of Slavery (Cambridge: Cambridge University Press, 2016).

20 See, for example, Paul Lashmar and Jonathan Smith, "My Forefathers Did Something Horribly Wrong: British Slave Owners' Family to Apologise and Pay Reparations", *The Observer*, 4 February 2023.

Chapter 25. The Struggle for Reparations in the United States

1   Thomas J. Davis, "Emancipation Rhetoric, Natural Rights, and Revolutionary New England: A Note on Four Black Petitions in Massachusetts, 1773–1777", *New England Quarterly*, vol. 62, no. 2, June 1989, pp. 248–263.

2   Ana Lucia Araujo, *Reparations for Slavery and the Slave Trade: A Transnational and Comparative History* (New York: Bloomsbury, 2017), pp. 49–50.

3   Araujo, *Reparations for Slavery and the Slave Trade*, pp. 49–50.

4   Andrew Weintraub, "The Economics of Lincoln's Proposal for Compensated Emancipation", *American Journal of Economics and Sociology*, vol. 32, no. 8, April 1973, p. 171.

5   William A. Darity Jr and A. Kirsten Mullen, *From Here to Equality: Reparations for Black Americans in the Twenty-First Century* (Chapel Hill: University of North Carolina Press, 2020), p. 98.

6   Darity and Mullen, *From Here to Equality*, p. 100.

7   Darity and Mullen, *From Here to Equality*, p. 102.

8   Akiko Ochiai, "The Port Royal Experiment Revisited: Northern Visions and the Land Question", *New England Quarterly*, vol. 74, no. 1, March 2001, p. 94.

9   Ochiai, "The Port Royal Experiment Revisited", p. 100.

10 Jeffrey R. Kerr-Ritchie, "Forty Acres, or, An Act of Bad Faith", in Michael T. Martin and Marilyn Yaquinto (eds.), *Redress for Historical Injustices in the United States: On Reparations, Slavery, Jim Crow, and Their Legacies* (Durham: Duke University Press, 2007), p. 223.

11 Ritchie, "Forty Acres, or, An Act of Bad Faith", p. 224.

12 This included a Congressional Bill to provide formerly enslaved with small payments and pensions in 1866. This bill was passed by the US Congress, but vetoed by President Andrew Johnson. Similarly, between 1890 and 1900, nine bills were presented to provide pensions for the formerly enslaved of African descent, but were struck down before they could be passed by Congress. See Melissa R. Michelson, "Black Reparations Movement: Public Opinion and Congressional Policy Making", *Journal of Black Studies*, vol. 32, no. 5, May 2002, pp. 575–576; Walter B. Hill, Jr, "The Ex-Slave Pension Movement: Some Historical and Genealogical Notes", *Negro History Bulletin*, Special Issue on Black Genealogy, vol. 59, no. 4, 1996, pp. 7–11.

13 Ritchie, "Forty Acres, or, An Act of Bad Faith", pp. 234–235.

14 Robert L. Allen, "Past Due: The African American Quest for Reparations", *Black Scholar*, vol. 28, no. 2, Summer 1998, p. 7.

15 Adjoa A. Aiyetoro, "The National Coalition of Blacks for Reparations in American (N'Cobra): Its Creation and Contribution to the Reparations Movement", in Raymond A. Winbush (ed.), *Should America Pay? Slavery and the Raging Debate on Reparations* (New York: HarperCollins Publishers, 2003), p. 209.

16 Mary Frances Berry, *My Face Is Black Is True: Callie House and the Struggle for Ex-Slave Reparations* (New York: Vintage, 2006); and Randall Robinson, *The Debt: What America Owes to Blacks* (New York: Dutton Press, 2000), p. 206.

17 While this has been discussed in several works, this is best outlined in Ta-Nehisi Coates, "The Case for Reparations: Two hundred fifty years of slavery. Ninety years of Jim Crow. Sixty years of separate but equal. Thirty-five years of racist housing policy. Until we reckon with our compounding moral debts, America will never be whole", *The Atlantic*, June 2014, https://www.theatlantic.com/magazine/archive/2014/06/the-case-for-reparations/361631/.

18 This is seen in the speeches and writings of Henry McNeal Turner, in the Georgia legislature, 3 September 1868. This is also seen when Henrietta Wood sued the man who sold her into slavery, Zebulon Ward, and was compensated to the tune of $20,000 in 1878. In 1920, the Universal Negro Improvement Association in their "Declaration of the Rights of the Negro People of the World" also demanded that they "place on record our most solemn determination to reclaim the treasures and possession of the vast continent of our forefathers". This was echoed by black leaders of the early twentieth century like Marcus Garvey and venerable Queen Mother Moore. See Allen, "Past Due", pp. 7–8.

19 Ewart Guinier, "The Negro Depression: A Warning for All America", *National Guardian*, 14 June 1950; and Address by Whitney M. Young Jr at the National Conference of the Urban League, New York, 1963.

20 Melissa R. Michelson, "Black Reparations Movement: Public Opinion and Congressional Policy Making", *Journal of Black Studies*, vol. 32, no. 5, May 2002, p. 576.

21 Martin Luther King Jr, "The American Negro: A Bill of Rights for the Disadvantaged", *New York Times*, 12 November 1967; and Denise M. Bostdorff and Steven R. Goldzwig, "History, Collective Memory, and the Appropriation of Martin Luther King, Jr: Reagan's Rhetorical Legacy", *Presidential Studies Quarterly*, vol. 35, no. 4, December, 2005, p. 667.

22 Allen, "Past Due", p. 8.

23 Keith Dye, "The Black Manifesto for Reparations in Detroit: Challenge and Response, 1969", *Michigan Historical Review*, vol. 35, no. 2, Fall 2008, p. 55.

24 "The Black Manifesto" in Martin and Yaquinto, *Redress for Historical Injustices in the United States*, pp. 593–599.

25 "The Black Manifesto", pp. 593–599.

26 "The Black Manifesto", pp. 593–599.

27 Robin D.G. Kelley, "A Day of Reckoning", in Martin and Yaquinto, *Redress for Historical Injustices in the United States*, pp. 212–213.

28 Allen, "Past Due", p. 9.

29 Allen, "Past Due", p. 10.

30 Boris I. Bittker, *The Case for Black Reparations* (Boston: Beacon Press, 2003) p. ix.

31 Bittker, *The Case for Black Reparations*, p. xiii.

32 Bittker, *The Case for Black Reparations*, p. 28.

33 Bittker, *The Case for Black Reparations*, p. 71.

34 Allen J. Davis, "A Historical Timeline of Reparations Payments Made from 1783 through 2023 by the United States Government, States, Cities, Religious Institutions, Universities, Corporations, and Communities", University of Massachusetts Library, last modified January 2023, https://guides.library.umass.edu/reparations.

35 Davis, "A Historical Timeline of Reparations Payments Made".

36 This is discussed in Robert Westley's "Many Billions Gone: Is It Time to Reconsider

the Case for Black Reparations?", in Raymond A. Winbush, (ed.), *Should America Pay? Slavery and the Raging Debate on Reparations* (New York: HarperCollins Publishers, 2003), pp. 108–134.

37   N'Cobra's history is chronicled in Aiyetoro, "The National Coalition of Blacks for Reparations in American (N'Cobra)", pp. 209–236.

38   Allen, "Past Due", p. 12.

39   Allen, "Past Due", p. 12.

40   Sheila Flemming-Hunter, "Conversations about Reparations for Blacks in America: A 21st Century Model in Civic Responsibility and Engagement", *Phylon*, vol. 53, no. 2, Winter 2016, p. 100.

41   John F. Harris, "Clinton Says US Wronged Africa", *Washington Post*, 25 March 1998, https://www.washingtonpost.com/archive/politics/1998/03/25/clinton-says-us-wronged-africa/ca090cd0-bdb8-4e33-9dfc-e66fdc2e59b6/.

42   Charles P. Henry, *Long Overdue: The Politics of Racial Reparations* (New York: New York University Press, 2007), p. 3.

43   Darity and Mullen, *From Here to Equality*, pp. 16–17.

44   Omar Jimenez and Rebekah Reiss, "Oklahoma judge dismisses Tulsa race massacre reparations case filed by last known survivors", CNN, 8 July 2023, https://www.cnn.com/2023/07/08/us/tulsa-race-massacre-reparations-case/index.html.

45   Ken Miller, "Judge: Tulsa Race Massacre Victims' Descendants Can't Sue", Associated Press, 4 August 2022.

46   Michael C. Dawson and Rovana Popoff, "Reparations: Justice and Greed in Black and White", *Du Bois Review*, vol. 1, no. 1, 2004, p. 11.

47   David Horowitz expands these arguments from his ad within the monograph *Uncivil Wars: The Controversy over Reparations for Slavery* (San Francisco: Encounter Books, 2002).

48   Examples of this include Raymond A. Winbush, *Should America Pay? Slavery and the Raging Debate on Reparations* (New York: Amistad, 2003); Roy L. Brooks, *Atonement and Forgiveness: A New Model for Black Reparations* (Berkeley: University of California Press, 2004); Alfred L. Brophy, *Reparations: Pro & Con* (Oxford: Oxford University Press, 2006); Henry, *Long Overdue;* Michael T. Martin and Marilyn Yaquinto, *Redress for Historical Injustices in the United States: On Reparations for Slavery Jim Crow and Their Legacies* (Durham: Duke University Press, 2007); Iris Marion Young, *Responsibility for Justice* (Oxford: Oxford University Press, 2011); Pamela Brandwein, *Rethinking the Judicial Settlement of Reconstruction* (Cambridge: Cambridge University Press, 2011); Ana Lucia Araujo, *Reparations for Slavery and the Slave Trade: A Transnational and Comparative History* (London: Bloomsbury Academic, 2017); Michael T. Martin and Marilyn Yaquinto (eds.), *Redress for Historical Injustices in the United States* (Durham: Duke University Press, 2017); and Darity and Mullen, *From Here to Equality*.

49   "Slavery and Justice: Report of the Brown University Steering Committee on Slavery and Justice", 2006, https://slaveryandjustice.brown.edu/sites/default/files/reports/SlaveryAndJustice2006.pdf.

50   "Slavery and Justice".

51   Leslie M. Harris, James T. Campbell, and Alfred L. Brophy (eds.), *Slavery and the University: Histories and Legacies* (Athens: University of Georgia Press, 2019), pp. vii–viii.

52   The President's Commission on Universities Studying Slavery, "Homepage",

accessed 1 January 2023, https://slavery.virginia.edu/universities-studying-slavery/.

53   Sarah J. Jackson, Moya Bailey, and Brooke Foucault Welles, *#Hashtag Activism: Networks of Race and Gender Justice* (Cambridge: Massachusetts Institute of Technology Press, 2020), p. 99.

54   Black Lives Matter, "About", accessed 1 January 2023, https://blacklivesmatter.com/about/.

55   Ta-Nehisi Coates, "The Case for Reparations", https://www.theatlantic.com/magazine/archive/2014/06/the-case-for-reparations/361631/.

56   James T. Campbell, Leslie M. Harris, and Alfred L. Brophy, "Introduction", in Harris, Campbell, and Alfred, *Slavery and the University*, pp. 1–2.

57   Lindsey K. Walters, "Slavery and the American University: Discourses of Retrospective Justice at Harvard and Brown", *Slavery & Abolition: A Journal of Slave and Post-Slave Studies*, vol. 38, no. 4, 2017, p. 737.

58   Katherine Shaver, "Georgetown University to Rename Two Buildings That Reflect School's Ties to Slavery", *Washington Post*, 15 November 2015, https://www.washingtonpost.com/local/georgetown-university-to-rename-two-buildings-that-reflect-schools-ties-to-slavery/2015/11/15/e36edd32-8bb7-11e5-acff-673ae92ddd2b_story.html.

59   Andy Newman and Vivian Wang, "Calhoun Who? Yale Drops Name of Slavery Advocate for Computer Pioneer", *New York Times*, 3 September 2017, https://www.nytimes.com/2017/09/03/nyregion/yale-calhoun-college-grace-hopper.html.

60   Jackson, Bailey, and Foucault Welles, *#Hashtag Activism*, p. 130.

61   Jackson, Bailey, and Foucault Welles, *#Hashtag Activism*, p. 124.

62   Reis Thebault, "Travon Martin's Death Set Off a Moment That Shaped a Decade's Defining Moments", *Washington Post*, 25 February 2022.

63   Davis, "A Historical Timeline of Reparations Payments Made", https://guides.library.umass.edu/reparations.

64   Will Wright, "Seminary Built on Slavery and Jim Crow Labor Has Begun Paying Reparations", *Washington Post*, 31 May 2021, https://www.nytimes.com/2021/05/31/us/reparations-virginia-theological-seminary.html.

65   Ed Shanahan, "$27 Million for Reparations over Slave Ties Pledged by Seminary", *New York Times*, 21 October 2019.

66   Davis, "A Historical Timeline of Reparations Payments Made".

67   David Paulsen, "As Dioceses Pursue Reparations, General Convention Poised for Churchwide Racial Justice Discussion", *Episcopal News Service*, 9 June 2022, https://www.episcopalnewsservice.org/2022/06/09/as-dioceses-pursue-reparations-general-convention-poised-for-churchwide-racial-justice-discussion/.

68   Nate Tinner-Williams, "Nikole Hannah-Jones Joins Delegation to Vatican Pressing for Slavery Reparations", *Black Catholic Messenger*, 20 July 2022, https://www.blackcatholicmessenger.com/reparations-delegation-at-vatican-07-2022/.

69   Kiran Misra, "Illinois City's Reparations Plan Was Heralded, but Locals Say It's a Cautionary Tale", *The Guardian* (London), 18 August 2021, https://www.theguardian.com/us-news/2021/aug/18/evanston-illinois-reparations-plan-cautionary-tale.

70   Neil Vigdor, "North Carolina City Approves Reparations for Black Residents", *New York Times*, 16 June 2020, https://www.nytimes.com/2020/07/16/us/reparations-asheville-nc.html.

71   Scott Merzbach, "Amherst Panel Backs New Fund for Reparations for Black Residents", *Amherst Bulletin*, 28 June 2021, https://www.amherstbulletin.com/Finance-Committee-in-Amherst-recommends-new-fund-for-reparations-for-Black-residents-40989888.

72   Kurtis Lee, "California Panel Calls for Billions in Reparations for Black Residents", *New York Times*, 6 May 2023, https://www.nytimes.com/2023/05/06/business/economy/california-reparations.html.

73   *California Task Force to Study and Develop Reparation Proposals for African Americans: Final Report*, https://oag.ca.gov/system/files/media/full-ca-reparations.pdf.

74   *California Task Force to Study and Develop Reparation Proposals for African Americans: Executive Summary*, https://www.oag.ca.gov/system/files/media/exec-summary-ca-reparations.pdf.

75   *San Francisco Reparations Plan 2023: A Submission from the San Francisco African American Reparations Advisory Committee*, https://sf.gov/sites/default/files/2023-07/AARAC%20Reparations%20Final%20Report%20July%207%2C%202023.pdf.

76   Task forces have appeared in Burlington (Vermont), Durham (North Carolina), Washington (District of Columbia), St Petersburg (Florida), Boston (Massachusetts), and St Paul (Minnesota). See Davis, "A Historical Timeline of Reparations Payments Made".

77   Charlie Innis, "Durham Calls for US Reparations for the Descendants of Enslaved People", *News & Observer*, 6 October 2020, https://www.newsobserver.com/news/local/counties/durham-county/article246245235.html. It should be noted that a 2021 Pew Research Center poll remarks that of those that support reparations, 75 per cent state that responsibility lies with the Federal Government. See Carrie Blazina and Kiana Cox, "Black and White Americans Are Far Apart in Their Views of Reparations for Slavery", Pew Research Center, https://www.pewresearch.org/short-reads/2022/11/28/black-and-white-americans-are-far-apart-in-their-views-of-reparations-for-slavery/.

78   H.R.40 – 118th Congress (2023–2024): Commission to Study and Develop Reparation Proposals for African Americans Act, 9 January 2023, https://www.congress.gov/bill/118th-congress/house-bill/40.

79   P.R. Lockhart, "America Is Having an Unprecedented Debate about Reparations. What Comes Next?", *Vox*, 20 June 2019, https://www.vox.com/identities/2019/6/20/18692949/congress-reparations-slavery-discrimination-hr-40-coates-glover.

80   "How Not to Repair America: California's Reparations Scheme Is Bad Policy and Worse Politics", *The Economist*, vol. 447, no. 9350, 10–16 June 2023, pp. 10–11; and Adekeye Adebajo, "Unmasking Anglo-Saxon Anti-Reparations", *Business Day* (South Africa), 3 July 2023.

Chapter 26. The Struggle for Reparations in Britain

1   This move was initiated by Rising Up, a network of activists committed to civil disobedience. For more information, see https://www.facebook.com/RisingUpUK/.

2   Esther Stanford-Xosei, "The Long Road of Pan-African Liberation to Reparatory Justice", in Hakim Adi (ed.), *British Black History: New Perspectives* (London: Zed Books, 2019), pp. 176–198.

3   Stanford-Xosei, "The Long Road of Pan-African Liberation to Reparatory Justice",

p. 177.

4 See, in particular, Eric Williams, *Capitalism and Slavery* (North Carolina: North Carolina Press, 1994).

5 Hilary McD. Beckles, *Britain's Black Debt: Reparations for Caribbean Slavery and Native Genocide* (Jamaica: University of the West Indies Press, 2013), p. 3.

6 Beckles, *Britain's Black Debt*, p. 21.

7 See, for example, Hugh Tinker, *A New System of Slavery: Export of Indian Labour Overseas, 1830-1920* (Oxford: Oxford University Press, 1974).

8 Kris Manjapra, "When Will Britain Face Up to its Crimes against Humanity", *The Guardian* (London), 29 March 2018, https://www.theguardian.com/news/2018/mar/29/slavery-abolition-compensation-when-will-britain-face-up-to-its-crimes-against-humanity (accessed 18 September 2020).

9 Marcus Wood, *The Horrible Gift of Freedom: Atlantic Slavery and the Representation of Emancipation* (Georgia: University of Georgia Press, 2010), pp. 9–10.

10 Wood, *The Horrible Gift of Freedom*, p. 10.

11 University College London, Legacies of British Slave-Ownership, https://www.ucl.ac.uk/lbs/ (accessed 18 September 2020).

12 David Olusoga, "The History of British Slave Ownership Has Been Buried: Now Its Scale Can Be Revealed", *The Guardian* (London), 12 July 2015, https://www.theguardian.com/world/2015/jul/12/british-history-slavery-buried-scale-revealed (accessed 11 February 2020).

13 Beckles, *Britain's Black Debt*, p. 201.

14 For more on the bicentenary, see Wood, *The Horrible Gift of Freedom*, pp. 296–353.

15 David Smith, "200 Years on, the Queen Is Told to Say Sorry for Britain's Role in Slave Trade", *The Guardian* (London), 5 December 2004.

16 Smith, "200 Years on".

17 Patrick Wintour, "Blair Fights Shy of Full Apology for Slave Trade", *The Guardian*, 27 November 2006, https://www.theguardian.com/politics/2006/nov/27/uk.race (accessed 4 January 2021).

18 Kehinde Andrews, "The Psychosis of Whiteness: The Celluloid Hallucinations of Amazing Graze and Belle", *Journal of Black Studies*, vol. 47, 2016, pp. 443–444.

19 Andrews, "The Psychosis of Whiteness", p. 447.

20 Andrews, "The Psychosis of Whiteness".

21 Full details of the ten-point plan can be found on the Caricom website: "CARICOM Ten Point Plan for Reparatory Justice", https://caricom.org/caricom-ten-point-plan-for-reparatory-justice/ (accessed 9 November 2020).

22 Michel-Rolph Trouillot, *Silencing the Past: Power and the Production of History* (Boston: Beacon Press, 1995).

23 Maatubuntumitawo-Global Afrikan Family Reunion International Council was responsible for proposing and initiating work on the "Pan-African Reparatory Justice Law of Holistic Rematriation/Repatriation" in response to the desire of rematriation coming from the diaspora.

24 See Adekeye Adebajo, *The Pan-African Pantheon: Prophets, Poets, and Philosophers* (Johannesburg: Jacana, 2020; and Manchester: Manchester University Press, 2021).

25 See, for example, Adi's definition in Hakim Adi, "Introduction", *British Black History*, pp. 1–14.

26 Cited in Stanford-Xosei, *The Long Road of Pan-African Liberation to Reparatory*

Justice, p. 181.

27   Cited in Stanford-Xosei, *The Long Road of Pan-African Liberation to Reparatory Justice*, p. 181.

28   Walter Rodney, *How Europe Underdeveloped Africa* (Baltimore: Black Classic Press, 2011 [1972]), p. 81.

29   Note that the original letter is referenced in John Atkins's account of *A Voyage to Guinea, Brasil and the West Indies; in His Majesty's Ships, the Swallow and Weymouth* (London: Ward and Chandler, 1735), https://archive.org/details/voyagetoguineabr00atki/page/n7 (accessed 10 July 2019). In this text, Atkins describes Agaja's (the King of Dahomey) conquest as motivated by a desire to rescue his own people from slavery and as having waged a revolution against the "Slave Trade"; Atkins, *Voyage*, pp. 119–122. It is for this reason that Akinjogbin describes Agaja as a leader inspired by a desire to put an end to slavery (despite the fact that, in later life, Agaja was forced back into trafficking as a means of self-defence); I.A. Akinjogbin, *Dahomey and Its Neighbours, 1708–1818* (Cambridge: Cambridge University Press, 1967). Note that the translation of the original letter that arrived several years later in Britain, and was presented before Parliament, was deemed to be a fraud, suggesting that Bulfinch Lambe had betrayed Agaja's proposal. See Robin Law, "Further Light on Bulfinch Lambe and the 'Emperor of Pawpaw': King Agaja of Dahomey's Letter to King George I of England, 1726", *History in Africa*, vol. 17, 1990, pp. 211–226.

30   Stanford-Xosei, *The Long Road of Pan-African Liberation to Reparatory Justice*, p. 183.

31   Quobna Ottobah Cugoano, *Thoughts and Sentiments on the Evil and Wicked Traffic of the Slavery and Commerce of the Human Species, etc.* (London and New York: Penguin Books, 1999 [1787]).

32   Stanford-Xosei, *The Long Road of Pan-African Liberation to Reparatory Justice*, p. 184.

33   See also Hakim Adi and Marika Sherwood, *The 1945 Manchester Pan-African Congress Revisited* (London: New Beacon, 1995).

34   Rhoda E. Howard-Hassmann, "Reparations to Africa and the Group of Eminent Persons", *Cahier d'Études Africaines*, vol. 44, 2004, pp. 81–97.

35   "The Abuja Proclamation", http://ncobra.org/resources/pdf/TheAbujaProclamation.pdf (accessed 22 August 2017).

36   Michael T. Martin and Marilyn Yaquinto, "Reparations for 'America's Holocaust': Activism for Global Justice", *Race and Class*, vol. 45, 2004, pp. 1–25.

37   Bernie Grant, "Early Day Motion 1987: Abuja Proclamation", 10 May 1993, http://www.parliament.uk/business/publications/business-papers/commons/early-day-motions/edm-detail1/?edmnumber=1987&session=1992-93 (accessed 22 August 2017).

38   Africa Reparations Movement UK, "Birmingham Declaration", 1 January 1994, https://www.inosaar.llc.ed.ac.uk/sites/default/files/atoms/files/1994_birmingham_declaration.pdf (accessed 4 January 2021).

39   Stanford-Xosei, "The Long Road of Pan-African Liberation to Reparatory Justice", p. 186.

40   Office of the United Nations High Commissioner for Human Rights, "Basic Principles and Guidelines on the Right to a Remedy and Reparation for Victims of Gross Violations of International Human Rights Law and Serious Violations of International Humanitarian Law", 16 December 2005, https://www.ohchr.org/EN/ProfessionalInterest/Pages/RemedyAndReparation.aspx (accessed 10 November

2020).

41   The human rights law firm Leigh Day won a case on behalf of the Kenyan Mau Mau for the atrocities perpetrated against them during the anti-colonial uprising (1952–1963). The British government was ordered to pay £19.9 million in compensation to over 5,000 claimants, amounting to £3,980 per person. Alex Wessely, "The Mau Mau Case: Five Years On", 6 October 2017, https://www.leighday.co.uk/Blog/October-2017/Kenyan-colonial-abuses-apology-five-years-on (accessed 6 November 2020).

42   Maulana Karenga, "The Ethics of Reparations: Engaging the Holocaust of Enslavement", The National Coalition of Blacks for Reparations in America (NCOBRA) Convention, Baton Rouge, Louisiana, 22 June to 23 June 2001, http://ncobra.org/resources/pdf/Karenga%20-THE%20ETHICS%20OF%20REPARATIONS.pdf (accessed 6 November 2020).

43   Ubuntudunia (Ubuntu+dunia) is a combined Nguni and Kiswahili word which means a Multipolar World of Global Justice.

44   Coined from the conjunction of "Maat" (the holistic justice concept from Kemet, ancient Egypt) with "Ubuntu" (the Bantu concept of the communion of humanity from southern Africa) and "Oman" (the Akan concept of egalitarian polity from West Africa), Maatubuntuman promotes the concept of a Global African polity ("Oman"), which is an organic embodiment of "Maat" and therefore practises "Ubuntu" in relation to her own citizens and the entirety of Humanity, Mother Earth, and the Universe.

45   Open meetings were held in London between 2005 and 2007, and the group produced the 2007 Cross-Community e-bulletin three times a year, including comment pieces about the significance of 2007. Task action groups were set up such as the Cross-Community Dialogue Action Group on Education (CCODAGE), jointly hosted by the Council for Education in World Citizenship and the School of Education at Kingston University. A Global Justice Forum was developed out of the 2007 cross-community forums in order to advance this work beyond 2007. Antislavery Usable Past, http://antislavery.ac.uk/items/show/497 (accessed 9 November 2020).

46   UNESCO's Associated Schools Project, "Breaking the Silence: The Transatlantic Slave Trade Educational Project", 2004, https://unesdoc.unesco.org/ark:/48223/pf0000137805 (accessed 18 September 2020).

47   Home Office, "Commemorating the Struggle Against Slavery and Its Abolition", 12 August 2004, http://www.ligali.org/pdf/Commemorating%20The%20Struggle%20Against%20Slavery%20And%20Its%20Abolition.pdf (accessed 9 November 2020).

48   "Struggle Against Slavery", 14 October 2004, Hansard, col. 143WH, https://publications.parliament.uk/pa/cm200304/cmhansrd/vo041014/halltext/41014h01.htm (accessed 9 November 2020).

49   Stanford-Xosei, "The Long Road of Pan-African Liberation to Reparatory Justice", p. 188. Stanford-Xosei was part of the ten-member Central Organising Committee that planned the African and African Descendants World Conference Against Racism and coordinated Britain's delegation of over 80 delegates to attend this conference.

50   Stanford-Xosei, "The Long Road of Pan-African Liberation to Reparatory Justice", p. 188.

51   Stanford-Xosei, "The Long Road of Pan-African Liberation to Reparatory Justice",

p. 188.

52   Stanford-Xosei, "The Long Road of Pan-African Liberation to Reparatory Justice",
      p. 188.

53   Stanford-Xosei, "The Long Road of Pan-African Liberation to Reparatory Justice",
      p. 189.

54   "The Queen and Law", https://www.royal.uk/queen-and-law (accessed 26 June
      2019).

55   Kofi Mawuli Klu, "Charting an Afrikan Self-Determined Path of Legal Struggle for
      Reparations", draft paper for presentation at the Birmingham Working Conference of
      the Africa Reparations Movement, UK, 11 December 1993.

56   Stop the Maangamizi, "Backgrounder: About the All-Party Parliamentary
      Commission of Inquiry for Truth and Reparatory Justice", 17 October 2020,
      https://stopthemaangamizi.com/2020/10/17/about-the-all-party-parliamentary-
      commission-of-inquiry-for-truth-reparatory-justice-appcitarj/   (accessed   30
      September 2022).

57   Kim Pamela Stanton, "Truth Commissions and Public Enquiries: Investigating
      Historical Injustices in Established Democracies" (Thesis submission, University
      of Toronto 2010), https://tspace.library.utoronto.ca/bitstream/1807/24886/1/
      Stanton_Kim_P_201006_SJD_thesis.pdf. See also Jeremy Sarkin (ed.), *The Global
      Impact and Legacy of Truth Commissions* (Cambridge: Intersentia, 2019).

58   Stop the Maangamizi, "About the All-Party Parliamentary Commission of Inquiry
      for Truth and Reparatory Justice (APPCITARJ)", 12 October 2015, https://
      stopthemaangamizi.com/2015/10/12/about-the-commission-of-inquiry-appcitarj/.

59   "Stop the Maangamizi: We Charge Genocide/ Ecocide Petition", https://www.
      change.org/p/stop-the-maangamizi-we-charge-genocide-ecocide. In 2018, the
      campaign received a response from Lord Ahmad of Wimbledon, Minister for the
      Commonwealth, which also rejected reparations, stating that "The United Nations
      General Assembly Resolution 60/147 of 16 December 2005 and the Rome Statute
      of the International Criminal Court … were not negotiated with the intention of
      being applied to historic events such as the Transatlantic slave trade". Letter from
      the Foreign and Commonwealth Office, 25 March 2018, https://stopthemaangamizi.
      com/2018/04/06/response-to-stop-the-maangamizi-petition-from-fco-minister-
      lord-ahmad/ (accessed 9 November 2020).

60   "Motion 5: Labour/Green: Atonement and Reparations for the United Kingdom's
      Transatlantic Traffic in Enslaved Africans", 15 July 2020, https://moderngov.
      lambeth.gov.uk/mgAi.aspx?ID=46459 (accessed 23 October 2020).

61   Stop the Maangamizi, "M.E.T. Proposal for the APPG on African Reparations
      (APPGAR)", 23 September 2021, https://stopthemaangamizi.com/2021/09/23/m-
      e-t-proposal-for-the-appg-on-african-reparations/ (accessed 7 October 2021).

62   Afrikan Reparations APPG, 17 November 2021, https://www.parallelparliament.
      co.uk/APPG/afrikan-reparations (accessed 3 October 2022).

63   Hilary Beckles, symposium on "Restorative Justice and Societal Repair: Global Racism
      and Reparations", 21 February 2020, Boston University. In his book, Beckles also
      points to the antagonisms between activists and scholars, the latter having repeatedly
      been engaged by state officials to provide them with "scholarly ammunition … to
      deny and deflect culpability". Beckles, *Britain's Black Debt*, pp. 12–13. In Britain, the
      International Network of Scholars and Activists for Afrikan Reparations (INOSAAR)

network was created precisely to challenge and overcome these historical tensions and develop strong alliances between academics and activists. INOSAAR, "Global Report", September 2019, https://www.inosaar.llc.ed.ac.uk/sites/default/files/atoms/files/inosaar_global_report_sept_2019_final.pdf (accessed 27 October 2020).

64   Extinction Rebellion Internationalist Solidarity Network (XRISN), https://www.xrisn.earth/ (accessed 9 November 2020).

65   Esther Stanford-Xosei, "Why I as a Reparations Activist Participated on XR's Rebellion Day", 10 June 2020, https://www.xrisn.earth/post/why-i-as-a-reparations-activist-participated-on-xrs-rebellion-day (accessed 10 November 2020).

Chapter 27. The Struggle for Reparations in Africa

1   Colin Legum, *Pan-Africanism* (London: Pall Mall Press, 1962).

2   See, for example, Adekeye Adebajo, *The Curse of Berlin: Africa after the Cold War* (New York: Oxford University Press, 2013 [2010]; Hurst: London, 2010; and Scottsville: University of KwaZulu-Natal Press, 2010).

3   J.F. Ade Ajayi, "The Crusade for Reparations", in Toyin Falola (ed.), *Tradition and Change in Africa: The Essays of J.F. Ade Ajayi* (Trenton and Asmara: Africa World Press, 2000), p. 339.

4   Ajayi, "The Crusade for Reparations", p. 346.

5   Ajayi, "The Crusade for Reparations", p. 344.

6   Ajayi, "The Crusade for Reparations", pp. 337–349.

7   Ali A. Mazrui, *Black Reparations in the Era of Globalization* (Binghamton: Institute of Global Cultural Studies, 2002), p. 88.

8   Figure cited in "Evolution of Debt Landscape over the Past 10 Years in Africa: Keynote Speech by Dr Akinwumi A. Adesina, President, African Development Bank Group, delivered at the Paris Club, June 20, 2023", https://www.afdb.org/en/news-and-events/speeches/evolution-debt-landscape-over-past-10-years-africa-keynote-speech-dr-akinwumi-adesina-president-african-development-bank-group-delivered-paris-club-june-20-2023-62308.

9   Mazrui, *Black Reparations in the Era of Globalization*, pp. 61–68.

10   Quoted in Hakim Adi, *Pan-Africanism: A History* (London: Bloomsbury, 2018), p. 218.

11   Cited in Mazrui, *Black Reparations in the Era of Globalization*, p. 135.

12   Cited in Mazrui, *Black Reparations in the Era of Globalization*, p. 136.

13   See the OAU Abuja Declaration, 27–29 April 1993, http://www.shaka.mistral.co.uk/abujaProclamation.htm.

14   "The Accra Declaration on Reparations and Repatriation", 12 August 1999, reproduced in Mazrui, *Black Reparations in the Era of Globalization*, pp. 139–143.

15   See, for example, Chandra Lekha Sriram and Suren Pillay (eds.), *Peace versus Justice? The Dilemma of Transitional Justice in Africa* (Scottsville: University of KwaZulu-Natal Press, 2009).

16   Wole Soyinka, *The Burden of Memory, the Muse of Forgiveness* (Oxford and New York: Oxford University Press, 1999), pp. 12–22; 45; 63–64.

17   Soyinka, *The Burden of Memory*, p. 86.

18   Soyinka, *The Burden of Memory*, p. 38.

19   Soyinka, *The Burden of Memory*, p. 39.

20   Soyinka, *The Burden of Memory*, pp. 83–85.

21   Cited in Adi, *Pan-Africanism*, pp. 219–220.

22   See Adekeye Adebajo, "Thabo Mbeki: The Pan-African Philosopher-King", in Adekeye Adebajo (ed.), *The Pan-African Pantheon: Prophets, Poets, and Philosophers* (Johannesburg: Jacana, 2020), pp. 167–181.

23   Thabo Mbeki, "Ending Racism in the World", World Conference Against Racism, Racial Discrimination, Xenophobia and Related Intolerance, Durban, 31 August 2001, in Thabo Mbeki, *Mahube: The Dawning of the Dawn; Speeches, Lectures, and Tributes* (Braamfontein: Skotaville Media, 2001), pp. 129–130.

24   Mbeki, "Ending Racism in The World", p. 130.

25   Hilary Beckles, "The Great Durban Betrayal: Global Africa, Reparations, and the End of Pan-Africanism", in Adebajo, *The Pan-African Pantheon*, pp. 58–69.

26   Beckles, "The Great Durban Betrayal", pp. 64–65.

27   Adom Getachew, "Reparations and the Recasting of Eric Williams's *Capitalism and Slavery*", *Items*, 22 February 2017, https://items.ssrc.org/reading-racial-conflict/reparations-and-the-recasting-of-eric-williamss-capitalism-and-slavery/.

28   On the concept of "global apartheid", see, for example, Ali Mazrui, "Global Apartheid: Structural and Overt", *Alternatives: Global, Local, Political*, vol. 19, no. 2, Spring 1994, pp. 185–187; and Adekeye Adebajo (ed.), *From Global Apartheid to Global Village: Africa and the United Nations* (Scottsville: University of KwaZulu-Natal Press, 2009).

29   The information in this and the preceding paragraph was drawn from United Nations, "World Conference Against Racism, Racial Discrimination, Xenophobia and Related Intolerance Declaration and Programme of Action", UN Department of Public Information, 2002, chrome-extension://efaidnbmnnnibpcajpcglclefindmkaj/https://www.ohchr.org/sites/default/files/Documents/Publications/Durban_text_en.pdf.

30   Beckles, "The Great Durban Betrayal", pp. 58–69.

31   See "President Akufo-Addo Holds Bilateral Discussions with Prime Minister Mottley", https://www.facebook.com/nakufoaddo/videos/video-president-akufo-addo-holds-bilateral-discussions-with-prime-minister-mia-m/344273466190392/.

32   Ray Chickrie, "Ghana's President Promotes 'Year of Return' to Five Caribbean Nations", *VisitGhana*, 18 June 2019, https://visitghana.com; and Paul Williams, "Ghanaian President Urges Stronger Trade, Ancestral Ties", *The Gleaner* (Jamaica), 19 June 2019.

33   African Union, "Building a United Front to Promote the Cause of Justice and Payment of Reparations to Africans", Executive Council, 44th Ordinary Session, 15 January – 15 February 2024, Addis Ababa, Ethiopia, EX.CL/1501 (XLIV), annex, p. 2.

34   Cited in Amelia Gentleman, "Africa and Caribbean Nations Agree Move to Seek Reparations for Slavery", *The Guardian* (London), 17 November 2023, www.theguardian.com.

35   Cited in Gentleman, "Africa and Caribbean Nations Agree Move to Seek Reparations for Slavery".

36   Cited in African Union, "Building a United Front to Promote the Cause of Justice and Payment of Reparations to Africans", p. 3.

37   African Union, "Building a United Front to Promote the Cause of Justice and Payment of Reparations to Africans", pp. 1–8.

38   African Union, "Building a United Front to Promote the Cause of Justice and

Payment of Reparations to Africans", pp. 1–9, and annex.

39 African Union, "Concept Note on the African Union Theme of the Year for 2025", 45th Ordinary Session of the Executive Council, EX.CL/1528 (XLV) Rev.1, 19 June – 19 July 2024, Accra, Ghana.)

40 This paragraph and the one below benefited from Piers Brendon, "The Kaiser's Holocaust by David Olusoga and Casper W. Erichsen: Review", *The Guardian* (London), 4 December 2010; David Olusoga, "Germany Comes to Terms with Its Forgotten Namibian Death Camps", *The Guardian* (London), 15 January 2017; Norimitsu Onishi and Melissa Eddy, "A Forgotten Genocide: What Germany Did in Namibia, and What It's Saying", *New York Times*, 28 May 2021; European Centre for Constitutional and Human Rights, "The 'Reconciliation Agreement': A Lost Opportunity", June 2021; and Joint Declaration by the Federal Republic of Germany and the Republic of Namibia, "United in Remembrance of Our Colonial Past, United in Our Will to Reconcile, United in Our Vision of the Future", June 2021.

41 Quoted in Jermain Ostiana, "Why the Dutch Apology for Slavery Leaves a Bitter Taste in My Mouth", *The Guardian* (London), 14 January 2023.

42 Quoted in Donna Ferguson, "Dutch King Apologises for Country's Historical Involvement in Slavery", *The Guardian* (London), 1 July 2023.

43 Cited in Ferguson, "Dutch King Apologises for Country's Historical Involvement in Slavery".

44 On France, see Frantz Fanon, *The Wretched of the Earth* (New York: Grove Press, 1963 [1961]); Alistair Horne, *A Savage War of Peace: Algeria, 1954–1962* (London: Macmillan, 1977); Guy Martin, *Africa in World Politics: A Pan-African Perspective* (Asmara: Africa World Press, 2002); and Victor T. Le Vine, *Politics in Francophone Africa* (Boulder: Lynne Rienner, 2007).

45 On Britain, see Caroline Elkins, *Legacy of Violence: A History of the British Empire* (New York: Alfred A. Knopf, 2022); Paul Maylam, *The Cult of Rhodes: Remembering an Imperialist in Africa* (Cape Town: David Philip, 2005); Stanlake Samkange, *What Rhodes Really Said about Africans* (Harare: Harare Publishing House, 1982); and Antony Thomas, *Rhodes: The Race for Africa* (Johannesburg: Jonathan Ball, 1996).

46 See Adam Hochschild, *King Leopold's Ghost: A Story of Greed, Terror, and Heroism in Colonial Africa* (London: Pan Macmillan, 1998).

47 See, for example, Miguel Bandeira Jerónimo, "Portuguese Colonialism in Africa", *Oxford Research Encyclopedia of African History* (Oxford: Oxford University Press, 2018); and Warwick Anderson, Ricardo Roque, and Ricardo Ventura Santos (eds.), *Luso-Tropicalism and Its Discontents* (Oxford and New York: Berghahn Books, 2019),

48 See, for example, Ali Abdullatif Ahmida, *Genocide in Libya: Shar, a Hidden Colonial History* (London and New York: Routledge, 2021); Bahru Zewde, *A History of Modern Ethiopia, 1855–1974* (Addis Ababa: Addis Ababa University Press, 1991); Ian Campbell, *The Addis Ababa Massacre: Italy's National Shame* (Oxford: Oxford University Press, 2017); and Giulia Barrera, "Dangerous Liaisons: Colonial Concubinage in Eritrea, 1890–1941", Northwestern University, Programme of African Studies Working Papers 1, 1996.

49 See, for example, Sebastian Balfour, *Deadly Embrace: Morocco and the Road to the Spanish Civil War* (Oxford: Oxford University Press, 2002); and Yolanda Aixelà-Cabré, "Colonial Memories and Contemporary Narratives from the Rif: Spanishness, Amazighness, and Moroccaness Seen from Al-Hoceima and Spain", *Interventions:*

International Journal of Postcolonial Studies, 21, 6, 2018, pp. 856–873.

50   See, for example, Adekeye Adebajo, "The Shadows of Empire: African Perceptions of Europe and the EU", in Christopher Hill, Michael Smith, and Sophie Vanhoonacker (eds.), *International Relations and the European Union* (4th edn, Oxford: Oxford University Press, 2023), pp. 259–280.

Chapter 28. The Struggle for Reparations in Latin America

1   Margaret Popkin and Naomi Roht-Arriaza, "Truth as Justice: Investigatory Commissions in Latin America", *Law and Social Inquiry*, vol. 20, no. 1, 1995, pp. 79–116.

2   Popkin and Roht-Arriaza, "Truth as Justice", p. 86.

3   Popkin and Roht-Arriaza, "Truth as Justice", p. 105.

4   Charles River Editors, *The Arawak: The History and Legacy of the Indigenous Natives in South America and the Caribbean* (Kindle edition, 2019), p. 34.

5   Sarah Deer, *The Beginning and End of Rape* (Minneapolis: University of Minnesota Press, 2015).

6   The United Nations Declaration on the Rights of Indigenous Peoples, 2007, Article 11:2, p. 6.

7   The Declaration was supported by 144 members, 4 objected, and 11 abstained. Subsequently 4 countries changed their votes to support the declaration.

8   "Celebrating 13 Years of the UN Declaration on the Rights of Indigenous Peoples", 12 September 2020, Cultural Survival, p. 1, www.culturalsurvival.org.

9   See Scott Wallace, "Death Stalks the Amazon as Tribes and Their Defenders Come under Attack", *National Geographic*, 15 November 2019.

10   Paul Ramirez, "Indigenous Latino Heritage: Destruction, Invisibility, Appropriation, Revival, Survivance", in Veysel Apaydin (ed.), *Critical Perspectives on Cultural Memory and Heritage: Construction, Transformation and Destruction* (London: University College London Press, 2020), p. 157.

11   Tomas Alberto Avila (ed.), *Black Caribs–Garifuna: Saint Vincent's Exiled People and the Roots of Garifuna; A Historical Compilation* (San Salvador: Milenio Associates, 2009), p. 88.

12   Christopher Taylor, *The Black Carib Wars: Freedom, Survival, and the Making of the Garifuna* (New York: St Martin's Press, 2012), p. 3.

13   Avila, *Black Caribs–Garifuna*, p. 36.

14   Taylor, *The Black Carib Wars*, p. 4.

15   See "Garifuna People, History and Culture: Global Sherpa", globalsherpa.org.

16   Taylor, *The Black Carib Wars*, p. 158.

17   Henry Louis Gates Jr, *Black in Latin America* (New York: New York University Press. 2011), p. 10.

18   Marisol de la Cadena, "Reconstructing Race: Racism, Culture and Mestizaje in Latin America", *Nacla*, September 2007, p. 1.

19   Gates Jr, *Black in Latin America*, p. 10.

20   Gates Jr, *Black in Latin America*, pp. 5 and 40.

21   Ramirez, "Indigenous Latino Heritage", p. 164.

22   Anadelia A. Romo, "Rethinking Race and Culture in Brazil's First Afro-Brazilian Congress of 1934", *Journal of Latin American Studies*, vol. 39, no. 1, 2007, pp. 31–54, https://www.jstor.org/stable/4491775.

23   Tommy J. Curry, "The Political Economy of Reparations: An Anti-ethical Consideration of Atonement and Racial Reconciliation under Colonial Moralism", *Race, Gender and Class*, 2011, pp. 125–146, www.jstor.org/stable/23884871.

24   Edward Telles, "Racial Discrimination and Miscegenation: The Experience in Brazil", *UN Chronicle*, vol. 44, no. 3, 2008, p. 1, https://www.un.org/en/chronicle/article/racial-discrimination-and-miscegenation-experience-brazil.

25   Terrence McCoy and Heloísa Traiano, "He Grew Up White. Now He Identifies as Black. Brazil Grapples with Racial Redefinition", *Washington Post*, 15 November 2020.

26   Frank Jack Daniel, "Can Truth Panel Help Mexico with Slavery Legacy?", *Newsamericas*, 14 February 2021, p. 1.

27   Daniel, "Can Truth Panel Help Mexico with Slavery Legacy?", p. 1.

28   Ana Lucia Araujo, *Reparations for Slavery and the Slave Trade: A Transnational and Comparative History* (London: Bloomsbury Publishing, 2017), p. 3.

29   Araujo, *Reparations for Slavery and the Slave Trade*, p. 3.

30   Niyi Afolabi, "Reversing Dislocations: African Contributions to Brazil in the Words of Manuel Querino, 1890–1920", *History Compass*, vol. 11, no. 4, 2013, pp. 259–267.

31   Fernando Duarte, "The Controversial Debate over Reparations for Slavery in Brazil", *Black Brazil Today*, vol. 19, April 2019, p. 1.

32   Araujo, *Reparations for Slavery and the Slave Trade*, p. 3.

33   Michael Albertus, Thomas Brambor, and Ricardo Ceneviva, "Land Inequality and Rural Unrest: Theory and Evidence from Brazil", *Journal of Conflict Resolution*, vol. 62, no. 3, 2018, p. 1, https://dx.doi.org/10.2139/ssrn.2442943.

34   Albertus, Brambor, and Ceneviva, "Land Inequality and Rural Unrest".

35   Albertus, Brambor, and Ceneviva, "Land Inequality and Rural Unrest", p. 2.

36   See Curry, "The Political Economy of Reparations", which notes that there were up to 1.17 *quilombos* in Brazil, p. 51.

37   Edward E. Telles "Discrimination and Affirmative Action in Brazil", 2009, wnet.org.

38   Miguel Teubal and Mariana Ortegais Breña, "Agrarian Reform and Social Movements in the Age of Globalisation: Latin America at the Dawn of the Twenty-First Century", *Latin American Perspectives*, vol. 36, no. 4, 2009, pp. 18, www.jstor.org/stable/20684655.

39   Caricom Reparations Commission, https://caricomreparations.org/.

40   Hilary Beckles, *Britain's Black Debt: Reparations for Slavery and Native Genocide* (Jamaica: University of West Indies Press, 2013), p. 76.

41   Eric Williams, *Capitalism and Slavery* (Chapel Hill: University of North Carolina, 1944), p. iv.

42   Williams, *Capitalism and Slavery*, p. 210.

43   The Convention establishing the Association of Caribbean States occurred in July 1994. The 25 members of the ACS are: Antigua and Barbuda, Bahamas, Barbados, Belize, Colombia, Costa Rica, Cuba, Dominica, Dominican Republic, El Salvador, Grenada, Guatemala, Guyana, Haiti, Honduras, Jamaica, Mexico, Nicaragua, Panama, St Kitts and Nevis, St Lucia, St Vincent and the Grenadines, Suriname, Trinidad and Tobago, and Venezuela.

44   The observer states of the ACS are: Argentina, Bolivia, Brazil, Chile, Ecuador, Peru, and Uruguay.

45   Association of Caribbean States, "The Declaration of Havana", 2016.

46   Association of Caribbean States, "The Declaration of Managua", 2019.

47   Bradford E. Burns, "Manuel Querino's Interpretation of the African Contribution to Brazil", *Journal of Negro History*, vol. 59, no.1, 1974, pp. 78–86.

48   Gates Jr, *Black in Latin America*, p. 58.

49   "Truth Commission on Black Slavery in Brazil: Public Hearings", 23 May 2019.

50   The Caricom Reparations Commission, "The Global Reparations Movement", https://caricomreparations.org/.

Index